Robert Louis Stevenson

# Robert Louis Stevenson
## *Life, Literature and the Silver Screen*

SCOTT ALLEN NOLLEN

McFarland & Company, Inc., Publishers
*Jefferson, North Carolina, and London*

ALSO BY SCOTT ALLEN NOLLEN AND FROM MCFARLAND: *Louis Armstrong: The Life, Music and Screen Career* (2004; paperback 2010); *Paul Robeson: Film Pioneer* (2010); *Abbott and Costello on the Home Front: A Critical Study of the Wartime Films* (2009); *Robin Hood: A Cinematic History of the English Outlaw and His Scottish Counterparts* (1999; paperback 2008); *Boris Karloff: A Critical Account of His Screen, Stage, Radio, Television and Recording Work* (1991; paperback 2008); *Warners Wiseguys: All 112 Films That Robinson, Cagney and Bogart Made for the Studio* (2008); *Sir Arthur Conan Doyle at the Cinema: A Critical Study of the Film Adaptations* (1996; paperback 2005); *Jethro Tull: A History of the Band, 1968–2001* (2002); *The Boys: The Cinematic World of Laurel and Hardy* (1989; paperback 2001)

Frontispiece: Robert Louis Stevenson, circa 1885

> The present work is a reprint of the library bound edition of Robert Louis Stevenson: Life, Literature and the Silver Screen, *first published in 1994 by McFarland.*

LIBRARY OF CONGRESS CATALOGUING-IN-PUBLICATION DATA

Nollen, Scott Allen.
  Robert Louis Stevenson : life, literature and the silver screen / Scott Allen Nollen.
     p.    cm.
  Includes bibliographical references and index.

  ISBN 978-0-7864-6712-9
  softcover : acid free paper ∞

  1. Stevenson, Robert Louis, 1850–1894—Film and video adaptations.  2. Scottish fiction—Film and video adaptations.  3. Motion pictures—History and criticism.  I. Title.
PR5497.N65 2012
828'.809—dc20                                            94-17785

BRITISH LIBRARY CATALOGUING DATA ARE AVAILABLE

© 1994 Scott Allen Nollen. All rights reserved

*No part of this book may be reproduced or transmitted in any form or by any means, electronic or mechanical, including photocopying or recording, or by any information storage and retrieval system, without permission in writing from the publisher.*

Front cover image: Charlton Heston as Long John Silver in *Treasure Island*, 1990 (Photofest); cover design by David K. Landis (Shake It Loose Graphics)

Manufactured in the United States of America

*McFarland & Company, Inc., Publishers*
  *Box 611, Jefferson, North Carolina 28640*
  *www.mcfarlandpub.com*

for Donald Craig Nance,

who likes a dram of single malt,
a Highland pipe tune,
and a rattling good sea yarn
as much as I do

# Contents

| | |
|---|---|
| *Preface* | ix |
| *Introduction: Uncharted Waters* | 1 |
| 1 The Word Versus the Image: Fiction into Film | 5 |
| 2 Teller of Tales: Robert Louis Stevenson | 9 |
| 3 A Window Opened to a Different View: The Art of RLS | 38 |
| 4 A Little Piece of Ingenuity: "The Sire de Maletroit's Door" | 48 |
| 5 Bound Together by a Formidable Oath: "The Suicide Club" | 55 |
| 6 Dead Mariners and Sea Disasters: "The Pavilion on the Links" | 64 |
| 7 The Lions and the Lambs: "The Body-Snatcher" | 68 |
| 8 There's a Breeze Coming, Jim: *Treasure Island* | 83 |
| 9 Like Figures in a Dream: *The Silverado Squatters* | 120 |
| 10 Temperate Nature: "The Treasure of Franchard" | 130 |
| 11 Foremost in the Ranks of War: *The Black Arrow: A Tale of the Two Roses* | 138 |
| 12 The War in the Members: *The Strange Case of Dr. Jekyll and Mr. Hyde* | 155 |
| 13 Into the Highlands: *Kidnapped* and *Catriona* | 227 |
| 14 The Twa Corbies: *The Master of Ballantrae* | 281 |
| 15 Judicious Levity: *The Wrong Box* | 298 |

| | | |
|---|---|---|
| 16 | The Commonplace Ghosts of Sailormen: *The Ebb-Tide: A Trio and Quartette* | 309 |
| 17 | No Bagatelle: *St. Ives* | 325 |
| 18 | Dr. Jekyll's Potion: A Conclusion | 338 |

*Appendices*

| | | |
|---|---|---|
| A. | Published Prose Writings (1873–94) | 349 |
| B. | Posthumously Published Prose Writings | 367 |
| C. | Published Poetry | 373 |
| D. | Silent Film Adaptations | 377 |
| E. | Sound Film Adaptations | 380 |
| F. | Film "Continuations" | 392 |
| G. | Jekyll-and-Hyde Parodies | 394 |
| H. | Films Inspired by *Treasure Island* and *The Strange Case of Dr. Jekyll and Mr. Hyde* | 397 |
| I. | Television Adaptations | 401 |
| J. | Radio Programs | 410 |
| K. | Educational Films | 417 |
| L. | Television and Radio Documentaries | 418 |
| M. | Record Albums | 421 |
| N. | Further Manifestations | 423 |

| | |
|---|---|
| *Glossary* | 427 |
| *Notes* | 429 |
| *Bibliography* | 441 |
| *Index* | 449 |

# Preface

Robert Louis Stevenson's life and work have been examined by past authors, but very little has been written about the film and other media adaptations of his short stories and novels. A few brief essays on Paramount's *Dr. Jekyll and Mr. Hyde* (1931) and the various versions of *Treasure Island* and *Kidnapped* have appeared in collections of film criticism, but these focus primarily on the cinematic representations, while virtually ignoring the literary originals.

From 1908 through June 1994, there have been 15 Stevenson works adapted for the motion picture screen (the total is at least 54 when all television, radio, and spoken-word adaptations are included). Yet, no film critic or historian has written a book on the subject. This volume is the first such work, a critical history compiled without the aid of a prototype or a previous filmography.

Although a proper presentation of the subject requires lengthy summaries and quoting, this material should not be used as a substitute for Stevenson's works. Accustomed to the various plots made famous by film versions, many people are unfamiliar with the content and style of the original stories. A good survey of relevant history is also important: in 1960, a reviewer for *Variety* criticized Walt Disney's adaptation of *Kidnapped* for being too Scottish! He claimed, "This part of history is apt to be pretty dim to most Americans (and possibly a good many Britons)."[1]

This study would not have been possible without the previous work of several Stevenson scholars, most of whom have had the advantage of living and working in Scotland. J. C. Furnas's *Voyage to Windward: The Life of Robert Louis Stevenson* (1951) and James Pope Hennessy's *Robert Louis Stevenson* (1974) were very helpful, and the more recent work of Jenni Calder, who has written a biography and a literary study, proved invaluable. David Daiches's several books on Stevenson and other aspects of Scottish culture also were useful. The bibliographical information provided by Roger G. Swearingen's *The Prose Writings of Robert Louis Stevenson* (1980) nearly was matched by Alanna Knight's listings of general Stevensoniana and British television and radio productions in *The Robert Louis Stevenson Treasury* (1985).

The text includes a history and analysis of each adapted story and all major American and European film adaptations. The appendices list all major and minor adaptations, mutations, and permutations, but there may be films, television programs, or radio shows (based on, loosely adapted from, or claiming to be inspired by Stevenson's work) that are not discussed or listed. If something has been left out, it proves that there are always obscure and forsaken sources lurking around out there! Analyses of a few films that could not be located were prepared from pressbook information, previous reviews in trade papers and newspapers, and lingering memories.

In general, would-be collaborators let me sail the sea of Stevenson as a solo effort. Unable to gather the equivalent of the mutineers in *Treasure Island*, I was forced to captain this ship with the tiniest of skeleton crews! Unaccustomed to the ways of modern piracy, I had forgotten that even cursory assistance requires a handful of doubloons and an oath in blood. Oh, these hard times!

While most institutional and corporate concerns ignored my quest, some kind individuals helped raise the Stevensonian standard. As always, the love, understanding, and tolerance of Karla Kay Nollen, me ain bonny rose, helped bring this project to completion. Also worthy of note is Sean Ian Nollen, me ain wee laddie, who now lives close to where a few boats sail. Any day now, he'll be hearing the rousing adventures of Long John Silver as he rests safely beneath the coverlet.

The folks whom we visited during our 1990 trip to Great Britain deserve mention. For starting us off on the right path (with suggestions, music, and good English ale), I must thank Dave Pegg ("Peggy"), jolly bassist-mandolinist for Jethro Tull and Fairport Convention, fantastic bands that ignited my interest in British culture many years ago and provided inspiration for many long writing sessions.

Helpful Scots include Mrs. P. Ciupik of Polton Bank, Edinburgh, who flawlessly directed us to several Stevenson locations in the area; Mrs. C. Fraser of beautiful Borlum House, Scaniport, who pointed us toward Jacobite historical sites and materials in Inverness and Fort William; the people on Edinburgh streets who helped us find various locales; and, finally, all those who patronize the legendary Deacon Brodie's Tavern!

Ellen Shaffer, late curator of the Silverado Museum, was instrumental in locating historic photographs of Stevenson and his family. Situated in St. Helena, California, the museum, which houses over 8,000 Stevensonian items, was built by the Vailima Foundation, an organization established by Mr. and Mrs. Norman H. Strouse in 1968. Since May 1979, the museum has been located at 1490 Library Lane in St. Helena and is open to the public.

While completing the manuscript, I fortuitously acquired a rare letter, written by Stevenson at the age of 26. With the kind assistance of Stevenson scholars Ernest Mehew of Stanmore, Middlesex, and Robin A. Hill of Edinburgh, I learned the exact date and pertinent details of the missive. (Stevenson was notorious for leaving his correspondence undated, and several scholars, including Mehew, deserve credit for their detective methods.) The document, which is reproduced for the first time in chapter three, was indeed an "undiscovered" treasure; in gratitude to Mehew, I happily agreed to include it in his new, multivolume edition of Stevenson's letters, published by Yale University. Furthermore, I would like to thank Timothy Walch, who drew my attention to the sale of "a Stevenson letter" and, in jocose fashion, suggested that I buy it. I, of studious bent and humble wallet, nearly went mad disposing of "unessential" items to raise the funds!

Boyd Magers of Video West in Albuquerque, New Mexico, donated a copy of *Adventures in Silverado,* an obscure 1948 B western that ranks as the only theatrical feature film to include Stevenson as a character. Fred J. Desjarlais and Scott Wilson also provided some hard-to-find films.

The following individuals and organizations located films, reference materials, and illustrations, provided information and encouragement, or simply took the time to answer my letters: Amaranth Books, Ian Anderson, Ray Bradbury, Seamus Carney, Jim Detlefsen, Alice Ferrante, The Haunted Bookshop, John E. Jensen, The Movie/Entertainment Book Club, Jerry Ohlinger's Movie Material Store, Tom A. Pennock, Stephen Sally, Gabe Taverney, the University of Iowa Main Library, and Peter G. Vasey of the Scottish Record Office, Edinburgh.

For ineffable inspiration, I must pay my respects to Martin Allcock, Battlefield Band, Robert Burns, the Chieftains, Johnny and Phil Cunningham, Manus Lunny, Dougie MacLean, Brian McNeill, Simon Nicol, Dave Pegg, Steeleye Span, Andy M. Stewart, the Tannahill Weavers, and Richard Thompson. Stevenson derived great enjoyment from music (a subject that is given its due in the following pages), and he probably would have appreciated the work of these wonderful musician-composers (we know, of course, that he liked Burns). I must also acknowledge Arthur M. Guinness and Son and the GlenMoray-Glenlivet Distillery.

Finally, I would like to thank you, the reader, for your attention to this book. This has not been a voyage without squalls, but spending four and one-half years with Stevenson was a challenging, incomparable pleasure. I hope you enjoy the experience as much as I have.

—SCOTT ALLEN NOLLEN
*Glenfiddich House,
near Lake MacBride, Iowa
June 1994*

# Introduction: Uncharted Waters

*To know what you prefer, instead of humbly saying Amen to what the world tells you ought to prefer, is to have kept your soul alive*—ROBERT LOUIS STEVENSON, *An Inland Voyage* (1878).

Robert Louis Stevenson never saw a movie. If he had lived into the twentieth century, at least long enough to witness the Great War and the first film adaptations of his stories, he might have had difficulty deciding which of the two he disliked the most. And if he could return to peruse this book, he might be surprised, perhaps horrified, to see that his name has been attached to so many cinematic entertainments.

But this volume goes beyond describing silver-screen images inspired by literary antecedents. An in-depth critical history of Stevenson's influence on the popular art of the twentieth century is accompanied by an examination of the forces that influenced his life and work: the beliefs of his parents, his educational background, his social habits and acquaintances, the intellectual currents of the Victorian era, and the turbulent history and distinct culture of the Scottish nation.

As with many popular authors, Stevenson's literary reputation has fluctuated since his death in 1894. For more than two decades, he was canonized by readers who often distorted his personal and literary achievements. One book-length celebration, Richard Rice's *Stevenson: How to Know Him* (1916), paints him as an incomparable artistic genius and a citizen of the world.[1] A reevaluation of Stevenson that ensued during the 1920s was a basic reaction to his celebrated image. One of the first revisionist studies, Frank Swinnerton's *Robert Louis Stevenson: A Critical Study* (1914), is "a reflex action against excessive promotion," and received little attention when it first appeared.[2]

A counterreaction to Swinnerton and others, Doris N. Dalglish's *Presbyterian Pirate: A Portrait of Stevenson* (1937), is a self-indulgent work of the hero-worship school. Although some interesting literary insights are included, the volume

1

resembles a belated love letter from an overwrought admirer.

More than half a century after Stevenson's death a sound critical appraisal began to take shape. Robert Kiely's *Robert Louis Stevenson and the Fiction of Adventure* (1964) is one of the most well-balanced and perceptive studies from the period. In his introduction, Kiely addresses a major problem that has detracted from Stevenson's literary credibility:

> The posthumous reputation of a novelist who has been very popular in his own lifetime is invariably distorted, and often seriously damaged, by that popularity. And if his fame rested largely on romance and high adventure, he risks, like Scott, Dickens, Melville, Twain, and Conrad, being placed in children's libraries. There is nothing unjust in that fact by itself. Each of these authors wrote books which are appealing—and, up to a point, comprehensible—to the young. The mistake, which in these five cases has been rectified in the last few decades, is to assume that a novelist who can entertain an adolescent cannot possibly have much of value to say to an adult.

That is essentially the modern attitude toward Robert Louis Stevenson. He is not held in disrepute. Most readers look back on their first encounter with *Treasure Island*, *Kidnapped*, and *A Child's Garden of Verses* with pleasure and nostalgia.... He was the author of a great many books, and the two or three we remember from childhood represent relatively early efforts in a career which extended over nearly a quarter of a century. Even when his juvenilia were at the height of their popularity, he was regarded by his contemporaries as a gifted and serious artist, and thought by many to be the greatest living master of English prose.[3]

Recent evaluations also have attacked the misconception that Stevenson's work can appeal only to the young. J. R. Hammond's *A Robert Louis Stevenson Companion* (1984) is an excellent survey of his fictional output. Referring to this popular image, Hammond writes: "So well known have been these aspects of his work, and so constantly in demand, that his more solid achievement as a novelist and short story writer has tended to be overlooked."[4]

The city of Edinburgh has recognized Stevenson's achievements by posting plaques on both his birthplace and boyhood home. Although there is no huge memorial to match those honoring Robert Burns and Sir Walter Scott, a brief biography is included on a Heriot Row information sign, and he may be mentioned by bus drivers who take tourists past a small museum along the Royal Mile.

Stevenson's current importance as an author may benefit from the timeless nature of some of his works. His pre–Freudian thoughts on psychology in *The Strange Case of Dr. Jekyll and Mr. Hyde* have been discussed for decades, but few people know of the interesting material included in "The Suicide Club," one of his earlier fictional efforts. As this tale (which deals with "ruined" people who need help to end their lives) was being scrutinized for this study, the controversy over the right to die and a doctor's "suicide machine" raged in headlines and on television news programs across the United States —over 100 years after Stevenson addressed the subject in an exciting piece of macabre storytelling! A few weeks later, a banker's illegal investment of deposits in "The Pavilion on the Links" was paralleled by American media reports of the massive savings and loan bail-out planned and begun by the George Bush administration.

The publication of this volume coincides with the centenary of Stevenson's death, and it follows on the heels of *Dreams of Exile*, an excellent new biography, by journalist Ian Bell. One hundred years after he was laid to rest on a Samoan mountaintop, Stevenson's words still speak to us.

• ONE •

# The Word Versus the Image: Fiction into Film

> *What ... is the object, what the method, of an art, and what the source of its power? The whole secret is that no art does "compete with life." Man's one method, whether he reasons or creates, is to half-shut his eyes against the dazzle and confusion of reality. The arts, like arithmetic and geometry, turn away their eyes from the gross, coloured and mobile nature at our feet, and regard instead a certain figmentary abstraction.* —RLS, "A Humble Remonstrance" (1884).

The study of motion pictures adapted from literature is an underdeveloped discipline. Since the publication of George Bluestone's *Novels into Film* in 1957, only a few scholarly volumes on fiction into film, focusing alternately on general theories and the specific works of various authors, have appeared. Edgar Allan Poe, Charles Dickens, and Mark Twain are obvious candidates for in-depth studies, but almost nothing has been written about their adapted stories. Even popular studies of films featuring Sir Arthur Conan Doyle's Sherlock Holmes virtually ignore the literary originals. The inspiration for over 80 theatrical films (and scores of television and radio productions), Robert Louis Stevenson is a logical choice for scrutiny.

Bluestone claims that a literary work cannot be transferred faithfully to the screen because the two media "belong to separate artistic genera": fiction is a linguistic medium, while cinema is a technological one.[1] Each medium has its own immutable conventions: "In the last analysis, each is autonomous, and each is characterized by unique and specific properties."[2] Therefore, Bluestone views the novel as a point of departure for the filmmaker, who exercises his own integrity when creating an artistic work.

Predating the romantic notions of 1960s auteur critics, Bluestone writes that a novel usually is created by one person working in isolation, while a film is the product of a collaborative team of artists or workers.

And, whereas a fictional work thrives on a limited and specific audience, a cinematic one must reach a mass audience to achieve financial success: "The product of a commercial society, the Hollywood commodity must make a profit; to make a profit, it must please consumers."[3]

Bluestone concludes that the work of the "film adapter," or director, does not represent the original text:

> What happens ... when the filmist undertakes the adaptation of a novel, given the inevitable mutation, is that he does not convert the novel at all. What he adapts is a kind of paraphrase of the novel—the novel viewed as raw material. He looks not to the organic novel, whose language is inseparable from its theme, but to characters and incidents which have somehow detached themselves from language and like the heroes of folk legends, have achieved a mythic life of their own. Because this is possible, we often find that the film adapter has not even read the book, that he has depended instead on a paraphrase by his secretary or his screen writer. That is why there is no necessary correspondence between the excellence of a novel and the quality of the film in which the novel is recorded.[4]

Implicit in Bluestone's theory is his belief that literature is the superior medium; while this assumption may be valid, it also reveals a critical bias. As subsequent theorists have pointed out, his paradigm cannot be applied to all film adaptations.

In her 1985 book *Double Exposure: Fiction into Film*, Joy Gould Boyum refutes Bluestone's idea that a film adaptation is a betrayal of the original text. She points out that *Novels into Film* was written "during a period of great concern with the effects of mass culture on high culture," and claims that Bluestone's bias may have been provoked, in part, by inferior Hollywood product (the dearth of 3-D horror melodramas, Biblical epics, and teen films released during the 1950s).[5] She offers as evidence Bluestone's neglect of *Great Expectations* (1946) and *Oliver Twist* (1948), two excellent Dickens adaptations cowritten and directed in England by David Lean, and theorist Andre Bazin's quote that an adaptation may achieve "an almost dizzy height of fidelity."[6]

Boyum writes that, while the narrative cinema has incorporated aspects of all art forms, it has appropriated a majority (plot, character, setting, dialogue, imagery, and manipulation of space and time) from literature—a fact that breeds contempt:

> In short, nobody loves an adaptation. Not literary enough in that it proceeds through pictures, not cinematic enough in that it has its origins in words, it finds itself in a no-man's-land, caught somewhere between a series of conflicting aesthetic claims and rivalries. For if film threatens literature, literature also threatens film, and nowhere so powerfully, in either instance, as in the form of adaptation. What makes matters worse is that desperate as both arts are—film for status and legitimacy; literature for mere survival—both overstate their case. Defenders on both sides fail to see how many of their positions follow from doctrinaire notions about the nature and role of art, from simple bias toward one medium or the

other, and from—dare one say it?—sheer hysteria.⁷

Boyum, in part, suggests that people do not read as often as they used to; rather than picking up the original text, many choose to take the lazy route of watching a film or television adaptation. (Consider the high school student who tosses aside his assigned book, rents a videocassette, and then writes an inaccurate term paper.) And, in an age of evolving electronic technology and reasonably priced paraphernalia (video games may be the best example), many Americans, particularly young people, *never* read a work of quality literature. Boyum adds, however, that a film adaptation "tends to encourage reading rather than discourage it—just as the fact that we've read the novel encourages us to see the film."⁸

In his introduction to the cleverly titled *No, But I Saw the Movie* (1989), a volume featuring reprints of 18 adapted stories (including Stevenson's "The Body-Snatcher"), editor David Wheeler claims that novels, particularly classics, have benefited greatly from their film versions: "Older established works are continually brought back into print, glossily repackaged and marketed to coincide with their appearance on the big screen."⁹ Wheeler incorporates Alfred Hitchcock's comment that "the nearest art form to the motion picture is ... the short story. It's the only form when you ask the audience to sit down and read it in one sitting."¹⁰ To be sure, short stories and films often are similar in structure, depth of characterization, and length; and the use of short stories as cinematic raw material, frequently obtained from national magazines and newspapers, has been a common practice in Hollywood since its pioneering days.

Gabriel Miller, author of *Screening the Novel: Rediscovered American Fiction in Film* (1980), offers some reasonable conclusions. Referring to the films discussed in his volume, he points out that cinematic adaptations usually *simplify* the scope of novels (he does not include short stories). This simplification is necessary to establish and maintain proper cinematic movement: "This streamlining process has the added advantage of focusing and accentuating the development of one or two central figures, a concentration of story interest that facilitates the fast pace and visual mode of film narrative."¹¹

In a general sense, the novel is too long to be adapted faithfully, and the short story may not be long enough. So the critic of the adaptation must maintain an open mind while hoping to find the greatest degree of loyalty to the original text—a method contingent upon the adaptability of the author in question.

A comprehensive study of the life, literature, and silver-screen influences of Robert Louis Stevenson provides a fascinating look at a vast artistic spectrum. The literary fidelity of each adaptation is a primary critical concern, but overall cinematic quality also is considered. Films claiming a great degree of faithfulness (billed as "Robert Louis Stevenson's" or "based on the story by Robert Louis Stevenson") should deliver what they promise, whereas those "suggested by the story" are not expected to include as much textual material. Finally, this study does not spring from generalized notions about the preeminence of a particular artistic medium; however, in specific cases, a literary work, for various reasons, will prove to be superior to its cinematic counterpart (and, in at least one instance, the opposite also is true). Perhaps David Wheeler puts it best: "In the final analysis, a story, a film, or any work of art for that matter, is good or bad on its own terms."[12]

• Two •
# Teller of Tales: Robert Louis Stevenson

*Bright is the ring of words*
  *When the right man rings them,*
*Fair the fall of songs*
  *When the singer sings them.*
*Still they are carolled and said—*
  *On wings they are carried—*
*After the singer is dead*
  *And the maker is buried*
—RLS, first stanza of poem 15,
*Songs of Travel and Other Verses*
(1887–91).

Robert Lewis Balfour Stevenson was born November 13, 1850, at 8 Howard Place, Edinburgh. The only child of Thomas and Margaret Isabella Balfour Stevenson, Lewis (as he was called throughout his life) spent his early years "amid elegant streets inhabited by genteel professional families."[1]

Born in 1818, Thomas Stevenson had followed in the footsteps of his father, Robert Stevenson (1772–1850), a successful engineer who developed many innovations for the lighthouses of Scotland. The Bell Rock Lighthouse, built over a 5-year span (1807–12) and located east of St. Andrews Bay in the North Sea, is his most noted construction.

Thomas extended his father's work by developing new methods of illumination that allowed navigators to steer safer courses into port, particularly through the narrow Irish Sea. In 1853, he became joint engineer for the Board of Northern Lights, a post he successfully maintained until 1885.

Margaret's ancestors, the Balfours of Pilrig (located between Edinburgh's Old Town and Leith), were a landed family of substantial means who had contributed to major events in Scottish history. In 1679, when the Presbyterian Covenanters rebelled against the religious intolerance of King Charles II, a Balfour fought at Bothwell Brig, the decisive battle in

8 Howard Place, Edinburgh. Stevenson was born here on November 13, 1850. (1990 photograph by S. A. Nollen.)

which the Duke of Monmouth's forces crushed the uprising.

In 1698–99, a Balfour invested a substantial sum of money in the Darien scheme, a series of two Scottish expeditions to the Isthmus of Panama. Created in defiance of the English Navigation Acts, a series of protectionist laws restricting Scottish trade to the West Indies and American colonies, the scheme was to provide the Scots with their own trading company. The expeditions alarmed the British East India Company and also incurred the wrath of the Spanish, who had a legitimate claim to the Darien area. Financed at a total cost of £400,000, both ventures were quashed by Spanish forces.

The "Robert" in young Stevenson's name was a tribute to Robert Stevenson, who died a few months before he was born, and "Lewis" honored Margaret's father, Lewis Balfour. Some years later, the spelling of Lewis was changed to "Louis." One theory suggests that Thomas, a strict Calvinist and Tory, made the change after a radical Edinburgh politician named Lewis offended him. (However, the French pronunciation of Louis with a silent "s" was never used.)

A tiny and physically underdeveloped child, Louis was given the colloquial Scots nickname "Smout" by his parents, who likened his size to that of a "small fry" salmon. From the age of two, he began to suffer from various maladies, particularly coughs and fevers that developed into bronchial infections. This tendency, referred to as a "lung weakness," was inherited from the Balfours, who had a history of respiratory disorders: Lewis and Margaret experienced attacks of coughing and chills, and these problems were passed on to the young Louis, who spent much of his first nine years in bed. Also troubled by gastric infections, he often suffered from insomnia and was forced to rely upon a vivid imagination to pass the long nighttime hours. Reinforced by stories recited by his nurse, Alison Cunningham, who was hired when Louis was 18 months old, his creative impulses evolved at an amazing rate.

"Cummy" (as Louis called her) was an inseparable companion during these developmental years. She often sat at his bedside, reading from the Bible and offering Calvinist sermons for his enjoyment and instruction. Historian Jenni Calder writes: "She condemned dramatically the works of the devil, amongst which were included the theatre and the novel, and fed Louis on a literary diet of the Bible and the more vivid and bloody stories of religious dedication and martyrdom."[2]

In 1853 the Stevensons moved across the road to the corner of Inverleith Terrace, a location from which Louis could gaze out the back windows toward Edinburgh Castle and Arthur's Seat. Ten days after his sixth birthday he began dictating an essay to his mother. Influenced by Cummy's tutelage, he titled this first literary effort "The History of Moses" and, three months later, followed it with "The Book of Joseph."

In the spring of 1857 Thomas Stevenson purchased 17 Heriot Row, a terrace in the center of Edinburgh's New Town. Louis continued his close relationship with Cummy, but his educational interests began to extend beyond the Bible and other religious material. He entered preparatory school at Canonmills, where his studies were interrupted by poor health and taunting classmates. Later that year his parents enrolled him at Henderson's School in India Street, but he departed a few weeks later. In September 1858 he was bedridden with a lengthy and intense illness that drastically affected his ability to eat, sleep, and sit up, and he did not return to Henderson's until October 1859.

At the age of nine Louis no longer needed to be reminded that he was a small and feeble lad. "Smout" began to irritate him and he protested vocally, demanding a fine of one penny from any person who uttered the dreaded nickname.[3] Realizing that he had outgrown his childhood epithet, Thomas and Margaret began to call him "Lou," a diminutive that stuck.

During family holidays on the Berwickshire coast, Louis enjoyed capering amid the sea and sand, playing pirates and treasure hunters with other boys his age. Visits to Allan Water, near Stirling, also excited him, and his fascination with Scotland's turbulent past was enhanced by sojourns to the nearby battlefields of Bannockburn (where Robert the Bruce and his forces routed the English in 1314) and Sherriffmuir (the site of the Jacobite army's defeat in 1715).

Beginning in 1861 Louis shuffled about from one school to another. He entered Edinburgh Academy

Inverleith Terrace, Edinburgh. From 1853 until the spring of 1857, young Stevenson lived in a corner house on this block, located just west of Howard Place. He often gazed out the back windows, southward toward the majestic rises of Edinburgh Castle and Arthur's Seat. (1990 photograph by S. A. Nollen.)

(founded in 1824 by Sir Walter Scott and others), where he remained for two years, and then attended a boarding school in Spring Grove, Isleworth, Middlesex, for a brief time in 1863. Complementing formal instruction with his own muses, he dictated ideas and stories to Cummy, who recorded them in her diary from January 7 to February 25, 1863. After his brief experience in Spring Grove, he then moved to a school in Edinburgh's Frederick Street, where he studied from 1864 to 1867.

Educational confinement often was remedied by excursions in the country. At Peebles Louis rode horses with his cousins, Bob and Katherine Stevenson, and exercised his frolicsome nature by naming the equines "Heaven," "Hell," and "Purgatory." During the autumn of 1863 he accompanied Thomas on a tour of lighthouses along the coast of Fife; in the summer of 1865 he repeated the experience when they sailed up the coast to Wick Harbor in the eastern Highlands.

Around the time of his seventeenth birthday, Louis was accepted by Edinburgh University. Although he wanted to write, Thomas expected him to follow in the family profession of lighthouse and harbor engineering. When he realized that his son was too frail for this type of work, Thomas relented and allowed him to study for the bar. Louis technically enrolled to learn the finer points of British law but spent more time reading Scottish

17 Heriot Row, Edinburgh. Thomas Stevenson purchased this New Town terrace in the spring of 1857, when Louis was six years old. It remained Stevenson's official home until his marriage to Fanny Osbourne in 1880. (1990 photograph by S. A. Nollen.)

history, French literature, and the controversial works of thinkers such as Herbert Spencer and Charles Darwin. It was during this period that he began to develop the bohemian attitude and lifestyle that has been the subject of much discussion and publication.

Far from accepting Thomas's genteel thinking, Louis expressed himself in ways that were "disturbingly iconoclastic."[4] He sought an escape from the conventional lifestyle prized by Edinburgh's upper class, and he initially challenged this attitude by wearing odd attire and frequenting the taverns and "howffs" on the Water of Leith, where he interacted with beggars, criminals, and prostitutes. His growing familiarity with philosophical and fictional literature may have inspired him to seek such company, but his interest in Scotland's historical rebels also had a strong impact. Fascinated by the events and personalities of the Covenanting and Jacobite rebellions, Louis pursued "avenues leading to a less 'respectable' way of life, and first found them, without leaving home, in the 'howffs' of Lothian Road, and the dark purlieus of Calton Hill."[5] In a short time many respectable people became used to seeing the thin, gleaming-eyed Louis striding through the streets, sporting a black shirt and neckerchief under a garish velvet jacket, and speaking in strange, decorous language.

Occurring when it did, Stevenson's period of revolt was due, in part, to the rebellious stage that many youths experience during their late teen years. However, as Victorian scholar David Daiches suggests, youthful passion was not the sole component: "There was more than one crisis between Stevenson and his family which left its mark on both father and son. When Stevenson embraced the bohemian way of life it was not a fad but a profession of faith ... an attitude and a way of life which he had come to believe in as a result of much genuine heart-searching and a great deal of very real unhappiness."[6]

In his 1950 study of Stevenson's Edinburgh years, Moray McLaren explains why he sought the company of lowlife individuals:

Eccentricities—those like deep drinking, running after loose women were all habits that could be allowed to the established and the middle-aged in a quite prosaic fashion. They must not, however, be romanticized. Young men, as the wiseacres of mid–Victorian Edinburgh knew, were inclined to invest their irregularities with a specious romance, even to sentimentalize them. ... It was not ... permitted for the young men of the city to imitate their elders. ... It was in such an atmosphere that the young Robert Louis Stevenson began his own career of eccentricity and bohemianism. All Edinburgh, both the conventional and the permittedly unconventional, were naturally opposed to him. It was only in the true underworld, amongst the unselfconsciously unconventional, that Robert Louis Stevenson of the velvet coat was accepted without question.[7]

Stevenson's bohemianism found little support among his cohorts at the university. Many students considered unconventional attitudes a waste of time, an offensive practice that detracted from a proper education. Calder writes: "In Scotland university education had traditionally been open to the sons of families that in England would never have dreamt of the possibility. For that reason learning was regarded with the greatest respect and seriousness. Stevenson's irresponsible, cavalier attitude, his scoffing at precisely the authorities and institutions that offered opportunities for achievement to the poor but decent, was not popular."[8]

In February 1869 Louis was elected to the Speculative Society, an intellectual group whose former members included Walter Scott and French author Benjamin Constant. While many undergraduates attended "Spec" meetings to skirt the university's prohibition of smoking, Louis enjoyed the company of other unconventional and literary-minded students. Outside the Spec, he made very few friends but, in 1870, he renewed his relationship with Bob Stevenson, whose experiences as an art student and social activist at Cambridge exerted a strong influence over him. During the summers of 1869 and 1870 he joined his father on voyages amid the Orkney and Hebridean islands; their three-week stay on Earraid during the latter trip made a strong impression on Louis, who later used the tidal islet as a setting in two of his finest Scottish stories.

In early 1873 Thomas was shocked to find the written constitution of the "Liberty, Justice, and Reverence" society among Louis's documents. Created by Bob Stevenson, this antiestablishment organization required its members to "disregard everything our parents have taught us." Thomas's discovery of the manifesto led to a discussion of religion and the realization that his son was, in his words, a "horrible atheist." Never one to hold extremist opinions, Louis instead formulated a rational agnosticism. David Daiches reports:

> Thomas blamed Bob for leading his son astray, and meeting him in the street accused him, as Louis put it, "of having ruined his house and his son." Bob replied that he did not know where Louis had found out that the Christian religion was not true, but it was not from him. ... Louis tried to explain his ideas about the differences between morality and religious institutions and to persuade his father that he accepted the ideals of Christian morality while repudiating the Church and the behavior of most people who called themselves Christians. But his parents were touched on a most sensitive spot, and the thought that their son was an infidel was beyond the reach of rational distinctions.[9]

During this bohemian period, Stevenson wrote a cynical poem that clearly defined his social and religious views:

> HAIL! Childish slaves of social rules
>   You had yourselves a hand in the making
> How I could shake your faith, ye fools,
>   If but I thought it worth the shaking.
> I see, and pity you; and then
>   Go, casting off the idle pity,
> In search of better, braver men,
>   My own way freely through the city.
>
> My own way freely, and not yours;
>   And, careless of a town's abusing,

Seek real friendship that endures
  Among the friends of my own
    choosing.
I'll choose my friends myself, do
    you hear?
  And won't let Mrs. Grundy do
    it,
Tho' all I honour and hold dear
  And all I hope should move me
    to it.

I take my old coat from the shelf—
  I am a man of little breeding,
And only dress to please myself—
  I own, a very strange proceeding.
I smoke a pipe abroad, because
  To all cigars I much prefer it,
And as I scorn your social laws
  My choice has nothing to deter
    it.

Gladly I trudge the footpath way,
  While you and yours roll by in
    coaches
In all the pride of fine array,
  Through all the city's thronged
    approaches
O fine, religious, decent folk,
  In Virtue's flaunting gold and
    scarlet,
I sneer between two puffs of
    smoke,—
  Give me the publican and harlot.

Ye dainty-spoken, stiff, severe
  Seed of the migrated Philistian,
One whispered question in your
    ear—
  Pray, what was Christ, if you be
    Christian?
If Christ were only here just now,
  Among the city's wynds and
    gables
Teaching the life he taught us, how
  Would he be welcome to your
    tables?

I go and leave your logic-straws,
  Your former-friends with face
    averted,
Your petty ways and narrow laws,
  Your Grundy and your God, de-
    serted.
From your frail ark of lies, I flee
  I know not where, like Noah's
    raven.
Full to the broad, unsounded sea
  I swim from your dishonest
    haven.

Alone on that unsounded deep,
  Poor waif, it may be I shall
    perish,
Far from the course I thought to
    keep,
  Far from the friends I hoped to
    cherish.
It may be I shall sink, and yet
  Hear, thro' all taunt and scornful
    laughter,
Through all defeat and all regret,
  The stronger swimmers coming
    after.

Undoubtedly written in a state of youthful fervor, this poem is one of several that contains Stevenson's views on Victorian conventions. Other efforts, however, are more subtle and artistic. The following three-stanza poem, written in a pleasant, singsong rhythm, avoids the didacticism of the above example while delivering a similarly powerful indictment:

I am a hunchback, yellow faced,—
  A hateful sight to see,—
'Tis all that other men can do
  To pass and let me be.

I am a woman,—my hair is white—
  I was a drunkard's lass;
The gin dances in my head,—
  I stumble as I pass.

I am a man that God made at first,
  And teachers tried to harm;
Here, hunchback, take my friendly
    hand,—
  Good woman, take my arm.

Stevenson's recognition of the ambiguous nature of human behavior and morality would serve him well when he began to write fiction professionally in the late 1870s. Although his denial of religion elicited strong reactionary outbursts from his father, a permanent rift between the two never occurred. Over the years, Thomas often provided his aspiring but economically insufficient son with financial assistance. Initially, however, Louis's rationalist position was vehemently rejected by Thomas's Calvinist theology. Calder writes: "What made it all doubly painful was this feeling that if he had lied it would have been preferable, that his parents actually wished that he had lied to spare them having to confront the horror of the fact that Louis could find no proof of the existence of God."[10] Even considering his father's extreme position, Louis did not let it alter the respect he had for his family:

> For all his criticisms and rebellion and his open disrespect at times Louis dearly loved his parents, and he was agonized at their distress. When his father hysterically declared that he wished he had never married, had never had a son, or wished his son dead rather than an atheist it was amazing that Louis' own distress remained tempered by affection. Although there were times when he felt it best to keep his distance, he did not turn his back on his parents.[11]

Stevenson occasionally enjoyed fine wine, ale, or malt whisky, and he may have experimented with drugs at one point. Calder notes:

> Louis found he could cure his depression and suppress his cough by taking opium and sometimes relished the effect it could have on him. "I had a day of extraordinary happiness; and when I went to bed there was something almost terrifying in the pleasures that beseiged me in the darkness." . . . There is no evidence that Louis experimented extensively with drug-taking, although addiction to laudanum and morphine was quite common in the Victorian period, and many victims were unaware that they were in effect addicts. . . . There are occasional letters written by Louis whose delightful incoherence suggests the possible effects of opium, but they could just as well be the effects of alcohol in immodest quantity or of sheer high spirits. But Louis took both his work and his health too seriously to risk seriously jeopardising either.[12]

During the summer of 1873 Thomas suggested that Louis spend a lengthy holiday in the village of Cockfield, near Bury St. Edmunds, in Suffolk. Biographer James Pope Hennessy suggests that this move may have been prompted by the elder Stevenson's "desire to place Louis for some weeks in a safely religious household"—that of Margaret Stevenson's niece, Maud Balfour, who had married the Reverend Churchill Babington, a wealthy English vicar.[13] On July 26 Louis's walk to the Babington household was a memorable one, "for watching him from the rectory window was a young and almost notoriously beautiful woman."[14] Far above the status of the fallen women with whom Louis experienced early sexual encounters, Mrs. Frances Sitwell, a cultured Irish lady of 34 who was separated from her clergyman husband and had helplessly watched one of her two young sons die a few months earlier, infatuated the 22-year-old Stevenson and "changed the whole tenor of his youth and life."[15]

Louis enjoyed long conversations with "Fanny," whose strong personality dominated his thoughts for the next two years, and he delighted in frolicking with Bertie, her surviving son, who tragically would die of tuberculosis in the spring of 1880. Through Fanny he began a lifelong friendship with Sidney Colvin, the Cambridge professor who later acted as keeper of the Department of Prints and Drawings at the British Museum. Although Stevenson expressed his feelings for Fanny in a voluminous series of love letters, she was devoted to Colvin and finally married him after her husband died in 1903.

On October 7, 1873, Louis expressed his despair in a letter to his friend, Miss E. R. Crosby:

> [M]y life is a very distressing one at home, so distressing that I have a great difficulty in keeping up a good heart at all or even in keeping my health together. For nearly a year back, I have lived in the most miserable contention with my parents on the subject of religion. I can do nothing myself, but hold my peace and try to steer away from dangerous subjects; but even with all this, fires break out every now and again and I am driven to the most wretched state. To be continually told that you have utterly wrecked the lives of your father and mother, and to see that much of this is true—the wretched truth—, is not you must grant, a very favourable circumstance for cheerful thought.[16]

During this same period, Louis traveled abroad for his health (from November 1873 to April 1874), was elected to London's Savile Club (in June 1874), resumed law classes at Edinburgh University (in November 1874), and began "The Two Falconers of Cairnstane," a story that he later rewrote as "An Old Song." A busy year, 1875 brought several momentous events his way. In February publisher Leslie Stephen took him to the Edinburgh Infirmary, where he met his friend and collaborator W. E. Henley, an amputee who was undergoing the painful antiseptic treatments of Joseph Lister. In May he played Orsino in Professor Fleeming Jenkin's production of William Shakespeare's *Twelfth Night,* and in July he was admitted to the Scottish bar. During the summer he joined his friend Sir Walter Simpson on a walking tour along France's Loire River, only to be arrested as a vagrant at Chatillon: after spending 30 minutes in the local gendarmerie, he was freed by his noble companion!

In the early summer of 1876 Louis accompanied Bob Stevenson to France, where romantic thoughts of Frances Sitwell soon would be replaced by the attractions of another older, married woman also called Fanny. At Barbizon the young men received information that two American women were vacationing at Grez-sur-Loing, but Louis failed to express much interest at the outset. As Hennessy notes, "It was decided that Bob had better go to Grez to scout out the ground and to determine whether the American ladies were tolerable or not."[17]

Upon arrival, Bob was introduced to the two women: one of them was certainly "tolerable"— Frances Matilda Vandegrift Osbourne, 35 years old and separated from her husband—but the other, Isobel Osbourne, was only a teenager and, more importantly, Frances's daughter! Also present was Frances's 7-year-old son, Samuel Lloyd. (A second son, 4-year-old Hervey, had died that April after suffering terribly from tuberculosis.) Joined by Walter Simpson, Bob immediately caught Fanny's eye but consistently spoke of Louis's great talent for witty conversation. After several days of being portrayed as a heroic figure by Bob, Simpson, and other artists who were lodging in the same hotel, Louis arrived on the scene—an event reported in somewhat romanticized fashion by Hennessy:

> In the dusk of a July evening, as the company at the Hotel Chevillon were seated at dinner at the long *table d'hôte*, there was a sudden flurry at one of the high windows which gave on to the street. In vaulted a tall, thin young man, with a healthy reddish complexion, flowing light-brown hair and a small drooping tawny moustache. He was carrying a dusty knapsack. The men in the dining-room rose to their feet in clamorous welcome. Louis Stevenson had arrived. The stranger said that he had dined but would have a cup of coffee. There was an empty chair next to Mrs. Osbourne and here he settled.[18]

At this stage in his career Stevenson had been writing literary essays and reviews for about three years. From the time of his first published work in the December 1873 issue of *The Portfolio* to his acquaintance with Fanny Osbourne in the summer of 1876, he had completed approximately 20 critical pieces for periodicals such as *Cornhill Magazine*, *The Academy*, *Vanity Fair*, and *MacMillan's Magazine*. The subject of his first book-length work, *An Inland Voyage* (1878), was provided by a September–October 1876 canoe trip on the canals of Belgium and France with Walter Simpson.

After joining Fanny and Lloyd in Paris during the autumn of 1876, Stevenson returned to Edinburgh, where he wrote the emotionally charged "On Falling in Love." Completed in November, the essay features some keen observations:

> Falling in love is the one illogical adventure, the one thing of which we are tempted to think as supernatural, in our trite and reasonable world. The effect is out of all proportion with the cause. Two persons, neither of them, it may be, very amiable or very beautiful, meet, speak a little, and look a little into each other's eyes. That has been a dozen or so times in the experience of either with no great result. But on this occasion all is different.

At the age of 26 Stevenson had proved a romantic but, as the conclusion of "On Falling in Love" demonstrates, "a realist as well":

> When the generation is gone, when the play is over, when the thirty years' panorama has been withdrawn in tatters from the stage of the world, we may ask what has become of these great, weighty and undying loves, and the sweethearts who despised mortal conditions in a fine credulity; and they can only show us a few songs in a byegone taste, a few actions worth remembering, and a few children who have retained some happy stamp from the disposition of their parents.[19]

This integration of romanticism and realism in "On Falling in

Love" would be displayed time and again in Stevenson's fiction.

In early 1877 "An Old Song" became his first published fictional work when it appeared anonymously in *London* magazine. That summer he returned to Grez and, in September, again joined the Osbournes in Paris. Until August 1878, when Fanny returned to her California home, he spent as much time as he could on French holidays, either enjoying the Osbournes' company or finding "legitimate" work. During a Paris International Exhibition held in June 1878, he acted as secretary to Fleeming Jenkin (who later became the subject of three Stevenson compositions written between June 1885 and March 1887).

Stevenson continued to write fiction, selling stories such as "Will o' the Mill" and "The Sire de Maletroit's Door" to various periodicals. *An Inland Voyage* was published in May 1878 and soon was followed by similar travelogues: "Edinburgh: Picturesque Notes" (December 1878) and *Travels with a Donkey in the Cévennes* (June 1879), an account of his September–October 1878 walking tour in southern France; the final section of the latter, "The Country of the Camisards," includes descriptions of the French Presbyterian rebels whom he calls "southern Covenanters."

On August 7, 1879, Stevenson sailed from Greenock in a second-class cabin aboard the 4,270-ton steamer *Devonia*, intending to meet the Osbournes in Monterey, California, where Fanny was recovering from an illness. For ten days he observed the many emigrants from Great Britain, Ireland, and mainland Europe who populated the ship's steerage. *The Amateur Emigrant,* his written narrative of the journey (which would be published as "Across the Plains" in an abridged periodical version [1883] and later as a book [1895], including "From the Clyde to Sandy Hook" and "Across the Plains") features documentary accounts that influenced his later fictional works. (In particular, his perception of emigration would resurface in one of *Kidnapped*'s more unforgettable passages.) Early in part one, chapter two, he notes:

> As I walked the deck and looked round upon my fellow passengers, thus curiously assorted from all northern Europe, I began for the first time to understand the nature of emigration. Day by day throughout the passage, and thenceforward across all the States, and on to the shores of the Pacific, this knowledge grew more clear and melancholy. Emigration, from a word of the most cheerful import, came to sound most dismally in my ear. There is nothing more agreeable to picture and nothing more pathetic to behold.

Stevenson arrived in New York during the afternoon of Sunday, August 16, and was told to present himself at the ferry depot of the railroad at 5 A.M. the following morning. From here he sailed aboard a river boat to Jersey City, where he began an 11-day rail journey with emigrants crossing the United States for the first time. He greatly enjoyed the "rich, poetical, humorous, and picturesque" nomenclature of the United States, found Chicago to be "great and gloomy," and had some interesting

*Letter from RLS to Robert Young, written at Swanston Cottage, July 27, 1877.* Thomas Stevenson leased Swanston, a two-story cottage in the Pentland Hills, in the summer of 1867. For several years, Louis joined his parents there during the summer months, and he often enjoyed walking through the hills to meet friends in Edinburgh.  ¶At Swanston, Louis met Robert Young, a quixotic horticulturist, who passed away, aged 72, on February 22, 1870. The following year, Louis eulogized Young in his university essay "An Old Scotch Gardener": "a man keenly alive to the beauty of all that was bygone."  ¶In July 1877, Louis interrupted his stay in France to attend his close friend Charles Baxter's wedding. While lodging at Swanston on Friday, July 27, he wrote this letter to Robert Young, son of the late gardener, whose mother, Mrs. Margaret Dickson Young, had passed away two days earlier.  ¶Concluding "An Old Scotch Gardener," Louis observes, "The earth, that he had digged so much in his life, was dug out by another for himself; and the flowers that he had tended drew their life from him, but in a new and nearer way." (From an original in the author's collection.)

experiences in Iowa, including a "hearty breakfast ... at Burlington on the Mississippi," a conversation with a "drunken man" named Cromwell in Creston, and an "inane misunderstanding" at the Union Pacific Hotel in Council Bluffs. While traveling across the plains of Nebraska, he sat atop a fruit car, searching "in vain for something new," and was deeply disappointed by the topography of the West:

> I longed for the Black Hills of Wyoming, which I knew we were soon to enter, like an ice-bound whaler for the spring. Alas! and it was a worse country than the other. All Sunday and Monday we travelled through these sad mountains, or over the main ridge of the Rockies, which is a fair match to them for misery of aspect. ... The plains have a grandeur of their own; but here there is nothing but a contorted smallness. Except for the air, which was light and stimulating, there was not one good circumstance in that God-forsaken land.

Stevenson's lack of social prejudice, which allowed him to interact with the lowlife of Edinburgh, was demonstrated in "his readiness to muck in with any of his working-class fellows on boat or train, his passionate and almost child-like interest in them, and his acceptance of them as his equals."[20] He was offended by the way his fellow Caucasians treated the members of nonwhite races, particularly the Chinese, who were being accused of spreading a foul odor throughout the train:

> These judgements are typical of the feeling in all Western America. The Chinese are considered stupid because they are imperfectly acquainted with English. They are held to be base because their dexterity and frugality enable them to underbid the lazy, luxurious Caucasian. They are said to be thieves; I am sure they have no monopoly of that. They are called cruel; the Anglo-Saxon and the cheerful Irishman may each reflect before he bears the accusation. I am told, again, that they are of the race of river pirates, and belong to the most despised and dangerous class in the Celestial Empire. But if this be so, what remarkable pirates have we here! and what must be the virtues, the industry, the education, and the intelligence of their superiors at home!

Stevenson also was disgusted by the derision aimed at Native Americans. After hearing his fellow passengers mock "the noble red man of the old story," he "was ashamed for the thing we call civilisation." In the chapter "Despised Races," he concludes:

> If oppression drives a wise man mad, what should be raging in the hearts of these poor tribes, who had been driven back and back, step after step, their promised reservations torn from them one after another as the States extended westward, until at length they are shut up into these hideous mountain deserts of the centre—and even there find themselves invaded, insulted, and hunted out by ruffianly diggers? The eviction of the Cherokees (to name but an instance), the extortion of Indian agents, the outrages of the wicked, the ill-faith of all, nay, down to the ridicule of such poor beings as were here with me upon the train, make up a chapter of injustice and indignity such as man must be in some ways base if his heart will suffer him to pardon or forget.

Three weeks of cramped and dusty travel were capped by his arrival in Monterey at the end of August. One of Fanny's surviving letters from this period states, "My literary friend from Scotland has accepted an engagement to come to America and lecture." As Stevenson scholar James Hart has written, "The children, like everyone else, saw through this easily enough."[21] Stevenson's love for Fanny, however, was complicated by his poor health: the frantic and unsanitary nature of the journey to California, irregular sleep, bad weather, and a lack of nutritional food worsened his sensitive bronchial condition.

Irritated by the frequent sea fogs that rolled into Monterey, Stevenson rode into the Santa Lucia Mountains in mid-September. His illness worsening by the minute, he "lay out under a tree in a sort of stupor" for two nights before he was found by an aged bear hunter. Transported to a nearby goat ranch, where the hunter lived with a Native American companion, he was nursed "in an upper chamber nearly naked, with flies crawling all over me and a clinking of goat bells in my ears" before he was strong enough to return to town.[22]

Undaunted by his weak physical state, Stevenson wrote for hours each day, frequently hiking into the surrounding woods where, on one occasion, he accidentally started a small-scale forest fire. The opening of *The Amateur Emigrant* took shape during this period, as well as the short story "The Pavilion on the Links," the first draft of *Prince Otto*, and the beginnings of a Californian novel: considering two titles, "A Chapter in the Experience of Arizona Breckonridge" and "A Vendetta in the West," he finished approximately half of the story before abandoning it.

During Fanny's absences he frequented a saloon operated by Adulpho Sanchez, a young Hispanic engaged to Fanny's sister, Nellie Vandegrift, and a French restaurant called Simoneau's. While visiting, he often met Crevole Bronson, editor of the *Monterey Californian,* who paid him $2 per week to write newspaper articles. After Fanny returned to her Oakland home, hoping to gain an amicable divorce from her husband, Samuel Osbourne, a former Civil War soldier, miner, and itinerant worker, Stevenson moved to San Francisco in mid-December.

At the rooming house of Mrs. Carson, a kindly Irishwoman, Stevenson fought poor health while living on meager finances and food. Continual rains throughout the spring of 1880 made matters worse and, when Mrs. Carson's four-year-old son, Robbie, contracted pneumonia, he spent countless hours helping her care for the child. James Hart describes the events:

When Robbie recovered, his older namesake collapsed. With his background of malaria and malnutrition, Stevenson fell into what he called a galloping consumption, which was marked by a high fever, cold sweats, frustrating attacks of coughing, and sinking fits in which he wholly lost the power of speech. As he wrote to Colvin, "I was near the other side of Jordan." Even after he began to recover under the dedicated nursing of Fanny and

Mrs. Carson, [local author Charles Warren] Stoddard said that his "itinerary was very limited; he usually travelled from his couch to his lounge, possibly touching at the arm-chair on the way."[23]

Stevenson continued to write, however, jotting down copious notes about his San Francisco experiences and turning out essays on Henry David Thoreau, Benjamin Franklin, and Sir William Penn. He also began an autobiography and composed the first draft of his famous poem "Requiem":

> Under the wide and starry sky,
>   Dig the grave and let me lie.
> Glad did I live and gladly die,
>   And I laid me down with a will.
>
> This be the verse you grave for me:
> *Here he lies where he longed to be,*
> *Home is the sailor, home from sea,*
>   *And the hunter home from the hill.*

Concerned about his wretched state, Fanny moved Louis to a hotel in Oakland, where she planned to nurse him back to health. Rather than showing signs of recovery, he experienced a serious lung hemorrhage. Hennessy explains, "After this first haemorrhage Louis Stevenson lived for the rest of his life under the threat of recurrence, a threat in fact of sudden death." Several medical professionals agreed that he suffered from tuberculosis, but the actual illness was never pinpointed with certainty: "At all events, after the Oakland bleeding, Louis had to live his life as if he were tubercular, greatly aided by Fanny, who combined a morbid interest in illness for its own sake with a pronounced gift for nursing it."[24]

Soon after this shocking development, which Stevenson referred to as "Bluidy Jack," Fanny allowed him to move into the parlor of her cottage, where she was able to monitor his health. As he recovered, his thoughts were focused on marriage and the financial burden that the union would entail; he wrote to Charles Baxter, asking his friend to sell the books he had left in Edinburgh, but in late April he was surprised by a cable from Thomas, who promised him an annual allowance of £250. Hart notes:

> Whether Fanny wrote surreptitiously to the senior Stevensons to tell them of their son's health and the impending marriage, as has sometimes been assumed, or whether Baxter or another friend gave them the details of his sickness and poverty, they responded remarkably. All of a sudden in late April his father's reserve melted. ... Since the divorce and the cable were received at about the same time, Stevenson and Fanny were at last able to marry.[25]

On May 19, 1880, Louis and Fanny were wed at the San Francisco home of the Reverend William A. Scott, a Scottish Presbyterian minister. Indulging their adventurous spirits, they honeymooned near the Calistoga Gold and Silver Mine at Silverado, 2,000 feet up Mount Saint Helena in California's Napa Valley, until the end of July. Louis was excited by the location, and documented their experiences in a journal called *The Silverado Squatters* (which eventually was revised and published in 1883).

In early August Louis, Fanny, and Lloyd boarded a Pullman train bound for New York. Intending to return to Scotland after a one-year absence, Stevenson purchased first-class tickets for an August 7 departure on the *City of Chester*. Ten days later the ship docked at Liverpool.

Initially, Thomas and Margaret Stevenson disapproved of Fanny, whose age and independence did not comport with their traditional conservative ideology. Louis's friends, too, began to question his social attitudes. Calder writes:

> Louis rejected the idea of a marriage of unassuming respectability. He was troubled by the subordination of women, which the accepted style of Victorian marriage implied. He had much sympathetic curiosity about the lives of women and attitudes to women. ... Marriage, he decided, required an impossible compromise and inevitable duplicity. Given the usual moral imperfections of young men, he saw it as "inexcusable that they should draw another's life into their own" ... far from being prepared by education and experience to live together, men and women, he felt, were encouraged to be as different as possible, with the result that the idea of sharing their lives together on common ground becomes ridiculous.[26]

In Scotland Louis sought various ways to improve his ill health. During the winter of 1880–81 he took Fanny and Lloyd to Davos, Switzerland, where a new resort area had been established for consumptives. At the end of April they returned to Scotland and, during the summer, stayed with Louis's parents in rented cottages at Pitlochry and Braemar, near Balmoral; it was within the latter dwelling that *Treasure Island* was conceived.

At the request of Thomas, Louis applied for a legitimate position at Edinburgh University when the chair of history and constitutional law became vacant in 1881. He did not possess the necessary qualifications, but the gesture pleased the elder Stevenson and reflected his "real and increasing interest in Scottish history."[27]

The following winter Stevenson and family again moved to Davos, where, in the spring of 1882, Dr. Karl Ruedi suggested that he seek permanent residence in the south of France, "fifteen miles from the sea and near a pine forest."[28] The high altitude of the Swiss Alps was no longer required for his slowly improving condition, but, rather than accepting the doctor's prescription, he followed the advice of his parents, who longed to see him back in Scotland.

During 1882 he sought lodgings in London, Edinburgh, and the Scottish countryside. Although he should have known better, his exposure to the cool, damp climate worsened his condition and he began hemorrhaging again. As Hennessy points out, "most of the good of the long months under Dr. Ruedi's intelligent care at Davos was undone."[29]

The Stevensons returned to France in September 1882 and briefly lived at Campagne Defli, St. Marcel, a suburb of Marseilles, before Fanny, fearing a breakout of typhus, sent Louis to Nice while she packed their belongings. Several days later railway officials told her that the ailing Louis probably had died, but she eventually found him lounging in a Nice hotel. In March 1883 they began a 9-month residence at La Solitude, a chalet at Hyeres, but the change of climate did nothing to improve Louis's rapidly worsening condition; another near-fatal hemorrhage rendered his right arm useless as he spent several days propped up in bed, writing portions of *A Child's Garden of Verses* with his left hand. He later developed sciatica (a neuralgia of the sensory and motor nerve that runs through the pelvis and upper leg) and Egyptian ophthalmia, a malady that quickly spread throughout the village. Able to leave his bed for only short periods of time, he worked on the manuscripts for two novels, *The Black Arrow*, a romantic tale set during the Wars of the Roses, and *Prince Otto*.

While at Hyeres, Louis benefited from the devotion of Valentine Roch, a French Swiss girl whom Fanny hired as their new housemaid. Treated as one of the family, Valentine served them for six years, frequently nursing Louis when he fell ill. She raised a few Victorian eyebrows when it became known that she slept in the same room with Louis, who often referred to her as "Jo" (the Scots word for sweetheart), during Fanny's absences.

Following brief stays at Vichy, Clermont-Ferrand, and Royat during the spring and summer of 1883, the Stevensons returned to Hyeres. In January 1884 they joined W. E. Henley and Charles Baxter in Nice, where Louis became so ill that he could not speak without spilling blood onto his clothes. From Hyeres they again traveled to Royat and, during the summer, moved to Bournemouth on the west cliff in southern England.

Shortly after *A Child's Garden of Verses* was published in March 1885, they settled into Skerryvore, a home Louis named after Uncle Alan Stevenson's lighthouse located west of the Isle of Mull on Dhu Heartach. In return for her cooperation in Thomas's effort to keep Louis in Great Britain, Fanny received the house as a belated wedding present. Lloyd Osbourne described Skerryvore as "unusually attractive" but claimed that it was little more than a prison for his invalid stepfather:

> His health throughout was at its lowest ebb; never was he so spectral, so emaciated, so unkempt and tragic a figure. His long hair, his eyes so abnormally brilliant in his wasted face, his sick-room garb, which he picked up at random and to which he gave no thought—all are ineffaceably pictured in my mind; and with the picture is an ineffable pity. . . . He had horrifying hemorrhages; long spells when he was doomed to lie motionless on his bed lest the slightest movement would re-start the flow; when he would speak in whispers, and one sat beside him and tried to be entertaining—in the room he was only too likely to leave in his coffin.[30]

Although he suffered physically during his two-year residence at Skerryvore, Stevenson wrote some of his best and most influential works. *The Strange Case of Dr. Jekyll and Mr. Hyde* and *Kidnapped*, stories that established his international literary reputation, were both penned while he sought refuge from England's cool, damp climate.

He also indulged his love of Celtic music, and the poetry and songwriting of Robert Burns in part fueled his interest in traditional Scottish songs, particularly those written during or shortly after the 1745 Jacobite Rebellion. Calder writes: "Music continued to absorb him, but that would never be a success. He sent his efforts at composition to Bob for comment. He and Lloyd—'You should hear Lloyd on the penny whistle, and me on the piano! Dear powers, what a concerto!'—were sending their neighbors, he alleged, 'in quest of brighter climes.' It was all part of the need for expression."[31] In *The Strange Case of Dr. Jekyll and Mr. Hyde*, Richard Enfield opines that a "cut and dry apothecary" is "about as emotional as a bagpipe." Here, Stevenson's remark about the pipes may indicate this English character's ethnocentrism; in his 1887 story, "The Misadventures of John Nicholson," the Edinburgh protagonist whistles a different tune: "The band was playing down in the valley under the castle; and when it came to the turn of the pipers, he heard their wild sounds with a stirring of the blood." (Indeed, the Highland pipes can be very expressive, and the Scottish small pipes, as well as the Irish uilleann pipes and Northumbrian small pipes, are particularly pleasurable.) Other than the piano, Stevenson's favorite instruments included the tin whistle and the a capella voice, as many of his novelistic passages demonstrate, and the flageolet, a small fipple flute that he liked to play while sitting in bed.

Poor health often prevented him from playing his musical instruments, while his many friends were limited to brief conversations and, in the case of Henley, minimal drams of malt whisky.[32] Fanny wrote that "evenings of interesting, clever, and brilliant talk were amongst the pleasantest experiences of my husband's life," particularly when American novelist Henry James dropped in.[33] In the autumn of 1885 they ventured out to visit Thomas Hardy in Dorchester but, during the return trip, Louis became seriously ill at an Exeter hotel.

After two years of college, Lloyd Osbourne, intent on becoming an author, returned to Skerryvore but was shocked to find his stepfather more somber than usual. During Lloyd's absence, Louis became fascinated with Leo Tolstoy and other Russian novelists whose gloomy, philosophical works stirred his philanthropic concerns. Obsessed with alleviating the suffering of Irish citizens who were being starved, brutalized, and evicted from their farms by the British government, Louis developed a "typically Russian" method of aiding them. Lloyd later wrote:

> R.L.S.'s plan, though nightmarish, was quite simple. We were all to go to Ireland, rent one of these farms, and be murdered in due course. As R.L.S. expressed it with an oratorical flourish: "The murder of a distinguished English literary man and his family, thus engaged in the assertion of human rights, will arrest the horror of the whole civilized world, and bring down its odium on these miscreants."[34]

In May 1887 life at Skerryvore was interrupted by news of Thomas Stevenson's rapidly deteriorating health. Abandoning his "absurd"

Tolstoyist ideas, Louis rushed to Edinburgh with Fanny and was shocked when his father failed to recognize him. Although Hennessy claims that Louis saw a "mindless zombie,"[35] J. C. Furnas has written that Thomas "was still dressed and upright."[36] Disgusted at the prospect of dying in bed, Thomas wished to be attired properly while smoking his beloved pipe. A private funeral was scheduled but became "the largest such ... occasion that Edinburgh had ever seen."[37] Having caught a serious cold, Louis was barred from the cemetery by his uncle, Dr. George Balfour. Rather than mourning at the graveside, he paid his respects by completing "Ticonderoga," a ballad he recently had discussed with Thomas.

A few months after he returned to Skerryvore, Stevenson's doctors advised him that he could no longer reside in Great Britain without risking further, perhaps fatal, illnesses. He considered a resort for consumptives in Colorado and, accompanied by Fanny, Lloyd, Valentine, and Margaret Stevenson, sailed from London aboard the *Ludgate Hill* on August 22, 1887. From that moment, he never revisited his native land.

Upon reaching New York in mid-September, Louis was flabbergasted by the warm reception he received from admirers and enthusiastic interviewers. Living within the confines of Skerryvore, he had not been aware of the international acclaim his recent novels had established. Writing to Sidney Colvin, he admitted, "My reception here was idiotic to the last degree."[38] Hennessy notes:

[H]e was approached by several publishers who offered him what seemed extravagant sums for weekly or monthly articles. He finally settled with Mr. Burlingame, editor of *Scribner's*, to supply a monthly article for twelve months at 3,500 a year—about 700 pounds. The subjects of the articles were entirely up to him, and the results, though he found it hard going, were some of the best of his essays. At first startled, then tantalized by his fame, Louis soon had a healthy reaction against it all. ... He was even embarrassed by the size of the sums of money offered him. "I tell you I do dislike this battle of the dollars," he wrote to Burlingame. "I feel sure you all pay too much here in America; and I beg you not to spoil me any more. For I am getting spoiled; I do not want wealth, and I feel these big sums demoralize me."[39]

After accepting the *Scribner's* offer, Stevenson wrote to his friend William Archer:

I am a bourgeois now; I am to write a weekly paper ... at a scale of payment which makes my teeth ache for shame and diffidence. ... I am like to be a millionaire if this goes on, and be publicly hanged (on two counts, now, for this and for Skerryvore) at the social revolution: well, I would prefer that to dying in my bed; and it would be a godsend to my biographer, if ever I have one.[40]

In October the Stevensons settled at Saranac Lake in the New York Adirondacks. Deciding that a trip to Colorado would prove disastrous for his health, Louis enjoyed the surrounding forests near the Canadian border. During this eight-month residence, he experienced no major illnesses and his "tuber-

**Cold Winter at Saranac, 1887–88. Valentine Roch, Mrs. Baker, landlady of the cottage, Lloyd Osbourne, Fanny Stevenson, RLS, and Sport, the dog. (From the original in the Silverado Museum, St. Helena, California.)**

culosis" was diagnosed as "arrested" by Dr. Edward Livingstone Trudeau.[41] Inspired by the turn in his health, he began writing *The Master of Ballantrae*, a novel of familial conflict engendered by the 1745 Rebellion.

During the spring of 1888 he contemplated another change of climate as the weather turned increasingly colder. An additional impetus was provided by the *New York World*'s Sam McClure, who previously had offered $10,000 per year in exchange for a weekly newspaper column. Undaunted by Stevenson's initial refusal, McClure "encouraged the idea of an exotic voyage in a chartered yacht, to be paid for, he suggested, by monthly letters from Louis on their experiences, letters which McClure undertook to syndicate."[42]

In March Fanny left for San Francisco, where she planned to rent a yacht suitable for a South Seas voyage. Closing the door of the Saranac cottage in late April, Louis traveled to New York with Lloyd, Margaret, and Valentine. While lodging at the Hotel St. Stephen, he ventured out one sunny afternoon to meet Mark Twain in Washington Square. Here the two authors sat on a park bench, discussing their art. When

Louis grew tired of the hotel, Will H. Low, an American painter he had befriended in Paris, suggested that he move south to Manasquan, New Jersey. Pleased to be near water again, he joined Low in several catboating excursions on the Manasquan River.

After a six-week effort, an ailing Fanny telegraphed that she had located the *Casco,* a 95 foot, 70 ton topsail schooner, anchored in San Francisco harbor. On May 31 Louis and "family" boarded a New York Pullman to begin the week long journey to Sacramento. Hired for $750 per month, the *Casco* was captained by A. H. Otis, who stood by while Fanny, who was hospitalized briefly, and Margaret secured necessary provisions for a six-month tour. On June 28 the yacht left San Francisco with Louis, Fanny, Lloyd, Margaret, Valentine, Captain Otis, and a crew of five on board.

After 30 days at sea the party visited the Marquesas Islands and then sailed on to Fakarava Atoll and Tahiti (where Paul Gauguin, another bohemian of the same era, lived from 1891–93), before arriving in Honolulu in late January 1889. For the next four and one-half months they settled into a house on Waikiki Beach, where Louis completed *The Master of Ballantrae* and a revised draft of *The Wrong Box,* a farcical novel originally begun by Lloyd in October 1887. Leisure activities included a reunion with Fanny's daughter, Isobel, and her unreliable husband, Joe Strong, both struggling artists living in Honolulu with their eight-year-old son, Austin, and lengthy "champagne parties" with King Kalakaua, the last of Hawaii's monarchs, who often imbibed several bottles before dinner.

Anxious to continue his island-hopping activities, Louis began searching for another vessel, as the *Casco* and her crew had proved less than reliable. Margaret returned to Edinburgh and Fanny dismissed Valentine, who apparently had engaged in an indiscreet affair with a crewman. In Honolulu Louis arranged a charter with Mr. Wightman, owner of the *Equator,* a new San Francisco–based trading schooner scheduled to pick up copra throughout Micronesia. Prior to departing with Fanny, Lloyd and Joe in late June (Isobel opted to take Austin with her to Sydney, where she would await further instructions), Louis spent seven days at the leper colony on Molokai, where the controversial Belgian missionary, Father Damien de Veuster (1840–89), recently had died of the disease. Refusing to wear gloves, Louis played with the children and ate meals served by leper girls.

Back in Honolulu he wrote to Charles Baxter about the projected length of the *Equator* voyage, advising him not to worry "till you get some certainty we have gone to Davie Jones in a squall, or graced the feast of some barbarian in the character of Long Pig."[43] The provisions taken on board included a magic lantern and several musical instruments: Louis's flageolet, Joe's accordion, Lloyd's ukulele, Fanny's guitar, and a portable organ. The *Equator*'s skipper, Denis Reid, a young Scot who wore a bonnet in the tropical heat, insisted on singing "Annie Laurie" and "In the

Luau with King Kalakaua, Honolulu, 1889. Kalakaua, the last of Hawaii's monarchs, was as fond of the Stevensons as he was of champagne. Here, Louis enjoys poi, beer, and the company of Princess Liliuokalani, Kalakaua, and Fanny Stevenson (seen in foreground). (From the original in the Silverado Museum, St. Helena, California.)

Gloaming," the only two songs he knew, whenever a session took place.

Pleased with his previous collaboration with Lloyd, Louis joined him in coauthoring the draft of another novel, *The Wrecker*, a maritime detective tale based on actual incidents. During the early stages of the voyage, Louis expressed a desire to remain in the South Seas, hopefully aboard his own yacht to be christened the *Northern Light*. He planned to use profits from *The Wrecker* to purchase the craft, appoint Reid as captain, and, together with Lloyd, start an island trading partnership called Jekyll, Hyde and Company.[44] The scheme eventually was scuttled after Stevenson caught wind of the deceitful tactics used by many South Sea traders.

After a six-week stay at Butaritari in the Gilbert Islands, the *Equator* docked at Apemama, where the party was stranded for two months while Reid and his crew sailed off to gather copra. Menaced by hordes of flies and a dwindling food supply, Louis and his companions benefited from the hospitality of "King" Tembinoka, a local despot who initially was reluctant to let them stay.

Threading its way through the remainder of the Gilbert atolls, the *Equator* braved a terrible storm before docking at Upolu in Samoa on December 7, 1889. Intent on collecting additional information for his book *In the South Seas,* Stevenson planned to stay for two months before returning to England, but he quickly grew attached to the location. A few weeks after their arrival he purchased 400 acres of land, including a cacao plantation, above the town of Apia and ordered a new home to be built. Except for a cruise aboard the *Janet Nichol* to the Gilbert, Marshall, and New Caledonian Islands from April to August 1890, and a few excursions to Sydney, the Stevensons remained in Samoa.

During October 1890 Louis and Fanny settled into a temporary four-room cottage. Here they drew plans for Vailima, a large home named after the five streams that flowed through their estate. Louis joined in the strenuous work of hacking through the jungle bush, and 15 acres eventually were cleared. Enormous sums of money were spent on shipping their belongings from Skerryvore and Heriot Row, general upkeep, crops, livestock, and feasts for native chiefs and the complements of visiting British warships. The estate subsequently housed Isobel, Joe, and Austin Strong (who all moved into the original cottage), Lloyd, Margaret, and seven Samoan aides, some of whom, on ceremonial occasions, donned the official uniform of Vailima: a loincloth of Royal Stewart tartan![45]

Although Stevenson concentrated on new writing projects (including the completion of *The Wrecker*) and the details of Vailima, he also joined in musical sessions with Lloyd and Isobel (incorporating such instruments as flageolet, piano, mandolin, and banjo), learned the Samoan language, and became involved in local political affairs. During 1892–93 he alternated the writing of *David Balfour* (titled *Catriona* in Great Britain), his sequel to *Kidnapped,* and *The Ebb-Tide,* a South Seas novel originally begun by Lloyd in the spring of 1889, with his participation in local tribal causes. When the "little war" broke out between rival factions in 1893, he supported Mataafa, a popular anti-imperialist rebel favored by the United States and, to some extent, Great Britain, against Malietoa Laupepa, a puppet leader installed by the German government. Detesting the activities of European consuls, Louis attempted to negotiate a reconciliation between the two chiefs; after Mataafa and his major supporters were banished to the German-occupied Marshall Islands, other tribal chiefs were incarcerated in an undistinguished prison in Apia until Louis and his family made a public visit.

Stevenson joined the prisoners inside the jail, ate with them, and vowed to secure their release. After the promise was fulfilled, the tribesmen honored him by constructing the "Road of the Loving Hearts," a grassy path that shortened the distance between Apia and Vailima. Considered a hero by the chiefs, Stevenson was known in Samoa as "Tusitala" (basic translation: "Teller of Tales"), a name that quickly came into general usage (although historians are uncertain as to when the name first was applied to him).

During this same period Stevenson wrote several letters to local

The Stevenson Household, Vailima, July 31, 1892. Lloyd Osbourne, Isobel Strong, Austin Strong (front); Margaret Stevenson, RLS, Fanny Stevenson, Joe Strong (back). (Note the cockatoo on Joe's shoulder.) (From the original in the Silverado Museum, St. Helena, California.)

newspapers in which he spoke out on various Samoan and South Sea matters, including the death of Father Damien, whose ethics had been criticized in the press by the Reverend C. M. Hyde of Hawaii. Though Damien had not lived within the priestly Catholic boundaries he swore to recognize, Stevenson admired his determination to care for the unfortunate individuals of the Molokai colony. Calder writes: "In a sense Damien was what Louis had always been looking for, the man who on conventional social and moral terms was to be condemned, but who in terms that really counted—that counted for Louis and, he was sure, for humanity—was a true hero."[46] After Damien's accuser read the "Open Letter to the Reverend Dr. Hyde of Honolulu," a harsh rejoinder published at no profit to Stevenson, the clergyman recriminated him for being a "bohemian crank ... a negligible person whose opinion signified nothing."[47]

Assessing Stevenson's political views, David Daiches notes:

> Paternalistic yet individualistic, conservative yet anti-imperialist, Stevenson's views on Samoan affairs represent a synthesis easily understandable by anyone who follows the development of his attitude from his bohemian youth to that final period of his life when his views on all problems of conduct had blended into the simple and generous morality to which he gave full expression in "A Christmas Sermon."[48]

Published in 1888, "A Christmas

Sermon" contains Stevenson's assessment of Victorian morality and his blueprint for a more tolerant, practicable code of ethics:

> Gentleness and cheerfulness, these come before all morality; they are the perfect duties. And it is the trouble with moral men that they have neither one nor other. It was the moral man, the Pharisee, whom Christ could not away with. If your morals make you dreary, depend upon it they are wrong. I do not say "give them up," for they may be all you have; but conceal them like a vice, lest they should spoil the lives of better and simpler people. ... There is an idea abroad among moral people that they should make their neighbors good. One person I have to make good: myself. But my duty to my neighbor is much more nearly expressed by saying that I have to make him happy—if I may.

At Vailima, Stevenson finished *Catriona*, *The Ebb-Tide*, and several short stories, including "The Beach of Falesá" (1892). He also began two complex novels, *Weir of Hermiston* (in October 1892) and *St. Ives* (in January 1893). Originally titled "The Justice Clerk," *Weir of Hermiston* includes a brilliant vision of Scotland conjured up in the midst of his new Samoan surroundings. Considered by many to be his finest work, this unfinished novel fell by the wayside when he turned to *St. Ives*, but he did revert to the earlier effort from time to time.

Having suffered a severe attack of writer's cramp during the summer of 1892, Stevenson began dictating his work to Isobel, who had moved in with them after separating from Joe (they were divorced in July 1892). The Samoan weather allowed Louis a respite from the respiratory problems which had plagued him in Europe and the United States, but his health continued to deteriorate. The thematics of his fiction became more somber, as did his correspondence with trusted friends. Writing to Sidney Colvin on August 23, 1893, Louis revealed "Life is not all Beer and Skittles; and mine is closing in dark enough. What is left, my God, in such a welter? When does blame come in? Nowhere, I believe, or very little. Only the inherent tragedy of things works itself out from white to black and blacker, and the poor things of a day look ruefully on."[49]

On December 3, 1894, while taking a break from dictating *Weir of Hermiston* to Isobel, Louis decided to help Fanny in the kitchen: bringing a bottle of burgundy from the cellar, he added cooking oil to a mayonnaise that she was preparing for dinner. After walking onto the verandah, he spoke, suddenly clasped his hands to his head, and cried out excitedly. (Various accounts state that he uttered, "Oh, my head," "What's that?" or "What a pain!") Turning to Fanny, he painfully asked, "Do I look strange?" Fanny grabbed one of his arms and, aided by Sosimo, their native valet, guided him into an armchair in the hall. Losing consciousness, Louis never recovered and, though his doctor arrived a short time later, he died from a cerebral hemorrhage at 8:10 P.M., aged 44 years, 3 weeks.

Stevenson's death shocked admirers throughout the world, but perhaps his Samoan friends were

**RLS in the Library at Vailima, 1892. Stevenson dictates to Isobel Strong, who was known as "Teuila" in Samoa. (From the original in the Silverado Museum, St. Helena, California.)**

affected to the greatest extent. Having revered him as a type of Samoan laird, many natives took part in his unconventional funeral service. Lloyd acquired necessary tools in Apia and sent messages to several island chiefs who, together with their workers, cleared a path to the top of Mount Vaea, the spot Louis had chosen as his final resting place. About 50 strong natives took turns carrying the coffin up the steep mountainside, while Fanny, Isobel, and Margaret watched from the verandah of Vailima.

Sixty natives and 19 European friends attended the service read by the Reverend Clarke, a missionary who had been among the first to welcome Stevenson to his new home. After a brief eulogy was delivered in Samoan by the Reverend Newell, the mourners made their way back down the mountain. Turning toward the grave, an aged chief added, "Tofa Tusitala, Tofa Tusitala." ("Sleep, Teller of Tales.")[50] Later a stone memorial, resembling a Samoan chief's monument, was erected upon the sepulchre: included in the engravings are a thistle and a hibiscus flower (the national emblems of Scotland and Samoa, respectively), a tiger lily (representing the independence of Fanny Stevenson, whose ashes were buried there about a year after her death on February 18, 1914), and both verses of "Requiem."

In 1878, while writing his sermonic essay "Aes Triplex," Stevenson, age 27, presaged some of the conditions of his subsequent life and earthly departure:

> Being a true lover of living, a fellow with something pushing and spontaneous in his inside, he must, like any other soldier, in any other stirring, deadly warfare, push on at his best pace until he touch the goal. "A peerage or Westminster Abbey!" cried Nelson in his bright, boyish, heroic manner. These are great incentives; not for any of these, but for the plain satisfaction of living, of being about their business in some sort or other, do the brave, serviceable men of every nation tread down the nettle danger, and pass flyingly over all the stumbling-blocks of prudence. Think of the heroism of Johnson, think of that superb indifference to mortal limitation that set him upon his dictionary, and carried him through triumphantly until the end! Who, if he were wisely considerate of things at large, would ever embark upon any work much more considerable than a halfpenny post-card? Who would project a serial novel, after Thackeray and Dickens had each fallen in mid-course? Who would find heart enough to begin to live, if he dallied with the consideration of death?
>
> And, after all, what sorry and pitiful quibbling all this is! To forego all the issues of living in a parlour with a regulated temperature—as if that were not to die a hundred times over, and for ten years at a stretch! As if it were not to die in one's own lifetime, and without even the sad immunities of death! As if it were not to die, and yet be the patient spectators of our own pitiable change! The Permanent Possibility is preserved, but the sensations carefully held at arm's length, as if one kept a photographic plate in a dark chamber. It is better to lose health like a spendthrift than to waste it like a miser. It is better to live and be done with it than to die daily in the sick-room. By all means begin your folio; even if the doctor does not give you a year, even if he hesitates about a month, make one brave push and see what can be accomplished in a week. It is not only in finished undertakings that we ought to honor useful labor. A spirit goes out of the man who means execution, which outlives the most untimely ending. All who have meant good work with their whole hearts, have done good work, although they may die before they have the time to sign it. Every heart that has beat strong and cheerfully has left a hopeful impulse behind it in the world, and bettered the tradition of mankind. And even if death catch people, like an open pitfall, and in mid-career, laying out vast projects, and planning monstrous foundations, flushed with hope, and tripped up and silenced: is there not something brave and spirited in such a termination? and does not life go down with a better grace, foaming with a full body over a precipice, than miserably straggling to an end in sandy deltas? When the Greeks made their fine saying that those whom the gods love die young, I cannot help believing they had this sort of death also in their eye. For surely, at whatever age it overtake the man, this is to die young. Death has not been suffered to take so much as an illusion from his hearth. In the hot-fit of life, a tip-toe on the highest point of being, he passes at a bound onto the

**RLS, at forty-two, Sydney, 1893.**

other side. The noise of the mallet and the chisel is scarcely quenched, the trumpets are hardly done blowing, when, trailing with him clouds of glory, this happy-starred, full-blooded spirit shoots into the spiritual land.

• THREE •

# A Window Opened to a Different View: The Art of RLS

> *In anything fit to be called by the name of reading, the process itself should be absorbing and voluptuous; we should gloat over a book, be rapt clean out of ourselves, and rise from the perusal, our mind filled with the busiest, kaleidoscopic dance of images, incapable of sleep or of continuous thought. The words, if the book be eloquent, should run thenceforward in our ears like the noise of breakers, and the story, if it be a story, repeat itself in a thousand coloured pictures to the eye.* —RLS, "A Gossip on Romance" (1882).

Robert Louis Stevenson's literary output reflects the singular nature of his life. His love of "clean, open air adventure"[1] was engendered by the vivid imagination he developed as a child, and, during his later wayfaring efforts to forestall the death that chronic illness would bring, he evolved into one of the most original and versatile writers in the English language.

Stevenson began his professional literary career penning essays and reviews on a variety of artistic, cultural, philosophical, and historical subjects. By his mid-twenties he already had displayed elements of the diversity that would distinguish his later fictional efforts. He wrote of Scottish topography, history, and song, the works of great European and American authors, and offered his views on idleness, friendship, relations between the sexes, and other social topics. His earliest endeavors are occasionally trivial and pedantic, but they allowed him to experiment with content, style, and structure; his entire output benefited from this early apprenticeship, and he continued to write essays, travelogues, and journalistic pieces throughout his career.

Some of his didactic essays offer a portrait of Stevenson the philosopher, the bohemian whose rebelliousness was tempered by an acute understanding of human behavior and society. "Crabbed Age and Youth" (1878), for example, foreshadows his future use of young fictional protagonists and brilliantly demonstrates the moral rationale that permeates his stories:

> You need repent none of your youthful vagaries. They may have been over the score on one side, just as those of age are probably over the score on the other. But they had a point; they not only befitted your age and expressed its attitude and passions, but they had a relation to what was outside of you, and implied criticisms on the existing state of things, which you need not allow to have been undeserved, because you now see that they were partial. All error, not merely verbal, is a strong way of stating that the current truth is incomplete. The follies of youth have a basis in sound reason, just as much as the embarrassing questions put by babes and sucklings. Their most anti-social acts indicate the defects of our society. When the torrent sweeps the man against a boulder, you must expect him to scream, and you need not be surprised if the scream is sometimes a theory. Shelley, chafing at the Church of England, discovered the cure of all evils in universal atheism. Generous lads irritated at the injustices of society, see nothing for it but the abolishment of everything and Kingdom Come of anarchy. Shelley was a young fool; so are these cock-sparrow revolutionaries. But it is better to be a fool than to be dead. It is better to emit a scream in the shape of a theory than to be entirely insensible to the jars and incongruities of life and take everything as it comes in a forlorn stupidity. Some people swallow the universe like a pill; they travel on through the world, like smiling images pushed from behind. For God's sake give me the young man who has brains enough to make a fool of himself!

In 1888 journalist and aspiring novelist James Barrie wrote: "Of living authors none perhaps bewitches the reader more than Mr. Stevenson, who plays upon words as if they were a musical instrument. To follow the music is less difficult than to place the musician."[2] Stevenson worked diligently to develop a unique and elegant prose style, but, with few exceptions, his stories are not mere examples of technique, as some hasty dilettantes have claimed. In a 1951 lecture at Yale University, David Daiches commented:

> An anonymous person reviewing my little book on Stevenson in a magazine called *Time* thought fit to rebuke me for making Stevenson out to be a serious writer, offering the original observation that Stevenson was a fine writer of rollicking tales of adventure and could not therefore (presumably) merit consideration on any more serious literary standard. But I think we have been fooled long enough by stereotypes of Stevenson which simply do not correspond to the facts.[3]

With very few exceptions, Stevenson's characterizations and themes are not lost amid stylistic virtuosity, as Joseph Conrad once suggested.[4] Daiches argued that Stevenson's early work does not lack substance but has an "unevenness of texture": "And contrary to what is often thought, it is not the fault of a man with nothing to say and lots of fancy ways of saying it, but of a man with more to say than he quite knows how to handle."[5]

Some realistically minded critics

assume that Stevenson's adventures exist only in a bygone era when romance and escapism were the rule of the day. But Stevenson held no illusions that literature, or any art, could reproduce reality. In "A Humble Remonstrance," his 1884 rejoinder to Henry James's "The Art of Fiction," he writes:

> Life is monstrous, infinite, illogical, abrupt and poignant; a work of art, in comparison, is neat, finite, self-contained, rational, flowing and emaculate. Life imposes by brute energy, like inarticulate thunder; art catches the ear among the far louder noises of experience, like an air artificially made by a discreet musician. ... The novel, which is a work of art, exists, not by its resemblances to life, which are forced and material, as a shoe must still consist of leather, but by its immeasurable difference from life, which is designed and significant, and is both the method and the meaning of the work.

In a December 1884 letter to James, Stevenson argues:

> People suppose it is the "stuff" that interests them; they think, for instance, that the prodigious fine thoughts and sentiments in Shakespeare impress by their own weight, not understanding that the unpolished diamond is but a stone. They think that striking situations, or good dialogue, are got by studying life; they will not rise to understand that they are prepared by deliberate artifice and set off by painful suppressions.[6]

Stevenson was a brilliant stylist, but he did not believe that beautiful prose was the sine qua non of literature: "From all its chapters, from all its pages, from all its sentences, the well-written novel echoes and re-echoes its one creative and controlling thought; to this must every incident and character contribute; the style must have been pitched in unison with this; and if there is anywhere a word that looks another way, the book would be stronger, clearer, and (I had almost said) fuller without it." "Thrawn Janet" (1881), *Treasure Island,* and "The Merry Men" (1882) are among the most unified of Stevenson's early stories. Wordiness dominates on rare occasions, as in portions of *Prince Otto* (1885), but his later, more mature works reinforce his literary ideal: *Kidnapped, The Ebb-Tide,* "The Beach of Falesa," and the majority of *The Master of Ballantrae* are powerful examples of artistic unison, and *Weir of Hermiston,* even in its unfinished form, is a harmonious masterwork that literally sings off the page.

Stevenson occasionally borrowed an idea or device from the stories of his favorite authors, but he was not content to emulate others. As Edwin Eigner writes, he "did not base his art on the daydream literature of Scott, but on the artistically and intellectually controlled romances of Victor Hugo, for whom 'the moral significance,' Stevenson wrote, 'is the essence of the romance; it is the organizing principle.'"[7] In "A Gossip on Romance" Stevenson refers to Scott as "out and away the king of the romantics," but admits that he could be "slovenly" and "ungrammatical," a man with "splendid romantic ... and tragic gifts" who "could so often fob us off with languid, inarticulate twaddle."[8] Throughout his fictional canon, Stevenson's carefully detailed prose follows a logical structure; Scott, he claims, could be "utterly careless" in creating a scene. To illustrate his observations, Stevenson quotes a sentence from Scott's 1815 novel *Guy Mannering*:

"A damsel, who, close behind a fine spring about half-way down the descent and which had once supplied the castle with water, was engaged in bleaching linen." A man who gave in such copy would be discharged from the staff of a daily paper. Scott has forgotten to prepare the reader for the presence of the "damsel"; he has forgotten to mention the spring and its relation to the ruin; and now, face to face with his omission, instead of trying back and starting fair, crams all this matter, tail foremost into a single shambling sentence. It is not merely bad English, or bad style; it is abominably bad narrative besides.

In his 1888 essay on Stevenson, Henry James observes, "Each of his books is an independent effort—a window opened to a different view."[9] Stevenson consistently experimented with style, structure, setting, and characterization, and he used his versatility to explore several basic themes. Influenced by the tales of historical and religious strife he had heard during his youth, he was fascinated by human conflict—simultaneously the struggle between rival social and political factions, individuals, and the opposing forces operating within the human psyche. His serious illnesses reinforced his understanding and appreciation of perseverance, a concept first instilled in him by his Calvinist parents and nurse. His interest in evil began during childhood, and his literary endeavors illustrate an evolution in his ability to depict the complexity of human behavior and interaction. His characters are neither good nor evil; while each may lean toward one of these moral extremes, all exhibit degrees of both. The abilities of a primarily "evil" person are often as appealing as those of a "heroic" one, and his blurring of moral boundaries maintains dramatic tension until the very end, when the struggle either is resolved or, in some cases, continues. He is careful to stress that solutions to major problems are usually costly and tenuous at best. In his 1887 essay on a novel by Alexandre Dumas, he writes, "There is no quite good book without a good morality; but the world is wide, and so are morals."[10]

While Stevenson's frequent depiction of resourceful young characters has led many to believe that he was a children's author, this motif is one of the keys to understanding the thematics of his fiction. The significance of imperfect young protagonists like Jim Hawkins and David Balfour is at least fourfold: they reflect the author's desire to seek adventure and freedom from physical and societal restraints, but they also symbolize the human quest to control the environment, portray the human ability to mature in the face of adversity, and provide a contrast to the self-serving, unpredictable, and ambivalent behavior of adults, many of whom possess the psychological duality that Stevenson presents most vividly in *The Strange Case of Dr. Jekyll and Mr. Hyde*. The determination of inexperienced young people is often superior to that of seasoned veterans who, in several instances, benefit from the efforts of their youthful cohorts.

The trial-and-error actions of Stevenson's young characters may be viewed as a function of his overall moral vision. In his fictional milieu the behavior and values of both children and adults often are dictated by specific circumstances, and their fluctuating moral views help to maintain narrative interest and movement. In his best stories, his prose style is an outgrowth of this and other thematic elements, and, partly for this reason, his plots rarely become staid or predictable.

Many of his stories lack visible female characters, but he did not ignore women out of prejudice or indifference, as some critics have charged. Robert Kiely's assertion that he "shunned dealing with any but the most superficial relationships between the sexes"[11] is refuted by passages in *The Black Arrow*, *Prince Otto*, "The Beach of Falesa," and *Weir of Hermiston*. The scarcity of major females in his early stories may be attributed to several factors: the dearth of realistic sexual elements in Victorian popular fiction, the traditional absence of women in the adventure genre, the male-dominated historical eras in which the tales are set, and the audience for which he was writing. The stories first appeared in periodicals and boys' adventure magazines that were read predominantly by males. During the mid- to late 1880s his readership expanded and, as his literary talent continued to evolve, stronger and more interesting women began to appear.

Stevenson freely recognized his literary shortcomings; in 1890 he wrote that only two of his female creations pleased him.[12] But, even as late as 1892, when an editor sought to expurgate "The Beach of Falesa," his attempts at female characterization were constricted by Victorian prudishness. On January 31 of that year he wrote to Sidney Colvin: "This is a poison-bad world for the romancer, this Anglo-Saxon world; I usually get out of it by not having any women in it at all; but when I remember I had "The Treasure of Franchard" refused as unfit for a family magazine, I feel despair weigh upon my wrists."[13] While most of Stevenson's women are not fully developed personalities, a majority are attractive, proud, and intelligent, and it can be argued that the unconventional behavior of a few offsets the stilted love scenes that occasionally mar his work. Married to an independent and canny woman, he thought little of men who treated the lasses as sex objects. In his 1879 essay "Some Aspects of Robert Burns," he writes of the great bard's decision to marry a pregnant lover: "It is the punishment of Don Juanism to create continually false positions— relations in life which are wrong in themselves, and which it is equally wrong to break or to perpetuate. This was such a case. Worldly Wiseman would have laughed and gone his way; let us be glad that Burns was better counselled by his heart." In another passage Stevenson's reference to Burns's "dual" nature predates many of his fictional explorations: "If he had been strong enough to refrain or bad enough to persevere in evil; if he had only not been Don Juan at all, or been Don Juan altogether, there had been some possible road for him throughout this troublesome world; but a man, alas! who is equally at the call of his worse and better instincts, stands among changing events without foundation or resource."

Several of Stevenson's best stories are rooted in his own experiences, and autobiographical references can be found throughout his work. Beset by illness and relative isolation during his early years, he developed many of his artistic and social ideas through independent study—a fact that, in part, accounts for the self-absorption and egoism that some of his biographers have referred to. In a general sense, his love of the outdoors and his brilliant remembrances of topographical detail permeate all of his work, while specific autobiographical motifs include familial strife and estrangement and major characters that he patterned after himself. The human duality that he continually explored is symbolized vividly by conservative fathers who disown their rebellious sons in "The Misadventures of John Nicholson" and *Weir of Hermiston,* and by brothers who are torn apart by disagreements over politics, riches, and women in *The Master of Ballantrae.*

Stevenson's well-drawn characters have been underrated by critics who view his work as a series of striking and memorable incidents. In "A Humble Remonstrance" Stevenson defines three specific novelistic genres: the novel of adventure, the novel of character, and the dramatic novel. The adventure, he claims, includes a limited amount of characterization and appeals to "sensual and quite illogical tendencies":

> Danger is the matter with which this class of novel deals; fear, the passion with which it idly trifles; and the characters are portrayed only so far as they realize the sense of danger and provoke the sympathy of fear. To add more traits, to be too clever, to start the hare of moral or intellectual interest while we are running the fox of material interest, is not to enrich but to stultify your tale. The stupid reader will only be offended, and the clever reader lose the scent.

By contrast, the novel of character requires no coherency of plot: "It turns on the humours of the persons represented; these are, to be sure, embodied in incidents, but the incidents themselves, being tributary, need not march in a progression; and the characters may be statically shown." The dramatic novel, he writes, is sometimes misconceived as incident-related: "The actors may come anyhow upon the stage: we do not care; the point is, that, before they leave it, they shall become transfigured and raised out of themselves by passion. A novel of this class may be even great, and yet contain no individual figure." The majority of Stevenson's fiction combines elements of the second genre with those of the first; his adventures appeal to the reader's sensual tendencies, but they also offer characterizations and themes of various complexities. It comes as no surprise that his tales have endured while those of more conventional writers have been forgotten. On the other hand, his dramatic efforts, namely the four rather pedestrian plays he cowrote with W. E. Henley, have been consigned to dusty library shelves for more than a century.

Stevenson's supernatural stories, ranging from grim historical melodramas to parabolic fantasies of South Sea genies, are among his most famous works, but his forays into levity are recognized infrequently. The dark, farcical work, *The Wrong Box,* is his most obvious attempt at humor, but subtle and observant wit graces many of his tales.

Regardless of genre, Stevenson sometimes found it difficult to write a satisfactory ending for a long story or novel, and his tendency to grow tired of one project and turn to another contributed to this problem. Many of his most convincing plots are set in Scotland, a heath to which he became more attached as his "exile" continued. More than one-third of his published fictional works, whole or in part, take place there, and his fervent interest in the history, culture, and traditional dialect of his homeland imbues them with a unique ambience. Gordon Donaldson and Robert Morpeth write: "For his short working life and his poor health, his output was remarkable, and his works, besides their admirable style, show an appreciation of Scottish life and a sense of Scottish history which no writer has surpassed."[14]

In his 1882 essay "The Foreigner at Home," Stevenson, while generalizing about Scottish youth, recalls some of his own early experiences:

> A Scottish child hears much of shipwreck, outlying iron skerries, pitiless breakers, and great sealights; much of heathery mountains, wild clans, and hunted Covenanters. Breaths come to him in song of the distant Cheviots and the ring of foraying hoofs. He glories in his hard-fisted forefathers, of the iron girdle and the handful of oatmeal, who rode as swiftly and lived so sparely on their raids. Poverty, ill-luck, enterprise, and constant resolution are the fibres of the legend of his country's history.

Stevenson attempted to discover a Highland ancestry for his family and, at the request of his father, did research in 1880 for a projected history of the region. Neither endeavor was completed successfully, but his studies proved invaluable during the composition of several tales, particularly *Kidnapped* and *Catriona.*

But Stevenson's attitude toward Scotland was not a wholly positive one: the damp climate and even colder religious and social values of Victorian Edinburgh troubled him both physically and morally. His bohemian rejection of conventional wisdom was as much a product of Scottish culture as was his affection for the nation's history and awe-inspiring natural beauty; and his fascination with rebels like Allan Breck and Bonnie Prince Charlie reflected both of these factors—complex feelings that helped spur the ambivalent moral tone of his fiction.

Stevenson's 1878 essay "Edinburgh: Picturesque Notes" features his first-hand impressions of the legendary city. Early in chapter one, a passage describing the palace of Holyroodhouse illustrates his faith in the enduring significance of the Scottish past:

The palace of Holyrood has been left aside in the growth of Edinburgh; and stands grey and silent in a workman's quarter and among breweries and gas works. It is a house of many memories. Great people of yore, kings and queens, buffoons and grave ambassadors, played their stately farce for centuries in Holyrood. Wars have been plotted, dancing has lasted deep into the night, murder has been done in its chambers. There Prince Charlie held his phantom levees, and in a very gallant manner represented a fallen dynasty for some hours. Now, all these things of clay are mingled with the dust, the king's crown itself is shown for sixpence to the vulgar; but the stone palace has outlived these changes.

Here, Stevenson presents deathless elements that live on in the modern, industrial era—a portrait that anticipates the thematics of his Scottish stories. Excepting "The Misadventures of John Nicholson," which takes place during his own lifetime, all of the Scottish tales offer fictionalized depictions of the past in which ageless conflicts are explored. His incorporation of historical events does not date his work, but imbues it with a transcendental quality. In chapter four of "Edinburgh" ("Legends"), he explains: "The character of a place is often most perfectly expressed in its associations. An event strikes root and grows into a legend, when it has happened amongst congenial surroundings. Ugly actions, above all in ugly places, have the true romantic quality, and become an undying property of their scene."

Macabre works such as "Thrawn Janet," his first thoroughly Scottish story, and the only one written entirely in the Scots dialect, "The Body-Snatcher" (1881), and "The Merry Men" mirror his opinion that the Scots "stand ... highest among nations in the matter of grimly illustrating death":

> We seem to love for their own sake the emblems of time and the great change; and even around country churches you will find a wonderful exhibition of skulls, and crossbones, and noseless angels, and trumpets pealing for the Judgement Day. Every mason was a pedestrian Holbein: he had a deep consciousness of death, and loved to put its terrors pithily before the churchyard loiterer; he was brimful of rough hints upon mortality, and any dead farmer was seized upon to be a text.[15]

Stevenson strengthened his historical settings and characterizations with convincing doses of Scots dialogue and excerpts from Scottish poems and songs. Several passages in *Kidnapped* and *The Master of Ballantrae* are enhanced by his use of Jacobite music, a genre that was still popular in nineteenth-century Scotland. Over two dozen of Stevenson's Scots poems, some of which were based on traditional songs, have been published. Like Robert Burns, he enjoyed writing words for Scottish airs, including "Wandering Willie" (poem 17 in *Songs of Travel*) and "Over the Sea to Skye" (unpublished verses found in the Vailima library after his death). "Over the Water to Chairlie," a poem that commemorates Stevenson's trip to Malie in 1892, was inspired by Burns's Jacobite ode "O'er the Water to Charlie," but it also bears similarities to a later Jacobite song, "Wha'll Be King But Cherlie?" by

Caroline Oliphant (Lady Nairne), whose father had been aide de camp to Bonnie Prince Charlie during the 1745 Rebellion. The first line of the poem is borrowed from Burns, and the remainder closely follows the meter of Lady Nairne's composition.

Stevenson's poems were inspired, in part, by Burns (1759–96) and Robert Fergusson (1750–74), a tragic bard who admirably depicted Edinburgh's "sordid pleasures"; acclaimed by Stevenson as "Burns's master in his art," Fergusson died in an asylum "while yet a stripling."[16] While discussing the respective accomplishments of these two poets in "Some Aspects of Robert Burns," Stevenson voices his appreciation of the Scots language:

> [W]henever Scotch poets left their laborious imitations of bad English verses, and fell back on their own dialect, their style would kindle, and they would write of their convivial and somewhat gross existences with pith and point. In [Allan] Ramsay, and far more in the poor lad Fergusson, there was mettle, humour, literary courage, and a power of saying what they wished to say definitely and brightly. . . . Had Burns died at the same age as Fergusson, he would have left us literally nothing worth remark. To Ramsay and to Fergusson, then, he was indebted in a very uncommon degree, not only following their tradition and using their measures, but directly and avowedly imitating their pieces.

In 1987 the members of Battlefield Band, a traditional Scottish group, noted, "Each wave of emigration in our country's history seems to wash home the seeds of the next one. Generations of this process have bred a kind of Scot who is driven to roam, a compulsive traveller whose personality becomes more identifiably Scottish the further it gets from home."[17] A century earlier Stevenson, roving among the islands of the South Pacific, experienced this phenomenon as his literary talent continued to evolve. His recollections of Scotland, and particularly Edinburgh, were vibrant and plentiful, and they set the stage upon which triumph and tragedy are played. He derived tremendous inspiration from his surroundings and, as his non–Scottish stories also demonstrate, the cultures of regions in which he lived and traveled—including France, the United States, and the South Seas—are well represented in his fiction. In the conclusion of "Edinburgh" he writes:

> [E]very place is a centre to the earth, whence highways radiate or ships set sail for foreign ports; the limit of a parish is not more imaginary than the frontier of an empire; and as a man sitting at home in his cabinet and swiftly writing books, so a city sends abroad an influence and a portrait of herself. There is no Edinburgh emigrant, far or near, from China to Peru, but he or she carries some lively pictures of the mind, some sunset behind the Castle cliffs, some snow scene, some maze of city lamps, indelible in the memory and delightful to study in the intervals of toil.

At the time of his death, Stevenson's thoughts were turned toward Scotland: *Weir of Hermiston* remained unfinished, as did *Heathercat*, a novel fragment set during the Covenanting resistances of the late seventeenth century, and *The*

*Young Chevalier,* a fragment focusing on Bonnie Prince Charlie's life in France after the 1745 Rebellion. Reminiscent of Prince Charlie's desperate escape from Scotland in 1746, poem 44 of *Songs of Travel,* written in the South Seas, symbolizes Stevenson's captivation with his Scottish heritage:

> Sing me a song of a lad that is
>     gone,
>   Say, could that lad be I?
> Merry of soul he sailed on a day
>   Over the sea to Skye.
>
> Mull was astern, Rum on the port,
>   Eigg on the starboard bow;
> Glory of youth glowed in his soul:
>   Where is that glory now?
>
> Sing me a song of a lad that is
>     gone,
>   Say, could that lad be I?
> Merry of soul he sailed on a day
>   Over the sea to Skye.
>
> Give me again all that was there,
>   Give me the sun that shown!
> Give me the eyes, give me the soul,
>   Give me the lad that's gone!
>
> Sing me a song of a lad that is
>     gone,
>   Say, could that lad be I?
> Merry of soul he sailed on a day
>   Over the sea to Skye.
>
> Billow and breeze, islands and
>     seas,
>   Mountains of rain and sun,
> All that was good, all that was fair,
>   All that was me is gone.

• FOUR •

# A Little Piece of Ingenuity: "The Sire de Maletroit's Door" (1877)

> *Lads were early formed in that rough, warfaring epoch; and when one has been in a pitched battle and a dozen raids, has killed one's man in an honourable fashion, and knows a thing or two about strategy and mankind, a certain swagger in the gait is surely to be pardoned.* —From the opening paragraph of "The Sire de Maletroit's Door."

In September 1429, 21-year-old cavalier Denis de Beaulieu is allowed safe conduct by a mixed command of Burgundian and English troops as he travels through the French countryside. Turning out of the rainy weather into the home of a friend, he stays long after the midnight hour. Disoriented by a night "as black as the grave," Beaulieu attempts to find his lodgings but stumbles into a narrow, walled passage in which he is confronted by a band of roving men-at-arms. He gropes along the wall, leans against a mysterious door, and enters the hidden portal of a house "of some pretentions." Unable to reopen the door from the inside, he finds himself in "a large apartment of polished stone" where he is greeted by the inhospitable Alain, Sire de Maletroit, whose niece, Blanche, has become involved in a premarital love affair. Misidentified as her lover, Beaulieu is told that he will be hanged if he does not marry her immediately. He considers dueling his way out but is prevented by the Sire, who acquaints him with a "dusky passage full of armed men."

Maletroit leaves the two "lovers" alone in a private chapel, allowing Beaulieu two hours to decide whether he will marry or be hanged. First choosing to fight and die, Beaulieu impresses Blanche when he proposes marriage, forgetting the previous love affair that so enraged the Sire. Pleased with the young cavalier's decision, Maletroit welcomes him into the family.

Stevenson's first published story,

"An Old Song," appeared anonymously as four installments in *London* from February 24 to March 17, 1877. During the ensuing spring and summer he wrote "A Lodging for the Night: A Story of François Villon," an exciting tale of theft, murder, and social conflict which was published in the October 1877 issue of *Temple Bar*. His third professional fictional effort, "Will o' the Mill," was written from June to July 1877, and during the following month he wrote "The Sire de Maletroit's Door"; in January 1878 both of these stories appeared in print, the former in *Cornhill Magazine* and the latter in *Temple Bar*.

"The Sire de Maletroit's Door" is a simple but fantastic adventure tale depicting a protagonist who loses his way in unfamiliar territory; forced to escape from an unpleasant situation, he finds himself in an even worse predicament. Throughout the tale and particularly at its climax, Denis de Beaulieu must surmount the challenges of a harsh environment (surviving in less than ideal conditions—a Stevenson motif.)

Stevenson's interest in French medieval history is apparent in the story's early stages. Although he does not mention a specific armed conflict, the tale is set during the Hundred Years' War (1337–1453), in which the English repeatedly invaded and occupied France. Claiming that their kings had a legitimate right to the French throne, Englishmen devastated crops, sacked towns and castles, and made large fortunes from the spoils of war. In 1429 (the year in which the story is set), Joan of Arc was on the march, relieving Orléans from English occupation and attempting to recapture Paris. A year later she was captured and tortured by the English, who, in 1431, burned her to death at Rouen for being a "witch" and a "relapsed heretic."

In 1407 the French split into two opposing camps: the Armagnacs, who supported the royal establishment, and the Burgundians, who offered military aid to the English in exchange for troops. When the story begins, the (unidentified) town is commanded by a coalition of English and Burgundians. Upon viewing the Maletroit home, Beaulieu is reminded of "a town house of his own at Bourges," the location of the French dauphin, King Charles VII's court during the 1420s. Although "The Sire de Maletroit's Door" is a romantic adventure tale, Stevenson weaves fictional events into a quasi-realistic setting.

Beaulieu and Maletroit are driven by the code of chivalry, which advocated the protection of a noble maiden's premarital honor. Beaulieu respectfully agrees to marry Blanche but tells her, "I love you better than the whole world" (which is not surprising, considering the way the rest of the world treats him). Maletroit is driven by chivalrous intent and by family honor, the latter a concept important to the nobility of fifteenth-century Europe. After demanding that Beaulieu marry his niece, the Sire explains:

> Your family, Monsieur de Beaulieu, is very well in its way; but if you sprang from Charlemagne, you should not refuse the hand of a

Maletroit with impunity—not if she had been as common as the Paris road—not if she were as hideous as the gargoyle over my door. Neither my niece, nor you, nor my own private feelings, move me at all in this matter. The honor of my house has been compromised; I believe you to be the guilty person, at least you are now in the secret; and you can hardly wonder if I request you to wipe out the stain. If you will not, your blood be on your own head! It will be no great satisfaction to me to have your interesting relics kicking their heels in the breeze below my windows, but half a loaf is better than no bread, and if I cannot cure the dishonor, I shall at least stop the scandal.

Here Maletroit shows that the external rituals of noble society override any individual concerns that each of them may have. To uphold the code of chivalry Beaulieu must aid Blanche, and either die for her and the family honor or marry only at her request. An unpleasant and suspenseful dilemma is resolved when Beaulieu accepts the demands of society and preserves the nobility of the Maletroits.

Stevenson uses detailed description throughout the story: the geography of the town, the appearance of Maletroit's estate, and the characterizations are incorporated into a highly visual, adventurous whole. His portrait of the Sire is a particular highlight:

> On a high chair beside the chimney, and directly facing Denis as he entered, sat a little old gentleman in a fur tippet. He sat with his legs crossed and his hands folded, and a cup of spiced wine stood by his elbow on a bracket on the wall. His countenance had a strongly masculine cast; not properly human, but such as we see in a bull, the goat or the domestic boar; something equivocal and wheedling, something greedy, brutal, and dangerous. The upper lip was inordinately full, as though swollen by a blow or a toothache; and the smile, the peaked eyebrows, and the small strong eyes were quaintly and almost comically evil in expression. Beautiful white hair hung straight all round his head, like a saint's, and fell in a single curl upon the tippet. His beard and moustache were the pink of venerable sweetness. Age, probably in consequence of inordinate precautions, had left no mark upon his hands; and the Maletroit hand was famous. It would be difficult to imagine anything at once so fleshy and so delicate in design; the taper, sensual fingers were like those of one of Leonardo's women; the fork of the thumb made a dimpled protuberance when closed; the nails were perfectly shaped, and of a dead, surprising whiteness. It rendered his aspect tenfold more redoubtable, that a man with hands like these should keep them devoutly folded like a virgin martyr—that a man with so intent and startling an expression of face should sit patiently on his seat and contemplate people with an unwinking stare, like a god, or a god's statue. His quiescence seemed ironical and treacherous, it fitted so poorly with his looks.

In this passage Stevenson's moral objectivity is demonstrated through his use of style and content. Rather than presenting a one-dimensional villain, he imbues the Sire with both bad and good qualities: Maletroit is "not properly human," "greedy," "brutal," and "treacherous," but he also possessed attributes that are "beautiful," "like a saint's," "the pink of venerable sweetness," and "like a virgin martyr." Stevenson weaves animalistic qualities ("the bull, the goat, or the domestic boar") with those that are more gentle and aesthetic ("like those of one of Leonardo's women"). In a single paragraph he creates a fascinating, ambivalent character and an account of great literary beauty and power. Even the Sire's later behavior does not destroy this earlier depiction.

Stevenson also displays detailed yet unadorned prose when he combines physical description with Beaulieu's troubled psychological state:

> There he sat playing with the guard of his rapier, and wishing himself dead a thousand times over, and buried in the nastiest kitchen-heap in France. His eyes wandered round the apartment, but found nothing to arrest them. There were such wide spaces between the furniture, the light fell so badly and cheerlessly over all, the dark outside air looked in so coldly through the windows that he thought he had never seen a church so vast, nor a tomb so melancholy. The regular sobs of Blanche de Maletroit measured out the time like the ticking of a clock. He read the device upon the shield over and over again, until his eyes became obscured; he stared into shadowy corners until he imagined they were swarming with horrible animals; and every now and again he awoke with a start, to remember that his last two hours were running, and death was on the march.

Although some situations are deliberately fantastic, Stevenson's romantic style, sense of movement (both somewhat reminiscent of Edgar Allan Poe), and use of history add credibility to the tale. As Richard Rice observed in 1916, "in no other spot in all Stevenson will you so nearly find the acme of adventure as you do in those twenty pages."[1]

## *The Strange Door* (Universal-International, 1951)

Released in November 1951, Universal-International's *The Strange Door* does not represent "the acme of adventure." The film incorporates the marriage subplot from the story, but Jerry Sackheim's "eighteenth-century" screenplay is a hackneyed mess, devoid of characterization and narrative development. All references to the Hundred Years' War are discarded, an aspect that greatly affects the intent and actions of the characters. (Perhaps setting the tale three centuries later saved the studio money, considering that Hollywood produced scores of eighteenth-century costume melodramas, and prop material could be found readily.)

As the first scene opens, the Sire (Charles Laughton) arrives at the Red Lion tavern, where he plots with two henchman to snare Denis de Beaulieu (Richard Stapley), a brash, obnoxious young man who is forcing himself upon a woman at the bar. After angering the rogue, one of the hirelings feigns death while dueling with him. Beaulieu then exits the tavern and hails a coach driven by another of Maletroit's confidants. Soon he arrives at "the strange door."

At this point, Stevenson's plot is followed for about five minutes, but much of the character motivation is destroyed. The Sire is depicted not as a man attempting to maintain his family honor but as a self-serving maniac seeking revenge against Blanche (Sally Forrest) and other Maletroits dreamed up by Sackheim. The theme of the story is altered when Laughton's bloated and outrageous Sire describes his vengeful intent: to destroy Blanche, whose birth caused the death of her mother (a woman whom he had loved, but who had married his brother, Edmond, instead), he sets out to marry her to Beaulieu. Having imprisoned Edmond (Paul Cavanagh) in a subterranean dungeon shortly after Blanche's birth, the Sire schemes to complete the last stage of his plan.

Though the subplot incorporates Stevenson's motif of familial conflict, it is simplistic and contrived: Edmond, planning to escape, feigns insanity to allay his brother's suspicions; aided by his faithful servant, Voltan (Boris Karloff), he awaits an opportunity. The forced marriage takes place, but after the couple attempts to flee the Sire throws them into Edmond's cell and sets an outdoor mill wheel in motion. Engaging a series of gears, the wheel powers the dungeon walls, which close in on the three helpless prisoners. Seriously wounded (stabbed, shot, then stabbed again by the Sire and his accomplices), Voltan swims the moat, tosses Maletroit to his death and, crawling along the dungeon floor as he takes his final breath, slides a key into the cell. In the nick of time, Edmond and the loving couple escape a terrible death.

More incredible than Sackheim's script are the opening credits, which read, "Robert Louis Stevenson's *The Strange Door*." Stevenson wrote neither a story with that title nor the insipid and time-worn elements worked into the narrative by Sackheim and director Joseph Pevney. Even accounting for the cinematic metamorphosis and the problems involved with stretching a short story to feature film length, *The Strange Door* is arguably one of Hollywood's worst adaptations of a literary work.

In the early scenes the film replaces Stevenson's morally ambiguous Sire with a deranged and vengeful character who refers to the marriage of Blanche and Beaulieu not as a token of the Maletroit honor but as a "game." "I know my uncle is an evil man," Blanche tells her fiancé (a man far more odious than the Stevenson character) at one point, noting "some fiendish reason" for his behavior. Her "young captain" (called Armand) is mentioned, but a love affair is never alluded to. The Sire fears that his niece will become an old maid but describes Armand as "neglectful" and unworthy of her hand. Allowing Blanche and Beaulieu 24 hours to make their decision, he tells a lackey that her husband must be a "blackguard and scoundrel," and later admits to Blanche that he has killed Armand. Laughton's Sire is thoroughly disgusting, a man who possesses no positive qualities. "He's a madman," Blanche remarks at one point, and even Maletroit himself speaks of his wicked personality:

*The Strange Door* (1951). Edmond de Maletroit (Paul Cavanagh) and Voltan (Boris Karloff), the "malevolent" servant, in Universal-International's insipid adaptation of "The Sire de Maletroit's Door."

"In my secluded dominion, villainy binds men together."

Beaulieu's appearance at the Maletroit estate does not result from an accidental meeting with (presumably Armagnac) men-at-arms; instead, the young cavalier is driven and chased to "the strange door" by the Sire's armed scoundrels. Stevenson conceptualizes a character affected by historical forces, while the film offers a simplistic Hollywood cliché involving a mad nobleman and an unsuspecting adventurer.

Unable to take the project seriously, Laughton is somewhat subdued in the early scenes but overacts outrageously throughout the film's second half. Frequently shouting his dialogue before breaking into a ridiculous horse laugh, he gorges himself at the dinner table: writhing in labored hilarity, he yells, "This mutton's good!" as he bites into a roasted chop. It is not difficult to imagine why the actor took this approach, particularly when Sackheim gave him such lines as "I'm in the mood for relaxation. Let's visit the dungeons."

The literary Denis de Beaulieu does not appear in the screenplay: Stevenson's wandering cavalier demonstrates sensitivity and chivalry, but Sackheim's character (portrayed by the lackluster Stapley) is as repulsive as the pompous Sire. Early in the film, he is shown killing a man, and later, Maletroit speaks of his unsavory "reputation." Hearing of the marriage plot, Beaulieu states, "This lady is too pure, too noble, for a man of my tastes—a far cry from Stevenson's prose: "though I will die for you blithely, it would be like all the joys of Paradise to live on and spend my life in your service." When the cinematic Beaulieu meets Blanche in his bedroom at night, he violently grabs and kisses her before stating, "I was expecting a toothless hag."

One of the film's most hackneyed moments occurs when the Sire first threatens Beaulieu. Insisting that the young man marry his niece, he draws a red-hot poker from the fire and holds up the end to the unemotional rogue's face. He then withdraws it, extinguishes the glow in a tankard of wine, and empties the liquid onto Beaulieu's head. But Beaulieu's anachronistic reply to the marriage offer is even worse: "I'm not the domestic type," he quips.

The cinematic characters extraneous to the story are superfluous, appearing sporadically to break the monotony of the stilted and overlong narrative. The addition of Edmond de Maletroit, although well acted by Paul Cavanagh, detracts from the literary premise, and Boris Karloff's tongue-in-cheek Voltan merely is grafted into certain scenes, a character created strictly for marquee value. Saddled with limited expression and ridiculous dialogue, Karloff plays a one-dimensional horror stooge (albeit with redeeming features) in an adaptation of a story that by no means belongs in the horror genre.

Ironically, Universal appears to have spent more money on their advertising campaign than on the film, including the hype "Robert Louis Stevenson's Masterpiece of Terror!" on several colorful, very attractive posters (all of which are visually superior to Joseph Pevney's cramped and static direction). Perhaps the most interesting aspect of the film is the fact that while Edmond, living in a filthy, stinking dungeon for 20 years, maintains his sanity, the Sire, lounging in the wealth and luxury of the ancestral castle, becomes a raving lunatic.

## "The Sire de Maletroit's Door" on Television

In 1951 BBC 1 aired an English television adaptation of "The Sire de Maletroit's Door." The only small-screen version of the tale, it was broadcast a few months before Universal-International released *The Strange Door.*

• FIVE •

# Bound Together by a Formidable Oath: "The Suicide Club" (1878)

> *"I cannot put a pistol to my head and draw the trigger; for something stronger than myself withholds the act; and although I loathe life, I have not the strength enough in my body to take hold of death and be done with it."*—The young man with the cream tarts in "The Suicide Club."

## "Story of the Young Man with the Cream Tarts"

One March evening in London the incognito Prince Florizel of Bohemia and his confidant, Master of the Horse Colonel Geraldine, venture into a Leicester Square oyster bar. The prince soon tires of his surroundings, but he is impressed by an eccentric young man and two commissionaires who carry covered dishes of cream tarts into the tavern. The man offers a pastry to each of the patrons but, upon refusal, eats one and moves on. Claiming that several more must be disposed of before the night is out, he appeals to Florizel's unbridled sense of adventure.

After visiting three more taverns, the man reveals that his jest concealed an ulterior motive: a recruitment of members for a secret organization known as the Suicide Club. Florizel (using the pseudonym "Mr. Godall") learns that "ruined" men may join the organization for a one-time fee of £40; in exchange, the person unable to commit suicide may have his life ended institutionally.

Florizel and Geraldine accompany the man to a "rather dark court," where they are introduced to the president of the Suicide Club. During a macabre card game, the president determines which member will die. An "honorary" member, the paralytic Mr. Malthus, turns up the death card and is killed by "the official of the night"—the young man with the cream tarts—later that evening.

The next morning Florizel reads about the "accident" and plans to stop the insidious president's murderous activities. During a second game that night, he receives the death card and awaits the appearance of his "murderer" in Box Court. Thrust into a carriage, he is surprised to meet Geraldine and two companions. Florizel then vows to help the "foolish and wicked" members of the club, and he exiles the president to "a little tour of the Continent" in the company of Geraldine's younger brother, an officer and accomplished marksman.

## "Story of the Physician and the Saratoga Trunk"

Silas Q. Scuddamore, a young American vacationing in Paris, becomes interested in Madame Zephyrine, a mysterious woman who occupies a neighboring hotel room. Hoping to meet her, he accepts an anonymous invitation to a gala ball and, subsequently, agrees to rendezvous near the Luxembourg Gardens the following evening.

Silas arrives at the tryst but finds no one there. Back at the hotel, he is startled by a porter who inquires about the "short, blond young man" in his room. Silas searches through the dark until he feels the outline of a human leg in his bed. Discovering a dead body, he recoils in terror and, unable to formulate a plan, falls asleep. Soon he is awakened by Dr. Noel, an acquaintance who offers to help dispose of the body.

Advising Silas to pack the corpse in his Saratoga trunk, Noel gives him two sealed envelopes: one, large and bulky, to be delivered, along with the trunk, to a London address indicated in the second, smaller enclosure. The doctor then admits that he was once "chieftain" of a criminal organization "bound together by a formidable oath, and working to the same purposes; the trade of the association was in murder"; the person to whom the trunk must be delivered was once an underling in this organization.

Booking an incognito passage with Prince Florizel of Bohemia and Colonel Geraldine, Noel sends Scuddamore on his way. In London, Scuddamore and the prince open the trunk and discover the corpse of Geraldine's younger brother. Florizel instructs Silas to avoid further contact with Dr. Noel and reveals that, through some feat of "generous inspiration," Noel has delivered the body to the address of "the actual criminal": the president of the Suicide Club.

## "The Adventure of the Hansom Cab"

Lieutenant Brackenbury Rich, an Indian war hero, arrives at a London military club during the early spring. Disappointed that his exploits have attracted little attention, he seeks adventure in "the great battlefield of mankind." While walking, Rich is hailed by a hansom cabman who drives to a villa gate and reveals that he has been hired to "kidnap single gentlemen in evening dress ... military officers by preference." Told to address a Mr. Morris, Rich enters a lavish home and meets a group of "dashing and capable" men; when Morris confronts them, only Rich and O'Rooke, "an old red-nosed cavalry Major," agree to meet Mr. T. Godall, his prestigious employer, and "rid the earth of an insidious and bloody villain." The adventurers then accompany Morris to Rochester House, where they are joined by Prince Florizel of Bohemia and Dr. Noel. When a knife-carrying figure leaps into the room, he is halted by Florizel, who beats Morris (aka Colonel Geraldine) to the punch.

"Gentlemen . . . this is a fellow who has long eluded me, but whom, thanks to Dr. Noel, I now have tightly by the heels," Florizel admits as he challenges the president of the Suicide Club to a duel. On the grounds of the house Florizel runs through his opponent in the presence of Rich and O'Rooke, as Noel and Geraldine watch from an upstairs window.

Stevenson's fourth professional fictional work, "Latter-Day Arabian Nights," was written between March and September 1878. The three stories comprising "The Suicide Club" were published as eight weekly installments in *London* from June 8 to July 27, 1878. Four additional stories ("Story of the Bandbox," "Story of the Young Man in Holy Orders," "Story of the House with the Green Blinds," and "The Adventure of Prince Florizel and the Detective"), included under the title "The Rajah's Diamond," also were published as ten weekly installments in 1878 *London* issues (August 3, 10, 17, and 31; September 7, 14, and 28; and October 12, 19, and 26). These latter tales further describe the heroic and adventurous exploits of Prince Florizel of Bohemia, who foils several greedy individuals involved in the theft of a priceless diamond.

In 1882 all seven stories were published in *New Arabian Nights*. Also included in this edition are other Stevenson tales previously included in magazines: "A Lodging for the Night: A Story of François Villon," "The Sire de Maletroit's Door," "Providence and the Guitar" (originally published as "Leon Berthelini's Guitar" in four consecutive issues of *London* in November 1878), and "The Pavilion on the Links" (1880).

Similar to critical attitudes given to other early Stevenson stories, very little attention has been paid to "The Suicide Club." Perhaps the fantastical events included in the tales have turned critics away (and all three are very much like other contemporary stories that Stevenson admired). Here his self-admitted tendency to "ape" favorite authors occasionally is apparent. Although the obvious influences reach back to 1606 (his paraphrase of Shakespeare's *Macbeth* in "Story of the Young Man with the Cream Tarts": "Now we know that life is only a stage to play the fool upon as long as the part amuses us"), the specter of Edgar Allan Poe permeates "Story of the Physician and the Saratoga Trunk," particularly through the presence of the concealed corpse.

Instead of featuring the same protagonist in each story, Stevenson crafted the second and third tales around other characters who encounter Florizel and Geraldine. This technique (which he repeats in "The Rajah's Diamond") may seem contrived, but it fits the overall style of the trilogy. The method of weaving together strands of seemingly unconnected subplots influenced Sir Arthur Conan Doyle, an admitted admirer of Stevenson, who created a similar style in several of his Sherlock Holmes stories, including the superb *The Valley of Fear* (1914–15).

Stevenson based the trilogy on an idea by Bob Stevenson. The overall structure of "Latter-Day Arabian Nights" was to follow "the old *Thousand and One Nights* frame-story, and the tales themselves a parody of popular adventure fiction of the day."[1] Stevenson intended to weave a satire of fashionable literary figures into the more obvious adventures of Prince Florizel. Kiely writes: "the tale is not a fragment of foolishness for its own sake, but a rather broad and amusing spoof of the professional pessimists and aesthetes of the 70s and 80s: the exquisite and morbid young men portrayed and epitomized by [Algernon Charles] Swinburne and Oscar Wilde, with whom Stevenson, in the most public of his various moods, had so little patience."[2]

Although "The Suicide Club" relies more on action and incident than on depth of characterization, it benefits from economical prose and attention to detail, elements well demonstrated in "Story of the Young Man with the Cream Tarts," when Florizel and Geraldine sup with their new acquaintance:

> In a small French restaurant in Soho, which had enjoyed an exaggerated reputation for some little while, but had already begun to be forgotten, and in a private room up two pair of stairs, the three companions made a very elegant supper, and drank three or four bottles of champagne, talking the while upon indifferent subjects. The young man was fluent and gay, but he laughed louder than was natural in a person of polite breeding; his hands trembled violently, and his voice took sudden and surprising inflections, which seemed to be independent of his will.

Here Stevenson opens with a long, descriptive sentence which advances the plot and provides a look at the characters' immediate surroundings; he then repeats the technique to describe the young man, whose strange behavior foreshadows the trilogy's macabre proceedings.

## Early Film Adaptations (1909–32)

Two short adaptations of "The Suicide Club" were produced during the silent era. Very little is known about American Mutoscope-Biograph's *The Suicide Club* (1909), but a few credits remain for the British and Colonial Kinematograph Company's four-reel version released in 1914. Also titled *The Suicide Club,* the latter film was directed by Maurice Elvey and featured Montagu Love, Elizabeth Risdon, Fred Groves, and M. Gray Murray. Unfortunately, no prints of either film are known to exist.

In 1919 a German adaptation, *Unheimliche Geschichten,* was released in Europe. The film was remade, under the same title, as a sound feature in 1932.

## *Trouble for Two* (MGM, 1936)

Seventy-five minutes of Hollywood hokum, MGM's *Trouble for*

*Two* (1936) focuses on the contrived relationship between Prince Florizel of "Karovia" (Robert Montgomery, in a remarkably bad performance) and Princess Brenda (Rosalind Russell), his intended bride from "Irania," a neighboring kingdom. Scattered incidents from "Story of the Young Man with the Cream Tarts" and "The Adventure of the Hansom Cab" are included in the film, but "Story of the Physician and the Saratoga Trunk" virtually is ignored. The script of Manuel Seff and Edward E. Paramore, Jr., is a never-ending parade of clichés which incorporate a few snippets of Stevenson's dialogue to justify billing his name in the credits.

The film opens at the palace of Florizel's father, the King of Karovia (E. E. Clive), one of many vapid characters who does not appear in the story. Pompous and conservative, the king informs his court that he has spent 15 years negotiating the marriage of his son and Princess Brenda. Prince Florizel states that he will take no part in such royal opportunism, due to his lasting memory of Brenda's childhood appearance: "in pigtails" and wearing "a horse bit in her mouth."

When "The Suicide Club" begins, the prince is in London, seeking adventure and a break from the monotony of royal life. Having nothing in common with the story, the first 20 minutes of the film are dedicated to the invented marriage plot: Florizel does not choose to ramble; he is ordered by his father to take a month-long holiday. The king believes that London will prove revelatory and his son will return, ready to marry the princess. Colonel Geraldine (Frank Morgan, in another inane performance) also receives a royal command: he will be executed if he does not accompany Florizel and put him right! Further absurdity is added when Florizel refers to Geraldine as "Jerry" (a patently American nickname for a "Karovian" military man).

In "The Suicide Club" Prince Florizel is a royal countenance to be respected, even revered. Montgomery's interpretation (no doubt prompted by the turgid script) is one of frequent apathy and occasional foolishness. His first appearance occurs a few minutes into the film, when he is shown clumsily whirling about on a pair of stilts! This image is a far cry from Stevenson's initial description of the character: "He was a remarkable man even by what was known of him; and that was but a small part of what he actually did."

The contrivances snowball when Florizel and Geraldine (using the literary pseudonyms "Mr. Godall" and "Major Hammersmith") set sail for England. The romantic subplot immediately takes over as Florizel comes face to face with Miss Vandeleur (actually Princess Brenda, who happens to be on the same ship, evading the forced marriage; of course, she doesn't reveal her true identity to Florizel until much later). In her cabin she entrusts an envelope to the prince and escapes the clutches of Sergei (Pedro de Cordoba), an unsavory villain, who rushes in moments later. After the ship docks in London, Florizel waits for her exit but finds an empty cabin and a steward who reports that no one had occupied it during the voyage. Soon Miss Vandeleur is shown spying on Florizel and Geraldine from an adjacent hotel room! (The surname "Vandeleur" is the film's sole connection to "The Rajah's Diamond.")

Following this 20 minutes of hoke is a loosely adapted version of "The Young Man with the Cream Tarts" (portrayed by Louis Hayward, a talented light actor who is given little motivation by director J. Walter Ruben). Unceremoniously entering the tavern, where his offer is refused, the young man bites into a tart and moves to Florizel's table. Containing none of Stevenson's literary intrigue, the scene features an angry prince and colonel who accuse him of aiming his jest at them. The young man admits that the stunt is a "mockery" and that he is at "the end of his life." Receiving no further explanation, Florizel suggests that he divide the remaining tarts between them, and a coin is flipped to decide the fate of one that is left over!

The cinematic episode with the tarts is a fleeting event, instead of the desperate and macabre incident created by Stevenson: rather than visiting more taverns (as in the story), the trio moves on to supper, during which the young man explains his actions and the significance of the Suicide Club. The story's supper scene is abandoned in favor of a brief discussion: after the young man speaks ambiguously of the club, Florizel states that they should go "into the next world" together. No explanation is included and, as the men leave the inn, two figures pop up from behind the furniture: Miss Vandeleur and the mysterious Sergei!

Following their interview with the president of the Suicide Club (Reginald Owen, donning a badly affixed skinhead wig), Florizel and Geraldine sign a register (inexplicably, the president knows that "Mr. Godall" and "Major Hammersmith" are pseudonyms) and enter the main room. The entrance of Miss Vandeleur immediately follows!

The subtleties of Stevenson's card game are purged by the script, which includes the gloating president referring to the ace of clubs as "the executioner." Predictably, the young man receives the ace of spades; he is dealt the ace of clubs in the story, but the film assigns it to Miss Vandeleur. (The invalid, Mr. Malthus, is mentioned and briefly shown, but he never comes close to either card.) The following morning the newspaper contains the young man's death notice.

Lovestriken, Florizel returns to the club the next night and (antithetical to the story) is accompanied by Geraldine. Beyond probability, Miss Vandeleur again receives the "executioner," while the "death card" is dealt to Florizel. Whisking him into the countryside, she explains that he will be mauled to death by lions at the Malden Zoo! This is, perhaps, the nadir of a film that continually sinks to new levels of absurdity. But at the last moment she cannot go through with it: she drags Florizel to a nearby cabin, reveals her true identity, and describes her flight from the marriage. In a fine example of Seff and Paramore's infantile dialogue, she babbles, "On the channel boat, I ran into the thing I was running away from." Moments later, Geraldine stumbles into the cabin and explains that he had tailed the president of the Suicide Club, who got lost during the pursuit.

The next scene shows the three sitting in a hotel room, eating breakfast the following morning. Soon a room-service attendant pleads with Florizel to defend his *dog* against a murder charge! Evidently, the mad beast killed a parrot and is being railroaded to his death. Incomprehensibly, Florizel's sense of adventure and justice cause him to be taken in by this folderol, and he walks back into the clutches of the evil president.

In a weak reference to "Saratoga Trunk" and "Hansom Cab," the president reveals that he is Dr. Franz Noel, a Karovian revolutionary seeking to eliminate the monarchy. (The king does refer to the growth of surrounding "republics" in an early scene, an element that has more in common with *Prince Otto* than with "The Suicide Club.") Noel accuses Florizel of treason and sentences him to hang in a "private chamber" (actually an empty room containing a noose). While Geraldine attempts a ruse— "I have a bomb!"—the prince runs for help; returning with a constable, he finds an abandoned building.

The next scene features a stilted near-love scene between Florizel and Brenda, and the receipt of a ransom note from Noel: "For a chance to kill you, I am willing to give you a chance to kill me" (yet another terrible sentence from the pens of Seff and Paramore). In exchange for murdering the prince, the doctor will refrain from hanging Geraldine.

Prior to appearing at the rural location designated by Noel, Florizel takes a cab to a London military club, where he picks up two officers. Here the plot of "Hansom Cab" is distilled into a nonsensical two-minute sequence: while driving Major O'Rook (the spelling has no "e" in the film credits) and Captain Rich to the home of the nonexistent Mr. Morris, Florizel blurts his story through the roof of the vehicle; obviously, Colonel Geraldine cannot masquerade as Mr. Morris, because he has been kidnapped by Noel and his anarchistic henchmen! (Seff and Paramore attempted to squeeze in more of the story here, but it adds nothing to the film's content or pace.)

At the rustic cottage the "treasonous" Florizel is told that he will be hanged, due to Noel's aversion to dueling. As the noose is proffered, Florizel's troops miraculously burst through the doorway. When the two archenemies brandish rapiers, the remaining men vacate the room, allowing them to engage in a very claustrophobic, indoor duel. Florizel forces Noel outside, impales him, and knocks him into a handily located grave.

This arrant nonsense drags to a halt as the wedding of Prince Florizel and Princess Brenda occurs in the king's Karovian palace. Here the couple's climactic embrace satisfies Hollywood convention and the Production Code of 1934. Whereas Stevenson's stories include none of the heavy royalist overtones found in this "joining of two kingdoms" sequence, the film suggests that monarchy is alive and well and a good thing, too! Aside from his somewhat heroic depiction of the prince, only one of Stevenson's sentences (in "Saratoga Trunk") contains material of a political nature, and this pertains not to the U.S. system of government but to its culture:

> He reflected pathetically over his ambitious designs for the future; he should not now become the hero and spokesman of his native place of Bangor, Maine; he should not, as he had fondly anticipated, move on from office to office, from honor to honor; he might as well divest himself at once of all hope of being acclaimed President of the United States, and leaving behind him a statue, in the worst possible style of art, to adorn the Capitol at Washington.

As an adaptation of literature, *Trouble for Two* is an abomination, but it also must be judged a bad film from any critical perspective. Even the music of Franz Waxman (who composed some of Hollywood's greatest film scores), with its sluggish melodic motifs and instrumentation, fails to add a tinge of quality to the production. The MGM studio's classic slogan was *ars gratia artis* (art for art's sake); to call *Trouble for Two* art would require an impossible stretch of the imagination, even though the studio's usual glossy production values are evident. Considering that Stevenson made the above comment about art in America, he assuredly would not have thought very highly of MGM's cinematic "adaptation."

A glance at two 1936 reviews indicates how the film was received by some contemporary critics. Aside from a few select writers (Pare Lorentz, James Agee, Graham Greene), many early critics of cinema concerned themselves with plot and acting, while paying little attention to other elements. Reviews of *Trouble for Two* in *Variety* and the *New York Times* prove how inadequate 1930s critical commentary could be. Before the days of scholarly studies and full-length books on the cinema, criticism was relegated primarily to brief articles in newspapers and magazines, usually written in haste to meet daily deadlines; this fact may account for the errors in perception and analysis in the following: "Mechanics of Stevenson's plots make farfetched probabilities on the screen. The coincidences, particularly those which bring the incognito prince and princess together, don't seem to jell. Good direction and casting and the rich mounting the production has received aren't strong enough to completely overcome these defections" ("Odec.").[3] Obviously, "Odec." never read the story, since the "farfetched probabilities" and "coincidences" came not from the author but from Seff and Paramore's script (almost none of Stevenson's events are featured in the film; and the princess is not one of his characters), and his positive appraisal of Ruben's direction belies any sufficient knowledge of film technique or acting.

Columnist Frank S. Nugent offers a startlingly positive review:

> J. Walter Ruben has filmed his story with an extraordinarily keen sense of melodramatic value and frequently achieves results with a finesse which we have come to

consider a stylistic trade-mark of England's master melodramatist, Alfred Hitchcock. The screenplay by Manuel Seff and Edward E. Paramore Jr. similarly is the product of superior craftsmanship. Only that could have made us accept another story about a mythical kingdom.[4]

It can be assumed that Nugent did not read "The Suicide Club" either; his comments about the direction and the screenplay in particular defy comprehension. Judging Seff and Paramore's work to be "superior craftsmanship" is analogous to calling a teen romance novel "great literature."

Prior to MGM's dismal effort, "The Suicide Club" could possibly have been adapted into a good adventure-suspense film. In 1933 the Carl Laemmle regime at Universal considered filming the stories with Boris Karloff in a starring role. Discussed briefly, the project fell through (along with a host of others) when Karloff experienced contractual problems and left to make *The Ghoul* in England.

The prospect of making *The Suicide Club* resurfaced in 1934, when Universal offered a three-picture deal (*The Black Cat, Dracula's Daughter,* and the Stevenson trilogy) to Karloff's horror rival, Bela Lugosi. After the Karloff-Lugosi film *The Black Cat* was a huge success, plans were made to feature both stars in *The Suicide Club.* (Although the character possesses none of the "redeeming features" that he usually invested in his terror roles, Karloff would seem an obvious choice for the evil president. In a moment of inspiration Laemmle could have cast the stately, mid–European Lugosi as Prince Florizel, thus making him the hero of the piece.) But one can only speculate about the success of a Universal "Suicide Club," perhaps directed by James Whale, the studio's official "ace" during the early to mid-1930s and a true master of the macabre. Unfortunately, the MGM production is the sole sound English-language adaptation of "The Suicide Club" to date. (A 1987 potboiler, *The Suicide Club,* starring Mariel Hemingway, borrows Stevenson's title but does not incorporate any significant literary material.)

## *New Arabian Nights* on Television

Although "The Suicide Club" has not been adapted for television, the four vignettes comprising its "sequel," "The Rajah's Diamond," were developed as a small-screen opera by British producer J. Mervyn Williams in 1979. Commissioned by the BBC, in association with the Welsh Arts Council, "The Rajah's Diamond" features music by Alun Hoddinott and libretto by Myfanwy Piper.

• SIX •

# Dead Mariners and Sea Disasters: "The Pavilion on the Links" (1880)

*The night set in pitch dark. The wind came off the sea in squalls, like the firing of a battery of cannon; now and then there was a flaw of rain, and the surf rolled heavier with the rising tide.* —FRANK CASSILIS, in "The Pavilion on the Links."

Frank Cassilis, a misanthropic Englishman, drops out of university life to seek a more adventurous existence. Traveling to Scotland with the unsociable R. Northmour, he spends the winter months in a pavilion at Graden Easter. Attacked by Northmour during an argument, Cassilis vacates and roams the countryside.

Seeking "desolate corners," Cassilis wanders for nine years before revisiting the "Pavilion on the Links," which he finds quiet and uninhabited. He sets up camp in a nearby wood and naps before setting forth into the night. At the pavilion he spots a light "passing from one window to another, as though someone were reviewing the different apartments with a lamp or candle."

The following morning Cassilis, believing that burglars have broken into the house, enters through an upstairs window but finds nothing of import. He spends the next few days observing a schooner yacht lying "some miles to the northeast," and he surveys its crew members after a small boat brings them ashore. He spies five yachtsmen carrying two sea chests and an intriguing female accompanied by "an unusually tall man" and another seaman. As the boat returns seaward, Cassilis discovers his old acquaintance, Northmour, walking toward the house. Startling him, Cassilis is repelled by a knife wound to the shoulder.

Three days later Cassilis arranges secret meetings with the young woman, who identifies herself as Clara, daughter of Bernard Huddlestone, a ruined banker accused of illegally investing his clients' funds. Northmour, she reveals, has offered her father protection and a safe voyage from Britain in exchange for her hand in marriage.

Cassilis confronts Northmour but is waylaid by a group of Italian *carbonari* seeking retribution for stolen revolutionary currency. After the Italians set fire to the house and shoot Huddlestone, Cassilis and Northmour argue over the young woman. Unwilling to be domesticated by Clara, Northmour hands Cassilis his pistol and boards the *Red Earl*, which has arrived "twelve hours too late." Closing his narrative, Cassilis admits, "Years after, Northmour was killed fighting under the colors of Garibaldi for the liberation of Tyrol."

After writing the initial draft of *Travels with a Donkey in the Cévennes* in September and October 1878, and beginning his collaboration with Henley on *Deacon Brodie* during the latter month, Stevenson turned to short fiction in November. Fascinated by the Scottish coastlines he had seen on lighthouse tours and family outings, he chose an area near North Berwick, a small town northeast of Edinburgh on the Firth of Forth, as a backdrop for the melodramatic adventure plot that dominates "The Pavilion on the Links." Involved in various personal affairs, including his "emigrant" voyage to meet Fanny in California, he finished the atmospheric but disjointed story in Monterey during November 1879. It was published as two installments in the September and October 1880 issues of *Cornhill Magazine* and reprinted in *New Arabian Nights* in 1882.

The first few pages of the story contain elegant visualizations of Scottish terrain, and Stevenson's description of the shoreline at Graden Easter is unforgettable: "On summer days the outlook was bright and even gladsome; but at sundown in September, with a high wind, and a heavy surf rolling in close along the links, the place told of nothing but dead mariners and sea disasters. A ship beating to windward on the horizon, and a huge truncheon of wreck half buried in the sands at my feet, completed the innuendo of the scene."

The initial chapter is an interesting, well-paced narrative, but the remaining eight chapters fail to match the early literary and dramatic qualities. When the particulars of the Northmour-Huddlestone affair enter the picture, the intrigue of Cassilis's earlier experiences is lost amid his disordered reminiscences: he often reveals the end result of an action (for example, his marriage to Clara Huddlestone) before describing the circumstances that prompted it (for example, his first memorable glimpse of her). Clara is a strong female character, but her personality is dulled by Cassilis's frequent recollections about their past relationship. Stevenson fails to create an interesting romance; he merely tells the reader what will happen, including the fact that Clara is dead (revealed 20 pages into the story).

Stevenson's tendency to grow tired of a project is apparent in "The Pavilion on the Links"; he evidently began writing the tale with great interest but, by the time he finished it on another continent a year later, the atmosphere and drama had fallen by the wayside. The quality of the first chapter suggests that the story's picturesque setting excited him, but the predictable climax (Huddlestone's murder) and final scene (the uniting of the lovers) do not match the intensity of his initial vision. (However, the "happy ending" is offset by earlier remarks about Clara's death.) David Daiches writes, "'The Pavilion on the Links' ... is a not altogether unsuccessful attempt to use a flamboyant and melodramatic episode as a means of suggesting the quality of the Scottish east coast near North Berwick. As a result, the effective handling of realistic detail in the first part ... loses part of its force in the face of an action which is on a wholly different level of probability."[1]

## The White Circle
## (Paramount, 1920)

Paramount's *The White Circle*, directed by Maurice Tourneur in 1920, is the only cinematic version of "The Pavilion on the Links." Adapted by screenwriter Jules Furthman and silent star John Gilbert (who also portrays Cassilis), the film, set in 1860, maintains Stevenson's melodramatic plot and features several of its most dramatic moments: most admirable is a scene in which Northmour (Harry B. Northrup) stands before a window to determine whether the *carbonari* are seeking to kill only Bernard Huddlestone (Spottiswoode Aitken) or the entire party. Here, Furthman and Tourneur's visualization closely follows Stevenson's passage:

Suddenly, as I was thus closely watching his expression and prepared against the worst, I saw a change, a flash, a look of relief, upon his face. He took up the lamp which stood beside him on the table, and turned to us with an air of some excitement.

"There is but one point that we must know," said he. "Are they going to butcher the lot of us, or only Huddlestone? Did they take you for him, or fire at you for your own *beaux yeux*?"

"They took me for him, for certain," I replied. "I am near as tall, and my head is fair."

"I am going to make sure," returned Northmour; and he stepped up to the window, holding the lamp above his head, and stood there, quietly affronting death, for half a minute.

Clara sought to rush forward and pull him from the place of danger; but I had the pardonable selfishness to hold her back by force.

"Yes," said Northmour, turning cooly from the window; "it's only Huddlestone they want."

The event that fuels the conflict between Cassilis and Northmour is altered in the film, which replaces their argument-cum-fight with a gun duel. Failing to drop his "companion" with one shot, Cassilis is spared but ordered to return to the pavilion once yearly so that Northmour may retaliate. During these annual visits, both men become acquainted with Clara Huddlestone. Here, the screenplay changes Cassilis's intent (his reappearance at Graden Easter is prompted by coercion), but both Stevenson's and Furthman's devices seem equally contrived.

One of the silent cinema's most

capable pictorialists, Tourneur, aided by cinematographer Alfred Ortlieb, created several stunning compositions (including location shots) for *The White Circle*, but the film, like the story, possesses an uneven quality: occasional thrills are interspersed with dramatically disappointing events. A faithful reproduction of the final pages includes Northmour's visions of marriage and domestic life, an element that briefly encourages identification with Cassilis's rival, but, as *Variety* notes, theater patrons must have been disappointed by this ending:

> What could be more dissatisfying a conclusion, although its very abruptness really has some effect in bringing the audience back to reality, because it is quite a compelling production as far as it goes and commands strict attention. However, the audience up to now is tensed for the expectant climax, for the interest is ever on the ascension. The "break" has not yet arrived, and, as matters develop, never will.[2]

Less attention is given to Clara Huddlestone (Janis Wilson), who acts as a pawn in the feud between Cassilis and Northmour, but the performances are uniformly good. Several memorable sequences are accentuated by the acting of John Gilbert (billed here as Jack Gilbert), who, at age 25, was years away from the MGM studio politics that would hasten his descent into alcoholism and an untimely death in 1936, and Spottiswoode Aitken, who appeared in several D. W. Griffith productions, including *The Birth of a Nation* (1915) and *Intolerance* (1916).

• SEVEN •

# The Lions and the Lambs: "The Body-Snatcher" (1881)

*"You can't begin and then stop. If you begin, you must keep on beginning; that's the truth. No rest for the wicked."* —DR. WOLFE MACFARLANE, in "The Body-Snatcher."

Donald Fettes, an old, rum-swilling Scotsman, sits with three friends in the parlor of the George Inn at Debenham. When Dr. Wolfe Macfarlane arrives to treat a neighbor, Fettes comes face-to-face with an old acquaintance. "Toddy Macfarlane!" he shouts, surprising the doctor, who offers the hospitality of his Edinburgh home. Fettes refuses, whispering, "Have you seen it again?" Aghast, Macfarlane cries out, strikes Fettes across the face, and flees the inn.

Intrigued by this meeting, Fettes's companions investigate his past associations with the "great rich London doctor." In a flashback describing Fettes's "young days," he is shown as a talented medical student in the schools of Edinburgh. As an assistant in the dissection laboratory of Dr. K---, he is influenced by Dr. Macfarlane, his immediate superior and aide in Dr. K---'s anatomy class. Together, they accept "subjects" for dissection from "resurrection men" who call during the dark hours of the night. Admitting that the subjects are being murdered due to a short supply of cadavers, Macfarlane kills Gray, an associate in body-snatching. Warned not to reveal this secret, Fettes distributes Gray's "parts" for student dissection.

On a pitch-black and stormy night, Fettes and Macfarlane disinter a woman's corpse in an old graveyard at Glencorse. Driving back to Edinburgh, they are made uneasy by the body, which continually falls against them as the gig careens on the wet, windswept road. "This is not a woman," Macfarlane frantically states as Fettes holds a lantern up to the corpse's face. Screaming out in fright, both men abandon the gig as the lantern crashes to the ground. The horse bolts, galloping toward Edinburgh with its sole occupant: "the body of the dead and long-dissected Gray."

The summer of 1881 proved to be a literarily terrifying one for Stevenson. Engulfed in Highland rain at Pitlochry, he wrote three Scottish stories, all powerful thrillers, in picturesque Kinnaird Cottage, where he and Fanny enjoyed a roaring fire and the ghoulish folk tales of Mrs. Sim, their hostess. In June he completed "Thrawn Janet" and began "The Body-Snatcher" and "The Merry Men," both of which occupied him well into the following month. He initially thought "The Body-Snatcher" "too horrid" for publication, but three and one-half years later it was included in the December 1884 *Pall Mall Christmas Extra*.[1] Appearing on the public scene shortly after the success of *Treasure Island*, it was dismissed as a piece of sensationalistic horror. Although the story rarely goes beyond a sketch of two characters involved in a specific series of events, it provides a fictionalized portrait of grisly crimes that shocked Edinburgh and much of Great Britain in 1828–29.

William Burke and William Hare, two men whose names quickly became synonymous with the act of grave robbing (although they never actually robbed any graves), were Irish Catholics who moved to Edinburgh around 1818. Both men originally sought navy work, but joined forces when Burke and his mistress, Helen MacDougal, moved into Log's, a boarding house in Tanner's Close owned by Hare and his wife.

Learning that several anatomists in the city were hampered by a paucity of dissection subjects, Burke and Hare subsequently murdered 16 people and sold the corpses to Dr. Robert Knox (the "Dr. K---" in Stevenson's story). The victims, often female, were lured with the promise of liquor and sex. The method of murder used, a suffocation technique, left no detectable signs of violence upon the body. One of their victims, a bonny 18-year-old lass named Mary Paterson, was recognized by an anatomy student who received the body from Burke. When questioned about her demise, the cold-blooded killer replied that she had died from "the drink." Strongly affected by the dead girl's stunning appearance, several students sketched her body before it was dissected by Dr. Knox. Knox's knowledge of this murder and that of Daft Jamie, a well-known Edinburgh halfwit, weighed heavily against him after Burke and Hare were arrested.

The sixteenth murder, that of an elderly pauper named Mary Docherty, was discovered before the delivery was made to Knox's assistant, David Paterson. Burke murdered the old mendicant during a drunken Halloween party, hid her naked body beneath some straw under his bed, and then poured whisky all over the room to disguise the odor. Worried by Mary's disappearance, Mrs. Gray, a lodger, discovered the corpse and, together with her husband, escaped Burke's wrath in time to inform the police.

After a long inquest and trial, Burke was convicted and sentenced to death for the murder of Mary Docherty, the only corpse that had not been dissected by Knox and his associates. Making two lengthy confessions while in prison, Burke cleared his mistress and his partner's wife, but a case was made against Hare. Due to the participation of counselors Sir James Moncreiff and Henry Cockburn, Liberals who sought to discredit the current Tory administration, the proceedings against Hare were aborted.

On January 28, 1829, William Burke was hanged in the midst of a crowd estimated at 25,000, including a portion who loudly chanted, "Burke him!" before the body dropped. After some in the gathering and a group of students protested, the body was displayed publicly on January 29 and 30, when nearly 30,000 spectators filed by to view it. Burke's ultimate destiny was the dissection table of Knox's greatest rival, Professor Alexander Munro, then serving as chairman of the Anatomy Department at Edinburgh University. His skeleton is still on display in the Anatomical Museum.

Threatened by organized vigilante mobs, Hare escaped to England with the aid of the mail service. While stopping in London for a drink, he nearly was killed by a mob of 8,000 but was protected by the police. He last was seen walking on a road near Carlisle, and was never heard of again. There is no known documentation of his birth or death.

Dr. Robert Knox, author of the dubious 1850 work *Races of Men*, studied anatomy in the hope of proving the superiority of the Scandinavian race. A pre-Darwinian believer in the "survival of the fittest" philosophy, Knox was "the real founder of British racism and one of the key figures in the general Western movement toward a dogmatic pseudo-scientific racism."[2] Educated at Edinburgh High School, Knox took the examination for anatomy in 1814 and pursued further study in Paris. Experiencing the shortage of corpses during a high point in student enrollment (504) during 1828–29, he was forced to solicit Burke and Hare.

Much like his attitude toward the "dark races"—"Destined by the nature of their race to run like all other animals, a certain limited course of existence, it matters little how their extinction is brought about"[3]—Knox believed that murdering "useless" individuals was a humane practice. Scottish historian Owen Dudley Edwards writes: "Knox simply did not regard the Burke and Hare murders as criminal: on the contrary, he looked on them as an enlightened method of disposing of worthless individuals with the ultimate betterment to the more desirable segments of humanity by reason of the benefits conferred to the study of anatomy."[4]

After the prosecution of the crimes, Knox maintained his position in Edinburgh for several years, until a younger generation, "frightened by the story of Burke and Hare," came of age.[5] He moved to Glasgow in 1844 to attract new students, but his career slowed to a near standstill. (Today, Edinburgh tour guides readily point out the location of Knox's laboratory and the nearby graveyard from which several bodies were stolen.)

The affairs of Burke, Hare, and Knox are past history at the outset of "The Body-Snatcher." By using

Fettes's story as a vehicle, Stevenson gives the reader some thinly disguised, historically accurate information about the anatomist:

> There was, at that period, a certain extramural teacher of anatomy, whom I shall designate by the letter K. His name was subsequently too well known. The man who bore it skulked through the streets of Edinburgh in disguise, while the mob that applauded at the execution of Burke called loudly for the blood of his employer. But Mr. K--- was then at the top of his vogue; he enjoyed a popularity due partly to his own talent and address, partly to the incapacity of his rival, the university professor. The students, at least swore by his name, and Fettes believed himself, and was believed by others, to have laid the foundations of success when he had acquired the favour of this meteorically famous man.

Prior to the mention of Fettes, this passage could be included in an encyclopedia entry on the Burke and Hare murders. In fact, Stevenson mentions the murderous duo in his earlier "Edinburgh: Picturesque Notes": "people hush their voices over Burke and Hare; over drugs and violated graves, and the resurrection-men smothering their victims with their knees." Of course, the "university professor" is Alexander Munro. Another of Stevenson's references to Burke and Hare comes a few pages later, when Fettes hears "grumbling Irish voices" emanating from the men who have brought him the corpse of Jane Galbraith, the well-known street singer.

Like "The Sire de Maletroit's Door," "The Body-Snatcher" weaves history with fictional characters and somewhat fantastical events; and the locations—actual sites in Edinburgh and the Pentland Hills—lend an authentic atmosphere to the gruesome proceedings. Penicuik, a village five miles south of the city, still features the Fisher's Tryst and rustic kirkyard where Macfarlane and Fettes hide their grave-digging implements in the story. Located up the hill from the tryst, Glencorse kirk, a site occasionally visited by Stevenson, still holds Sunday morning services, and the official graveyard, described in the story as "solemn and isolated" and "buried fathoms deep in the foliage of six cedar trees," is called "Burying Ground of the People of Glencorse, 1885" and postdates the story by about four years. (Glencorse kirkyard is now surrounded by a British military installation.) And the name "Fettes" graces at least four sites in Edinburgh, including Fettes Row, a street located between Howard Place and Heriot Row that was familiar to Stevenson. (His friends, Professor and Mrs. Fleeming Jenkin, settled on Fettes Row when they moved to Edinburgh in 1868.)

Similar in structure to "The Sire de Maletroit's Door," the narrative moves at a fast pace and is highlighted by descriptive and poetic prose. When Macfarlane eludes Fettes at the George, Stevenson almost allows the reader to *see* the doctor's actions: "He crouched together, brushing on the wainscot, and made a dart like a serpent, striking for the door."

*Top:* Penicuik Cemetery. "Bottle and all, it was a sad and silent drive as far as Penicuik, where they were to spend the evening. They stopped once, to hide their implements in a thick bush not far from the churchyard...." (1990 photograph by S. A. Nollen.) *Bottom:* The Fisher's Tryst, Penicuik. "...and once again at the Fisher's Tryst, to have a toast before the kitchen fire and vary their nips of whisky with a glass of ale." (1990 photograph by S. A. Nollen.)

"Burying Ground of the Parish of Glencorse." "In the sunken woods that traverse the neighborhood of the burying-ground the last glimmer failed them, and it became necessary to kindle a match and reilluminate one of the lanterns of the gig. Thus, under dripping trees, and environed by huge and moving shadows, they reached the scene of their unhallowed labours." (1990 photograph by Karla Nollen.)

*The Body Snatcher*
(RKO-Radio, 1945)

The visual grace that distinguishes portions of Stevenson's story is found in abundance in Val Lewton's cinematic adaptation. A rare artistic achievement, *The Body Snatcher* is an improvement upon the literary original. Using the pseudonym Carlos Keith, Lewton and collaborator Philip MacDonald fashioned a screenplay that provides a fuller realization of the events created by Stevenson.

From 1942 to 1946 Val Lewton's producing efforts almost single-handedly rescued the horror-film genre from a state of total absurdity. While Universal Studios was grinding out pale imitations of its successful horror classics of the early to mid–1930s, Lewton and his low-budget production team at RKO-Radio created a new type of screen terror: a style that relied on suggestive, eerie visuals and sound effects, understated acting, and spare, literate writing, rather than a straightforward depiction of supernatural monsters and physical action. Lewton, who referred to his films as psychological or historical thrillers, researched each of them extensively, often incorporating actual events into the narratives.

Lewton's ability to adapt literary material for the screen was considerable, and before becoming a story editor for David O. Selznick in 1933, he wrote and published nine novels, six nonfiction works, a collection of poetry, and *Jasmine*, a pornographic book. In May 1936 he was the first person at Selznick International to read Margaret Mitchell's then unfinished *Gone with the Wind*. Reporting his opinions to Selznick, he described the lengthy story as "ponderous trash."[6]

In 1942 studio executives at RKO-Radio created a low-budget horror unit. Choosing Lewton as its creative force, Chares Koerner, head of studio production, dictated that the unit produce horror "programmers" to cost no more than $150,000 each and run no longer than 75 minutes. Though he was limited by miniscule budgets and restrictive running times, Lewton and his associates created some of the most thoughtful and artistically powerful horror films of the 1940s or any other decade. Quite different from what theater patrons expected, the extremely successful *Cat People* (1942) initiated a series that includes *I Walked with a Zombie* (1943), *The Leopard Man* (1943), *The Seventh Victim* (1943), *The Ghost Ship* (1943), *Curse of the Cat People* (1944), *The Body Snatcher* (1945), *Isle of the Dead* (1945), and *Bedlam* (1946). Of these productions, *The Body Snatcher* is the only one based on a classic literary work.

The film omits the story's opening scene, in which the aged Fettes meets Macfarlane at the George. Instead, the narrative begins in 1831, two years after the affairs of Burke, Hare, and Knox. The character of "Toddy" MacFarlane (Henry Daniell; the "f" is capitalized in the film's credits) replaces Dr. K--- as head of the anatomy school and Fettes (Russell Wade) is appointed as his assistant. Well researched, Lewton and MacDonald's script assigns many of Dr. Robert Knox's qualities to MacFarlane, while Fettes's characterization is enlarged from the original; Knox is referred to by name but has fled to London, leaving MacFarlane in power. Although the character roles are altered in the film, many of Stevenson's passages are included in expanded form.

Several new characters are featured, including three females and Joseph (Bela Lugosi), an additional servant. But the major improvement on the tale is Lewton's enlargement of Gray (Boris Karloff), the hansom cab driver who moonlights as a body snatcher.

Meeting Gray for the first time, Fettes becomes involved in the hideous crimes. Soon he promises a young widow (Rita Corday) that MacFarlane will operate on her disabled daughter (Sharyn Moffet) but is informed that the procedure is impossible due to a lack of experimental subjects. Soliciting Gray, the young assistant inadvertently prompts the murder of a young street singer (Donna Lee), who subsequently is dissected by MacFarlane's students.

After hearing the doctor and Fettes discussing the murder, Joseph threatens to expose Gray: "Give me money," he demands as the grave robber tells the tale of Burke and Hare. Pouring brandy, Gray asks Joseph to join him in a similar enterprise: "We will, so to speak, 'Burke them,'" he says, placing his hands over the drunken servant's nose and mouth, ultimately suffocating him.

Discovering Joseph's corpse in his laboratory vat, MacFarlane confronts and bludgeons Gray to death, dissects him, and sells his cab and horses to a resident of Penicuik. Before returning to Edinburgh, he and Fettes rob the old woman's grave at Glencorse. While driving through a torrential rainstorm, MacFarlane hears voices and, upon examining the face of the corpse, sees the visage of Gray: an image that sends the horses bolting and the doctor to his death at the bottom of a gorge. Fettes runs to the scene of the accident, searches for MacFarlane's vital signs, lifts the shroud from the corpse, and sees only the old woman's lifeless face.

Loosely based on James Gray, who testified against Burke, the aptly named "resurrection man" appears very briefly, but memorably, in a few paragraphs of Stevenson's story. He speaks with MacFarlane and Fettes in only one scene but provides the psychological motivation for their comeuppance at the story's end.

In the film Gray's presence is felt continually, whether or not he is on-screen. Introduced in long shot, delivering a patient to MacFarlane's home, he is depicted as a complex character. Holding Georgina Marsh, the disabled girl, in his arms, the grandfatherly cabman acquaints her with his horse while simultaneously appearing sinister when noticed at the door by MacFarlane's wife (Edith Atwater).

This moral ambiguity is a part of the literary Gray (since he does appear "evil" in life but ultimately "punishes" other evildoers after he dies), a quality wisely stressed by Lewton and MacDonald's writing and the alternately powerful and subtle direction of Robert Wise.

Karloff's magnificent portrayal of Gray occasionally is reminiscent of Stevenson's Long John Silver, a literary creation possessing a great range of both good and bad qualities. Like Silver, Gray performs morally evil actions incited by his environment: to a certain extent, he cannot help the situation he has fallen into, due to the society in which he was raised with its rigid class distinctions and considerable poverty. Perhaps his most heinous crime in *The Body Snatcher* occurs in the first "resurrection" sequence, when he enters Greyfriars kirkyard and kills a small dog guarding the grave of its recently interred master. His tendency toward murder in the line of duty (working to supply "humane" researchers with subjects) may exonerate him from his later murder of the street singer (an element adapted from the story that contains very subtle, dramatic suspense). When MacFarlane attempts to bribe Gray with enough money to live a "respectable" life, he replies: "I am a small man, a humble man, and being poor, I have had to do much that I did not want to do. But so long as the great Dr. MacFarlane jumps at my whistle, that long am I a man—and if I have not that, I have nothing. Then I am only a cabman and a grave robber."

Gray often exhibits sincere gestures of kindness, even gentleness,

*The Body Snatcher* (1945). Gray (Boris Karloff) taunts "Toddy" MacFarlane (Henry Daniell) "for auld lang syne," as Joseph (Bela Lugosi) brews thoughts of blackmail, in RKO-Radio's superb, literate thriller.

caring for Georgina Marsh and requesting that the indifferent Mac-Farlane perform the corrective operation on her spine. This personality trait also is suggested after he has smothered the inebriated Joseph. During an earlier conversation with Fettes, Gray is shown tenderly petting his cat (an interesting contrast to his previous killing of the dog). This image recurs, in more subtle form, as Joseph lies expired upon the floor: in a moment of inspired direction and performance, Gray removes his hands from Joseph's mouth and gently reaches over to pet the cat, allowing the animal's tail to slide slowly through his palm. (The cat is called "Brother," which suggests the degree of Gray's identification with the animal, a cunning creature capable of stalking silently through the night.)

The character of Gray proves that a film adaptation does not have to adhere slavishly to every word of a literary original to do it artistic justice. With *The Body Snatcher* Val Lewton and company took Stevenson's ideas and made them more clear and interesting to both the reader and film viewer. Stevenson's tendency to create morally ambiguous characters is only sporadically evident in the story; Macfarlane, in particular, believes that the human race is composed of two distinct types of people: "Why man, do you know what this life is? There are two squads of us—the lions and the lambs. If you're a lamb, you'll come to lie on these tables like Gray or Jane Galbraith; if you're a lion, you'll live and drive a horse like me, like K---, like all the world with any wit or courage." Perhaps Stevenson felt that this distinction would link Macfarlane with the racist Robert Knox, or would drive home the effectiveness of the story's ending. But moral complexity is a stronger component in the film version. Arguably, Lewton's *The Body Snatcher* can be viewed as the sole example of a film adaptation being more faithful to Stevenson's general style than the literary work itself. (However, Stevenson wrote "The Body-Snatcher" early in his fictional career, at a time when he was beginning to develop a distinctive style. Obviously, Lewton had access to all of Stevenson's later works as well.)

Stevenson depicts Macfarlane as a lion, but the cinematic character is less rigid. Rather than expressing himself in Stevenson's terms, he frequently appears angst-ridden and unable to pursue objectives that will bring him personal and public success. At several points the audience is allowed to empathize with him, particularly when sharing his view of Gray's dead face at the end. MacFarlane and Gray often appear to be two parts of one larger entity, with neither of them being able to function without the other—a factor reinforced by Henry Daniell's incisive and powerful portrayal of MacFarlane, a performance that perfectly complements Karloff's.

"You and I have two bodies," Gray tells MacFarlane, "aye, very different sorts of bodies, but they are closer than if we were in the same skin—for I saved that skin of yours once, and you'll not forget it." Reminding the doctor of an incident during the Burke and Hare trials when he "testified for him" in the witness box, Gray uses blackmail to keep MacFarlane under his thumb; this coercion, combined with the doctor's dependence upon the cabman's "resurrection" abilities, does not allow MacFarlane any escape from his antagonistic alter ego.

When Gray confronts the drunken MacFarlane shortly before their last fateful encounter, he attempts, in a very powerful manner, to explain the doctor's spiritual deficiencies. While MacFarlane wallows in self-pity because of his failed surgery on the Marsh girl, Gray cuts to the heart of the problem.

Placing the bowl of one champagne glass on top of another, MacFarlane explains how he repaired the girl's spine. He is interrupted, however, by Gray's dashing of the glasses to the floor.

*Gray:* You can't build life the way you put blocks together, Toddy.
*MacFarlane:* What the devil are you talking about? I'm an anatomist. I know the body. I know how it works.
*Gray:* You're a fool, Toddy, and no doctor. It's only the dead ones you know.
*MacFarlane:* I am a doctor. I teach medicine.
*Gray:* Like Knox taught you? Like I taught you? In cellars? In graveyards? Did Knox teach you what makes the blood flow?

*MacFarlane:* The heart pumps it.

*Gray:* Did he tell you how thoughts come and go—and why things are remembered, and forgot?

*MacFarlane:* The nerve center—the brain.

*Gray:* What makes a thought start?

*MacFarlane:* The brain, I tell you—I know.

*Gray:* You don't know, and you'll never know or understand, Toddy. Not from Knox or me would you learn those things. Look.

Gray turns MacFarlane toward a mirror on the wall beside the table. The camera shifts to the "point of view" of the mirror, as cinematographer Robert De Grasse's evocative chiaroscuro lighting highlights the reptilian look on Boris Karloff's face.

Gray then continues, "Look at yourself. Could you be a doctor, a healing man, with the things those eyes have seen? There's a lot of knowledge in those eyes, but no understanding. You'd not get that from me."

Though Gray states that he is incapable of teaching "understanding" to MacFarlane, he does so in this scene. He observes that the doctor has the intellectual capacity required for medical technique, but that he does *not* possess the human feeling to carry it out. In a later scene Fettes reinforces this claim when he tells Mrs. Marsh that MacFarlane "taught me the mathematics of anatomy, but he couldn't teach me the poetry of medicine." In *The Body Snatcher* MacFarlane is primarily the healing agent and Gray is seen as preying on both the living and the dead, but the distinctions are blurred consistently. The poor resurrection man Gray actually possesses a greater understanding of humanity than the learned Dr. MacFarlane does.

The cinematic Gray is a far cry from the "coarse, vulgar, and stupid" character described in the story. Not only does he convince MacFarlane to perform the surgery and then provide him with a necessary research subject, his kindness to Georgina ultimately inspires her to walk: as the girl is sitting on a rooftop with her mother and Fettes, she hears a cab in the street below; thinking that the horse may be Gray's, she rises from her wheelchair and takes a step forward.

Throughout the film Gray and MacFarlane appear to exchange elements of their personalities: while the former contributes to Georgina's cure, the latter becomes a manipulative and self-serving grave robber. When MacFarlane boasts that he is "rid of him forever" and then tells Fettes that he will no longer require the services of "reptilian creatures like Gray," he has become the very thing he is trying to destroy. His ultimate disregard for others is foreshadowed in an earlier scene, when his wife, Meg, tells Fettes that he has forced her to pose as his maid. Here Lewton alludes to the class distinctions of Victorian Edinburgh by depicting the marriage of a rural Highlander (Meg Cameron) to a respectable Lowlander (MacFarlane) who must hide the truth to maintain his standing in upper-class society.

Much of Stevenson's dialogue is reproduced in the film. Gray's lone appearance in the story is taken verbatim and slightly expanded upon, when MacFarlane and Fettes encounter him at the tavern. "A fine specimen, isn't he, Toddy?" asks an off-camera Gray, as the two men eye a pig roasting in the fireplace. Taking a seat at the cabman's table, they are captivated by his curious power and sarcastic charm.

> *Gray:* I'm a pretty bad fellow myself, but MacFarlane's the boy—Toddy MacFarlane, I call him. Toddy, order your friend another glass. *(looking at Fettes)* Toddy hates me.
> *MacFarlane:* Don't call me by that confounded name.
> *Gray:* Hear him! Did you ever see the lads play knife? *(thrusting a knife into a loaf of bread)* Toddy would like to do that all over my body.
> *Fettes:* We medicals have a better way than that. When we dislike a friend of ours, we dissect him.

At this point in the story a meal is briefly mentioned, with Gray forcing Macfarlane to pay the bill. However, in the film, Gray adds, "You'll never get rid of me that way, Toddy"—a remark that becomes the verbal leitmotif for the remainder of the drama. After hearing Gray state it another time, MacFarlane, having performed the dissection of the corpse and still haunted by the remark, is driven to paranoia and death.

As directed by Robert Wise, Stevenson's harrowing climax is one of the most frightening four-minute sequences ever filmed. After Gray's sepulchral voice induces MacFarlane to stop the coach, the light from Fettes's lantern falls upon the corpse. Here, a shot from MacFarlane's point of view shows the doctor (and the audience) that the corpse *has* changed. MacFarlane's yell spooks the horse into a rapid charge, sending the doctor to his death. The imagery used during MacFarlane's hallucination is particularly strong, with the emaciated Gray appearing to embrace him as the coach speeds off.

These 4 minutes contain 64 cuts that utilize 26 different camera setups. The shots form a montage not unlike a musical crescendo, increasing dramatically as it progresses. Wise's editing talent is apparent (he cut *Citizen Kane* in 1941), as the tempo of the scene never draws attention to itself. Shots of the exterior of the gig (always photographed in medium long shot) are strategically placed within the scene. The first setup, an establishing shot of the gig on the road, is followed by 10 shots of the characters within the gig. This structure is repeated 4 times, after which shots of the gig on the road and shots of the characters are alternated, lasting less screen time at each interval. This method of balanced editing, culminating with rapidly cut alternating shots, creates a very frenzied, uneasy atmosphere.

MacFarlane and Fettes are photographed consistently with the camera placed outside the coach, a technique which adds to the claustrophobic mood of the scene. Prior to the accident, Fettes's point of view is never shown, and the camera is placed to the right of MacFarlane, with the doctor in the foreground and Fettes in the background. Long shots are not included, even when the coach is shown on the road; these images are photographed in medium or medium long shot, helping to maintain the oppressive ambience. MacFarlane's point of view is featured only when Gray's face appears, providing the height of the doctor's terror and a dramatic climax; the close of the scene includes the same type of composition from Fettes's viewpoint, proving that MacFarlane was slain by his troubled conscience.

In the story Stevenson has both Macfarlane and Fettes see the face of Gray before they frantically abandon the gig. Unlike the film's resolution of killing the doctor, Stevenson allows him to live, only to be haunted by the memory of Gray's spirit (hence his strong reaction when Fettes asks, "Did you see it again?"). Stevenson presents Fettes as a worn-out, broken drunkard, an unfeeling man who also has been punished by the apparition of Gray. Not only did he follow Macfarlane's orders while working for Dr. K--- but he also chose to become a "lion," even after expressing reservations about accepting the corpses of both the street singer and Gray. While sharing a meal with Macfarlane at the Fisher's Tryst, Fettes boasts openly:

> When they reached their journey's end the gig was housed, the horse was fed and comforted, and the two young doctors in a private room sat down to the best dinner and the best wine the house afforded. The lights, the fire, the beating rain upon the window, the cold, incongruous work that lay before them, added zest to their enjoyment of the meal. With every glass their cordiality increased. Soon Macfarlane handed a little pile of gold to his companion.
>
> "A compliment," he said. "Between friends these little d---d accommodations ought to fly like pipe lights."
>
> Fettes pocketed the money, and applauded the sentiment to the echo. "You are a philosopher," he cried. "I was an ass till I met you. You and K--- between you, by the Lord Harry! but you'll make a man of me."
>
> "Of course we shall," applauded Macfarlane. "A man? I tell you, it required a man to back me up the other morning. There are some big, brawling, forty-year-old cowards who would have turned sick at the look of the d---d thing; but not you—you kept your head. I watched you."
>
> "Well, and why not?" Fettes thus vaunted himself. "It was no affair of mine. There was nothing to gain on the one side but disturbance, and on the other I could count on your gratitude, don't you see?" And he slapped his pocket till the gold pieces rang.
>
> Macfarlane somehow felt a certain touch of alarm at these unpleasant words. He may have regretted that he had taught his young companion so successfully, but he had no time to interfere, for the other noisily continued in this boastful strain:
>
> "The great thing is not to be afraid. Now, between you and me, I don't want to hang—that's practical; but for all cant, Macfarlane, I was born with a contempt. Hell, God, devil, right, wrong, sin, crime, and all that old gallery of curiosities—they may frighten boys, but men of the world, like you and me, despise them. Here's to the memory of Gray!"

The cinematic Fettes is neither lion nor lamb, but a confused medical student involved in circumstances beyond his control. He feels personally responsible when Gray delivers the body of the street singer; in the story the men "with Irish voices" bring the girl's body without being commissioned. Although he later becomes hardened toward the murders, Stevenson's Fettes does feel a brief tinge of remorse. The film telescopes the two grave robbers into the character of Gray, but the following passage is faithfully reproduced:

> "I know her, I tell you," he continued. "She was alive and hearty only yesterday. It's impossible she can be dead; it's impossible you should have got this body fairly."
> 
> "Sure, sir, you're mistaken entirely," said one of the men.
> 
> But the other looked Fettes darkly in the eyes, and demanded money on the spot.

This episode is Stevenson's version of the Mary Paterson murder, an incident highlighted by Lewton, who based the cinematic Fettes on David Paterson and other Knox students. In the film, when Fettes joins MacFarlane at Penicuik, he desires not to rob graves but to inform the doctor of the successful surgery; in the story, Dr. K--- orders both men to rifle the grave at Glencorse. The idea of Georgina's back problems may have come from another of Burke's atrocities, in which he snapped the spine of a deaf, mute 12-year-old boy and then delivered the body to Knox in a herring barrel.

Somewhat naive in the film, Fettes is well played by Russell Wade, as are the other supporting roles, particularly Meg, a strong female character given credibility by the understated acting of Edith Atwater. In the brief role of the doomed Joseph (who appears to have been based, in part, on Daft Jamie), Bela Lugosi gives a convincing and somewhat moving performance, particularly in his scene with Karloff (making *The Body Snatcher* the last of eight films in which both actors appeared).

Although the entire film was shot on the RKO lot, Lewton evokes a convincing mid-nineteenth-century Scottish atmosphere, particularly through the use of Robert De Grasse's inventive compositions and lighting and Roy Webb's outstanding music. Shots of Edinburgh Castle are integrated successfully into the initial scene, and the re-creations of the Fisher's Tryst at Penicuik and Glencorse cemetery lend an authentic ambience. But the most impressive geographical element is the location that Lewton chose for the climactic sequence, a remarkable approximation of the Pentland Hills. The observant viewer may spot some heather in the medium long shots featuring the gig, and the final shot, showing Fettes walking up the road toward some rain-drenched braes, is particularly impressive.

Perhaps Lewton's most horrific use of Scottish history is his variation of an event that occurred in mid-nineteenth-century Edinburgh. After Gray kills the dog at Greyfriars, Fettes meets Mrs. Mac-Bride (Mary Gordon) as she carries its corpse from the kirkyard. "They killed me poor little Robbie, too," she tearfully informs him. Here Lewton perpetrates some cruel black humor by having the body snatcher slay one of Scotland's most beloved historical figures: "Greyfriars Bobby," the little terrier who diligently guarded the grave of its beloved master! (In Edinburgh today, there is a pub called Greyfriars Bobby, located across from the kirkyard, where tour guides invariably spend a great deal of time describing this sentimental tale to visitors. Perhaps Lewton had heard the story one time too many.)

Incorporating several traditional Scottish songs (an element that would have pleased Stevenson), Webb's score includes "We'd Better Bide a Wee," "When Ye Gang Awa', Jamie," and the Jacobite classic "Will Ye No Cam Back Again?" (all sung by the street singer), "Spit Song" (sung by a boy in the street, portrayed by Jack Welch), and Sir Walter Scott's "The Bonnets of Bonny Dundee" (sung by a quartet of men at the Fisher's Tryst). Other characters also engage in musical expression, including Fettes, who whistles his way through the Edinburgh streets, and Gray, who sings to Joseph about the murderous activities of Burke and Hare.

• EIGHT •

# There's a Breeze Coming, Jim: *Treasure Island* (1881)

*"Now, you mark me. I ask no questions, nor I won't let others. I know when a game's up, I do; and I know a lad that's staunch. Ah, you that's young—you and me might have done a power of good together!"*—LONG JOHN SILVER to Jim Hawkins, in *Treasure Island.*

The setting of this tale is described by young Jim Hawkins:

> Squire Trelawney, Dr. Livesey, and the rest of these gentlemen having asked me to write down the whole particulars about Treasure Island, from the beginning to the end, keeping nothing back but the bearings of the island, and that only because there is treasure not yet lifted, I take up my pen in the year of grace 17-- and go back to the time when my father kept the Admiral Benbow inn and the brown old seaman with the sabre cut first took up lodging under our roof.

Gravely ill, Billy Bones resides at the Admiral Benbow for "many months." The "brown old seaman" strikes fear into patrons' hearts as he consumes dangerous quantities of rum and sings an old sea ditty:

> Fifteen men on the dead man's chest—
> Yo-ho-ho, and a bottle of rum!
> Drink and the devil had done for the rest—
> Yo-ho-ho, and a bottle of rum!

Bones warns Jim to keep his "weather-eye open for a seafaring man with one leg" and relates tales of piracy and other foul deeds on the Spanish Main. One evening, while guzzling rum, he is reprimanded by Dr. Livesey, who has arrived to examine Jim's dying father. A short time later, Black Dog, a mysterious "tallowy creature," frightens Jim into revealing the whereabouts of Bones. Following a brief sword duel with the "Dog," the old seaman is visited by Blind Pew, another of his old shipmates, who delivers the "black spot," a death summons used by seafarers. Soon after, Bones succumbs to a fatal attack of apoplexy. Jim and his mother run to a nearby village, where the inhabitants unanimously refuse to help. Just before the pirates reach the inn, the inn, Jim removes a key from the corpse and grabs an oilskin packet from the captain's old sea chest. While the brigands frantically sack Bones's belongings, Jim and his mother hide under a nearby bridge. Unable to find "Flint's fist," the pirates escape, leaving Pew behind to be fatally trampled by horsemen from the village.

At the home of Squire Trelawney, Jim delivers the packet to Dr. Livesey. "This is the black-hearted hound's account book," the squire observes after the oilskin is removed. Passing over figures and course headings, the men turn to a second enclosure, a map of Captain John Flint's treasure island. Trelawney experiences an uncontrollable fit of excitement, vows to secure the best ship in England, and commands Livesey and Jim to accompany him on a treasure-hunting voyage.

Several weeks later Trelawney hires Long John Silver, a one-legged seaman and cook, and a salty band of sailors. At Bristol the crew weighs anchor and the *Hispaniola* begins its journey. Becoming acquainted with the charismatic sea cook, who totes a pet parrot named "Captain Flint," Jim is surprised when, hiding in an apple barrel on deck, he overhears Silver conspiring with crewmates Israel Hands and young Dick to take the ship once the treasure is carried aboard.

After land is sighted, a battle ensues between Captain Smollett's royal forces and Silver's swarthy knaves. Jim escapes ashore and falls in with Ben Gunn, an unfortunate seaman who was marooned by Captain Flint three years earlier. Treading the boundary between the opposing camps, Jim wins the confidence of Gunn (who leads Dr. Livesey to the treasure, which the marooned sailor has transferred to his secret cave) and recaptures the *Hispaniola* after cutting her hawser and sending Israel Hands to his death at the bottom of the sea.

Following a near-fatal experience with the surviving pirates (who arrogantly tip their leader the black spot and then rescind it), Jim accompanies Silver on the treasure hunt. When the angry rogues discover that the treasure has been removed, Silver shoots George Merry (the rebellious rascal who had deposed him the previous evening). Firing musket balls from the surrounding trees, Dr. Livesey, Squire Trelawney, and Ben Gunn force the remaining freebooters into the hinterlands.

Trelawney and his crew stow the treasure safely in the *Hispaniola*'s hold and leave provisions for the marooned pirates before setting sail for England. During a brief stop at a South American port, Silver, who faces trial and execution, steals a sack of coins and escapes over the rail.

Jim Hawkins concludes:

> Of Silver we have heard no more. That formidable seafaring man with one leg has at last gone clean out of my life; but I dare say he met his old Negress, and perhaps still lives in comfort with her and Captain Flint. It is to be hoped so, I suppose, for his chances of comfort in another world are very small.
>
> The bar silver and the arms still lie, for all that I know, where Flint buried them; and certainly they shall lie there for me. Oxen and

wain-ropes would not bring me back again to that accursed island; and the worst dreams that I ever have are when I hear the surf booming about its coasts or start upright in bed with the sharp voice of Captain Flint still ringing in my ears: "Pieces of eight! Pieces of eight!"

Late in August 1881 Stevenson conceived "The Sea Cook: A Story for Boys" in a rented cottage at Braemar. Again troubled by wet, windy weather, he remained indoors, where he and Lloyd experimented with a box of paints, passing the time by sketching a map of an "imaginary island." Stevenson later wrote:

> [A]s I paused upon my map of "Treasure Island," the future character of the book began to appear there visibly among imaginary woods; and their brown faces and bright weapons peeped out upon me from unexpected quarters, as they passed to and fro, fighting and hunting treasure, on these few square miles of a flat projection. The next thing I knew I had some papers before me and was writing out a list of chapters. How often have I done so, and the thing gone no further! But there seemed elements of success about this enterprise. It was to be a story for boys; no need of psychology or fine writing; and I had a boy at hand to be a touchstone. Women were excluded. I was unable to handle a brig (which the *Hispaniola* should have been), but I thought I could make shift to sail her as a schooner without public shame. And then I had an idea for Long John Silver from which I promised myself funds of entertainment; to take an admired friend of mine . . . to deprive him of all his finer qualities and higher graces of temperament, to leave him with nothing but his strength, his courage, his quickness, and his magnificent geniality, and to try to express these in terms of the culture of a raw tarpaulin. . . . On a chill September morning, by the cheek of a brisk fire, and the rain drumming on the window, I began *The Sea Cook*, for that was the original title.[1]

Completing 15 chapters in as many days, Stevenson was interrupted by illness and, after leaving Scotland, continued working on the first draft at Weybridge, outside London, and during a two-week session at his winter home in Davos. Lloyd had inspired him to write a boys' adventure story, but an additional impetus was provided by his father, who discussed various points of the tale and suggested the scene of Jim in the apple barrel, the specific contents of Billy Bones's sea chest, and the name *Walrus* for Captain Flint's old ship.[2]

Of this particular creative experience, Stevenson wrote, "It's quite silly and horrid fun, and what I want is the *best* book about the Buccaneers that can be had."[3] Though he used the word "buccaneer" in this instance, he utilizes both "buccaneer" and "pirate" to describe Long John Silver and his crew in the novel. In reality, these terms represent two distinct types of seafaring men who sailed during the seventeenth and eighteenth centuries.

Buccaneers (from the French word *boucaniers*, meaning "smokers of meat") were specific groups of French and English free-trading sailors who created a black market in an effort to skirt Spain's trading monopoly. It was their policy "to sell to the Spanish colonies what the settlers must have but could not get legally."[4] Eventually, they evolved into carousing freebooters who attacked and looted Spanish ships and ports. Establishing bases in Hispaniola and Tortuga Island, they held influence throughout the West Indies and into Central America. Historian and former naval officer Harold Francis Watson writes that they "were a rough lot ... guilty of drunkenness, rape, torture, and murder; but they occasionally rose to rather noble heights of chivalry and loyalty."[5]

In 1697 European trading nations signed the Peace of Ryswick, an international agreement which eliminated the excesses of the buccaneers but consequently raised the sail for another group of maritime criminals. These men, less disciplined and prone to fight among themselves for personal gain, were known as pirates. Concentrating most of their attacks in eastern seas, they settled in Madagascar and plundered extensively in Porto Bello and Zanzibar. Among the most famous pirates were Henry Avery (aka "Long Ben"), William Kidd (aka "Captain Kidd," a former privateer and pirate hunter who also used the names Robert, Richard, and John), and Edward Teach (aka "Blackbeard").

Watson describes the pirates' distinguishable characteristics:

> [T]he cloak of patriotism could not be used, as it was by the buccaneers, to cover all sorts of depredations. Hence, probably a larger portion of the pirates found themselves sun-dried at Corso Castle, or less exotically at Execution Dock, Wapping ... it was these eighteenth century freebooters who evolved the Jolly Roger, and used such expressions as "gentlemen of fortune" and "on the account."[6]

The piratical presence was felt in various parts of the globe (including the Southeastern United States) until the early nineteenth century. Watson adds: "Jean LaFitte, who became practical ruler of the Gulf of Mexico and dictator of Galveston in time to take part in our War of 1812, was about the last of the picturesque scoundrels of the old school."[7]

Stevenson blurs the distinction between the two groups by using their names interchangeably. However, by creating an ambiguous "good badman" personality for Silver (bearing similarities to the buccaneer style of behavior), he sets him apart from the selfish, cutthroat crew (who are cast more in the piratical vein).

Two general types of sea novels were popular during the nineteenth century: the navy yarn, which places a capable officer in adventurous situations amid realistic settings and historical events; and the desert island romance, which features shipwrecked or marooned characters confronted by treasure-seeking pirates or angry natives. Around 1815 the latter genre became one of the most popular fictional styles in Great Britain. Watson suggests that this interest may have been created, in part, by "the contemporary interest in the 'noble savage' of Rousseau and Chateaubriand, derived ultimately from the Greek pastoral. ... It is obvious of course that *Treasure Island* belongs to this development."[8]

The growth of the desert island genre can be traced back to 1719, when Daniel Defoe's legendary *Robinson Crusoe* was published. A century later, novels such as S. H. Burney's *The Shipwreck* (1816), Sir Walter Scott's *The Pirate* (1822), and Allan Cunningham's three-volume *Paul Jones* (1826) expanded upon the "almost monopolistic influence" of Defoe's classic.[9] Other period tales include John Howison's "The Island" (1830) and Jane Porter's verbosely titled *Sir Edward Seaward's Narrative of his Shipwreck and consequent discovery of certain islands in the Caribbean Sea with a detail of many extraordinary and highly interesting events in his life, from the year 1733 to 1749 as written in his own diary* (1831)!

Novels dealing with the macabre subject of "ghost" ships appeared toward the end of the 1830s, with Captain Frederick Marryat's *The Phantom Ship* (1839) and Nelson Neale's *The Flying Dutchman or a Legend of the High Seas* (1840) being two notable examples. Tales of piracy and shipwreck remained popular through the late 1860s, when, as Watson claims, Douglas Stewart's *The Pirate Queen* (1867) marked the nadir of the genre.[10]

Authors in the United States also contributed their share of maritime adventure stories. James Fenimore Cooper's *The Pilot* (1823), "the first major example of an American naval yarn," describes the exploits of Nantucket harpooner "Long Tom Coffin," a character that may have been familiar to Stevenson. However, as Watson writes, "If *The Pilot* had any influence at all on *Treasure Island*, possibly Long Tom contributed a detail or two, including perhaps Silver's nickname of Long John; and this, it should be emphasized, in view of the comparatively common use of the designation for a tall man in England, is supremely doubtful."[11] ("Long John" is also a brand of blended Scotch whisky, named after Long John MacDonald and established at Glasgow's Long John Distillery in 1825. Although Stevenson was fond of single malt whiskies, he probably was acquainted with blended varieties as well.)

Cooper contributed other sea tales, including *The Red Rover* (1827), *The Two Admirals* (1842), and *The Crater* (1847), which feature elements of the desert island romance. During the same period Edgar Allan Poe wrote the short classic, "MS Found in a Bottle" (1833), the fascinating novella, *The Narrative of Arthur Gordon Pym* (1837–38), and the intriguing tale of buried treasure, "The Gold-Bug" (1843). The 1830s and early 1840s also included the freebooting tales of Joseph Holt Ingraham, who penned *Lafitte, the Pirate of the Gulf* (1836), *Captain Kyd, or the Wizard of the Sea* (1838–39), and *The Spanish Galleon, or the Pirate of the Mediterranean* (1845).

Herman Melville, a major influence on the entire spectrum of contemporary literature, wrote many adventurous and powerful sea stories. Before he completed *Moby Dick* in 1851, he penned *Typee* (1846), *Omoo* (1847), *Mardi* (1849), *Redburn: His First Voyage* (1849), and *White Jacket* (1850).

In creating specific characters and devices for *Treasure Island*, Stevenson consciously borrowed material from previous authors. In a July 1884 letter to Sidney Colvin, he writes, "'Treasure Island' came out of Kingsley's 'At Last,' where I got the Dead Man's Chest—and that was the seed—and out of the great Captain Johnson's 'History of the Notorious Pirates.'"[12] In a 1934 essay Charles Starrett notes that "Deadman's Chest" is "an islet about half way along the southern coast of Puerto Rico, called on modern maps Isla de Caja de Muertos, i.e., Coffin Island." Watson adds, "[T]he name was carelessly transferred, at least by Charles Kingsley, to what on the old maps and modern charts I have examined appears invariably as Dead Chest Island. ... There is no reason to suppose that Stevenson was familiar with anything but the name."[13]

Stevenson admitted that he took the idea of Captain Flint's skeleton pointer from Poe's "The Gold-Bug," and he constructed Billy Bones's history from the pages of Washington Irving, another of his favorite writers. In his 1894 essay "My First Book," he mentions these literary influences—"some recollections of canoeing on the high seas, and the map itself, with its infinite and eloquent suggestion"—as being his major impetuses for writing the novel.[14]

One month after he conceived "The Sea Cook," chapters began to appear in the pages of *Young Folks* magazine. Eventually, the entire novel ran in 17 weekly installments from October 1, 1881, through January 28, 1882. Stevenson declined to use his real name, and titled the serialized novel "Treasure Island; or, The Mutiny of the Hispaniola. By Captain George North." *Young Folks* originally promised £100 for the serialization, but later calculated the amount by the page: he received only £34. 7s. 6d., but was allowed to maintain the copyright.

In a September 1881 letter the confident author writes, "I'll make this boy's business pay; but I have to make a beginning. When I'm done with 'Young Folks,' I'll try Routledge or some one. I feel pretty sure the 'Sea Cook' will do to reprint, and bring something decent at that."[15]

On November 14, 1883, Cassell and Company published the novel as *Treasure Island,* and Boston's Roberts Brothers released the American edition three months later. Sales in Great Britain proved good enough to necessitate a second Cassell edition in August 1885.

Although the *Young Folks* serialization did not elicit the response that Stevenson expected, British critics were nearly unanimous in their positive appraisal of the novel. Among the most ardent admirers of *Treasure Island* was William Gladstone (1809–1898), the zealous Liberal politician who served four terms as British prime minister between 1868 and 1894.

In his 1964 analysis Robert Kiely writes, "*Treasure Island* is one of the most satisfying adventure stories ever told primarily because it is the most unhampered. The great pleasure in reading the first few chapters depends not only on the gathering mystery, but on the exhilarating sense of *casting off* which Stevenson gives us."[16]

*Treasure Island* is arguably one of the greatest works of storytelling in the English language. Stevenson created subsequent novels with greater depth and insight, but he rarely surpassed the combination of pacing, color, and poetic prose that distinguishes his tale of piracy and boyhood adventure. Single, short sentences almost allow the reader to see the landscape and feel the atmosphere; for example, "Not a man, not a sail, upon the sea; the very largeness of the view increased the sense of solitude."

Stevenson includes believable dialogue in his early short stories, but his use of distinct dialects in *Treasure Island* is developed further. Not only does the reader experience the formal English of Squire Trelawney and, to some extent, Jim Hawkins but also the metaphorical and rhythmic jargon of the less-educated pirates. Long John Silver's dialogue, in particular, often flows in a lyrical manner. In chapter 11 ("What I Heard in the Apple Barrel"), Jim overhears a fine example of pirate speech:

> "Billy was the man for that," said Israel. "'Dead men don't bite.' says he. Well, he's dead now hisself; he knows the long and short on it now; and if ever a rough hand come to port, it was Billy."
>
> "Right you are," said Silver; "rough and ready. But mark you here, I'm an easy man—I'm quite the gentleman, says you; but this time it's serious. Dooty is dooty, mates. I give my vote—death. When I'm in Parlyment and riding in my coach, I don't want none of these sea lawyers in the cabin a-coming home, unlooked for, like the devil at prayers. Wait is what I say; but when the time comes, why, let her rip!"

The pirates' love of music further enhances their unique manner of expression. Billy Bones's legendary "Dead Man's Chest" song is a leitmotif, and the pirates' whistling of "Lillibulero," a traditional song favored by Whigs, provides an ironic political counterpoint to Captain Smollett's whistling of the Scottish melody "Come Lasses and Lads" after Silver attempts to bargain with him. These subtle references add to the unpredictable nature of the characters.

Although he is a larger-than-life creation, Long John Silver was inspired by Henley. Having lost a leg, Henley provided a physical disability that would become an eternal part of pirate lore. And at least one critic has written that the character's surname was suggested during Stevenson's honeymoon at the Silverado mine.[17] It is possible that other characters have historical precursors, including Ben Gunn (Benjamin Gun of Rio Pungo), Blind Pew (Thomas Tew, admiral of the pirate fleet at Madagascar), and Darby McGraw (Darby Mullins, who was hanged with Captain Kidd on May 23, 1701).[18]

*Treasure Island* is a prime example of Stevenson's refusal to champion any particular moral or social code. Evil is just as resourceful and likeable as good, and he weaves both concepts into the character of his pirate captain. "I was not a little proud of John Silver," he wrote, "and to this day rather admire that smooth and formidable adventurer."[19] Daiches describes the classical adventure-story structure Stevenson used to create this aspect of the novel:

> The problem to be faced by any writer of a boys' adventure story of this kind is that, while the struggle has to be essentially between the

good and the bad, the real romantic interest tends to lie with the bad. Picturesque villainy is naturally more appealing in such a context than everyday virtue, and the author's task is to enlist the sympathies of the reader at the same time on the side of virtue and the picturesque.[20]

Daiches suggests that moral ambiguity is a stylistic component of the novel. Regardless of Stevenson's intent, several scholars agree on his philosophical tone. While Dennis Butts writes that "Stevenson constantly reminds us of the inconsistencies of human behavior,"[21] Robert Kiely notes that Silver's escape "seems justified": "To have killed him would have implied a punishment, a moral judgement Stevenson apparently did not want to make in his book. By the same token, to have rewarded him too generously or to have brought about his conversion would also have introduced a moral element not anticipated by anything earlier in the novel and therefore hardly appropriate at the conclusion."[22]

Silver's personality confuses the "good" characters (Jim Hawkins, Dr. Livesey, and, in some respects, Squire Trelawney), but it seems clear-cut to the motley band of pirates: while they observe the same ambivalence in Silver's nature, they know that obedience is necessary in a chain of command, particularly toward a man who is both resourceful and brutal. Considering their captain to be preternatural (in the same way that they view the deceased Captain Flint), the pirates fear and obey him until late in the story, when they tip him the black spot; and even then, Silver gains the upper hand by calling attention to their desecration of a Bible. The usage of the affectionate nickname "Barbecue" is indicative of a familiarity and personal attachment which some of the pirates have experienced. Not only does Silver's power reign on the sea but also in his restaurant, where he successfully tends to the customers and the kettle over the fire.

In chapter ten ("The Voyage"), the insidious Israel Hands admits a reverence for the captain: "'He's no common man, Barbecue,' said the coxswain to me. 'He had good schooling in his young days and can speak like a book when so minded; and brave—a lion's nothing alongside of Long John! I seen him grapple four and knock their heads together—him unarmed." Jim notices that the remainder of the crew shares Hands's assessment, and he soon begins to feel it himself: "All the crew respected and even obeyed him. He had a way of talking to each and doing everybody some particular service. To me he was unweariedly kind, and always glad to see me in the galley, which he kept as clean as a new pin, the dishes hanging up burnished and his parrot in a cage in one corner." Silver's relationship with Jim reveals the depth of his personality. He is not a one-dimensional pirate figure killing his way toward treasure, but one of Stevenson's thoughtfully crafted "dual" characters.

*Treasure Island* has been praised for its depiction of Jim Hawkins, a boy who is forced to grow up quickly in the face of extraordinary circumstances. After the efforts of

Captain Smollett, Squire Trelawney, and Dr. Livesey prove ineffectual, Jim saves the ship and, with Ben Gunn's help, the treasure. This element may account for the novel's reputation as a children's favorite: while adult wisdom and authority fail to solve a problem, a resourceful and vigorous youth (aided by a half-crazed marooned sailor) succeeds. J. R. Hammond refers to Jim as Stevenson's "acute understanding of a child's outlook on the adult world,"[23] while Daiches views him as an essential element of the genre: "it is characteristic of the adventure story that the hero does not take control until a fairly late stage in the story: at first he is *swept* into the story, and only later is he able—since he is the hero—to establish a measure of control."[24]

Stevenson's depiction of Jim is thoroughly believable: though he performs adult feats, he is still a boy who becomes frightened and emotional. Daiches adds:

> Jim has courage and resourcefulness, but it is not these qualities alone that enable him to save himself and his friends. He has a kind of beginners luck. ... He is the ordinary boy thrown into the midst of adventure by pure chance and acquitting himself very creditably. In the course of the story he develops from a purely passive character into an experienced and resourceful campaigner. This development takes place under the reader's eyes, and the reader can see it as natural and inevitable in the circumstances. With his outwitting of Israel Hands Jim achieves his full stature as a man of action, just as in his refusal to go back on his word and escape from Silver and his men with Dr. Livesey he achieves his full moral stature.[25]

Unlike the popular conception of the character (created primarily by filmic depictions), Jim Hawkins is not a small boy, but a lad of 13 or 14. He is forced to become a man sooner than expected, due to his father's illness and the responsibilities of operating the Admiral Benbow, but he still displays actions traditionally viewed as "weak." At two points in the novel he weeps briefly, once in the face of death and, later, when he is accused of cowardice by Dr. Livesey.

Through his interactions with Jim, Billy Bones also displays relatively complex behavior. During his stay at the Admiral Benbow the doomed seaman alternately evokes fear and sympathy in the lad—a phenomenon graphically illustrated in chapter three ("The Black Spot") when, immediately after receiving the death summons from Blind Pew, he suffers his fatal apoplectic attack:

> "Ten o'clock!" he cried. "Six hours. We'll do them yet," and he sprang to his feet.
> Even as he did so, he reeled, put his hand to his throat, stood swaying for a moment, and then, with a peculiar sound, fell from his whole height face foremost to the floor.
> I ran to him at once, calling to my mother. But haste was all in vain. The captain had been struck dead by thundering apoplexy. It is a curious thing to understand, for I had certainly never liked the man, though of late I had begun to pity him, but as soon as I saw that he was dead, I burst into a flood of tears. It was the second death I had known, and the sorrow of the first was still fresh in my heart.

Stevenson's persuasive characterization of Jim is demonstrated during the recapture of the *Hispaniola*. The lad does not intend to pilot the ship but plans to set it adrift to circumvent the pirates' plunderous designs. After cutting the hawser, he is swept into the current and forced to spend the night drifting in the coracle. He does not think of sailing the ship to the north inlet until it stares him in the face the next morning; finding only one injured man aboard, he chooses to beach her.

Jim's relationship with Silver is drawn full circle when they join forces during the treasure hunt. In chapter 28 ("In the Enemy's Camp"), Silver admits his debt to the boy:

> "Now, look you here, Jim Hawkins," he said in a steady whisper that was no more than audible, "you're within half a plank of death, and what's a long sight worse, of torture. They're going to throw me off. But, you mark, I stand by you through thick and thin. I didn't mean to; no, not till you spoke up. I was about desperate to lose that much blunt, and be hanged into the bargain. But I see you was the right sort. I says to myself, you stand by Hawkins, John, and Hawkins'll stand by you. You're his last card, and by the living thunder, John, he's yours! Back to back, says I. You save your witness, and he'll save your neck!"
>
> I began dimly to understand.
>
> "You mean all's lost?" I asked.
>
> "Aye, by gum, I do!" he answered. "Ship gone, neck gone—that's the size of it. Once I looked into that bay, Jim Hawkins, and seen no schooner—well, I'm tough, but I gave out. As for that lot and their council, mark me, they're outright fools and cowards. I'll save your life—if so be as I can—from them. But see here, Jim—tit for tat—you save Long John from swinging."
>
> I was bewildered; it seemed a thing so hopeless he was asking—he, the old buccaneer, the ringleader throughout.
>
> "What I can do, that I'll do," I said.
>
> "It's a bargain!" cried Long John. "You speak up plucky and, by thunder, I've a chance!"

Perhaps Silver's most powerful display occurs in chapter 29 ("The Black Spot Again"), immediately after he is deposed by his mutinous crew. Here Stevenson includes a dramatic passage graced with colorful pirate jargon and a keen sense of rhythm. Accused of botching the mission, Silver lashes out at the pirates, disassociating himself from their self-interest and invincible stupidity:

> "Well now, look here, I'll answer these four p'ints; one after another I'll answer 'em. I made a hash o' this cruise, did I? Well now, you all know what I wanted, and you all know if that had been done that we'd a been aboard the *Hispaniola* this night as ever was, every man of us alive, fit, and full of good plum-duff, and the treasure in the hold of her, by thunder! Well, who crossed me? Who forced my hand, as was the lawful cap'n? Who tipped me the black spot the day we landed and began this dance? Ah, it's a fine dance—I'm with you there—and looks mighty like a hornpipe in a rope's end at Execution Dock by London town, it does. But who done it? Why, it was Anderson, and Hands, and you, George Merry! And you're the last above board of that same meddling crew; and you have the Davy

Jones's insolence to up and stand for cap'n over me—you that sank the lot us! By the powers! But this tops the stiffest yarn to nothing."

Stevenson referred to *Treasure Island* as a boys' adventure tale, but its subsequent reputation as a children's novel has damaged its credibility as a major nineteenth-century work. In his 1951 biography of Stevenson, J. C. Furnas strongly criticizes this categorization, laying a portion of the blame at cinema's door: "The movies usually completed the sabotage by casting Jim as a child of nine or ten instead of as a boy in his teens conceivably capable of snatching up a cutlass in the melee at the blockhouse."[26]

Film historian Tony Thomas writes, "*Treasure Island* is such a perfectly constructed yarn that it defies doing badly."[27] Only the first half of Thomas's claim is true: the novel is ideally suited to visualization but, as the cinematic record shows, it has been "done badly." In fact, it took 82 years and 8 major attempts before the novel received a satisfying and faithful treatment.

## Early Film Adaptations (1908–18)

The first film version of *Treasure Island*, a one-reel silent featuring select passages from the novel, was released by Vitagraph in 1908. A second short, directed by J. Searle Dawley and released by Edison, appeared in 1912. No prints of either film are known to exist.

In 1918 Fox released a six-reel "Kiddie" adaptation. Codirected by C. M. and S. A. Franklin, the film opens with a pirate attack on the Admiral Benbow and then segues into a dream experienced by Jim Hawkins (Francis Carpenter). Portions of Stevenson's plot are integrated into the dream sequence, which features child actors as Long John Silver, Ben Gunn, and others. An additional character, Virginia (Virginia Lee Corbin), the daughter of Squire Trelawney, was added to attract a wider children's audience. Not only did Fox fabricate a female character (Mrs. Hawkins is the only woman who appears in the novel), but the studio cast a girl (Violet Radcliffe) in the role of Silver!

## *Treasure Island* (Paramount, 1920)

The first serious feature adaptation of *Treasure Island* was directed by Maurice Tourneur in late 1919 and released by Paramount the following spring. Perhaps following Fox's lead, the studio cast a girl in a conspicuous male role. On April 20, 1920, a day after the film premiered at the Rivoli in New York City, the *New York Times* reported, "The first false note is struck when Miss Shirley Mason appears as Jim Hawkins. She does all a girl can with the part and in a number of scenes has something of boyish charm, but at no time is she the sturdy lad depicted by Stevenson, and every now and then her distinctly feminine mannerisms destroy the last illusion."[28]

Several contemporary reviews criticized Jules Furthman's excursive screenplay. Combined with Shirley Mason's performance, Furthman's approach destroys the credibility of Jim Hawkins: he is depicted not as a lad who matures in the face of adversity but as a pawn in the schemes of Dr. Livesey and other adults. The *New York Times* noted that this alteration presents Jim as "a convenient agent for bringing about predetermined results."[29] The recapture of the *Hispaniola* is not executed by Jim, but results from a series of accidents that occur after he is sent on an errand by Dr. Livesey. Other deviations from the novel involve Jim's experience in the apple barrel (he spends the entire month-long voyage inside it!) and a change in the narrative point of view: Jim does not recount the events; he is merely one of several characters affected by them.

Taken on its own terms, the film is composed vividly by the action-oriented Tourneur (who again would collaborate with Furthman, on Paramount's *The White Circle*, later that year) and cinematographer Rene Guissart. As Long John Silver, Charles Ogle primarily concentrates on the evil side of the character, but Lon Chaney, Sr., who appears as both Blind Pew and George Merry, lends a curious element to the production. Still a few years away from his starring roles in Universal's *The Hunchback of Notre Dame* (1923) and *The Phantom of the Opera* (1925), Chaney created two original make-ups to add to his evolving gallery of "a thousand faces."

## *Treasure Island* (MGM, 1934)

The first sound adaptation of the novel, MGM's *Treasure Island* (1934), is also the most famous, produced by the glossiest of Hollywood studios and featuring an all-star cast of American and British character actors. The review in *Variety*, however, mentions the pitfalls of such a lustrous approach:

> It's pretty dangerous to put an old classic as popular as is this Stevenson yarn on the screen. So many millions have read the story that they all have preconceived notions of the casting necessary and the manner in which the story should be told. With the manner there is, in this instance, no quarrel; it is as pretentious and swashbuckling as it could be. But the casting, despite the quality of the people used, leaves something to be desired.[30]

Again, the story is told without narration from Jim Hawkins (Jackie Cooper), whose father is dead when the action begins. A large crowd (inconceivable at this point in the novel) is celebrating outside a brightly lit studio version of the Admiral Benbow as Jim sentimentally bakes his mother a birthday cake! The early scenes, including Billy Bones's arrival, follow the novel's outline rather closely, but little of Stevenson's memorable dialogue is included and none of the actors attempt to conceal their American accents (a factor that adds to the artificiality of the entire production). Lionel Barrymore overplays his turn as Bones, making absurd nose-blowing sounds as he wheezes about the premises. (Bones does blow his nose in the novel.) He succumbs immediately after the black spot is delivered by Blind Pew (William V. Mong), who is trampled (not by horses but by a wagon) in a graphically composed shot by cinematographer Ray June.

Although some adults have no idea who wrote the novel, they may

*Treasure Island* (1920). Lon Chaney, Sr., as pirate-mutineer George Merry, one of his two roles in Paramount's unconvincing adaptation of the legendary pirate novel.

recall the name of Wallace Beery when its title is mentioned. This is unfortunate, considering that even *Variety* noted the actor's apparent disinterest. Placing Jackie Cooper's portrayal of Jim Hawkins in the same category, the review claims that "neither of the two completely convinces; neither seems to be aware of the seriousness and danger of the situations they get into."[31]

*Treasure Island* (1920). Lon Chaney, Sr. (in makeup as Blind Pew), director Maurice Tourneur, and Shirley Mason (in makeup as Jim Hawkins!) on an outdoor set.

Silver's first appearance is uneventful, as he is shown standing beside Squire Trelawney (Nigel Bruce) on the deck of the *Hispaniola*. The atmosphere and intrigue of Jim's visit to the Spy-Glass tavern is abandoned, apparently in an attempt to advance the plot (which still plods along). Stevenson's rapid but carefully crafted pace is purged in favor of contrivances that establish an implausible alliance between Jim and Silver. Shortly after the voyage begins, both characters are seen at the wheel of the ship (Captain Smollet [Lewis Stone] seems to be lax in his duties) and, soon after, a weepy Jim asks the pirate leader to move in with him! "We'll always be mates, won't we," the boy simpers.

Large doses of Hollywood costume-drama hokum pervade the Silver-Hawkins relationship. Silver's parrot receives more attention here than in the novel, and the comic bantering between the pirate and the bird is a nuisance. Several of Stevenson's colorful pirate phrases are overused, including the "Dead Man's Chest" song (first sung by Billy Bones) and "pieces of eight" (repeatedly babbled by the parrot). Stevenson's "Dead men don't bite" becomes the more verbose "Dead men don't bite, nor tell no tales, says he," stated by Silver during Jim's sojourn in the apple barrel.

This tendency to overplay some of the novel's elements is demonstrated further when Jim reports the mutiny to Captain Smollett and Squire Trelawney. After repeating Silver's plan to take the ship, Jim weeps, claiming that his lifelong friend has deceived him. This extended Jackie Cooper take foreshadows several mawkish scenes which occur later.

Similar to the liberties taken by the 1920 version, this film assumes that plot exposition and credibility are a waste of time. Wholesale contrivances occur after the *Hispaniola* reaches the island: events just *happen* and no effort is taken to depict the action leading up to them. The battle aboard the ship is omitted and, later, Jim (getting the idea from Smollett) recaptures her with very little effort. The battle at the stockade, ragingly depicted by Stevenson, is stilted, with the action alternating between the "heroes" and the pirates. The interior of the stockade is not shown, and the fight seems to end before it has begun. These narrative and stylistic choices, made by both director Victor Fleming and screenwriter John Lee Mahin, maintain a pace that drags throughout most of the 109-minute running time.

One of the novel's finest passages, the mutiny of Silver's crew at the stockade, is handled poorly. The scene of the pirates tipping Silver the black spot is ignored, and the following morning, when Dr. Livesey (Otto Kruger) arrives, Jim grovels and weeps.

The final scenes move toward an inevitable conclusion. Unlike the novel, which develops Jim and Silver's relationship into a mutual need for survival, the film concludes with them engaging in absurd comedy and sentimentality. Hearing that the pirate will stand trial and hang, Jim cries and, while Ben Gunn is preoccupied with an enormous piece of cheese, releases his friend from the brig. Incredibly, Silver pleads, "No, no, no! I'm ticklish—under my arm!" This last gasp of Hollywood humor is followed by Silver's escape over the rail. Handing Jim his parrot, the pirate again sets the lad weeping as he speaks of how they will be treasure-hunting mates in the future.

The two stars do very little to improve the deficiences of the screenplay. Beery's Silver is slightly comic and *very* lovable and Cooper's Jim is indelibly maudlin—both are artless variations of characters they created for *The Champ* (1931) and *The Bowery* (1933), two costarring vehicles produced at MGM. The artificiality of their relationship is made even worse by the glossy lighting of June and the sentimental musical score by Herbert Stothart. Perry Nodelman comments on this filmic simplification:

> Under Victor Fleming's direction Jackie Cooper's Jim Hawkins and Wallace Beery's Long John Silver are unambiguous caricatures of boyish innocence and unattractive evil. Imperviously innocent, Cooper's Jim perceives a charm in Beery's charmless Silver invisible to everyone else, including the audience. The film has it both ways: it asks us both to despise Silver and to admire Jim's ability not to notice how despicable Silver is. Neither Jim's innocence nor Silver's evil is the least bit ambiguous.[32]

Referred to as a "terminally ingenuous heartwringer" by Nodelman, Jackie Cooper's Jim is difficult to accept on any level. A large portion of the blame, however, must fall on Louis B. Mayer, who insisted that Cooper play several tearful scenes, and Mahin, whose script repeatedly mocks the period language used in the novel. Stevenson's expert integration of dialects used in eighteenth-century England and, particularly, in maritime circles, becomes another silly Hollywood gag. At several points Cooper repeats a phrase to make it sound as ridiculous as possible: gazing at Silver on one occasion, he hoots, "Says you! Says I! Says you!" and, when surprised (a state he frequently experiences), he babbles, "Bless my soul" or "Upon my soul" with a cute, wide-eyed gleam.

There are a few watchable elements. Wallace Beery rarely becomes hammy (a tendency that some performers have not been able to resist), although he appears lethargic in most of his scenes. Unlike the star performers, the supporting players are the film's redeeming feature. As Squire Trelawney, Nigel Bruce portrays a pompous aristocrat without slipping into his usual blowsy style (most obviously demonstrated in his 14 appearances as Dr. Watson to Basil Rathbone's Sherlock Holmes in the 1939–46 20th Century–Fox/Universal series). But the finest characterizations are Douglas Dumbrille's believably evil Israel Hands and Lewis Stone's determined Captain Smollett. Though most of the action is unconvincing, there are a few aboard-ship shots which lend a picturesque atmosphere.

Unfortunately, this film was the only English-language adaptation of *Treasure Island* made during the 1930s. In 1937 a feature version, starring Osip Abdulov as Long John Silver, was produced in the USSR.

## *Treasure Island* (Walt Disney, 1950); *Long John Silver's Return to Treasure Island* (DCA, 1954)

*Treasure Island*'s reputation as a children's novel can be attributed, in part, to the popularity of Walt Disney's 1950 film version. Like the 1934 adaptation, it abandons plot exposition and detail for an abridged narrative, one-dimensional characterizations, and fabricated dialogue. The $1.8 million budget rarely shows on the screen, and the visual style, rendered by director Byron Haskin and cinematographer F. A. Young, is often cramped and static, relying primarily on the medium two-shot and the medium long shot. There are a number of striking silhouette shots (depicting men, horses, and ships' riggings against the night sky), but these do little to balance the artificial and claustrophobic atmosphere.

Prior to *Treasure Island,* Walt Disney had never produced a live-action film—a fact that may account for the cartoon-like screenplay and performances. To utilize "frozen" British revenues, Disney chose to shoot the film in England and, together with RKO-Radio, maintained a sound commercial strategy by treading close to the puerile content of his animated productions. Catering to popular

***Treasure Island*** (1934). Jim Hawkins (Jackie Cooper), Long John Silver (Wallace Beery), and "Captain Flint," in MGM's maudlin adaptation.

taste, he cast 12-year-old, Iowa-born Bobby Driscoll as Jim Hawkins and shipped him to the shores of Old Blighty, where he soon appeared (with dubious "period" clothing and Midwest American accent) amid a company of English character actors.

Lawrence E. Watkin's script follows the basic outline of the novel, but many specific incidents, nearly all of the colorful period dialogue and, most distressingly, Jim's first-person narration are eliminated. As the film begins, Billy Bones (here called Captain Bones [Finlay Currie]) is at the Admiral Benbow, lying near death as Black Dog (Francis de Wolff) is sent away by Jim (who appears to be a tiny tot of about nine). Soon the captain stumbles down the stairs, asking for rum to steady his tremulous condition. When the old sea dog guzzles the foul liquor, Jim runs out to fetch Dr. Livesey (Denis O'Dea) but is stopped in his tracks by the evil Pew (John Laurie). Bones receives the black spot (which features the ambiguous warning "until dark"), opens his sea chest, and shoves the treasure map into Jim's shirt before falling dead on the floor. Stevenson's fascinating Bones becomes inconsequential: Currie's characterization is neither menacing nor capable of arousing the viewer's sympathy. And Mrs. Hawkins and Jim's ailing (or deceased) father are eliminated; apparently, the wee lad has been operating the Admiral Benbow all by himself!

For the remainder of the film, characters telegraph the results of events before they happen—a narrative blunder created by Watkin's hackneyed screenplay and Haskin's frenetic pacing. Before Long John Silver (Robert Newton) is introduced, Jim, Dr. Livesey, and Squire Trelawney (Walter Fitzgerald) stroll into the Spy-Glass inn and discuss the apples that they will take on the voyage! And, shortly after Silver's first appearance, he and Jim, facing each other in the back room, eagerly shake hands "as shipmates." When the *Hispaniola* reaches the island, Jim escapes Silver's clutches and, chased by some of the pirates, immediately runs into Ben Gunn (Geoffrey Wilkinson), who leaps down from a craggy hill.

The action sequences pale in comparison to those in the 1934 version: the mutiny aboard the *Hispaniola* amounts to little (land is sighted as Jim, hiding in the apple barrel, overhears Silver's plans), and the battle at the stockade culminates in a montage of close-ups that alternates between Captain Smollet's (Basil Sydney) men and Silver's cutthroats. Silver stands at the fence, leering and grimacing, before shooting the captain and running back toward the beach. Jim's recapture of the *Hispaniola* is even worse. After accepting the treasure map from Dr. Livesey and sneaking off into the night, he sends Israel Hands (Geoffrey Keen) to Davy Jones and, instead of sailing the ship to the northern inlet, beaches her on the sand, in plain sight of the pirates. Remarkably, he does strike the Jolly Roger and raise the Union Jack before returning to the stockade, where he falls into Silver's hands.

The pirates' mutiny against Silver is one of the film's better sequences, although much of Stevenson's dialogue is discarded. The majority of the scene is well staged and acted, but the childish impotence of Driscoll's performance (and Watkin's script) mars the overall effect. After Silver barks his resignation to the men, he turns and winks at Jim, who is apparently too stupid to understand the proceedings. When they reach the looted treasure spot (the hunt lasts exactly two minutes), the villains are dispatched and Jim pleads for Silver's life. Soon Jim and Dr. Livesey state that they will testify at his "fair trial in England." (Incredibly, when the men bear the treasure from the island, it is stored in one small sea chest!)

All appears neat and tidy until Silver wrests two pistols away from Trelawney and Jim as they row out to the ship. Tossing the other men into the water, the determined pirate forces Jim to steer the boat across the channel to the beach, where he plans to blow out the frightened little boy's brains. Silver is unable to pull the trigger, however, and Jim helps him shove off into the open sea. Reaching the shore in another skiff, the others watch as Silver raises his sail. With the closing credits looming, Dr. Livesey offers his best wishes as Jim waves.

The most satisfying moments (as in the 1934 version) are supplied by the supporting actors. As Captain Smollett, Basil Sydney turns in the most believable performance and is nearly matched by Denis O'Dea's restrained and distinguished Dr. Livesey. The two featured performances, however, fail to capture much of the Silver-Hawkins rapport. While Bobby Driscoll's Jim is stilted and lethargic, Robert Newton's Silver is too blustery and overblown: his bizarre pronunciations (particularly his tendency to add a "hard R" sound to certain words; he pronounces "amen" as "armen," for example), coupled with his eye-rolling and incessant grimaces, add to the unconvincing atmosphere. Newton is more subdued in some scenes but is limited by the one-dimensional script. Silver and Jim have no relationship, but merely recite starchy dialogue to one another from time to time.

The cartoon-like style is reinforced by Clifton Parker's musical score, particularly in the scenes featuring Ben Gunn: each time the marooned sailor leaps into Jim's path, he is accompanied by an absurd xylophone flourish. Another of Stevenson's colorful characters, Gunn matters little here: after his encounter with Jim, he briefly reappears at the treasure site and in the background when Dr. Livesey and Jim bid farewell to Silver. After spending five years alone on the island (three years in the novel), poor old Ben is not included among those who row out to the *Hispaniola* (in fact, all of the characters, except Silver, are still standing on the island when the final scene fades). The triviality of this character is only one example of Haskin's and Watkin's shallow presentation. Select events from the novel, animated by actors blurting out stale approximations of Stevenson's dialogue, occur without motivation or explanation.

Without question, Walt Disney produced some of the most entertaining and technically marvelous films of Hollywood's golden age, but most of his live-action efforts pale in the shadow of his animated classics. His *Treasure Island* will appeal primarily to children below the age of 12 and, for this age group, it provides a pleasant diversion. But, after seeing the film, any child would benefit from a bedtime reading of the original text.

Disney-inclined critics such as Leonard Maltin have praised this adaptation as a great adventure film. His assessment suggests that he viewed it through rose-colored glasses, and his reading of the Silver-Hawkins relationship is highly dubious:

> [C]entral to the book, and emphasized in the film, is the relationship between young Jim and Long John Silver. Jim is rather mature for his age, and is beyond the fairy-tale stage of hero-worshipping pirates. But he is still a boy, and he relishes the opportunity to go to sea on a great adventure. He *does* get taken in by Long John's facade of good humor and courtliness, but this is not due so much to Jim's naiveté as to Silver's convincingness.[33]

Maltin's comments provide a reasonably accurate picture of the novel, but there is no evidence in the Disney film to justify these statements. The cinematic characterizations never go beyond a surface reading of the text, and they are not "mature" or "convincing." Maltin mistakes studio glass shots and unremitting claustrophia for "authenticity"; he justifies Robert

*Treasure Island* (1950). On board the *Hispaniola*, Jim Hawkins (Bobby Driscoll) attempts to escape the clutches of the evil Israel Hands (Geoffrey Keen).

Newton's overacting as a quality which "remains in the memory long after everything else about the film has been forgotten"; he calls Bobby Driscoll's performance "masterful"; and he incomprehensibly praises Watkin for a finale that "builds on Stevenson's foundation": "Although this changes Stevenson's finale . . . it is most assuredly in keeping with the spirit of the author's work, and enhances the already fascinating relationship between these two characters."[34]

Maltin's most egregious error occurs when he blames Stevenson for Newton's histrionic caricature: "The film . . . belongs to Robert Newton, as Long John Silver. Rereading Stevenson, one finds that Newton *is* Long John, and the 'hamminess' that many found over- bearing in the performance is really as much Stevenson as it is Newton."[35] If Maltin had reread the novel *before* seeing the film, he may have developed a different opinion about Newton's performance. Turning to the novel afterward, he probably found what he was looking for, rather than what Stevenson intended. Newton's one-dimensional pirate possesses none of the moral ambiguity of Stevenson's creation and only a brief display of what Maltin calls a "facade of good humor and courtliness."

Byron Haskin, as well as Newton and Watkin, bears some of the responsibility for the trivial depiction of Silver. Claiming that "Long John was very near the top in flamboyant playing," Haskin "could do little more than let him 'rip'" while on-screen: "I cast Ralph Truman in the role of George Merry ... giving him full scope to out-ham Newton whenever he could. At times, Newton, by contrast, looked downright underplayed!"[36]

A talented cinematographer and special-effects artist, Haskin was a technically adept filmmaker but poorly qualified to direct a literary adaptation. (Three years later he directed Paramount's adaptation of H. G. Wells's *War of the Worlds;* though the film is technically impressive, it is acted badly, and Barre Lyndon's screenplay includes very little of Wells's text.) The general quality of *Treasure Island* can be attributed to his misinterpretation of the novel: "Anyhow, the film was a children's story, told by Stevenson to children. Kids don't go in much for subtleties."[37] According to Haskin's insulting comment, Stevenson did not *write* *Treasure Island,* but *told* a melodramatic yarn to little children who were too stupid to understand anything more artful. Considering Haskin's attitude, it is no wonder that Jim Hawkins is so dense and frightened in the film.

Some of Haskin's technical choices can be criticized as well. As mentioned previously, the static, visual style is occasionally broken up by silhouette shots, but his one attempt at a picturesque long shot, depicting a sweeping vista, is framed from the wrong perspective: rather than showing the island from the point of view of a character on the *Hispaniola,* the scene shows the ship from the viewpoint of the island! (Since Ben Gunn has yet to be introduced, his point of view [which is never used as a visual or narrative device] cannot be considered as a possibility.) Of course, Leonard Maltin praises Haskin "for bringing out the full potential of each situation."[38]

Walt Disney cannot be blamed for all of the film's deficiencies, but he was responsible for allowing Haskin and Watkin free reign during the production, both on location and at Denham Studios in England. Critical reaction to the film's release on July 19, 1950, was negative on both sides of the Atlantic, and box-office receipts fell far below what Disney anticipated. Due to its lukewarm reception, the film was not reissued, and Disney waited a decade before producing another (and much better) Stevenson adaptation. (*Treasure Island* was later broadcast, in its entirety, on the *Wonderful World of Disney* television program. An edited version of the film was reissued to theaters in 1975.)

Robert Newton and Byron Haskin, however, could not resist reteaming for a sequel. Sporting the verbose title, *Long John Silver's Return to Treasure Island,* this 1954 Australian film (aka *Long John Silver*) expands the worst qualities of the Disney production. The artificiality of Newton's earlier performance seems realistic when contrasted with his drink-sodden, snarling, and goggle-eyed turn in this overlong and pedestrian exercise.

Supposedly beginning some years after Silver's escape from Trelawney and company, the film depicts the once cunning pirate as the agent of an island governor! Hired to rescue the politician's daughter from "El Toro," a

Spanish cutthroat, Silver sops up large quantities of rum and inordinately growls, "Aaaaarrrrgh!" and laughs, "Heh, heh, heh, heh," to those around him. Together with his bosom companion, Jim Hawkins (13-year-old Kit Taylor, who looks much younger), Silver foils "El Toro" and sails back to Treasure Island, where he plans to discover an additional £900,000 that Captain Flint had buried there!

Some scattered references to the novel are included (Silver's usage of "smart as paint" and "Them's that dies'll be the lucky ones!"), but the only major Stevenson incident is a poor paraphrase of Jim's experience in the apple barrel. While at sea, the lad discovers yet another Silver-inspired plot to steal a ship and hunt for buried treasure; while ducking into the galley to get some salt, he conveniently overhears the pirate's plan. After the ship arrives at the island, the pace drags interminably as Silver and his crew search for the loot. Inexplicably, Israel Hands (Rod Taylor) is among them, having arisen from Davy Jones's locker to become a grotesque, blind madman. Thirsting for revenge, "El Toro" arrives but, after some poorly staged action sequences, both Jim and Silver emerge as heroic figures. The final scene shows the pirate being chased by Purity Pinker (Connie Gilchrist), an old, plump, blonde woman who proposes marriage, presumably to end his adventurous, eye-rolling, and tongue-lolling lifestyle.

The first Australian film shot in Cinemascope, *Long John Silver's Return to Treasure Island* is neither artful nor entertaining. Bad direction, writing, acting, cinematography, editing, art and costume direction, and 1950s Latin music combine to create a thoroughly inane viewing experience. Jim's sentimental devotion to Silver (the lad declares, "Squire Trelawney will defend you!" at one point) is matched by the use of cheap, miniature ships, absurd plot twists, and banal comedy relief. Even Robert Newton did not deserve scenes involving a ridiculous, stereotyped female character who forces him to drink milk, dunks his head into a barrel of water, and chases him through the streets! Incredibly, the film was advertised in the United States as "Robert Louis Stevenson's *Long John Silver*."

To promote its "first major attraction," the fledgling Distributors Corporation of America (DCA) included large doses of propaganda in the official pressbook. One article, titled "Adventure Saga in CinemaScope Captures Spirit of Pirate Era," states that screenwriter Martin Rackin "worked on a logical account of Silver's later adventures, examining every authentic detail, every fable of the Spanish Main, for background and color."[39] The most outlandish hype, however, was DCA's claim that the "rigidly trained" group of extras who appeared as pirates in the film included "a former master of dueling, a former trainer of duelists, two judo experts and four commandos"![40] (With these formidable fighters at his side, Byron Haskin should have created more exciting action scenes.)

Apparently undaunted by the poor quality of this film, Newton

*Long John Silver's Return to Treasure Island* (1954). An original advertisement for DCA's Australian "sequel" to Walt Disney's *Treasure Island*. Robert Newton's facial expression is indicative of his intolerably obnoxious performance, in a film whose origin was actually credited to Stevenson!

portrayed Silver in a subsequent Australian television series before heavy drinking hastened his death at the age of 50 on March 25, 1956. Although he was a notorious scene-stealer in his later films, he did give memorable performances as Pistol in Laurence Olivier's adaptation of Shakespeare's *Henry V* (1944), as Lukey in the Carol Reed-directed *Odd Man Out* (1947), and as Bill Sykes in David

Lean's and Stanley Haynes's adaptation of Dickens's *Oliver Twist* (1948).

Tragically, Bobby Driscoll became one of Hollywood's many child stars to meet an untimely end. He appeared in only five films after *Treasure Island* and, by 1958, his career was over. After being arrested for drug possession on a number of occasions, he moved to New York City in 1965, where his body was found in an abandoned tenement three years later. Occlusive coronary arteriosclerosis (hardening of the arteries) was diagnosed as the cause of death and the body was buried in a pauper's grave, but positive identification was not made until 1969. Though he had received an Academy Award as "the outstanding juvenile actor of 1949" (for his performance in the Ted Tetzlaff-directed *The Window*), Driscoll was a has-been at the age of 21 and he was only 31 when he died. Without question, Driscoll and the other elements that make up the 1950 *Treasure Island* do not constitute a faithful adaptation of Stevenson, but they are infinitely preferable to anything in the next two cinematic excursions.

## *Return to Treasure Island* (World/United Artists, 1954)

*Return to Treasure Island* (1954), World Films' "continuation" of the novel, should receive a special award for being the worst motion picture based on or suggested by a Stevenson work. Produced and written by Aubrey Wisberg and Jack Pollexfen, this abysmal excuse for entertainment stars Dawn Addams as "Jamesina" Hawkins, a direct descendant of Jim Hawkins, and Tab Hunter as Clive Stone, an archaeologist searching for the remainder of Captain Flint's treasure.

Featuring a voice-over narration by Hunter, the "story begins some two-hundred years after Robert Louis Stevenson's tale of adventure on Treasure Island ends." Moments into the opening scene, a hackneyed flashback incorporates brief images of Long John Silver (Robert Long) and Captain Flint (Dayton Lummis), who, contrary to Stevenson, was still alive when Trelawney's expedition landed on the island! In fact, the film claims that Stevenson was wrong about many things and depicts a simpering, infantile Silver being gunned down by the insidious Flint, who then turns his pistols on the entire crew, including (the long-dead) Darby McGraw.

The next scene is set at a low-budget version of the Admiral Benbow, where Miss Hawkins, now called "Jamie," is visited by an archaeologist (Porter Hall) who introduces himself as Clive Stone. Speaking of his interest in pirates, "Stone" asks to see Captain Flint's old treasure map and Bible, both of which were left at the inn by her famous ancestor. Jamie is intrigued by the map and agrees to accompany "Stone" (actually a criminal named Maximillian Harris) to Treasure Island, where a group of "pirates," led by the blind James Seay (Felix Newman), plan to steal Flint's buried loot.

In a badly adapted version of the apple barrel incident, Jamie overhears members of Harris's gang discussing the impending treasure hunt. One of the film's most laughable sequences, it shows the swimsuit-clad Dawn Addams (whose ample physical attributes are highlighted by William Bradford's Pathecolor camerawork) descending a ladder into a studio approximation of the Atlantic ocean. As the boat (which supposedly is sailing to the island) remains anchored in a stagnant water tank, Addams listens through a porthole. Referred to as a schooner by the characters, the boat is actually a small yacht, but stock footage of an authentic schooner is cut in on occasion. This bad editing technique recurs when the real Clive Stone attempts to find a passage out of Ben Gunn's cave: as Tab Hunter babbles to himself, the scene alternates between medium shots filmed in a studio cave and medium close-ups shot on a bright, sunlit backlot location.

A visual disgrace, *Return to Treasure Island* features some of the worst acting ever filmed. Receiving the majority of screen time, Dawn Addams is particularly bad when she rattles off the names of Stevenson's characters: "They were all here," she tells Stone (as Wisberg and Pollexfen's script attempts to work in "material" from the novel). An English-born nonactress who later appeared in Charles Chaplin's absurdly pretentious *A King in New York* (1957) and several low-budget horror films (including a Dr. Jekyll and Mr. Hyde adaptation), Addams merely adds some topographical splendor to the lackluster art direction. In one of his early film roles, 1950s beefcake star Tab Hunter turns in a truly appalling performance. His mechanical delivery and tendency to stumble over every line is made even worse by director E. A. Dupont's insistence that he play every scene without a shirt.

The German-born Dupont, who wrote and directed *Variety* (1925), one of the European silent cinema's true masterpieces, spent his later career making mediocre programmers in Hollywood. Although *The Neanderthal Man* (1953), another Wisberg-Pollexfen production for World Films, is one of his worst directorial outings, *Return to Treasure Island* rivals the work of Edward D. Wood, Jr. (who wrote and directed his "classics," *Glen or Glenda* [1953], *Bride of the Monster* [1955], and *Plan 9 from Outer Space* [1956] during the same period), for sheer cinematic incompetence. However, unlike Wood's films, which are entertaining in a masochistic way, *Return to Treasure Island* is simply a ridiculous, offensive bore. Fortunately, for poor Dupont, responsibility cannot be placed entirely on his shoulders: equally guilty is Jack Pollexfen, who contributed his ineptitude to three Stevenson "continuations" during the 1950s.

## *Treasure Island* (National General, 1972)

Each adaptation of a literary work incorporates the stylistic tenets of the studio or collaborative team that produces it. The 1934 *Treasure Island* is MGM's glossy vision of the novel, while the 1950 version is Stevenson filtered through the eyes of Walt Disney and company. An adaptation produced in the USSR in 1971, starring

Boris Andreyev as Long John Silver and Aare Laanemets as Jim Hawkins, undoubtedly reflects its studio of origin. But the 1972 National General release (coproduced by British, Spanish, French, and German companies) can be described as having no style at all or, perhaps, a conglomeration of styles that nullify one another.

After seeing this film, viewers may wonder why Orson Welles played such a major role in degrading a classic novel. (His wine commercials and appearance in a documentary about the prophecies of "Nostradamus" benefit by comparison.) More hackneyed than the 1934 and 1950 versions combined, the script telegraphs every turn in the plot, as if Welles, using the pseudonym O. W. Jeeves, and Wolf Mankowitz (like Lawrence Watkin before them) assumed that the audience would be too stupid to understand the narrative of a popular adventure tale. But since all the characters appear terminally ignorant, perhaps this strategy made sense to them.

As Billy Bones (Lionel Stander) lies near death, he tells Jim (Kim Burfield) to find the oilskin packet in his sea chest: "That's it, take it, guard it with your life!" The lad has no opportunity to discover the treasure map or decide what course of action to take; he already has been led down the path (as is the audience throughout the film).

Combined with John Hough's direction, the script makes a shambles of Jim's recapture of the *Hispaniola*. Expecting the treasure-hunters to arrange a pardon for him, Ben Gunn (Jean Lefebvre) leads Jim to the coracle, in which the lad rows out to the ship in broad daylight! Not bothering to cut the hawser, he climbs over the rail, sets the wheel spinning, and the ship automatically drifts toward the island. The harrowing battle with Israel Hands (Aldo Sambrell) lasts only a few seconds, and Jim miraculously maneuvers the ship onto the beach. There is no exposition and, therefore, no reason to believe that any of this has happened.

The *Hispaniola* sequence is one example of the film's general style. All persons responsible appear to have completed the production hastily and with very little effort. A lethargic atmosphere, wholesale condensation of the novel's situations, and pointless paraphrasing of Stevenson's dialogue permeate every frame.

Without a doubt, Welles's Long John Silver is the worst on film. It is nearly inconceivable that the creator of *Citizen Kane* (1941), *The Lady from Shanghai* (1949), and *Touch of Evil* (1958) could give a performance described by *Variety* as an alternation "between utter intelligibility and the croaks of a yawning lion with an Irish brogue, if such can be imagined."[41] Written by "Murf," this observation is close to the mark, as Welles babbles and whispers his way through the entire film. Whole passages of his dialogue are impossible to understand, and one wonders if he used this technique in lieu of a convincing English accent.

Little, if anything, can be said about the Silver-Hawkins relationship; it simply does not exist. Perry Nodelman writes:

Orson Welles does sweat a little.

But considering his bulk, that's not surprising; his performance gives no evidence that he's exerting himself much. Wearing a Gauguin-ish straw hat, he mumbles his way incomprehensibly through scene after weary scene; and he bulks so large and moves so rarely that he seems more like a cathedral with laryngitis than a pirate. It's no wonder that Jim's response to this Long John is so vague—there really isn't anything for him to respond to.[42]

Welles's performance may seem perversely amusing if the spectator views the film as a parody. The scene in which Jim meets Silver at the Spy-Glass tavern is particularly absurd due, in part, to Welles's incoherent babbling, but also for one of his statements that can be decifered. "Barbecue, they calls me," Silver mumbles, making a self-conscious reference to his own nickname. A term of affection used by the pirates, it is mentioned by the literary Silver, but in a more straightforward manner: in chapter 31 ("The Treasure Hunt: Flint's Pointer"), he tells his crew, "Aye mates, it's lucky you have Barbecue to think for you with this here head."

Even more ridiculous (and perhaps the lowest ebb of Welles's hulking incompetence) is Silver's initial appearance at the stockade (which, unbelievably, is made of stone; presumably, Flint's men managed to locate and quarry enough sedimentary rock to construct an entire building!). Hobbling toward the structure (in medium close-up, above the waist; his "one-legged" nature is visualized only during the end credits), the incapacitated pirate stops but never tries to enter.

Kim Burfield's interpretation of Jim Hawkins does not match Welles's impotence, but the character rarely figures into the action. Once again, Jim is not a teenager but an unintelligent, naive boy who appears to be eight or nine years old. Possessing none of the insight and ability of his prototype, Jim's importance is slight, even in the apple-barrel scene, which is relegated to about one minute of screen time. He learns nothing about the details of the mutiny, leaving one of Stevenson's best passages untapped.

The remaining characterizations are equally forgettable, particularly Lionel Stander's stilted Billy Bones, who appears to read his lines off the Admiral Benbow wall, and Paul Muller's Blind Pew, who delivers the black spot and then falls beside the horses as they gallop past the inn. One unique element is the inclusion of Silver's black wife, referred to as "his old Negress" in the novel. Never depicted or even mentioned in any of the other adaptations, Mrs. Silver (Alibe) appears briefly in the tavern scene.

There are some beautiful Eastmancolor compositions (used mainly as establishing shots) contributed by Cecilio Paniagua, but these do not compensate for the one-dimensional caricatures that walk through them. The mumbling of the actors is matched by Natal Massara's inappropriate musical score, which features noisy sound effects and anachronistic instrumentation: an overdriven electric guitar frequently adds some 1970s art-rock distortion to poorly chosen folk melodies. Included are the traditional English song "Scarborough Fair" (many contemporary audience members probably were familiar with Simon and Garfunkel's 1967 pop rendition used in the soundtrack for *The Graduate*) and a theme that would be more at home in a John Wayne western of the early 1970s. (The combination of electric guitar and western-like melodies suggests that Massara may have attempted to capitalize on the popularity of Ennio Morricone's innovative spaghetti-western scores.)

The art direction is perhaps the final degradation. Not only is the stockade made of stone, but the treasure, which consists of costume-jewelry doubloons and necklaces, is buried in Ben Gunn's cave (he does not find it and carry it there, as in the novel), and the black spot delivered to Billy Bones is merely a painted blotch in the center of what looks like typing paper!

One "adaptation," reputedly based on "a story" by Stevenson and containing elements of *Treasure Island,* was produced in 1973. Marking Kirk Douglas's directorial debut, *Scalawag* was shot in Yugoslavia and released by Paramount in mid–October of that year. Set on California's Baja Peninsula during 1840, Albert Maltz and Sid Fleischman's screenplay depicts the adventures of "Peg," a one-legged, treasure-seeking pirate, his cutthroat crew, and a pair of marooned siblings. Primarily enacted by Yugoslav performers whose dialogue later was dubbed into English, the entire production is a disjointed fiasco. As Peg, Kirk Douglas is supported abysmally by early 1970s child star Mark Lester, a young Lesley-Anne Down, a prestardom Danny De Vito, and the voice of Mel Blanc as an alcoholic parrot! Incredibly, a scene near the end of the film depicts the protagonists escaping in a hot-air balloon (an event perhaps borrowed from Stevenson's unfinished novel, *St. Ives*). The anachronistic costume design (including Lester's omnipresent 1970s haircut and bell-bottom trousers) may be the film's most absurd element. The second of two Stevenson abominations that Douglas contributed during 1973, *Scalawag* died a quick death at the box office. *Variety*'s "Beau" derided the film as follows:

> *Scalawag,* a Bryna Co. film for which Paramount made no advance payment to secure distribution rights, is a lame and boring attempt to resurrect the pirate genre. Inane plotting and inept technical work are qualitatively matched by Kirk Douglas' directorial debut. Kiddie matinees seem the likeliest market. ... Douglas strains hard to impersonate a peg-legged bandit who befriends young Mark Lester and sister, newcomer Lesley Anne Down. Both Lester and Down sport British accents that are no more improbable than her heavy mascara job, the awkwardly inserted John Cameron ballad or young lead George Eastman's insistent display of pearl-white teeth. Douglas directed the proceedings lethargically, while his wife Anne produced. Their dog, Shaft Douglas, makes a billed appearance as Lester's loyal pet. So much for togetherness.[43]

Although many of "Beau"'s comments are justifiable, he failed to realize that both Mark Lester and

Lesley-Anne Down were born in England!

The *Scalawag* promotional campaign was even worse than the film. A pop number called "The Scalawag Song," performed by Frankie Valli and the Four Seasons and released through Motown, was accompanied by posters featuring a raucous, pistol-toting Douglas and the following copy: "He's Long John Silver and Jesse James rolled into one! His name is Captain Peg and he wasn't born to die in bed!" Ironically, all advertising material included the credit, "Based on a story by Robert Louis Stevenson."

## *Treasure Island* (Agamemnon Films/Turner Network Television, 1990)

> *Treasure Island* is one of the greatest adventure novels of all time. When we set out to film it for TNT, we wanted to make the most exciting, realistic and cinematic version ever filmed of Robert Louis Stevenson's masterwork. We hope this film will be every bit as vibrant and captivating for today's audience as the novel was when it first appeared.
>
> Fraser C. Heston
> Writer/Director/Producer
> of *Treasure Island*[44]

One viewing of Agamemnon's *Treasure Island* proves that a filmmaker finally read the novel carefully and in its entirety. The intentions of an artist seldom are realized in an exact fashion, but with this film, Fraser Heston came very close to fulfilling that goal. His effort is the best version of *Treasure Island* to date and, perhaps, one of the most faithful adaptations ever produced. This feat is fairly remarkable considering that the film was the first ever directed by Heston, who also served as producer and screenwriter.

"My father read the book to me when I was five years old, and, since then, it has always been a dream of mine to make it into a film," Heston claims.[45] Of course, his father is Charlton Heston, who created the first authentic Long John Silver, expertly interpreting Stevenson's dialogue and physical description.

Although the 1934 and 1950 versions have been praised by past critics (who, perhaps, were unfamiliar with the nuances of the novel), Fraser Heston's endeavor is the only one to do *Treasure Island* the service it deserves. Other than TNT's television advertisements, the film did not receive much media attention prior to its January 22, 1990, premiere. Perhaps a certain portion of the American public, having seen past versions, just ignored it. A prime misinterpretation was created by a *TV Guide* reviewer who gave Charlton Heston a facetious "Yo, Ho, Ho and a Bottle of Rum" award for "his exuberantly hammy portrayal."[46] Nothing could be farther from the truth: Heston is Stevenson's Silver incarnate; when he appears to overplay certain lines, this intensity comes from the prose, not from a deliberate intention to "ham." (But *TV Guide* considers *Return to Treasure Island* to be "good escapist entertainment."[47] Calling Heston "exuberantly hammy" is as wrongheaded as Leonard Maltin's belief that Robert Newton *is* Silver.)

Remaining faithful to the novel, the younger Heston shot the film in as many realistic locations as possible. Production designer Tony Woollard claims, "Today's audiences are much more sophisticated than when *Treasure Island* was brought to the screen in the '30s and the '50s, and I believe they appreciate authenticity."[48] While the principal photography was done at England's Pinewood Studios, several important set pieces were filmed in Baysingtoke and along the Devon coast. The scenes set aboard the *Hispaniola* (actually the HMS *Bounty*, a replica of an eighteenth-century three-master built for MGM's 1962 *Mutiny on the Bounty* and acquired by Ted Turner when he purchased the studio in 1985) were filmed during a voyage to Jamaica, where some of the island sequences were staged (others were completed in Florida). Fraser Heston adds, "It's hard to believe that the earlier film versions of *Treasure Island* were made without a real ship."[49] (Here, Heston is mistaken: Walt Disney chartered an actual sailing ship for portions of the 1950 production.)

The majority of the film's sequences are direct visualizations of Stevenson's prose. All 34 chapters are represented, but a few are condensed (to maintain the pacing necessary for a successful 130-minute film). Two specific episodes conclude more quickly: Billy Bones's stay at the Admiral Benbow and Jim's voyage in the coracle. (Perhaps to make the lad seem more heroic, the film echoes earlier adaptations by depicting the recapture of the *Hispaniola* not as a last-minute decision but as a premeditation.)

Pirate vernacular that has become clichéd (due to the overindulgence of past films, particularly the 1934 version) is omitted in Heston's script. Though Stevenson uses them several times, the expressions "shiver my timbers" and "pieces of eight" are utilized sparingly and strategically in the film. Footage of Silver's parrot is integrated subtly into the action, and its most important function—alerting Jim to the pirates' presence at the stockade—is made more effective, since the audience has not grown tired of its squawking (a "comic" motif in the 1934 film). Stevenson's "Dead men don't bite," however, is transformed into the more familiar (and rhythmic) "Dead men tell no tales."

The footage of the *Hispaniola* sailing from Bristol dock is the film's most realistic sequence, an exciting visualization of Stevenson's account in chapter ten:

"Now, Barbecue, tip us a stave," cried one voice.

"The old one," cried another.

"Aye, aye, mates," said Long John, who was standing by, with his crutch under his arm, and at once broke out in the air and words I knew so well:

"Fifteen men on the dead man's chest—" And then the whole crew bore chorus:—"Yo-ho-ho, and a bottle of rum!" And at the third "Ho!" drove the bars before them with a will.

Even at that exciting moment it carried me back to the old Admiral Benbow in a second, and I seemed to hear the voice of the captain piping in the chorus. But soon the anchor was short up; soon it was hanging dripping at the bows; soon the sails began to draw, and the land and shipping to flit by on either side; and before I could lie down to snatch an hour of slumber the *Hispaniola* had begun her voyage to the Isle of Treasure.

I am not going to relate that voyage in detail. It was fairly prosperous. The ship proved to be a good ship, the crew were capable seamen, and the captain thoroughly understood his business. But before we came the length of Treasure Island, two or three things had happened which require to be known.

Primarily serving as cabin boy in the novel, Jim (Christian Bale) becomes a more tolerable seaman in the film. When Captain Smollett (Clive Wood) gives the order to sail from Bristol, the crew is seen laboring diligently on deck, weighing anchor and raising the sails. Silver, who seems to appreciate Jim's determination and strength, suggests that the boy, too, take a hand at the ropes. Jim is surprised by the physical exertion required but quickly grows accustomed to the toil. This material, which shows Jim receiving the equivalent of a sailor's apprenticeship, lends a realistic element to his later recapturing of the ship. A further touch of credibility is added by a brief galley scene in which Jim swings to and fro in a hammock. Attempting to raise the lad's spirits, Silver shoves a bowl of salt-pork stew under his nose, causing him to vomit into a nearby bucket. In the novel Jim never becomes violently ill, but, upon arrival at the island in chapter 13 ("How My Shore Adventure Begins"), he mentions, "I had to cling tightly to the backstay, and the world turned giddily before my eyes, for though I was a good enough sailor when there was way on, this standing still and being rolled about like a bottle was a thing I never learned to stand without a qualm or so, above all in the morning, on an empty stomach."

The battle at the stockade is one of the film's visual and dramatic highlights. Realistically photographed and edited, the scene shows the points of view of both groups but is shot primarily from Jim's and his comrades' positions inside the structure (this time constructed of logs). Musket balls ricochet, cannon balls explode the surrounding terrain and fill the stockade with dust, and (most graphically) a sword is thrust through an unfortunate pirate's abdomen. In fact, the cinematic battle is more intense than the literary one, as the pirates drag one of the ship's cannons up the hillside, and Smollett's men possess a smaller, portable gun (neither of these weapons figures into the novelistic battle).

Most importantly, the Silver-Hawkins relationship is represented correctly for the first time. Charlton Heston maintains Silver's moral ambiguity ("[he] ... is a complex character ... a charming, extraordinary and able man. If he weren't a murderer, a thief, a thug and a liar, he could have been an Admiral ... and a good one"[50]), and is reinforced by his son's outstanding screenplay, which carefully includes the variations in the pirate leader's attitude and actions. The duality displayed by Silver is reminiscent of Boris Karloff's Gray in *The Body Snatcher* and, in fact, Heston delivers a few lines (particularly, "I'm going to get that loot!" at the climax of the treasure hunt) in a distinctly Karloff style. Unlike the efforts of Charles Ogle, Wallace Beery, and Robert Newton, Heston's Silver is not the fabrication of a collective actor-studio style, but an accurate representation of the character.

Amazingly, every other actor matches the depth and believability of Heston's performance. Born in Pembrokeshire, West Wales, on January 30, 1974, Christian Bale appeared in the BBC television production "Heart of the Country," the NBC miniseries "Anastasia: The Mystery of Anna" (1986), and the Steven Spielberg–directed *Empire of the Sun* (1987) before landing the role of Jim Hawkins. Claiming that "the idea of hanging out on a ship with a bunch of pirates was very appealing,"[51] Bale created a convincing characterization (and the first of an approximately accurate age and intelligence). While the novel includes the death of Jim's father in its early pages (to show that the boy must, at that point, assume a greater degree of responsibility), he is already dead when the film begins. Therefore, Bale's Jim has developed a degree of maturity and strength at the outset; he never resorts to tears but combines emotions of fear and surprise with solid qualities of strength and resourcefulness.

Heston's script adds some picturesque touches to Stevenson's conclusion. Whereas the novelistic pirate escapes while the crew is ashore, the film depicts one last conversation on board. Expressing his fear of hanging, Silver humbly asks Jim to testify for him, adding, "What a pair we could've made."

"You should have thought of that before you turned to piracy," the lad replies. (Heston adapted portions of this discussion from chapter 28, in which Silver, fearing he will be deposed by the mutineers, asks for Jim's help and then speculates, "Ah, you that's young—you and me might have done a power of good together!")

After stealing a sack of doubloons and a gold bar from the hold, Silver quietly claps a knife to the throat of Ben Gunn, who is more than willing to let "Barbecue" escape over the rail. As Captain Smollett, Dr. Livesey (Julian Glover), and Squire Trelawney (Richard Johnson) relax in the cabin below, Silver climbs past an open window, grinning slightly as he descends into a dinghy. Some time later Smollett discovers the escape, but the laughing pirate has sailed out of reach. Raising his cocked hat into the salty air, Silver bids his captors farewell. Jim Hawkins then narrates a faithful paraphrase of Stevenson's last two paragraphs.

The first character to appear, Oliver Reed's thundering Billy Bones immediately establishes the tone of the film. Drifting in on a small craft, he drags his sea chest ashore and walks the wooded road to the Admiral Benbow. (The opening image, depicting Bones standing upright as the boat sails toward the beach is paralleled directly by the closing shot of Silver's boat on the misty horizon.) Disguising his well-known voice with a Scottish burr, Reed gives a powerful and often painful performance as the dying sea dog. Consistently demanding the rum that

*Treasure Island* (1990). Charlton Heston, as the cinema's first authentic Long John Silver, in Agamemnon/TNT's outstanding adaptation.

will end his life, his physical state is revealed with startling realism: as he coughs, the congestion and blood can be heard in his throat, and the final attack of apoplexy brings his brief but memorable appearance to a dramatic climax.

Julian Glover and Richard Johnson, both distinguished British character actors, present faithful interpretations of Dr. Livesey and Squire Trelawney, respectively, and Christopher Lee enacts a nightmarish Blind Pew that rivals his most effective horror-film characterizations. Undergoing a two-hour makeup process, Lee became the hideously scarred villain whose disability allows Jim and his mother to escape his attack. "I should have put his eyes out!" Pew cries in anger as he stumbles outside to be trampled horrifically (in one of the film's more grotesque moments). Lee has said, "Blind Pew is the messenger of death whose very name strikes fear into the hearts of his fellow pirates. The violent impact of his confrontations with Captain Billy Bones propels the story of *Treasure Island*. It is not a role one can hope to underplay."[52]

The most intense performance in the film, Lee's Pew is played with a great deal of believable gusto.

Silver's pirate crew is well represented by Michael Halsey as the rodent-like Israel Hands, Peter Postlethwaite as the ambitious and back-stabbing George Merry, James Coyle as old Tom Morgan, and Steven MacKintosh as the naive Dick. Their usage of Silver's nickname properly reflects the five times it appears in the novel, particularly when the pirates realize that tipping him the black spot could hinder their discovery of the treasure. After Silver lashes out at them, they begin to whistle a different tune:

> "That's fair enow," said the old man Morgan.
> "Fair, I reckon so," said the seacook. "You lost the ship; I found the treasure. Who's the better man at that? And now I resign, by thunder! Elect whom you please to be your cap'n now; I'm done with it."
> "Silver!" they cried. "Barbecue forever! Barbecue for cap'n!"

This passage is faithfully represented, but Heston's Silver reaches a more intense level of anger: "I'll eat your liver for breakfast, George Merry ... you miserable son of a whore!"

Mrs. Hawkins (Isla Blair) is presented as an amazingly strong eighteenth-century woman. Although Stevenson paints her as fairly determined, he also has her faint during the pirates' initial attack. Blair's Mrs. Hawkins first stands up to Billy Bones and then valiantly battles with Pew and his men. (At one point, she violently bashes Pew's mutilated face with the butt of a musket.) One of the film's few representations of modern values (Jim's reference to the immorality of piracy is another), this cinematic Mrs. Hawkins may be more a woman of the late 1980s than of "the year of grace 17--."

Technically, the film is almost flawless. The visual scope is rendered on a grand scale by cinematographer Robert Steadman, who captures the excitement and mystery of the sea and island settings while maintaining a realistic physical atmosphere. When the pirates are shown aboard ship or engaged in battle, the viewer is allowed to see their machinations and interactions, due to a well-balanced style of composition and editing. The action is not cut into rapid, studio-bound montages (as are sequences in earlier versions) but often is depicted in long shot (when the entire group may be seen), giving some scenes a near documentary quality. This technique is used in at least two shots that show a full-figure (and one-legged) Silver hobbling about on his crutch.

Rarely has music perfectly complemented the action and ambience of a motion picture. Composed by Paddy Moloney, the score is integrated within the entire cinematic experience (a feat accomplished by very few films). A combination of original themes and traditional Celtic tunes (including the Irish classic "The Star of County Down") played by The Chieftains and an orchestra conducted by Gerald Grant, the score is derived from the period depicted in the film (an aspect that parallels Stevenson's use of period tunes in the novel). Traditionally, scores for adventure films have been patterned after the romantic symphonic music of the late nineteenth century (Erich Wolfgang Korngold and Max Steiner's music for the Errol Flynn-Warner Bros. classics, for example, in which the influence of Tchaikovsky and Richard Strauss can be heard). Historical locales such as those depicted in *Treasure Island* (the Admiral Benbow, the Spy-Glass tavern, the ship's deck) could have been venues for music similar to Moloney's (but the sites graced by Flynn in *Captain Blood* [1935] and *The Sea Hawk* [1940] hardly could have featured the soaring melodies and occasional bombast of a full symphony orchestra).

Prior to creating the *Treasure Island* score, which he called "my longest, most challenging and most exciting film project to date,"[53] Moloney officially founded The Chieftains (referred to as "the most famous exponents of traditional Irish music in the world"[54]) in 1969. (They had played together since 1963 and recorded an album in 1965.) Accompanied by them, Moloney contributed to the scores for *Barry Lyndon* (1976) and *The Grey Fox* (1982) as well as composing the music for the television productions *Year of the French* (1982) and *Ballad of the Irish Horse* (1985). On the *Treasure Island* score, Moloney's virtuoso uilleann pipes and tin whistle are joined by fellow Chieftains Martin Fay and Seane Keane (fiddles), Derek Bell (harp), Kevin Conneff (bodhran), and Matt Malloy (flute). (Since the premiere of *Treasure Island*, The Chieftains have recorded the tune "Lillibulero," paired with a political opposite, the Jacobite tune "The White Cockade," on two albums.)

## *Treasure Island* on Television

The first television adaptation of *Treasure Island* was written by Fletcher Markle and aired by the Canadian Broadcasting Corporation in 1947. In 1951, two versions, a feature and a seven-part serial, were produced in England and aired on BBC 1.

The first "Treasure Island" television series, a "continuation" called "The Adventures of Long John Silver," was produced in Australia during the 1955-56 season. Beginning where the 1954 film, *Long John Silver's Return to Treasure Island* leaves off, the series includes 26 episodes of 30 minutes produced by Isola del'Oro and Joseph Kaufman. Many of the same cast members, including Robert Newton, Kit Taylor, Connie Gilchrist, and Rod Taylor, repeat their one-dimensional cinematic roles.

In 1957 BBC 1 aired another English production, "The Old Buccaneer," on the "For the Children" program; and in 1960 an American adaptation was produced by David Susskind for the "Dupont Show of the Month" program. Broadcast by CBS on March 5, this 90-minute presentation features Hugh Griffith as Long John Silver and Richard O'Sullivan (in his television debut) as Jim Hawkins. Viewed more than 30 years later, it displays the cramped sets and lighting that were a standard feature of live studio productions. Griffith and Sullivan, as well as Michael Gough (Dr. Livesey), Douglas Campbell (Squire Trelawney), and Barry

Morse (Captain Smollett), appear somewhat lethargic, due to the claustrophobic atmosphere.

The acting highlight is provided by a thunderous Boris Karloff, who occasionally goes "over the top" in a guest-star spot as Billy Bones. Although the dramatization itself runs only 75 minutes (allowing 15 for Dupont commercials), the Bones character receives more screen time than in any of the theatrical versions. (Susskind, who also produced a Karloff television series, undoubtedly wanted to keep his star happy.) The depiction of the brown old seaman's stay at the Admiral Benbow follows the novel very closely, showing Bones drinking and singing amid the patrons and, later, being visited by Dr. Livesey.

Another interesting element is the background music, which proves that Agamemnon's adaptation was not the first to feature a score by Irish musicians. Several songs were provided by the Clancy Brothers and Tommy Makem, individuals famous for performing traditional material at that time. The arrangements are more American pop than Celtic in nature, however, and this aspect adds to the artificiality of the production.

An English "continuation," "Billy Bones," was produced as a series in 1968 and aired on BBC 1, while the novel was expanded by Franco London Films for a 13-part Canadian (CBC) serial the following year. In 1974 a feature-length adaptation appeared on New Zealand Television, and in 1977 BBC 1 aired yet another English effort: produced by Barry Letts and adapted by John Lucarotti, this four-part serial features Alfred Lynch, Anthony Bate, Patrick Troughton, and Jack Watson. Seven years after their feature attempt, New Zealand Television broadcast a serial version in 1981.

Thirty-five years after the release of the Robert Newton-Bobby Driscoll film, Disney Studios produced a ten-part series, "Return to Treasure Island," to be broadcast on their cable network (and subsequently sold on videocassette). The first *Treasure Island* adaptation produced in the United States since 1960, this continuation begins ten years after Long John Silver's escape. As the first episode, "The Map," opens, 22-year-old Jim Hawkins (Christopher Guard) is welcomed home from Oxford by Mrs. Hawkins (Charlotte Mitchell) and his comrades from the *Hispaniola:* Squire Trelawney (Bruce Purchase), Dr. Livesey (Peter Copley), Captain Smollett (Richard Beale), and Ben Gunn (Ken Colley). Moments later, Long John Silver (Brian Blessed) rows ashore near the Admiral Benbow and rouses Jim from a dream.

Against his mother's wishes, Jim insists on sailing to Jamaica to begin his law practice. Before he makes preparations, however, he testifies at Silver's trial. Condemned to serve as a slave in the American colonies, Silver is put aboard the ship that Jim and Ben Gunn have hired for their passage. Not surprisingly, the pirate is freed, and the merry trio row away to search for more loot on Treasure Island.

As with other continuations of the novel, "Return to Treasure Island" destroys Long John Silver's timeless mystique by involving him in additional, conventional exploits. When he escapes at the end of the novel, he sails into immortality; the reader is allowed to devise countless possibilities for his ultimate fate. But when the viewer sees him brought back to relive poor imitations of literary events and conflicts, his mythical persona is destroyed. In the initial episode there is no reason for Silver to arrive at the Admiral Benbow, except to appear in a sequel that transforms him into a stereotypical scoundrel searching for hidden booty.

Every plot turn in the series is contrived, and the older Jim Hawkins possesses none of the daring, youthful qualities which make the original character so interesting (his 1980s blow-dried hairstyle does not help), but the series may prove a pleasant diversion for children and young adults. The acting, period costumes, and art direction create a reasonably convincing atmosphere, but the narrative content and pacing often becomes tedious (an inevitable outcome for a series that stretches a few ideas into a running time of nearly six hours).

• NINE •

# Like Figures in a Dream: *The Silverado Squatters* (1883)

> *All things in this new land are moving farther on: the wine-vats and the miner's blasting tools but picket for a night, like Bedouin pavilions; and tomorrow, to fresh woods! This stir of change and these perpetual echoes of the moving footfall haunt the land. Men move eternally, still chasing Fortune; and, Fortune found, still wander.* —RLS, chapter four, *The Silverado Squatters.*

Originally written in journal form, *The Silverado Squatters* documents the Stevensons' honeymoon trip to the Calistoga Gold and Silver Mine during June and July 1880. After they were married on May 19, the newlyweds spent a few days in San Francisco before seeking a more agreeable climate for Louis's health. They considered a summer house situated on a spur of Mount Saint Helena but settled into a small cottage on the grounds of the Hot Springs Hotel at Calistoga, where Louis quickly tired of the lavish accommodations and $20 per week rent. Following visits to several sites in the Napa Valley, Louis, Fanny, and Lloyd were directed to the Toll House Hotel, located "right up the mountain" from Calistoga. Here, they were presented to the Hansons, a local family who operated the hotel and kept an eye on the abandoned Silverado mine.

Stevenson's 15-chapter narrative begins with a detailed description of Mount Saint Helena and its environs. Displaying an admirable knowledge of the area, he outlines basic geographical characteristics, flora and fauna, dwellings, commercial buildings, and transportation routes before describing the town of Calistoga and its inhabitants. Here he mentions "a land of stagedrivers and highwaymen: a land, in that sense, like England a hundred years ago":

> The highway robber—road-agent, he is quaintly called—is still busy in these parts. The fame of Vasquez is still young.[1] Only a few years ago, the Lakeport stage was robbed a mile or two from Calistoga. In 1879, the dentist of Mendocino City, fifty miles away upon

the coast, suddenly threw off the garments of his trade, like Grindoff, in *The Miller and His Men,* and flamed forth in his second dress as a captain of banditti.[2] A great robbery was followed by a long chase, a chase of days, if not weeks, among the intricate hill-country; and the chase was followed by much desultory fighting, in which several—and the dentist, I believe, amongst the number—bit the dust. The grass was springing for the first time, nourished upon their blood, when I arrived in Calistoga. "He had been unwell," so ran his humorous defence, "and the doctor told him to take something, so he took the express-box."

Later, when Stevenson describes Rufe, patriarch of the Hanson family, he again mentions a highway crime: "It was he who pursued Russel and Dollar, the robbers of the Lakeport stage, and captured them the very morning after the exploit, while they were still sleeping in a hay-field. Russel, a drunken Scots carpenter, was even an acquaintance of his own, and he expressed much grave commiseration for his fate." (Although Stevenson includes few details, his comments apparently refer to two separate incidents of stagecoach robbery: the first account describes a lengthy chase, while the second relates a brief incident.)

Sketches of Stevenson's experiences in a petrified forest and some Napa vineyards precede "The Scot Abroad," a generalized portrait of his homeland and its people. Returning to the subject of Calistoga, he describes a family of Russian Jews whose patriarch drove them to the Toll House Hotel and introduced them to the Hansons and other residents. Informed that the only dwelling, a dilapidated house containing an assayer's office and miner's barracks, stood near the abandoned tunnel, the newlyweds chose to remain at the rent-free site.

The next morning the adventurous pair were driven back to Calistoga, where they collected Lloyd, Chuchu, their dog, and the necessary supplies for a return trip. Occasionally aided by Rufe Hanson and Irvine Lovelands—Mrs. Hanson's "unmitigated Caliban" brother—Louis and Fanny attempted to mix relaxation with the difficult work of repairing the house, gathering water, and avoiding indigenous pests.

Chapter 11 ("The Sea Fogs") features Stevenson's stunning recollections of a natural occurrence that startled him at 5 A.M. one Sunday morning:

> The sun was still concealed below the opposite hill-tops, though it was shining already, not twenty feet above my head, on our mountain slope. But the scene, beyond a few near features, was entirely changed. Napa Valley was gone; gone were all the lower slopes and woody foothills of the range; and in their place, not a thousand feet below me, rolled a great level ocean. It was as though I had gone to bed the night before, safe in a nook of inland mountains, and had awakened in a bay upon the coast. I had seen these inundations from below; at Calistoga I had risen and gone abroad in the early morning, coughing and sneezing, under fathoms on fathoms of grey sea-vapor, like a cloudy sky—a dull sight for the artist, and a painful experience for the invalid. But to sit aloft one's

**The Stevensons at Silverado. Woodcut by Joe Strong, used as a frontispiece for *The Silverado Squatters*.**

self in the pure air and under the unclouded dome of heaven, and thus look down on the submergence of the valley, was strangely different, and even delightful to the eyes. Far away were hill-tops like little islands. Nearer, a smoky surf beat about the foot of precipices and poured into all the coves of these rough mountains. The colour of that fog-ocean was a thing never to be forgotten. For an instant, among the Hebrides and just about sundown, I have seen something like it on the sea itself. But the white was not so opaline; nor was there, what surprisingly increased the effect, that breathless, crystal stillness over all. Even in its gentlest moods the salt sea travails, moaning among the weeds or lisping on the sand; but that vast fog-ocean lay in a trance of silence, nor did the sweet air of the morning tremble with a sound.

Stevenson eluded the threatening fog, but Fanny and Lloyd contracted diphtheria and, on the sixth day of their stay, all three were forced to return to Calistoga. Louis selected Joe Strong as their new aide and, about one week later, the entire party returned to Silverado. Informed that the owner of the mine would lose his rights on June 30, 1880, Stevenson drew up a new notice for the Hansons, who promptly jumped the claim "for water purposes."[3]

In the final chapter ("Toils and Pleasures"), Stevenson recounts "some notion of our life, of how the days passed and what pleasure we took from them, of what there was to do and how we set about doing it, in our mountain hermitage." He describes his early morning chores, the arduous task of walking amid the rough terrain, his experiences with rattlesnakes (about which they were ill-informed) and, ultimately, "the pleasure that we took in the approach of evening":

I was the last to go to bed, as I was still the first to rise. Many a night I have strolled about the platform, taking a bath of darkness before I slept. The rest would be in bed, and even from the forge I could hear them talking together from bunk to bunk. A single candle in the neck of a pint bottle was their only illumination; and yet the old cracked house seemed literally bursting with the light. It shone keen as a knife through all the vertical chinks; it struck upward through the broken shingles; and through the eastern door and window it fell in a great splash upon the thicket and the overhanging rock. You would have said a conflagration, or at least a roaring forge; and behold it was but a candle. Or perhaps it was yet more strange to see the procession moving bedwards round the corner of the house, and up the plank that brought us to the bedroom door; under the immense spread of the starry heavens, down in a crevice of the giant mountain, these few human shapes, with their unshielded taper, made so disproportionate a figure in the eye and mind. But the more he is alone with nature, the greater man and his doings bulk in the consideration of his fellow-men. Miles and miles away upon the opposite hill-tops, if there were any hunter belated or any traveller who had lost his way, he must have stood, and watched and wondered, from the time the candle issued from the door of the assayer's office till it had mounted the plank and disappeared again into the miner's dormitory.

At the end of July 1880 the Stevenson party returned to San Francisco. A few days later Louis was well enough to begin the rail trip to New York, where he, Fanny, and Lloyd boarded the *City of Chester* on August 7. Back in Scotland, Louis laid his journal aside and concentrated on other literary projects.

Completed in April 1882, "The Silverado Squatters: Sketches from a California Mountain" appeared as two installments in the November and December 1883 issues of *Century Illustrated Monthly Magazine*. It was first published in book form as *The Silverado Squatters* by Chatto and Windus on January 8, 1884. The U.S. edition, published by Boston's Roberts Brothers, appeared later that month.

Although *The Silverado Squatters* is a work of nonfiction, it often reads like a romantic adventure tale. In the opening chapter Stevenson's account of the voyage across San Francisco bay recalls some of Jim Hawkins's descriptive narration in *Treasure Island* and looks ahead to the impressions of David Balfour in *Kidnapped:*

> In all the contractions and expansions of that inland sea, the Bay of San Francisco, there can be few drearier scenes than the Vallejo Ferry. Bald shores and a low, bald islet enclose the sea; through the narrows the tide bubbles, muddy like a river. When we made the passage (bound, although yet we knew it not, for Silverado) the steamer jumped, and the black buoys were dancing in the jabble; the ocean breeze blew killing chill; and, although the upper sky was still unflecked with vapour, the sea fogs were pouring in from seaward, over the hill-tops of Marin County, in one great, shapeless, silver cloud.

In "The Sea Fogs" his brilliant descriptions often flow like the salty vapor itself:

> We were set just out of the wind, and but just above the fog; we could listen to the voice of the one as to music on the stage; we could plunge our eyes down into the other as into some flowing stream from over the parapet of a bridge; thus we looked on upon a strange, impetuous, silent, shifting exhibition of the powers of nature, and saw the familiar landscape changing from moment to moment like figures in a dream.

This single-sentence account is a literary highlight, a powerful vision that would not seem out of place in an Edgar Allan Poe fantasy.

The people whom Stevenson met during his stay at the mine are depicted with great skill. His ability to create vivid yet believable characters is demonstrated when he recalls an incident that took place at the Toll House Hotel:

> Here I beheld one man, already famous, or infamous, a centre of pistol-shots: and another who, if not yet known to rumour, will fill a column of the Sunday paper when he comes to hang—a burly, thickset, powerful Chinese desperado, six long bristles upon either lip; redolent of whisky, playing cards, and pistols; swaggering in the bar with the lowest assumption of the lowest European manners; rapping out blackguard English oaths in his canorous Oriental voice; and combining in one person the depravities of two races and two civilizations. For all his lust and vigour he seemed to look cold upon me from the valley of the shadow of the gal-

lows. He imagined a vain thing; and while he drained his cocktail, Holbein's Death was at his elbow.

Some of Stevenson's recollections are enhanced by analogies drawn from lifelong interests. His fascination with the sea, for example, creates a memorable image of Silverado's lone, ramshackle dwelling:

> Late at night, by Silverado reckoning, and after we were all abed, Mrs. Hanson returned to give us the newest of her news. It was like a scene in a ship's steerage: all of us abed in our different tiers, the single candle struggling with the darkness, and this plump, handsome woman, seated on an upturned valise beside the bunks, talking and showing her fine teeth, and laughing till the rafters rang. Any ship, to be sure, with a hundredth part as many holes in it as our barrack, must long ago have gone to her last port.

The most humorous passage is colored by Stevenson's love of music:

> Nor was it only vegetable life that prospered. We had, indeed, few birds, and none that had much of a voice or anything worthy to be called a song. My morning comrade had a thin chirp, unmusical and monotonous, but friendly and pleasant to hear. He had but one rival: a fellow with an ostentatious cry of near an octave descending, not one note of which properly followed another. This is the only bird I ever knew with a wrong ear; but there was something enthralling about his performance. You listened and listened, thinking each time he must surely get it right; but no, it was always wrong, and always wrong the same way. Yet he seemed proud of his song, delivered it with execution and a manner of his own, and was charming to his mate. A very incorrect, incessant human whistler had thus a chance of knowing how his own music pleased the world.

Though *The Silverado Squatters* is a documentary record of his experiences in northern California, Stevenson often works Scottish terms into the text: mountains become "highlands," a valley is a "glen" or "strath," rocks are "scaurs" and "cairns," and, at one point, he calls a section of the valley "haughland." These references add to the personal tone of the narrative, a story recounting portions of an unusual and picturesque honeymoon excursion. Unlike Stevenson's fictional tales, which filter his attitudes through various characterizations, *The Silverado Squatters*, like his essays and other travelogues, directly communicates his remarks to the reader. His feelings about Scottish and American culture, human behavior, adventure and the outdoor life, commercial practices, transportation, food, and various forms of art are integrated into a vivid and entertaining account of his travels.

## *Adventures in Silverado* (Columbia, 1948)

A B western produced by a minor studio, *Adventures in Silverado* is perhaps the most unique Stevenson adaptation. Suggested by a few paragraphs in chapter two ("Calistoga"), it is the only fictional cinematic work to include Stevenson as a character.

Set in 1880, the film opens with Stevenson's (Edgar Barrier) passage to Silverado aboard a stagecoach. As the establishing shot fades in to show the coach winding along a dusty road, Barrier, in a voice-over, paraphrases Stevenson's words: "If there be a story in this new country, then I shall find it, and write it for the world to read. It must be remembered that we are here in a land of stage drivers and highwaymen—a land, in that sense, like England, a hundred years ago." When the scene cuts to an interior shot of the coach, Stevenson (using Americanized English) addresses the stranger (Edgar Buchanan) seated across from him.

*Stevenson:* Are we nearing Silverado, sir?
*Stranger:* Yes, we should be there in a few minutes.
*Stevenson:* Beautiful state, your California.
*Stranger:* Your first visit?
*Stevenson:* Yes, my health hasn't been any too good. I thought a change of climate might help.
*Stranger:* Sometimes does. You're English, aren't you?
*Stevenson:* I'm a Scot.
*Stranger:* Forgive me if I seem inquisitive, but what are you always writing in that book?
*Stevenson:* Notes—I sling ink.
*Stranger:* You sling ink?
*Stevenson:* I'm a sort of writer.
*Stranger:* Oh—ha, ha, ha, ha. What kind of things do you write?
*Stevenson:* Oh, a bit of everything—verse, essays, fiction.
*Stranger:* You'll find plenty to write about here. By the way, we haven't introduced ourselves. My name's Henderson—Doc Henderson. I live in Silverado.
*Stevenson:* Stevenson is my name, sir. Robert Louis Stevenson.

In Silverado driver Bill Foss (William Bishop) is met by hostile citizens who refuse his bid to establish a second stage line. While Stevenson scribbles in his notebook, Foss is challenged to a race by Zeke (Forrest Tucker), head driver for the Silverado Stage Line, a business operated by Jeanie (Gloria Henry). Stevenson wagers "a pound on the stranger" as the two men speed into a Ben Hur-style contest. When Zeke grinds an axle hub into the spokes of Foss's left rear wheel, the latter loses control, injures his horse, and is forced to pay a steep bet.

Later, a saloon patron speaks of Calistoga and a notorious bandit who has stolen his gold. After Doc Henderson visits a family of farmers at Squatter Flats, a sun-scorched area controlled by McHugh, a big businessman, the Silverado stage is robbed by "the Monk." That evening Zeke spreads rumors that Bill Foss and "the Monk" may be partners in a criminal scheme. Soon Mike, a representative of the Last Dog mine, claims that Foss earlier had killed a man in Salt Lake City. Seated at the bar, Stevenson continues to note his experiences.

The next day Jeanie acknowledges Foss's admission that the killing was accidental. Meanwhile, Stevenson accompanies Doc Henderson to a birthday party for Lucy (Patti Brady), the insightful daughter of the squatter family. Stevenson offers her a present but cannot match Henderson's gift of a pony and a promise to build an irrigation dam, half of which will be paid for by the dreaded McHugh.

To prove that Zeke is in cahoots with "the Monk," Foss tells Jeanie to assign a gold shipment to him and then secretly place the strongbox on Zeke's coach. Zeke suspects nothing and follows Foss; as the two men fight, "the Monk" appears. Foss's shot clips the bandit in the shoulder, and Zeke returns to Silverado, claiming that Foss warned "the Monk" away. Soon the townspeople form a lynch mob, but Stevenson grabs a shotgun, insists that they have no evidence against Foss, and suggests that they find "a man with a wounded shoulder." After the mob leaves the saloon, Stevenson turns to a Chinese servant and admits, "I wouldn't have had the courage to hold a room of ruffians at bay if I hadn't had a loaded firearm."

While examining Doc Henderson's stove, Foss discovers a charred shirt sleeve. Henderson admits that he is "the Monk," a western Robin Hood who is stealing gold from McHugh and giving it to the squatters. When Zeke barges into the room, Foss knocks Doc unconscious to prevent his confession from being overheard. Reassembled, the mob drags Foss back into the street, but Stevenson again interrupts their vengeful plans.

The following day, Foss rides to Calistoga, where he offers to trade "the Monk" for McHugh's financing of the dam. McHugh agrees to a lenient settlement, but Foss is chased back to Silverado by Zeke's posse. Foss readies his coach and enlists Jeanie and Stevenson, who again wields a shotgun. Halfway between Silverado and Calistoga, Foss finds Doc Henderson disguised as "the Monk." Just as Doc accepts Foss's plan, a member of Zeke's posse guns him down.

Knowing of McHugh's agreement, Foss marries Jeanie. Prior to leaving for a honeymoon in San Francisco, he accepts a rematch with Zeke, who tosses him the prize money from the previous race. After Zeke lets Foss win, the scene cuts to Stevenson, who looks up at Doc Henderson's placard and concludes: "I found my story in Silverado. I saw its beginning, I saw its growth. As all men must, he paid the penalty for his crime. But we cannot condemn him too harshly, for, above all laws, he held the welfare of his fellow men."

*Adventures in Silverado* may be one of the most unusual low-budget films of the 1940s. The melding of B-western plotting with elements of the Robin Hood legend was not new in 1948, and the presence of a robust and somewhat overweight Stevenson is awkward and far-fetched, but these components lend a curious charm to a film that is no more inaccurate and manipulative than other Hollywood productions purportedly based on his works.

The material involving the heroic stagecoach driver has a precedent in chapter two. After Stevenson recalls the activities of the Californian highwaymen, he writes of a famous driver whom he met on one occasion:

> The cultus of the stagecoachman always flourishes highest where there are thieves on the road, and where the guard travels unarmed, and the stage is not only a link between country and city, and the vehicle of news, but has a faint warfaring aroma, like a man who should be brother to a soldier. California boasts her famous stage drivers, and among the famous Foss is not forgotten. Along the

unfenced, abominable mountain roads, he launches his team with small regard to human life or the doctrine of probabilities. Flinching travellers, who behold themselves coasting eternity at every corner, look with natural admiration at their driver's huge, impassive, fleshy countenance. He has the very face for the driver in Sam Weller's anecdote, who upset the election party at the required point.[4] Wonderful tales are current of his readiness and skill. One in particular, of how one of his horses fell at a ticklish passage of the road, and how Foss let slip the reins, and, driving over the fallen animal, arrived at the next stage with only three. This I relate as I heard it, without guarantee.

I only saw Foss once, though, strange as it may sound, I have twice talked to him. He lives out of Calistoga, at a ranche called Fossville. One evening, after he was long gone home, I dropped into Cheeseborough's, and was asked if I should like to speak with Mr. Foss. Supposing that the interview was impossible, and that I was merely called upon to subscribe the general sentiment, I boldly answered "Yes." Next moment, I had one instrument at my ear, another at my mouth, and found myself, with nothing in the world to say, conversing with a man several miles off among desolate hills. Foss rapidly and somewhat plaintively brought the conversation to an end; and he returned to his night's grog at Fossville, while I strolled forth again at Calistoga high street. But it was an odd thing that here, on what we are accustomed to consider the very skirts of civilization, I should have used the telephone for the first time in my civilized career. So it goes in these young countries; telephones, and telegraphs, and newspapers, and advertisements running far ahead among the Indians and the grizzly bears.

Stevenson was 29 when he visited Silverado; New York–born Edgar Barrier, who bears no physical resemblance to him, was 41 when *Adventures in Silverado* was filmed at Columbia Studios. References to *The Silverado Squatters* include Barrier's pseudo–Stevensonian appearance, the fictionalized version of Foss, the squatters who camp outside the town, and Doc Henderson's claim that he possesses "some of the finest wine from Napa Valley." Henderson was inspired by the "dentist of Mendocino City" described by Stevenson; ironically, actor Edgar Buchanan, born in Missouri in 1903, worked as a dentist before drifting to Hollywood in 1940! The film also represents, to a degree, the strong-willed independence of Fanny Stevenson: Jeanie is not a typical western heroine but a woman who operates a business, drives a thundering team of horses, and stands up to the chauvinistic Zeke.

Director Phil Karlson, who helmed a few intriguing low-budget westerns during the late 1940s and early 1950s, began his career as a cinematic jack-of-all-trades at Universal. In the mid–1950s he received critical praise for his direction of several gritty crime films, including *Five Against the House* (1955) and *The Brothers Rico* (1957). While shooting *The Phenix City Story* (1955), a drama about small-town corruption, in Alabama, Karlson uncovered evidence that led to the conviction of murder suspects who were on trial there.

## *The Silverado Squatters* on Television

In 1977 BBC Scotland aired an abridged television adaptation of *The Silverado Squatters*. To date, this production is the only small-screen version of Stevenson's fascinating travelogue.

• TEN •

# Temperate Nature: "The Treasure of Franchard" (1883)

*"All the world imagine they will be exceptional when they grow wealthy; but possession is debasing, new desires spring up; and the silly taste for ostentation eats out the heart of pleasure."*—DOCTOR HENRI DESPREZ, in "The Treasure of Franchard."

Doctor Henri Desprez, an avowed atheist and self-proclaimed philosopher, is summoned from Gretz to the bedside of a dying mountebank. Unable to save the charlatan, Desprez becomes interested in his servant, a bright, 14-year-old gypsy tumbler named Jean-Marie. Convincing his wife, Anastasie, to adopt the child, Desprez offers Jean-Marie food, clothing, and an education in exchange for his services as stable boy: "I propose no wages, but if ever you take a thought to leave me, the door shall be open, and I will give you a hundred francs to start the world upon."

Jean-Marie moves into the attic of the Desprez's 400-year-old, two-story house. During the mornings the doctor composes the "Comparative Pharmacopoeia, or Historical Dictionary of all Medicines" but spends the afternoons walking with his adopted son. Though the boy retains little of his formal education, he is fascinated by Desprez's peripatetic lectures: "My system, my beliefs, my medicines, are resumed in one phrase—to avoid excess. Blessed nature, healthy, temperate nature, abhors and exterminates excess." Desprez speaks of his former wealth and profligate gambling in Paris, and he claims that cities and riches are debasing influences. Jean-Marie, however, does not agree that a particular location "should so transform the most excellent of men": "Paris, he protested, was even an agreeable place of residence."

Referring to his current lifestyle of moderation, the doctor describes his former indulgences, admitting, "I long for Paris, for my wallowing in the mire." To denude himself, he offers Jean-Marie money to squander on childish pleasures: "Save me from that part of myself which I disown. If you see me falter, do not hesitate; if necessary, wreck the train! I speak, of course, by a parable. Any extremity were better than for me to reach Paris alive."

While walking one afternoon, Jean-Marie asks if riches may be put to positive use. "In theory, yes," Desprez replies. "But it is found in experience that no one does so." When the boy suggests that less wealth may make Desprez a better man, the doctor nervously adds, "I have formed my life for my present income. It is not good for men of my years to be violently dissevered from their habits." Though the boy is influenced by Desprez, he often spends his days in a cave near Acheres, displaying mental independence, the convictions of "a spirit wholly abstracted."

Early one morning Desprez and Jean-Marie drive toward Franchard in a two-wheeled gig. Intending to collect botanical specimens, Desprez summarizes the adventurous history of their destination, "a hermitage and chapel" which were destroyed during the English wars of the Middle Ages. Before the buildings were sacked, however, the hermits had concealed their priceless sacrificial vessels in an outdoor niche. Desprez speaks of the life such wealth could create, but when Jean-Marie counters, "It is only money. ... It would do harm," the doctor scolds the boy for misapplying his philosophy.

At Franchard, Desprez locates the treasure, and he rants about material goods and a return to Paris as they load it into the trunk (boot) of the gig. After driving to Fountainebleau, the doctor dispatches a telegram to Casimir, Anastasie's businessman brother, and purchases expensive foods and gifts.

At Gretz the sight of the treasure overpowers Anastasie. Disappointed, Jean-Marie escapes into the night, lamenting the possibility of a new life in Paris. As he ponders the corrupting influences that will alter his beloved guardians, he recalls "the Doctor's prophecies of evil": "If this were the first day, what would be the last? 'If necessary, wreck the train,' thought he, remembering the Doctor's parable. He looked round on the delightful scene; he drank deep of the charmed night air, laden with the scent of hay. 'If necessary, wreck the train,' he repeated. And he rose and returned to the house."

The next morning, Desprez awakens to find a rifled dining-room cupboard and no traces of his newly found wealth. At 11 A.M. Casimir arrives and, learning of the robbery and Jean-Marie's background, rudely questions the boy. When the broker requests that Desprez sell the Turkish bonds in which he has invested his "small fortune," the doctor refuses. At Anastasie's behest, Desprez agrees to forget about the treasure, the robbery, and any suspicions of Jean-Marie's involvement.

During the winter, on the evening of Gunpowder Day (November 5), a savage storm lashes against Desprez's aged house. As the structure begins to fall in, the doctor grabs Anastasie and awakens Jean-Marie and Aline, the servant girl. In the arbor, the four terrified occupants watch the house "rock on its foundation" and crash to the ground. When Anastasie is embarrassed by her appearance, Desprez hands her a pair of his velveteen trousers, but she refuses to wear such undignified attire. Welcomed into a neighbor's home, they remain until daylight. Desprez then hires a sentry to guard the ruins while he acquires a room at Tentaillon's Inn.

On the third day of their exile Jean-Marie returns to the inn with a spade and the remains of the doctor's snow-covered trousers. In one of the pockets, Desprez discovers a letter he had received from Casimir on the day of the disaster; he unfolds the wet missive, peruses it, tosses it into the fire and, mentioning Paris, shouts "Ottoman Bonds!" as he rushes out the door.

The following morning the doctor is escorted back to the inn by Casimir, who informs Anastasie that she has been ruined by her "sinister husband." Undaunted by this attack, Desprez guarantees Jean-Marie his 100 francs, but the boy begins to sob and is ordered outside by Casimir. A few hours later Jean-Marie returns to the inn, "staggering under a large hamper":

> "Jean-Marie," cried the Doctor, in a voice that was only too seraphic to be called hysterical, "is it—? It is!" he cried. "O, my son, my son!" And he sat down upon the hamper and sobbed like a little child.
> "You will not go to Paris, now," said Jean-Marie sheepishly.
> "Casimir," said Desprez, raising his wet face, "do you see that boy, that angel boy? he is the thief; he took the treasure from a man unfit to be entrusted with its use; he brings it back to me when I am sobered and humbled. These,

Casimir, are the Fruits of my Teaching, and this moment is the Reward of my Life."
> *"Tiens,"* said Casimir.

From November 1881, when *Treasure Island* was completed, until August 1882, Stevenson took a respite from fiction writing. During this interim, he finished the final draft of *The Silverado Squatters*, penned several essays, selected a group of his previously published short stories for the *New Arabian Nights* collection, and suffered through a round of hemorrhages. When the romantic muse finally returned, he began "The Treasure of Franchard," another tale of buried riches which alter the behavior of those who discover them. Completed in November 1882, it was published as two monthly installments in the April and May 1883 issues of *Longman's Magazine* and later was included in the 1887 collection *The Merry Men and Other Tales and Fables*.

A detailed and rather ornate morality play, "The Treasure of Franchard" differs thematically from much of Stevenson's fiction. Although Doctor Henri Desprez, the dualistic protagonist, demonstrates enough ambiguity to offset the parabolic ending, the story may be viewed as a forerunner to the "Fables" that Stevenson wrote during 1893–94. (Some sources date the origin of the "Fables" to 1874.) David Daiches writes:

> "The Treasure of Franchard" is the most like "Will o' the Mill" ... not in theme but in treatment, for here, too, the details of the narrative go beyond what are necessary to present the allegorical

meaning effectively, so that the allegory fades out as we read the story, and more and more we read it as a rather charming study of French provincial life at its most attractive, saved from sentimentality by a generous sprinkling of goodnatured irony.[1]

The allegorical thread does not "fade out" of the tale, but Daiches's observations about narrative details and the French settings are on the mark. Like "The Sire de Maletroit's Door," "The Treasure of Franchard" incorporates specific French locations (based on Stevenson's memories of Gretz and Fontainebleau) and several references to the Hundred Years' War. But, while the former story is set during the conflict (1429), the latter deals with nineteenth-century events. During one of his walks with Jean-Marie, Desprez ethnocentrically describes how warfare affected the area around his home:

[I]t was once a walled city; thriving, full of furred burgesses and men in armour, humming with affairs;—with tall spires, for aught that I know, and portly towers along the battlements. A thousand chimneys ceased smoking at the curfew bell. There were gibbets at the gate as thick as scarecrows. In time of war, the assault swarmed against it with ladders, the arrows fell like leaves, the defenders sallied hotly over the drawbridge, each side uttered its cry as they plied their weapons. Do you know that the walls extended as far as the Commanderie? Tradition so reports. Alas, what a long way off is all this confusion—nothing left of it but my quiet words spoken in your ear—and the town itself shrunk to the hamlet underneath us! By-and-by came the English wars—you shall hear more of the English, a stupid people, who sometimes blundered into good—and Gretz was taken, sacked, and burned. It is the history of many towns; but Gretz never rose again; it was never rebuilt; its ruins were a quarry to serve the growth of rivals; and the stones of Gretz are now erect along the streets of Nemours. It gratifies me that our old house was the first to rise after the calamity; when the town had come to an end, it inaugurated the hamlet.

Desprez's sudden moral change is an indirect result of the Hundred Years' War, during which impending English plunder induced the Franchard hermits to bury their treasure. Like other Stevenson characters, Desprez alternates between two opposing personalities: the good (the teacher of Jean-Marie who abhors excess and enjoys philosophy and country life) and the bad (the crapulous big-city socialite and gambler). While his wife provides the impetus for his good side ("Those who had known the Doctor in bachelor days, when he had aired quite as many theories, but of a different order, attributed his present philosophy to the study of Anastasie."), the treasure brings out the bad.

Anastasie is one of Stevenson's more visible female characters. She saves Desprez from a life of self-interest and overindulgence, but is also a "typical" Victorian woman: she consistently defers to her husband and becomes hysterically vain during her outdoor appearance in nightclothes. In an August 19, 1890, letter to Marcel Schwob, Stevenson writes: "I have never pleased myself with any women of mine save two character parts, one of only a few lines—the Countess of Rosen [in *Prince Otto*], and Madame Desprez in 'The Treasure of Franchard.'"⁹

The ending is foreshadowed in chapter four ("The Education of a Philosopher"), when Jean-Marie suggests that Desprez might be a better man if he had less wealth. When the doctor answers, "It is not good for men of my years to be violently dissevered from their habits," he teaches the boy a concept that inspires the later retrieval of the treasure. After the winter storm and lost Turkish bonds combine to destroy Desprez's habitual lifestyle, Jean-Marie, "that angel boy," rewards the doctor with "the Fruits of (his) teaching."

At one point Desprez declares, "If millions are offered me, I wave them back. . . . Hygiene—hygiene and mediocrity of fortune—these be your watchwords during life!" Stevenson echoed this sentiment in his 1887 letter to *Scribner's* editor E. L. Burlingame: "I do not want wealth, and I feel these big sums demoralize me."³

After the robbery is discovered in chapter six ("A Criminal Investigation, in Two Parts"), Desprez utilizes "inductive science" in his investigation. Here Stevenson appears to imitate Edgar Allan Poe, who includes a similar process in "Murders in the Rue Morgue" and "The Gold Bug." It also suggests Stevenson's influence on Conan Doyle's Sherlock Holmes tales. (Conan Doyle calls Holmes's method "deductive" science, although it would have been more accurate to use "inductive," as Stevenson does.) More obvious Poe influences appear in chapter seven. The title "The Fall of the House of Desprez" is Stevenson's version of "The Fall of the House of Usher," a macabre tale that culminates with the collapse of an ancient home.

Poesque references and buried riches are two of several elements that recall *Treasure Island*. Doctor Desprez, like Long John Silver, is an interesting character who commands attention, but it is the 14-year-old Jean-Marie who, like Jim Hawkins, emerges as the hero of the tale: both lads perform valiant deeds, demonstrate clever, independent thinking, and ultimately save their adult mentors from ruin. In "The Treasure of Franchard" Stevenson again demonstrates his interest in the abilities of young people but is careful to make Jean-Marie appear confused and frustrated on several occasions.

Doctor Desprez is rescued at the end of the story, but he is not a character who always commands sympathy: he calls an entire nation of people "stupid," alternates a longing for self-gratification with an endorsement of the opposite, and dogmatically dismisses the opinions of others. During his peripatetic discussion with Jean-Marie, he contradicts his philosophy of moderation when he declares, "Any extremity were better than for me to reach Paris alive." Described as "so agile a dialectician that he could trace his nonsense, when challenged, back to some root in sense, and prove it to be a sort of flower upon his system," Desprez does not accept responsibility for his behavior but blames wealth and the environment for his acts of indulgence and waste. A precursor to Joseph Finsbury in *The Wrong Box,* the doctor delights in delivering arcane lectures to those around him:

> That gentleman never wearied of the sound of his own voice, which was, to say the truth, agreeable enough to hear. He now had a listener, who was not so cynically indifferent as Anastasie, and who sometimes put him on his mettle by the most relevant objections. Besides, was he not educating the boy? And education, philosophers are agreed, is the most philosophical of duties. What can be more heavenly to poor mankind than to have one's hobby grow into a duty to the State?

After Desprez's home and fortune are lost, his philosophy is utilized successfully by Jean-Marie. Stevenson admirably creates an arrogant character who is "sobered and humbled" by a boy who exercises self-control. In chapter four Desprez commands, "If you see me falter, do not hesitate; if necessary, wreck the train!" But the doctor's recovery is not created by his teaching alone; Jean-Marie's remarkable "divine right" convictions play a large role in his salvation.

When "The Treasure of Franchard" was reprinted in *The Merry Men and Other Tales and Fables,* some critics singled out the story as the best of the lot. In his March 12, 1887, *Spectator* review, R. H. Hutton notes as follows:

> [I]t is in The Treasure of Franchard that Mr. Stevenson shows us how dramatic is his humour, and how humourous his drama can be. Two more brilliantly painted figures than Dr. Desprez and his wife our English fiction could hardly produce,—two stranger mixtures of selfishness and kindliness, of materialism and a gasconading kind of idealism, of egotism and disinterestedness. . . . We do not think it would be easy . . . to make any figures live more truly than Mr. Stevenson makes these live within the narrow limits of eighty not very full pages. . . . No man without the most definite genius could have written this tale, or, indeed, for that matter, much the greater part of this little volume.[4]

## *The Treasure of Lost Canyon* (Universal-International, 1951)

Specific portions of "The Treasure of Franchard" seem tailor-made for cinematic adaptation. The opening chapter includes a paragraph that rivals the atmosphere and visual power of the best German expressionist silents:

> It was a large place, lighted only by a single candle set upon the floor. The mountebank lay on his back upon a pallet; a large man, with a Quixotic nose inflamed with drinking. Madame Tentaillon stooped over him, applying a hot water and mustard embrocation to his feet; and on a chair close by sat a little fellow of eleven or twelve, with his feet dangling. These three were the only occupants, except the shadows. But the shadows were a company in themselves; the extent of the room exaggerated them to a gigantic size, and from the low position of the candle the light struck upwards and produced deformed foreshortenings. The mountebank's profile was enlarged upon the wall in caricature, and it was strange to see his nose shorten and lengthen as the flame was blown about by draughts. As for

Madame Tentaillon, her shadow was no more than a gross hump of shoulders, with now and again a hemisphere of head. The chair legs were spindled out as long as stilts, and the boy sat perched atop of them, like a cloud, in the corner of the roof.

The physical aspects of this passage, particularly the distorted shadows and postures of the characters, evoke the stark and moody black and white styles of German filmmakers Fritz Lang, F. W. Murnau, and Karl Freund.

Like Freund, Los Angeles-born director Ted Tetzlaff began his career as a successful cinematographer. When he was selected by Universal-International to direct an adaptation of "The Treasure of Franchard" in 1951, he unfortunately was given yet another screenplay that replaces Stevenson's prose with fabricated Hollywood mediocrity.

Earlier that year Universal-International produced the sole film adaptation of "The Sire de Maletroit's Door." Apparently unsatisfied with bastardizing only one of Stevenson's French tales, the studio assigned screenwriters Brainerd Duffield and Emerson Crocker to adapt "The Treasure of Franchard." The duo then discarded most of the plot and characters, and replaced provincial France with the American Southwest! (Released one month before *The Treasure of Lost Canyon*, *The Strange Door* at least maintains Stevenson's setting.)

As directed by Tetzlaff, *The Treasure of Lost Canyon* centers on Doc Homer Brown (William Powell), a small-town Californian physician. When Lucius Cooke (Henry Hull), an unscrupulous lawyer, leaves David (Tommy Ivo), a young orphan, with a traveling medicine show, Brown rescues him. After moving in with the doctor and his wife, Samuella (Rosemary de Camp), David's newfound happiness is disrupted when the doctor discovers an ancient treasure chest full of priceless gems and coins. To prevent Brown from returning to a life of indulgence in San Francisco (and Cooke from getting his hands on any of the valuables), David hides the chest under a waterfall. When Brown promises to remain in the country, David helps him recover the treasure.

*The Treasure of Lost Canyon* includes a simplistic outline of Stevenson's story, but the characterizations are either pale imitations of the originals or total fabrications: Lucius Cooke, the one-dimensional, evil attorney; Jim Anderson (Charles Drake), the local lawman; and Myra Wade (Julia Adams), the lovely, token female. Anastasie Desprez is an interesting woman, but Samuella Brown is a typical Hollywood frontier homemaker.

Returning to the screen after a three-year hiatus, William Powell could not mask his apathy. As written by Duffield and Crocker, his characterization is an ingenuous variation on Dr. Desprez, a mere caricature of Stevenson's fascinating and complex philosopher. As Cooke, Henry Hull turns in his usual quota of histrionics, and Julia Adams adds natural beauty to the admirable Technicolor lensing of Russell Metty.

The best performance is given by

*The Treasure of Lost Canyon* (1951). David (Tommy Ivo) and Doc Brown (William Powell, flashing his trademark lip purse) enjoy trout fishing in a California stream.

young Tommy Ivo, who portrayed juvenile roles in many westerns, adventure films, and dramas (including the Billy Wilder–directed *Sunset Boulevard* [1950]) during the late 1940s and early 1950s. His David contains a few glimpses of Stevenson's Jean-Marie, but he cannot overcome the implausible, clichéd nature of many situations (particularly the underwater treasure hunt).

"Wear." writes in *Variety*, "Story of an orphaned youngster fleeced by a San Francisco attorney, until given a home by a kindly, small-town medico, contains typical Stevenson suspense."[5] Wear.'s comment proves that he neglected to read "The Treasure of Franchard"; try as he may, the reader will find no suspense in the story. This reviewer's assumption that Stevenson relied on a conventional stylistic method is surpassed in absurdity by his comment that "The Treasure of Franchard" is a "Robert Louis Stevenson pioneer western story"!

• ELEVEN •

# Foremost in the Ranks of War: *The Black Arrow: A Tale of the Two Roses* (1883)

*"It is the ruin of this kind land. If the barons live at war, ploughfolk must eat roots."*—Peasant woman, in *The Black Arrow.*

During the reign of King Henry VI, Tunstall hamlet is menaced by the black-shafted arrows of John Amend-All, a formidable outlaw. While the Wars of the Roses continue to polarize the English lords into opposing Yorkist and Lancastrian camps, Master Richard Shelton, ward of Sir Daniel Brackley, a political chameleon who currently favors the House of Lancaster, is ordered to command the reinforcement of Tunstall.

At Kettley, Dick delivers a packet from Sir Oliver Oates, the parson of Tunstall. Following an inspection of his troops, Sir Daniel opens the package and reads a poem that John Amend-All had tacked to the Tunstall church door. Stating that Sir Oliver killed Dick's father, Harry Shelton, the poem troubles the knight, who orders Dick to carry a reply back to the hamlet. Prior to Dick's departure, Master John Matcham, Sir Daniel's young companion, is seen "stealthily creeping from the room."

About one mile from Kettley, Dick spies Matcham "peering from a clump of reeds." The lad reveals that he was kidnapped by Sir Daniel, who plans to marry Dick to Joan Sedley, a young woman who disapproves of her prospective bridegroom. Dick then agrees to escort him to Holywood Abbey.

Near the River Till, Dick climbs a tall oak and surveys the forest. He spots a small troop, quickly escorts Matcham into a thicket, and points to a sentry who is spying from a neighboring fir tree. Ten minutes later they resume their flight and take cover in a ruined house, where they overhear two armed men discussing the activities of John Amend-All. Soon a score of "tall, likely fellows" arrive for dinner. Ellis Duckworth, "a tall, lusty fellow, somewhat grizzled, and as brown as a smoked ham,"

138

addresses the gathering. Vowing to lead his 50 archers in a successful campaign against Sir Daniel, Duckworth claims, "I have a writ here at my belt that, please the saints, shall conquer him." The archers then recount recent acts of highway robbery and prepare to relax for the evening. Suddenly, the whistle of an arrow startles Dick and Matcham, who hold their ground while Duckworth shouts, "I have three men whom I will bitterly avenge—Harry Shelton, Simon Malmesbury, and ... Ellis Duckworth, by the mass!" Following this affirmation, "the men of the Black Arrow" scatter throughout the forest.

When Dick pledges to aid Sir Daniel's men, Matcham mentions the death of Harry Shelton, demanding that he complete the journey to Holywood. Dick leaps, knocks Matcham to the ground, and draws a deadly shaft. Soon after Dick lowers his bow, Sir Daniel's troops are attacked by the outlaws. Dick and Matcham flee the scene but are confronted by "a stout fellow in green" who aims an arrow at their heads. Matcham halts, but Dick runs straight at the forester and plunges a dagger into his heart. Matcham accuses Dick of committing unnecessary murder, and they seek shelter in a sandy pit.

The next morning they are awakened by a blind leper making his way through the forest. When the unfortunate outcast chases them and drags Matcham to the ground, Dick draws his crossbow but is surprised to find Sir Daniel's face under the leper's hood.

At Tunstall Moat House, Dick discovers that 12 of Sir Daniel's men have survived the battle. After Sir Daniel orders a messenger to deliver a letter to an influential friend, Dick asks questions about his father's death. Later Dick is summoned to the hall by the knight, who scolds the lad for being ungrateful: "Upon my word of honour, upon the eternal welfare of my spirit, and as I shall answer for my deeds hereafter, I had no hand nor portion in your father's death."

Just as Sir Daniel orders Sir Oliver to take a similar oath, the priest is terrified by a black arrow that crashes through the window and pierces the top of a long table. Sir Oliver faints, but Sir Daniel and Dick rush to join the sentries. Back in the hall, the knight tells the priest that Dick, whom he has ordered to sleep "in the chamber above the chapel," may soon "join his father." When Dick returns, Sir Oliver attempts to save the lad by swearing that he took no part in Harry Shelton's death. The priest leaves the room, but Dick notices a winking eye in a strange tapestry hanging on the wall above.

That evening Dick is visited by Matcham, who warns that the house "is full of spies." Moments later an assassin attempts to enter through a trap door but is interrupted by shouts. When Dick hears Sir Daniel's voice repeating the name "Joanna," he realizes that Jack Matcham is actually Joanna Sedley, the young woman who had refused to marry him.

Sir Daniel's men ram the door while Dick and Joanna escape into a passage below the trap. Joanna explains that she was kidnapped by the knight, who forced her to wear men's clothes. As Dick reconnoiters, Bennett Hatch appears at the far end of the passage; under pain of death, Hatch reveals the location of another trap door. Dick quickly lifts a stone slab and escorts Joanna to the room where the messenger had descended earlier in the day. When Joanna declines to take the rope, Sir Daniel's men rush in to seize Dick, who grabs the knotted cord and jumps out of the window, spinning "round and round in mid-air like a criminal upon a gibbet" as he makes his way toward the moat. "Soused head over ears into the icy water," he is assaulted by a thick flight of arrows: one strikes his shoulder as another grazes his head.

The next morning Dick awakens to find a corpse "hanging from the bough of a tall oak." He cuts it down, recognizes the face of the messenger, and removes Sir Daniel's letter as he is discovered by Lawless and Greensheve, two men of the Black Arrow. In the outlaws' camp Dick meets Ellis Duckworth, who vows to help Dick avenge the death of Harry Shelton and rescue "the wench" from Sir Daniel.

During the ensuing months, the Lancastrians triumph over the Yorkists. At Shoreby-on-the-Till, Sir Daniel enjoys a guard of threescore men while "growing rich on confiscations." On a "black, bitter cold evening in the first week of January," Dick and two companions follow the knight to his house near the sea. When Sir Daniel stops to speak with a party of four men, Dick overhears his plan to wed Joanna to old Lord Shoreby, "a man of infamous reputation." Reinforcements arrive, and Dick attempts to rescue Joanna, but his men lay down their weapons after a group of well-armed "strangers" engage them in a fierce battle. Soon Dick is greeted by one of the strangers, an "unfriend" of Sir Daniel's and a distinguished lord, who calls for a meeting "at point of day at St. Bride's Cross."

The next morning Dick arrives at the cross, moments before his new acquaintance appears. Introducing himself as Lord Foxham, the stranger informs Dick that he is Joanna's true guardian: "if between us we regain the maid, upon my knightly honour, she shall marry you!"

Acting upon Foxham's plan to free Joanna "with one bold stroke that evening," Dick and Lawless propose to steal a ship and attack from the shore behind Sir Daniel's house. While Lawless accompanies Arblaster, an old sea captain, and Tom, his mate, to a nearby alehouse, Dick sends word to Foxham of the impending theft of the *Good Hope* of Dartmouth, Arblaster's "stout boat." A storm begins to brew, but Dick welcomes the lord and about 40 outlaws before returning to the alehouse, where he ambushes the two drunken seamen.

Though many of the men sicken during the voyage, Dick helms the *Good Hope* to a pier behind the house. Besieged by "a shower of arrows" and their own improvidence, the men retreat after a brief melee. Lawless attempts to steer the ship back into the stormy sea but is hit by a tremendous swell. Several men drown, while the injured Foxham is laid upon a berth in the cabin. Near death, he tells Dick to meet with Richard, Duke of Gloucester, at St. Bride's Cross "on Sunday, an hour before noon."

The next morning Dick bids farewell to Foxham's men and accompanies Lawless into the forest near Holywood. "Under a grove of lofty and contorted oaks," the two comrades enter Lawless's "burrow in the earth," where they enjoy a fire and some strong wine as they plan to dress as friars and attend Sir Daniel's court.

The following afternoon two "monks" join a merry group at Sir Daniel's mansion in Shoreby. Here Dick learns that Joanna is to wed the old lord the next morning. After the young woman goes to dinner, Rutter, a dwarfish servant, enters the chamber and examines the wall hangings and furniture; he finds one of Dick's girdle tassels on the floor and appears to exit the room but is interrupted by the stuporous Lawless. Dick rushes out to quiet the drunken monk, thrusts a poniard into the dwarf's chest, removes the tassel from his wallet, and discovers a letter proving Lord Shoreby's treacherous dealings with the House of York. Dick then replaces the letter with a warning from John Amend-All.

That evening Dick watches as Sir Daniel and Lord Shoreby examine the body. Moments later the knight posts sentries throughout the house and garden. Dick resumes his disguise and is escorted to the abbey by four guards. In the church Dick is approached by Sir Oliver, who offers him protection. During Rutter's wake, Dick again asks the priest about the death of his father. "A man may be innocently guilty," Sir Oliver replies. "He may be set blindfolded upon a mission, ignorant of its true scope. So it was with me. I did decoy your father to his death; but as Heaven sees us in this sacred place, I knew not what I did."

Shortly after dawn Lawless appears, still clad in his monk's habit. As the procession begins and Joanna appears in the church, Lord Shoreby is pierced by two black arrows. "Pale with horror," Sir Oliver betrays Dick and Lawless, who are seized by a party of archers. Dick's bloodied poniard is discovered, but he calls for sanctuary and accuses Sir Daniel of murdering his father. Joanna enters the fray, revealing the truth about the forced marriage and her love for Richard Shelton; when her companion reinforces her claims with frank testimony, Earl Risingham begins a proper investigation.

In a house on the edge of Shoreby, Dick is brought before Risingham, who admits, "I knew your father, who was a man of honour, and this inclineth me to be more lenient." When Dick produces the letter containing Shoreby's plan to seize Risingham's estate, the lord releases him. Dick then explains Lawless's participation in the "crimes," and Risingham agrees to spare him as well.

While heading back to the Goat and Bagpipes tavern under cover of darkness, Dick and Lawless run afoul of Arblaster and two of his men. Lawless escapes, but Dick is trussed "like a basting turkey" and savagely kicked by the three drunken sailors. In the alehouse Dick cozens the ignorant seamen with an Ali Baba–style tale of untold riches. Freeing his arms, he hurls the table at them and escapes "into the moonlit night."

At sunrise Dick sets out for Lawless's den, where he plans to collect Lord Foxham's papers before returning to meet the Duke of Gloucester at the Cross of St. Bride. Halfway between Shoreby and the forest, he is startled by a trumpet blast and the sound of clashing steel. On the hill above he witnesses one man battling against "seven or eight assailants" and is drawn quickly into the skirmish. When reinforcements arrive and the assailants throw down their weapons, the young victor scrutinizes his new comrade. Dick, in turn, is surprised to discover "a lad no older than himself—slightly deformed, with one shoulder higher than the other, and of a pale, painful, and distorted countenance." After the five survivors are hanged, Richard of Gloucester rallies his forces and, accompanied by Dick, heads toward Shoreby.

The Battle of Shoreby provides Dick with an opportunity to win glory for Richard and the House of York. He proves his mettle early in the contest, and Gloucester dubs him a knight of the realm. When the war cry of York is trumpeted from the outskirts of town, Dick rides to Shoreby Church, where he spies Sir Daniel's company making its way through the snow "upon the margin of the woods."

Offered a reward by Gloucester, Dick requests that he and 50 men be allowed to pursue Sir Daniel. The duke grants his wish but refers to it as "fresh service" and "no reward." Gazing upon a small group of prisoners, Dick recognizes the face of the unfortunate Arblaster. "I have found my reward," Dick tells Gloucester. "Grant me the life and liberty of yon old shipman." The duke criticizes his companion's merciful qualities but agrees to free the captain.

"About halfway between the town and the forest" Dick spots Joanna's friend, Alicia Risingham, alive among the corpses scattered along the road. "She is farther on," Alicia states. "Ride—ride fast!" Revived by a strong cordial, she is lifted onto Dick's saddlebow.

That evening Dick and his men trail Sir Daniel's entourage through the snow-laden forest. When darkness falls, the men halt, post sentries, and, as Dick and Alicia argue about their past meeting, clear enough snow to build a roaring blaze. The young woman accuses Dick of murdering her kinsman, Earl Risingham, and suggests that he offer marriage as a reparation for the crime. "Madam," he replies, "I will go into a cloister, an ye please to bid me; but to wed with anyone in this big world besides Joanna Sedley is what I will consent to neither for man's force nor yet for lady's pleasure."

After Dick spots the glow of Sir Daniel's campfire, he sets out with Alicia and 40 of his men. He orders Bennett Hatch to surrender, but the stout fighter hails his retinue as Joanna runs to her lover's side. Meeting strong resistance, Dick's archers drop Hatch with a host of fatal arrows. With Joanna in tow, Dick heads into the forest. Alicia arrives moments later and accompanies them to Holywood, where the Duke of Gloucester is celebrating the defeat of the Lancastrian forces.

Before dawn the next morning

Dick impatiently walks through the forest. Sir Daniel, "arrayed like a pilgrim," arrives seeking sanctuary within the walls of Holywood. "I carry arms for York, and will suffer no spy within their lines," Dick replies, threatening to call the guard. The knight berates Dick for his harsh behavior and begins to walk back into the forest but is pierced by a deadly black shaft. Dick prays over the body and is joined by Ellis Duckworth, who vows that "the Black Arrow flieth nevermore—the fellowship is broken."

At 9:00 A.M. Dick and Joanna speak with the Duke of Gloucester, who offers his official blessing. Moments after the wedding, the "ambitious hunchback" leaves Holywood "towards his brief kingdom and his lasting infamy." While the loving couple experience a life "apart from alarms in the green forest where their love began," the faithful Lawless and the pitiable Arblaster enjoy "pensions in great prosperity and peace."

Commissioned by *Young Folks* editor James Henderson as a follow-up to *Treasure Island*, "The Black Arrow: A Tale of Tunstall Forest" was written at La Solitude in Hyeres during the summer of 1883. Like Stevenson's previous adventure novel, this new effort, published in 17 weekly installments, began to appear before it was completed; he conceived the tale on May 26, and on June 30 the first episode by "Captain George North" was on the stands.

"It's great sport to write tushery," Stevenson wrote to Sidney Colvin in October 1883.[1]

Though he had written an adventure tale for a particular market, he was surprised by Fanny's harsh reaction. When the book version, *The Black Arrow: A Tale of the Two Roses,* was published by Charles Scribner's Sons in 1888, he added a dedication to the "Critic on the Hearth," in which he mentions his wife's uncompromising attitude: "I have watched with interest, with pain, and at length with amusement, your unavailing attempts to peruse *The Black Arrow;* and I think I should lack humour indeed, if I let the occasion slip and did not place your name in the fly-leaf of the only book of mine that you have never read—and will never read." Scribner's June 16 publication was followed by Cassell's British edition on August 2.

In an 1894 letter to William Archer, Stevenson writes, "I find few greater pleasures than reading my own works, but I never, O, I never read *The Black Arrow.*"[2] By joining his wife in shunning the novel, Stevenson reflected the opinions of others who considered it an episodic hack work devoid of depth and characterization. Patterned after the adventure tales of Alfred R. Phillips, who also wrote for *Young Folks, The Black Arrow* actually helped to increase the magazine's circulation and was much more popular than *Treasure Island.* In his 1888 dedication Stevenson concludes:

> I could not, indeed, displace Mr. Phillips from his well-won priority; but in the eyes of readers who thought less than nothing of *Treasure Island, The Black Arrow* was supposed to mark a clear advance.

Those who read volumes and those who read story papers belong to different worlds. The verdict on *Treasure Island* was reversed in the other court; I wonder, will it be the same with its successor?

The *Black Arrow* has been ignored by some Stevenson critics, but the author's own verdict of "tushery" should be thrown out of any literary court. As J. R. Hammond writes, "it bears upon it the stamp of Stevenson's personality and embodies a number of his most characteristic preoccupations."³ There are several finely crafted characters who possess degrees of moral and physical ambiguity; the less than heroic personality of Richard Shelton, the androgynous nature of Joanna Sedley, the dual personality of the young Richard of Gloucester, and the inclusion of elements from the Robin Hood legend are some of the novel's most intriguing components.

The Wars of the Roses occurred in England during the years 1455 to 1485. A civil conflict between the Plantagenet heirs of King Edward III, the wars began when Richard, Duke of York, rebelled against the authority of the Lancastrian king, Henry VI.

In 1377 Edward III was succeeded by his grandson, Richard II, who subsequently was deposed by his cousin, Henry Bolingbroke, the son of John of Gaunt, Duke of Lancaster, in 1399. Bolingbroke declared himself Henry IV and was succeeded by his son, Henry V, in 1413, and his grandson, Henry VI, in 1422.

A mere infant when he ascended the throne, Henry VI proved to be an ineffectual ruler. When the Hundred Years' War with France concluded in 1453, he was dubbed "Mad Henry" because of his unstable mental faculties. After several small battles, Henry VI was ousted by Edward, Earl of March, the son of Richard, Duke of York, in 1461. Although Henry and Queen Margaret fled to Scotland, they were captured and imprisoned in the Tower of London in 1466. In 1470 Henry was restored to the throne by his brother, Richard, Earl of Warwick ("the Kingmaker"), and Edward IV's brother, George, Duke of Clarence, but this second reign was short-lived.

*The Black Arrow* is set during this latter period, "in the reign of old King Henry VI." Stevenson creates vivid characters and situations which capture the tumultuous events of 1470–71, and he is particularly adept at portraying the fluctuating political affiliations of the nobility and the effect that the wars had on England's civilian population. Early in the prologue he describes Sir Daniel Brackley as a man who "had changed sides continually in the troubles of that period, and every change had brought him some increase of fortune." Brackley's (and later, Richard Shelton's) tendency to use political allegiance for personal gain accurately symbolizes the behavior of many nobles during the wars. Historian Jeremy Potter writes:

> During the Wars of the Roses there was not much warfare and precious little display of heraldic roses. Estimates of total time occupied in active campaigning dur-

ing the entire period between 1455 and 1487 vary from three months to 428 days, and few of the armed encounters between members of the nobility and gentry and their retainers merit description as a battle. ... Those participating in the conflict were more concerned with their own private disputes over landed property and legal rights than with whether York or Lancaster should wear the crown. ... The objective of most of the nobility, in council or in arms, was not to commit themselves irrevocably to either side.[4]

Richard Shelton is a far cry from the one-dimensional heroes that populate boys' adventure tales. Stevenson occasionally depicts him as an impetuous bungler, a young man who makes bad decisions and treats his companions with disrespect. His feats of derring-do often become botched escapes or unsuccessful attempts to rescue his beloved lady in distress. His inept command of the *Good Hope* is an unqualified disaster, and it paves the way for one of the novel's most poignant episodes. Arblaster's reappearance in book five, chapter four ("The Sack of Shoreby") gives Dick a chance to reexamine his own selfish, mercenary actions. Stevenson's description of the destitute sailor creates an unforgettable image: "a tall, shambling, grizzled old shipman, between drunk and sober, and with a dog whimpering and jumping at his heels." When Dick calls for Arblaster's freedom, he performs a true act of heroism, disputing the orders of the formidable Duke of Gloucester. But the old sea captain views his actions differently:

"An I had had my ship," said Arblaster, "I would 'a' been forth and safe on the high seas—I and my man Tom. But ye took my ship, gossip, and I'm a beggar; and for my man Tom, a knave fellow in russet shot him down. 'Murrain!' quoth he, and spake never again. 'Murrain' was the last of his words, and the poor spirit of him passed. 'A will never sail no more, will my Tom."

Dick was seized with unavailing penitence and pity; he sought to take the skipper's hand, but Arblaster avoided his touch.

"Nay," said he, "let be. Y' have played the devil with me, and let that content you."

The words died in Richard's throat. He saw, through tears, the poor old man, bemused with liquor and sorrow, go shambling away, with bowed head, across the snow, and the unnoticed dog whimpering at his heels, and for the first time began to understand the desperate game that we play in life; and how a thing once done is not to be changed or remedied, by any penitence.

Later, when Dick speaks with Alicia Risingham in the forest, he freely admits:

I do partly see mine error. I have made too much haste; I have been busy before my time. Already I stole a ship—thinking, I do swear it, to do well—and thereby brought about the death of many innocent, and the grief and ruin of a poor old man whose face this very day hath stabbed me like a dagger. And for this morning, I did but design to do myself credit, and get fame to marry with, and, behold! I have brought about the death of your kinsman that was good to me. And what besides, I know not. For, alas! I may have set York upon the throne, and that may be the worser cause, and may do hurt to England. O, madam, I do see my sin. I am unfit for life.

The relationship between Dick and Joanna Sedley is Stevenson's earliest attempt to portray romantic love in a novel. To his credit, he eschews clichés in favor of confusion and conflict, particularly in the chapters in which Joanna masquerades as "a sturdy boy." In book one, chapter six ("To the Day's End"), Stevenson simultaneously reveals Dick's self-interested weakness and Joanna's moral strength when the former brutally murders the forester. "And wherefore did ye slay him, the poor soul?" Matcham asks. "He drew his arrow, but he let not fly; he held you in his hand, and spared you! 'Tis as brave to kill a kitten, as a man that not defends himself." The combination of Dick's naiveté and Joanna's masculinity adds an interesting component to the early chapters that occasionally are bogged down by an overabundance of plot exposition. Stevenson continues to depict the weakness of his hero in book five, chapter six ("Night in the Woods [concluded]: Dick and Joan"), when Dick narrowly rescues Joanna during his botched attack upon Sir Daniel's men.

Alicia Risingham is also a stalwart female creation. In book four, chapter three ("The Dead Spy"), Dick boasts of his ability to free Joanna from Sir Daniel's Shoreby residence: "if the deep sea were there, I would straight through it; if the way were full of lions, I would scatter them like mice." Later, after Dick slays the spy, Joanna still fears that she will be wed according to Sir Daniel's plan. Mocking Dick's earlier claim, Alicia observes, "And here is our paladin that driveth lions like mice! Ye have little faith, of a surety. But come, lion-driver, give us some comfort, speak, and let us hear bold counsels."

Stevenson patterned his Richard of Gloucester after the "crookbacked" Elizabethan villain of William Shakespeare's play *The Tragedy of Richard III* (published in 1597), but he added conflicting personality traits which offer a less predictable and, ultimately, more realistic characterization. While revisionist scholars have argued that Richard III's deformities are part of a larger myth created by Tudor historians and reinforced by Shakespeare's powerful melodrama, Stevenson's inventive variation virtually has been ignored.

Shakespeare based his play, in large part, upon two major studies: *Anglicae Historiae* (1534), a Tudor account by Polydore Vergil (Henry VII's official historian) and *The History of King Richard the Third* (written about 1513, published posthumously in 1543) by Sir Thomas More. Jeremy Potter writes:

> Richard's hunchback and withered arm were the figments of Thomas More's fertile imagination. They represented a distortion apposite to the burden of his homily and were perhaps not intended to be understood as historical truth. Their *raison d'être* was the common superstition of the period that a warped body signified an evil character. Deformity was a sign of the devil's own or at least the mark of God's disfavour. From More and for this reason Shakespeare developed his famous lump of foul

deformity, and the tradition continued to develop under its own impetus.[5]

The historical Richard III was born on October 2, 1452, at Fotheringay in Northamptonshire. In 1461, when his father, Richard, Duke of York, and his elder brother, Edmund, were killed by Lancastrians at Wakefield, Edward of March, his eldest brother, dubbed him "Duke of Gloucester" after wresting the crown from Mad Henry. During the summer of 1469, young Richard became interested in English politics when the king declared war on Warwick the Kingmaker.

Although Richard did not ascend the throne until 1483, after Edward IV had died, and George, Duke of Clarence, his other surviving brother, and Edward's young sons, Edward V and Richard, had been disposed of, Stevenson integrates many of the king's later traits into his younger, less experienced character. When the Yorkist cause appeared defeated in 1470, Richard did not join the traitorous Clarence and Warwick but fled abroad with Edward IV, only to return a short time later to renew the offensive against the Lancastrians. It is at this point that Stevenson introduces Richard as the "active and dexterous" fighter who, in book five, chapter one ("The Shrill Trumpet"), holds his own with "seven or eight assailants" at the Cross of St. Bride. (Here, Stevenson describes the "slightly deformed" lad who is "no older" than Dick and, in a footnote, reveals that he has altered history for dramatic reasons; not only does he refer to the character as "Richard Crookback," but he admits that Gloucester "would have been really far younger at this date.")

Throughout book five ("Crookback"), Stevenson portrays Richard as being both treacherous and grateful. He is "painful," "distorted," and "pale as linen," but his eyes shine "like some strange jewel" and his voice breaks "with the exultation of battle and success." The "ugly hunchback" who smiles "upon one side" when viewing the hideous aftermath of battle shakes Dick's hand but nearly squeezes the blood from his palm while doing so:

> Dick quailed before his eyes. The insane excitement, the courage, and the cruelty that he read therein filled him with dismay about the future. This young duke's was indeed a gallant spirit, to ride foremost in the ranks of war; but after the battle, in the days of peace and in the circle of his trusted friends, that mind, it was to be dreaded, would continue to bring forth the fruits of death.

This chilling passage foreshadows Dick's later misgivings about his own self-interested behavior and political allegiances. Richard III's multifaceted personality is a larger symbol of the conflict and ambivalence that rage within Richard Shelton's soul. In his October 1883 letter to Colvin, Stevenson writes: "I am pleased you like Crookback; he is a fellow whose hellish energy has always fixed my attention. I wish Shakespeare had written the play after he had learned some of the rudiments of literature and art rather than before."[6]

Stevenson successfully incorporates the Wars of the Roses into the background of *The Black Arrow*, but many specific events are patterned after various legends about Robin Hood and his merry men. The romantic conception of Hood as a gallant defender of the downtrodden was a popular invention of the early nineteenth century, and by the time Stevenson wrote *The Black Arrow* in 1883, readers had seen Sir Walter Scott's *Ivanhoe* (1819), Thomas Love Peacock's *Maid Marion* (1822), and Pierce Egan's *Robin Hood and Little John* (1840), "the first comprehensive story [about Hood] deliberately written for children."[7] In his 1982 study of Robin Hood fact and fiction, J. C. Holt compares the earliest stories of the outlaw with the later, heroic conception:

> What the original story was really like, how the plant took root and grew in what sort of soil, are matters for patient reconstruction. But when the work is done a further task remains. The fancy present in all legends falsifies, and fancy saturates the tale of Robin Hood. It made heroes of outlaws. It confused violence and crime with justice and charity. In bridging the gap between the real and the ideal world it presented some of the social problems of the Middle Ages as sharply cut issues of right and wrong. In this it achieved an enduring confidence trick. Playwrights may surrender to it. Sociologists may compound it. We can all enjoy it. But it is also useful to uncover it and understand what made it possible.[8]

Stevenson reinforces the romantic depiction of the heroic outlaw in *The Black Arrow*, but he tempers it with well-drawn characters who are often unreliable. Dick's occasional ineptitude, Lawless's mercenariness, Alicia's dual personality, and the general atmosphere of fluctuating political allegiances add depth to the morally simplistic Robin Hood story. But there are plenty of direct parallels with the legend of Locksley: John Amend-All's quest for "justice" and his skill with a bow and arrow; the outlaws' camp where Amend-All/Duckworth speaks to his men; Dick and Lawless's incognito adventure in which they dress as friars; Dick's efforts to rescue Joanna from the clutches of the self-seeking Brackley; and the lovers' successful reunion at the end of the tale. (The historical "John Amend-All," Jack Cade, was an Irish rogue who led the men of Kent in a rebellion against Henry VI's government in May 1450. After his band freed prisoners in Marshalsea, they stormed the Tower of London and fought a battle on London Bridge. Cade was pursued to Sussex and killed.) If Duckworth and Dick Shelton are, in part, Stevenson's collective version of Robin Hood, then Joanna is Maid Marian, Lawless is Little John, and Sir Daniel is Prince John. (The similarities between the Robin Hood legend and *The Black Arrow* are echoed in Warner Bros.' classic 1938 film, *The Adventures of Robin Hood*, when one of the outlaw's [Errol Flynn] arrows flies into Prince John's [Claude Rains] castle, pinning a death warrant to a table between the sire and Sir Guy of Gisbourne [Basil Rathbone].)

*The Black Arrow* contains a wealth of cinematic possibilities. Dramatic events often are complemented by descriptive prose that is breathtaking in its imagery and ambience. In book two, chapter three ("The Room Over the Chapel"), Stevenson includes a prototype for a scene that appears in scores of Hollywood adventure and mystery films: "Presently the steps began again, and then, all of a sudden, a chink of light appeared in the planking of the room in a far corner. It widened; a trap-door was being opened, letting in a gush of light. They could see the strong hand pushing it up; and Dick raised his crossbow, waiting for the hand to follow."

The theft of the *Good Hope*, Richard of Gloucester's sword duel, and the fierce Battle of Shoreby are the stuff of which great adventures are made, but one of the most powerful vignettes occurs when Dick surveys the battlefield from the church tower in book five, chapter four:

> A confused, growling uproar reached him from the streets, and now and then, but very rarely, the clash of steel. Not a ship, not so much as a skiff remained in harbour; but the sea was dotted with sails and rowboats laden with fugitives. On shore, too, the surface of the snowy meadows was broken up with bands of horsemen, some cutting their way towards the borders of the forest, others, who were doubtless of the Yorkist side, stoutly interposing and beating them back upon the tower. Over all the open ground there lay a prodigious quantity of fallen men and horses, clearly defined upon the snow.

The novel's most stunning image occurs in book five, chapter five ("Night in the Woods"), during a tense but more peaceful time:

"Dick drew bridle in despair. The short winter's day was near an end; the sun, a dull red orange, shorn of rays, swam low among the leafless thickets; the shadows were a mile long upon the snow; the frost bit cruelly at the finger-nails; and the breath and steam of the horses mounted in a cloud."

Stevenson also includes such atmospheric elements as drunken sailors "tuning up an old, pitiful sea-ditty, to the chorus of the wailing of the gale" (book three, chapter four: "The *Good Hope*"); locals who mistake Dick and his men for notorious French pirates (book three, chapter six: "The *Good Hope* [concluded]"); and in the prologue a poem by John Amend-All outlining the outlaw's plan of action:

> I had four blak arrows under my belt,
> Four for the greefs that I have felt,
> Four for the number of ill menne
> That have opressid me now and then.
>
> One is gone; one is wele sped;
> Old Apulyaird is ded.
>
> One is for Maister Bennet Hatch,
> That burned Grimstone, walls and thatch.
>
> One is for Sir Oliver Oates,
> That cut Sir Henry Shelton's throat.
>
> Sir Daniel, ye shull have the fourt;
> We shall think it fair sport.
>
> Ye shull each have your own part,
> A blak arrow in each blak heart.
> Get ye to your knees for to pray:
> Ye are ded theeves, by yea and nay!
>
>       Jon Amend-All
>       of the Green Wood,
>       And his jolly fellaweship

Referring to Richard Shelton's

comment that "a thing once done is not to be changed or remedied by any penitence," Hammond concludes:

> This theme ... underlies much of the action of *The Black Arrow*. Richard finally achieves happiness and is reunited with his heroine but at a cost of much travail and bloodshed. The reader identifies with the hero and sympathises with him in his changing fortunes yet is simultaneously aware of the unhappiness and death which are the lot of others. It is a world in which moral judgements must be constantly weighed in the balance, a world where a course of action embarked upon for the loftiest motives can redound on the instigator and bring havoc in its train.[9]

Hammond's analysis recalls the comment made by the peasant woman in the prologue who, along with the rest of England's ploughfolk, must resort to scavenging while the rival houses continue their bloody campaigns.

## *The Black Arrow* (Edward Small/Columbia, 1948)

The original pressbook for Columbia's *The Black Arrow* (1948) heralds, "Robert Louis Stevenson's Immortal Adventure Novel! . . . Now on the screen in all its fiery glory." While the film is not the faithful visualization promised by studio publicity, it is an entertaining and stylishly produced melodrama.

Constricted by Edward Small's budget, screenwriters Richard Schayer, David P. Sheppard and Thomas Seller were selective in adapting Stevenson's material. To avoid costly battle scenes, they decided to open the film with Sir Richard Shelton's (Louis Hayward) return to "Sedley Manor" after the Wars of the Roses have ended. Confiscated by King Edward IV and Richard, Duke of Gloucester (Lowell Gilmore), the estate is overseen by Sir Daniel Brackley (George Macready), who murdered Harry Shelton and blamed John Sedley (Paul Cavanagh) for the crime. Upon arrival, the younger Shelton is startled by a black arrow that carries a warning from "John Amend-All," a Lancastrian outlaw.

Appointed guardian of Joanna Sedley (Janet Blair), Sir Daniel orders Richard to fetch her from a nearby monastery. Joanna informs Richard that she supports the Lancastrians and that her father, believed dead by the Yorkists, is actually John Amend-All. Meanwhile, Lawless (Edgar Buchanan), Amend-All's deadly archer, avenges Harry Shelton by attacking the men involved in the murder; he shoots a black arrow through the heart of Nick Appleyard (Ray Teal), Sir Daniel's executioner, and then repeats the act upon Sir Oliver Oates (Walter Kingsford) during Sir Daniel and Joanna's aborted wedding ceremony.

Having been wounded during his escape from Sedley Manor, Richard kills Bennett Hatch (Rhys Williams) in a dagger duel and later returns to the castle to rescue Joanna and the recaptured John Sedley. He is imprisoned in a dungeon with Sedley and the intoxicated Lawless, but manages to break out and confront Gloucester, who endorses his chivalrous decision to face Sir Daniel in mortal combat. Armed with broadsword, battle axe, mace, and lance, the two knights engage in a brutal contest. Nearly bludgeoned to death, Richard impales Sir Daniel with a broken lance, receives Gloucester's praise, and kisses Joanna as the final scene fades to black.

Only a few passages from the novel are depicted in the film, but events such as Dick's theft of the *Good Hope* and the Battle of Shoreby could not be staged realistically by an independent producer working with a limited budget. Scenes of armed combat are small-scale affairs, enhanced by Louis Hayward's swordsmanship and the technical advice of master fencer Fred Cavens: two highlights are the well-staged dagger duel between Richard and Bennett Hatch and the climactic battle sequence. Although the latter event does not appear in the novel, it is a well-edited combat scene that includes realistic jousting footage and several grueling close-ups of Sir Daniel pummeling Richard with a mace. However, the final series of shots, in which Richard impales Sir Daniel, depend solely on editing and fail to present a convincing picture of an arduous feat.

Passages adapted for the film include Richard's questioning of a dying man (Carter in the novel, Appleyard in the film); Sir Oliver's denial of responsibility for Harry Shelton's death; Richard's duel with Bennett Hatch in the castle corridor; Richard's escape into the moat, where he is struck by an arrow; Lawless and Greensheve's discovery and rescue of the injured Richard; and Richard and the drunken Lawless's incognito adventure at the castle.

With the exception of the Duke of Gloucester, whose complex personality is displayed briefly, Stevenson's characters become unambiguous Hollywood types. Sir Oliver Oates, who expresses remorse in the novel, maintains a villainous demeanor, and Lawless, whom the literary Richard never trusts completely, becomes a dependable and somewhat lovable outlaw.

Stevenson presents Richard Shelton as a confused and regretful young man, but the cinematic version is a stock heroic adventure character. Louis Hayward, who enacts the title roles in earlier Edward Small swashbucklers—including the James Whale–directed *The Man in the Iron Mask* (1939) and the Rowland V. Lee–directed *The Son of Monte Cristo* (1940)—gives a good performance, though at 39 he is much older than the "boy" described in both the novel and the film. Portraying his second Stevensonian character (his first was the young man with the cream tarts in *Trouble for Two;* his third [pseudo–Stevensonian] role would occur three years later in *The Son of Dr. Jekyll* [1951]), Hayward endured several dangerous shooting situations, including the jousting scene, which took one week to rehearse and six days to film in southern California's 100-degree summer heat.

As portrayed by the striking Janet Blair, the cinematic Joanna Sedley lacks the androgynous attributes of her literary counterpart, but she briefly rises above her stereotypical ingenue status. When Richard compliments her, "I bow to your brains, m'lady," she replies, "It's about time somebody appreciated women. England will never be

*The Black Arrow* (1948). Louis Hayward and Janet Blair, in an original advertisement for Columbia's abridged adaptation, set in the days following the Wars of the Roses.

great until she's had a queen or two." Touted as an admirer of historical novels and a proficient archer, Blair was excited about the role but disappointed that she had no chance to display her talent with a bow and arrow.[10]

Even though the film follows the general outline of the novel, it lacks the complex relationships and political milieu depicted so vividly by Stevenson. None of the characters shift their allegiances or question their actions, particularly Sir

Daniel, who enjoys the official endorsement of the Duke of Gloucester; awarded the Sedley estate, he maintains a self-indulgent lifestyle of coercion and murder. Gloucester will not consider withdrawing his support, even when Richard and Joanna reveal the truth about Sir Daniel's crimes. The screenplay presents him as a thoroughly evil villain who murders for personal gain (Harry Shelton is described as his half brother) and then lusts after the daughter and possessions of the victim.

The film often reinforces the similarities between Stevenson's characters and events and the Robin Hood legends. The gravel-voiced Edgar Buchanan (making one of his two Stevensonian appearances of 1948) recalls Eugene Pallette's Friar Tuck in *The Adventures of Robin Hood*, and the depiction of the noble John Sedley as a political rebel is a variation on the Sir Robin of Locksley theme. One self-reflective scene actually includes Richard's admission that "I used to play Robin Hood in these passages, if I haven't forgotten them."

The film is superior to many other genre productions of the era, but it could have been improved by a larger budget and a more faithful script. The cast is one of the finest ever assembled for a Stevenson adaptation and includes several British veterans of the Hollywood adventure and historical drama genres: Paul Cavanagh, Walter Kingsford, Rhys Williams, Halliwell Hobbes, Harry Cording, and silent-screen comic Billy Bevan.

During *The Black Arrow*'s initial run, Columbia overplayed the film's fidelity to the novel but compensated with a multifaceted publicity campaign that acquainted audiences with Stevenson's literary output. Publicists encouraged exhibitors to hide tickets and dollar bills in library copies of his books, to accept books as tickets (to be donated subsequently to local hospitals and orphanages), to offer cash prizes to students who wrote essays comparing the novel and the film or discussing a favorite Stevenson story, to ask local booksellers to create window displays, and to persuade local mayors to proclaim a "Robert Louis Stevenson Week" (to coincide with the film's opening date).

Edward Small's adaptation may not be Stevenson's *The Black Arrow*, but it is an agreeable way to spend 76 minutes. The direction, performances, art direction, and photography (save for one badly staged sword thrust) are top-notch in a film that was probably the first to depict Richard of Gloucester as anything but a hunchbacked monstrosity.

## *The Black Arrow* on Television

Produced for the Disney cable network, "Black Arrow" (1984) is a lame variation on the Robin Hood tale, with a few of Stevenson's characters and situations added to justify the use of his name above the title. Cinematographer John Cabrera and art director Jose Maria Alarcon are the real stars of this version, but their work fails to compensate for a simplistic script and one-dimensional characterizations that waste the talents of a distinguished cast.

Oliver Reed portrays Sir Daniel Brackley squarely in the "Prince John" tradition, exacting harsh taxes from his subjects and plotting the death of his ward and nephew, Richard (Benedict Taylor). The Wars of the Roses have concluded in victory for York, and "Black Arrow" (not John Amend-All), a Lancastrian rebel (Stephan Chase), sets out to avenge himself upon Sir Daniel and his retinue, who have confiscated his lands and daughter, Joanna (Georgia Stowe).

Rife with contrivances, the script maintains many adventure clichés while ignoring the historical detail and epic drama of the novel. Worst of all, Richard of Gloucester is neither seen nor mentioned. Though most of the characters are clear-cut heroes or villains, Taylor's Richard (he has no surname) exhibits moments of confusion, particularly when Joanna (in Matcham fashion) steals his clothes and escapes from Sir Daniel's castle. Anxious to be reunited with her father (his actual name is never revealed), Joanna is a strong female who outdoes Richard in several harrowing situations.

All of Stevenson's complex character relationships are replaced by comic-book alliances: the depiction of Richard's father as Sir Daniel's brother, Joanna as Black Arrow's daughter, and Oates (Donald Pleasence) as a nonclerical mercenary. In fact, "Black Arrow" may contain the worst bastardization of a Stevenson character: At one point, the Earl of Warwick (Fernando Rey) refers to the young hero as "Richard ... whatever your name is"! Why screenwriters David Pursall and Peter Welbeck included this insulting line, instead of using the surname Shelton, boggles the mind.

After all villains have been disposed of by Black Arrow (who confronts them in western-style showdowns), the film concludes with the wedding of Richard and Joanna, who miraculously join the rival houses of York and Lancaster; if these two lovers had met at an earlier date, the Wars of the Roses could have ended much sooner!

Disney's "adaptation" proves that, in this case, literature is the superior medium. While filmmakers require large sums of money (a reality that producers Harry Alan Towers and Michael John Biber avoided by discarding the novel), an author such as Stevenson could create an epic drama with an inexpensive pen, a sheaf of paper, and an imaginative intelligence. In today's marketplace a faithful adaptation of *The Black Arrow* would cost at least $100 million, and it is doubtful (considering that Hollywood probably would demand that Kevin Costner play Richard Shelton like one of the trees in Tunstall Forest) that the film would recoup its cost. Fortunately, only a few people, with a subscription to the Disney Channel and nothing better to do, suffered through this tiresome film.

• TWELVE •

# The War in the Members: *The Strange Case of Dr. Jekyll and Mr. Hyde* (1885)

> It's ill to loose the bands that God decreed to bind;
> Still will we be the children of the heather and the wind;
> Far away from home, O it's still for you and me
> That the broom is blowing bonnie in the north countrie.
> —Stevenson's dedication to Katharine (Stevenson) de Mattos, *The Strange Case of Dr. Jekyll and Mr. Hyde.*

Richard Enfield, "the well-known man about town," and Mr. Utterson, a distinguished lawyer, ramble down a by-street in a dingy London neighborhood. Near a "certain sinister block of building" Utterson pauses to listen to his companion's strange recollection of "some damned Juggernaut" that trampled a small girl and "left her screaming on the ground." Following this "hellish" spectacle, Enfield restrained the man and escorted him back to the scene, where a local "sawbones" examined the girl. When Enfield insisted that restitution be made to the child's parents, the man walked to a door, entered with a key and obtained "another man's cheque for close upon a hundred pounds." After cashing the draft the following day, Enfield let the matter drop.

His curiosity piqued, Utterson demands to know the name of the ruffian who injured the child. "It was a man of the name of Hyde," Enfield replies, adding that "there is something wrong with his appearance; something displeasing."

Realizing who occupies the building with the by-street door, Utterson returns to his home and removes the will of Henry Jekyll, M.D., D.C.L., LL.D., F.R.S., and so forth, from his safe. The document states that in the event of Jekyll's demise, "all his possessions (are) to pass into the hands of his 'friend and benefactor Edward Hyde'; but that in case of Dr. Jekyll's 'disappearance or unexplained absence for any period exceeding three calendar months,' the said Edward Hyde should step into the said Henry Jekyll's shoes without further delay." Utterson returns the "obnoxious paper" to the safe and visits his friend, Dr. Hastie Lanyon, who, over the past ten years, has developed a severe distaste for Jekyll's unorthodox scientific theories. Lanyon admits that he knows nothing of Mr. Hyde, and Utterson returns home; following a fitful night of sleep, the lawyer vows to solve the mystery.

One frosty evening some time later, Utterson confronts a small, plainly dressed figure approaching the by-street door. "Mr. Hyde, I think?" he declares, revealing his identity and place of residence. During a brief discussion, Hyde offers his own address before disappearing into the house.

Two weeks later, Utterson is invited to dine at Jekyll's home; after the other guests depart, he probes for information about Hyde. Claiming that he cannot change the provisions of his will, Jekyll insists that his "strange position" prevents him from talking about the matter. He does, however, assure the lawyer that "the moment I choose, I can be rid of Mr. Hyde." As Utterson prepares to leave, Jekyll reaffirms his testament.

Nearly a year passes before Utterson hears of Mr. Hyde again. During the month of October 18--, all of London is shocked by the brutal murder of Sir Danvers Carew, a prominent M.P. A maidservant, sitting in her window, witnessed a very small gentleman— "a certain Mr. Hyde, who had once visited her master"— club Carew to death with a cane. At 2:00 A.M. she summoned the police, who found Carew "in the middle of the lane, incredibly mangled" and a splintered half of the cane in a nearby gutter. Searching further, they discovered a sealed and stamped envelope addressed to Mr. Utterson.

While viewing the corpse and the murder weapon fragment, Utterson recognizes the cane he had presented to Henry Jekyll some years before. He then accompanies Inspector Newcomen to Hyde's Soho residence, where he finds the other half of the cane and the butt end of a burned green checkbook; a visit to the indicated bank reveals that Mr. Hyde has several thousand pounds deposited in his name. Newcomen states that he will soon capture the murderer, but the authorities are unable to obtain further information.

That afternoon Utterson visits Dr. Jekyll, who has heard reports of the murder. Asked if he is sheltering Hyde, the doctor swears that he "will never set eyes on him again." To allay Utterson's suspicions, Jekyll presents a letter from "Edward Hyde" stating that the doctor is in no danger, due to a "means of escape on which he placed a sure dependence." Later Utterson shows the letter to Mr. Guest, his head clerk and trusted confidant, who possesses a keen knowledge of handwriting. Fortuitously, a servant enters with a dinner invitation from Dr. Jekyll, and Guest is able to compare the two signatures: "Well sir ... there's a rather singular resemblance; the two hands are in many points identical: only differently sloped." That night Utterson locks the note in his safe and surmises that Jekyll forged the letter attributed to Hyde.

The police make a thorough

search and thousands of pounds are offered in reward, but Mr. Hyde is never found. Freed from Hyde's "evil" influence, Dr. Jekyll emerges from his laboratory, interacts with friends and colleagues, and renews his interest in charity work. However, after two months pass, his door is closed to visitors. Poole, Jekyll's trusted butler, claims that his master has been confined and can see no one. Repeatedly turned away, Utterson pays another visit to Lanyon, who suddenly has become ill. "I have had a shock," Lanyon admits, "and I shall never recover. It is a question of weeks." When Utterson mentions that Jekyll, too, is ill, Lanyon concludes, "I am quite done with that person, and I beg that you will spare me any allusion to one whom I regard as dead."

Worried by Lanyon's appearance, Utterson writes a letter of protest to Jekyll, who reaffirms his need for seclusion. Less than two weeks later, Lanyon dies in bed, prompting Utterson to examine a sealed envelope from the deceased: "PRIVATE: for the hands of J. G. Utterson *alone,* and in case of his predecease *to be destroyed unread."* Utterson breaks the seal and extracts another enclosure marked "Not to be opened till the death or disappearance of Dr. Henry Jekyll."

On a following Sunday Utterson again walks the by-street with Richard Enfield. Glancing at a half-open window, they spot the despondent Dr. Jekyll, whose face registers a bloodcurdling expression. Some days later Utterson is visited by Poole, who claims that Dr. Jekyll has fallen victim to "foul play." Soon Utterson discovers that all of Jekyll's servants are hysterical, huddling together "like a flock of sheep." Poole knocks on the laboratory door and beckons the lawyer to heed the voice coming from within.

Utterson suggests that Jekyll may have been murdered but questions why the culprit would remain in the laboratory. Poole reveals that "him or it, or whatever it is" has left several notes during the week, asking him to purchase a specific drug from various London chemists. "Crying night and day" for this medicine, "it" has rejected each delivery because of impurities. During one of his visits, Poole observed that the "thing was not my master. . . . My master . . . is a tall, fine build of a man, and this was more of a dwarf." Joined by Bradshaw, the footman, they break down the laboratory door. Utterson enters to find Edward Hyde grasping a crushed phial, his body "sorely contorted and still twitching." Unable to locate Dr. Jekyll, they find Hyde's broken and rusty key lying on the floor beneath the backdoor lock. Utterson then discovers a large envelope, addressed to him in Jekyll's hand, on the business table. Several enclosures fall out, including another will, naming Edward Hyde the beneficiary, and a short note instructing Utterson to read Lanyon's narrative and, if he desires, "the confession of Your unworthy and unhappy friend, Henry Jekyll."

Dr. Lanyon's narrative reveals that on December 10, 18--, he received a registered letter from Henry Jekyll requesting that he obtain "some powders, a phial, and a paper book" from Jekyll's laboratory and take them to his consulting room, where a messenger would meet him at midnight. Precisely at 12 o'clock the messenger arrived, frantically mixed the chemicals in a graduated glass, and asked if he could leave, but Lanyon demanded that he remain. The messenger then drank the mixture and, much to Lanyon's horror, underwent a series of transformations until Henry Jekyll appeared, "like a man restored from death."

Lanyon refused to repeat Jekyll's revelation, fearing that his terror would culminate in premature death, but he concluded, "The creature who crept into my house that night was, on Jekyll's own confession, known by the name of Hyde and hunted for in every corner of the land as the murderer of Carew."

Utterson then turns to Jekyll's narrative and learns the details of the case. The statement opens with the doctor's theory that "man is not truly one, but truly two" and a description of his efforts to separate this "primitive duality" for the good of mankind. After purchasing "a large quantity of a particular salt" from a wholesale chemist, he compounded it with other elements and, "with a strong glow of courage, drank off the potion." Swept through an agonizing attack, he felt "conscious of a heady recklessness, a current of disordered sensual images running like a mill race in my fancy, a solution of the bonds of obligation, and unknown but not an innocent freedom of the soul." Judging his alter ego, "Edward Hyde," to be a representative of "pure evil," Jekyll indulged sensual urges that he had sublimated to appease "respectable" London society: "I was the first that could thus plod in the public eye with a load of genial respectability, and in a moment, like a schoolboy, strip off these lendings and spring headlong into the sea of liberty." After several excursions as Hyde, Jekyll noticed that his own "good" personality had less control over the transformed, "evil" one. Determined to end his dreadful experiment, he was shocked by his inability to prevent the murder of Carew and, some days later, an unsolicited transformation into Hyde. He then sought one batch of salt after another but was unable to re-create the original mixture. Fearing that Hyde would discover his narrative and "tear it to pieces," Jekyll concluded, "Will Hyde die upon the scaffold? or will he find the courage to release himself at the last moment? God knows; I am careless. This is my true hour of death, and what is to follow concerns another than myself. Here, then, as I lay down the pen and proceed to seal up my confession, I bring the life of that unhappy Henry Jekyll to an end."

During an evening's sleep at Skerryvore in September 1885, Stevenson dreamed "a fine bogy tale." Screaming loudly, he became infuriated when Fanny awakened him. At dawn he began to document his memories of the nightmare and, a few days later, rushed downstairs to read his new 30,000-word narrative to Lloyd and Fanny, who dismissed the tale as a piece of sensationalistic horror: the idea of a dual personality needed a strong allegorical element, she insisted.

Lloyd recalled: "Stevenson was beside himself with anger. He trembled; his hand shook on the manuscript; he was intolerably chagrined. His voice, bitter and challenging, overrode my mother's in a fury of resentment. Never had I seen him so impassioned, so outraged, and the scene became so painful that I went away, unable to bear it any longer."[1] Lloyd later returned to find Fanny sitting alone by the fireplace. After some apparent reflection, Louis descended the stairs and, admitting that Fanny was right, tossed the manuscript into the fire. He then spent the next six days writing a new version of *The Strange Case of Dr. Jekyll and Mr. Hyde*. While Lloyd claimed that this draft ran 64,000 words, the published novella runs about 25,000. Even so, Stevenson's average of more than 4,000 words per day far outdistanced the 1,000 considered a standard quota for contemporary writers of fiction—an effort Lloyd called "an astounding feat, from whatever aspect it may be regarded."[2]

The second draft of the story included the allegorical overtones suggested by Fanny, who, after hearing a recitation, gave her approval. Following six weeks of proofreading and editing, Stevenson mailed the manuscript to Longmans, Green, and Company in London. Incredibly, his Jekyll-and-Hyde experience was repeated in November, when he transformed another nightmare into "Olalla," an eerie short story that was published in the Christmas 1885 issue of *Court and Society Review*. On January 9, 1886, *The Strange Case of Dr. Jekyll and Mr. Hyde* was published in Great Britain, four days after Charles Scribner's Sons of New York distributed the U.S. version.

When essayist John Addington Symonds wrote to criticize the novella's "picture of victorious evil," Stevenson replied that he had attempted to address "that damned old business of the war in the members."[3] In her preface to a 1905 edition, Fanny describes other public reactions that followed early printings:

> Many peculiar letters were received by my husband, more particularly from spiritualists and theosophists, who fancied he must have had some supernatural guidance in his portrayal of the double life. In one letter, from a German countess, the writer asked if the story were really the result of a dream, assuring him that if this were the case he was in a very precarious position, as the forces of "white and black magic" were contending for his soul. The countess implored him to accept the truths of theosophy, otherwise the forces of black magic would obtain the mastery, when, as she assured him, "the consequences would be most disastrous."[4]

In 1916 Richard A. Rice wrote that *The Strange Case of Dr. Jekyll and Mr. Hyde* was an "especially personal" project for Stevenson, for "a dream is the very essence of spontaneity."[5] Many biographers and literary scholars have speculated about Stevenson's inspiration for the dual personality, usually noting the influence of his strict Calvinist upbringing, his use of various prescribed drugs, and the effects of his lifelong illnesses. Prior to writing the story, he had witnessed his distinguished friend, Walter Ferrier, succumb to alcoholism, and he also was familiar with the story of Edinburgh cabinetmaker Deacon Brodie (1741–88), who had been hanged for leading a double life. Brodie, who specialized in robbing respectable citizens' homes after inviting them to parties, had provided the raw material for Stevenson and Henley's 1880 play, *Deacon Brodie,* which was revised in 1888.

Some scholars have criticized Stevenson's concept that a man could be transformed physically by a drug. J. R. Hammond writes: "A number of critics drew attention to this point on publication but were compelled to acknowledge that the power and conviction of the narrative were such as to override this technical weakness."[6] Stevenson presents his ideas as an allegory, utilizing the physical transformation to show a clear-cut difference between the good and evil sides of human beings. Even in a brilliantly written psychological novel, it would be difficult to depict such a behavioral dichotomy and, in 1885, this style had not been developed to any significant extent. Stevenson chose the most direct way to display a person's dual nature and combined it with an imaginatively plotted mystery.

As described by Dr. Jekyll, his growing enslavement to the desires of his evil half is similar to a person's addiction to narcotics or alcohol. Like the addict who gradually becomes dependent on heavier doses and then is unable to shake the habit, Dr. Jekyll is incapable of freeing himself from the influence of Mr. Hyde and, after a time, cannot achieve the desired effect, even when administering heavier doses of the drug. He begins to change into his evil half without the aid of chemical stimulants. Following his two-month respite from the ravages of Hyde, Jekyll again requires a "fix": "But time began at last to obliterate the freshness of my alarm; the praises of conscience began to grow into a thing of course; I began to be tortured with throes and longings, as of Hyde struggling after freedom; and at last, in an hour of moral weakness, I once again compounded and swallowed the transforming draught."

Two months before the murder of Sir Danvers Carew, Jekyll awakened in "the little room in Soho where [he] was accustomed to sleep in the body of Edward Hyde." Confused, he rushed to the mirror, where his blood was chilled: "Yes, I had gone to bed Henry Jekyll, I had awakened Edward Hyde. How was this to be explained?" Here, Jekyll's inability to fight off the lingering Hyde is akin to a severe alcoholic hangover.

Harry M. Geduld writes: "Mr. Hyde is, of course, the product of pharmacological experiment. Notwithstanding DeQuincey's Opium Eater, Dr. Jekyll was probably the first significant literary creation to dabble with personality-changing drugs. This alone is likely to make his tale more disturbingly plausible to the modern reader than Frankenstein's work with galvanic batteries and corpses."[7]

In the 1990s Stevenson's use of the physical transformation may not seem as implausible as some critics have suggested. Alcohol and drug abuse, while not transforming a person completely, often alters the addict's appearance. Regardless of how this aspect is analyzed, Stevenson's realization of the dual personality predated similar theories advanced by European psychologists.

More than seven years after *The Strange Case of Dr. Jekyll and Mr. Hyde* became a public sensation, Sigmund Freud and Josef Breuer published their first paper on hysteria. Geduld notes: "In this and the papers that followed, Freud examined the reasons why hysterics split off pieces of consciousness and forget them: the pieces contain painful or socially unacceptable or infantile ideas and wishes. (Clearly, in this instance, Stevenson anticipated Freud by allowing Hyde to represent the unacceptable ideas of Jekyll.)"[8]

Unlike the Henry Jekyll of many film adaptations, Stevenson's character is concerned primarily with his own pleasures. Realizing that the two sides can be separated, Jekyll uses Hyde to escape the Victorian code of respectability—as a way of expressing his evil urges. Stevenson's first draft of the story depicted a Dr. Jekyll whose only intention was to create Hyde as a disguise in which he could carry out his carnal desires. After Fanny expressed her disgust and the manuscript was burned, Stevenson then added the moralistic material (including the regret Jekyll expresses throughout his "Statement of the Case").

Edwin M. Eigner has written that Henry Jekyll's inability to exhibit virtuous behavior identifies him as a thoroughly selfish character:

The only goodness Stevenson seems capable of rendering in his fiction is the act of renunciation, and sacrifice seems hardly to be Henry Jekyll's strong point. . . . Jekyll disappears for the last time, absolutely careless as to what wickedness Hyde may perform with his body. The benevolence in Jekyll seems to stem not from any innate springs of virtue, but, as he admits, from an "imperious desire to carry my head high, and wear a more than commonly grave countenance before the public."[9]

Eigner's analysis may be a bit extreme. Prior to the first signs of his unorthodox behavior, Jekyll "had always been known for charities" (chapter six, "Remarkable Incident of Dr. Lanyon"), and in chapter ten ("Henry Jekyll's Full Statement of the Case") he reminds Lanyon of "how earnestly in the last months of last year I laboured to relieve suffering; you know that much was done for others." Jekyll is eclipsed by Hyde, but he is not merely careless; he is unable to halt the inevitable outcome of his experiment. When the final transformation occurs, he prevents further mayhem by taking his own life. Jekyll is another refreshingly ambiguous creation: his actions are not filled with goodness, but he is not amoral, either.

There are obvious similarities between Stevenson's thematics and those expressed by Mary Shelley in *Frankenstein*, written nearly 70 years earlier. Eigner adds: "In writing such a story of a creature turned diabolic in response to the hatred and rejection afforded him by society and by the man to whom he owes his life, Stevenson must have been aware of similarities to the first important monster story of the century."[10]

Stevenson's use of multiple points of view is an admirable stylistic element. The actions of Utterson and Enfield are relayed in an impersonal style before Utterson narrates a third-person account (sometimes observing the action directly and at other times hearing events described by others). Stevenson then uses the final two chapters to reveal the first-person narratives of Dr. Lanyon and Dr. Jekyll. This style allows the reader to take part in the experiences of several different characters rather than being relegated to a single perspective.

Stevenson's narrative structure maintains a sense of mystery; readers in 1886 did not realize that Jekyll and Hyde were *one* man until the latter stages of the story. Mr. Hyde is described in chapter one ("Story of the Door") and appears in chapter two ("Search for Mr. Hyde"), while Dr. Jekyll does not appear until chapter three ("Dr. Jekyll Was Quite at Ease"). The reader is not given proof that Hyde *is* Jekyll until chapter nine ("Dr. Lanyon's Narrative"), and Jekyll's transformations are not elaborated upon until chapter ten. (It is unlikely that this structure could be transferred adequately to a stage or screen adaptation; to date, no film has incorporated it.)

The novella is set in London, but much of the geography seems more Scottish than English. In 1950 Edinburgh historian Moray McLaren wrote that "there is a distinctly un–London flavour about it":

Dr. Jekyll and Mr. Hyde's town *is* Edinburgh. The dark contrast between the dark evil and the almost equally ill-lit virtue is pure Edinburgh. The black old streets in which Hyde slinks on his evil path amidst carefully undescribed squalor and committing, for the most part, carefully unspecified sins, are *Edinburgh* streets. The heavily furnished, lampshaded interior of Dr. Jekyll's unostentatiously prosperous house is the inside of any well-to-do professional man's home in the New Town of Edinburgh. The contrast is not so much between black evil and golden goodness as between dark dirt and gloomy respectability. The stage throughout is only half lit. It is an Edinburgh Winter's Night tale.[11]

Stevenson's dialogue contains Scottish phrases, and some of the characters, as McLaren suggests, speak with "the accents of the Edinburgh upper classes."[12]

The influence of the Jekyll-and-Hyde story has been immense, and even after Freud and others have developed sophisticated theories about the multiple personality, the fascination with Stevenson's concept still remains. Popular literature, particularly the work of Oscar Wilde, H. G. Wells, and Sir Arthur Conan Doyle, has shown this impact. Stevenson himself continued to explore the duality theme in many future novels and stories.

## Early Theatrical Adaptations (1886–1931)

Soon after Stevenson arrived in New York during the summer of 1887, he was sought out by Richard Mansfield, the English-born character actor who had achieved suc-

RLS at age thirty-six, 1887.

cess on the American stage, particularly in the operas of Gilbert and Sullivan. Mansfield currently was portraying Jekyll and Hyde in the first serious theatrical adaptation of the novella. Adapted by Thomas Russell Sullivan, *Dr. Jekyll and Mr. Hyde* was staged at the Boston Museum from May 9 to 13, and at the Madison Square Theatre in New York City from September 12 to October 1. This first run met with critical and public acclaim, but Mansfield's attempts to see Stevenson were unavailing. The actor recalled:

> It happened that he was not at home when I called on him, and it happened that I was not at home when he called on me. At last, one day, I was fortunate, as I thought. I sent in my name, and a person

whom I understood to be Mr. Stevenson's adopted son presently appeared, and, after the customary exchange of civilities, said that Mr. Stevenson wished to know whether I had a cold, because, if I had, he could not venture to see me. I told him to tell Mr. Stevenson, with my kindest regards, that I had an exceedingly bad cold, which I should be most happy to communicate to him, and so took my leave. We did not meet. Later I heard that Mr. Stevenson had promptly left town—probably to escape infection,—and me!"[13]

Regarding this reminiscence, Mansfield biographer William Winter comments, "That incident is characteristic of Mansfield's eccentricity, but no words can express the humor with which he related it."

After touring the United States from October 3, 1887, to June 25, 1888, Mansfield's company sailed to England, where Howard Poole took over production at Croydon's Theatre Royal on July 26. Unable to reproduce his American success, Mansfield "attracted no attention and made no impression" on British audiences.[14] On August 4 the play moved to London's Lyceum Theatre, where it fared somewhat better with audiences and critics. A review in the September 1, 1888, issue of London's *The Theatre* notes: "No one who has seen Mr. Sullivan's version of R. L. Stevenson's weird story will for a moment speak of it as making a good play—in fact it would have been almost impossible out of the material at command to produce an effective drama."[15]

*The Strange Case of Dr. Jekyll and Mr. Hyde* contains no major female characters. In fact, only four women are mentioned in the novella: the maidservant who witnesses the Carew murder, a match-girl who is "smote in the face" by Mr. Hyde, and Dr. Jekyll's housemaid and cook, who are frightened by the strange sounds emanating from the laboratory. The Sullivan-Mansfield play is responsible for adding principal females: Mrs. Lanyon (Kate Ryan in the United States and Helen Glidden in Great Britain); Agnes Carew, daughter of Sir Danvers (Isabelle Evesson in the United States and Beatrice Cameron in Great Britain); and Rebecca Moore (Emma Sheridan in both). This addition has been integrated, through various characterizations, into most subsequent stage and film adaptations; considering that popular theater and the infant cinema both relied on sex for a portion of their success, it was inevitable that women would play a major role in Mr. Hyde's debauched existence.

In act 1 of Sullivan and Mansfield's play, Agnes Carew was presented as the fiancée of the nervous Dr. Jekyll. Mr. Hyde also appeared in this initial movement, slithering into the house and demanding to see Miss Carew. Refusing, Sir Danvers (U.S. play, Boyd Putnam; British play, Mr. Holland) immediately was mauled and choked to death.

Act 2 contained two scenes, showed a brandy-drinking Hyde confronted by Sir Danvers's ghost, and Hyde's escape from the London police. The movement ended with Hyde entering Dr. Jekyll's laboratory, where he was accosted by Mr. Utterson (U.S. play, Frazer

Coulter; British play, John T. Sullivan).

Act 3 included Hyde's swallowing of the potion and transformation in Dr. Lanyon's house, and act 4 concluded with Hyde's suicide. Pleading with Lanyon (U.S. play, Alfred Hudson; British play, D. H. Harkins) to bring Agnes within his sight, Jekyll, involuntarily transforming into Hyde, was forced to take his own life after being discovered by Utterson and the police.

Although the adaptation drew little acclaim, the acting in the British version was singled out by *The Theatre*. Mansfield was lauded for transforming "without mechanical means or leaving the stage" (a claim that Paramount would make for John Barrymore in its 1920 film version). Beatrice Cameron and Emma Sheridan "ably filled" their parts, while W. H. Compton (Inspector Newcomen) and J. C. Burrows (Poole) displayed "distinctive and clever originality."[16]

In his 1910 assessment of this first attempt to dramatize the novella, William Winter discusses Sullivan's approach and its relation to literature and the visual arts:

> In order to build a play upon the allegory of imagined, emblematic experience it was necessary, first, to reject the intention to reproduce the exact, literal substance of the book, and secondly, to devise a scheme of innovation upon the original. There is a narrow order of the critical mind which, in a case of this kind, seems to feel a savage delight at finding discrepancies betwixt a play and a novel upon which the play is founded. Of course, there are discrepancies. They exist in every similar case; they are inevitable, and, furthermore, they are essential. A lecturer is not an actor, although each may treat a dramatic theme. A novel is not a play, although both may relate to the same subject. The novel describes. The play exhibits. The novel is character in picture, clothed with description. The play is character in action, clothed with scenery. Sometimes a novel is so dramatic that it can, with only a few touches, be converted into a play. More often the novel must be greatly altered before its dramatic aspects can be released. Portions of its material frequently must be rejected, to make way for material absolutely new. That was necessary in dealing with *Dr. Jekyll and Mr. Hyde*. The dramatist used the central idea of the story, its ground plan and some of its incidents; but he modified its characters, he displayed them under changed conditions, and he environed the *The Strange Case* as well with an atmosphere of domestic life and love as with the otherwise unrelieved investiture of horror.[17]

Almost a year before Mansfield's first performance a parody, *The Strange Case of a Hyde and Seekyl*, premiered at L. C. Toole's Theatre in London on May 18, 1886 (just four months after the novella was published). Another burlesque, *Dr. Freckle and Mr. Snide*, was performed at Dockstader's Minstrel Hall in New York City on October 3, 1887 (two days after Mansfield gave his last performance at the Madison Square Theatre).

A second serious adaptation, also titled *Dr. Jekyll and Mr. Hyde*, premiered in New York City during Mansfield's American tour. On March 12, 1888, Daniel Bandmann (who also wrote the play) trod the boards at Niblo's Garden and again at Brooklyn's Amphion Academy on March 19. This version (featuring five major female characters) incorporated much of Sullivan's plotting with several scenes of intrusive comedy relief. After a short New York run, the play resurfaced at London's Opera Comique on August 6, where it closed after two dismal performances. The *Theatre* noted:

> It is of course impossible to say whether Mr. Bandmann's version which he is said to have played in America is a good one; there can be but one verdict as to the version produced here—that it was bad. ... Mr. Bandmann's Dr. Jekyll was a canting, sanctimonious humbug of Pecksniffian appearance; his Mr. Hyde a malevolent dwarf-like creature with large teeth, that was ridiculous from its monkey-like tricks, which only produced laughter and derision where they should have inspired terror.[18]

The inferior quality of Bandmann's version was not the only reason for its two-day run. When Stevenson's publisher, Longmans, Green, and Company, caught wind of it, they cited Bandmann with copyright infringement and forced him to close. In fact, the Bandmann fiasco would not have existed if Mansfield and Sullivan had been protected by an American copyright. Attempting to exhibit his play before Mansfield opened on August 4, Bandmann did not get under way until August 6, and by that time his production was doomed.

Bandmann managed a performance at the Opera House in Savannah, Georgia, in 1902, but was left in a cloud of Mansfield's dust. Reviving the Sullivan play on January 1, 1890, Mansfield continued to portray the dual character until March 21, 1907, when he made his final bow at New York's New Amsterdam Theatre.

In 1893 the English rights to the theatrical production were purchased by Henry Irving, who intended to make the dual role one of his greatest achievements. Mansfield was distressed by this development: "Mr. Irving's last action was to buy 'Dr. Jekyll and Mr. Hyde,' to prevent me from playing it in London."[19] By the time Irving first appeared in the Comyns Carr adaptation at London's Queen's Theatre on January 29, 1910, at least 13 other serious versions and a musical farce had been performed on U.S. and British stages.

An admirer of Harry S Truman has reported that the late president attended a touring production of *Dr. Jekyll and Mr. Hyde* during its run at the Auditorium Theatre in Independence, Missouri, circa 1902–03. Then an employee of the Kansas City Commerce Bank, Truman apparently took in an evening's performance, only to be "scared all the way out to his boarding house after the play."[20]

In 1923 another New York dramatization was followed by three more London attempts (two in 1927 and one in 1931). There are at least two known adaptations of *The Strange Case of Dr. Jekyll and Mr. Hyde* that were never produced (an unpublished 1910 manuscript and a 1956 version published in London's *Plays of the Year*).

## Early Film Adaptations (1908–20)

The first motion pictures were exhibited during 1894–96 by various pioneers in the United States, France, Germany, and England. As film historian A. R. Fulton has written, however, "the attempt to represent the illusion of motion by pictures is older than civilization."[21] Devices such as Leonardo da Vinci's camera obscura (late 1400s), Christian Huygens's magic lantern (circa 1655), Joseph Plateau's Phenakistiscope (1828), and the first Zoetrope, the Daedaleum (1833), invented by British mathematician William George Horner, are notable examples.

A decade before the birth of films, Stevenson, too, had his own "cinematic" vision. After dreaming the "bogy tale" that would become *The Strange Case of Dr. Jekyll and Mr. Hyde,* he incorporated a similar experience into the story. Piqued by Enfield's recollections of Mr. Hyde, Utterson retires for the night, but his sleep is accompanied by a vivid dream:

> Six o'clock struck on the bells of the church that was so conveniently near to Mr. Utterson's dwelling, and still he was digging at the problem. Hitherto it had touched him on the intellectual side alone, but now his imagination also was engaged, or rather enslaved; and as he lay and tossed in the gross darkness of the night and the curtained room, Mr. Enfield's tale went by before his mind in a scroll of lighted pictures. He would be aware of the great field of lamps of a nocturnal city; then of the figure of a man walking swiftly; then of a child running from the doctor's; and then these met, and that human Juggernaut trod the child down and passed on regardless of her screams. Or else he would see a room in a rich house, where his friend lay asleep, dreaming and smiling at his dreams; and then the door of that room would be opened, the curtains of the bed plucked apart, the sleeper recalled, and, lo! there would stand by his side a figure to whom power was given, and even at that dead hour he must rise and do its bidding. The figure in these two phases haunted the lawyer all night; and if at any time he dozed over, it was but to see it glide more stealthily through sleeping houses, or move the more swiftly and still the more swiftly, even to dizziness, through wider labyrinths of lamplighted city, and at every street corner crush a child and leave her screaming.

A talented filmmaker could not wish for better raw material. Stevenson's inclusion of the phrase "scroll of lighted pictures"—a literal description of a film—sets the stage for Utterson's dream, the structure of which resembles a cinematic montage: a series of scenes that culminates with Mr. Hyde moving "swiftly and still the more swiftly." This brilliant passage could be used as a blueprint for a film sequence; the semicolons even provide probable locations for edits. (Though Stevenson did not live long enough to see a film, he was familiar with the precursory magic lantern and its slides.) Considering that *The Strange Case of Dr. Jekyll and Mr. Hyde* has inspired numerous adaptations, it seems odd that no one has attempted a faithful visualization of Utterson's slumberous phantasm.

The macabre elements of the novella have fascinated screenwriters since the early days of cinema. In fact, Stevenson may be credited, for better or worse, as the spiritual father of the American horror-film genre. Based on an 1897 Luella Forepaugh–George F. Fish stage adaptation that toured the United States, the Polyscope Company's *Dr. Jekyll and Mr. Hyde* (also known as *The Modern Dr. Jekyll*) reached nickelodeon screens in 1908. Directed by Otis Turner and produced by Colonel William Selig, who saw the play in Chicago on its final night, this primal horror film was a condensed version of the four-act stage script and featured the same actors, including Hobart Bosworth and Betty Harte. A Kalem Company adaptation, directed by Sidney Olcott and featuring Gene Gauntier and Frank Rose, also was released that year.

In 1909 Nordisk of Copenhagen released *Den Skaebnesvangre Opfindelse*, directed by August Blom and starring Alvin Neuss (as Jekyll and Hyde), Emilie Sannon, and Oda Alstrup. During the same period, Neuss also played Conan Doyle's Dr. Watson in Nordisk's Sherlock Holmes series. Today, Nordisk and Neuss are remembered primarily for their involvement in both the earliest Holmes series and the first European Jekyll-and-Hyde film. After portraying Stevenson's dual character, Neuss became the first actor to play both Dr. Watson and Sherlock Holmes (when he switched costumes for *Millionobligationen* in 1911; he was succeeded in these roles by Reginald Owen and Jeremy Brett). *Den Skaebnesvangre Opfindelse* was the first adaptation to write off Jekyll's hideous experience as a dream.

A 1910 British release, Wrench Films' *The Duality of Man*, features some of Stevenson's more action-oriented passages. In the closing scenes Hyde evades the police, transforms into Jekyll, and courts his fiancée; turning back into Hyde, he murders her father before swallowing a phial of poison.

The first widely released *Dr. Jekyll and Mr. Hyde* was Thanhouser's 1911 version, directed by Lucius Henderson and starring James Cruze (as Dr. Jekyll) and Marguerite Snow (as "the Minister's daughter"). Closely resembling the Sullivan-Mansfield stage version, this one-reeler features quick-dissolve transformation scenes (photographed in static medium shot) and Hyde's attacks on a small girl and his sweetheart's father (a simplistic visualization of the Sir Danvers Carew murder). For years film historians and horror fans assumed that Cruze (who later became a distinguished director) also appears as Mr. Hyde but, in 1963, a little-known actor named Harry Benham, then in his eighties, admitted that he had donned the monstrous Hyde makeup. Apparently saving time (and perhaps Cruze's vanity), Benham's interpretation is that of a snarling, tongue-lolling gargoyle.

In 1913 Stevenson's novella became the first tale of terror to be filmed in color. A two-reel adaptation, shot in Charles Urban's U.S. studio, was released by Kineto-Kinemacolor of Great Britain, a company that marketed a crude two-strip color process. Few theaters showed the film, however, due to the bulky and expensive equipment that the process required: a special projector, running at twice the normal speed, and a system of revolving red and green filters had to be installed prior to exhibition. Like many of the early Jekyll-and-Hyde adaptations, no prints of this film are known to exist.

Another 1913 release, Imp's *Dr. Jekyll and Mr. Hyde*, was produced by Hollywood pioneer Carl Laemmle, who included the film in his successful King Baggot series. A former stage star, Baggot began appearing in Laemmle productions in 1910, after his touring theatrical company folded. Acting in a one-reel drama each week, Baggot was catapulted to international stardom and increasingly better roles in two-reelers. Supported by Jane Gail, Matt Snyder, Howard Crampton, and William Sarell, Baggot played both Jekyll and Hyde and (according to some sources) also directed the film.

Several two-reel versions followed Laemmle's effort. Two 1914 releases, Starlight's *Dr. Jekyll and Mr. Hyde* and Warner's *Dr. Jekyll and Mr. Hyde Done to a Frazzle*, were parodies. Lubin's *Horrible Hyde* (1915), featuring Jerold T. Horner, Billy Reeves, and Mae Hotely, was directed by Arthur Hotaling, while Vitagraph's *Miss Jekyll and Madame Hyde* (1915), starring Helen Gardner and directed by Charles L. Gaskill, was the first adaptation to change the doctor's gender.

Three serious adaptations and two parodies were produced in 1920. Directed by F. W. Murnau, Lipow Film's *Der Januskopf* (U.S. titles, *Janus-Faced*, *The Head of Janus*, or *Love's Mockery*) was German expressionism's entry in the Jekyll-and-Hyde saga. Before production began, the intractable Murnau refused to secure copyright clearance and altered the story (an act he repeated while transforming Bram Stoker's *Dracula* into *Nosferatu* the following year), drawing his title from the myth of Janus, the two-faced Roman god. For the dual role of "Dr. Warren and Mr. O'Connor," Murnau chose Conrad Veidt, who had proved a sensation as Cesare, the somnambulist, in the Robert Wiene–directed *The Cabinet of Dr. Caligari* (1919). Obsessed with his bust of Janus, Warren became the perverted, bestial O'Connor and, in a Stevenson-inspired sequence, trampled a small girl in the street. Another scene featured O'Connor dragging Warren's fiancée (Margarete Schlegel) into a sleazy brothel. Further quoting the novella, the film ended with Warren poisoning himself. Written by Hans Janowitz (who coauthored *Caligari* with Carl Mayer) and photographed by Carl Hoffman, Carl Weiss, and the legendary Karl Freund, the film also featured Bela Lugosi (as Dr. Warren's butler). Unfortunately, no prints of *Der Januskopf* have ever been located (only an original script and a few stills are known to exist).

## *Dr. Jekyll and Mr. Hyde* (Paramount-Artcraft, 1920)

In 1920 matinee idol John Barrymore was reaching the height of his theatrical popularity. On April 9, 1919, he had joined his elder brother, Lionel, on stage at New

York's Plymouth Theatre to begin a 77-performance run of *The Jest,* an American adaptation of Sam Benelli's Italian play *La Cena delle Beffe.* In its opening night review the *New York Times* raved that "*The Jest* has fallen across the sky of the declining season like a burst of sunset color."[22]

While avoiding adoring females who crowded outside the stage door, Barrymore honored a three-picture contract with Adolph Zukor, who, in 1916, had merged his own company, Famous Players, with Paramount. At the time these films were released in 1919, legitimate critics had begun to take a serious interest in motion pictures. Referring to *The Test of Honor,* Barrymore's twelfth film (but the first to feature him in a serious dramatic role), *Photoplay* stated, "The piece is a very ordinary melodrama, but Mr. Barrymore's performance is magnificent."[23] Continuing his profitable association with Barrymore, Zukor convinced him to star in the first feature-length adaptation of Stevenson's novella. Remarkably, his performance in *The Jest* was a perfect forerunner for his turn as Jekyll and Hyde. In his 1951 memoir, *We Barrymores,* Lionel Barrymore writes:

> He was supposed to be an esthetic, almost effeminate boy who achieved an enormous thrill out of being in personal danger. Then, as his character develops before your eyes, you see a person who is not physically supreme triumph over and kick the daylights out of a brute. This was Jack's personal interpretation of the part and his contribution to the writing of the role. He made his Giannetto bring about the absolute demolition of the great roaring heel Neri—then quailed when he saw how completely he had destroyed him.[24]

In his review of the film, Edward Weitzel praises Stevenson's work, claiming that many of his stories are perfectly suited for the "Silver Sheet":

> *Dr. Jekyll and Mr. Hyde* is Stevenson's unique contribution to the imperishable literature of the world and of all his writings the tale that is best adapted to being told on the shadow stage. Its compact plot, the frank employment of the supernatural, the breadth and engrossing power of its theme, the dread fascination of its dark moments and the truth and impressiveness of its terrible lesson give it dramatic values that utilize every resource of film art.
>
> Such a story demands the highest skill in each phase of its making. The dual role of the scientist and the Nemesis of his own creating is one to test the talents of the greatest masters of acting. Happily for the screen it has fallen to an actor who measures up to the full task to embody the two characters in the Paramount-Artcraft production. By its selection of John Barrymore, the Famous Players–Lasky Company has guaranteed the moving picture public the services of the foremost tragic actor of this country in a part that allows him to be seen at his best. All the intellectual force, glow of imagination and command of the preternatural that are Barrymore's to such an unusual degree find complete expression in *Dr. Jekyll and Mr. Hyde.*[25]

Nearly 75 years later, Weitzel's assessment still rings true. Though the film incorporates material extraneous to the story, it remains one of the most faithful adaptations and, arguably, one of the finest productions of the American silent period.

The first major departure is the depiction of Henry Jekyll as a "do-gooder" who runs a free clinic for the London poor. The initial title card reads: "John Barrymore as Henry Jekyll, idealist and philanthropist—by profession, a doctor of medicine." This information is followed by a medium close-up of Jekyll (Barrymore in profile) carefully tending to a patient. Behind him is Dr. Richard Lanyon (Charles Lane), described by a title card as conservative and unbending in his disdain for Jekyll's progressive idea that scientific research is the road to ultimate knowledge. This romanticized portrait of Jekyll adds heroic overtones to a character who, in the novella, displays a sporadic interest in charitable work.

In the film Jekyll does not develop the theory of human duality on his own. While dining at the home of Sir George Carew (Brandon Hurst), the father of his "beloved" Millicent (Martha Mansfield), Jekyll is informed of "man's dual nature" by his host, who suggests that the good doctor spend less time helping others and more on his own pursuits. Although Stevenson depicts (Danvers) Carew as an M.P. who is murdered "with apelike fury," screenwriter Clara S. Beranger incorporated into the Carew character the personality of Lord Henry Wotton, the cynical aristocrat from Oscar Wilde's *The Picture of Dorian Gray* (1891). Far from being a typical prospective father-in-law, Carew takes the chaste Jekyll to a local music hall and solicits Therese (or Miss Gina—as she is called in the Blackhawk print—played by Nita Naldi), an exotic dancer, to seduce him. This incident prompts Jekyll to experiment with freeing his "good" side from the "evil" one. A title card reads: "For the first time in his life, Jekyll had wakened to a sense of his baser nature."

The inclusion of rigidly defined good and evil female characters who act as visual metaphors for the Jekyll-and-Hyde duality was pioneered by Berenger. Earlier stage and screen versions had introduced and expanded the character of Jekyll's pure, virginal fiancée, but sexuality, in the form of a more libidinous female, had been ignored (an aspect that remained more faithful to Stevenson's asexual depiction of Jekyll). Barrymore's Mr. Hyde was the first to indulge in sexual depravity rather than mere viciousness (child abuse, for example). Nita Naldi's Therese is an incredibly erotic vision, shot in suggestive close-ups during her initial appearance as she dances with upraised arms and amply displayed cleavage. A daring inclusion for an American silent film, this salacious image is the catalyst for Jekyll's investigation of the evil side (another aspect that recalls *Dorian Gray*).

Most of the scenes represent material in the novella, although events are not depicted in the same order. Dr. Jekyll is the first character to appear, with Hyde emerging during the initial transformation scene. Like its stage and screen predecessors, the film does not allow the audience to solve the mystery (the other on-screen characters, however, do not discover Hyde's true identity until the conclusion). Specific passages are visualized, including Jekyll's discussion of his will with Utterson and Hyde's trampling of a small child in the by-street (unlike Stevenson's plotting, this incident occurs not at the beginning of the narrative but near the end). Hyde brutally steps on the child's spine and is confronted by several people (including Sir George Carew and Utterson) who demand compensation. He then withdraws a key, opens a door in the by-street, and returns with a £100 check signed "Henry Jekyll"; to assure his accusers of its legitimacy, he leads them to a nearby bank. Questioned by Carew, Poole (George Stevens) admits that Hyde holds the only key to the laboratory door.

Plotted as a mystery, the novella does not allow the reader to experience one of Jekyll's transformations until the final chapter; Barrymore's performance and John S. Robertson's direction gave audiences the first elaborate Jekyll-into-Hyde metamorphosis. After Jekyll proposes his new theory to Lanyon, he spends "days and nights" in the laboratory (the actual scene lasts only a few seconds), attempting to discover a chemical mixture that will split his two personae.

The transformation scene is photographed and paced beautifully. The first image shows Jekyll, in long shot, stirring the potion; preparing to drink, he places the flask on the table and walks away. Contemplating his next move, he is taunted by the memory of Carew's "evil" influence (a close-up image of Carew's face is superimposed over the action); unable to resist, he soon retrieves the flask. A cut to a medium shot is followed by Jekyll's drinking of the contents: he convulses violently, undergoes a series of intense contortions, and raises his face toward the camera. Here, the scene cuts to a close-up of the face, which is now that of the grotesque Hyde, before another cut leads to a close-up of his left hand (which, through a lap-dissolve process, becomes elongated and darker in color). A cut to another close-up then shows him raising the long-nailed hand to his face.

Barrymore's remarkable skill allowed him to perform the initial transformation without the use of make-up (the medium shot shows Hyde's face *before* the scene cuts). Following his performance in this scene, makeup was applied gradually to make Hyde's physical appearance match his mental descent into debauchery and murder.

As Hyde sinks deeper into drinking and illicit sex with Therese (one scene in his Soho flat shows him ordering her out—"I'm through with you," he tells her), Barrymore's interpretation becomes a hybrid of Shakespeare's hunchbacked Richard III (a role he was playing concurrently on Broadway) and a huge arachnid. His long, spider-like hands are accompanied by a pointed head (first seen midway through the film when he removes his hat), long, oily hair, and a distended face (some reports claim that Barrymore dislocated his jaw to achieve this effect). One scene shows Jekyll asleep, while a giant spider crawls across the floor and onto his bed; merging with the doctor's body, the arachnid causes him to change into the hideous

Hyde. Accomplished with little cutting and a smoothly superimposed spider, this scene is a stunning visual representation of Jekyll's inability to overcome Hyde's growing control.

Another powerful transformation occurs when Jekyll is visited by Carew, who (like Utterson in the novella) becomes interested in the activities of Hyde; he demands to know the extent of Jekyll's involvement with the brute and threatens to call off Millicent's engagement. Accusing Carew of turning him toward temptation and the exploration of evil, Jekyll metamorphoses into the roaring beast, chases the old man into the courtyard, and brutally bludgeons him to death with a heavy walking stick. This savage act is rendered graphically by Robertson, cinematographer Roy Overbaugh, and Barrymore, who becomes one of the most terrifying specters ever to grace the screen.

The climactic scenes contain a large amount of Stevenson's material, including Utterson and the police searching Hyde's Soho flat, Poole's inability to obtain the proper drugs for Jekyll, and Jekyll's servants cowering in the hall as the doctor confines himself within the laboratory. Having exhausted all traces of the transforming drug, Jekyll realizes that he cannot save himself from Hyde's malignant control. As Millicent approaches the door, he feels the initial effects of the metamorphosis and quickly extracts a substance from his ring (an Italian relic containing poison, earlier seen in close-up on Therese's finger) before changing into Hyde. He chases Millicent around the room but soon convulses and falls dead into a chair. As she leaves the room, Lanyon arrives in time to see Hyde change back into Jekyll (Stevenson's passage, set in Lanyon's home, is not represented). Realizing that Jekyll has atoned for his crimes, Lanyon consoles Millicent: "Hyde has killed Dr. Jekyll," he tells her. After Millicent kneels beside Jekyll's body, the scene cuts to a close-up of his lifeless profile (a reversal of the film's opening shot) before fading to black.

Many of Stevenson's incidents are visualized, but his characters either are modified or play a small role in the proceedings. Most obviously, Jekyll's motivation is altered: instead of exploring duality to vent his selfish, depraved desires, he is a pillar of society led astray by Sir George Carew, who has nothing in common with Stevenson's Sir Danvers (therefore, Hyde's murder of Carew in the film almost seems justified). Utterson and Richard Enfield (who appear briefly) bear almost no resemblance to their literary forebears. Utterson is the most visible character in the novella, but Beranger's screenplay telescopes him and *Dorian Gray*'s Sir Henry into the Carew character. The female characters are inventions who transform Jekyll's intent from defying Victorian conventions into a desire for sex (a development that would be included in most future adaptations). Lanyon is the only character who treads close to Stevenson's conception (he does not die, however, but lives to witness Jekyll's fate in the final reel).

One of the more faithful moments occurs when Jekyll takes his own life. In the novella Jekyll no longer exists when Hyde commits suicide, but Beranger and Barrymore's approach is close to the mark (and does not include the police breaking in to shoot him, as do many subsequent adaptations).

Beranger's alteration of Stevenson's intent is equaled by the presence of the handsome John Barrymore. The physical opposite of "a large, well-made, smooth-faced man of fifty," the 38-year-old actor alternates between youthful idealist and repulsive demon. Perhaps the first great "monster" of the American fantasy cinema, Barrymore's uncanny physical interpretation incorporates enough realism to make it fascinating more than 70 years later. Unlike the famous freak characterizations of Lon Chaney, Sr., in the mid–1920s, Barrymore's conception does not rely on a literal mask of makeup and histrionic pantomime. (Although Chaney was an undisputed master of innovative makeup techniques, his characters appear more curious than plausible.) Concluding his 1920 assessment of Barrymore, Edward Weitzel claims that his performance "is worthy to rank along side of the Mephistopheles of Henry Irving and the Bertuccio of Edwin Booth. The screen has never before known such great acting."[26]

Critics and audiences were nearly unanimous in their praise. New York City's Rivoli Theatre enjoyed a huge first-run success while the *New York Times* observed: "While Mr. Barrymore is achieving greatness as Richard III on the stage ... a great many more people will see *Dr. Jekyll and Mr. Hyde,* and have through it their only opportunity of knowing what Mr. Barrymore can do. This is true for today and more importantly true for the future."[27] Unfortunately, great reviews did nothing for Barrymore's physical and mental condition. Exhausted from his *Richard III* performances, the filming of the strenuous Jekyll-and-Hyde sequences, and studying for his forthcoming interpretation of *Hamlet,* the actor suffered a nervous breakdown which was complicated by serious marital and drinking problems.

Paramount's *Dr. Jekyll and Mr. Hyde* deviates considerably from the novella, yet it remains one of the most faithful adaptations. With its compact screenplay, consistent pace, and tendency to relate the story in visual terms (very few title cards appear throughout its seven reels), it ranks as one of the few definitive cinematic interpretations of a Stevenson work.

## Dr. Jekyll and Mr. Hyde (Pioneer, 1920)

Even in 1920, success in the American film industry bred quick imitation. Due to a loophole in Paramount-Artcraft's copyright, a cheap travesty of the Robertson-Barrymore effort was produced by Louis B. Mayer, who then was operating the Pioneer Film Corporation. A poor excuse for entertainment, Mayer's *Dr. Jekyll and Mr. Hyde* is not an adaptation of the Stevenson novella but a fabricated potboiler incorporating serial-like action and religious propaganda. To discourage comparisons with the Paramount production, Mayer set his story in the present

**Dr. Jekyll and Mr. Hyde** (1920). The lecherous Mr. Hyde (John Barrymore) accosts Millicent Carew (Martha Mansfield) in Dr. Jekyll's study.

day, a move that destroyed the story's period atmosphere and introduced many ludicrous images into the film's plotless movement.

As portrayed by serial actor Sheldon Lewis, Dr. Jekyll borders on the insignificant. Appearing in the film's opening shot, Lewis's Jekyll mixes chemicals and cares for sick children. A title card reads, "Through years of labor he has acquired a fortune which allows him

***Dr. Jekyll and Mr. Hyde*** **(1920). John Barrymore's arachnidian Mr. Hyde remains one of the horror cinema's most grotesque creations.**

to devote the greater part of his time to the poor and afflicted." Described as a free clinic, Jekyll's domain has a precedent not in the novella but in the previous film (even the staging, photography, and editing in this scene resemble the earlier release).

In the next sequence the remaining characters are introduced in a stagey manner. A hasty shot of Dr. Lanyon (Alexander Shannon), Jekyll's "lifelong friend," is followed by brief images of Mrs. Lanyon (Dora Mills Adams), Edward Utterson (Harold Forshay), and Bernice (Gladys Field), Lanyon's niece and Jekyll's fiancée, all of whom have gathered at the Lanyon home for a card game (a cut-rate and unimaginative exposition for characters who are never developed). Soon Danvers Carew (Leslie Austin), a handsome young man introduced as "Bernice's chum since childhood," walks in to muddle the proceedings. Told primarily by cumbersome title cards, the story becomes visually and narratively static after the first five minutes. The location is never revealed (it is not London, but somewhere in the United States, circa 1920). The absurdity of the card game is outdone moments later, when Bernice arrives at Jekyll's laboratory: sauntering in, she reminds the doctor that he had promised to play golf with her! These elements are indicative of the general content: "filler" combined with Hyde's constant scurrying about the neighborhood. (Most of the film was shot outdoors, incorporating an alley and a few street locations.)

Jekyll develops the duality theory independently in this version, but his intent differs from that of Stevenson's character: the doctor's driving force is an atheism which tempts him to prove "that there is no soul." (The viewer may grasp the premise at this point, but a lengthy tedium must be endured before the film grinds to a halt.)

The first transformation scene, a poor introduction to the Hyde character, is amateurish and stilted. Photographed in medium shot, Jekyll drinks the frothing brew, raises his right hand to his forehead, turns his back to the camera, and walks to the back of the room.

A cut to a location outside the lab shows Poole readying the doctor's coat and hat (a visit to the opera has been planned) before the scene cuts back inside to a frantic Hyde. Donning a slicker overcoat and a Buster Keaton–style hat, the hunched-over, leering beast resembles an extra wearing an inexpensive Halloween mask. He scampers into a nearby alley, attacks and robs a woman, fights with some workers, and hides in a sewer to elude the police (his actual escape is not shown).

Recovering from his first Hyde excursion, Jekyll pleads, "Oh God help me!—save me from the penalty of my unbelief—help—help—Oh God!" Here the moral ambiguity of Stevenson's character is abandoned for a simplistic religious sermon (Jekyll has become Hyde because he is not a Christian!).

Tired of waiting for the preoccupied Jekyll, Bernice calls off their engagement. Vengeance ridden, Hyde torches the Lanyon home as the scene cuts to bad stock footage of fire engines and men battling the blaze. After a brief nod to Stevenson is made (Jekyll adds the Hyde provision to his will), Hyde returns to the (apparently unscathed) house, where he witnesses the marriage proposal of Danvers Carew. When Bernice conveniently walks upstairs to speak with her uncle, Hyde speeds in, throttles poor Danvers, and beats him to death. Back at Jekyll's lab, the beast absurdly fondles and kisses a human skull before the scene fades to black.

In a later sequence Hyde is shown in his "tenement" digs, where he is visited by Carew's ghost. After this episode peters out, the enraged monster repeats his throttling act on the hapless landlady. Inexplicably, the police run in, initiating a chase that constitutes the final one-third of the film. Briefly becoming himself again, Jekyll hastily scrawls a confession to Bernice, who subsequently arrives to find a crazed monster waiting for her. (Here, a title card states that Jekyll "involuntarily" becomes Hyde, although he already has been experiencing this effect for some time.)

Hyde is arrested by the police and incarcerated at the local station. Before he can be questioned, he changes back into Jekyll (off-screen). Given "the third degree" (as a title card states), the abused doctor is overcome by yet another Hyde attack (bad editing, depicting the officers' astounded faces, accounts for this transformation). Having confessed the entire truth, Jekyll/Hyde is condemned to die in the electric chair. (A title card states, "A life for a life"; now the viewer knows that the story is set not in England but in the United States.)

One last poverty-row stunt occurs as Hyde is being strapped into the chair. Before the switch can be thrown, the scene dissolves to show Jekyll awakening from a dream; he is not about to die, but on his way to the opera! "Bernice—Bernice," he emotes, "I believe in God—I have a soul—and—and I still have you." Here the final propaganda message assures the viewer that the formerly heathenish Jekyll has been punished by his horrible subconscious experience. This scene brings a perfectly dreadful film to an end.

In his review of the film Louis Reeves Harrison writes: "Sheldon Lewis has made a careful and intelligent study of his dual role. In his portrayal there is displayed an ability to get at the essence of nobility in Jekyll quite as well as the hideous perversion of Hyde."[28] Considering that Harrison lists London as the film's location and makes no mention of the updated setting, one may assume that he paid little attention to a film containing no intelligence, plot, or visual interest. Rather than making a "careful study" of his role, it appears that Lewis, along with everyone else concerned, neglected to read the novella. Louis B. Mayer, failing to provide even a ghost of the superior Paramount offering (although Harrison claims that the film would "prove a winner for both producer and exhibitor"), created what is arguably the worst cinematic adaptation of *The Strange Case of Dr. Jekyll and Mr. Hyde*. Two 1920 parodies, Arrow Film's *Dr. Jekyll and Mr. Hyde*, featuring Hank Mann, and Aywon's *When Quackel Did Hyde*, cannot be less faithful.

Perhaps impressed by the Paramount version (or discouraged by Mayer's dismal effort), serious screenwriters shied away from the Jekyll-and-Hyde domain for the next 11 years. The only productions inspired by the novella during this period were two short parodies. Produced by Joe Rock and directed by Percy Pembroke, the two-reel *Dr. Pyckle and Mr. Pryde* (1925) features a pre–Hardy Stan Laurel dashing around a set built for Universal's *The Hunchback of Notre Dame* (1923). According to biographer Fred Lawrence Guiles, Laurel was drinking heavily and going without sleep during the production,[29] a fact that may have enlivened his dual performance. Released the same year, Standard's *Dr. Jekyll and Mr. Hyde* provided another comic interpretation.

## *Dr. Jekyll and Mr. Hyde* (Paramount, 1931)

The creators of Paramount's 1931 *Dr. Jekyll and Mr. Hyde* drew as much of their inspiration from previous screenplays as they did from Stevenson, but this adaptation captures the very mood and philosophical essence of the novella. Combining an outstanding array of technical achievements with powerful acting and a brilliant script, this film is one of the classic American cinema's true masterpieces and, when viewed over 60 years later, still seems modern and innovative.

Eleven years had elapsed since Paramount released its silent adaptation, but growing public interest in horror films, in part, enticed the studio to take another stab at Stevenson's tale. Released on Valentine's Day, 1931, Universal's *Dracula,* starring Bela Lugosi and Helen Chandler, had been a major hit, and in August, Carl Laemmle's regime, under the clever directorial hand of James Whale, had begun filming *Frankenstein,* a thriller that would break box-office records throughout the country and propel its monster, Boris Karloff, to international stardom. Not only did these two films create a horror vogue, but they proved that adaptations of nineteenth-century Gothic novels could be immensely popular (a trend that would continue until pressure groups and the Production Code of 1934 consigned the genre to an early, albeit temporary, grave during the mid–1930s).

The first mention of a new version of *Dr. Jekyll and Mr. Hyde* came on April 15, 1931, when David O. Selznick, then executive assistant to Ben Schulberg, Paramount's managing director of production in Hollywood, wrote a memo suggesting that Emil Jannings be cast as the dual character. The memo was never sent, however, and talk of the film did not resurface until the summer, when Rouben Mamoulian was assigned to helm the project.

A Paramount star director and one of Hollywood's few intellectual filmmakers, Mamoulian was born in Tiflis, Georgia, Russia, in 1898, and later studied criminology at the University of Moscow and Stanislavskian dramatic technique at the Moscow Art Theatre. In 1918 he developed his own drama studio and two years later toured England with the Russian Repertory Theatre. In 1922 he studied drama at the University of London and directed his first play. According to film historian Ephraim Katz, Mamoulian's initial attempt favored "the traditional Russian naturalistic style but from then on disavowed realism in favor of a stylized, rhythmic, lyrical impressionism."[30]

In 1923 Mamoulian immigrated to the United States, where he directed operas and operettas at the George Eastman Theatre in Rochester, New York, before landing a teaching and production position with the New York Theatre

Guild in 1926. He scored his first Broadway hit with *Porgy* the following year, but his stage success was interrupted when Paramount executives, impressed with his innovative and powerful dramatic style, hired him to direct *Applause* (1929), a film scheduled to be shot at their studio in Astoria. An early example of Mamoulian's cinematic prowess, *Applause* became one of the first technically adept sound productions. In 1975 film historian Richard J. Anobile perceptively wrote:

> Despite his theater background Mamoulian possessed an intense curiosity for film and while other stagebound directors merely recorded scenes, Mamoulian strived for new ways to use the film medium. He had a total grasp of the freedom afforded by the camera and fully explored film technique.
>
> I consider Mamoulian a pioneer and as important a personage to the development of the modern cinema as D. W. Griffith. Like Griffith, he has contributed to film technique what today are considered basic elements of directorial acumen.[31]

With *Applause*, Mamoulian freed the camera from the microphone "stranglehold" so prevalent during the first years of sound production. The fluid cinematography that would grace his later films is demonstrated here, in an otherwise tedious and maudlin burlesque story starring Helen Morgan. His second Paramount assignment, *City Streets* (1931), a powerful gangster film starring Gary Cooper and Sylvia Sidney, allowed Mamoulian to experiment further with moving camera and sound techniques. Utilizing a subjective sound method he called "audience thoughts," Mamoulian developed the voice-over and combined striking imagery and movement with a dynamic editing style.

Preferring to suggest rather than depict the more amorous and violent aspects demanded by his screenplays, Mamoulian established himself as a stylist who often appeared to champion imagery over content (a tendency that more realistically minded critics have reproved over the years). In a November 1972 interview Mamoulian spoke of his decision to incite the viewer's imagination:

> [*City Streets*] was made during the period of gangster films, such as *Little Caesar* and *Scarface,* in which you had murders and bodies being thrown out of cars and machine guns splattering and so on. I had several murders in *City Streets,* but I never showed one, except indirectly. People said, "What kind of gangster film is this? People love to see these things?" I said, "I don't think so." The film was enormously successful, and much more interesting.
>
> As a matter of fact, after *City Streets,* I had staged a couple of plays and I went to Chicago with a play—I think it was *Solid South*—for a pre–Broadway tryout. People were very hospitable there, you know, and they took me to dinners and parties and whatnot. One night they took me to a nightclub in Chicago, and as word spread, people were coming over and shaking hands with me and being very nice. This little guy came over and sat down and said, "Mr. Mamoulian, my brother just loves *City Streets.* He thinks it is the only film that is worth seeing. He's seen it

six times. He thinks that it has got such class." And he carried on in that vein, and I asked, "Who on earth is his brother?" The answer was Al Capone. That was Sidney Capone. You know, at first it puzzled me. Why should Capone like *City Streets*? It's completely stylized and doesn't show a single murder. Then I thought that's precisely why he likes the film. It's "clean," it's in "good taste." I don't show the dirty work, I "tactfully" skirt around it.[32]

The narrative of the 1931 *Dr. Jekyll and Mr. Hyde* roughly parallels the 1920 Paramount version, with portions of the original "Dr. Lanyon's Narrative" and several Mamoulian flourishes added. Dr. Jekyll is depicted as a noble scientist who cares for the poor while seeking a division of the two selves which will bring out the goodness in human beings. When Dr. Lanyon (Holmes Herbert) tells Jekyll (Fredric March) that he must admit his "indecent self" and accept "certain things," Jekyll replies, "I don't want to accept them. I want to be clean not only in my conduct but in my innermost thoughts and desires."

When Paramount selected *Dr. Jekyll and Mr. Hyde* for Mamoulian's third film project, the studio planned to cast Irving Pichel in the leading role. Mamoulian recalled:

I thought the idea was atrocious, and I said that I wouldn't be interested in doing the film with him. They said that he would make such a wonderful Hyde. "I'm not worried about Hyde," I said. "I'm worried about Jekyll. I want Jekyll to be young and handsome, and Mr. Pichel can't play that." I wanted to use Freddie March who was at that time a light comedian. He had just done a film called *Laughter*. They said, "You're crazy. How can March play this part?" I told them that if I couldn't use Freddie March, I wouldn't do the film. I'd never even met March, I'd just seen him on the screen. Finally the studio gave in, and March won an Academy Award for his performance.[33]

Mamoulian's vision of a "young and handsome" Jekyll is indicative of his overall approach to the character. He borrowed Stevenson's ideas of the dual personality and the scientist's exploration of the evil self, incorporated the earlier film depiction of the philanthropic doctor, and tied all three elements together with his own personal interpretation. Again Stevenson's mystery structure was abandoned in favor of encouraging viewer identification with Jekyll (an element emphasized by Samuel Hoffenstein and Percy Heath's screenplay and Karl Struss's subjective camera technique, which places the viewer inside Jekyll's head in the opening scene and at various other points).

Mamoulian erred in thinking that the novella includes a sexual component, but he carefully elaborated upon his rationale:

In Stevenson's original work, which might be called a horror story, Dr. Jekyll is a florid man of 55—a big, plump guy who is irked by the restrictions of morality. I wouldn't even say Victorian morality—just morality. He'd like to indulge in all sorts of sexual excess and debauchery but can't do it as Dr. Jekyll, without losing face. His aim is to separate the two parts of his nature so he can have one hell of a good time and still keep up his hypocritical virtuous facade. I thought this interpretation was not interesting enough and not pertinent enough to the spectators who were going to see the film. I thought that a more interesting dilemma would be not that of good versus evil or moral versus immoral but that of the spiritual versus the animalistic which are present in all of us. That is our common dilemma. God knows we struggle and battle constantly with ourselves about which instinct to follow.

Therefore, as a prototype for Hyde, I didn't take a monster but our common ancestor, the Neanderthal man. Mr. Hyde is a replica of the Neanderthal man. He is not a monster or animal of another species but primeval man—closest to the earth, the soil. When the first transformation takes place, Jekyll turns into Hyde who is the animal in him. Not the evil but the animal. Animals know no evil; they're completely innocent and much better morally than we are. Animals never kill except to eat. They don't torture each other. The first Hyde is this young animal released from the stifling manners and conventions of the Victorian period. He is like a kitten, a pup, full of vim and energy. He knows no evil, he simply gives vent to all his instincts. . . .

But, of course, he's not only an animal. He's partly a human being, and a human being—let's face it—is a very perverse creature. So because he is part human and possesses a human brain, which on the one hand reaches heaven and on the other wallows in depravity, he begins to refine his unorthodox pleasures—cruelty, sadism, and murder. Gradually Hyde changes from an innocent animal into a vicious—I won't say beast because beasts are not vicious—human monster, a monster that is part of us but which we usually keep under control. Throughout the film you see Hyde getting worse, both physically and psychologically; and you also see Jekyll, instead of becoming liberated as he had hoped, deteriorating with Hyde. It's a sad story.[34]

Although Mamoulian's claim that "beasts are not vicious" is no longer a valid generalization about nonhuman animals (recent studies have proved that chimpanzees, the closest human relative, are often brutal and murderous), his approach to the Hyde character remains fascinating and innovative.

The inclusion of two morally opposite female characters again parallels the spiritual and animalistic sides of the Jekyll character. Muriel Carew (Rose Hobart), daughter of Brigadier General Carew (Halliwell Hobbes) and fiancée of Jekyll, represents the unattainable good woman whose desirable attributes are kept at a distance by her father. Jekyll wishes to be married as soon as possible but is prevented by Carew's rigid conservatism. On the other hand, Ivy Pierson (Miriam Hopkins), dance-hall singer and prostitute, represents the sensual urges that plague Jekyll and are enjoyed by Hyde.

In an early scene Jekyll delivers a lecture at St. Simon's Hospital. Prior to his address, the tone of the film is established by four spectators:

*Student One:* I hope Jekyll's in form today.

*Student Two:* He's always in form. The old codgers are in for another joke.

*Older Professor:* Obviously our friend has something up his sleeve again, Dr. Lanyon.

*Dr. Lanyon:* Jekyll is always sensational, always indulging in spectacular theories.

Within a few seconds the division between Victorian conservatism (the old-guard professoriate) and progressive liberalism (the younger generation of students) is suggested. As Jekyll begins to speak, this dichotomy is established:

> Gentlemen, London is so full of fog that it has penetrated our minds, set boundaries on our vision. As men of science we should be curious and bold enough to peer beyond it into the many wonders it conceals. I shall not dwell today on the secrets of the human body, in sickness and in health. Today I want to talk to you of a greater marvel, the soul of man. My analysis of the soul, the human psyche, leads me to believe man is not truly one, but truly two. One of him strives for nobility. This we call the good self. The other self seeks an expression of impulses that binds him to some dim animal relation with the earth. This we may call the bad. These two carry on an eternal struggle in the nature of man, yet they are chained together and that chain spells repression to the evil, remorse to the good. Now, if these two selves could be separated from each other, how much freer the good in us would be. What heights it might scale, and the so called evil, once liberated, would fulfill itself and trouble us no more. I believe the day is not far off when this separation will be possible. In my experiments I have found that certain chemicals have the power...

At the outset Mamoulian, Hoffenstein, and Heath emphasize the conflict between the individual thinker and society at large and set the stage for Jekyll's (and soon Hyde's) attempts to combat stifling conservative pressures. Unlike Stevenson's Jekyll, Mamoulian's character is the ultimate idealist (even more of a utopianist than those depicted in earlier film versions) who wishes to eradicate the bad self from the human psyche. When he fails to obtain support from the establishment (particularly represented by Lanyon and Carew), Jekyll assumes the role of lone scientist and experiments upon himself (and, in turn, Hyde obtains the sexual gratification that Jekyll has been unable to get from Muriel). Jekyll wants to be "clean in his thoughts and desires," but it is these sentiments that separate him from the upright, stilted world which surrounds him.

Outside the lecture hall Lanyon mentions Jekyll's scheduled meeting with the Duchess Densmores and criticizes him for spending too much time in the free ward: "My dear fellow, be reasonable. You know how insistent the Duchess was on your coming. Well, heaven knows why. You can't neglect her for a lot of charity cases."

"Can't I, Lanyon?" Jekyll confidently asks. "It's the things one can't do that always tempt me."

Later, after attending a dinner party and dance at Carew's, Jekyll asks the general if he will set an earlier date for the wedding. Responding that the wedding will take place on the anniversary of his own marriage, Carew fumes, "Hang it all man, it isn't done—it isn't done!" and he calls Jekyll's request "eccentric" and "positively indecent."

Lanyon exits the house, fearing that Jekyll has offended the general:

> *Jekyll:* Offended him? It's a pity I didn't strangle the old walrus. Did you hear him? "Wait. Wait." What the devil does one wait for?
>
> *Lanyon:* Well, I hope the responsibilities of marriage will sober you up.
>
> *Jekyll:* I'm not marrying to be sober. I'm marrying to be drunk. Drunk with love and life and experiment.
>
> *Lanyon:* Your experiment is absurd, my dear fellow.
>
> *Jekyll:* You have no interest in science at all. You have no dreams, no curiosity.
>
> *Lanyon:* There are bounds beyond which one should not go.
>
> *Jekyll:* Yes, it isn't done I suppose. I tell you there are no bounds, Lanyon.

As Jekyll describes the possibility of replacing London's primitive gas lamps with futuristic incandescence, he is interrupted by a woman's scream; he runs down an alley, rescues Ivy Pierson from the clutches of a mauling brute, and carries her up a flight of stairs to her room, where she undresses and insists that he examine her bruises. Here, the overtones are demonstrated clearly when Ivy's sensuality briefly overtakes Jekyll's senses. Tossing her stockings and garter at his feet (which he fondles with his walking stick), she entices him to sit on her bed, where she gives him a passionate kiss. (The scene is daring for a 1931 film: as the naked Ivy embraces Jekyll, she is shown in profile; while the bed covers conceal her from the waist down, only Jekyll's cape hides her breasts from view. An astonished Lanyon then enters to witness Jekyll's ungentlemanly act.)

Until his death on December 4, 1987, Mamoulian considered this scene to be one of his favorites. His approach is an excellent example of the style he employed in future films (including *Blood and Sand* [1941], in which Rita Hayworth attempts to seduce Tyrone Power but instead puts him to sleep!). From a 1972 perspective, Mamoulian explained:

> You know, they say nature abhors a vacuum. For me, art abhors the obvious. There is a great difference between sex as pornography and as eroticism. Eroticism is certainly an important part of human nature and the arts. There are a great many paintings and works of literature that are erotic but not pornographic. Actually the definition of obscenity by our Supreme Court, I think, is somewhat cock-eyed in that it condemns an appeal to the prurient interest. Well, the prurient interest is the erotic interest. There is nothing wrong with the appeal to eroticism in us any more than there is to an appeal to beauty, to goodness, to anything of that sort. But then eroticism is always indirect. It doesn't hit you on the head with an axe, it's oblique, and thereby much more interesting. In all my films you will notice that the interesting part of a love scene, of every love scene I've made, is what precedes a kiss and then what follows the sexual activity, but never the activity itself. All these films that concentrate on two people kissing for 120 feet, you know, are plain dull and much less

*Dr. Jekyll and Mr. Hyde* (1931). Fredric March as a noble Dr. Jekyll, in Paramount and director Rouben Mamoulian's brilliant variation on the novella.

erotic than simply showing what leads up to sex and what follows. The rest you can imagine easily enough.[35]

One of Mamoulian's innovations is the Freudian subtext that accounts for Dr. Jekyll's behavior (though some film critics have cited MGM's *Dr. Jekyll and Mr. Hyde* [1941] as the first Freudian version of the story). Fredric March's Jekyll possesses a healthy libido, and his

***Dr. Jekyll and Mr. Hyde*** **(1931). Dr. Jekyll (Fredric March) is aroused by the bedroom striptease of prostitute Ivy Pierson (Miriam Hopkins), in one of "golden age" Hollywood's most erotic (albeit censored) scenes.**

attempts to control primal urges are overcome by his transformations into Hyde. He continually requests a speedy marriage but is rebuffed by the general who, in a way, provokes his indulgences of the evil side. (This aspect recalls Brandon Hurst's Carew in the 1920 Paramount version, although the two characters differ in philosophy and intent.)

Prior to Hyde's first tryst with Ivy, he enters the dance hall, demands a table, scoffs at other patrons, and is aroused by scantily clad dancing girls (a medium two-shot shows the legs and derrieres of two somewhat acrobatic ladies). "What are you waiting for?" Hyde rudely asks the waiter. "A tip, eh? Get out!" Undaunted by Hyde's Neanderthal appearance, the waiter sneers, "Blighter!" as he descends a small flight of stairs. Hyde quickly grabs his cane, thrusts it through a railing, and sends the waiter crashing to the floor. Releasing his animalistic tension, Hyde leers at the prostitute, who breaks into the song "Champagne Ivy."

Hailing the waiter he nearly had beaten to death, Hyde demands, "Tell that lady in black to come over and have a bottle of wine with me." Ivy agrees to "take a chance" but is repelled by the cut of Hyde's gibe. "Ah, but you are pretty," Hyde compliments, "and, ah, what a figure." He refuses to let her leave, explains that she should live in a place befitting her beauty, and removes the shawl from her shoulders. "You should have a place that would set off that fine body of yours," he adds as she looks down at her breasts.

Offered clothes, jewelry, and champagne, Ivy asks, "And how am I to get it?"

"How do you think you're going to get it, my bright little burden?" Hyde replies sarcastically. Admitting that he is "no beauty," he implies that she may be more comfortable with "one of those fine mannered, virtuous and honorable gentlemen—one of those panting hypocrites who like your legs but talk about your garters." Hyde threatens to kill another suitor before he tells Ivy that he loves her. (Here, a tight, eerily lit close-up shows Hyde's face moving *into* the camera to kiss Ivy and, indirectly, the viewer!)

The first meeting of this couple is only one of several erotic scenes that merge sensuality with male domination. Later, when Hyde visits Ivy in the garish apartment he has rented, he stuffs an entire sandwich into his mouth and kicks a bear rug before he embraces her. Interested in observing her reaction, he places his cheek against her right breast. "I've got bad news for you, my dear. Very bad," he taunts. "I'm going away for a few days." When she looks pleased, he rears up. "Remember you belong to me, do you hear!" he shouts. "You belong to me. And if you do one little thing that I don't approve of while I'm gone, the least little thing mind you, I'll show you what horror means." Faced with such an ultimatum, Ivy defers to Hyde, who calls her "my little bird" and kisses her on the chest. The scene fades out when Hyde embraces her on the bed.

Some of Stevenson's material is included at this point, when Jekyll decides to end Hyde's existence; his reason for doing so differs, however. In the novella Jekyll, horrified by the murder of Sir Danvers Carew, begins "a new life" that lasts for two months: he locks the back entrance to the laboratory, grinds the key under his heel, and then attempts to compensate for Hyde's evil deeds. In the film the return of the vacationing Muriel prompts his actions. "See this key, Poole?" he asks the butler (Edgar Norton). "I'll have no further use for it. From now on I'll use only the front door."

Apparently freed from Hyde's influence, Jekyll sends £50 to Ivy, whose flogged back is being attended to by Mrs. Hawkins (Tempe Pigott), the landlady. Before Poole arrives with the envelope, Hawkins tells Ivy to inform the police about her abusive lover. "They'd fix his hide, ma'am," she assures.

"No, no. I'm afraid," Ivy admits. "There ain't nobody to help me. Nobody. Who cares what becomes of the likes of me?" Upon receipt of the money, Ivy is persuaded by Mrs. Hawkins to visit "the celebrated Dr. Jekyll" and "thank the gentleman proper": "Then you could tell him all about this 'ere Hyde business. He'll tell that blighter what's what. You see if he don't."

One of Mamoulian's innovative visual techniques occurs in this scene: a diagonal split screen shows both Ivy in her apartment (upper frame left) and Muriel in the Carew home (lower frame right).

As Ivy considers visiting Jekyll, the screen widens (upper left) to show Muriel speaking with Jekyll. Here the technique powerfully reinforces the narrative content and indicates that Mamoulian was not only a stylist but also a visual artist who utilized style to tell a story.

Jekyll again pleads for an early marriage and, following the usual objections, he and Muriel finally convince General Carew to set a date. "Very well, you shall be married next month," the old man acquiesces. "Come to dinner tomorrow, eh? And we'll make a formal announcement to our friends."

Jekyll rushes home to tell Poole the good news. As the butler congratulates him (with a smile strangely framed in tight close-up), Jekyll replies enthusiastically, "If music be the food of love, play on!" and takes a seat at the organ, where he plies the keys with near-orgasmic glee. A montage of seven quickly cut close-ups follows, linking Jekyll's ecstatic profile, his hands on the keyboard, a candelabrum, a full-figure statue, a sculpture of a grinning face, Poole's similarly grinning face, and the flaming fireplace logs. This bizarre juxtaposition is capped by Poole's announcement that "Miss Pierson is waiting for you in the consulting room." Jekyll is sobered immediately, and he asks Poole to escort her in.

Astonished to find the man she had kissed in her bed, Ivy returns the £50 and begins to remove her blouse. "Pretty, ain't it?" she fearfully asks. "It's a whip, that's what it is. A whip!" Jekyll attempts to reason with her, but she cries, "He ain't a man. He's a devil. ... If he knows I've been here today, I don't know what he'll do. It won't be anything human, sir." She pleads for his help and drops to her knees. "You're an angel, sir. I'll do anything you like. I ain't as bad as you think—and I ain't a bad looker, either. I'll work for you. I'll slave for you. I'll love you."

"I give you my word that you will never be troubled by Hyde again," Jekyll replies in an attempt to convince both Ivy and himself. Sending her home, he drops into a chair as the scene fades out.

At this point the film's concluding sequences have been foreshadowed by Jekyll's respective meetings with the two women: he has made heartfelt promises to both but will keep neither. The remaining footage moves very quickly and incorporates several literary passages.

While walking to Carew's dinner party the next day, Jekyll stops to rest on a park bench. Prior to sitting down, he enjoys the chirping of a bird, but his pleasure is interrupted by a cat that scampers across a branch and kills it (the attack is suggested, not shown). Jekyll glances at his hands, grabs his throat, throws both hands over his face, and transforms into Mr. Hyde: the thought of marrying his loved one, the memory of the relationship with Ivy Pierson, and the animalistic action of the cat combine to create an involuntary metamorphosis. Here, Mamoulian powerfully merges Stevenson's material with the sexual component, while still remaining faithful to the original prose:

> It was a fine, clear January day, wet under foot where the frost had melted, but cloudless overhead;

and the Regent's Park was full of winter chirrupings and sweet with spring odours. I sat in the sun on a bench; the animal within me licking the chops of memory; the spiritual side a little drowsed, promising subsequent penitence, but not yet moved to begin. After all, I reflected I was like my neighbours; and then I smiled, comparing myself with other men, comparing my active good will with the lazy cruelty of their neglect. And at that very moment of that vainglorious thought, a qualm came over me, a horrid nausea, and the most deadly shuddering. These passed away, and left me faint; and then as in its turn the faintness subsided, I began to be aware of a change in the temper of my thoughts—a greater boldness, a contempt of danger, a solution of the bonds of obligation. I looked down: my clothes hung formlessly on my shrunken limbs; the hand that lay on my knee was corded and hairy. I was once more Edward Hyde.

Stevenson's Hyde seeks a room at the Portland Hotel, but Mamoulian's character scurries to Ivy's apartment. Shown in a split screen with Muriel, who is worried by Jekyll's lateness, Ivy is drinking champagne bought with the kind doctor's money. In front of a dressing table she speaks to her reflection in the mirror: "Here's hoping that Hyde rots wherever he is—and burns where he ought to be. And here's hoping that Doctor Jekyll will think of Ivy once in a while. He's an angel, he is." As the last few words are spoken, a chiaroscuro image of Hyde is seen in the mirror: he closes the door, descends the stairs, and backs Ivy against a wall. Repeating the words she spoke to Jekyll the previous day, Hyde concludes, "You wanted him to love you, didn't you? Well, I'll give you a lover now. His name is death."

Ivy runs but falls onto a nearby sofa: "You must be the devil. There was nobody there but me and Doctor Jekyll. He wouldn't have told you. No, he wouldn't."

Hyde glowers in her face: "Wouldn't he though? Wouldn't he? Listen, my dear, listen. I'm going to let you into a secret. A secret so great that those who share it with me cannot live. I *am* Jekyll! I am the angel whom you wanted to slave for and love. I'm going to take you in my arms now and hold you close. Close, my little lamb. My dove. My bird."

Ivy dashes for the door, but Hyde leaps over the railing and chases her into the bedroom. Throttling her, he slowly lowers her limp body onto the floor beside the bed. The camera remains, in medium close-up, on a statue, Antonio Canova's "Psyche and Eros," sitting on a table behind them. Sculpted in white marble, the statue depicts Eros, the winged Greek god, making love to Psyche, Greek maiden and subsequent personification of the human soul. Two paintings of nude females are also visible. "There my sweet. There my dove. There my little bride," Hyde calmly sneers. "Isn't Hyde a lover after your own heart?" As other tenants arrive to investigate, Hyde frantically exits the apartment and speeds toward the back entrance of Jekyll's laboratory. Realizing that he no longer has the key, he rings at the front door but is sent away instantly by Poole.

In one of the few essays published on this film, Janice Welsch comments on some of the sexual overtones: "Underscoring [Hyde's] animal likeness are the terms of endearment with which [he] brutally and sadistically assaults Ivy, for they emphatically point to her vulnerability as well as his feral nature."[36] Welsch's observation correctly identifies Hyde's many verbal references, but she goes too far when pointing out that "There is no similar underscoring in Stevenson." There would be no reason for any such inclusion: Stevenson created no comparable female characters to underscore!

Welsch notes that Ivy's "flirtatious lambency" toward Jekyll quickly entraps her when she is dominated by the violent Hyde: "The change is seen in the apartment Hyde furnishes for her. It is an apartment filled with fetishistic statues and pictures of nudes as well as with plush, baroque drapes and heavy ornate furniture, an apartment from which there is no escape. The despair created there for Ivy parallels that experienced by Jekyll."[37] While Welsch does point out the erotic symbols adorning the apartment, she may exaggerate the narrative importance of the art direction. Expensive Victorian apartments might contain plush tapestries and furniture, and Ivy's original room includes a conspicuous painting of two nude women (hanging on the wall beside her bed).

The scene featuring Jekyll's first meeting with Ivy was somewhat longer in the original print. (In fact, four major edits, accounting for ten minutes of footage, were ordered when the film was reissued in the late 1930s. Thought lost forever, nearly all of the excised material was restored for MGM/UA's 1988 videocassette release. However, the expurgated footage from the seduction scene is still missing.) Mamoulian commented:

> The beginning and end are there, but what's missing is her gradual undressing behind the blanket. You never see any part of her. From under the blanket she keeps throwing away the stockings, the garters, then the brassiere, the panties. The scene builds, and you don't see Jekyll's face, just his feet pointed towards her. So you know he's looking. Well, they cut the whole middle out of the scene—probably for the ancient censorship reasons. Today it would be totally innocent.[38]

If the original scene still existed, it probably would be one of the classic cinema's most artfully erotic scenes. As it stands, Jekyll's brief poking of Ivy's garter with his walking stick jump-cuts to a shot of her pulling the bed covers over her nude body (which is partially exposed later in the scene). Even considering censorial destruction, it is still an effective sequence that demonstrates Mamoulian's tasteful approach to cinematic sex.

By comparison, the romantic scenes featuring Jekyll and Muriel are overlong, verbose, and artificial—interludes that often slow the movement of a primarily well-paced film. Perhaps Mamoulian did this intentionally, to contrast their stilted relationship with the more natural, earthy quality exuded by Ivy, but all of these sequences resemble similar material in other contemporary films. (The visual style, however, is far superior to that of many 1931–32 releases.) Their first meeting in the Carew garden is photographed and edited beautifully (several striking close-ups highlight faces and eyes), but it quickly bogs down with Jekyll's redundant love declarations. "Now, my darling; chide me, mock me, hate me! But don't send me away," he spouts at one point. The most interesting moment occurs when their lovemaking is interrupted: tilting down to a statue and water lilies in a fountain, the camera pans across the slate patio before focusing on a man's feet; tilting up, it reveals the butler, who requests that Muriel return to the house. Janice Welsch refers to this garden setting as "fairyland" and a visual introduction to their limited relationship: "For Jekyll, Muriel is a goddess, the Unknown, the idealized woman. She is kept, however, in a gilded cage by an ever watchful father who periodically places her on a pedestal to be admired and desired. She remains unattainable."[39]

After Jekyll fails to arrive at the Carew dinner party (due to Hyde's murder of Ivy), the general declares, "I'll kill that scoundrel, Jekyll, if I ever set eyes on him again." While Muriel protests a split-screen technique is used, this time showing Hyde in a barroom (frame left) and the general (frame right). Appearing to stare directly into Hyde's face, Carew orders, "Muriel, you will have nothing more to do with that man."

"Get me a pencil and paper, quick," Hyde demands to the bartender; poking about with his walking stick, he hires a waiter to deliver a message. A lap dissolve then shifts the scene to the home of Dr. Lanyon, where the butler enters with the note:

Dear Lanyon:
I am in mortal distress, and I beg you to do what I ask.
Hasten to my laboratory and there from a cabinet marked E, take the phials listed below and bring them to your home.
Remain there *alone*. At midnight a man will call for the package. Place it in his hands. In God's name, do not fail me.
                    Henry Jekyll
Phials marked A.H.S.T.R.M.

The following sequence is another faithful visualization. As Lanyon walks out of the front door the scene dissolves to show Hyde entering through the front gate; accepted by Lanyon, he tramps into the study. Lanyon hands him the package and draws a pistol: "Take me to Doctor Jekyll or you'll not leave this room." Hyde pleads for release, but his host refuses. "Very well, Lanyon. This be on your own head," Hyde accuses as he tears open the package; mixing the various chemicals in a graduated flask, he raises it to his mouth. Here, Stevenson's dialogue is paraphrased and embellished:

*Hyde:* Now, Lanyon, will you let me take this flask and leave without further questions?
*Lanyon:* I've gone too far not to see this through to the end.
*Hyde:* Think before you decide, I tell you. Do you want to be left as you are or do you want your eyes and your soul to be blasted by a sight that would stagger the devil himself?
*Lanyon:* I'm not to be persuaded by this rigamarole.

*Hyde:* Very well then. Remember your vows to your profession. What you are about to see is a secret you are sworn not to reveal. And now, you who have denied the power of man to look into his soul; you who have derided your superiors. Look! Look!

Lanyon stares in amazement as Hyde downs the mixture and falls into a chair. A medium shot of Lanyon cuts to a close-up of Hyde's face, and a reverse transformation (via a series of lap dissolves) begins. A close-up of the aghast Lanyon then cuts back to Hyde as Jekyll fully appears. In the novella this event is narrated in two separate installments by Lanyon (who is too shocked to relay any particulars) and Jekyll (who merely states that he received Lanyon's "condemnation"), respectively. The film, however, provides a dramatic conclusion. One of Mamoulian's many excellent transitions (in close-up, a burning candle, through a lap dissolve, melts to half its original height) indicates that Jekyll has revealed the details of his terrible ordeal:

*Lanyon:* I can't believe what I've seen. I don't understand.
*Jekyll:* I'm in your hands to do with as you wish.
*Lanyon:* Horrible. Horrible.
*Jekyll:* I'm a murderer, Lanyon. Help me! Help me!
*Lanyon:* There is no help for you, Jekyll. You've committed the supreme blasphemy. I've warned you! I told you that no man could violate the tradition of his kind and not be damned.
*Jekyll:* That I still do not believe. Don't be my inquisitor, Lanyon. Don't judge me. Help me if you will. I'm at your mercy.
*Lanyon:* There is no help for you here. Nor mercy beyond. You're a rebel and see what it has done for you. You are in the power of this monster that you've created.
*Jekyll:* I'll never take that drug again.
*Lanyon:* Yes, but you told me that you became that monster tonight. Not of your own accord. It will happen again.
*Jekyll:* Never. I'm sure of it. I'll fight it. I'll conquer it.
*Lanyon:* Too late, you cannot conquer it. It has conquered you.
*Jekyll:* No, no, no. I'll fight it. I know it will not happen again. Oh, help me!
*Lanyon:* You promise at least never to mix this drug again?
*Jekyll:* With all my heart.
*Lanyon:* And what about Muriel?
*Jekyll:* I'll give her a ... I'll go to her tomorrow. Set her free.

This well-played, powerfully photographed sequence is similar to a scene in *Frankenstein,* which hit theatres only a few weeks before *Dr. Jekyll and Mr. Hyde* went into general release. In the former Dr. Henry Frankenstein (Colin Clive) is warned by Professor Waldman (Edward Van Sloan) that "You have created a monster and it will destroy you." Both films feature science versus society thematics and opposing conservative and free-thinking characters.

The morning after his dramatic meeting with Lanyon, Jekyll reads of Ivy's murder. Here the religious component featured in earlier films resurfaces as the guilt-ridden doctor pleads, "Oh God, this I did not intend. I saw a light but I could not see where it was leading. I have trespassed on your domain. I've gone further than man should go. Forgive me! Help me!" After failing to obtain help from Lanyon

# The Strange Case of Dr. Jekyll and Mr. Hyde

***Dr. Jekyll and Mr. Hyde* (1931). The image of Queen Victoria hovers over Dr. Lanyon (Holmes Herbert) and the tormented Mr. Hyde (Fredric March), in an outstanding visualization of Stevenson's original scene.**

(the mortal representative of tradition and morality), it is logical that Jekyll would ask a similar favor from his deity.

Later in the day Jekyll calls at the Carew home. "I can offer you no welcome, sir," the general pompously declares. "If the matter'd been left in my hands, I would have turned you from the door." In an awkward and overplayed sequence, Jekyll tells Muriel that she is free from his claim. Leaving through the front door, he walks around to the back of the house and peers in at her: weeping and despondent, she has fallen onto the piano keyboard. Shuddering, Jekyll again transforms involuntarily. "Oh, God! Oh, God, don't let me," he begs. "Don't let me. Save me! Save me!" God does not honor his request, however, and Hyde quietly steals into the room. Looking more debauched than ever, he catches Muriel in a lustful embrace as Carew runs in. Hyde pivots and crashes through the window but is followed by Carew and the butler. Rendering the butler unconscious, he then bludgeons Carew to death with his walking stick (the actual blows fall below camera range). Again, the murder of Carew (this time a general with no first name) is based on material in earlier adaptations (particularly the 1920 Paramount version).

Hyde's demise is depicted as the culmination of an exciting police chase. Pursued to Jekyll's laboratory, he changes back into the good doctor in time to fool a detective and his assistant. "Wait!" Lanyon commands as the two officers prepare to leave. "Your man has not escaped." Pointing to Jekyll, he adds, "There, there he is. There's your man. ... Look!" Consumed by Hyde's personality, Jekyll transforms a final time, climbs the walls, and swings like an ape from lab equipment before he is gunned down. Falling onto a table, the decrepit, perverted Hyde changes back into the young, handsome Jekyll. Lanyon does not die (as he does in the novella) but lives to condemn Jekyll to death; the Enfield and Utterson characters are eliminated (Jekyll's will is never mentioned), but a few of Utterson's actions are performed by Lanyon.

Six decades after its original release, Paramount's *Dr. Jekyll and Mr. Hyde* remains a technically impressive film and an outstanding example of what was cinematically possible in early 1930s Hollywood. Accused of being a mere stylist, Mamoulian achieved a near-perfect marriage of aesthetics and narrative content by blending an intelligent screenplay and masterful performances with striking framing and chiaroscuro lighting techniques. Mamoulian commented:

> You'll find that in every film and play I've ever done, I believe that everything on the screen and on the stage must be controlled by a dramatic point of view rather than by pure aesthetics. Pure aesthetics may be decorative and pleasant to look at, but it can also be meaningless. In the theatre or in film, just as in great painting or sculpture, art must go beyond aesthetics. It must convey a certain idea

or dramatic impulse. So I don't use shadows simply because they are decorative. ... In certain scenes the shadows can intensify the dramatic meaning. In the scene where Hyde is running away through the streets, for instance, the batlike shadows on the walls make it much more exciting.[40]

Fredric March's initial transformation into Mr. Hyde has been lauded as a unique achievement by several film historians. Although the scene is the best of its particular kind, it has been misrepresented in past analyses. Rather than creating the transforming effect through a series of lap dissolves, Mamoulian, Struss, and makeup artist Wally Westmore pioneered a new process. In 1975 Richard Anobile wrote, "Mamoulian has yet to divulge what lights and makeup he used for the effect but no doubt it was accomplished with infrared light,"[41] but horror aficionado Alan Frank notes: "the actor's features were covered with special makeup which showed up on film only when photographed through filters of either red or green, while the shot was lit in one or the other colours."[42]

Due to the deliberate suppression of the film by MGM in 1940, *Dr. Jekyll and Mr. Hyde* was not screened for decades. In 1974 William Everson wrote:

> During those years, it received no exhibition at all, except—infrequently—at European archives and, as so often happens with "lost" films, generations who had not seen it began to build its reputation in absentia. Fortunately, the film was good enough to survive even this; when it did become available again in the early 1970s,

albeit, with a couple of censor cuts ... it more than lived up to its reputation, and even managed to surpass it.⁴³

In a general sense the film does live up to its reputation but, specifically, the transformation sequences may disappoint some first-time viewers. Books and periodicals, particularly those on the horror film, often have hinted that the *entire* metamorphosis was achieved with filters and lighting which revealed a previously applied makeup. Regardless of the actual technical process used, only the early stages of the transformation were captured on film in a continuous take. March's face gradually becomes darker, his lips and nostrils turn black, and his eyebrows become bushier (the appearance of the take suggests that infrared light was used). The remaining stages were achieved in various ways, including editing and lap dissolves (after heavier layers of makeup were applied).

Jekyll's first Hyde experience lasts only a few minutes. Alone in the laboratory, he mixes the final combination of chemicals, glances over at a nearby skeleton (the camera pans over to it and back again), and writes a short note:

> My darling Muriel,
> If I die—it is in the cause of science. I shall love you always—through eternity.
> 
> Harry

Raising the flask to eye level, he peers into it (a tight close-up registers his point of view and then focuses on a mirror in front of him) before downing the contents. He grimaces, grabs his throat (first with one hand, then with both), gropes about, and falls to the floor. The scene depicts the first (unedited) stages of the transformation before cutting to a surrealistic hallucination sequence, in which Jekyll sees whirling images of Muriel and himself in the garden, the mocking faces of Lanyon and General Carew, and Ivy sitting on her bed. Sounds of his heartbeat are interspersed with Carew's "positively indecent. ... It isn't done, it isn't done," and Lanyon's "Your conduct is disgusting. ... You're mad, mad!" The hallucination concludes when Ivy seductively offers, "Come back soon, won't you, come back, come back, come back."

As the scene focuses on a pot in the fireplace (still Jekyll's point of view), the camera pans and tracks back over to the mirror, where Hyde soon appears. "Free! Free at last!" he shouts. "Ah! Mad—eh, Lanyon? Eh, Carew! Ah, you hypocrites, deniers of life. If you could see me now, what would you think?" He stretches, laughs, walks around in apish fashion, and ties on a cape before a knock at the door interrupts his pleasure. The scene cuts outside to Poole as the door opens and Jekyll appears. Assuring the butler that his friend, "Mr. Hyde," has left through the back entrance, Jekyll checks his appearance in the mirror and returns to the lab table as the scene fades out.

Mamoulian revealed some of the techniques used to create Jekyll's subconscious state:

> That transformation scene was a breakthrough in terms of sound. Here you have a totally unrealistic event. Well, pictorially I knew how

to do it. To capture the feeling of Jekyll's vertigo, I had the camera revolve around on its axis 360 degrees, the first time this was done on the screen. One cameraman had to sit on the floor, and the man holding the focus—luckily a very small guy who looked like a jockey—was tied with ropes on top of the camera box, so that he could control it from the top. Because the camera revolved, the whole set had to be lighted which was a real tough job.

With such a fantastic transformation what sound do you use? Do you put music in here? God, it's coming out of your ears, the scoring. I thought the only way to match the event and create this incredible reality would be to concoct a melange of sounds that do not exist in nature, that a human ear cannot hear. I said, "Let's photograph light." We photographed the light of a candle in various frequencies of intensity directly transforming light into sound. Then I said, "Let's record the beat of a gong, cut off the impact, run it backwards." And we recorded other things like that. But when we ran it, the whole thing lacked rhythm. I'm a great believer in the importance of rhythm. I said, "We need some kind of a beat." So they brought in all sorts of drums, a bass drum, a snare drum, a Hawaiian drum, Indian tom-toms. But no matter what we used, it always sounded like what it was—a drum. Finally in exasperation I got this wonderful idea. I ran up and down the stairway for a few minutes, and then I put a microphone to my heart and said, "Record it." And that's what is used as the basic rhythm in the scene—the thumping noise which is like no drum on earth because it's the heart beat, my own heartbeat. So

when I say my heart is in *Dr. Jekyll and Mr. Hyde,* I mean it literally.[44]

After a brief scene in which the libidinous Jekyll asks Muriel to elope, the action again shifts to the laboratory. Poole now notices that his master is a bit nervous, so he suggests that Jekyll go out and amuse himself at one of London's gentlemanly attractions. "Gentlemen like me have to be very careful about what they do and say," Jekyll replies. When Poole leaves, Jekyll's sexual tension is punctuated by a series of close-ups which show his fingers drumming on the table, his foot tapping on the hardwood floor, and the fireplace kettle blowing its lid! Surrendering to temptation, he drinks a second dose of potion. This time the full metamorphosis is shown in what appears to be a continuous take, with the camera panning back and forth between March's face and hands as he sits in a chair. However, close inspection reveals two edits that piece the sequence together (the cuts occur as the camera moves from hand to face). The early stages again are shown in close-up, with the filtering process revealing darker skin and harsher facial features, but the heavier makeup appears in two successive takes (when the camera pans from the left hand to the face, and again from the right hand to the face). Although it is not the marvel of technology hailed by past historians, the sequence is rendered superbly by Struss's mobile camera and William Shea's near-seamless editing.

Back in his primitive state, Hyde displays simian movements, dons his cape, and exits through the back door. Outside, he raises his face to the pouring rain and drinks, grinning happily, before heading toward Ivy Pierson's apartment.

These first two transformation scenes are an excellent introduction to the Hyde character, but they were seen only during the original 1931–32 release. Perhaps the Production Code Administration (PCA) did not care for the suggestive images of Jekyll's desires, but, whatever the reason, the second scene was completely excised (along with the intervening Jekyll-Muriel sequence) for the reissued version. The beginning of the first scene and the end of the second were edited together: shortly after Hyde emerges from the hallucination, a lap dissolve shows him outside in the rain (Jekyll's motivation for becoming Hyde, so importantly illustrated in the second scene, was removed!).

Thankfully, the 1988 video version includes both transformations and Jekyll's elopement offer. Two other scenes also benefited from the restoration, most importantly Jekyll's involuntary transformation in the park. As edited by PCA censors, the scene showed Jekyll briefly glancing at the bird before transforming; this made no narrative sense, but believability was not the PCA's concern. Once considered too violent, the cat running across the branch is now back where it belongs. The opening sequence, important for creating viewer identification with the doomed protagonist, also has been replaced: Jekyll plays the organ, dresses for the lecture, and helps a disabled girl to walk at the free clinic. The censored film began when Jekyll walked into St. Simon's to deliver his lecture.

The cinematography, editing, and sound components are complemented by Mamoulian's innovative use of the musical score. Few films released in 1931 include incidental music, but *Dr. Jekyll and Mr. Hyde* features background scoring in some scenes. Mamoulian revealed:

> [I] love the use of counterpoint. The orthodox way of scoring any motion picture is that a happy scene has happy music, a tragic scene has sad music. I don't think this is as dramatically expressive as using the music in counterpoint to the scene. When Jekyll comes and tells Muriel that he is going to give her up, a completely tragic scene, the music heard is the waltz when they were happy, waltzing around the room. The music goes against the mood which, of course, makes the despair much more poignant. ... Also, when Hyde kills Ivy, you don't see the murder. It happens below the camera. What you see is Canova's Psyche and Eros, the complete visual counterpoint. These things sharpen the situation and make it much more interesting.[45]

The film relies heavily on Fredric March's outstanding performance. Other actors have created distinctions between the good and evil sides of Dr. Jekyll, but March is the only one who has separated the two while still maintaining a convincing linkage between them. He overplays Jekyll at times (particularly in the scenes with Muriel), but his Hyde is a flawless realization of Mamoulian's approach.

Similar to Boris Karloff's grueling monster sessions with Jack P.

Pierce at Universal, March had to suffer long, somewhat experimental, makeup applications: "For six weeks I had to arrive at the studios each morning at 6 A.M., so that Wally Westmore could spend four hours building pieces on my nose and cheeks, sticking fangs in my mouth, and pushing cotton wool up my nostrils."[46] Some historians have criticized Mamoulian and Westmore for making Hyde look too monstrous, but his devolution from a virile, sprightly animal to "a weary, pouchy, hairy old pervert," as the late Leslie Halliwell wrote,[47] is rendered perfectly by the makeup and March's considerable talent: his ability to alter his voice, speech patterns, gait, and bodily gestures created a landmark characterization and the only horror-genre performance to win an Academy Award.

Other performers in the film take a back seat to March (due, in large part, to a screenplay that eliminates many of Stevenson's characters and spends little time developing those who do appear), but Miriam Hopkins brings intensity, sensuality, and subtlety to a role that she originally refused. Mamoulian commented:

> [S]he's a marvelous actress. . . . I called her in and said, "I have a part for you in *Dr. Jekyll and Mr. Hyde*." "I'd love to work with you," she said. "Which part is it?" I told her Ivy and gave her the script to read. She came back the next day and said, "I don't want to do that part. I'd rather be Muriel, the good girl." I said, "Miriam, are you crazy? Look, it will be very easy for me to get somebody to do Ivy, it's a marvelous part. It will be difficult for me to get somebody who would want to play Muriel, and yet you want to play Muriel." "Yes," she said. "I don't want to play that little tart." "Miriam, I give you my word. If you play Ivy, you will make a sensation and become a star. If you play Muriel, nobody will notice you." "No," she said. "I'd rather play Muriel." "That's fine," I said. "No more argument. Muriel is your part. Goodbye." She started walking out, stopped at the doorway, and said, "Now wait a minute." "I don't want to wait for anything. You've got Muriel." "Now look, wait a minute, Rouben," she said, "You really think that I. . . ." "I've said all I'm going to say. You've made up your mind, that's it." Then Miriam said, "Let me do it your way." So she played Ivy and what a superb performance she gave.[48]

Holmes Herbert, a distinguished British character actor who appeared in approximately 200 Hollywood silents and talkies, admirably portrays a rigidly conservative yet believable Lanyon. After *Dr. Jekyll and Mr. Hyde* he enacted roles (usually reputable British officials or professional men) in *Mystery of the Wax Museum* (1933), *The Invisible Man* (1933), *Mark of the Vampire* (1935), *Captain Blood* (1935), *The Life of Emile Zola* (1937), *The Adventures of Robin Hood* (1938), and six of the Basil Rathbone–Nigel Bruce Sherlock Holmes films (1939–46).

When production wrapped up during the first week of November 1931, Mamoulian honored the contributions of 100 cast and crew members with a lavish party at the Russian-American Club in Los Angeles. On November 9 *Variety* reported that Mamoulian's gesture was becoming "a more and more infrequent custom" practiced by Hollywood directors.[49] At the dinner table March mimicked Mamoulian, a camera was passed around to demonstrate the moving shots used in the film, Karl Struss modeled ladies' hats, and Edgar Norton and Halliwell Hobbes performed their own version of the Jekyll-and-Hyde tale.

Released on December 26, 1931, *Dr. Jekyll and Mr. Hyde* benefited from the current horror vogue. *Frankenstein,* which had been drawing record crowds for three weeks, was seen as competition in some areas of the United States, but the film quickly became a major attraction in most large cities. When it opened in Detroit, a local critic remarked that *Frankenstein* was "a comedy" by comparison.[50] Theaters held Jekyll-and-Hyde contests and offered prizes to children who gave the best impression of each character. On January 5, 1932, *Variety* ran a full-page ad featuring a large photo of Hyde (Paramount, perhaps wishing to play up the horror angle, did not keep the Hyde makeup a secret). Mamoulian's name was displayed far above that of Stevenson, which appeared, in fine print, at the bottom of the page![51]

Paramount proudly referred to Mamoulian as the auteur of the 1931 adaptation; after all, he understood the dramatic possibilities of the novella better than previous playwrights and filmmakers:

> I think the destiny of mankind lies in our ability to control certain basic elements in our nature. We seem to succeed in all sorts of miraculous achievements, but we fail to dominate ourselves—which is why we have murders and war—because it's difficult to control the primitive elements in ourselves. Any ideal that a man may have about achieving this control is noble.
>
> You'll notice in the film I occasionally use the image of a boiling pot surrounded with flames—the turmoil within a human being, within a man like Jekyll. Yet the flame is a pure thing, a clean thing. At the end, after his death and the last transformation, Hyde returns back to Jekyll who is a handsome, young man. His experiment failed, but his aim was noble.[52]

## *Dr. Jekyll and Mr. Hyde* (Metro-Goldwyn-Mayer, 1941)

In 1940 the powers that be at MGM committed an artistic atrocity. Anxious to produce another surefire moneymaker, studio executives and producer-director Victor Fleming decided to give *Dr. Jekyll and Mr. Hyde* their own "prestige" treatment. To ensure its investment MGM purchased the rights to Paramount's 1931 masterpiece and exiled it to the depths of a film vault for the next three decades. In its place the studio released a pretentious, overlong, and dramatically bankrupt imitation featuring three non–English stars who are miscast dreadfully.

As Franz Waxman's bombastic theme music dies down, the opening scene fades in on a church spire (actually a model that sets the stage for the next 127 minutes of relentless artificiality). Sir C. Aubrey Smith begins his brief performance as a pontificating bishop, reciting a line of dialogue that should have been heeded by Fleming before filming got under way: "With purity in our hearts, with right-thinking in our minds, we arm ourselves with intolerance of all evil." The bishop continues, "So it is, on this glorious Sabbath morning, in this momentous year of 1887, we naturally turn our thoughts toward that way of life as exemplified by Victoria, our beloved queen." Incredibly stilted, this introduction pummels the viewer with unnecessary exposition. (Anyone remotely familiar with the novella or previous adaptations would have *some* notion about the setting depicted in the film!)

The scene continues to tutor the audience (the bishop rambles on about Victoria's "forces of good" conquering the "forces of evil") as a parishioner begins to mock the sermon. Seated a few pews ahead of the hysterical man, the eminent Dr. Harry Jekyll (Spencer Tracy) turns around to observe the spectacle. Although he is engaged in "pious reverence" with his fiancée, Beatrix Emery (Lana Turner), and her father, Sir Charles (Donald Crisp), Jekyll is fascinated by the unfortunate man's evil behavior. Outside the cathedral, Jekyll kisses Beatrix, much to the chagrin of Sir Charles, who objects to public demonstrations of affection. "Now, father, don't be pompous," Beatrix scolds in a very un–Victorian manner.

At the hospital Jekyll confers with his superior, Dr. Heath (Frederic Worlock), who refuses to let him administer experimental drugs to the "insane" man. "There might be trouble," Heath warns.

These brief opening scenes are screenwriter John Lee Mahin's claim to originality (there are no precedents in the novella or in previous screenplays). At this point the film becomes a scene-for-scene remake of the 1931 version, with occasional moments of creative license thrown in. (One viewing proves that MGM purchased Paramount's rights so Mahin could plagiarize without fear of a nasty lawsuit. Louis B. Mayer, who had capitalized upon Paramount's 1920 success by producing the Sheldon Lewis–Pioneer Film release, again had a hand in bastardizing a superior Jekyll-and-Hyde adaptation.) Receiving sole credit for the screenplay, Mahin was no stranger to Fleming, who had used him to give the Hollywood treatment to *Treasure Island* in 1934.

Only three characters from the novella remain: Jekyll, Poole (Peter Godfrey), and Lanyon (Ian Hunter), who makes very few appearances. The Carew character is represented by Sir Charles Emery, who objects to his daughter's relationship with Jekyll. Emery also displays attributes previously assigned to Lanyon (attacking Jekyll with his conservative beliefs) in both the novella and film versions.

To allow for Ingrid Bergman's indelible Swedish accent, Mahin changed the character of Ivy Pierson to Ivy Peterson, a confusing mixture of Cockney barmaid and Stockholm beauty. Consistently shot in MGM glossy close-ups, Bergman attempts to overcome the generic studio style and Fleming's lifeless, badly paced direction.

Ivy's first meeting with Jekyll is a drawn-out affair. Bergman radiates

*Dr. Jekyll and Mr. Hyde* (1941). The stuffy and staid Dr. Jekyll (Spencer Tracy), at the home of Beatrix Emery (Lana Turner), his chaste fiancée, in MGM's pompous bastardization of the 1931 Paramount film.

sensuality, but an intrusive close-up frequently breaks the mood created by her performance. Later, when Hyde accosts her at the music hall, Tracy and Bergman merely go through the motions: Hyde trips the waiter, Ivy sings and tries to escape Hyde's clutches, and so on. A new addition is Hyde's initiation of a full-scale brawl in which he takes no active part. Observing the proceedings, he rants and laughs (Tracy, in hair dye and bushy eyebrows, issues forth his one sneer and slightly altered voice) before paying the publican to fire Ivy. Practically tossed into the street, Ivy is forced to accept Hyde's offer (rendered somewhat ambiguous by PCA requirements).

Many scenes from the 1931 film are re-created, but only the framework is there; none of the atmosphere, visual elegance, or acting skill engendered by Mamoulian is captured by Fleming and his cohorts. Except for Bergman's enticing bedroom performance, the sexual overtones so crucial to the success of the familiar cinematic story are nowhere in evidence. Jekyll has the same pair of women—the good and the bad—to arouse him, but Tracy's leaden performance fails to generate much interest or excitement. In one brief sequence Jekyll asks to set a wedding date, but he shows none of the sexual angst needed to provoke his subsequent metamorphosis into Hyde.

The structure of the initial transformation scene is lifted from the 1931 film. Due to the death of the "insane" man, Jekyll is unable to test his drug (the development of which is shown in an unnecessary montage sequence); back in the laboratory, he impatiently guzzles the mixture himself. As he gasps and chokes, the scene shifts into a Freudian hallucination in which he sees himself frantically whipping horses that transform into naked images of Ivy and Beatrix (framed in medium close-up); as the hallucination ebbs, Hyde walks to the mirror, and none of the transformation is shown. This climax is perhaps justified, since Tracy's Hyde does not look much different than his Jekyll. Fleming and makeup man Jack Dawn may have chosen a less animalistic appearance for Hyde, but it requires a huge stretch of the imagination to believe that Lanyon, Ivy, and Beatrix do not see Jekyll when Hyde approaches them.

As in the previous film, Hyde is interrupted by a knock, and as the scene cuts outside to Poole, Jekyll opens the door. Having experienced a premonitory dream, Beatrix is waiting in the study. As the two lovers kiss, Sir Charles intervenes, announcing that he will take Beatrix to Europe at once. When Beatrix requests that Jekyll see her off at the train station, his libido briefly surges as Tracy clumsily replies, "Better have two engines—I might try to hold it back."

The next scene blatantly imitates the 1931 film. The first shot, a close-up of water trickling down the laboratory window, widens to show Jekyll peering out into the rainy darkness. His brooding is interrupted by Poole, who delivers a letter from Beatrix, relating the news that her holiday has been extended for another four weeks. Noting his master's depression, Poole suggests that he take in a "comical and daring" show at the Vanity Fair. As the butler leaves the room, Jekyll picks up the garter that Ivy offered as "payment" for his services; he gives no physical indication that he is aroused but soon pours the potion and drinks it down. Apparently unsatisfied with only one hallucination sequence, Fleming offers yet another Freudian excursion (designed by Slavko Vorkapitch) in which Ivy's head is now the cork in a liquor bottle. Reaching the limits of absurdity, the action culminates when a hand (presumably Jekyll's) reaches in with a corkscrew and tears her head off! Again, no transformation is shown before Hyde appears; further quoting the earlier film, he dons a cape and top hat before walking into the pouring rain (Tracy grins and shakes his head a little).

One on-screen transformation occurs late in the film when Jekyll, determined to abandon his experiments, is walking toward the Emery home (persuaded by Beatrix, Sir Charles has agreed to announce their official engagement). Feeling ill, Jekyll rests on a nearby bench, where he (with no apparent provocation) becomes Hyde. Through a series of lap dissolves, the viewer finally sees Tracy acquire his slightly darker skin, jutting jaw, and bushy eyebrows.

The next sequence shows Ivy in front of her mirror, toasting Jekyll's health (she paid her call, to thank him for the £50, the previous evening). Here the dialogue previously spoken by Miriam Hopkins is overplayed by Bergman, who screams hysterically after Hyde appears and chases her around the room. Again the action is ruined by an overabundance of glossy close-ups, including one of Hyde spewing pretentious dialogue as he strangles her.

The meeting with Lanyon, in which Hyde obtains the antidote, is also a claustrophobic exercise, consisting of alternated close-ups of the two characters. Though it is one of the 1931 film's most dramatic moments, the scene falls flat here, with Lanyon registering little surprise as he witnesses the reverse transformation.

Jekyll's subsequent visit to Beatrix and Hyde's murder of her father are also stilted exercises. Required to become hysterical, Lana Turner simply does not deliver, and Donald Crisp hardly can be seen as his character is pummeled to death by Mr. Hyde. Badly acted and directed, this scene should have been an embarrassment to Fleming, but it maintains the overall style of the film: MGM stars and supporting players go through the motions while a studio cinematographer (Joseph Ruttenberg, in this case) creates the usual mise-en-scène.

When Fleming first considered the project in 1940, MGM had selected British actor Robert Donat for the lead role, but during preproduction Donat was ousted in favor of the more bankable Tracy.

Tracy biographer Larry Swindell writes: "Tracy tried and failed to get out of the Jekyll-Hyde assignment. He said candidly that he had no business doing it, but the studio worked on his vanity. They wouldn't make the picture without him, he was the only actor they had who could play the double role."[53]

To keep Tracy's "shocking" appearance a secret, Fleming ordered that no publicity stills of Hyde be issued. He also insisted that the Hyde scenes be filmed on closed sets, but at least one visitor broke through this wall of security: British author Somerset Maugham, who, upon observing Tracy's performance, whispered into Fleming's ear, "Which one is he now, Jekyll or Hyde?"[54]

Most contemporary reviewers panned the film and Tracy's performance. The *New York Times* reported:

> Mr. Tracy has taken the short end of the stick by choice. Though his facial changes, as he alternates between Dr. Jekyll and his evil alter ego, may be a trifle subtler than his predecessors in the role, Mr. Tracy's portrait of Hyde is not so much evil incarnate as it is the ham rampant. When his eyes roll in a fine frenzy like loose marbles in his head he is more ludicrous than dreadful. When he blows grapeskins upon the fair cheek of Miss Bergman ... it is an affront to good taste rather than a serious, and thereby acceptable, study in sadism.[55]

Recognizing his limitations, Tracy may have given his best effort, but that counts for little when the film is viewed back-to-back with the 1931 version. According to Larry Swindell, Fredric March generously recalled: "I thought Spence did a fine job, as he always does. His Jekyll and Hyde weren't anything like mine, but why should they be? After all, we're two different actors, aren't we? I'm sure Spence would never look at a performance and try to copy it."[56]

It can be assumed that March was being less than objective when making this statement. Even the self-effacing Tracy refused to accept it. Swindell claims that when March telephoned, Tracy laughed and said, "Why, Fred, you son of a bitch, I've just done you the biggest professional favor you'll ever have!"[57] Unfortunately, filmgoers were unable to see March's performance until the (edited) film resurfaced 30 years later.

After agreeing to play the dual role, Tracy proposed some of his own creative ideas to Victor Fleming. Suggesting that the two female personalities be integrated into a single character, the actor thought it would be more interesting to have Jekyll see the good side and Hyde see the bad side of the same woman; and with his beloved Katharine Hepburn portraying this character, he would have felt more comfortable in a difficult assignment. But Fleming bought none of it and rigidly aped the structure and characterizations of the 1931 film.

When casting began, Fleming ran into a problem similar to that experienced by Mamoulian and Miriam Hopkins ten years earlier. Ingrid Bergman jumped at the chance to appear with Spencer Tracy in her fourth American film, but she refused to play the role Fleming offered. In 1980 she recalled:

> Naturally, as always, I'd been given the part of the sweet fiancée because now I had played three parts almost the same. ... I really was fed up having to play it again. I went to Mr. Fleming and I said, "Couldn't we switch, and let Lana Turner play the fiancée, and I play the little tart in the bar, the naughty little Ivy?"
> 
> He laughed. "That's impossible. How can you with your looks? It's not to be believed."[58]

After shooting a screen test, Fleming changed his mind but had to convince Bergman's agent, David O. Selznick, who wanted to maintain her image as a "Hollywood peaches-and-cream girl."

Many publications, including *Variety* and the *New York World-Telegram,* criticized the film but were kind to Bergman. In one review Cecelia Ager wrote:

> *Dr. Jekyll and Mr. Hyde* is handsome, stuffy, pompous hoke, with nothing new to say and therefore no reason, save hunger, to say it again. Indeed, to rattle its decent Victorian bones today is most unkind. For it turns out that they're not bones at all, just hollow clumps of papier-mache ... Mr. Hyde does go a little far; he kills a few people. But at least he waits till the end of the picture to kill Ingrid Bergman, so everybody has a good chance to gaze upon her lovely face.[59]

Recounting the production, Bergman spoke of Tracy's acting limitations:

> Spencer Tracy wasn't really very happy—not because of me, we got on well—but because he didn't like

doing these two characterizations: the sane doctor and the monster Mr. Hyde. He wanted to play himself, his own personality, which of course was the warm and marvelous personality that had made him a great movie star. He hated playing this double-natured character, showing the hideous reality of the brutal and evil man living within Dr. Jekyll.

Spencer didn't like some of the scenes, especially the one where he had to race up the stairs carrying me off to the bedroom for his immoral purposes. Victor Fleming demonstrated. Big and strong, he picked me up and ran up the stairs as if I weighed nothing. Spencer wailed, "What about my hernia?" So they rigged up a sling which supported me so they could hoist me upward while Spencer hung on and raced up behind me looking as if he were carrying me.

But it wasn't that easy. First they hauled me up so fast that Spencer just couldn't keep up, and Victor Fleming said, "Take her up at a natural pace. Let's try again." It was most difficult. Up and down, up and down, for the whole rehearsal time. Then, on the twentieth attempt, the rope broke. I dropped down into Spencer's arms. He couldn't hold me, and we went rolling head over heels to the bottom of the stairs. How either of us was not injured I'll never know. It was just a miracle. But there we were at the bottom helpless with laughter, roaring with laughter, while Victor came racing up, all sympathy and concern, but really so relieved that both his stars were not hurt and could continue to work.[60]

Bergman's comments explain Tracy's apathetic display. If Stevenson had been a prophet as well as an innovative author, he could have given both Jekyll and Hyde the personality of Spencer Tracy; then Tracy could have given a good performance as himself. In the opening credits a separate panel states, "Based on the novel by Robert Louis Stevenson." It should read, "Based on the 1931 film directed by Rouben Mamoulian."

Perhaps the *New York Times* review provides the best summation:

> Of all the actors, only Miss Bergman has emerged with some measure of honor. Lana Turner, as Dr. Jekyll's pure little fiancée; Donald Crisp, as her stiff-spined parent; Ian Hunter, as Jekyll's bewildered friend—all these move like well-behaved puppets around the periphery of Mr. Tracy's nightmare. But the fault lies deeper than the performances. Out of ham and hokum the adaptors have tried to create a study of a man caught at bay by the devil he has released within himself. And it doesn't come off either as hokum, significant drama or entertainment.[61]

## Offspring and Offshoots (1951–57)

By 1943 the sons of King Kong, Frankenstein, and Dracula had wreaked cinematic havoc (even Dracula's daughter had made a somewhat hostile appearance in 1936). During World War II, Hollywood depicted Sherlock Holmes, Tarzan, and the Invisible Man battling cinematic Nazis and "Japs," and one wonders why a spry son of Dr. Jekyll was not enlisted to change the personalities of those evil monsters.

In 1951 an Argentinian company released *El Extraneo Caso del Hom-*

bre y la Bestia (U.S. title, *The Doctor Jekyll*), a feature directed by and starring Mario Soffici. After MGM's pompous spectacle, major Hollywood studios steered away from Stevenson's horror tale, which, by the early 1950s, had become fodder for the popular B-film market. For Columbia's *The Son of Dr. Jekyll* (1951), screenwriters Mortimer Braus and Jack Pollexfen blessed Jekyll with a male descendant and, in turn, added to the Hollywood myth that the poor doctor was a sex-crazed maniac. Retaining the female character motif, they gave Hyde a wife and, of course, a son who eventually acts like dear old dad! None of the events leading up to Hyde's marriage are explained (Jekyll maintains his own home and identity while keeping the Soho apartment for Mrs. Hyde!), but the written prologue makes it clear that the woman was his wife and not just a "live-in" (thus remaining true to the PCA):

> Hyde, the monster, terror of all London, climaxed his many acts of violence by murdering his wife in their Soho flat.
> Chased by an enraged mob, he fled toward his Mayfair home—his only thought to take the potion that would change him back to the respected Dr. Henry Jekyll.

As the words fade, Hyde is pursued through the streets and burned to death by a torch-wielding gang. This action, combined with references such as "monster" and "many acts of violence," owes more to Universal's Frankenstein series than to Stevenson's prose. In fact, nothing in the film has a precedent in the novella. The appearances of Universal veterans Lester Matthews, Gavin Muir, and Paul Cavanagh in character roles further suggest other horror and mystery influences.

Situating Jekyll's death in 1860, the film focuses on Edward, the doctor's infant son, who is entrusted to Dr. Curtis Lanyon (Alexander Knox). Named executor and guardian by Jekyll's will, Lanyon claims that his bachelor status excuses him from responsibility, so care of the child is assumed by John Utterson (Lester Matthews), a close friend of Lanyon and the late Jekyll.

After this brief exposition, the film jumps ahead to 1890. Now 30 years old, Edward (portrayed by 42-year-old Louis Hayward) is a student at the Royal Academy of Science. Described as flaunting the "authority of his superiors" and engaging in "experiments bordering on witchcraft," he is dismissed from the institution by angry administrators. Having no knowledge of his origins (Utterson thought it best to withhold the information), Edward is driven by a strong genetic connection to his iconoclastic father. Upon claiming his inheritance, he learns the truth.

As Morris Stoloff's syrupy musical score swells on the soundtrack, Edward becomes convinced that over the years the public attitudes about his father have "made more of a monster out of him than when he was alive." Determined to "fight prejudice," young Jekyll moves into the ancestral home and reenacts his father's experiments. He is hounded by members of the press, police officers, and the general public, all of whom share a feverish lynch-mob mentality, but he is successful after Lanyon secretly adds a chemical to his potion.

Following a disastrous public demonstration, Edward's actions are misconstrued as those of a fiend, and he is declared mentally incompetent by Lanyon, who is not the loyal friend he appears to be. Desiring the Jekyll fortune for himself, he has manipulated public opinion, forged a bogus version of Henry Jekyll's notes, and masqueraded as a Hyde-like monster to frame Edward. Concluding the disordered, poorly written screenplay, Lanyon admits, "My association with your father almost ruined me. I had to use the Jekyll estate to get back what I'd lost." When Edward accuses him of keeping the original Jekyll notes for his own use, he reveals, "All I need to create a monster is a penny worth of paint and a lot of hysteria." He then lunges for Edward's throat and sets the entire house ablaze (the shots of the fire look conspicuously like those at the beginning of the film). Incredibly, Edward reaches safety, but Lanyon, repeating Jekyll's actions of 30 years earlier, jumps to his death from the roof.

A thoroughly infantile sequel to earlier films, *The Son of Dr. Jekyll* grafts many of Stevenson's character names onto new, one-dimensional personalities. The worst of these is Lanyon, Henry Jekyll's assistant, who supported him while "others were laughing." When Edward attempts to prove that his father discovered a new personality-splitting chemical, Lanyon claims that society caused the Hyde transformation, "not some mysterious, unknown drug." Unlike Stevenson's Lanyon, who is the ideological opposite of Jekyll, this character is merely an opportunist who knows the truth but lies to protect himself; he insists that Edward, like his father, will be driven insane by a reactionary mob.

The technical aspects of the film are on a par with the comic-book plot. One amateurish transformation, occurring when Edward first takes the drug, includes a close-up of his right hand growing clumps of black hair and absurd canine claws. After he tumbles to the floor (in a laughable shot in which Hayward rises from the chair and nearly falls into the camera), his face becomes darker and more heavily featured (via a makeup that resembles blackface).

The screenplay and Seymour Friedman's direction emphasize a pseudo-documentary style (the use of a written prologue and voice-over narration), but the result is ludicrous. Wrapping up 77 minutes of tedium, the badly written epilogue reads: "The fiery death of Dr. Lanyon ended the Jekyll-Hyde legend. Both the original manuscript and the fake copy went into Scotland Yard files to go down in history with other tales of bizarre crimes."

*The Son of Dr. Jekyll* is far-fetched and incredibly dull but, within its own genre, it works as well as MGM's bloated prestige effort. Although the next Hollywood offshoot would feature burlesque routines, it also offered entertaining situations and performances.

Billed beneath a popular comedy team and doubled by a masked stunt man, Boris Karloff plays the dual role in Universal-International's *Abbott and Costello Meet Dr. Jekyll and Mr. Hyde* (1953). After giving one of his finest performances in *The Body Snatcher* and rambling about as a fabricated villain in *The Strange Door*, he agreed to appear amid tried-and-true comic material in his third Stevensonian outing (his fourth, and final, would be the 1960 television version of *Treasure Island*).

For the most part, director Charles Lamont wisely repeated the structure used by Charles T. Barton in *Abbott and Costello Meet Frankenstein* (1948) and allowed Karloff to build a semblance of characterization while relegating the patter and pratfalls to Abbott and Costello. This decision was dictated, in part, by Sidney Fields and Grant Garrett's original treatment, which incorporated the story of two bumbling policemen with elements from the novella. Perhaps familiar with earlier parodies, writers Lee Loeb and John Grant created a final screenplay of some originality.

Abbott and Costello portray Slim and Tubby, American officers assigned to study British crime control methods in turn-of-the-century London. Failing to quell a riot, they are tossed into jail and subsequently expelled from the force by an angry inspector (Reginald Denny). In the meantime the recent murder of Dr. Stephen Poole, a reputable physician, and numerous reports of a terrorizing monster named Mr. Hyde continue to shock the populace. Hoping to be reinstated, the two bumblers track down the beast and Tubby cages him in a wax museum. When the inspector arrives to take the monster into custody, he finds the noted Dr. Henry Jekyll behind bars.

Humiliated again, Slim and Tubby are paid £5 to act as Jekyll's bodyguards. During their sojourn in the doctor's home, they take part in a series of altercations with Jekyll and his hulking assistant, Batley (John Dierkes). Suspicious of Jekyll's experiments and subterranean laboratory, Tubby drinks a potion that transforms him into a giant mouse, and he is injected later with a serum. Simultaneously transformed into monsters, he and Jekyll provoke a police chase that culminates with the doctor's death and Tubby's capture. Believing he has the real monster, the inspector (along with his assistants) is bitten savagely. The film ends with all of the officers turning into monsters.

A total farce, *Abbott and Costello Meet Dr. Jekyll and Mr. Hyde* features an interesting variation on earlier cinematic depictions of Jekyll. Shortly after the character is introduced, he shares a hansom cab with his ward, Vicky Edwards (Helen Westcott), and Bruce Adams (Craig Stevens), an amorous (and very American) newspaper reporter, who inquires about his work. The discovery of "what makes men evil," according to Jekyll, will bring lasting world peace. (However naive his belief may be, it is quite lofty for an Abbott and Costello film.)

Surrounded by respectable period detail, Karloff plays his scenes with more conviction than one would expect in a film of this type. Borrowing the sexual-angst motif from earlier films, Loeb and Grant

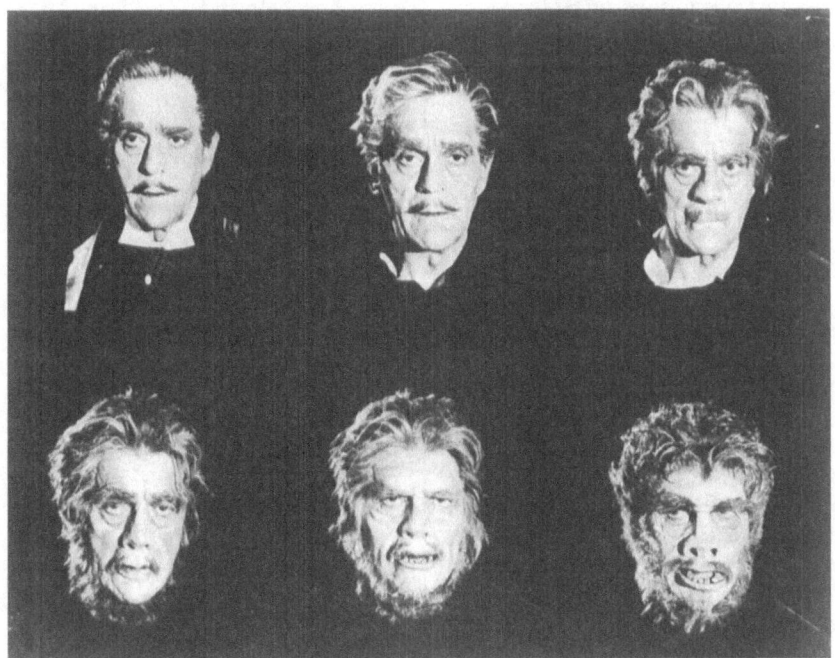

*Abbott and Costello Meet Dr. Jekyll and Mr. Hyde* (1953). Dr. Jekyll (Boris Karloff) transforms into a rubberized, Neanderthal Mr. Hyde in this publicity still from Universal-International's silly but surprisingly effective burlesque.

injected a new element—the depiction of Jekyll as a man who already possesses some of Hyde's traits—into the screenplay. Jekyll claims to strive for "world peace" but is too self-indulgent to maintain his own household; in love with his ward, he ignores the wishes of others and often treats his assistant with conscious brutality. Karloff's Hyde, however, is limited to a few transformations, ably rendered by makeup man Bud Westmore and cinematographer George Robinson. Edwin Parker, stunt veteran of countless Universal horror films, filled in for the 65-year-old star during the action sequences.

Jekyll possesses a degree of depth, but Hyde is a comic prop. Reduced to buffoonery in the overlong and repetitive chase scene (Jekyll and Tubby's monsters display identical behavior), Hyde bears the brunt of several slapstick escapades before he falls to his death from one of Jekyll's windows.

The opening scene, in which Vicky Edwards leads a suffragette rally in Hyde Park, is a highlight. One of the very few peacetime political references to appear in an Abbott and Costello picture (most of their early films are World War II propaganda efforts, and Costello himself was a staunch right-wing patriot and friend of Joseph McCarthy), it culminates with a brawl between the radical women and several male bystanders (including the most ubiquitous of Hollywood character actors, Harry Cording). Never lauded for its historical accuracy (in fact, most critics hated the film), *Abbott and Costello Meet Dr. Jekyll and Mr. Hyde* melds an aspect of early 1900s Britain with American slapstick. Particularly in London, these years were politically and socially tumultuous, and the suffragette movement often became heated and violent. Some historians link the considerable efforts of the Women's Social and Political Union, under the leadership of Emmeline Pankhurst and her daughters, with the difficulties experienced by the Liberal Party and Parliament itself.

By the early 1950s Abbott and Costello's popularity had begun to fade; they had met just about every villain and visited every conceivable location that Universal had up its sleeve. When *Meet Dr. Jekyll and Mr. Hyde* was released in August 1953, no one at the studio expected a huge success, but the box-office combination of Bud, Lou, and Boris packed many theatres throughout the country.

Some serious devotees of literature may consider a meeting with Abbott and Costello to be an unkind fate for Stevenson's tale, but things can, and did, get much worse. Not content with the son he had given Dr. Jekyll, Jack Pollexfen rewrote his absurd 1951 screenplay and sold it to Allied Artists as *The Daughter of Dr. Jekyll* (1957). For good measure, he also produced the fiasco and dragged in the formerly stylish Edgar G. Ulmer to direct it. After assisting some of Germany's greatest expressionist filmmakers, including F. W. Murnau, and helming *The Black Cat* (1934) with Boris Karloff and Bela Lugosi, *Bluebeard* (1944), and *Detour* (1946), Ulmer spent the latter part of his career grinding out B-film schlock. Some auteur critics have overrated him as a low-budget genius, but a few of his efforts from the 1940s and 1950s include stylish moments. The reputation of *The Daughter of Dr. Jekyll*, however, cannot be saved by even the most adamant auteurist.

The film opens with a glowering, hirsute face and some of the most preposterous narration ever conceived:

> One of the early masterpieces of science and horror is Robert Louis Stevenson's immortal *Dr. Jekyll and Mr. Hyde,* the thought-provoking story of how a strange experiment transforms a benevolent doctor into Mr. Hyde, a human werewolf. When the news of the death of this monster came, there was a nationwide sigh of relief. No longer would the sound of every strange footstep mean terror. The evil thing would never prowl the dark again.

Just before the titles appear, the badly lit face inquires, "Are you sure?" Indicative of the entire screenplay, this prologue proves that Jack Pollexfen was one of the worst writers in cinema history. Not only did he neglect to include the full title of the novella, he apparently knew little about lycanthropic legends; after all, a non-human werewolf is only a wolf. (Betwixt conceiving the two Jekyll progeny, Pollexfen, it should be remembered, sired Jim Hawkins's descendant, Jamesina, for *Return to Treasure Island.*)

Gloria Talbot stars as Janet

Smith, an orphaned Englishwoman who returns home to collect her sizable fortune. Informed by her guardian, Dr. Lomas (Arthur Shields), that her father was the infamous Dr. Jekyll, she is persecuted by Jacob (John Dierkes), a servant, and a horde of reactionary townspeople. Several murders occur, Janet dreams that she is a werewolf and, in the end, her clever fiancé, George Hastings (John Agar), discovers the real killer: Dr. Lomas, a greedy werewolf/vampire who blamed his earlier crimes on the unfortunate Dr. Jekyll! Lomas joins Hastings in a stilted fight, but Jacob, accompanied by his vigilante friends, impales the beast with a wooden stake.

Badly written, directed, photographed, and acted, this film is undoubtedly the nadir of Jekyll-and-Hyde offshoots. The cast is a treat for fans of bad cinema who may appreciate the pathetic performances of B-film notable John Agar (whose wardrobe consists of an undersized turtleneck and a hideous, striped sportcoat) and John Dierkes (whose vampire hunter is a change of pace from his assistant role in the Abbott and Costello film).

Ulmer's static compositions (most scenes contain no more than two or three shots) frame Agar as he delivers some of the worst dialogue ever scripted: "Wasn't that close to a man trying to be God?" he naively asks after hearing the story of Dr. Jekyll. The most entertaining aspect of the film, Agar's lines become more ridiculous as the narrative drags on. After calling his beloved Janet a "little idiot," he makes a series of grammatically inept observations: "The atmosphere of this place would get anybody down"; "The only thing I can think of is to get her out of here in a hurry"; "She is no condition to face an inquisition." But Pollexfen's incompetence shines most when Agar stammers, "We're not dealing with a man. We're not dealing with anything human. And if we don't get out of here quick, we won't be dealing with anything, ever again." Other laughable ingredients include Agar's perusal of a book entitled *Witch, Warlock and Werewolf* and Shields's comment that Hyde was Jekyll's "perverted mask of evil"!

Primarily playing the drive-in circuit, the film shared a double bill with the equally atrocious Allied Artists release *The Cyclops* (1957), starring Lon Chaney, Jr., and again, Gloria Talbot. *Variety's* "Kove" said it best: "At one point, co-star John Agar declares, 'This is ridiculous.' That sums up cheapie horror pic for the exploitation market."[62]

## British Variations (1959–71)

In the late 1950s England's Hammer Films was the world's leading producer of commercially successful horror films. Working with modest budgets, the studio revitalized the genre with garish and violent remakes of several 1930s Universal classics. In early 1957 *The Curse of Frankenstein*, directed by Terence Fisher and starring Peter Cushing and Christopher Lee, played to packed houses throughout Europe and the United States. Reinvesting some of the profits, Hammer again enlisted

Fisher, Cushing, and Lee for *Dracula* (U.S. title, *Horror of Dracula*), a minor masterpiece of the genre and one of the most exciting adaptations of Bram Stoker's tale of terror. Released in June 1958, it was followed by *The Revenge of Frankenstein* (1958), *The Hound of the Baskervilles* (1959), and *The Mummy* (1959).

Imitating every classic Hollywood horror film they could recall, producers Michael Carreras and Anthony Hinds quickly latched onto the Jekyll-and-Hyde story. Within a 15-month period the studio released two films inspired by the novella.

Directed by Lance Comfort, *The Ugly Duckling* (1959) features a Jekyll descendant named Henry (Bernard Bresslaw) in a lame attempt at parody. "Based on characters created by Robert Louis Stevenson," Sid Colin and Jack Davies's screenplay offers "Teddy" Hyde, an urbane jewel thief in the Raffles mold. Transforming back into Jekyll near the end of the film, he redeems himself by capturing a gang of robbers.

Faced with a long history of adaptations and variations, Hammer invented a new twist for their second, and more serious, Stevensonian effort. For *The Two Faces of Dr. Jekyll* (1960), screenwriter Wolf Mankowitz (who later joined Orson Welles in penning the turgid *Treasure Island* [1972]) chose to emphasize Hyde's moral degeneracy rather than deformity or ugliness. Physically, Henry Jekyll sports a heavy beard and drab dress, while Edward Hyde is a handsome man about town.

As portrayed by Canadian actor Paul Massie, who appeared in only a few films during the early 1960s, the dual character falls short of Mankowitz's concept. Like other Hammer films directed by Terence Fisher, a slow pace and brightly lit color compositions, as well as a reliance on reaction shots and editing in the "transformation" scenes, often mar the dramatic effect.

A staple ingredient in the Hammer horror formula, sex plays an important role in motivating the actions of Hyde. Whereas earlier adaptations feature a monster who obtains female contact through sheer force and brutality, Massie's Hyde is attractive enough to seduce Maria (Norma Marla), the snake dancer at the Sphinx, a glamorous nightclub. This aspect of Mankowitz's approach suggests that inner evil is not always accompanied by physical ugliness. Hyde's degenerate acts emanate from his personality, and his success relies in part on his ability to dupe others with his handsome appearance. (This material suggests the influence of Wilde's *The Picture of Dorian Gray,* an aspect the film shares with the 1920 Paramount version.)

Through experimentation, Jekyll wants to free the good in humans by controlling their personalities; of course, evil emerges when he selects himself as the test subject. Transformed into the striking Hyde, he visits the Sphinx, where he finds Jekyll's wife, Kitty (Dawn Addams), dancing with a close friend, Paul Allen (Christopher Lee). Unbeknownst to Jekyll, Allen, a gambler and womanizer, has been partaking of Kitty's favors

*The Two Faces of Dr. Jekyll* (1960). An unconvincingly hirsute Dr. Jekyll (Paul Massie, in an admirable performance) is approached by the swindling, womanizing Paul Allen (Christopher Lee), in Hammer's interesting but flawed variation.

for quite some time. At one point Allen admits to Hyde, "Women aren't a weakness, my dear friend—they're a recurrent necessity."

Confronted by his friend, Litauer (David Kossoff), who has discerned Hyde's true identity, Jekyll is persuaded to abandon the formula but is unable to control his evil impulses; soon he pays visits to a gin mill and an opium den. While carousing with prostitutes one evening, he is bludgeoned and left for dead. He awakens in a gutter and decides to create an antidote that will restore his gentle personality, but Kitty's affair with Allen prevents him from releasing the anger that begets Hyde. He then throws a party at the Sphinx, where Paul is crushed to death by a python and Kitty jumps to her death.

Hyde returns home, makes love to Maria, and strangles her as Jekyll's personality reemerges. Fully recovered, Jekyll peers into a laboratory mirror and sees the image of Hyde (in *Dorian Gray* style) speaking to him. Hyde then murders the stable boy and sets fire to the house; when the police arrive, he announces that Jekyll has killed himself. At the coroner's inquest Hyde tells Litauer of his decision to leave Britain. Before he can finish speaking, however, he metamorphoses into a haggard, prematurely aged Jekyll.

The idea of a gentle, scruffy

Jekyll indulging himself as the depraved, handsome Hyde and wearing himself out in the process is the film's most obvious connection with *Dorian Gray*. Over the years this integrative approach has failed to impress critics. Alan Frank expresses an opinion held by many: "As ever, Terence Fisher directed with his usual flair, eliciting good performances from Christopher Lee and Paul Massie, but the script by Wolf Mankowitz, turning the Jekyll character into a sinister, bearded, and taciturn scientist while his alter ego, Hyde, was clean shaven and charming as he wenched his way through the flesh pots of Victorian London, defeated both director and actors."[63] Christopher Lee has commented:

> This was a script by Wolf Mankowitz, a very good writer, and the part of Paul was written for me. A cad, sponger, swindler. The man who lives off women, and doesn't pay gambling debts. A rake. I think it was one of the best performances I've given.
>
> The idea behind *The Two Faces of Dr. Jekyll* was a very clever one, but it didn't work out: the idea being that when Jekyll becomes Hyde he turns from being a rather dreary professor into a handsome, vicious, evil young man, like Dorian Gray.
>
> It was a good picture, with beautiful clothes and wonderful to look at, but in my opinion the premise was wrong.[64]

As much of a failure as the doctor's experiment, *The Two Faces of Dr. Jekyll* contains nothing from the novella except the basic dual-personality concept and brief sequences in which Jekyll mistreats a little girl and writes of his decision to lock the laboratory door. Paul Massie successfully depicts two personalities by using different voices for Jekyll and Hyde, and is often moving as the former, but he cannot overcome a script that relies predominantly on sexual references and situations. The nightclub scenes are overly long, and Norma Marla's dance is merely an extended and lifeless remake of Nita Naldi's sensual performance in the 1920 Paramount film. Although most of the violence occurs off-screen, Hyde's rape of Kitty and bedroom murder of Maria (a scene obviously borrowed from the 1931 Paramount version) are tasteless gratuities.

The next British adaptation, *I, Monster* (1971), offered Christopher Lee a better opportunity to interpret Stevenson's prose. Released by Milton Subotsky and Max J. Rosenberg's Amicus Productions, a company that specialized in low-budget horror films during the 1960s and 1970s, *I, Monster* combines a large portion of the novella with Freudian theory.

Downplaying violence in favor of mood and intelligent dialogue, Milton Subotsky's screenplay remains the most faithful adaptation of the story. Most of Stevenson's characters are depicted, including Utterson (Peter Cushing), Dr. Lanyon (Richard Hearndell), Enfield (portrayed as a doctor by Mike Raven), Poole (George Merritt), and the small girl who is trampled in the by-street. While the initial one-third of the film centers on the doctor's experimentation with a drug that proves the validity of Freud's sexual repression theory, the remaining footage successfully paraphrases many of Stevenson's

## The Strange Case of Dr. Jekyll and Mr. Hyde

*I, Monster* (1971). Mr. Utterson (Peter Cushing) consults Dr. Marlowe (Christopher Lee), a Freudian variation on Dr. Jekyll, in Amicus' uneven but remarkably literate adaptation.

passages. Ironically, the dual character is called "Dr. Marlowe" and "Mr. Blake," and the lurid title (a variation on *I, Mobster,* a 1959 Roger Corman film) is followed by the credit, "Based on a story by Robert Louis Stevenson." (Perhaps Subotsky avoided copyright expenses by not mentioning the novella or the Jekyll and Hyde names.)

Some film buffs have mistaken *I, Monster* for a Hammer production, an error that may be attributed to the team of Lee and Cushing, who also appear in Amicus's *Dr. Terror's House of Horrors* (1964), but the similarity to Hammer's style and content ends with the two stars. In the mid–1970s Subotsky commented:

Amicus isn't really in competition with Hammer. I don't think we are in the same field, frankly. We make a different kind of film but both ours and theirs are unfortunately covered by the word *horror*. Ours, I think, are more fantastic films. What I'm interested in is not what they're interested in—I mean, they make films that are shocking and have a lot of blood and gore, and sometimes I envy their bad taste but I just can't do that sort of thing. Their films have punch but I find that, for me, their stories are boring. I mean, you could take big chunks out of any Hammer film and it wouldn't make any difference. You could take six reels out and just leave reels one and two, and nine and ten, and you've got a picture. All the rest are just extra murders and extra gore. . . .

But we try to make films that are

imaginative and relate to an audience in a different way. We never have any blood and gore in our films. You never see it, it's always suggested. . . .

The script is the most important thing in filmmaking—the script and the editing. The direction is not that important. I think the cult of the director came into being because the critics have to attach some name to a film and so they think the director is the man who makes the film, but he's not. I don't really think it's all that important who directs a picture. That's one of the reasons we've given so many people their first picture to direct. I think we've given more directors their first chance than any other company. One of the reasons you work with a novice is that you think that maybe he can give you something more interesting than someone who's stuck in the mud.[65]

Subotsky selected 22-year-old Stephen Weeks as director and insisted that he shoot *I, Monster* in 3-D. Totally inexperienced, Weeks failed to master the complicated process as he haphazardly filmed all of the scenes at Shepperton Studios in 1970. The footage was salvaged in the cutting room and released in Great Britain in 1971. Two years later it went into limited release in the United States and was soon sold to television.

The content and pacing are marred by awkward transitions, but despite its problematic origins, the film is successful on several levels. The highlight of Subotsky's screenplay is the Dr. Marlowe characterization: like Stevenson's Jekyll, he is middle-aged, progressive, and most importantly, asexual. Like Jekyll, Marlowe enjoys the freedom afforded by his alter ego; he carouses amid the lowlife world of taverns and tenements, but never seeks female companionship. In a scene inspired by Mamoulian, Blake shares some champagne with an amply developed slattern, but he shows no interest in making love to her. Later he chases the drunken woman through the streets and corners her in an alley. Assuming that he wants sex, she begins to undress, but he bludgeons her to death with his walking stick. Some feminist-minded critics may interpret this as a savage rape, but more realistically, the scene is a sensationalistic updating of the Danvers Carew murder. The next morning police officers find a fragment of the weapon, which is soon identified by Utterson. (In an earlier scene laced with contrived Freudianism, Marlowe tells Utterson that his father had used a gold-headed cane for "things other than walking"!)

The aversion to sex is a trait shared by both Marlowe and Blake. When first testing the new drug, Marlowe believes that he has discovered a way to reinforce Freud's division of the human psyche. Discussing the three components—the id, the ego, and the superego—with Dr. Lanyon, he claims that his drug can erase either the id or superego, depending upon which dominates a particular person's psyche. If a patient is morally upright and does not indulge in sensual, or evil, pleasures, the control of the superego can be altered to allow the id free rein, and vice versa. Given the ability to create a psychic equilibrium, Marlowe believes that his discovery will benefit mentally troubled individuals.

## The Strange Case of Dr. Jekyll and Mr. Hyde

*I, Monster* (1971). Prior to an evening of debauchery and murder, Mr. Blake (Christopher Lee) goes berserk in Dr. Marlowe's laboratory.

In one of his most successful experiments, Marlowe injects Diane (Susan Jameson), one of his female patients, whose neurosis, he believes, stems from sexual repression. In an effective sensual moment the young woman removes her clothes and, when Marlowe reenters the room, offers herself to him. Well staged and photographed, the scene is highly suggestive: with her back to the camera, Diane, draping a large black cape around her shoulders, faces Marlowe and opens it wide. Here, the result of her action is communicated to the viewer solely through Marlowe's facial reaction (and Christopher Lee's admirable underplaying). Unmoved, he administers an antidote and calmly informs her of the results. Blatantly symbolic, yet subtle in execution, this visual and dramatic highlight reinforces Marlowe's Freudian methods and reveals a great deal about his personal morality.

When Marlowe finally injects himself, his reserved qualities quickly disappear as he joyously toys with flaming burners and smashes glass equipment in the laboratory. Although he does not transform physically, subsequent injections progressively alter his appearance. Logging the ninth experiment, he barely is able to write as his alter ego takes over. As he shuffles out of the room, Blake's self-abusive and debauched personality is physically matched by his decrepit appearance. (The absence of Lee's perennial toupee is an effective touch.)

The early scenes cross-cut between Marlowe's experiments and the scientific and philosophical discussions held by Lanyon, Enfield, and Utterson: a narratively economic style that contrasts the progressive world of research with the more conservative Victorian drawing room. When Marlowe speaks of Freud's theories, Lanyon condemns them, adding, "Your ideas are even more dangerous." Closely patterned after Stevenson's characterization, Lanyon breaks all professional ties with Marlowe but later is summoned to obtain the chemicals from his lab. When Blake arrives to fetch the package, Lanyon witnesses the metamorphosis (Lee's shadow is framed in medium shot as he pantomimes the change). The following day Lanyon delivers his narrative of the event to Poole and dies soon after.

The final 50 minutes contain few digressions from the novella. Adapted passages include Blake's acquisition of a seedy Soho flat, his involuntary transformation in the park, and his many interactions with Utterson, a character who finally is given his due. Eliminated by some adaptations, and barely mentioned in most, Utterson appears in a semi-narrative capacity while observing the actions of both Marlowe and Blake; his stroll through the by-street with Enfield, the examination of Marlowe's will, the dream involving Blake's trampling of the little girl, the meeting with Blake at the laboratory door, the meeting with Marlowe to discuss the will, and the later meeting to discuss the disappearance of Blake are all gleaned from Stevenson.

The climactic scene, however, is a Subotsky creation. After transforming and destroying much of Marlowe's laboratory, Blake walks to Utterson's home, enters the upper story, attacks the unsuspecting doctor, and sets a raging fire. Utterson fights valiantly, knocks Blake into the flames, and sends him crashing down the stairs to his death. As Marlowe's features appear (in a lap-dissolve transformation), the credits begin to roll.

Unfortunately, the literary passages suffer from Weeks's lackluster direction, and the uniformly underplayed performances fail to generate much excitement. Contrary to Subotsky's comments about good taste, there are several tasteless moments: the opening titles fade in on a two-headed baby pickled in alcohol, Blake slits a street tough's throat during a violent fight, and the bludgeoning of the cleavage-ridden prostitute continues for some time. But these sensationalistic images do not negate the intelligent screenplay or Christopher Lee's credible acting. In an early 1980s interview Lee referred to *I, Monster* as "probably the most difficult picture I've ever done" and the Marlowe/Blake role as "one of the best performances I've given."[66]

*I, Monster* was the thirteenth serious English-language Jekyll-and-Hyde adaptation. After 63 years of filmizations, a screenwriter finally adapted the story instead of relying on his own fabrications. Regardless of its overall quality, the film provides one of the few opportunities to hear Stevenson's prose emanating from the screen.

While Amicus was sifting through Stephen Weeks's disjointed

footage, director Roy Ward Baker was helming another Jekyll-and-Hyde variation for Hammer. Released in mid–October 1971, *Dr. Jekyll and Sister Hyde* became the first feature film to portray Hyde as a woman. Vitagraph's 1915 short, *Miss Jekyll and Madame Hyde,* included a good female character who metamorphoses into an evil one, but the Hammer screenplay, penned by Brian Clemens, is the only adaptation that depicts Jekyll as a bisexual. Considering that the film was produced in the early 1970s by a studio known for its sexy horror films, such a development came as no surprise.

Prior to the release of *Dr. Jekyll and Sister Hyde,* Hammer had featured ample cleavage and straight sexual relationships in almost all of its horror releases, plus the added titillation of nudity and lesbianism in *The Vampire Lovers* (1970) and its sequel, the turgid and silly *Lust for a Vampire* (1971). As if Stevenson's asexual character had not experienced enough cinematic amour, Hammer explored the basic sexual elements that still remained, namely sadomasochism and male homosexuality. Needless to say, the novella fell by the wayside when Clemens decided to turn Dr. Jekyll into Jack the Ripper!

Instead of developing a serum by mixing various chemicals, Jekyll (Ralph Bates) murders young women and removes their organs. (Another Hammer motif, graphic dismemberment and decapitation, also is depicted in *Frankenstein Must Be Destroyed* [1969].) Like his cinematic predecessors, Jekyll is a scientist whose research is intended to benefit humanity. When his friend, Professor Robertson (Gerald Sim), warns him that he will not live long enough to perfect his antivirus, a drug that will eradicate all major viral diseases, Jekyll seeks an "elixir of life" that will allow him to experiment further. After he develops a formula from hormones extracted from female cadavers, he tests it on a fly that not only lives much longer than usual but also undergoes a gender transformation.

When the morgue runs out of female specimens, Jekyll hires Burke (Ivor Dean) and Hare (Tony Calvin) to murder young women. Soon he drinks the potion and changes into a beautiful woman (Martine Beswick). Queried by his new upstairs neighbors, Susan Spencer (Susan Brodrick) and her brother, Howard (Lewis Fiander), he describes the woman as his sister, "Mrs. Hyde, a widow." One night Burke and Hare are attacked by angry Whitechapel residents, who hang the former and toss the latter into a lime pit. Forced to commit murder to obtain more female organs, Dr. Jekyll romances Susan while his transsexual alter ego pursues her brother. All goes reasonably well until Jekyll, thinking that he is still in female form, makes a pass at Howard. Though he attempts to control his evil female half, Jekyll is interrupted by the police and a mob of vigilantes who force him onto the roof of his house. When he attempts to climb up an adjacent building, he transforms into the lovely Sister Hyde and falls to his death.

Admittedly, Clemens's approach to the subject is novel and inventive, and the dual role is portrayed

***Dr. Jekyll and Sister Hyde*** **(1971). Dr. Jekyll (Ralph Bates) and Sister Hyde (Martine Beswick), in a publicity still for Hammer's bisexual variation on the dual personality premise.**

excitingly by Ralph Bates (a fine actor who appeared in several Hammer horror films during the early 1970s) and the voluptuous Martine Beswick (who later starred in such grade-Z material as *The Happy Hooker Goes Hollywood* [1980], in which she engages in poolside relations with Batman himself, Adam West); but the screenplay, at best, is a clumsy patchwork of various historical characters and events and a few snippets from the novella.

Like earlier films, *Dr. Jekyll and Sister Hyde*'s opening credits claim that the narrative is "based on the story by Robert Louis Stevenson." Clemens's 30-year-old Dr. Jekyll has nothing in common with Stevenson's character, except a wish to destroy his iniquitous alter ego. Both Jekyll and Hyde choose to murder innocent prostitutes, and the doctor's personality changes very little until the last ten minutes of the film. A scene in which Sister Hyde attempts to kill Susan but is halted by the strength of Jekyll's personality, compensates for a contrived sequence featuring her seduction and murder of the curious Robertson.

Clemens's incorporation of the Burke and Hare murders transforms Jekyll into a Dr. Knox–like character—an element that recalls Dr. Macfarlane in "The Body-Snatcher." This content has nothing to do with the literary Dr.

Jekyll, and the idea of passing off his crimes as the Whitechapel Murders (which occurred during the autumn of 1888) is a hard pill to swallow. But the film is one of Hammer's more exciting offerings, thanks to Roy Ward Baker's atmospheric direction and the performances of Bates and Beswick. In a 1970s interview Baker commented:

> *Dr. Jekyll and Sister Hyde*—there you had a case where none of us realized how good Ralph Bates and Martine Beswick looked together. It was uncanny. And it was Jimmy Carreras who cast the girl, oddly enough, against the wishes of the producers, Albert Fennell and Brian Clemens. There was a controversy going on over three or four different girls though I didn't have much of an opinion about it one way or the other. Anyway, in the end, Hammer put his foot down and said you're going to have Martine Beswick, and she turned out to be an absolute crackerjack. I regret that I didn't make more out of the eroticism in the situation, and it needed above all things a confrontation scene between the man and the woman. But Brian Clemens was determined to be consistent with his logic and as they only had one body between them, you couldn't have a two-shot scene. We did a mirror scene at one point that went part of the way towards capturing the effect I wanted.[67]

## Parodies, "Quickies," and a Soviet Hyde (1976–87)

At present, *Dr. Jekyll and Sister Hyde* stands as the last "serious" cinematic adaptation of the story produced in the West. Since 1971 the only English-language theatrical films citing the novella as resource material have been ridiculous parodies and cheap exploitation "quickies." Perhaps the most entertaining of these is *Dr. Black and Mr. Hyde* (1976), a late entry in the 1970s "blaxploitation" genre. Originally titled *Dr. Black and Mr. White*, the film stars ex–Los Angeles Rams running back Bernie Casey as Dr. Pride, a respected California physician who becomes a psychotic, Caucasian killer after quaffing a powerful elixir. Delightfully absurd, the film culminates with a "tribute" to *King Kong* (1933): the crazed white monster climbs to the top of the Watts Towers and is gunned down! A film that many African Americans would like to forget, *Dr. Black and Mr. Hyde* followed such "blaxploitation classics" as *Blacula* (1972) and *Blackenstein* (1973). Released by Dimension, it was shown as *The Watts Monster* in some areas.

Written "with apologies to Robert Louis Stevenson" by Charles B. Griffith, *Dr. Heckyl and Mr. Hype* (1980) stars Oliver Reed as an unattractive podiatrist who attempts to kill himself with a chemical mixture. Failing to bring about the desired effect, the potion transforms Dr. Heckyl into the handsome and violent Mr. Hype. No stranger to the horror parody, Griffith had written the screenplays for some of Roger Corman's "quickies," including *A Bucket of Blood* (1959), *The Little Shoppe of Horrors* (1960), and *The Creature from the Haunted Sea* (1960). For this Menahem Golan and Yoram Globus extravaganza, he also doubled as director. Often funnier than one would expect, the film features a fine supporting cast, including Corinne Calvet and Jackie Coogan (in one of his last screen appearances).

The same cannot be said for Paramount's perfectly awful *Jekyll and Hyde ... Together Again* (1982), a "modernized adaptation" that focuses on early 1980s drug and punk-rock culture. In overblown comic style, Mark Blankfield portrays Jekyll, a surgeon and medical researcher who changes into "a disco refugee with New Wave tendencies" after accidentally snorting cocaine. Shunned by critics and audiences alike, *Jekyll and Hyde ... Together Again* actually includes Stevenson's name in the credits.

A handful of Soviets were the only feature filmmakers who took the novella seriously during the 1980s. In 1987 *The Strange Case of Dr. Jekyll and Mr. Hyde*, starring Innokenti Smoktunovsky as Jekyll and Alexander Feklistovh as Hyde, was released in the USSR.

## *The Strange Case of Dr. Jekyll and Mr. Hyde* on Television

The first television adaptation of the novella "Dr. Jekyll and Mr. Hyde" was broadcast live from New York on September 20, 1949. Directed and produced by Robert Stephens for CBS's "Suspense" program, this 60-minute episode featured Ralph Bell in the dual role. Constrained by the limitations of the live format, Stephens cut to Bell's hands during Jekyll's transformations and used a subjective camera technique to showcase Hyde's "warped mentality."[68]

Two serious adaptations and at least one major parody were broadcast on American television during the 1950s. "The Strange Case of Dr. Jekyll and Mr. Hyde" (1950), produced by Fred O'Donovan and adapted by John Keir Cross, was followed by a comic skit on the March 22, 1953, episode of CBS's "Jack Benny" program. The inimitable comedian's unique interpretations of doctor and demon did nothing to dissuade Gore Vidal from adapting the novella for CBS's 60-minute "Climax" program; first aired on July 28, 1955, this "Dr. Jekyll and Mr. Hyde," directed by Allen Reisner, starred Michael Rennie and Sir Cedric Hardwicke.

Originally broadcast in France, the film *Le Testament du Doctor Cordelier* (1959) was written and directed by Jean Renoir. Financed by the French government, this updating of Stevenson's tale is one of the legendary director's lesser efforts. Hampered by a static and murky visual style, the film fared poorly during its theatrical run in the United States. *Variety*'s "Mosk" reported:

> Here the doctor's changes are done via cuts and sans any special effects. Jean-Louis Barrault does some fine pantomiming as the clownish monster who is the evil in the doctor and his other self when released by the drug he has invented. But other actors are left to fend for themselves. Direction is simple and unassuming which makes the film lag and lose tempo at times.
>
> Renoir has tried to make a pic to please both mediums *[sic]* and hasn't quite brought it off. But the well-wearing tale could make this film worth slotting in a TV horror

series for the U.S. or for use in secondary situations. It lacks the weight and technical standards for art chances.[69]

American television producers avoided Jekyll-and-Hyde adaptations for many years, but elements of the novella occasionally were incorporated into a series episode. One of the most successful primetime efforts, penned by science-fiction veteran Richard Matheson, was telecast on October 6, 1966. The fifth official "Star Trek" episode, "The Enemy Within" opens with Captain Kirk (William Shatner) being split into two entities by the malfunctioning transporter. Causing widespread confusion aboard the USS *Enterprise,* the "evil" Kirk is fused with the "good" Kirk after Spock (Leonard Nimoy) discerns the facts and Scotty (James Doohan) performs his dependable transporter repairs. Matheson's teleplay is intelligent and innovative in its exploration of the "evil" side of humans; the idea that people draw requisite strength from their primitive and violent instincts is conceptualized by both Spock and Dr. McCoy (DeForest Kelley) who, for the first time, utters his legendary line, "He's dead, Jim."

A second-season "Star Trek" episode, "Wolf in the Fold," written by Robert Bloch and directed by Joseph Pevney (who helmed *The Strange Door*), also contains Jekyll-and-Hyde elements. Originally aired on December 22, 1967, it focuses on Scotty's apparent bouts with schizophrenia and murder, but ultimately reveals that the killings have been committed by the undying spirit of Jack the Ripper!

A feature-length television adaptation was presented by the Canadian Broadcasting Corporation in 1968. Titled "Robert Louis Stevenson's 'The Strange Case of Dr. Jekyll and Mr. Hyde,'" this two-part video drama was produced by Dan Curtis and directed by Charles Jarrott. As scripted by Ian McLellan Hunter, the story melds several of Stevenson's passages with fabricated characters and a large body count. The visual style is perpetually claustrophobic, but many of the scenes benefit from an excellent cast that includes Denholm Elliott as Devlin (a reworked version of Mr. Utterson), Leo Genn as Dr. Lanyon, and Billie Whitelaw as Gwyn (a prostitute patterned after Ivy in the 1931 film).

Later in his career Dan Curtis produced similar videotaped versions of Mary Shelley's *Frankenstein* (1972) and Bram Stoker's *Dracula* (1974). Both of these adaptations are drawn-out, boring affairs, but thanks to Jack Palance's surprisingly effective performance, "The Strange Case of Dr. Jekyll and Mr. Hyde" is more successful. Although Palance's Count Dracula in the 1974 telefilm is a pale Bela Lugosi imitation, his Dr. Jekyll and Mr. Hyde are quite unlike prior interpretations. Portraying the doctor as a gentle, understated, asexual scientist who occasionally loses his temper (particularly when he is mocked by a mob of reactionary colleagues in the opening scene), Palance often rises above the shoddy visual style (which includes several badly executed zooms) and exaggerated dialogue and situations. His Hyde chews the scenery now and then (he giggles too long after bludgeoning or murdering his victims), but Palance can be credited as the first actor to consistently emphasize the joyful glee experienced by Jekyll's evil side. (A personality trait suggested by Stevenson and mildly exhibited by Fredric March, this aspect also is displayed by Christopher Lee in *I, Monster*.)

Jekyll again is depicted as a researcher who wishes to aid humankind with his discovery: the opening scene includes his claim that the separation of the two selves will speed the process of evolution. But his colleagues, being non–Darwinian Christian dogmatists, scoff in his face and confirm his belief that men are half-animal entities. Dedicated to proving this theory, he absorbs himself in experimentation. After a few nocturnal excursions he begins to enjoy the evil side. When he brutally attacks Lanyon and kills Stryker (Oscar Homolka), an assistant who provided him with chemicals, he foregoes future experiments and destroys his equipment. For six months he treats the sick and teaches anatomy at the hospital, where his students and colleagues praise his devotion and amazing knowledge.

One evening Lanyon renews their friendship by inviting Jekyll to dinner, but the doctor is interrupted by Gwyn, who arrives to thank him for the money he has sent. (This scene, depicting Jekyll's restitution for Hyde's brutality, is another reworking of material from the 1931 film.) Convincing Jekyll to drive her home, Gwyn plies him with kisses and liquor before entering the boudoir to remove her clothes. Seated in front of a dressing table, she awaits Jekyll's embrace but is strangled by Hyde. After six months of normalcy, the doctor's asexual rationalism cannot overcome his motivated desire; and, again, an adaptation uses sex to bring out his savage alter ego.

Literary passages depicted in the teleplay are those most frequently visualized in prior film versions: Utterson (Devlin) questioning Jekyll about his relationship with Hyde; Jekyll awakening as Hyde in the morning; Jekyll's revision of his will; Jekyll "forging" a letter from Hyde; Jekyll's servants, including Poole (Gillie Fenwick), fretting over their master's strange behavior; and Lanyon's witnessing of Hyde's reverse transformation into Jekyll (although the script substitutes Devlin for Lanyon). Hunter's embellishments add some interesting twists to the story (the evolution concept and a late 1960s reference [spoken by Lanyon] about drugs getting "into the hands of young people"), but the final sequence follows in the footsteps of earlier versions: chased by the police, Jekyll is shot to death (in this instance by Devlin, his closest friend).

First broadcast in the United States by ABC on January 7, 1968, "The Strange Case of Dr. Jekyll and Mr. Hyde" was later shown by PBS. A conglomeration of adapted literature, crafty innovation, modern horror film violence, and cramped video style, it is worth at least one viewing, if only to see Jack Palance's interesting performance.

Very little information is available on "Dr. Jekyll and Mr. Hyde"

(1972), an adaptation aired on BBC 1, but Sherman Yellen's 1973 British teleplay, set in 1887 London and starring Kirk Douglas as a *singing* Jekyll and Hyde, has achieved infamy. The only filmed musical version of the story (a Broadway show was staged in 1989), Yellen's "Dr. Jekyll and Mr. Hyde" features songs by Lionel Bart, Mel Mandel, and Norman Sachs, and performances by a reputable cast, including Stanley Holloway as Poole, John Moore as Utterson, and Sir Michael Redgrave as Danvers.

Yellen's ludicrous adaptation, produced by Burt Rosen and directed by David Winters, is a farcical remake of the 1931 film (although the credits claim that it is "based on the classic story by Robert Louis Stevenson"). Only one incident from the novella, the murder of Danvers Carew, appears amid fatuous musical numbers and inane situations. Again Jekyll is depicted as a philanthropic research scientist; early in the film he declares that his drug will cure insanity. As author of "The Cause and Prevention of Mental Disorder," Jekyll disagrees with the local asylum master's claim that the insane are possessed by the devil. When he is prevented from experimenting on human subjects, Jekyll is inspired by Fred Smudge (Donald Pleasence), a devious pickpocket, who suggests that the doctor use himself as a guinea pig.

In an attempt to mask Kirk Douglas's American origins (and stilted performance), Yellen's script transforms Jekyll into a Canadian! During the first banal metamorphosis, the poor doctor talks to himself, noting his symptoms as the drug takes effect. As Hyde, he roams through a badly edited hallucination sequence in which he participates in a boxing match and hurls fruit at several peers of the realm during a session at the House of Lords.

Like the 1931 and 1941 film versions, Jekyll becomes involved with two women: Isabel (Susan Hampshire), the virginal fiancée, and Annie (Susan George), the sensuous prostitute. One ridiculous sequence features Douglas "playing" a piano and singing in the center of a graveyard. Finishing his abysmal performance, Hyde injects the hapless whore with Jekyll's drug and renders her terminally insane.

The most thoroughly preposterous sequence, however, centers on Jekyll's arrival at the home of Danvers, Isabel's arch-conservative father. Dressed in holiday touring attire, the singing Jekyll rides a bicycle *inside* the solarium before requesting an earlier wedding date! Later, he attends his engagement party and loses the respect of his peers when he espouses radical views and bad manners. Finally, he involuntarily transforms into Hyde and bludgeons Danvers with his walking stick. Chased by the police, Hyde changes back into Jekyll, but enraged by the accusations of Smudge, he becomes the monster one last time. He climbs a wall (à la Fredric March) and falls to his death on a laboratory table.

Yellen's script introduces characters who sing a few lines and then disappear into a cloud of obtrusive songs and choreography. With the exception of Susan George, Donald

Pleasence, and Judi Bowker as a young woman of the street, the primarily miscast actors appear uninterested in their roles. Arguably, Kirk Douglas gives the worst performance of his career (worse than Spencer Tracy's interpretation of the role, but slightly better than Sheldon Lewis's), and his singing will tax the patience of even the most tolerant viewers. The opening and end credits proudly proclaim that "Dr. Jekyll and Mr. Hyde" was "conceived and directed by David Winters"; all persons involved in its production probably wish that Winters had never courted the idea. First broadcast in the United States by NBC on March 8, 1973, this video fiasco quickly disappeared from the airwaves.

Three serious full-length television adaptations followed the musical farce. Originally produced for BBC 2 in 1980, "The Strange Case of Dr. Jekyll and Mr. Hyde," starring David Hemmings, was adapted by Gerald Savory and directed by Alistair Reid. Another claustrophobic video presentation, it aired in the United States as two installments of PBS's "Mystery" (January 6 and 13, 1981).

The most recent adaptations have been produced for U.S. television. In 1990 the Showtime cable network aired "The Strange Case of Dr. Jekyll and Mr. Hyde," a boring one-hour teleplay starring Anthony Andrews as a timid, tedious Jekyll and a pernicious, monotonic Hyde. Apart from the dual personality premise, this episode replaces Stevenson's prose with a myriad of female characters who satisfy Hyde's sexual and murderous desires.

Once again, Jekyll is a doctor who seeks to eradicate evil from the human psyche, a moth-eaten characterization made insufferable by Andrews's poker-faced, mumbling performance. Most of Hyde's activities are confined to a bordello where he taunts the prostitutes, fornicates with multiple partners, strangles a beautiful virgin, and endures the bad acting of Rue McClanahan, who plays a "European" madam. The script faithfully depicts Jekyll's asexuality (he consistently rebuffs Rebecca Laymon [Laura Dern], the daughter of a conservative professor whom Hyde bludgeons to death), but the remainder of the episode is a tasteless exercise in sadomasochism.

Originally broadcast by ABC on January 21, 1990, "Jekyll and Hyde" stars Michael Caine in the dual role and Cheryl Ladd as yet another fabricated love interest. This feature-length British teleplay, written and directed by David Wickes, primarily disregards the novella for inferior original material, and Caine (in his third Stevensonian outing) overacts badly as Hyde. Forced to wear an outrageous monster makeup, Caine resembles a radioactive refugee from a 1950s B film.

## • THIRTEEN •
# Into the Highlands: *Kidnapped* (1886) and *Catriona* (1893)

> *"The Hielands are what they call pacified. Small wonder, with never a gun or sword left from Cantyre to Cape Wrath, but what tenty folk have hidden in their thatch! But what I would like to ken, David, is just how long?"*
> —ALAN BRECK to David Balfour, in *Kidnapped*.

In June 1751, 18-year-old David Balfour is visited by Mr. Campbell, the minister of Essendean. "When your mother was gone," Campbell reveals, "and your father ... began to sicken for his end, he gave me in charge a certain letter, which he said was your inheritance." Instructed by the clergyman, David sets off on foot to meet his uncle, Ebenezer Balfour, at the house of Shaws near Cramond. Two days later he arrives in the area, but his inquiries are met with strange, ambiguous replies. Accompanied by Jennet Clouston, "a stout, dark, sour-looking woman," David is surprised to find the house in a ruined state. "That is the house of Shaws," she cries. "Blood built it; blood stopped the building of it; blood shall bring it down. See here! I spit upon the ground, and crack my thumb at it! Black be its fall!"

As the sun sets, David, with his "hair on end," approaches the estate. His first knock falls on deaf ears, but his second, louder rap produces "a man's head in a tall nightcap, and the bell mouth of a blunderbuss, at one of the first-storey windows." During the evening and the following day, David becomes acquainted with Ebenezer, his late father's only living relative, who offers to exchange a £37 inheritance for a favor. Told to retrieve a chest of papers that lies at the top of a five-story stair-tower, David nearly falls to his death but returns to startle his scheming uncle; as Ebenezer cringes, the lad demands to know the truth about his family.

The next morning Ebenezer mumbles an explanation but is interrupted by a knock at the door. Ransome, a "half-grown" boy, wearing sea clothes and dancing a hornpipe, enters with a message from Captain Hoseason, a man

Ebenezer describes as a business associate.

Soon the three set out for Queensferry on the Firth of Forth, where Hoseason's ship, the *Covenant,* is ready to sail. Anxious to meet Mr. Rankeillor, the Balfour family solicitor, David is waylaid by Hoseason, who entices him with a tour of the ship and a promise of safe passage to the lawyer's house. Aboard the *Covenant,* David, noticing that Ebenezer has not accompanied them, is knocked senseless; for several days he is subjected to seasickness, inclement weather, and the harsh lifestyle of Hoseason's crew. Late one night Ransome is killed by Mr. Shuan, one of the captain's mates. David is selected as the new cabin boy and ordered to work and sleep in the roundhouse, where he spends the following week. One evening the *Covenant,* sailing through a dense fog, strikes a boat and splits it down the middle; the crew drowns but one passenger survives by grabbing the brig's bowsprit.

Inside the roundhouse, Hoseason and David learn that the survivor is a prominent Jacobite who fought in the 1745 Rebellion. The man offers to pay Hoseason for safe passage to France, but the captain agrees only to set him ashore in Scotland. While the Jacobite rebel and the "good Whig" lad discuss their political differences, the captain speaks with his crew. Hoseason then attempts to bribe David with money and good treatment in Carolina; pretending to retrieve pistols and powder from the roundhouse, David informs the rebel of the captain's plans. "My name is Stewart," the Jacobite admits. "Alan Breck, they call me." Leaving the front door open to facilitate combat with Hoseason's 15 men, Alan brandishes a cutlass but hands the pistols and ammunition to David, who prepares to guard the back door and skylight. Moments later the siege of the roundhouse begins: after a furious melee, six of Hoseason's men lie dead and another four are wounded, while David and Alan emerge safe and sound.

At breakfast the next morning Alan gives David a silver button from his coat and then agrees to help Hoseason navigate the *Covenant* to Loch Linnhe. Back in the roundhouse, David speaks of his admiration for the Campbells while Alan describes the destruction of the Highland clan system and the harrowing of the glens that followed the Jacobite defeat at Culloden in 1746. Alan admits that he began fighting as a redcoat but eventually "deserted to the right side at Preston Pans." He describes King George's campaign to strip the Highland man of his powers and the tax collectors who carry out the monarch's plans. To Alan's clan, the Stewarts of Appin, the king's oppression is symbolized by the "Red Fox," Colin Roy Campbell of Glenure.

Late that evening Alan and Hoseason attempt to sail the *Covenant* through the treacherous Torran rocks, but a savage storm scuttles the ship against a reef. Tossed into the sea, David reaches a spare yard, which he uses as a raft. After kicking and splashing for more than an hour, he reaches Earraid. For four days he braves rain, wind, and rough, granite terrain as he heads eastward toward Mull.

On the third day he signals two fishermen in a small boat, but they shout in Gaelic and laugh before passing by. The following morning the fishermen return; though David cannot understand Gaelic, he discovers that Earraid, a tidal islet, "can be entered and left twice in every twenty-four hours, either dryshod, or at the most by wading."

On the Isle of Mull David tramps toward Ben More, a recognizable landmark. At a "low and longish" house he meets an old gentleman who knows of the shipwreck and the subsequent affairs of Alan Breck. "I have a word for you, that you are to follow your friend to his country, by Torosay," the old man tells him. The next day David begins his trek, viewing the poverty and disgrace that Alan had described. Aided by a few locals, David reaches Torosay on the Sound of Mull, and then ferries to Kinlochaline, Morven, on the mainland. Here he meets Henderson, a mysterious evangelist from the south country, who discusses the Highland situation and the activities of the Red Fox.

At Loch Linnhe David rows across to Appin with a local fisherman. In a wood of birches he meets four travelers: a red-headed man, a lawyer, a servant wearing the Campbell tartan, and a sheriff's officer. When one of the others calls the red-headed man "Glenure," the inexperienced lad realizes that he is standing face to face with Colin Roy Campbell, the Red Fox. As Campbell speaks, a shot rings out from the hill above and knocks him to the ground. "Take care of yourselves," he murmurs. "I am dead." David scrambles up the hill and cries, "The murderer! The murderer!" A dark figure—"a big man, in a black coat, with metal buttons"—moves up the hill as the others accuse David of complicity. A brigade of redcoats is signaled, and a frantic search begins.

Unsure of what course to take, David is surprised by a voice that advises him to duck into the trees. Here he finds Alan Breck holding a fishing rod. Moments later they are running along a mountainside toward Ballachulish. Stopping to rest in some heather, Alan declares his innocence and describes the aftermath of the shipwreck, in which Mr. Riach prevented Hoseason and the others from attacking him and stealing his money. Later that evening they reach the home of James Stewart. Convinced that a redcoat reprisal is imminent, James fears that his kinship with Alan will send him to the gallows. To protect himself, James must offer a public reward for Alan's capture and a general description of David, but he gives the two fugitives a change of clothing and sends them into the night.

David and Alan's flight in the heather continues for about ten days, in which they pass through Glencoe, hide among rocks in the mountains, grope in streams for fish, and engage in instructional sword duels. At Ben Alder they spend two days in "Cluny's Cage," the home of Cluny MacPherson, a prominent Jacobite exile. Here David observes the inner workings of a Highland clan and hears of Bonnie Prince Charlie's brief stay after the defeat of 1746, while Alan loses their money in a card game.

The next morning Cluny offers to return the money, but David accepts it only after expressing his disgust.

Led by one of Cluny's men, David and Alan cross Loch Errocht. Soon after they accuse each other of bungling various aspects of their escape. Exhausted and ill, David behaves childishly, but his actions are matched by Alan's stubborn conceit. When Alan criticizes David's beliefs, the young Lowlander asks, "Do you think it either wise or very witty to cast my politics in my teeth?" Alan whistles a Jacobite air and increases the pitch of the argument. David quickly draws his sword, but they soon realize the futility of their actions. Alan then helps David walk the remaining distance to the braes of Balquhidder. Populated by the broken remnants of Highland clans, the area offers a week's respite and a doctor who restores David's youthful health. At the home of the Maclarens Alan engages Robin Oig, one of the sons of Rob Roy MacGregor, in a piping duel. Displaying characteristic bravado, Alan is defeated by Robin, who corrects his opponent's mistakes before skirling a flawless pibroch.

Back on the road, Alan and David traverse the Highland line and head for Stirling, where they plan to cross the bridge into safety. When a guard appears, Alan convinces a local serving girl to help them. She steals a neighbor's boat and rows them across to the Lothian shore.

The next day Alan fends for himself while David consults Mr. Rankeillor in Queensferry. Telling the tale of his dangerous adventures, David is assured of his inheritance. Rankeillor explains how Ebenezer acquired the estate by allowing Alexander to marry Grace Pitarrow, a woman whom both men loved. At the house of Shaws the intrepid Alan hoodwinks Ebenezer into admitting his part in the kidnapping, and Rankeillor tends to the legal details. Promised two-thirds of Shaws's yearly income, David asks Rankeillor's permission to provide Alan with safe passage to France. On a hill overlooking Edinburgh the two friends part company. As David enters the city, he feels "a cold gnawing in my inside like a remorse for something wrong."

Continuing his association with *Young Folks* magazine, Stevenson began writing "David Balfour" Skerryvore in March 1885; after turning to *The Strange Case of Dr. Jekyll and Mr. Hyde* in September, he resumed the new novel after the "bogy tale" was published in January 1886. Three months later illness again took its toll, and Stevenson wrote to his father that he would end the story, while leaving room for a sequel. Completed in April or May 1886, "Kidnapped, or The Lad With the Silver Button. By Robert Louis Stevenson" was published as 14 weekly installments in the May 1 through July 31, 1886, issues of *Young Folks*. The entire manuscript was published in novel form on July 14, 1886, by Cassell in London and Charles Scribner's Sons in New York. By the time the book was available in stores, the popularity of *Dr. Jekyll and Mr. Hyde* had ensured a resounding success.

*Kidnapped* has been called "the sort of bridge by which Stevenson passed from the story of adventure to the serious historical novel."[1] By combining the excitement and imagery of *Treasure Island* with a specific historical milieu, detailed geography, and well-developed character psychology that contrasts the Lowland and Highland cultures, Stevenson demonstrated enormous growth as a novelist. Unlike other authors who tackled Scottish history in their works, Stevenson was interested in using events as a backdrop for the conflicts experienced by people in various cultural settings. Jenni Calder writes: "It was not only that the Scottish past fascinated him, but that certain features of Scottish history seemed to him particularly insistent, and the most insistent were undoubtedly the divisions and conflicts that had repeatedly riven the country." After discussing Stevenson's observations about the societal dichotomy in Edinburgh (the New Town professionals and the lower community of poverty and crime), Calder continues:

> Wherever Stevenson looked in the Scottish past, he found that the division was echoed. ... The Jacobite rebellion was ... [an] obvious episode of internal strife, and has commanded the attention of many novelists. It is interesting that in *Kidnapped*, Stevenson did not attempt to set the story during the time of the Rebellion itself, which would immediately have brought him into precisely the same territory as Scott's *Waverley*, but takes us into the Highlands when the bitter aftermath of that shabby conflict emphasized the barrier of the Highland line perhaps even more intensely.

It is unfortunate that it is *Kidnapped* which is most readily taken up by critics as the novel to compare with Scott: unfortunate because the comparison can do Stevenson little justice. He is not a historical novelist in the same sense as Scott, and it is misleading to look in his work for a similar treatment of historical subjects. Scott's sense of the movement of history, of the historical forces that shaped the lives of all levels of society, and of the close relationship between history and story, all contributed to his stature as an unrivalled historical novelist. Stevenson lacked all of these. What he had was a profound sense of the relationship between society and *character*, rather than between society and history. To get his history right, therefore, was less important to Stevenson than getting his psychology right, in terms of social influences and personality. He used the past to provide him with an authentic environment for his psychological insight.[2]

Henry James considered *Kidnapped* to be Stevenson's finest book, and he wrote elegantly of the impact Scottish history and culture had upon the story: "We know very little about a talent till we know where it grew up, and it would halt terribly at the start any account of the author of *Kidnapped* which should omit to insist promptly that he is a Scot of the Scots."[3] In this novel Stevenson explores the "duality" that contributed to his homeland's turbulent past; through the eyes of a Jacobite fighter and a Whig youth, he vividly examines the feelings experienced by Highlanders and Lowlanders five years after the bloody battle at Culloden.

As a political movement Jacobitism was initiated in late 1688 by Scots and English who supported the main line of the Stewart dynasty.[4] Upon gaining the throne in 1685, the Stewart king, James II of England and Ireland and VII of Scotland, intended to restore Roman Catholicism throughout both kingdoms. A great majority in Scotland and England opposed this development and, in November 1688, James II (VII) was overthrown by his Dutch son-in-law, Prince William of Orange.

Together with his wife, Mary, the eldest daughter of James II (VII) and his first wife, Anne Hyde, William of Orange reigned until his death in 1702. His mother, Mary Stuart, was the daughter of Charles I, who was executed by Oliver Cromwell's government in 1649. While the main line of the Stewart dynasty practiced Catholicism, James's elder brother, Charles II (who was proclaimed king in 1649, went into exile during the Cromwellian regime [1651–60], and returned to rule from 1660 to 1685), preferred Protestantism. At his command, both of James's daughters, Mary and Anne, had been raised as Protestants, and his insistence was compounded by Anne Hyde's own Protestant faith. Mary was heir presumptive to her father's throne until James's second wife, the Catholic princess Mary Modena of Italy, gave birth to a boy, James Francis Edward Stuart, Prince of Wales, in 1688.

Faced with rebellion and a Dutch invasion, James II (VII) entrusted the infant Prince of Wales to Mary of Modena, who sailed for France in late December 1688. Although his first escape attempt failed, James soon followed his wife and son into exile. During the spring of 1689 a Convention Parliament began to meet in Edinburgh; after reading letters from both William and James, the assemblage declared that James had forfeited the crown on April 4. Thereafter, the Scottish Stewart line, which had ruled Scotland since the ascension of Robert II in 1371, was supplanted by England's "Glorious Revolution," so named by Protestant Whigs who had objected to James's Catholicism and divine right political beliefs.

During the Convention, the supporters of James were referred to as Jacobites. Derived from the Latin name Jacobus, which means James, the term began to attract more attention when General John Graham of Claverhouse, Viscount Dundee (the "Bonnie Dundee" of Scott's song) raised James's standard against the Williamite government later in April. Although Dundee marshaled about 2,500 men for a brief Highland campaign, this first Jacobite rebellion was doomed to failure. The Highlanders' greatest success occurred on July 17, 1689, at Killiecrankie, just south of Blair Atholl, where they routed the Williamite forces; but Dundee was killed when a musket ball knocked him from his horse. His successor, Colonel Alexander Cannon, failed to carry the rebellion into the Lowlands, and his forces were devastated after four hours of savage street fighting in Dunkeld on August 21. After this defeat, the Jacobites rebelled four more times between 1689 and 1746.

In an attempt to bring the Highland clans under control, the government devised one of the most notorious events in Scottish history. Unwilling to commit large amounts of financial and military resources for a lengthy Highland campaign, the Williamites targeted a single Jacobite clan to use in a propaganda ploy. Secretary of State Sir John Dalrymple, Master of Stair, selected the MacDonalds of Glencoe, the Clan Iain Abrach, as the group that would defy King William and thereafter suffer military execution. Scottish historian Bruce Lenman writes, "In theory one such act of frightfulness might effectively terrorise the much larger ascendancies."[5]

To bait his trap, King William "set a date by which all Highland chiefs had to recognize his authority on pain of a renewed offensive, not only by land forces but also by naval units which were being moved into the waters of the Inner Hebrides."[6] A few days before the January 1, 1692, deadline, the Jacobite chiefs received approval from their exiled James VII. While most of the chiefs met the deadline, Alasdair MacDonald of Glencoe became the victim of a political snafu. After a bogus administrator took MacDonald's oath in late December, the confused chief was forced to travel through deep snow to the home of royal sheriff Sir Colin Campbell in Inverary. On January 2 MacDonald reached Inverary, but Campbell was still celebrating Hogmanay with relatives. By the time Campbell returned on January 5, he was outraged at MacDonald's late arrival but still administered the oath. When the government received it on January 6, the oath was considered invalid and the MacDonalds fell into the Master of Stair's trap.

At 5:00 A.M. on February 14, 1692, Campbell of Glenlyon and a large contingent from the Argyll regiment swept into the MacDonald homes. Without warning, 38 people, including the chief, two women, and a six-year-old child, were slaughtered (henceforth, known as the Massacre of Glencoe). The previous day two of the chief's sons and other members of the clan had escaped through the treacherous, snow-covered mountains surrounding Glencoe. This atrocious act failed to subjugate the clans, and antipathy toward King William increased throughout the Highlands. Many English Whigs joined in protesting the sadistic brutality of William's act. Lenman notes, "The whole mess was a propaganda gift of a high order to the exiled Stuarts, and was relentlessly exploited, first by the French and then by the English and Scots Jacobites."[7]

In 1700 James II (VII) died in exile. Fearing that the Catholic James Francis Edward, who had been proclaimed King James VIII (of Scotland) and III (of England and Ireland) by King Louis XIV of France, would gain support in Scotland, the Williamite government passed the Act of Settlement, which transferred the royal succession to the Hanoverian line of the Stewarts, in 1701. King William's sister-in-law (younger daughter of

James II), Princess Anne, became heir to the throne, and Sophia, Electress of Hanover, the nearest Protestant relative, was appointed as her successor. The act also declared that future monarchs must be Protestants and support the Church of England. When King William died in 1702, Anne was declared Queen of England and Scotland.

The Westminster government became even less popular with the Jacobites after the Scottish Parliament ratified the Act of Union on January 16, 1707. This act, which merged Scotland and England into the nation of Great Britain, abolished Scottish sovereignty, assured the Hanoverian line, and gave the Scots 45 seats in Parliament, while the English received 513 (a ratio of 1 : 10 in the House of Commons and 1 : 12 in the House of Lords).

When the Act of Union was passed, James Francis Edward Stuart, now 19, believed that his return to Scotland was imminent. Convinced that James, or "the Old Pretender," as he was later called, would rally a majority of Scots, King Louis XIV promised French support for an expedition to begin in March 1708. Although some Jacobite lairds answered the call to arms, the rebellion never got off the ground. James contracted measles and then seasickness; the military commander, the Comte de Gace, was pessimistic at the outset; and one of five warships was lost following a confrontation with a Royal Navy squadron.

In 1714 both Queen Anne and Sophia of Hanover passed away, making George Louis of Hanover the new British monarch. Proclaimed George I of England and Scotland, he aroused the enmity of many Jacobites who expected greater support for James. In fact, Jacobitism was at its height during this period: the large number of dedicated Scots now were being supplemented by discontented English Jacobites who opposed the new Hanoverian line. On September 6, 1715, John Erskine, the sixth Earl of Mar, backed by widespread Highland support, raised the Jacobite standard on the braes of Mar (Braemar).

On September 14 Mar's forces (estimates run as high as 5,000 troops, both foot and horse) captured Perth, where a Jacobite headquarters was established. By early October the army, now increased to 9,000 troops, fortified Perth before splitting up for simultaneous western and southern attacks. At Stirling, John Campbell, second Duke of Argyll, commander of the governmental forces, reinforced both his northern and southern flanks.

The Jacobite forces of the '15 (1715 Rebellion) never benefited from a strong central military leadership. Instead, the larger Highland group was supplemented by smaller risings, including one in the Scottish Borders and another, composed of Tories, Catholics, and High Anglicans, in northeast England. By November Mar commanded 10,000 men, many of them inadequately trained and attired, while Argyll countered with 4,000 well-paid, regimental soldiers. As in earlier rebellions, the Jacobites continually hoped for foreign aid, a reliance that again proved to be a major setback.

On November 13 both forces met at the indecisive battle of Sheriffmuir, above Dunblane. The following morning Argyll was amazed to find that Mar's forces had disappeared. Retreating back to Perth on November 15, Mar sought provisions, and the army was recalled two days later. Each side claimed victory at Sheriffmuir, but Mar's army never advanced farther southward. The southern Jacobite force, marching to Lancashire, opened fire at Preston, also on November 13, but surrendered to governmental troops the next day. By the time James Stuart finally landed at Peterhead on December 22, the Jacobites were fighting for a lost cause. A reinforced Argyll marched to Perth, and Mar's forces evacuated the town on January 30, 1716. On February 5, Mar, accompanied by the Old Pretender himself, sailed from Montrose toward the security of France. By February 14 the remaining Jacobite fighters headed for their respective homes. The government executed some Jacobites captured after the battle of Preston and a few noblemen who played conspicuous roles in the rebellion, but a general amnesty was granted to those who agreed to hand over weapons and provisions.

In 1719 the Spanish government, anxious to recover Italian lands lost to England in 1713, decided to use the Jacobites for its own ends. Cardinal Giulio Alberoni devised a plot in which Scottish Jacobites would provide a diversionary attack to draw British troops away from London while a Spanish army of 26,000 marched on the city. However, the "'19," as it was called, was only a small rising and proved to be a futile exercise for both the Jacobites and the Spanish.

While Jacobitism appeared to be obsolete as a political movement, the exiled James, now in Italy, provided a glimmer of hope for his loyal Scottish supporters. During the evening of December 31, 1720, his bride of two years, the 17-year-old Habsburg princess Maria Clementina Sobieska of Poland, gave birth to a child, Charles Edward Louis Philip Casimir Stuart. However, the majority of Jacobites remained inactive over the next two decades, and most clan chiefs were concerned primarily with governing their respective lands and livestock. Bruce Lenman writes:

> The very nature of Jacobite ideology tended to endorse a passive approach on the part of its adherents. They cultivated a ritual year, with celebrations of the Pretender's birthday, and they treasured Jacobite keepsakes and engraved glasses, but fundamentally they had a mystical belief ... that their dynasty represented a Right Moral Order. Its restoration to the British thrones was therefore a matter of cosmic justice. By definition such a restoration would solve all the tensions and troubles which alarmed their conservative souls when they looked round the British scene. The fact that it would have had no such effect—it would have solved some problems and created others—is neither here nor there. They believed in the redemptive nature of their sacral king with total conviction.[8]

Having no real military experience, the 23-year-old Charles

Edward Stuart, called the Young Pretender and, later, Bonnie Prince Charlie, decided to lead a major Jacobite rising in January 1744. Plans for the invasion were botched, however, and Charles stayed in northern France to raise the spirits of exiled followers.

Most Jacobite chiefs refused to support another rebellion without official French assistance. Unless Charles landed in Scotland with an equipped army, they stressed, he would receive little aid from Highlanders whose hopes had been dashed in previous campaigns. However, on July 5, 1745, Charles boarded *Le du Teillay* to begin an 18-day voyage to Scotland. Attacked by a British man-of-war on July 10, the frigate was saved by fire from *L'Elisabeth*, a French warship loaded with muskets, broadswords, 20 field pieces, and ammunition. After the British ship retreated, *L'Elisabeth* returned to port, but *Le du Teillay* continued around Ireland toward the Outer Hebrides. On July 23 the ship reached a harbor on the islet of Eriskay, where Charles met with Alexander MacDonald of Boisdale, chief of the MacLeod clan. Declining to join the venture, MacDonald told the prince to go home.

Charles, who was seeing Scotland for the first time, replied, "I am come home, sir, and I will entertain no notion at all of returning to that place from whence I came." Convinced that "his faithful Highlanders" would rally to his call, Charles raised the Jacobite standard at Glenfinnan, on the shores of Loch Shiel, on August 19, 1745. For the next five months the Jacobite army, which numbered about 1,500 men at the outset, met with considerable success in Scotland, including a stay at Holyrood after they marched into Edinburgh on September 17. On September 21 Charles led his troops eastward to Prestonpans, where they routed General Sir John Cope's army in eight minutes.

Although he had become master of Scotland, Charles mistakenly assumed that England also would fall under the weight of his army. Conferring with Lieutenant General Lord George Murray, Charles decided to march his troops to London by way of Carlisle. Hoping that English and Welsh Jacobites would join them, the army, numbering 5,000 foot and 600 horse, set out in two columns on November 1. They experienced little resistance at first and on November 15 Charles, atop a white steed, rode into Carlisle while a brigade of 100 pipers played a rousing Jacobite march.

After recruiting 300 more troops at Manchester, Charles marched south to Derby on December 4. Though he had come within 130 miles of London, where inhabitants feared a substantial attack, Charles was surrounded by government forces a few days later. The troops of William, Duke of Cumberland, were at Lichfield, about 25 miles to the south, while General George Wade's forces grouped at Wetherby, about 75 miles to the north. An inadequately trained defense militia also waited at Finchley, north of London. Prior to the march on Derby, Charles had insisted that many English Jacobites were ready to support the cause; after no assistance was received, his troops realized that their hero had played a con game, going so far as to claim that the Tories would rally behind them. Realistically, most English supporters were "drinking" Jacobites—men who toasted the cause—sipping wine from engraved Jacobite glasses while their northern "comrades" did most of the fighting. On December 6 the Jacobite army began its retreat.

On December 20 Charles and his troops, now numbering 3,600 foot and 500 horse, waded across the Esk into Scotland. They met with some success, including the capture of Stirling on January 8 and a surprise attack at Falkirk Moor on January 17, but by February 17 Charles and a motley band of remaining forces had retreated to Inverness. For two months the "bonnie prince" attended society functions in the town. After the government captured the Jacobite sloop *Prince Charles*, which had been carrying French supplies and money, the Duke of Cumberland's forces reached Nairn, about 12 miles south of Inverness, on April 14.

Preparing for an attack, Charles assembled his troops at Drumossie Moor, later called Culloden, on the morning of April 15. When Cumberland's army failed to appear, Lord George Murray suggested that the Highlanders prepare for a surprise nighttime raid. Cumberland was still in Nairn, celebrating his twenty-fifth birthday. Wishing to avoid open warfare on the moor, Murray preferred a predawn strike against unsuspecting and brandy-soaked men. Shortly after 8:00 P.M. Murray and the prince each led a column of men through heavy mist and darkness toward Cumberland's camp. Murray's men proved sluggish, however, and he was forced to stop at Kilvarock Castle, west of Nairn. Realizing that dawn would break before they marched the remaining few miles, both columns retreated.

At 5:00 A.M. on April 16 Cumberland roused his troops and, forming three columns, quickly followed the Jacobites back to Culloden. Charles ordered his 5,000 exhausted men to assemble on the moor, while Cumberland's 6,400 foot and 2,400 horse approached from the east. Once the battle began, the pitifully unprepared Jacobites were routed in less than an hour. Charles was dragged off the moor by Adjutant General John O'Sullivan, who had chosen Drumossie as the battle site, while his remaining Highlanders attempted to flee. Surgeons cared for the government wounded, but the wounded Jacobites, per Cumberland's order of "no quarter," were hacked and clubbed to death. When Cumberland's men finally left, the moor was covered with dismembered and scattered Jacobite bodies. Some innocent bystanders, including women and children, also were beaten and stabbed to death.

Cumberland's barbaric display at Culloden earned him the epithet "the Butcher." Of the 3,470 Jacobites taken prisoner by the government, 120 were executed (peers were beheaded, while others were hanged, drawn, and quartered), 936 were sent to the American colonies as bond slaves, 222 were exiled, 1,287 were released or exchanged, and 700 were not accounted for.

After leaving the battlefield, Bonnie Prince Charlie became a hunted fugitive. Aided by a few faithful Jacobites and others who respected his royal lineage, he roamed the Western Highlands and islands for nearly six months before escaping to France on September 19 and 20, 1746. He sailed aboard *L'Heureux* from Loch nan Uamh, the same spot at which he had arrived on the Scottish mainland 13 months earlier. He never returned to Scotland but lived a disappointing existence, wracked by unsuccessful marriages and excessive drinking, until he died in Italy in January 1788.

Charles escaped the government's retaliation, but many Highlanders were left without basic necessities. After the butchery at Culloden was finished, Hanoverian troops burned homes, stole and killed livestock, and plundered the belongings of rebels and nonrebels alike. The government then instituted a series of measures that literally destroyed the Highland way of life. Traditional dress, including the kilt, was outlawed, and the speaking of the Gaelic language was discouraged. In a vivid account of Charles's escape attempts, Eric Linklater writes: "That Bonnie Prince Charlie brought sorrow and ruin to the Highlands is incontestable; and yet, by a not uncommon paradox, he enriched them beyond measure by a story that lives, and probably will, among the great stories of the world."[9] David Daiches has also written of the Jacobite literary legacy:

> Anachronistic and historically meaningless as the Jacobite movement was, it nevertheless provided—for historical reasons which can be precisely identified—a focus for Scottish national feeling. The very fact that the cause was lost helped to turn Scottish national feeling into something elegiac and literary and is one reason—the other is the unassimilated effects of the industrial revolution on the Scottish imagination—for the incurable nostalgia of much Scottish literature, especially in the nineteenth century.[10]

The idea that Jacobitism was historically meaningless is debatable, but Daiches's comment that the movement was politically anachronistic is a view shared by many historians. In *Kidnapped* David Balfour and Alan Breck Stewart often display their different impressions of Jacobitism. While Alan clings to an anachronistic past to make sense out of the Highland way of life, David supports the more modern Whig heritage which has supplanted it.

Incorporating elements of Jacobite history and culture with topographical detail and well-developed characters, Stevenson apparently based portions of David and Alan's flight in the heather on two specific events in Bonnie Prince Charlie's six-month journey through western Scotland. David's arduous four-day experience on Earraid (where Stevenson himself spent three weeks during the summer of 1870) is similar to Charles's brief stay on a tidal island near Benbecula during late June 1746. Put ashore by fishermen, Charles and two companions feared they would starve until the tide ebbed and they were allowed to continue on their journey. During the latter stages of his escape, Charles successfully executed a real flight in the heather and, at one point, spent an entire night hiding atop a rock with his companions.

"Cluny's Cage" is Stevenson's depiction of the actual hideout of Ewan Macpherson Younger of Cluny on Ben Alder, a 3700-feet hill located about 25 miles east of Fort William. Charles stayed there for a week in early September 1746 before he escaped from Loch nan Uamh on September 19. The Cage "was concealed by a grove of holly, it afforded wide views, and was constructed, against the steepness of the ground, on two floors, and was roofed with turf. Against a great slab of grey rock behind it the smoke from its chimney was invisible, and with a fire to warm them six or seven people could find room to play cards and cook another meal."[11] In chapter 23 ("Cluny's Cage"), the hideout is described vividly by David:

> Quite at the top, and just before the rocky face of the cliff sprang above the foliage, we found that strange house which was known in the country as "Cluny's Cage." The trunks of several trees had been wattled across, the intervals strengthened with stakes, and the ground behind this barricade levelled up with earth to make the floor. A tree, which grew out from the hillside, was the living centre-beam of the roof. The walls were of wattle and covered with moss. The whole house had something of an egg shape; and it half hung, half stood in that steep, hillside thicket, like a wasp's nest in a green hawthorn.
>
> Within, it was large enough to shelter five or six persons with some comfort. A projection of the cliff had been cunningly employed to be the fireplace; and the smoke rising against the face of the rock, and being not dissimilar in colour, readily escaped notice from below.

Of course, Cluny tells David about his past association with the bonnie prince:

> All the while Cluny entertained us with stories of Prince Charlie's stay in the Cage, giving us the very words of the speakers, and rising from his place to show us where they stood. By these, I gathered the Prince was a gracious, spirited boy, like the son of a race of polite kings, but not so wise as Solomon. I gathered, too, that while he was in the Cage, he was often drunk; so the fault that has since, by all accounts, made such a wreck of him, had even begun to show itself.
>
> We were no sooner done eating than Cluny brought out an old, thumbed, greasy pack of cards, such as you may find in a mean inn; and his eyes brightened in his face as he proposed that we should fall to playing.

Stevenson's attention to historical detail is displayed throughout this chapter, but David's speculative comments about Prince Charles's drinking problem, which became evident some years later, suggest that he did not burden himself with precise factual information. In his 1886 dedication to Charles Baxter, he clearly outlines his intent:

> If you ever read this tale, you will likely ask yourself more questions than I should care to answer: as for instance how the Appin murder has come to fall in the year 1751, how the Torran rocks have crept so near to Earraid, or why the printed trial is silent as to all that touches David Balfour. These

are nuts beyond my ability to crack. But if you tried me on the point of Alan's guilt or innocence, I think I could defend the reading of the text. To this day you will find the tradition of Appin clear in Alan's favour. If you inquire, you may even hear that the descendants of "the other man" who fired the shot are in the country to this day. But that other man's name, inquire as you please, you shall not hear; for the Highlander values a secret for itself and for the congenial exercise of keeping it. I might go on for long to justify one point and own another indefensible; it is more honest to confess at once how little I am touched by the desire of accuracy. This is no furniture for the scholar's library, but a book for the winter evening school-room when the tasks are over and the hour for bed draws near; and honest Alan, who was a grim old fire-eater in his day, has in this new avatar no more desperate purpose than to steal some young gentleman's attention from his Ovid, carry him awhile into the Highlands and the last century, and pack him to bed with some engaging images to mingle with his dreams.

In chapter nine ("The Man with the Belt of Gold"), Alan Breck reveals: "I am one of those honest gentlemen that were in trouble about the years forty-five and six; and (to be still quite plain with ye) if I got into the hands of any of the red-coated gentry, it's like it would go hard with me. Now, sir, I was for France; and there was a French ship cruising here to pick me up; but she gave us the go-by in the fog."

In chapter 12 ("I Hear of the 'Red Fox'"), Alan mentions "the Butcher Cumberland" and tells David that after enlisting in the English army, he "deserted to the right side at Preston Pans—and that's some comfort." These references reveal specific facts that Stevenson worked into the story, including the exploits of the historical Allan Breck Stewart, who along with his kinsman James Stewart served in the Jacobite army during 1745–46.

In 1747 Allan Breck fled to France but returned to Scotland in December 1749. In May 1751 he again sailed to France. In the meantime, James Stewart, having made his peace with the Hanoverian government, remained in Appin to manage the Ardshiel estate. (His half brother, Charles Stewart, laird of Ardshiel, had fled to France after the '45 [the 1745 Rebellion].) On Hogmanay, December 31, 1751, James and other local Highlanders met and drank with Colin Roy Campbell of Glenure, crown factor (land agent) of Ardshiel, the Cameron estates of Callert, and part of Lochiel, in a tavern at Kintalline (Kentallen). In February 1752 Allan arrived in Edinburgh and in March was back in Appin, speaking "wildly of Glenure to Dugald Maccoll and others."[12] (Evidently, Campbell's canine sobriquet was uttered publicly by Allan during a boastful drinking spree a few weeks before the murder. After purchasing two pecks of meal for a pauper, Allan told the man that he would receive better if he could procure the skin of the Red Fox.)

In late March or early April 1752 Campbell obtained a Precept of Removing against five tenants of Ardshiel. On April 3 James Stewart rode to Edinburgh, where he obtained an injunction from Lord Dun, a solicitor who practiced before the Court of Session. On May 5 the bill was rejected by Lord Haining, and Campbell was given the authority to evict the tenants, an act to be enforced by May 15.

On the evening of May 8 Allan lodged with James's son, Charles, at Fasnacloich. While Campbell was in Maryburgh (Fort William) on May 11, Allan traveled to Acharn and borrowed some of James's clothing. Two days later he was in Ballachulish, where he spent the night.

At noon on May 14 James was in Acharn when Allan left Ballachulish House to go fishing. Between 5:00 and 6:00 P.M. Colin Campbell was murdered at Lettermore. As the gloaming fell, James's servants hid two guns under thatch while Allan was seen on a hillside by Ballachulish House. At 3:00 A.M. the following morning Allan woke the MacDonald chief, the laird of Glencoe, at Carnoch and bade him farewell. In the evening members of James's household hid Allan's French uniform and concealed guns and four swords on the nearby moor.

On the morning of May 17 a warrant for James's arrest was signed in Edinburgh. That evening Allan met with Alexander Stewart ("Sandy Bane"), one of James's messengers, at Koalisnacoan (Caolasnacon), where he collected his clothes and some money before departing for Arlarich. On May 22 members of the family were questioned by the sheriff, and the guns were discovered on the moor the following day. An examination of James, who had been in prison since May 19, began on June 2, but the warrant was not announced formally until July 6. Later in July Allan's borrowed black coat with yellow metal buttons (the silver-buttoned coat mentioned by David Balfour at several points in *Kidnapped* refers to Allan's French coat) and powder horn were found in the cleft of a rock at Koalisnacoan. (He was last seen in Invernahadden, Rannoch, in late May.)

On August 21 criminal letters were served on James in prison and, a few days later, on Allan—in absentia—at Acharn and Inverary, the seat of the Campbell clan. From 6:00 A.M. on September 21 until 7:00 A.M. on September 24 the trial of James Stewart was held, uninterrupted, at Inverary. Arraigned before a judge, who was also the clan chief, and a jury composed of 11 Campbells and four others, James "was sacrificed to political considerations."[13] (In a cruel twist of fate, the defense preparation of James and his counsel was cut drastically short when Britain, according to an act passed the previous year, adopted the Gregorian calendar in early September. One provision required that 11 days be excised from that month, with the second day being followed by the fourteenth.)

Convicted of hatching the murder plot, James was sentenced to death at 11:00 A.M. on September 25 and hanged at Cnap Chaolis Mhic Pharuig, Ballachulish, on November 8. Prior to his execution he was allowed to read a farewell speech, in which he emphatically protested his innocence. According to custom, his body was displayed publicly for more than two years. In January 1755 the corpse fell from the gibbet but was rechained soon after; Appin folklore suggests that, as the skeleton decayed, John Stewart of Ballachulish collected the bones and buried them in a coffin containing the remains of Margaret Stewart, James's wife, at Keil Chapel, where the grave may still be viewed.

As Stevenson mentions in the dedication to *Kidnapped*, his version of the Appin murder takes place in 1751, at least a year before the actual incident. The episode is witnessed by David Balfour, but the lad does not see who fires the fatal shot. (This device remains consistent with the historical evidence, since no one has identified the actual murderer.)[14] Like the historical Allan Breck, Stevenson's character (whose first name, Alan, is spelled with only one "l") is seen on a hill (in this instance, in the Wood of Lettermore), but by David, who questions him before taking flight in the heather. (In *The Killing of the Red Fox* [1989], the most recent and best account of the murder and trial, Irish author Seamus Carney identifies Allan Breck as the murderer and James Stewart's son, Allan Oig, and an anonymous accomplice as his co-conspirators. James, Carney asserts, was probably innocent of complicity.)

As part of his research, Stevenson read printed accounts of the murder, including a transcript of the trial that his father purchased in Inverness. David Daiches claims that his inclusion of this episode "introduces a sombre note quite different from anything in *Treasure Island* and from anything in the early part of *Kidnapped*. Structurally, the function ... is to provide David with a motive for his attempt to prove James Stewart's innocence on his return to Edinburgh."[15]

In chapter 12 ("I Hear of the Red Fox"), Alan tells David of the eviction of the Ardshiel tenants and the appointment of Colin Campbell:

"And who is the Red Fox?" I asked, daunted, but still curious.

"Who is he?" cried Alan. "Well, and I'll tell you that. When the men of the clans were broken at Culloden and the good cause went down, and the horses rode over the fetlocks in the best blood of the north, Ardshiel had to flee like a poor deer upon the mountains—he and his lady and his bairns. A sair job we had of it before we got him shipped; and while he still lay in the heather, the English rogues, that couldnae come at his life, were striking at his rights. They stripped him of his powers; they stripped him of his lands; they plucked the weapons from the hands of the clansmen, that had borne arms for thirty centuries; ay, and the very clothes off their backs—so that it's now a sin to wear a tartan plaid, and a man may be cast into a gaol if he has but a kilt about his legs. One thing they couldnae kill. That was the love the clansmen bore their chief. These guineas are the proof of it. And now, in there steps a man, a Campbell, red-headed Colin of Glenure—"

"Is that him you call the Red Fox?" said I.

"Will ye bring me his brush?" cries Alan, fiercely. "Ay, that's the man. In he steps, and gets papers from King George, to be so-called factor on the lands of Appin. And at first he sings small, and is hail-fellow-well-met with Sheamus—

that's James of the Glens, my chieftain's agent. But by-and-by, that came to his ears that I have just told you; how the poor commons of Appin, the farmers and the crofters and the boumen, were wringing their very plaids to get a second rent, and send it over-seas for Ardshiel and his poor bairns. What was it ye called it, when I told ye?"

"I called it noble, Alan," said I.

"And you little better than a common Whig!" cries Alan. "But when it came to Colin Roy, the black Campbell blood in him ran wild. He sat gnashing his teeth at the wine table. What! should a Stewart get a bite of bread, and him not be able to prevent it? Ah! Red Fox, if ever I hold you at a gun's end, the Lord will have pity on ye!"

Here Stevenson foreshadows the murder and reveals Alan's hatred of Colin Campbell. A short time later Alan reiterates his threat after David erroneously assumes that the Appin problem has been solved:

"Well, Alan," said I, "that is a strange story, and a fine one, too. And Whig as I may be, I am glad the man was beaten."

"Him beaten?" echoed Alan. "It's little ye ken of Campbells, and less of the Red Fox. Him beaten? No; nor will he be, till his blood's on the hillside! But if the day comes, David man, that I can find time and leisure for a bit of hunting, there grows not enough heather in all Scotland to hide him from my vengeance!"

By using the story of Ardshiel and the Red Fox, Stevenson begins to draw the social distinctions that separate Alan and David. When David points out that "Christianity forbids revenge," Alan leads the discussion into a more political direction:

"Ay," said he, "it's well seen it was a Campbell taught ye! It would be a convenient world for them and their sort, if there was no such thing as a lad and a gun behind a heather bush! But that's nothing to the point. This is what he did."

"Ay," said I, "come to that."

"Well, David," said he, "since he couldnae be rid of the royal commons by fair means, he swore he would be rid of them by foul. Ardshiel was to starve: that was the thing he aimed at. And since them that fed him in his exile wouldnae be brought out—right or wrong, he would drive them out. Therefore he sent lawyers, and papers, and red-coats to stand at his back. And the kindly folk of that country must all pack and tramp, every father's son out of his father's house, and out of the place where he was bred and fed, and played when he was a callant. And who are to succeed them? Bare-leggit beggars! King George is to whistle for his rents; he maun dow with less; he can spread his butter thinner: what cares Red Colin? If he can hurt Ardshiel, he has his wish; if he can pluck the meat from my chieftain's table, and the bit toys out of the children's hands, he will gang hame singing to Glenure!"

"Let me have a word," said I. "Be sure, if they take less rents, be sure Government has a finger in the pie. It's not this Campbell's fault, man—it's his orders. And if ye killed this Colin to-morrow, what better would ye be? There would be another factor in his shoes, as fast as spur can drive."

"Ye're a good lad in a fight," said Alan; "but, man! ye have Whig blood in ye!"

When David reaches the Western Highlands, he witnesses the poverty and hardship experienced by the tenantry. Chapter 16 ("The Lad with the Silver Button: Across Morven") contains one of Stevenson's most striking passages:

> There is a regular ferry from Torosay to Kinlochaline on the mainland. Both shores of the Sound are in the country of the strong clan of the Macleans, and the people that passed the ferry with me were almost all of that clan. The skipper of the boat, on the other hand, was called Neil Roy Macrob; and since Macrob was one of the names of Alan's clansmen, and Alan himself had sent me to that ferry, I was eager to come to private speech of Neil Roy.
>
> In the crowded boat this was of course impossible, and the passage was a very slow affair. There was no wind, and as the boat was wretchedly equipped, we could pull but two oars on one side, and one on the other. The men gave way, however, with a good will, the passengers taking spells to help them, and the whole company giving the time in Gaelic boat-songs. And what with the songs, and the sea-air, and the good-nature and spirit of all concerned, and the bright weather, the passage was a pretty thing to have seen.
>
> But there was one melancholy part. In the mouth of Loch Aline we found a great sea-going ship at anchor; and this I supposed at first to be one of the King's cruisers which were kept along that coast, both summer and winter, to prevent communication with the French. As we got a little nearer, it became plain she was a ship of merchandise; and what still more puzzled me, not only her decks, but the sea-beach also, were quite black with people, and skiffs were continually plying to and fro between them. Yet nearer, and there began to come to our ears a great sound of mourning, the people on board and those on the shore crying and lamenting one to another so as to pierce the heart.
>
> Then I understood this was an emigrant ship bound for the American colonies.
>
> We put the ferry-boat alongside, and the exiles leaned over the bulwarks, weeping and reaching out their hands to my fellow-passengers, among whom they counted some near friends. How long this might have gone on I do not know, for they seemed to have no sense of time: but at last the captain of the ship, who seemed near beside himself (and no great wonder) in the midst of this crying and confusion, came to the side and begged us to depart.
>
> Thereupon Neil sheered off; and the chief singer in our boat struck into a melancholy air, which was presently taken up by the emigrants and their friends upon the beach, so that it sounded from all sides like a lament for the dying. I saw the tears run down the cheeks of the men and women in the boat, even as they bent at the oars; and the circumstances and the music of the song (which is called "Lochaber no more") were highly affecting even to myself.

Here Stevenson depicts the sorrow many people experienced when they were forced to immigrate to the New World. In the early 1750s the American colonies comprised a wild and woolly frontier, a land alien to Scots familiar with the organized lifestyle of the Highland clan. During one of the summer tours with his father, Stevenson had seen despondent Highlanders huddling onto an immigrant ship, and the memories of his own 1879 immigration remained clear. His description and structure in the above passage are equally impressive: he follows David's account of the dispirited scene with a terse, one-sentence paragraph that directly identifies the ship and its cargo. His juxtaposition of the passengers' tear-covered faces with "Lochaber No More," a song attributed to Allan Ramsay, is an example of how powerful literature can be. (This passage could provide a talented filmmaker with a vivid scene: no dialogue is necessary to convey the sad plight of these people. Stevenson's prose is a literary precursor of cinematic style in that it combines a visual image with a piece of background music.)

The contrast between Alan Breck's Highlander and David Balfour's Lowlander gives *Kidnapped* an edge that often motivates its adventure aspects. Although David supports Whig culture and ideology, he also considers the beliefs and values of others. After he is abducted he lies aboard the *Covenant,* pondering the lifestyle of his captors:

> Yet I had not been many days shut up with them before I began to be ashamed of my first judgment, when I had drawn away from them at the Ferry pier, as though they had been unclean beasts. No class of men is altogether bad, but each has its own faults and virtues. They were kind when it occurred to them, simple even beyond the simplicity of a country lad like me, and had some glimmerings of honesty.

David's comment about the virtues of all classes reflects Stevenson's attitude toward the lower class with whom he often identified. Stevenson's use of Balfour, his mother's family name, is another autobiographical element. Daiches suggests that the character "is the author's projection of himself into a carefully chosen past."[16]

The introduction of Alan Breck in chapter nine acquaints David (and the reader) with the social and political differences between the Jacobite rebel and the Whig youth. At several points in the novel Alan bursts into a Jacobite song, reinforcing, sometimes in Gaelic, his dedication to the Stewart cause. The romanticized portrait of Jacobitism celebrated in songs written after the '45 is an element that Stevenson flawlessly incorporates into the narrative—a manifestation of a tradition established 140 years earlier. Daiches writes: "The Jacobite movement brought a new surge of song to Scotland; some of it springing up anonymously, some adaptations of earlier popular songs, some, like Burns's, cunning imitations or completions of true folk song, some by minor versifiers who sometimes caught the genuine spark because of the kind of tradition which the aftermath of the Jacobite movement brought into being."[17]

Alan Breck's flights into song represent one of Stevenson's most accessible usages of traditional music. After the fight in the roundhouse Alan composes an original Gaelic ditty. David's translation, "in the king's English," runs thus:

> This is the song of the sword of Alan;

The smith made it,
The fire set it;
Now it shines in the hand of Alan Breck.

Their eyes were many and bright,
Swift were they to behold,
Many the hands they guided:
The sword was alone.

The dun deer troop over the hill,
They are many, the hill is one;
The dun deer vanish,
The hill remains.

Come to me from the hills of heather,
Come from the isles of the sea.
O far-beholding eagles,
Here is your meat.

David is quick to comment about Alan's singing:

> Now this song which he made (both words and music) in the hour of our victory, is something less than just to me, who stood beside him in the tussle. Mr. Shuan and five more were either killed outright or thoroughly disabled; but of these, two fell by my hand, the two that came by the skylight. Four more were hurt, and of that number, one (and he not the least important) got his hurt from me. So that, altogether, I did my fair share both of the killing and the wounding, and might have claimed a place in Alan's verses. But poets have to think upon their rhymes; and in good prose talk, Alan always did me more than justice.

In chapter 24 ("The Flight in the Heather: The Quarrel"), Alan whistles the melody of "Johnnie Cope," a Jacobite song that mocks the English general's frantic retreat from the Battle of Prestonpans; and his most elaborate musical performance occurs in chapter 25 ("In Balquhidder"), during his piping duel with Robin Oig. (The historical Robin Oig, whose name figured in testimony fabricated by his brother, James More Macgregor Drummond, to discredit James Stewart, was condemned for abducting, forcibly marrying, and raping Jean Kay, a rich Edinburgh widow; he was hanged in 1754.) When Alan asks the girl to locate a boat for their passage across the Forth in chapter 26 ("End of the Flight: We Pass the Forth"), he whistles a few bars of the Jacobite song "Charlie Is My Darling." But it is his final musical reference that greatly affects David:

> At first I proposed I should give him for a signal the "Bonnie House of Airlie," which was a favorite of mine; but he objected that as the piece was very commonly known, any ploughman might whistle it by accident; and taught me instead a little fragment of a Highland air, which has run in my head from that day until this, and will likely run in my head when I lie dying. Every time it comes to me, it takes me off to that last day of my uncertainty, with Alan sitting up in the bottom of the den, whistling and beating the measure with a finger, and the grey of the dawn coming on his face.

Alan and David's differing beliefs build to a climax in chapter 24. Since the story is narrated by David, the reader experiences Alan's behavior through his eyes: Highland attitudes are filtered through a Lowland sensibility. Calder notes: "The story takes David from a comprehensible Lowland world to a disordered Highland world; from an environment where familiar precepts of Church and State appear to operate satisfactorily to one where they are reversed."[18] David experiences disorder before he reaches the Highlands, however: His near-fatal stay with the treacherous Ebenezer gives him a taste of the confusion and danger he will encounter later. But Alan Breck and his world are a much stronger challenge: Toward the end of their flight, Alan's taunts of "Whigamore" and "Whiggie" begin to wear on the exhausted David's nerves. As the argument escalates, David describes his physical condition:

> I felt I could drag myself but little farther; pretty soon, I must lie down and die on these wet mountains like a sheep or a fox, and my bones must whiten there like the bones of a beast. My head was light perhaps; but I began to love the prospect, I began to glory in the thought of such a death, alone in the desert, with the wild eagles besieging my last moments. Alan would repent then, I thought; he would remember, when I was dead, how much he owed me, and the remembrance would be torture. So I went like a sick, silly, and bad-hearted schoolboy, feeding my anger against a fellow-man, when I would have been better on my knees, crying on God for mercy.

Barely able to overcome the "flushes of heat" and "spasms of shuddering," David strikes out at the sarcastic Alan, who again calls him "Whig": "'Mr. Stewart,' said I, in a voice that quivered like a fiddle-string, 'you are older than I am, and should know your manners. Do you think it either very wise or very witty to cast my politics in my teeth? I thought, where folk differed, it was the part of gentlemen to differ civilly; and if I did not, I may tell you I could find a better taunt than some of yours.'"

When Alan whistles "Johnnie Cope," David orders him to "henceforth speak civilly of my King and my good friends the Campbells." Alan insists that his status as a Stewart forbids such behavior, so David insults him: "'O!' says I, 'I ken ye bear a king's name. But you are to remember, since I have been in the Highlands, I have seen a good many of those that bear it; and the best I can say of them is this, that they would be none the worse of washing.'"

Continuing his insults, David draws his sword on the unsuspecting Highlander, who refuses to fight: "I cannae draw upon ye, David. It's fair murder." Realizing that their differences cannot be solved by argument or force, Alan helps David walk the remaining distance to Balquhidder. When the two characters part at the end of the novel, one of Stevenson's basic points is demonstrated clearly: Though Alan and David come from different cultures and their respective ideologies often are opposed, they overlook these differences and remain friends. Neither character alters his opinions, but each realizes that he has survived with the other's help. Calder writes:

> It is important that, before Alan and David meet, David should already have proved himself a survivor: he outwits his uncle, who is trying to kill him; he aids Alan before Alan is in a position to help him. This balance lies at the centre of the book. . . . It is tempting to see David and Alan as the obverse of each other, to see them reflecting

not only the division between Highland and Lowland, Jacobite and Whig, wilderness and civilisation, but the "war in the members," as Stevenson himself described it, that he felt was at the root of the Scottish psyche, and at the centre of himself.[19]

In his best moments Alan Breck is charming and courageous, but in his worst he is pompous and childish. However, unlike the split personalities of earlier Stevenson characters, Alan's behavior is more complex, a trait often demonstrated through his use of humor, sometimes in dangerous and desperate situations. His sense of humor acts as a bridge between good and evil, and it blurs the distinctions that separate these traits. This aspect links the fictional Alan Breck with the historical Bonnie Prince Charlie, who fell to jesting during his harrowing flight in the heather. Linklater has written of a joke Charles told his aide, Flora MacDonald, before they escaped to the Isle of Skye. Dressed in drag, Charles worried that he would not be able to defend himself:

> Under his petticoat Charles wanted to wear a pistol, but Flora objected. If he were to be searched, she said, the discovery of a pistol would give him away, to which he answered, "Indeed, Miss, if we shall happen with any that will go so narrowly to work in searching me as what you mean, they will certainly discover me at any rate." ... That Charles could be dressed-up as Betty Burke, and make a joke of any sort while his embittered enemies were closing in on him, throws a light of agreeable gaiety on his spirit.[20]

As to Alan and David's relationship, Calder concludes: "Alan does indeed become his friend, but they are totally separate people, and at the end of the book it is only appropriate that the two should go their separate ways."[21]

Many uninformed readers categorize *Kidnapped* as a "children's story" or "boys' adventure tale," but the historical aspects and the characterizations allow the novel to work on many levels. Robert Kiely has written:

> [M]uch that at first appears to be obscure local color makes better sense in the context of Scottish history. Nevertheless, it remains a fact that *Kidnapped* has continued to be popular with young readers who probably know almost nothing about clan warfare in eighteenth-century Scotland. This does not mean that the historical setting is not important in the novel, but that it remains peculiarly detachable from the action in the foreground. In reading *Kidnapped* a child can quite easily leave "the bulk of the book unrealized," but fix on the rest and live it.[22]

In *Kidnapped* Alan and David rely on a "bonny lass" for their successful escape across the Firth of Forth. While the former admits, "David, it is a very fine lass," the latter fears that they have implicated her in their dangerous situation. Although her appearance accounts for only a few pages in the novel, the (nameless) girl leaves a loose end in the story: what happens to her after she rows back to the shores of Fife? Several years after *Kidnapped* was published, Stevenson answered this question, as well as others pertaining to the fortunes of Alan and David, in

*Catriona*, his official sequel. In his 1892 dedication to Charles Baxter, he writes: "It is the fate of sequels to disappoint those who have waited for them; and my David, having been left to kick his heels for more than a lustre in the British Linen Company's office, must expect his late reappearance to be greeted with hoots, if not with missles."

*Catriona* begins as David Balfour collects a portion of his inheritance in Edinburgh. Soon after buying clothing that befits his new position, he attempts to prove the innocence of James Stewart but is prevented by Lord Advocate Prestongrange, whose political allegiance outweighs the administration of justice. On his way to the advocate's, David meets Catriona Drummond, a beautiful gray-eyed girl, whose father, James More Drummond, a Jacobite who fought with Alan Breck in the '45, has been arrested. Having chartered a ship bound for France, David visits Catriona, rendezvous with Alan at Gillane Sands, and is kidnapped after his friend departs.

David's captors, hired through a conspiracy involving Prestongrange, Simon Fraser, and James More, keep him imprisoned on Bass Rock until the fate of James Stewart has been determined. Upon his release David rushes to Inverary but is too late to aid Stewart; he then accepts Prestongrange's assistance and decides to study for the bar at Leyden in Holland. Tutored in the ways of gentlemanly life by Barbara Grant, Prestongrange's sister, David sails for Holland on the *Rose*. Catriona is also on board and plans to meet with her exiled father in Helvoetsluys.

When Catriona's guardians refuse to leave the ship during inclement weather, David assumes responsibility for the girl's welfare. At Leyden he acquires two rooms and introduces Catriona as his sister. After James More arrives, David explains their compromising situation, but More insists that he marry Catriona. She refuses the ultimatum and departs with More, while David remains to complete his studies.

During a visit from Alan Breck, David and his old friend walk and then ride to Dunkirk, where they plan to meet James More. David again asks for Catriona's hand, while Alan keeps a watchful eye on her father. Spying the English ship *Seahorse* in the harbor, David discovers More's plan to betray Alan. Enraged, Alan duels with More and escapes, taking David and Catriona with him.

The young lovers are married in Paris but visit the dying More before returning to Shaws in Scotland. In an epilogue David tells of their two children, Alan and Barbara, and a late-night visit from a Mr. Jamieson: "the name they know him by now in France is the Chevalier Stewart."

Originally titled "David Balfour: Memoirs of His Adventures at Home and Abroad," *Catriona* was written at Vailima, February 13–September 30, 1892. The novel was published, under its original title, as ten monthly installments in *Atalanta* 6 (December 1892–September 1893). On September 1, 1893, Cassell and Company published it in book form as *Catriona: A Sequel to "Kidnapped" Being*

*Memoirs of the Further Adventures of David Balfour at Home and Abroad.* The U.S. version, published simultaneously by Charles Scribner's Sons, appeared under the original title.

Though he had not seen his native land since 1887, Stevenson's memories remained vivid as he sat down to write in his South Seas home. Calder notes: "[T]housands of miles from his origins Stevenson produced a novel which contains his most detailed fictional exploration of his native city. ... Stevenson simply allows his sense of Edinburgh—not an Edinburgh that he knew, for he is writing of a time almost a century before he was born—to permeate the action and the personalities."[23] *Catriona* demonstrates Stevenson's continued interest in Scottish history and culture, but the tale also includes episodes set in Holland and France.

While *Kidnapped* is a well-integrated blend of adventure, geography, history, and psychology, the sequel is occasionally disjointed and confusing. Part 1 ("The Lord Advocate") centers on the aftermath of the Appin murder and David's thwarted attempt to prove James Stewart's innocence, but part 2 ("Father and Daughter") leaves history and politics behind in favor of an uneasy adolescent romance. While the novel fails to re-create the pacing and excitement of its predecessor, it does contain several intriguing adventure passages, interesting and colorful language, a striking Scots "bogy" tale, and strong political overtones.

Stevenson's use of the Appin murder creates some dramatic and structural problems. At the midpoint of the tale James Stewart has been hanged and David's efforts to save him no longer affect the action. Stevenson could have expanded the first part of the story, discarded the romance angle, and retained the title "David Balfour" (as his friend Henry James suggested), but, accounting for his occasional difficulty in sustaining longer narratives, he may have shifted to David's courtship of Catriona when he ran out of Appin material. Each section of the novel does have its merits, however.

For several reasons David is unable to save James Stewart. Most obviously, the Whig politics of King George, reinforced by Prestongrange's involvement, create an insurmountable obstacle. (The historical Lord Advocate, William Grant of Prestongrange, was Scotland's chief prosecutor, a powerful man who personally conducted the Campbell-Stewart case.) Whereas politics remain in the background of *Kidnapped,* they are at the forefront of *Catriona.* In chapter four ("Lord Advocate Prestongrange"), David learns the truth about Stewart's arrest:

> "My lord," I said, "I am as free of the charge of considering my own interests in this matter as your lordship. As God judges me, I have but one design, and that is to see justice executed and the innocent go clear. If in pursuit of that I come to fall under your lordship's displeasure, I must bear it as I may."
> 
> At this he rose from his chair, lit a second candle, and for a while gazed upon me steadily. I was surprised to see a great change of gravity fallen upon his face, and I

could have almost thought he was a little pale.

"You are either very simple, or extremely the reverse, and I see that I must deal with you more confidentially," says he. "This is a political case—ah, yes, Mr. Balfour! whether we like it or no, the case is political—and I tremble when I think what issues may depend from it. To a political case, I need scarce tell a young man of your education, we approach with very different thoughts from one which is criminal only.

Prestongrange's generalized description becomes more specific when David reveals that he will testify on behalf of James and Alan:

> "I am a man nursing with both hands the interests of this country," he replied, "and I press on you a political necessity. Patriotism is not always moral in the formal sense. You might be glad of it I think: it is your own protection; the facts are heavy against you; and if I am still trying to except you from a very dangerous place, it is in part of course because I am not insensible to your honesty in coming here; in part because of Pilrig's letter; but in part, and in chief part, because I regard in this matter my political duty first and my judical duty only second. For the same reason—I repeat it to you in the same frank words—I do not want your testimony."

This passage embodies one of Stevenson's most powerful literary themes and reflects his feelings about the way people behave in the face of society and state. Here he joins other historians and writers (and a large number of ordinary folk over the last two centuries) by suggesting that James Stewart was sacrificed to political considerations. Later, after David has been kidnapped to prevent his appearance at the trial, the lad again appeals to Prestongrange, who replies, "James is a dead man; his life is given and taken—bought (if you like better) and sold.... Blow high, blow low, there will be no pardon for James Stewart."

Prestongrange reveals that knowledge of his association with David would precipitate his downfall: If he had taken "the ready and plain path" and sent "Mr. David to his grave or to the gallows," his position would be secure. At this point David abandons his quest to prove James's innocence (an act that would have placed suspicion upon Alan) in favor of supporting Prestongrange (an act that conceals the involvement of Catriona's father).

Forced to withhold the truth, David must rationalize his actions. By supporting Prestongrange he "is inevitably absorbed into that world which is truly his" and "the world of Highland adventures, is by implication severely renounced."[24] In chapter 20 ("I Continue to Move in Good Society"), Stevenson's attitudes color David's assessment of James Stewart's execution:

> So there was the final upshot of my politics! Innocent men have perished before James, and are like to keep on perishing (in spite of all our wisdom) till the end of time. And till the end of time young folk (who are not yet used with the duplicity of life and men) will struggle as I did, and make heroical resolves, and take long risks; and the course of events will push them upon the one side and go on like a marching army. James was hanged; and here was I dwelling in

the house of Prestongrange, and grateful to him for his fatherly attention. He was hanged; and behold! when I met Mr. Simon in the causeway, I was fain to pull off my beaver to him like a good little boy before his dominie. He had been hanged by fraud and violence, and the world wagged along, and there was not a pennyweight of difference; and the villains of that horrid plot were decent, kind, respectable fathers of families, who went to kirk and took the sacrament!

The "Mr. Simon" referred to here is Simon Fraser, son of Simon Fraser, twelfth Lord Lovat (1677–1747), a Jacobite colonel in the '45 who acted as a double agent for King George. Before he was arrested and executed in 1747, the elder Fraser sat for William Hogarth, who captured his gargantuan visage in a famous etching. The younger Fraser also played both sides of the political fence and acted as advocate-depute, or counsel for the private prosecutors, in the Appin trial. Later he recruited ex-Jacobites for the French and Indian War, a move that led to the restoration of the Fraser estates in 1774. Stevenson first mentions him in chapter six ("Umquhile the Master of Lovat"), when the ambitious official with "the sharp voice and the fat face" accuses David of being a paid accomplice in the murder.

Stevenson also based James More on a historical figure, the James More Drummond mentioned above—another of Rob Roy MacGregor's roguish sons. Imprisoned for aiding his brother in the abduction of Jean Kay, More fabricated evidence against James Stewart in an attempt to gain a pardon, but he eventually escaped from Edinburgh Castle with the help of his daughter, who entered while dressed in cobbler's clothing. In chapter 18 ("The Tee'd Ball"), Stevenson's fictionalized account of the prison break appears in a letter written by Prestongrange's eldest daughter:

"Here is all the town bizzing with a fine piece of work," she writes, "and what would make the thing more noted (if it were only known) the malefactor is a protege of his lordship my papa. I am sure your heart is too much in your duty (if it were nothing else) to have forgotten Grey Eyes. What does she do, but get a broad hat with the flaps open, a long hairy-like man's greatcoat, and a big gravatt; kilt her coats up to Gude kens whaur, clap two pair of boot-hose upon her legs, take a pair of clouted brogues in her hand, and off to the Castle! Here she gives herself out to be a soutar in the employ of James More, and gets admitted to his cell, the lieutenant (who seems to have been full of pleasantry) making sport among his soldiers of the soutar's greatcoat. Presently they hear disputation and the sound of blows inside. Out flies the cobbler, his coat flying, the flaps of his hat beat about his face, and the lieutenant and his soldiers mock at him as he runs off. They laughed not so hearty the next time they had occasion to visit the cell and found nobody but a tall, pretty, grey-eyed lass in the female habit! As for the cobbler, he was 'over the hills ayont Dumblane,' and it's thought that poor Scotland will have to console herself without him. I drank Catriona's health this night in public. Indeed the whole town admires her; and I think the beaux would wear bits of her garters in their button-holes if they could only get them."

Alan Breck is less interesting in *Catriona*, but he provides some colorful and adventurous moments. At the end of *Kidnapped* the reader may suspect that Alan will leave Scotland shortly, but at the beginning of *Catriona* he still is awaiting passage to France. In dealing with the fates of Alan and James, Stevenson incorporates several historical events, including the trial at Inverary (though he dates it Thursday, September 21, 1751, exactly one year earlier than the actual event), the presentation of Alan's criminal summons at the cross of Inverary, and James's execution (dated November 8, 1751, also one year earlier than the actual incident). And he indirectly refers to the two-year display of James's corpse in chapter three ("I Go to Pilrig"):

> My way lay over Mouter's Hill, and through an end of a clachan on the braeside among fields. There was a whirr of looms in it went from house to house; bees hummed in the gardens, the neighbors that I saw at the doorsteps talked in a strange tongue; and I found out later that this was Picardy, a village where the French weavers wrought for the Linen Company. Here I got a fresh direction for Pilrig, my destination; and a little beyond, on the wayside, came by a gibbet and two men hanged in chains. They were dipped in tar, as the manner is; the wind span by them, the chains clattered, and the birds hung about the uncanny jumping-jacks and cried. The sight coming on me suddenly, like an illustration of my fears, I could scarce be done with examining it and drinking in discomfort. And as I thus turned and turned about the gibbet, what should I strike on, but a weird old wife, that sat behind a leg of it, and nodded, and talked aloud to herself with becks and courtesies.

Here Stevenson creates an unforgettable macabre image by combining an unsavory historical practice with brilliant description. David's viewing of the gibbet occurs just before his meeting with Prestongrange and effectively symbolizes his fear. When the old wife appears to read David's mind, Stevenson, in a beautifully written one-sentence paragraph, adds another haunting image: "The two chance shots that seemed to point at Alan and the daughter of James More, struck me hard; and I fled from the eldritch creature, casting her a baubee, which she continued to sit and play with under the moving shadows of the hanged."

The quarrel between David and Alan that distinguishes much of *Kidnapped* is nowhere evident in *Catriona*. Since both men are now hunted outlaws, their bond of friendship is strengthened by a common need. After his meeting with Prestongrange and Simon Fraser, David calls on Charles Stewart, the Highland Writer, one of Alan and James's kinsmen whom the boy has paid to locate a ship for their escape to France. (Stevenson based this character on the historical Charles Stewart, a Maryburgh notary. James sent a letter to him, requesting assistance, on the day Colin Campbell was murdered. The official's son, also a notary named Charles, had aided James in his efforts to forestall the evictions.) When Charles promises to defend his condemned relative, David seems preoccupied with another matter:

> "One thing more," said I. "Can I no see Alan?"
>
> He seemed boggled. "Hech, I would rather you wouldnae," said he. "But I can never deny that Alan is extremely keen of it, and is to lie this night by Silvermills on purpose. If you're sure that you're not followed, Mr. Balfour—but make sure of that—lie in a good place and watch your road for a clear hour before ye risk it. It would be a dreadful business if both you and him was to miscarry!"

When Alan reappears in chapter 29 ("We Meet in Dunkirk") the pace increases dramatically: His characteristic perception and humor motivate the story's more adventurous aspects. The rousing climax is precipitated by Alan, who encourages David's marriage proposal and then duels with James More and his henchmen. Several recurrent female characters also set *Catriona* apart from *Kidnapped*. Stevenson had felt that honest depictions of male-female relationships were made impossible by conventional morality, but by 1892 he "wanted to suggest something of sexual feeling."[25] However, he avoids explicitness by creating characters who are both young and inexperienced. Some literary scholars have faulted him for depicting Catriona as a stereotypical female who is childish, quick-tempered, and frail, but this criticism is unfair: the lass is very young and has led a sheltered life. David's attitudes toward Catriona may be unrealistic—he frequently feigns disinterest to protect her virtue—but he is exploring unknown territory which is protected rigidly by societal conventions.

Catriona's first appearance, early in chapter one ("A Beggar on Horseback"), is a striking passage:

> It chanced the girl turned suddenly about, so that I saw her face for the first time. There is no greater wonder than the way the face of a young woman fits in a man's mind, and stays there, and he could never tell you why; it just seems it was the thing he wanted. She had wonderful bright eyes like stars, and I daresay the eyes had a part in it; but what I remember the most clearly was the way her lips were a trifle open as she turned. And whatever was the cause, I stood there staring like a fool. On her side, as she had not known there was anyone so near, she looked at me a little longer, and perhaps with more surprise, than was entirely civil.

Here, Stevenson honestly captures how a man may feel when he is attracted to a woman's appearance: "he could never tell you why; it just seems it was the thing he wanted." Later, when Catriona dresses in men's clothing to free her father from the castle (an act that recalls the similar actions of Joanna Sedley in *The Black Arrow* and the Countess von Rosen in *Prince Otto*), she is more than a pretty image in the mind of a romantic lad.

Barbara Grant, Prestongrange's sister, is a very interesting, less stereotypical female character. David meets her in chapter five ("In the Advocate's House") when Prestongrange introduces the boy to his daughters, "the three handsomest young women (I suppose) in Scotland." But Miss Grant is more than beautiful: she is adept at music, poetry, women's and men's fashions, etiquette, and romance. She is knowledgeable about the ways of the world, while Catriona is essentially innocent. Though Catriona immediately appeals to David, Miss Grant gives him his first taste of physical passion; at the end of chapter 20 she embraces and kisses him "with the best will in the world."

The girl who aids David and Alan in *Kidnapped* reappears briefly; she is unnamed in the earlier novel, but David now reveals her identity. While making escape plans with Charles Stewart, he acknowledges: "'Then there's the lass Alison Hastie, in Limekilns,' said I. 'Her that helped Alan and me across the Forth. I was thinking if I could get her a good Sunday gown, such as she could wear with decency in her degree, it would be an ease to my conscience; for the mere truth is, we owe her our two lives.'" Later David and Miss Grant visit Alison Hastie, who gratefully thanks "the tautit laddie" for his "grand present." Left wondering about her fate at the end of *Kidnapped*, the reader now sees the lass in fine health.

The reappearances of Alan Breck and Alison Hastie help to tie up the loose ends of *Kidnapped*. However, the characterization of David Balfour is altered slightly. Whereas he appears politically unchanged at the conclusion of *Kidnapped*, his dedication to Whiggery and King George in *Catriona* is not as extreme: he seeks justice for two notorious Jacobites and makes perceptive comments about conventional society. One of his observations occurs when Miss Grant and Prestongrange's daughters accompany him to Hope Park:

> Young folk in a company are like to savage animals: they fall upon or scorn a stranger without civility, or I may say, humanity; and I am sure, if I had been among baboons, they would have shown me quite as much of both. Some of the advocates set up to be wits, and some of the soldiers to be rattles; and I could not tell which of these extremes annoyed me most. All had a manner of handling their swords and coat-skirts, for the which (in mere black envy) I could have kicked them from that park. I daresay, upon their side, they grudged me extremely the fine company in which I had arrived; and altogether I had soon fallen behind, and stepped stiffly in the rear of all that merriment with my own thoughts.

David has progressed beyond the open-minded Whig depicted in *Kidnapped*. He appears to have absorbed some of the beliefs of his Jacobite friend, just as Stevenson, writing in his Samoan home, allowed his current political experiences to affect the characterizations and the overall tone of the novel.

In general, Stevenson abandons the geographical detail of *Kidnapped* in favor of finely tuned dialogue: his knowledge of various dialects and speech patterns is demonstrated throughout. Instead of relying on detailed physical description, he often allows the characters to reveal their own identities. When passages (particularly those featuring Alan) incorporate the detailed topography of *Kidnapped*, the reader is able to experience Stevenson's vivid memories of his native heath. Chapter 15 ("Black Andie's Tale of Tod Lapraik"), set on Bass Rock near North Berwick, includes an eerie tale of a "bogie" told to David by one of the Highland captors. Here, Stevenson's use of the Scots language and his depiction of the Caledonian fascination with evil and the supernatural brilliantly recall the terrifying "Thrawn Janet."

## *Kidnapped* (Forum/Edison, 1917)

The only silent adaptation of *Kidnapped* has been described as "much more faithful to the novel than all of the subsequent versions."[26] Released in 1917 by Forum/Edison, this five-reel condensation was adapted by Sumner Williams and directed by Alan Crosland, who later helmed the John Barrymore vehicle *Don Juan* (1926) and the part-talking *The Jazz Singer* (1927), a film that invariably disappoints when viewed today.

The majority of the narrative focuses on David Balfour's (Raymond McKee) kidnapping and subsequent shipboard adventures. The fight in the roundhouse, featuring Alan Breck (Robert Cain) and members of Captain Hoseason's (Franklin Hanna) crew, is a dramatic and visual highlight. Much of the novel is ignored, due to the brief running time, but portions are rendered accurately. In the *Variety* review, "Jolo" comments: "The 'atmosphere' is so marvelously carried out in to photodramatic version of the immortal tale that the spectator feels like a participant. . . . Stevenson's tale has been as closely followed as it is possible for a picturization, in straightaway narrative form without resorting to flashbacks."[27] Considering that the novel proceeds in "straightaway narrative form" and contains no flashbacks, this film at least respects Stevenson on that level. Unfortunately, prints of this lone silent are not available for viewing, ranking it as a possible lost film.

## *Kidnapped* (20th Century–Fox, 1938)

Darryl F. Zanuck's 1938 production of *Kidnapped* is the earliest version known to exist. Unfortunately, this 90-minute Hollywood concoction features only a few scenes that recall material from the novel, and these are poorly acted and directed; even discounting its lack of faithfulness, it is a dismal excuse for entertainment. The screenplay by Sonya Levien, Eleanor Harris, Ernest Pascal, and Edwin Blum ignores history, geography, cultural traits, and other realities of the Scottish nation. Zanuck's Scotland is a badly disguised 20th Century–Fox backlot populated by Americans and English gibbering stilted pseudo–Scots dialogue.

The first historical error occurs just after the title credits. A prologue states, "Highland clans had twice rebelled against English rule," obviously referring to 1715 and 1745, but oblivious to the other rebellions of 1689, 1708, and 1719. After the title card "Scotland, 1747" appears, the opening scene fades in to show Alan Breck (Warner Baxter) leading a group of insurgent clansmen toward Edinburgh. This incident has nothing to do with the novel and is one of the most ahistorical moments in the film: the '45 was the last fateful gasp of organized rebellion in Scotland. By 1747 no Highlander in his right mind would have suggested raising the standard again.

Soon the Duke of Argyll (whose castle, inexplicably, is located in Edinburgh) signs a proclamation for the arrest of Alan Breck. Meanwhile, young David Balfour (Freddie Bartholomew) sits in the school of Dominie Campbell (Halliwell Hobbes), who delivers a propagandistic speech against Alan and his brand of "lawbreakers." After the lecture ends with "God save King George!" some of the students rush outside, yell "Long live Scotland!" and toss handfuls of mud at a copy of the proclamation which hangs on a nearby tree. David defends Campbell's position but gets a face full of mud in return; he briefly brawls with one of the lads but returns to school, where Campbell tells him of his father's death. The narrative then shifts to material from the novel as Campbell preaches about "abiding the law": "Don't rebel against the world you have to live in." However, Stevenson's tale again disappears in the midst of hokum.

The ancestral house of Shaws is eliminated and, instead, David is told to deliver his late father's letter to his Uncle Ebenezer in Edinburgh. During his two-day walk to the city from his home (it is never referred to as Essendean), David passes through a village where he speaks to a man (E. E. Clive) who delivers a respectable Lowland brogue as he asks for snuff. Moments later the populace runs in terror as an ornate carriage pulls into the village square. The door opens and out steps the feared tax collector, the Red Fox (Leonard Mudie). (The character is not identified as Colin Roy Campbell, and the screenplay fails to provide any characterization other than calling him the Red Fox.) Why the factor (who removed the Ardshiel tenants) is terrorizing the Lowlands (Lothian, in particular) is never explained, but then, most of the events take place in, or near, Edinburgh! This contrivance is followed by yet another when Alan Breck and a group of his clansmen arrive. One of them, referred to as Jamie (James Stewart, no doubt [Ralph Forbes]), quickly shoots the Red Fox and, before he can retreat, is observed by David. (A tight close-up of David's face is followed by a point of view long shot of Jamie, who waits an inordinate length of time after he fires the gun. The action is stilted, and no one could possibly identify a person at such a distance. This is one of many spatial distortions created by director Alfred Werker and editor Allen McNeil.)

As an insurance policy, Alan whisks David aboard his horse and rides into the countryside, where he sternly reprimands Jamie for the murder. Claiming that he only wanted to steal the tax collector's money bag (is this Alan Breck or Robin Hood?), Alan suggests that Jamie flee to Glasgow, where he may board a ship bound for the

American colonies. When Jamie refuses to leave his sweetheart, Jean MacDonald (Arleen Whelan), who lives near Glencoe, Alan commands him to take her along on the voyage.

Later in the evening Alan and David camp out on a moor near Edinburgh. Having ordered Jamie to Glasgow, Alan plans to call on Miss MacDonald the next day. Exposing another of the screenwriters' blunders, Alan tells David that they will reach Glencoe (a location 100 miles to the northwest) by 12 noon! (Apparently, the writers forgot their earlier comment about David's *two-day* walk to Edinburgh from Dominie Campbell's school.) In the novel Alan and David's journey from Cluny's Cage on Ben Alder (a location slightly northeast of Glencoe, but roughly equidistant to Edinburgh) lasts several days. The characters have a horse in the film, but how a hunted fugitive like Alan Breck could speed through the countryside without being identified is never explained.

As the next scene fades in, the viewer is transported miraculously to the MacDonald home at Glencoe. This location is as close as the film gets to Alan's home turf of Appin, although the name is never referred to. In fact, Glencoe is the only Highland locale mentioned in the film, which matters little, since the MacDonald home looks more like a cabin on the American plains than a croft in the Western Highlands. After Neil MacDonald (Nigel Bruce, in one of the film's more convincing performances) arrives, he introduces his daughter, Jeanie, to Alan and David.

One of the film's most ludicrous attributes, Jeanie MacDonald was created solely as a token Hollywood love interest: The character bears no resemblance to anyone in the novel, not even Alison Hastie. Arleen Whelan debuted in this film, after Zanuck discovered her giving manicures in a Los Angeles beauty salon! Her stilted and emotionless performance is so bad that it makes one wonder how Gregg Toland could stand photographing her scenes. She speaks with an omnipresent Southwestern American accent and delivers garbled lines on more than one occasion. Even her soft-focus close-ups, which require little or no acting talent, are an embarrassment.

Alan disguises Jeanie as his wife and adopts the name "Mr. Mac-Kenzie" for their return journey to Lothian. (Why Alan decides to head back to Edinburgh, instead of delivering Jeanie to Jamie in Glasgow, is another inexplicable plot turn, but of course she has to hang around long enough to fall in love with him.) The trip lasts only a few seconds and is made even worse by the singing of Whelan, Baxter, and Bartholomew, who sit atop a cart while a noticeable backscreen churns away behind them. When they come across a redcoat patrol on the road, all three break into a lackluster version of "Loch Lomond." (The only Scottish folksong used to any extent in the soundtrack, its familiar melody [called "Red is the Rose" in Ireland] is repeated many times in various incarnations.) Alan fools the English soldiers (unbelievably, Baxter, who has used his own Ohio accent up to this point, now attempts a Highland brogue), and

***Kidnapped*** (1938). Ebenezer Balfour (Miles Mander) attempts to skirt the accusations of David Balfour (Freddie Bartholomew), in 20th Century–Fox's travesty of Stevenson's brilliant novel.

before heading to who knows where, he drops David on a road near Ebenezer's home (referred to as "Castle Balfour").

Material from the early stages of the novel begins to appear 36 minutes into the film. As David glances up at the kind of matte-painted Gothic castle that no Scotsman ever lived in, two commoners advise him to retreat. "Blood built that house—and blood stopped the building of it!" a witchy old woman tells him. Just as the unwary lad approaches the grounds, the film segues from adventure to horror: lightning and thunder crash around the battlements as David knocks on the door. Some moments later the door creaks open to reveal the face of Ebenezer Balfour (Miles Mander).

After ordering David to leave, the grizzled old man agrees to read the letter and offers him a bowl of pasty porridge and a few swallows of ale. (In one of the film's few effective touches, Ebenezer pours ale from his glass into David's, glances into David's glass, and then pours some of it back again.)

David eats his meal and examines a small book which includes the dedication, "To my brother Ebenezer on his fifth birthday." Soon Ebenezer informs David that he may sleep in a room "at the top of the stair-tower." A simplified version of a passage from the novel, this scene includes David's near-fatal climb up the crumbling stairs. (The film does not feature an exterior stair-tower, but a flight of stairs in the middle of the castle.)

David regains his footing and rushes down to accuse his uncle of stealing the estate from his father, the elder brother and rightful heir. Before the scene fades, the enraged lad forcefully calls Ebenezer a "yellow-belly" (a slang term previously used by Alan in several scenes but of course never spoken by Stevenson's character).

The next scene opens in Edinburgh, where David plans to call on Mr. Rankeiller (the spelling is changed in the film). While walking on the docks, Ebenezer blurts out a vague approximation of the story about David's mother and the younger brother's claim upon the inheritance. Soon Captain Hoseason (Reginald Owen) appears and with the aid of Ransome (Donald Haines), entices David aboard his ship. Here the lure is not a bowl of punch and a passage to the town pier near Rankeiller's house, but a piece of sugar cane! Below deck with Ransome, David spots his laughing uncle through a port window as the ship weighs anchor and pulls away from the dock. The literary Ransome's interesting personality and untimely death are ignored, and after a few vicious words from Hoseason, David is given a job as assistant cabin boy.

After a journey through the North Sea, past the Shetlands, and around to the Hebrides (lasting a few seconds of screen time, in which a black line moves across a map), Hoseason docks in the Western Highlands, where he is scheduled to pick up two passengers. In the film's most absurd contrivance, Alan and Jeanie, aka Mr. and Mrs. MacKenzie, step on board! Mr. MacKenzie announces that he and his wife wish to sail to Glasgow, and the ship departs. Even if the viewer has not read *Kidnapped* (and realized that the film has transformed Stevenson's prose into disjointed nonsense), he may notice the geographical ignorance displayed by the screenwriters. In this scene the ship docks at Invercraig (the map indicates a spot about 60 miles northwest of Glasgow). In the earlier scene described above, Alan and David ride the 100-plus miles from Edinburgh to Glencoe in a matter of hours, but now Alan wishes to *sail* 60 miles down the coast to Glasgow!

The entire incident aboard Hoseason's ship has nothing to do with Stevenson's brilliant tale of Alan Breck's failed escape to France and the subsequent shipwreck in which Alan and David are forced to fend for themselves in wild and stormy country. Instead, the film offers a preposterous situation that any alert eight-year-old should refuse to accept; with four screenwriters working on the script, at least one could have realized that the concept of Hoseason kidnapping David in the east, and then sailing around Scotland to pick up Alan Breck in the west just to throw the two characters back together again is an insult to the viewer.

None of Stevenson's material is used in the shipboard scenes, and only two consequential events affect David: He pretends he doesn't recognize Alan when he serves dinner, and he is threatened with a cat-o'-nine-tails by Hoseason, who demands to know MacKenzie's real identity. Alan later confronts David on deck.

Delivering dialogue only a hack screenwriter could fashion, he charges, "You told him I was Alan Breck!" as one of the crewmen listens nearby. Instantaneously, a fight breaks out between Alan and the entire crew, while David, aiding the inept, stereotypically female Jeanie, lowers a skiff into the sea. Alan escapes unscathed, jumps into the boat, and off they float into a lap dissolve. The next image shows all three characters, safe and sound, standing on a nearby shore as Hoseason's ship apparently sails toward Glasgow.

The sea voyage is a superfluous event, for Davis is never left alone to suffer and persevere, Alan is never in any real danger, and the tidal island of Earraid is neither seen nor mentioned. As the lad and the fugitive stand on the beach, Alan emotionally asks, "Shall we become true friends, to trust and help each other always?" Apparently, the screenwriters felt that this one line could substitute for Alan and David's eight-chapter trek in the novel.

Now that they have eliminated all differences of opinion (their one brief "political" discussion after the Red Fox's death substitutes for the novel's lengthy argument), the two "true friends" set a trap for Ebenezer in Rankeiller's office. Evidently, Alan walked into Edinburgh, unseen and unmolested, and then sat down to discuss the situation with the lawyer (none of these events are shown). Upon his arrival, Ebenezer is shocked to find that David has claimed the inheritance. (This outcome is another fabrication, as David does not become Laird of Shaws until Ebenezer's death in part 2 of *Catriona*. However, David refers to himself as the Laird of Balfour throughout the film.)

Ebenezer leaves Rankeiller's office and ducks into a tavern to meet Captain Hoseason himself! Somehow, the salty old sea dog has managed to sail back to Edinburgh in time to tell Ebenezer that Alan Breck, masquerading as MacKenzie, has arrived too. In a quickly edited sequence a group of redcoats arrest Alan and carry him off to jail. Jeanie offers to wring a confession from Jamie, but she is told that he has sailed for the colonies. Tried by a 15-man jury in Edinburgh, Alan is sentenced to hang— a verdict that incites the clan chiefs to rally in the courtroom.

Later the chiefs meet with the Duke of Argyll. Claiming that another rebellion will occur if Alan is hanged, one of them boasts that his group speaks "for all the clans in Scotland" and that "every Highlander supports Alan Breck." (None of the Highland rebellions benefited from clan solidarity, but historical and political impossibilities are this film's leitmotifs.)

As the gallows is built, Jeanie visits Alan in his cell (a syrupy "Loch Lomond" again swells on the soundtrack). Afterward she prays in a nearby chapel while David sneaks into Argyll's home. Before the wily lad approaches the duke, an underling announces that the hangman has "either turned-coat or (been) abducted by the clans." A bit of *Catriona* is tossed in here, as David speaks of Alan's innocence; he fails to strike a deal (in exchange for Alan's life, he will keep the fugitive out of Scotland) but appeals to Argyll's sense of patriotism. Convincing the duke that Alan and he are fighting for the same cause, the desperate lad declares, "You're so alike ... in your love for Scotland." Pondering the statement, Argyll's King George heart is melted instantly.

Prior to the execution, Argyll visits Alan in his cell. If Alan will make a speech to the people, asking them to avoid bloodshed, the duke says, his gesture will be repaid with new tax reforms for the people. When Alan's plea immediately quells all notions of revolt, Argyll commutes his sentence to exile and announces the film's final historical inaccuracy: "We are a people united for the first time." Wildly shouting, the crowd burns the gallows as God answers Jeanie's prayer.

Now that everything ends happily ever after for the characters and all of Great Britain, a brief epilogue shows Alan and Jeanie (who, by all appearances, are married) boarding a ship bound for France, while David, the new Laird of Balfour, swaggers back into Edinburgh. One last flourish of "Loch Lomond" accompanies him as "The End" mercifully appears.

A failure on almost every level, this version of *Kidnapped* vies with MGM's *Trouble for Two* as the worst Stevenson adaptation of Hollywood's golden age. (MGM's *Treasure Island* and *Dr. Jekyll and Mr. Hyde* [1941] benefit by comparison.) Screenwriters Levien, Harris, Pascal, and Blum should have realized that adapting a popular and widely read novel demands at least a modicum of faithfulness to balance 90 minutes of Hollywood hokum. Two of their worst sins are the depiction of James Stewart as a cold-hearted, murderous thug, and their inability to incorporate even a simplistic political subtext. (Since the terms Jacobite and Whig are never mentioned, the characters may as well be cowboys and Indians or cops and robbers.) Even worse, however, is the studio's (perhaps Zanuck's) inclusion in both the opening and closing credits of an 1887 sketch by American sculptor Augustus Saint-Gaudens which depicts Stevenson writing in bed. (Saint-Gaudens created a famous bas-relief medallion from his sketches; an enlarged copy hangs in St. Giles Cathedral, Edinburgh.)

During the film's original release in May 1938, most well-read critics gave no quarter to *Kidnapped*. Frank S. Nugent wrote:

> If it's a flagrant case of literary vandalism you're after, may we recommend the Twentieth Century–Fox version of Robert Louis Stevenson's "Kidnapped," which opened at the Roxy yesterday. There is just enough Stevenson left in the piece to give the producer technical immunity from prosecution for fraud. Morally he stands guilty of entrusting a beloved adventure tale to a quartet of movie-conscious hacks who have zealously tossed in a measure of romance, a dash of glamor and a gill of historic importance. ... Evidently they decided to have nothing to do with Stevenson after the midway mark and tacked on a brand new episode about Alan Breck's capture, his trial and his winning of Scottish freedom. It might well be a passable adventure tale stamped with Hollywood's seal of self-approval. But it is about as Scottish as a hot dog stand and about

as much Stevenson as Darryl Zanuck permitted it to be. We intend to read the book again and forget that the film version ever happened. Mr. Zanuck should read it, too.[28]

In an August 1938 review, the acerbic Graham Greene literally annihilated the film:

> They called it *Kidnapped*: that is what I resent most as Mr. Warner Baxter, with a gleam of those too prominent and even teeth of his, waves a sword among the sepia-tinted Highlanders and shouts—in an American accent—"On to Edinburgh," and Master Freddie Bartholomew, with his Fauntleroy features and Never-Never-Land voice, makes winsome remarks—to Jennie [sic] Macdonald. And who in Tusitala's name is she? She is the girl who loves Alan Breck (that is what they call Warner Baxter), and Breck is trying to restore her to her betrothed, James Stewart, whom he wants to ship out of the country because he has killed the Red Fox.... Do you catch strange echoes of a story you once read? There *was* a Red Fox, and a James Stewart, though neither killed the other, and as for Alan trying to get anyone but himself out of the country or loving a girl....
>
> I doubt if the summer will show a worse film than *Kidnapped*; the only fun you are likely to get from it is speculation, speculation on the astonishing ignorance of filmmakers who claim to know what the public wants. The public will certainly not want this *Kidnapped*, where all the adventures which made them read the book have been omitted. Is it even honest to bring in Stevenson's name? (There should be a society for protecting authors who may be out of copyright.) Apart from the title and the circumstances of David Balfour's kidnapping, there is practically nothing of the original story here—you will find no trace of the magnificent battle in the round house or of the flight in the heather. Alan Breck's character, with its cunning vanity, is not so much altered as lost—he is only an American voice shouting over and over again, "To Edinburgh" or "The Redcoats": he is only a set of teeth like those exhibited in the windows of cheap dentists. A little of David's priggishness is left (it comes easily to the actor), but none of that "darkness of despair and a sort of anger against all the world" which when we were young dragged us with him through the heather. All that remains is an odd echo—familiar names misused, lines out of the book misplaced, trivial incidents, which any competent scenarist would have cut, dragged in to take the place of—everything. All the great filmic scenes of battle and flight are eliminated, and a tiny incident without bearing on the story, like that of the minister who asked David for snuff, is retained. As for the girl with her great dewy eyes, her dimples and her tartan and her kissing mouth, she represents, I suppose, the love interest—as if there wasn't love enough in the original story to wither these wistful caresses and misunderstandings and virginal pursuits, the love of an exile for a particular scene and of a sick man for a life of action he couldn't lead.[29]

## *Kidnapped* (Monogram, 1948)

Recognized as one of Hollywood's better poverty-row studios, Monogram churned out low-budget westerns, mysteries, and horror programmers from 1930 to 1953, when the corporate name was

*Kidnapped* (1938). Two Californian Highlanders: Jeanie MacDonald (former manicurist Arleen Whelan) and Alan Breck (Warner Baxter, whose idea of Highland culture is singing "Loch Lomond" with a Columbus, Ohio, accent).

changed to Allied Artists Pictures. During the 1940s one of the studio's most prolific directors was William Beaudine, who began his film career in 1909 as a property boy for D. W. Griffith. Often derided as "One Shot" Beaudine, he is remembered primarily for a quartet of dreadful Bela Lugosi films (*The Ape Man* [1943], *Ghosts on the Loose* [1943], *Voodoo Man* [1944], and the outrageous *Bela Lugosi Meets a Brooklyn Gorilla* [1952]), four of Monogram's 17 Charlie Chan pictures (1947–48), and a series of East Side Kids/Bowery Boys outings in the 1940s and early 1950s. He also helmed two of the most notoriously bad horror westerns ever made, *Billy the Kid Vs. Dracula* and *Jesse James Meets Frankenstein's Daughter*, in 1966.

Amid a career of mediocre programmers and cinematic disgraces, Beaudine also directed a few quality films, including the Mary Pickford classics *Little Annie Rooney* (1925) and *Sparrows* (1926). One of his best sound films, a medium-budget version of *Kidnapped* released by Monogram in 1948, is an occasionally striking and generally well-acted production (although it does borrow a few devices from the 1938 20th Century–Fox version).

The strains of Scott's "Bonny Dundee" accompany the film's titles, which give the 19-year-old Roddy McDowall top billing and an associate producer's credit. The first scene then fades in to reveal a written prologue: "Scotland—1751: Bonnie Prince Charlie has lost his Scottish throne and fled to France but his Jacobite supporters in the Highlands still fan the smouldering fires of resistance to England's King George II and his Whig followers in the Lowlands." Although Bonnie Prince Charlie never had a Scottish throne to lose, the mention of the two opposing political parties is a noticeable improvement over the 1938 film's omission of specific historical references.

The prologue is followed by a graphic of the novel's first page and a voice-over narration of the initial paragraph. As the action begins, W. Scott Darling's screenplay and Beaudine's brisk direction offer a condensed version of *Kidnapped,* with snippets of *Catriona* added at various points. Darling's economical adaptation strays from the novel in the later scenes but also hits some high points along the way. Much of the dialogue is Stevenson's, as are most of the characters: Jennet (here spelled Janet) Clouston (Janet Murdoch), the old crone who tells David to avoid the house of Shaws; Ebenezer Balfour (realistically portrayed by Houseley Stevenson); Ransome, the cabin boy (Bobby Anderson, in one of the film's more Americanized performances); Captain Hoseason (Roland Winters, who was then making his final Charlie Chan films for Monogram); Mr. Shuan (a very nasty Jeff Corey); Colin Roy Campbell (Olaf Hytten); and, of course, Alan Breck (Irish-born Dan O'Herlihy, who at least could claim a Celtic origin).

Using a respectable Lowland brogue, Roddy McDowall creates a believable and appealing David Balfour. The first scene opens with David mentioning both Essendean and the house of Shaws as he treks toward his meeting with Ebenezer. As daylight beams down upon the house, Beaudine and cinematographer William Sickner resist the horror film trappings that invade the 1938 production. Inside, Ebenezer reads Alexander's letter (shown in close-up) and offers David a tower room for the night. (Again, Stevenson's suspenseful stair-tower passage is condensed. This sequence is one of several in the film that mimics the 1938 release, suggesting that Beaudine may have screened it before production began.) David escapes death (perhaps a bit too easily) and returns to surprise Ebenezer, who faints before revealing the truth about Alexander and the inheritance.

The next scene is a lightning-paced visualization of chapter six ("What Befell at the Queen's Ferry"). After Ebenezer concludes his brief meeting with Hoseason, David walks into the captain's office and is kidnapped immediately. Chapters seven ("I Go to Sea in the Brig 'Covenant' of Dysart") and eight ("The Round-House") are also abridged. After Ransome's lifeless body is laid upon his bunk, David is promoted to the rank of cabin boy. "He brought me a dirty pannikin!" the inebriated Shuan roars as David enters the roundhouse. The drunkard attempts to hit the lad with a rum bottle, but Hoseason knocks Shuan unconscious.

Alan Breck's first appearance is a concise paraphrase of Stevenson's prose. First seen rowing toward the *Covenant* in a skiff, Alan and a companion—believing that they are approaching a French ship—are capsized by a violent collision; though his comrade drowns, Alan manages to climb aboard. (Here the soundtrack includes an effective orchestration of "O'er the Sea to Skye," the beautiful Jacobite air commemorating Bonnie Prince Charlie's escape to the Isle of Skye.)

A great deal of Stevenson's dialogue is featured during David's first meeting with Alan. After Hoseason leaves them alone in the roundhouse, they argue about Jacobite and Whig politics before the famous battle begins. As Alan duels his way onto the deck, David jumps into the sea. The film's first major contrivance occurs here, when the scene fades out before the *Covenant* supposedly founders on the Torran Rocks. This low-budget avoidance of the wreck leads to the next scene, in which two Highlanders discover David lying on a shore near Appin. As the men rouse him, they speak of Alan Breck's whereabouts and, miraculously, finish the discussion that Alan had begun in the roundhouse! (Here Darling's screenplay becomes too "economical" as he replaces Stevenson's plot development with larger doses of fabricated material.)

The Appin murder occurs within a few minutes of David's shipwreck. As the Highlanders escort the lad into a village, a woman (Mary Gordon) informs them that the Red Fox has paid a call. The next scene depicts David's meeting with Colin Campbell and his three redcoat companions on a nearby road. When Campbell is shot dead, David spots the murderer and chases him up a hill; the redcoats follow, but David is pulled into a thicket by Alan, who swears that he is innocent. Though he claims to have seen the murderer, he adds, "I forgot what he looked like."

At this point the novel is abandoned for a romantic subplot which integrates small portions of *Catriona* with material from the 1938 film. American accents abound, particularly when David enters an inn on Loch Rannoch, located east of Appin, and is met by a young woman (Sue England). "You're a Lowlander ... and you're gentry," the girl remarks in a very American manner. "What's a Lowlander doing on a lonely road in the *Hee*lands, in times like these?" She introduces herself as Aileen Fairlie ("ferlie" is a Scots word meaning "wonder" or "marvel"), claims to know all about the murder, and expresses pleasure over the Red Fox's death. (Here the breakneck pace of the film gives no indication of how much time has passed since the murder occurred.)

When a small group of redcoats arrives, Aileen tells David to hide in her father's barn; kneeling down to milk a cow, she stiltedly sings "Bonny Dundee" and assures them that she has seen no fugitives. The soldiers leave, Alan Breck enters, and after he discusses the '45 and his current situation with Aileen's father (Alex Frazer), the girl introduces herself as "a true Jacobite." Moments later the old man runs out to inform the redcoats, but Aileen transports Alan and David across the loch. (Here Alison Hastie's heroic deed is moved into the Highlands, where the bad acting of Sue England detracts from several stunning location shots.)

The next scene, presumably set in the upper Lowlands, features a duel between Alan and David, and commentary by Aileen, who has tagged along as the lad's love interest. However, her presence does not interfere with a well-acted argument in which some of Stevenson's dialogue is highlighted (Alan's "Whiggie" references and claim that it would be "fair murder" to fight with David; and David's complaint that Alan has "cast my politics in my teeth"). When the disgusted Jacobite leaves the two young lovers to fend for themselves, David locates a nearby inn and introduces Aileen as his sister (another *Catriona* reference). Much to David's chagrin, Captain Hoseason is lodging there also! (This contrivance also recalls the 1938 film.)

Hoseason confronts David in the dining room and explains that he is heading back to Edinburgh to inform Ebenezer of the shipwreck. David offers him a bribe, but the captain replies by making a pass at Aileen. A duel commences, but Alan calmly walks down the stairs and saves David's skin. (No previous hint of Alan's whereabouts prepares the viewer for his heroic entrance.) Hoseason's prospects look dim until his entire crew, including the evil Shuan, saunters through the front door! A full-scale brawl occurs (perhaps Darling felt that the earlier roundhouse duel needed to be completed here), but the resourceful Alan locks all of the cutthroats in a store room and hitches a ride on a friendly local's hay cart. "Alan, you arrived just in the nick of time!" David cheers.

As the next scene fades in, Alan, David, and Aileen are describing their adventures to Mr. Rankeillor (Erskine Sanford). David speaks to the lawyer in Latin and learns that he has been cleared of any participation in the Appin murder. Conveniently, James Stewart has confessed to the crime. (This purely fictional plot turn detracts from the screenplay's earlier historical and literary accuracy.) The humbuggery keeps piling up when Hoseason appears again, this time at the house of Shaws. Arriving ahead of the rest, the wily captain attempts to extort more money from the fearful Ebenezer. "Hide in the tower room. You can escape by the stairs, if need be," the old man tells Hoseason as someone raps on the door.

The scene cuts to the exterior of the house, and Ebenezer, brandishing a blunderbuss, opens the window above the front door. In the yard below Alan enacts the ruse detailed in chapter 29 ("I Come into My Kingdom") while the others hide in the bushes. After the details are worked out, Aileen—the American Highlander—again blunders her way through a Scots phrase: "It's a *braw nicht*, Mr. Balfour."

Back inside, Ebenezer is menaced by the indestructible Hoseason, who draws his sword. The two men clamber up the stairs as they clumsily thrust and parry, but neither is triumphant, and they quickly fall to their deaths. Gazing upon the lifeless bodies, David remarks, "The fulfillment of Janet Clouston's curse." Here the film's heavily contrived second half climaxes in thoroughly insipid fashion.

A brief epilogue depicts Alan rowing out to a French ship while David and Aileen wave from the shore. One last arrangement of "Bonny Dundee" swells on the soundtrack as "The End" appears.

Although a few snippets of the flight in the heather are featured in this adaptation, the references to *Catriona* interfere with the plot and the relationship between Alan and David. Overall, material adapted from the novel outweighs the fabrications, but Darling's screenplay does not allow for sufficient plot development or the proper dramatic atmosphere. Entire chapters from the novel are either eliminated or represented by terse and ambiguous sequences.

Convincing location shots evoke the grandeur of certain sections of Scotland, and they are edited effectively into Beaudine and Sickner's basic visual style. But the highest honors must go to Roddy McDowall for his sensitive portrayal of David Balfour. Often saddled with stilted dialogue and little dramatic inspiration, the young actor rises above the material to evoke the complex personality of Stevenson's characterization. He displays courageous qualities, but his David is also naive, timid, and confused at times—a characterization that recalls some of the traits he created for young Huw Morgan in the John Ford–directed *How Green Was My Valley* (1941). Edward J. Kay's musical score is also a highlight, particularly in the scenes featuring Jacobite and other period melodies.

Incredibly, the *Variety* review of "Brog." describes the film as "telling its story with a too leisurely pace that keeps things at a walk for 81 minutes."[30] Perhaps if that writer had authored the script or edited the final print, even more literary material would have been eliminated. Admittedly, the action scenes (particularly the duels) are amateurish and unexciting, and the inclusion of the bland Aileen Fairlie character hampers the flow of the narrative, but the general pace of the film is fast and selective.

## *Kidnapped* (Walt Disney, 1960)

Although 20th Century–Fox and Monogram had advertised their films as "Robert Louis Stevenson's *Kidnapped*," Walt Disney's 1960 release was the first to deserve such a heading. Containing none of the scenery-chewing melodramatics of *Treasure Island* (1950), *Kidnapped* is the better of Disney's two Stevenson adaptations and an entertaining film in its own right.

During preproduction Disney screened the 1938 and 1948 releases, noting their weaknesses and deviations from the novel. In an interesting move, Walt Disney selected London-born filmmaker Robert Stevenson to write and direct the most faithful visualization that his budget would allow. Disney's publicity department issued an article titled "*Kidnapped* Author and Its Director Have More in Common Than Name" to suggest that both Robert Stevensons had experienced similar lifestyles: "The two Stevensons share the same young-in-heart approach to all facets of life; the same vivid memory of their own childhood;

the same stimulating and lively imagination which colors their creative work; the same inherent love of change and adaptability to strange surroundings."³¹

Disney may have believed that this paragraph would sell tickets, but Robert Stevenson did not need such hype to attract filmgoers. Educated at Cambridge, he began writing screenplays in 1930; by 1932 he was directing films for UFA in Germany and Gainsborough in England, and in 1936 he wrote and directed the classic fantasy film *The Man Who Changed His Mind*, starring Boris Karloff and Anna Lee, for Gaumont-British. In 1939 he signed a contract with David O. Selznick and soon became noted for his technical prowess and elegant visual style. He went on to direct several Hollywood films during the golden age, including *Tom Brown's Schooldays* (1940), Universal's remake of Fannie Hurst's *Back Street* (1941), and an adaptation of Charlotte Brontë's *Jane Eyre* (1944) starring Joan Fontaine, Orson Welles, and Henry Daniell. In 1957 he directed the Revolutionary War tale, *Johnny Tremain,* for Disney, and for the next 20 years helmed many of the studio's major box-office hits, including *Old Yeller* (1957), *Darby O'Gill and the Little People* (1959), *The Absent-Minded Professor* (1961), *Son of Flubber* (1963), *Mary Poppins* (1964), *That Darn Cat* (1964), *Blackbeard's Ghost* (1968), and *The Love Bug* (1969).

While Robert Stevenson was working on the *Kidnapped* screenplay, Walt Disney searched for the actual sites depicted in the novel; his decision to base the production in Great Britain gave the cast and crew the luxury of a faithful script and the proper dramatic and geographic atmosphere. In early 1959 shooting began at London's Pinewood Studios, where all of the interior scenes and special-effects sequences were completed. In April relevant cast members and 85 technicians trekked to Scotland, where exterior scenes were shot at historic locations.

From Ardgour equipment was carried by pack ponies to Lettermore Wood, where the murder of Colin Campbell was re-created upon the original site. Other scenes were shot at Ganavan Sands, Loch Nell, Easdale, Glen Nevis, Creagon, Onich Falls, Oban, and Ballachulish. One of the film's most powerful images is a beautifully composed long shot of Glencoe, where Alan (Peter Finch) and David (James MacArthur) stop for a brief rest.

The narrative follows the novel very closely, covering every incident except David's experiences on Earraid (this material is replaced by David's meeting with a sinister Highlander) and Alison Hastie's heroic effort on the Forth (instead, Alan's hoodwinking of an old woman allows them to cross the guarded bridge at Stirling). The flight in the heather is abridged, but well represented by sections lifted verbatim from the novel. Most importantly, there is no female love interest to slow the pace and interrupt the adventurous and political aspects of the story; other than the old crone at Stirling, Jennet Clouston is the only woman who appears.

All major characters depicted in the film resemble their literary

*Kidnapped* (1960). Original advertisement for Walt Disney's faithful, well-written adaptation shot on location in Scotland.

counterparts. Robert Stevenson's screenplay and Disney's casting work hand in hand to present careful re-creations that are both exciting and restrained. After a brief casting session in Hollywood, Disney selected the majority of his actors while at Pinewood. As Captain Hoseason, London-born Bernard Lee creates a character who is both self-serving and conscientious, while a young Peter O'Toole, born in Connemara, Ireland, turns in a brief but memorable performance as Robin Oig MacGregor. Scottish actors in the cast include Shake-

*Kidnapped* (1960). A publicity still depicting Alan Breck (Peter Finch), Mr. Shuan (Niall MacGinnis), David Balfour (James MacArthur), and Captain Hoseason (Bernard Lee) on board the *Covenant*. Posing together, the actors give no indication of the violent conflicts that separate their characters in the film.

spearean-trained John Laurie as Ebenezer Balfour, 81-year-old Finlay Currie as fearless Cluny MacPherson (Laurie and Currie also appear in Disney's *Treasure Island*), Andrew Cruikshank as a pompous and painted Colin Roy Campbell, Alex MacKenzie as the ferryman who escorts David to Appin, and Duncan MacRae as the murderous Highlander.

As David Balfour, 22-year-old

James MacArthur is too American at times, but he does give an acceptable performance. The adopted son of screenwriter-director Charles MacArthur (1895–1956) and actress Helen Hayes (1900–93), he debuted in RKO-Radio's *The Young Stranger* in 1957 before signing a contract with Disney the following year. Prior to *Kidnapped*, he starred in *The Light in the Forest* (1958) and *Third Man on the Mountain* (1959). After appearing in *Swiss Family Robinson* (1960), MacArthur acted in films for several Hollywood studios, but he is best known for his portrayal of Danny "Dano" Williams in the television series "Hawaii Five-0" (1968–79).

As Alan Breck, Peter Finch is outstanding, giving *Kidnapped* a performance equal to those of Fredric March in *Dr. Jekyll and Mr. Hyde*, Boris Karloff in *The Body Snatcher*, and Charlton Heston in *Treasure Island*. Born William Mitchell on September 28, 1916, in London, Finch lived in Australia from the age of ten and in 1935 began acting on the legitimate stage. He appeared in Australian films from 1936 to 1948 and then moved to London, as a protégé of Laurence Olivier, the following year. During the 1950s he became one of Great Britain's top stars and won the British Film Academy (BFA) best actor award four times. His riveting performance in *Network* (1976) earned him an Academy Award, but before he could be presented it he died of a massive heart attack during the film's promotional campaign in early 1977.

Before *Kidnapped* was released on March 25, 1960, Finch called Alan Breck "a role of tremendous power and by far the most exciting thing I've ever done." He commented:

> When I first read the *Kidnapped* script, I thought Alan Breck was an interesting character well within my range. When I read it again I saw the underlying traits and character quirks in the man and began to have my doubts. This wasn't going to be so easy after all.
>
> Breck is really a good fellow at heart, loyal to his cause, a good fighter, brave, quick-tempered, kind hearted—but he has a diabolical weakness for cards and he is tremendously boastful.[32]

To prepare himself for the role, Finch, aided by dialect adviser John Breslin, worked for six weeks to acquire a passable Highland brogue. He then left for Scotland, where he spent three weeks in the Western Highlands familiarizing himself with the geography and customs.

Finch perfectly captures Alan's personality traits, particularly his resourcefulness, intelligence in battle, and tempered bravado. While Warner Baxter and Dan O'Herlihy merely add some animation to a cardboard cutout of the character, Finch's interpretation brings Alan Breck to cinematic life. In the scenes set aboard the *Covenant*, he precisely and realistically conveys entire dialogue passages from the novel. When he describes his hatred for the Campbells, the battle at Culloden, and the activities of the Red Fox, the film captures the powerful drama of Stevenson's prose.

Finch is particularly good during the battle in the roundhouse. As in the novel, Alan plans all of his

*Kidnapped* (1960). Donald Dhu MacLaren (Abe Barker) suggests that Alan Breck (Peter Finch) and Robin Oig MacGregor (Peter O'Toole) settle their differences with the Highland bagpipes. One of the novel's most memorable passages, the pipe duel is re-created faithfully in the film.

strategy beforehand: with David positioned at the window, he stands in front of the open door to await his enemies. The inexperienced lad expresses concern, but Alan replies, "Ye see, I have but one face; but so long as that door is open and my face to it, the best part of my enemies will be in front of me, where I would aye wish to find them." After the battle is won, Alan gives David one of the silver buttons from his French greatcoat (making this film the first to include this symbol of Alan's friendship).

The scene in Cluny's Cage (called Cluny's "house" here) is a condensed version of chapter 23, which focuses on Alan's weakness for gambling. Bonnie Prince Charlie is not mentioned, but Cluny does pour a few drams before toasting "to the restoration of our own true king." Shortly after this celebration, David retires for the night, claiming that gambling is a poor pastime for gentlemen. Some time later Alan awakens him to ask for a loan, which is then lost to Cluny. Stevenson's passage describing David's unwillingness to accept charity money from the old Highland chief is presented admirably. The flight in the heather is abridged, but the political argument is emphasized. When the exhausted David loses his temper and draws his sword, Alan refuses to fight. Too ill to continue, David collapses at Alan's feet.

The next scene opens at the home of Donald Dhu MacLaren (Abe Barker), where David is convalescing. This sequence, featuring Alan's meeting with Robin Oig, is a dramatic highlight; when an argument escalates into armed conflict, Donald suggests that the two men prove their mettle with the Highland bagpipes. Alan takes the instrument in hand and swaggers around the room as he plays "The White Cockade," but his bravado ends when Robin skirls into a superior performance. Both Finch and O'Toole play the scene perfectly, with the latter (in one of his first screen appearances) playing the pipes in a very relaxed and effortless style. When Alan becomes visibly irritated, Robin then mimics the former's swaggering march. The inclusion of this scene adds an important element to the film's depiction of Alan Breck: At the outset of the duel he displays his usual boastful confidence, but after Robin begins to play, this facade melts away. (Another first for this film is the depiction of Alan's musical abilities.)

The scene at Stirling Bridge is well played by Finch as Alan offers the old crone money for her pipe, tobacco, and tinderbox. Lighting the bowl, he casually walks halfway across the bridge, where he stops to survey the Forth; David passes behind him and they both cross undisturbed as the sentries discuss the rewards which have been offered for their capture!

One of the most faithful scenes follows, in which David discusses his adventures with Rankeillor (English-born, multitalented Miles Malleson, who speaks with an impeccable Lowland brogue). Unlike earlier adaptations, in which the befuddled Ebenezer describes his brother's forfeiture of the estate, Rankeillor recounts the tale here. As in the novel, David describes his plan to the lawyer before they walk to the house of Shaws, where Alan tricks Ebenezer into confessing.

As David (now Laird of Shaws) and Alan bid each other farewell in the final scene, the film alters Stevenson's ending. Though the two men are not hampered by the presence of other characters (as they are in earlier adaptations), Alan prepares to board a French ship that lies in the Forth. Apparently, Robert Stevenson chose not to worry about the price on Alan's head (the ship is clearly anchored in open water) or David's uncertainty about his feelings for his Jacobite friend. James Stewart is mentioned (David asks Colin Campbell about the home of "James of the Glens"), but his part in the Appin incident is omitted: During their flight Alan and David do not visit James's home or cite his name. When Alan and David part, the former is free to go where he pleases and the latter has received his entire inheritance. However, since no references to *Catriona* appear in the film, this denouement is perfectly acceptable; it deviates from *Kidnapped*'s ambiguous conclusion but does not mar the film itself. (While Stevenson always had planned to write a sequel to *Kidnapped*, Walt Disney apparently did not wish to produce a cinematic continuation—and he never did.)

Technically, the film could be

better. Paul Beeson's cinematography is generally very good, but some of the scenes fail to take advantage of the Scottish locations that Disney and his crew worked so hard to find. Other than the magnificent shot at Glencoe and a few long shots of lochs and mountains during the redcoat chase, the visual style is marred by an overabundance of close-ups. During most of the Highland scenes, the viewer gets to see very little of the geographic detail that distinguishes the novel, and the picturesque grandeur of the area often is lost. Disney must be given high marks for taking the production to Scotland, but it is unfortunate that Robert Stevenson and Beeson failed to create a better mise-en-scène. The scenes set aboard the *Covenant* are also very cramped, and the miniatures and backscreen projection effects do nothing to improve the claustrophobic atmosphere.

As in many other Disney films, the mood often is dependent upon music. Cedric Thorpe Davie's thunderous and syrupy score, conducted by Muir Mathieson, contains very little traditional material, but "The White Cockade," a tune commemorating the white rosette worn by the Jacobite army during the '45, can be heard in several scenes.

An interesting component is Disney's subtle inclusion of his own moral message. In the novel David thinks about the men he has killed during the battle in the roundhouse but is interested primarily in matching Alan's prowess in combat. By contrast, Disney's David expresses a feeling of dismay after he kills a man. In a contemporary review, critic Arthur Knight praised the film because it "takes a forthright stand against killing, drinking and gambling without ever being mealy-mouthed or self-conscious about it."[33] Although Knight is correct in assessing Disney's position, *Kidnapped* would be a very different story without killing, drinking, and gambling. Throughout the novel Stevenson maintains his admirable ambiguity toward these practices, which were primary elements in much of the history and culture of Scotland in 1751.

Ironically, the qualities that make Disney's *Kidnapped* a good Stevenson adaptation actually kept patrons away from the box office. While most British critics praised the film for its fidelity to the novel, many American reviewers disliked it for the same reason. After viewing a February 12, 1960, preview at the studio, *Variety*'s "Powe." faulted the locations for paying off "too richly, with accents as thick as Scottish oatmeal."[34] Perhaps this ethnocentric critic would have preferred seeing Warner Baxter back in the Alan Breck role! However, the review may explain the poor audience turnout:

> A good deal of the plot revolves around the resistance by the Scots to the Hanoverian kings, and the Scots' devotion to the Stuarts. This part of history is apt to be pretty dim to most Americans (and possibly a good many Britons) and since the speech of the film is a commendable effort at consistency in speaking with the Highland burr, a good many of the fine points are altogether lost on the American ear.[35]

*Kidnapped* (1960). Walt Disney confers with members of his crew and cast, including James MacArthur, Peter Finch and John Laurie (in makeup as Ebenezer Balfour) at London's Pinewood Studios.

## *Kidnapped* (Omnibus–American International, 1971)

In 1968 an adaptation of *Kidnapped,* starring Thomas Weisberger as Alan Breck and Werner Kanitz as David Balfour, was produced in East Germany. Three years later an ambitious British version, combining material from both *Kidnapped* and *Catriona,* received good reviews on both sides of the Atlantic.

Directed by Delbert Mann, Omnibus's *Kidnapped* focuses on the political underpinnings of the novels. Screenwriter Jack Pulman chose to situate David Balfour's (Lawrence Douglas) trek to the house of Shaws in 1746, while the Jacobites were experiencing the last stages of their doomed uprising. After meeting Ebenezer (Donald Pleasence), David is kidnapped by Hoseason (Jack Hawkins), who rescues Alan Breck (Michael Caine) from the sea. Fleeing from Culloden, Breck assumes that the ship will transport him to France, where he plans to collect arms and men for another rebellion. After a furious battle Alan and David escape from Hoseason's men (the ship is not wrecked) and head for the home of James Stewart (Jack Watson). Here David is charmed by Stewart's daughter, Catriona (Vivien Heilbron), who accompanies them after redcoat leader Mungo Campbell (Terry Richards) is murdered. David and Alan leave Catriona with Cluny (Freddie

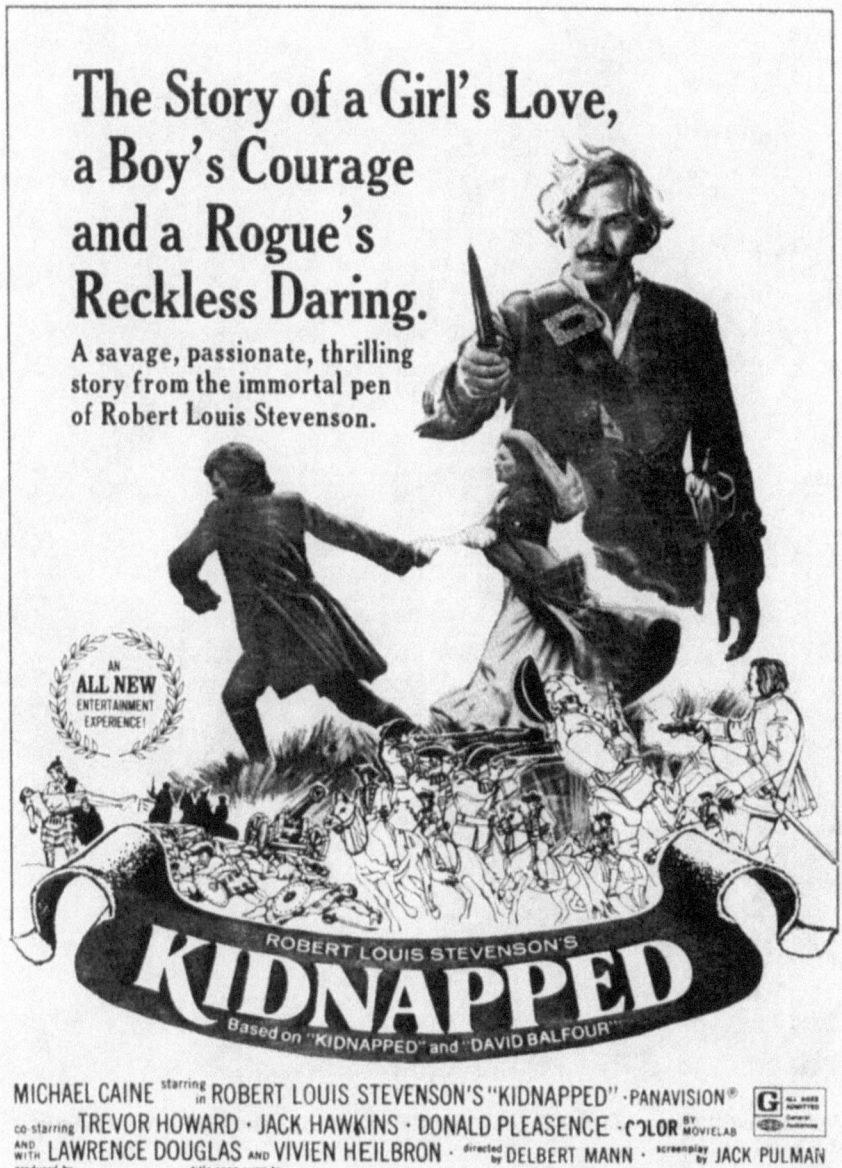

*Kidnapped* (1971). Original advertisement for Omnibus' integrative adaptation which spotlights the political elements of *Kidnapped* and *Catriona*.

*Kidnapped* (1971). Alan Breck (Michael Caine), during the harrowing flight in the heather.

Jones) before walking to Edinburgh, where the young woman later reveals that her wounded father is being held for the Campbell murder. Aided by Charles Stewart (Gordon Jackson), they force Ebenezer to grant David's inheritance, a portion of which will be used to transport Alan to France. David then meets with Lord Advocate Grant (Trevor Howard) and asks for permission to appear as a witness at James Stewart's trial. Grant refuses, claiming that political stability is more important than justice, and David and Alan barely escape from a redcoat troop. Catriona then meets with Alan and persuades him to forego another rebellion in favor of stopping the execution of her father. When Alan willfully surrenders to the redcoats, James is released and Catriona and David are free to marry.

Although the film, at 100 minutes, is a condensation of the two novels, it faithfully visualizes several key episodes from both. Shot on location in the Western Highlands, the well-paced narrative is enhanced by the atmospheric cinematography of Paul Beeson (who improved upon his compositions for the 1960 Disney version) and a first-rate cast of Scottish and English actors. Making his film debut, Lawrence Douglas, at 23, looks too old for his role but delivers a convincing interpretation of David. Educated at the Royal College of Dramatic Art in Glasgow, he portrayed Stevenson in "Heather on Fire," a Scottish television drama, and Robert Burns in a stage play before accepting the *Kidnapped* assignment. Trevor Howard, Jack Hawkins, and Freddie Jones all lend distinction to their roles, and Vivien Heilbron (another 23-year-old Scot making her film debut) is voluptuous and strong as the cinema's only (albeit altered) Catriona.

Michael Caine's Alan Breck is the highlight of the film, a dedicated Jacobite who abandons his cause to save a kinsman's life. A powerful variation on Stevenson's original character, Alan provides a link between David's personal quest and the battle against King George's oppression of the Highland people. At least one critic claimed that Mann and Pulman's emphasis on the political subplot was prompted by contemporary concerns, including the Vietnam War. (This observation is supported by the American International pressbook, which refers to the Jacobite campaigns as guerrilla wars.)[36] The final scene, showing Alan walking through the gates of Edinburgh Castle, is augmented by Caine's admirable performance and Mann and Beeson's compositions, one of which shows the political martyr pausing to glance toward the Highlands.

In an essay published in 1983, W. M. von Zharen claims that the film is superior because it "is far more rebellious and political than the two novels."[37] While von Zharen accurately interprets some of the film's elements, he criticizes Stevenson's work because it does not place enough emphasis upon strictly political concerns (a tendency that many socially oriented film scholars demonstrate). One reading of Stevenson's *Kidnapped* dedication makes his purpose clear. Apparently unbeknownst to von Zharen, *Catriona* is a novel that places great emphasis upon the political ramifications of the Colin Campbell murder.

While the Omnibus production is technically impressive, the political focus alters history (Alan's deliverance of James Stewart, for example) and simplifies or eliminates equally important components. Pulman integrated many of *Kidnapped*'s major episodes, but the only principal elements from *Catriona* are David's intention to testify at James Stewart's trial (the appearance of the lord advocate is a nice touch) and his romantic interest in the young woman. Von Zharen concludes: "If successful film adaptation means tight construction that omits little from the original text, then *Kidnapped* is an utter failure. However, if success depends on selecting ideas and essence from a novel with the intent of capturing its spirit and intended direction, then *Kidnapped* has met its goal."[38] Without question, this version of *Kidnapped* is one of the better films adapted from a Stevenson work. The screenplay does not faithfully reproduce both novels from which it sprang, but Mann and Pulman's approach is interesting and innovative, an interpretation that differs admirably from the entertaining Disney production of the previous decade. The fact that there are three passable versions of *Kidnapped* makes it the most successfully adapted Stevenson work.

## *Kidnapped* on Television

In 1949 the Canadian Broadcasting Corporation aired the first television production of "Kidnapped," an abridged version adapted by Andrew Allan. Over the next seven years the CBC aired three more adaptations: an abridged 1951 production for the "Fun with Books" program, a 1952 serial version, and a 1956 six-part "For the Children" serial.

The BBC also produced a "Kidnapped" adaptation in 1956. Three years before he was selected to portray Ebenezer Balfour in the Disney feature film, John Laurie played the character in this small-screen version.

In 1975 New Zealand Television broadcast a feature-length animated adaptation; and in 1980 BBC Scotland aired two versions: a feature produced by Tom Cotter and a serial.

## • FOURTEEN •

# The Twa Corbies: *The Master of Ballantrae* (1889)

> *Twa Duries in Durrisdeer,*
> *Ane to tie and ane to ride,*
> *An ill day for the groom*
> *And a waur day for the bride.*
> —Rhyme, attributed to Thomas of Erceldoune
> (Thomas the Rhymer), in *The Master of Ballantrae*

In 1745 Prince Charles Edward Stewart calls for Scots Jacobites to join his rebellion. At the house of Durrisdeer, near St. Brides on the Solway shore, the "old lord" agrees to send one of his sons to fight for Bonnie Prince Charlie while the other remains at home to support King George. After a coin is tossed, the elder brother, James Durie, Master of Ballantrae, rides north to join the rebels. Months later, news of Culloden and James's death reaches Durrisdeer, where Henry Durie woos and marries Alison Graeme, his late brother's fiancée.

Having escaped from the English forces, James and Colonel Francis Burke, an Irish comrade, are rescued by Teach, a notorious American pirate, after the French ship *Sainte-Marie-des-Anges* is lost at sea. Aboard the *Sarah*, James supplants Teach as captain when they reach the American colonies. Near Albany, in the province of New York, James buries his pirate loot in the depths of the wilderness before traveling to Paris with Burke.

In April 1749 Burke arrives at Durrisdeer with letters from the Master of Ballantrae. Henry and Alison are shocked, but the lord is pleased by the good news. For the next seven years James drains money from the estate, while Henry withholds the truth from his father. When Durrisdeer becomes "a mark and an eyesore in the neighborhood," Mackellar, land steward of the estate, informs Alison of James's avaricious activities.

In November 1756 James returns to Durrisdeer. The lord is concerned about his safety, but Henry is piqued by James's arrogant and insulting behavior. Soon a local

281

Jacobite sympathizer reveals that James is working secretly as a government spy.

On the wintry night of February 27, 1757, James's insults rival the frigid winds that blast the walls of Durrisdeer. When Henry strikes him in the mouth, he insists that his brother pay for the offense with blood. Continuing his taunts, James ignores the rules of fair play as they duel in the garden. Forced to accompany them, Mackellar watches as Henry plunges his sword through James's body. In haste, Mackellar rouses Alison and the old lord, who advises him to extinguish the candles that still burn in the garden. Alison follows Mackellar to the dueling spot, but only a sword and a pool of blood lie where the body had fallen.

Six months pass before Mackellar learns the truth about James's disappearance: Seriously wounded, he had mustered enough strength to hail some traiders who then transported him to France. Mackellar gathers James's papers and, together with a written explanation, presents them to Alison, who subsequently burns the entire bundle. Disgusted by this destruction of evidence, the steward capitulates when he learns that Henry will be castigated publicly if James, the rightful heir, is barred from the estate. Mentally affected, Henry remains in a lethargic state; after Mackellar explains that James may have survived, he declares, "Wherever I am, there will he be." Soon the old lord becomes torporific and dies in his sleep.

On July 17, 1757, a son, Alexander, is born to Alison and Henry, who spends all of his waking hours with the child. When the boy reaches the age "of six or seven," Mackellar is alarmed by Henry's description of the duel and his disregard for Alison and Katherine, their daughter. Meanwhile, Francis Burke has a chance meeting with James and his native companion, Secundra Dass, in war-torn India.

In April 1764 James, accompanied by Secundra, again returns to Durrisdeer. He demands money but is forestalled by Mr. Carlyle, a lawyer who draws a legal document entrusting the estates to Mackellar and himself. One night Henry and Alison, their two children, and a maid, aided by Mackellar and another servant, sneak out of the house. For three weeks Mackellar maintains silence but is foiled by Secundra, who has concealed his knowledge of English.

James, Secundra, and Mackellar sail from Glasgow aboard the *Nonesuch*. Mackellar prays that the "very ancient ship" will sink in a violent storm, but he lives to make an assassination attempt on James, who subsequently exhibits gestures of friendship and consideration. When the ship reaches New York on July 22, 1764, Mackellar, "resolved to steal a march upon the Master," rows off to locate Henry's new home.

Possessing evidence that James murdered a man after the '45, Henry awaits his brother's arrival. Snubbed by a gathering of provincial magnates, James establishes a tailor's shop in the "poor quarter of town," where he and Secundra, an accomplished goldsmith, plan to raise funds for an expedition. Henry continues to ridicule his brother; when James asks for a loan, he leaves him high and dry.

About one week later Henry and Mackellar voyage up the Hudson River. After a lengthy stay in Albany, where Henry drinks himself into stupors while anticipating news of his brother, they join Sir William Johnson on a diplomatic errand into the frosty northland. One night John Mountain, a trader who had accompanied James's party, enters the camp.

When the Master caught wind of a mutiny, Mountain reveals, he escaped while the others were asleep. He returned, however, and soon fell gravely ill. On the third day of his sickness he gave instructions to Mountain and Hastie, a former divinity student, before he died. The following morning the entire party watched as Secundra buried James's body. During their subsequent treasure hunt, all but one of these "dregs of colonial rascality" were murdered by Indians.

When Henry insists that his brother is not dead, Sir William reluctantly offers a boat and a complement of men, some of whom describe a safer route to the grave. Bereft of reason, Henry looks on as Secundra Dass digs furiously into the frozen ground. Questioned by the others, Secundra reveals that a Hindu burial method was used to save James from the mutineers. After the others light a fire to warm the body, Secundra works on the corpse for several hours before crying out. Fluttering briefly, the Master's eyes open to gaze upon the bewildered retinue. Henry does not survive the shock and is buried beside his brother in the frigid ground of the New York wilderness.

One cold night in December 1887 Stevenson listened to ice crackling in the river as he paced the veranda of his Saranac home. He had finished reading Frederick Marryat's *The Phantom Ship* for the "third or fourth" time and was "moved with the spirit of emulation."[1] Alone in the darkness, he conceived a tale unlike any he had written before—a story that portrays humanity in nonromantic, pessimistic and, ultimately, tragic terms.

Creating *The Master of Ballantrae* gave Stevenson "hours of unadulterated joy," but his interest in the novel ebbed when he began to plot his South Seas voyage a few months later.[2] He concentrated on the farcical *The Wrong Box* from March to May 1888 but returned to the more serious tale after the *Casco* arrived at Tahiti that autumn. The story began to appear in *Scribner's Magazine* in November 1888, six months before he completed it. The writing of the final chapters proved arduous, and after arriving in Honolulu in late January 1889, he again turned to *The Wrong Box*. He finished the Durie tragedy in May, just in time to honor his contract with *Scribner's*. (The last of 12 monthly installments appeared in the October 1889 issue.) On September 20, 1889, Cassell and Company published *The Master of Ballantrae: A Winter's Tale* in London, and the U.S. version, published by Charles Scribner's Sons, appeared the following day.

Several literary scholars have claimed that *The Master of Ballan-*

trae marks a radical change in Stevenson's literary style, that the dark tale of the Duries demonstrates the talents of a more mature and versatile novelist. While the novel's essence, established by remarkable character development and a thoroughly depressing view of life, differs from his earlier work, the story also contains elements previously explored in *Treasure Island, The Strange Case of Dr. Jekyll and Mr. Hyde,* and *Kidnapped.* Stevenson's incorporation of Scottish history, sea voyages, piracy, buried treasure, and psychological duality was not a new development, but his profound use of these elements revealed that his art was becoming more solemn and less picturesque. Three years after the novel was published, he admitted that it "lacked all pleasurableness."[3] Although J. R. Hammond exaggerates the differences between *The Master of Ballantrae* and Stevenson's other stories, he is correct in claiming that its fusion of various genres forms a "haunting tragedy on the theme of intolerance."[4]

As in *Treasure Island,* Stevenson uses two narrators to tell his tale. The chapters featuring excerpts from Francis Burke's memoirs allow the reader to witness James Durie from a comrade's viewpoint, while the remainder of the novel, narrated by Ephraim Mackellar, presents a prejudicial account by a steward who is faithful to the Master's brother. (In chapter eight ["The Enemy in the House"], Mackellar compares James to Satan in John Milton's *Paradise Lost.*) The complex relationships between these characters enhance the narrators' observations: James and Burke argue (like David and Alan in *Kidnapped*), Mackellar frequently criticizes the actions of Henry, and, later, during the passage to New York, the steward begins to temper his hatred of James with understanding.

David Daiches has praised Ephraim Mackellar as Stevenson's first "unheroic" narrator, an observer whose "adult insight" makes him superior to the adolescent storytellers in *Treasure Island* and *Kidnapped.*[5] Mackellar is middle-aged, but he shares certain traits with younger predecessors, namely his status as a commoner who serves aristocrats and soldiers, and his naive outlook on the world. Moreover, Stevenson's earlier narrators are not simple, heroic figures: both Jim Hawkins and David Balfour perform courageous feats but are far from being faultless paragons.

Stevenson's greatest achievement in *The Master of Ballantrae* is his depiction of the two estranged brothers. Here, his examination of the human capacity for evil eclipses the dual-personality premise in *The Strange Case of Dr. Jekyll and Mr. Hyde.* Henry Jekyll mentions that human beings may possess a myriad of personalities, but only two—the good and the evil—are characterized. Neither Durie brother is completely good or evil, but each is a fluctuating composite of these moral extremes. James performs more evil deeds than his brother does, but he is the one who loses his inheritance and is forced to flee from his homeland after the disastrous rebellion. Eventually, the vindictive and obsessive Henry, who has usurped James's wealth and lover, hires a gang of cutthroats to murder him. Believed dead on three separate occasions, the seemingly indestructible James stirs long enough to frighten Henry to death in the closing chapter. Unable to reconcile their differences while living, the brothers finally are joined in the grave.

Reminiscent of Mary Shelley's *Frankenstein,* in which the scientist and the monster pursue each other to their deaths in a frozen waste, the ending of *The Master of Ballantrae* is tragic and terrifying but, unlike Shelley's conclusion, deeply disappointing. The final two chapters seem tacked on and are filled with so many new, undeveloped characters that the novel becomes erratic and confusing. Stevenson was aware of this narrative defect, and later wrote to Sidney Colvin, "This cursed end of the Master hangs over me like the gallows."[6]

As in *Kidnapped,* Stevenson uses the '45 as a backdrop for intense personal conflict. Like Alan Breck, James Durie sacrifices his freedom and fortune for the Jacobite cause but in the end fares much worse. While *Kidnapped* alternates delight with despair and topographical beauty with perilous events, *The Master of Ballantrae* is consistently fatalistic: there are no moments of genuine comradeship, tenderness, or gaiety. Stevenson paints a romantic vision of Jacobite devotion in the earlier novel; in the latter he presents a doleful lament for the aftermath of Culloden.

Early in chapter three ("The Master's Wanderings"), Stevenson briefly interrupts the gloomy atmosphere with a self-reflective aside. In a passage that recalls a similar incident in *Kidnapped,* Francis Burke reports that, during their escape from Culloden, he and James met a famous personage:

> This was on the second day of our flight, after we had slept one night in the rain upon the inclination of a mountain. There was an Appin man, Alan Black Stewart (or some such name, but I have seen him since in France), who chanced to be passing the same way, and had a jealousy of my companion. Very uncivil expressions were exchanged; and Stewart calls upon the Master to alight and have it out.
> "Why, Mr. Stewart," says the Master, "I think at the present time I would prefer to run a race with you." And with the word claps spur to his horse.
> Stewart ran after us, a childish thing to do, for more than a mile; and I could not help laughing, as I looked back at last and saw him on a hill, holding his hand to his side, and nearly burst with running.

At the foot of the page Stevenson includes the following note: "*Note by Mr. Mackellar.* Should this not be Alan *Breck* Stewart, afterwards notorious as the Appin murderer? The Chevalier is sometimes very weak on names." This incident is simultaneously humorous and suggestive of the political differences between Alan Breck and James Durie. While the former is dedicated to Bonnie Prince Charlie's cause, the latter becomes a Jacobite at the toss of a coin.

The coin-tossing episode is indicative of James's politically chameleonic abilities. He becomes a Jacobite, a pirate leader, an Indian sahib, and an American craftsman with equal ease. While events primarily provide a background for the interaction of the characters, James's brief reign on Captain Teach's ship is a vivid and exciting incident. Reminiscent of material in *Treasure Island* and *Kidnapped*, Stevenson's picturesque introduction of Teach adds some welcome panache to the novel's somber mood: "Their leader was a horrible villain, with his face blacked and his hair curled in ringlets; Teach, his name, a most notorious pirate. He stamped about on the deck, raving and crying out that his name was Satan, and his ship was called Hell. There was something about him like a wicked child or a half-witted person, that daunted me beyond expression." Teach's exaggerated behavior is designed to frighten the drunken crew, but his treatment of captives and his own men often becomes murderous. He chews glass to make blood run down his cheeks, fatally stabs a man who accidentally kicks a barrel of rum overboard, and forces innocent passengers and women to walk the plank. Revolted by this piratical lifestyle, James humiliates Teach in front of the crew, who then depose the inebriated scoundrel.

Stevenson's use of the name "Teach" may lead readers to believe that the character is a fictionalized portrait of Edward Teach, aka "Blackbeard." However, Stevenson cleverly includes a footnote that denies this association: "*Note by Mr. Mackellar.* This Teach of the *Sarah* must not be confused with the celebrated *Blackbeard*. The dates and facts by no means tally. It is possible the second Teach may have borrowed the name and imitated the more excessive part of his manners from the first."

James's estrangement from his brother is complicated by Alison Graeme, the sixth major female character to appear in Stevenson's novels. According to James Pope Hennessy, she may have been inspired by the widow of General George Armstrong Custer, who twice visited Stevenson at Saranac. During an argument, Mrs. Custer suggested that he include more women in his stories.[7] While Hennessy calls Alison an "insipid" heroine, scholar M. R. Ridley claims that she is "a portrait of a woman for her own sake, not just ... a convenient super to bring out the quality of the men."[8] In fact, any insipidity that Alison demonstrates may be attributed to Mackellar's biased observations. In chapter four he is angered by her devotion to the evil Master:

I think there is a devil in women: all these years passed, never a sight of the man, little enough kindness to remember (by all accounts) even while she had him, the notion of his death intervening, his heartless rapacity laid bare to her; that all should not do, and she must still keep the best place in her heart for this accursed fellow, is a thing to make a plain man rage. I never had much natural sympathy for the passion of love; but this unreason in my patron's wife disgusted me outright with the whole matter.

In chapter six ("Summary of Events During the Master's Second Absence"), Mackellar rebukes Alison for burning the evidence against James, but she quickly turns the tables on the chauvinistic steward:

"I wonder to find you so simple, Mr. Mackellar," said Mrs. Henry. "What does this man value reputation? But he knows how we prize it; he knows we would rather die than make these letters public; and do you suppose he would not trade upon the knowledge? What you call your sword, Mr. Mackellar, and which had been one indeed against a man of any remnant of propriety, would have been but a sword of paper against him. He would smile in your face at such a threat. He stands upon this degradation, he makes that his strength: it is in vain to struggle with such characters."

*The Master of Ballantrae* is set on three continents, a feature that enhances its adventurous qualities but also adds to its disjointed plot structure. The chapter set in India is particularly awkward, a defect that Stevenson consciously incorporated. Years earlier, his uncle, Inspector-General John Balfour, had told him a story of an Indian fakir who was buried and then resuscitated. Stevenson used this memory as a springboard for the rest of the novel; he simply had to feature India as one of the major settings:

> My story was now world-wide enough: Scotland, India, and America being all obligatory scenes. But of these India was strange to me except in books; I had never known any living Indian save a Parsee, a member of my club in London, equally civilised, and (to all seeing) equally occidental with myself. It was plain, thus far, that I should have to get into India and out of it again upon a foot of fairy lightness; and I believe this first suggested to me the idea of the Chevalier Burke for a narrator.[9]

Not surprisingly, *The Master of Ballantrae* was Stevenson's first novel to include scenes set in North America. He had grown familiar with the New York wilderness during his ramblings into the forests surrounding Saranac, and his observance of the status of Native Americans added another element to the complex story. In chapter 12 ("The Journey in the Wilderness"), Mackellar, writing of Sir William Johnson's diplomatic expedition, draws an interesting parallel: "His standing with the painted braves may be compared to that of my Lord President Culloden among the chiefs of our own Highlanders at the 'Forty-five; that is as much to say, he was, to these men, reason's only speaking-trumpet, and counsels of peace and moderation, if they were to prevail at all, must prevail singly through his influence."

But *The Master of Ballantrae* is essentially a story about Scotland, a nation viewed from a distance by an author who would never return to its shores. In the preface to the novel Stevenson calls himself an exile, and in his May 17, 1889, dedication to Sir Percy Florence Shelley (the only surviving son of Percy Bysshe and Mary) and Lady Shelley, he writes:

> Here is a tale which extends over many years and travels into many countries. By a peculiar fitness of circumstance the writer began, continued it, and concluded it among distant and diverse scenes. Above all, he was much upon the sea. The character and fortune of the fraternal enemies, the hall and shrubbery of Durrisdeer, the problem of Mackellar's homespun and

how to shape it for superior flights; these were his company on deck in many star-reflecting harbours, ran often in his mind at sea to the tune of slatting canvas, and were dismissed (something of the suddenest) on the approach of squalls.

Hammond writes: "Begun in the icy cold of Saranac and completed in the heat of the Pacific islands, the novel breathes the atmosphere of Scotland: yet it is an atmosphere tinged with a perception of regret. This reaches its climax in the scene in which Henry leaves Scotland for the last time, en route for America."[10]

The novel is set in "many countries," but the house of Durrisdeer, Bonnie Prince Charlie and the '45, and the narration of Mackellar are elements that keep the novel rooted in Scottish soil. Stevenson wrote that it was "conceived in Highland rain, in the blend of the smell of heather and bog-plants, and with a mind full of Athole correspondence and the memories of the dumlicide Justice."[11] As in *Kidnapped*, his inclusion of traditional Celtic music adds to this atmosphere. Five incidents are accompanied by Scottish and Irish songs, whistled and sung by Colonel Burke, James, and Henry. In chapter three ("The Master's Wanderings"), Burke escapes Teach's wrath by dancing a jig and shouting "some ribaldry"; soon he regales the pirates with a fiddle that he finds on board. In chapter four ("Persecutions Endured by Mr. Henry"), Burke swaggers away from Mackellar, whistling "Shule Aroon," an air favored by Jacobite exiles in France; later in the chapter James sings the lyrics of the song, "a poor girl's aspirations for an exiled lover," to Mackellar and Henry:

O, I will dye my petticoat red,
With my dear boy I'll beg my bread,
Though all my friends should wish me dead,
  For Willie among the rushes, O!

The last two pieces of music are traditional Scottish songs. In chapter nine ("Mr. Mackellar's Journey with the Master"), Stevenson accompanies James's final departure from Scotland with the lament "Wandering Willie." This moving passage is made even more poignant by Mackellar's response to his sworn enemy:

The chaise came to the door in a strong drenching mist. We took our leave in silence: the house of Durrisdeer standing with dropping gutters and windows closed, like a place dedicate to melancholy. I observed the Master kept his head out, looking back on these splashed walls and glimmering roofs, till they were suddenly swallowed in the mist; and I must suppose some natural sadness fell upon the man at this departure; or was it some prevision of the end? At least, upon our mounting the long brae from Durrisdeer, as we walked side by side in the wet, he began first to whistle and then to sing the saddest of our country tunes, which sets folk weeping in a tavern, *Wandering Willie*. The set of words he used with it I have not heard elsewhere, and could never come by any copy; but some of them which were the most appropriate to our departure linger in my memory. One verse began:

Home was home then, my dear,
  full of kindly faces;
Home was home then, my dear,
  happy for the child.

And ended somewhat thus:

> Now, when day dawns on the brow of the moorland,
>> Lone stands the house, and the chimney-stone is cold.
> Lone let it stand, now the folks are all departed,
>> The kind hearts, the true hearts, that loved the place of old.

I could never be a judge of the merit of these verses; they were so hallowed by the melancholy of the air, and were sung (or rather "soothed") to me by a master-singer at a time so fitting. He looked in my face when he had done, and saw that my eyes watered.

"Ah! Mackellar," said he, "do you think I have never a regret?"

"I do not think you could be so bad a man," said I, "if you had not all the machinery to be a good one."

Here, Stevenson hints at Mackellar's changing attitude, but he also creates a literary parallel for the trepidation he must have felt during his own emigration from Scotland on August 22, 1887.

The final song is shrilled by Henry in chapter 11 ("The Journey in the Wilderness"). Returning home after one of his drunken escapades, he emits a "high, carolling utterance" similar to that "heard upon the lips of children, ere they learn shame." Here, Mackellar praises James for having "all the graces of the family," but Henry, possessing "no gift of music," sinks "into a degree of maudlin pathos that was to me scarce bearable" while singing the "Twa Corbies."

Stevenson's musical references do more than provide a pleasant ambience or emotional diversion. Although he works traditional songs into the thematics of *Treasure Island* and *Kidnapped,* his usage here is even more profound: By expressing themselves through the music of their native culture, his characters communicate their thoughts and feelings in a way that dialogue cannot provide. The "Twa Corbies," which translates as "two carrion crows" or "two ravens," symbolizes the Durie brothers' impending doom:

> And over his banes when they are bare
> The wind sall blaw for evermair!

*The Master of Ballantrae* is filled with detailed, descriptive prose. As in Stevenson's earlier stories, many passages appear tailor-made for cinematic adaptation. The escape of Henry and his family in chapter eight is a vivid example:

> All were dressed and waiting—my lord, my lady, Miss Katherine, Mr. Alexander, my lady's woman Christie; and I observed the effect of secrecy even upon quite innocent persons, that one after another showed in the chink of the door a face as white as paper. We slipped out of the side postern into a night of darkness, scarce broken by a star or two; so that at first we groped and stumbled and fell among the bushes. A few hundred yards up the wood-path Macconochie was waiting us with a great lantern; so the rest of the way we went easy enough, but still in a kind of guilty silence. A little beyond the abbey the path debouched on the main road; and some quarter of a mile farther, at the place called Eagles, where the moors begin, we saw the lights of the two carriages stand shining by the wayside. Scarce a word or two was uttered at our parting, and these regarded busi-

ness: a silent grasping of hands, a turning of faces aside, and the thing was over; the horses broke into a trot, the lamplight sped like Will-o'-the-Wisp upon the broken moorland, it dipped beyond Stony Brae; and there was Macconochie and I alone with our lantern on the road.

Chapter eight culminates with the insomniac Mackellar sitting alone in his room as he imagines the tragic events of Durrisdeer unfolding before him. Stevenson's prose in the final paragraph is among his most remarkable:

> When I got to the chamber, I sat there under a painful excitation, hearkening to the turmoil of the gale, which struck full upon that gable of the house. What with the pressure on my spirits, the eldritch cries of the wind among the turret-tops and the perpetual trepidation of the masoned house, sleep fled my eyelids utterly. I sat by my taper, looking on the black panes of the window, where the storm appeared continually on the point of bursting in its entrance; and upon that empty field I beheld a perspective of consequences that made the hair to rise upon my scalp. The child corrupted, the home broken up, my master dead. or worse than dead, my mistress plunged in desolation—all these I saw before me painted brightly in the darkness; and the outcry of the wind appeared to mock at my inaction.

Referring to several passages in the novel, Hammond writes:

> The effect of such literary touches as "my teeth smote each other in my mouth," "there was no breath stirring," "the blackness was like a roof over our heads," and "the cold of the night fell about me like a bucket of water" is to fix the scene indelibly on the reader's imagination. The scene is not only described, it is *felt*: there is an irresistible persuasion that here is an account of an episode actually experienced.[12]

*The Master of Ballantrae* enhanced the literary reputation that *The Strange Case of Dr. Jekyll and Mr. Hyde* and *Kidnapped* had established for Stevenson. Although the novel has flaws, the Durie brothers are among his most profound characterizations, the mark of an author whose style and thematics were continuing to evolve. As scholar Allen Bentley wrote in 1964, the novel makes us "aware only that we have been on a journey into the depths of human nature and have emerged, perhaps, with some clearer insight into the complexity of life."[13]

## *The Master of Ballantrae* (Warner Bros., 1953)

By the early 1950s adventure star Errol Flynn's carousing lifestyle had begun to take its toll on his health and appearance. From 1935, when his performance in *Captain Blood* made him one of Hollywood's most bankable properties, to the release of *The Adventures of Don Juan* in 1949, he had appeared exclusively for Warner Bros. in 31 feature films. But by the time the latter film was made in late 1948 his star was on the wane, and he spent the next ten years freelancing at MGM, Republic, Warners, Universal-International, and 20th Century–Fox. During this period he also appeared in a few independently produced films that were

*The Master of Ballantrae* (1953). This original advertisement misrepresents the novel by calling it "Robert Louis Stevenson's Masterwork of Adventure," but no one at Warner Bros. was concerned about false advertising: the studio delivered an Errol Flynn adventure film with the added attraction of location scenes shot in Scotland, England, and Sicily.

distributed by United Artists, Allied Artists, and William Marshall Productions.

*The Master of Ballantrae* (1953) is recognized as one of the best films of Flynn's final decade. And, if it is judged strictly as an Errol Flynn adventure, this assessment is close to the mark. However, Warner Bros.' assertion that the film is "Robert Louis Stevenson's Masterwork of Adventure" is a barefaced lie. Other studios have claimed that their films accurately represent Stevenson's work, but Warners' statement, featured in most of the advertising material, was simply a ploy to attract patrons into local theatres. The two Durie brothers (renamed Durisdeer; note the spelling difference with the house of Durrisdeer in the novel) are included in Herb Meadow and Harold Medford's contrived screenplay, but they bear almost no resemblance to Stevenson's characters. Mr. Mackellar and Colonel Burke are insignificant, and their observations are replaced by the omniscient narration of an unbilled actor. A few trivial events from the novel are depicted during the first 25 minutes, but the remaining 64 contain nothing written by Stevenson. Considering that *The Master of Ballantrae* is a pessimistic and depressing story, it is not surprising that the original Warners pressbook whitewashes it as "the lustiest and most vigorous tale of them all."[14]

The film opens with a historically accurate montage, accompanied by narration describing the '45, Bonnie Prince Charlie, and King George. Jamie Durisdeer (Errol Flynn) is summoned from the Ballantrae cottage of Jessie Brown (Yvonne Furneaux), a local wench, and he rides home to hear of the rebellion. At the castle MacKellar (Mervyn Johns) decides that only one of the Durisdeers should fight with the Stewarts. Henry (Anthony Steel) will not honor his brother's wishes, so Jamie tosses a coin; as he departs to join the Jacobite forces, Alison (Beatrice Campbell), his fiancée, gives him a white cockade.

Another montage and voice-over depict the capture of Edinburgh, the march to Derby, Culloden, and the rape of the Highlands. In a burned-out croft house, Jamie meets Colonel Francis Burke (Roger Livesey), a scoundrelly Irishman. Jamie tosses a coin to determine "whether they'll fight or be comrades," and they sit down to share a meal. Back in Ballantrae, Jamie is reunited with Henry and Alison at Jessie Brown's. Later he attempts to sail with Burke but is shot by a redcoat patrol. Lord Durisdeer (Felix Aylmer) declares Henry the new master, but later that evening Jamie appears at the estate and accuses his brother of betraying him to the English. During a sword duel Henry denies the accusation but falls and stabs Jamie with his dirk. When Henry and MacKellar examine the area a few minutes later, Jamie's body is gone.

Carried away from the castle by Burke, Jamie recuperates aboard the ship of Captain MacCauley (Moultrie Kelsall). En route to the West Indies, the ship is attacked by Arnaud (Jack Berthier), "an incredible French dandy," and his pirate crew. Jamie is wounded and captured but soon strikes a bargain with Arnaud. At Tortuga Jamie and his followers steal a treasure-filled Spanish galleon from Mendoza (Charles Goldner), an infamous pirate. Jamie kills Arnaud in a duel and, adopting the name "Mr. Bally," sails for Scotland, where he plans to be reunited with Alison.

Jamie and Burke enter the castle during a gala ball at which Henry announces his betrothal to Alison. Jamie lashes out at his brother and insults a group of redcoats, but when a duel begins, Henry tosses him a sword. To cap off his feats of derring-do, Jamie saves Henry from a redcoat bullet, and the two brothers are reconciled. However, Jamie and Burke are condemned to death, while Henry is acquitted

*The Master of Ballantrae* (1953). Jamie "Durisdeer" (Errol Flynn) engages in a bit of derring-do in the West Indies before sailing back to Scotland.

because he was faithful to King George.

Alison visits Jamie's cell and admits that she accepted his brother's proposal to be close to him, whom she presumed dead. Later Jessie Brown accosts the guard and unlocks the cell door. Shot by a redcoat, Jessie informs Jamie that it was she, in a fit of jealousy, who betrayed him to the English. Henry helps Jamie and Burke escape, and he provides them with horses and a hideout in the nearby "Smuggler's Cave." In return, Jamie tells his brother where the Spanish treasure is hidden before he, Burke, and his beloved Alison ride off into the Highland sunset.

During the summer of 1951 William Keighley, who had directed Flynn in *The Prince and the Pauper* (1937) and *The Adventures of Robin Hood,* flew to Great Britain to select locations for the film. The interiors were shot at Elstree Studios in London, while the exterior Scottish scenes were filmed at Newquay in Cornwall, in the Highlands at Dornie, Ballachulish, and Glencoe, and at Eilean Donan Castle. Keighley first selected Castle Beauly near Inverness but was snubbed by Lord Lovat, who was concerned that the film crew would "contaminate his fine herds."[15] Captain MacRae Gilstrap, Laird of Eilean Donan, also refused the production company's telegrams, letters, and phone calls, but he finally capitulated to a member of the location crew. Flynn enjoyed working in the castle, which added some authentic atmosphere to his formulaic performance. After the narrative shifts from Scotland to the West Indies (Keighley chose to shoot these scenes at Palermo, Sicily), the film becomes a typical Errol Flynn adventure outing. Beatrice Campbell recalled:

> I remember there was a love scene between Flynn and myself ... he hadn't been at rehearsal and we simply played it without his having prepared anything. I thought the scene went perfectly. But when the scene was over, Flynn went over and talked to Keighley for several minutes. The director called me aside and I said, "What's the matter?" He told me, "I think you should play the scene differently." I said, "We've discussed it and rehearsed it and we both agreed that this is the way it should be played." And he replied, "Well, it's like this. If you play it this way the camera follows you as you make your exit. Errol wants us to follow him instead." That way the audience remembered him at the end of the scene and wanted to know what he would do in the next scene. Nobody was to take one tiny bit of limelight away from him.
>
> It wasn't selfishness: the method of a selfish actor in the theatre who works only for himself to the detriment of the play. Everything in *The Master of Ballantrae* had to build up and support *Flynn*. He was clever enough to know that he mustn't give an inch, or he would lose that mile that made him a star.[16]

After the Sicilian scenes were completed, Flynn was supposed to return to London with the cast and crew, but he decided to remain for an extended holiday. When a cable from Jack Warner arrived, Flynn still refused to leave. Warner's second cable, "Get your ass to England," was answered by Flynn two weeks later: "Your cable fully understood and will follow instructions." However, Flynn waited another two weeks before he set sail for England aboard his private yacht.[17]

Although the film contains accurate historical material, a few scattered connections with the novel do not compensate for a simplistic plot and one-dimensional characters. At 89 minutes, it is overlong, and the pirate scenes are marred by filler footage of dancing girls and drunken mariners. As Mendoza, Charles Goldner overacts unmercifully, particularly during Marianne's (Gillian Lynne) exotic choreography. (Remarkably, this scene, which unabashedly showcases Lynne's prominent breasts, was not cut from the final print.) The scenes set in Scotland benefit from Jack Cardiff's stunning Technicolor cinematography, but Keighley's decision to confine the story to the Highlands, rather than incorporating the actual Ballantrae site in southwestern Scotland, detracts from the historical atmosphere. India and the American colonies are never mentioned, and the West Indies merely provide a backdrop for banal piratical adventures.

Discounting the film's infidelity to the novel, the depiction of the Durisdeer brothers still disappoints. The familial conflict is an example of the conventional love triangle featured in countless Hollywood films, a situation in which two brothers pursue the same woman. Audiences may not have accepted Errol Flynn had he played Stevenson's complex and tragic James Durie, and it is doubtful if the heroic movie star could have succeeded in the role. Warner Bros. played it safe, denying the novel's brooding pessimism by calling it "Robert Louis Stevenson's Masterpiece of Gallantry!"[18] As additional hype, the publicity department created sketches to be colored by audience members and suggested that theater owners admit, free of charge, anyone named Robert Stevenson!

## *The Master of Ballantrae* on Television

The first visual adaptation of *The Master of Ballantrae* was produced for television three years before Warner Bros. released its theatrical film. Written by Andrew Allan for the Canadian Broadcasting Corporation, this teleplay was aired in 1950. A second television version was broadcast in Scotland in 1962.

For several decades, the "Hallmark Hall of Fame" program has provided American television with quality literary adaptations. In conjunction with CBS, Hallmark broadcast a three-hour British version of "The Master of Ballantrae" on January 31, 1984. As scripted by William Bast, this telefilm faithfully represents every chapter of the novel; although some scenes summarize large sections of the plot, the characterizations and events are well developed and enacted by an outstanding cast. Director Douglas Hickox and cinematographer Bob Edwards shot the entire film on location in Scotland, England, and Wales, and their efforts create a realistic and breathtaking atmosphere. Only one other film—TNT's *Treasure Island*, which was also produced for television—recreates a Stevenson story with this degree of accuracy.

Aside from the final scene, in which Henry (Richard Thomas) witnesses the brief resurrection of James (Michael York) but lives to accompany Alison (Finola Hughes) and Alexander (Andrew Panton) back to Durrisdeer, the plot closely follows the structure of the novel. The role of Jessie Broun (Kim Hicks), the trollop impregnated by James, is expanded, but she possesses none of the artifice of Yvonne Furneaux's Jessie Brown in the 1953 film. Stevenson's minor characters, including John Paul (Donald Eccles), Macconochie (Robert James), Chew (Nick Brimble), and Mountain (Brian Coburn), are interpreted respectfully, as are Teach (thunderously rendered by Brian Blessed, who would play Long John Silver in Disney's *Return to Treasure Island* series the following year), Lord Durrisdeer (John Gielgud), Francis Burke (Timothy Dalton), Secundra Dass (Nickolas Grace) and, most importantly, Mackellar (Ian Richardson), who advises Henry throughout the narrative.

Bast's script includes an admirable amount of Stevenson's dialogue but keeps Hickox and Edwards' excellent mise-en-scène at the forefront. Unlike Meadow and Medford's 1953 screenplay, in which narration is used to *tell* the story of the '45 and some of Jamie's subsequent adventures, Bast's stylistic approach *shows* these events. The film opens with Bonnie Prince Charlie's arrival in Scotland,

and the battles at Culloden and aboard Teach's ship are dramatic highlights. Before James is wounded in the Jacobite defeat, he bravely warns Charlie off the bloody moor.

Michael York's portrayal captures many of the nuances of Stevenson's character. Most of James's actions are the product of an evil conceit, but the courage and resourcefulness he displays in dangerous situations (as well as his seemingly indestructable nature) add to his psychological complexity. York interprets a difficult role by combining charisma with quiet intensity; he never overplays his scenes. As the outwardly timid Henry, Richard Thomas reveals more of his character's personality as the narrative progresses. He is strong enough to confront James and emerge victorious in a duel, but he later succumbs to vengeance and illness. Thomas's Henry hires Captain Harris (John Hallam) and his band of cutthroats to murder James, but, unlike his literary counterpart, he admits that he loves his brother. Bast justifies Henry's survival by carefully depicting James as a man who will stop at nothing to destroy Henry. In the novel Henry's family fades into the background during the final chapters, but the film offers an image of them returning to Durrisdeer, where they are welcomed by the servants. (Katherine, Henry and Alison's daughter, does not appear in the film.)

As James passes away in the film, he whispers that he will haunt Henry long after his demise. This threat is more plausible than Henry's death from fright in the novel, and is reinforced during the concluding sequence: After the coach arrives at Durrisdeer, John Paul observes young Alexander and remarks that the lad is the very image of James. This eerie epilogue ends as Henry gazes up at the broken window through which James's coin had passed in 1745, when their tragic conflict began. Rather than burying him with his brother, as Stevenson does, Bast offers a Henry who will live with the memory of what he has done.

As portrayed by the fetching Finola Hughes, Alison is a woman frustrated by the behavior of the men who surround her. She continually sees her hopes dashed by hatred and violence but grows to love Henry, after realizing that she has been a pawn in James's quest for glory. When James first returns to Durrisdeer, Henry does not wish to fight but is forced to defend his wife's honor. Like Henry, Alison is persecuted by villagers who blame the Durie family for sending James to his possible death in the '45. In an effective scene gleaned from the novel, the pregnant Jessie Broun strikes Henry with a rock; when queried by Alison, he claims the attack was perpetrated by a man.

At 152 minutes "The Master of Ballantrae" moves at a leisurely rate—a factor that can be attributed to the novel. Some sequences either end too abruptly or begin with insufficient exposition, but additional longueurs only would have slackened the pace. Bast's decision to kill Burke during his chance meeting with James in India is more final (and dramatic) than the exit provided by Stevenson (in which the character simply disappears after Mackellar includes the Indian passage from his memoirs). The musical score by Bruce Broughton integrates some pleasant Celtic melodies and instrumentation, but the murky sound recording mars the overall effect.

The location shooting is uniformly outstanding, with one exception: a long shot in which James and Burke ride toward what appears to be a loch in the Scottish Highlands. Referring to one of Burke's previous comments, James admits, "This is England, man. I'm just as lost as you are."

The fine performances and exceptional visuals are enhanced by the detailed art direction of Derek Nice and the striking period costumes created by Olga Lehmann and Brenda Dabbs: Finola Hughes's many dresses and the tartan attire worn by Michael York in the early scenes are particularly stunning. All told, this version of "The Master of Ballantrae," produced by HTV Limited of England and distributed by Columbia Pictures television, is a good Stevenson adaptation and an interesting film in its own right.

• FIFTEEN •

# Judicious Levity: *The Wrong Box* (1889)

> *"Do you know how often the word whip occurs in the old Testament? One hundred and (if I remember exactly) forty-seven times."*—JOSEPH FINSBURY, in *The Wrong Box*.

When Joseph Finsbury and his brother Masterman were little lads in white-frilled trousers, their father—a well-to-do merchant in Cheapside—caused them to join a small but rich tontine of seven and thirty lives. A thousand pounds was the entrance fee; and Joseph Finsbury can remember to this day the visit to the lawyer's, where the members of the tontine—all children like himself—assembled together and sat in turn in the big office-chair, and signed their names with assistance of a kind old gentleman in spectacles and Wellington boots.

This tontine, a common-fund insurance plan, guarantees all shares to the last survivor. In 1840 the 37 members are still living, but by 1850 their number has been reduced to 31; in 1857, it is down to 22; and in 1870 the number is five. As the narrator begins his tale only three survivors remain, including the two septuagenarian Finsburys.

Retired from business, Masterman is viewed as a model of British respectability, while Joseph, an eccentric who enjoys lecturing to "the shallow-minded," is the guardian of orphans: Morris and John Finsbury, sons of his late brother, Jacob; and Julia Hazeltine, daughter of the late Henry Hazeltine. While Morris and John are still youngsters, Joseph invests their £30,000 fortune in his leather shop, hands the business reins to "a capable young Scot," and sets off for Europe and Asia Minor. Returning several years later, he discovers that the business is in the throes of bankruptcy. Faced with a £7,800 deficit, Morris threatens to sue his irresponsible uncle but is prevented by legal counsel. In return, Joseph signs over his interest in the tontine to Morris, who agrees to provide room and board for his uncle and Miss Hazeltine. John, "a gentleman with a taste for the banjo, the music-hall, the Gaiety bar, and the sporting papers," also resides there.

One evening Morris is pleased to

hear that Lieutenant General Sir Glascow Biggar, the third surviving member of the tontine, has passed away. "Beholding his seven thousand eight hundred pounds restored to him, and himself dismissed from the vicissitudes of the leather trade," Morris visits Masterman's son, Michael, to secure part of the tontine for himself. When Morris threatens to discuss the matter with Masterman, Michael stops him. Morris then surmises that the old man is dead and that Michael is keeping his death a secret.

After this incident, the medical baronet Sir Faraday Bond orders Joseph to move to Bournemouth for his health. One day, while traveling to London with Morris and John, Joseph is involved in a violent train wreck. Many people are injured, but Morris awakens to find himself and his brother unharmed. In a ditch beside the wreckage, Morris discovers a mutilated corpse: "everything . . . identified the body as that of Uncle Joseph." Aided by John, he drags it into a nearby wood and hastily digs a shallow grave; they then rent a cottage at Browndean and find a water barrel to fit the corpse.

(While the brothers are searching for their uncle and subsequently burying a cadaver in the woods, Joseph flees from the wreckage, runs into the woods, and falls asleep a few hundred yards from the spot where his nephews are concealing "the body of a total stranger"!)

The following morning Morris heads for London while John stays at Browndean. Meanwhile, Joseph walks to the highway and catches a ride on a parcel cart. At the Tregonwell Arms in Southampton, he sups and delivers another of his tedious lectures. Unable to pay his bill, Joseph offers to settle in "a day or two" when he can cash an £800 note. Tired of the old man's incessant discourse, the landlord orders him out.

Soon Joseph accosts the local stationmaster, who assigns him a first-class compartment on a train carrying a barrel addressed to "M. Finsbury, 16 John Street, Bloomsbury." At Winchester two men climb aboard the carriage as the train departs. Inside, the elder of the two recognizes Joseph and escapes into the luggage van. Here Michael Finsbury tells Wickham, his companion, that the "old boy in the carriage is worth a hundred thousand pounds to me." After a guard steps in, Michael moves into a compartment, but Wickham remains to "play billy" with the luggage labels.

At No. 16 John Street, Bloomsbury, Julia Hazeltine is visited by Gideon Forsyth, a young barrister, as she deals with a workman who has delivered "the largest packing-case in the county of Middlesex." Gideon removes the front door and enlists a group of bystanders to help him wedge the box into the house. Unable to withstand the suspense, they open the case and find a statue of Hercules that Gideon describes as "about the biggest and worst in Europe." Confused, Julia displays a letter from Morris which mentions the delivery of a barrel.

Soon Morris arrives to find an artistic atrocity staring him in the face. Back at the train station, he learns that a man called William Bent Pitman had arrived to claim a packing-case and was left with a barrel. Angered, he returns to John Street and smashes the statue with a coal axe. In the morning, he forges a check and attempts to withdraw funds from his uncle's account but is prevented by a bank official who claims that Joseph drew off the money the previous day.

At 7 Norfolk Street, King's Road, "W. D. Pitman, Artist," examines the mysterious water barrel. Later he is visited by his lawyer, Michael Finsbury, who tells him not to worry about the missing statue. They then dismantle the barrel and are shocked by the appearance of a blanket-swathed, mutilated corpse. Michael advises Pitman to bury the body in the garden but later decides to conceal it in his Broadwood grand piano and offer it as a gift to "a young gentleman whom I know by sight."

The next day Michael and Pitman disguise themselves and deliver the piano to Gideon Forsyth. Before departing, Michael carefully places the lid key within a "square tower of cigars." In the evening Michael orders a drink in a King's Road public house, where Joseph is delivering an impromptu lecture on the theatres of London. Certain that Morris and John are out of sight, the old man declares, "They must think me dead, and are trying to deceive the world for the chance of the tontine." Michael offers Joseph spending money and demands that he return the business funds to the bank. Fifteen minutes later the wily lawyer calls on Morris, who still insists that Joseph is recovering at Browndean.

As darkness falls, Gideon Forsyth returns home. Stumbling into a heavy object, he discovers the scratched and stained Broadwood grand, throws open the keyboard, and plays some soundless exercises. Later he finds the key and lifts the lid. "Limp and rumpled and bloodshot," Gideon decides to dump the body off a yacht.

The next morning Gideon, assuming the identity of Jimson, an operatic composer, rents an old houseboat at Padwick near the holiday residence of his uncle, Edward Hugh Bloomfield. The following afternoon he awaits the arrival of the piano but is startled by Julia Hazeltine and his uncle, who both offer to help him.

Not far from Padwick, Harker, a young driver playing a penny whistle, is approached by Color Sergeant Brand of the Blankth, who challenges him to a musical duel. After several visits to local public houses, the drunken lad passes out in a ditch and the military man speeds off in the cart: at Padwick, he flies past Gideon and Miss Hazeltine, who spot a piano in the back.

At 16 John Street, Morris receives a letter from his long-suffering brother; unable to send money, he posts some magazines before calling at his business. Here he is visited by a Jewish bill collector who accepts a postdated check. In an effort to locate some ready money, he then advertises for Pitman, who "must have some of that eight hundred left."

At Michael's request, Pitman accepts Joseph as a boarder. While perusing the Sunday paper, the old man reads Morris's advertisement and sends Pitman scurrying to the lawyer's. Incognito, Michael accompanies his client to Waterloo Station, where they meet the mysterious inquirer. Michael recognizes Morris and the truth is told, but when Gideon Forsyth arrives, a brawl ensues. Michael breaks free and joins Pitman in a hasty escape, while Gideon restrains Morris. Several remarks about the corpse are parried back and forth before Gideon admits "I have lost it myself," and then runs out of the station.

At home Morris is startled by John, who demands a sumptuous meal and threatens to expose his brother's scheme. When Morris claims that he is equally guilty, John counters, "Have I committed forgery? have I lied about Uncle Joseph? have I put idiotic advertisements in the comic papers? have I smashed other people's statues?" Momentarily, they are interrupted by a messenger who delivers a summons from Michael.

At 10:00 A.M. the next day the two brothers meet Joseph Finsbury and Gideon Forsyth in Michael's office. After Michael proves that Masterman is still alive, he advises Morris to relinquish the financial claim held upon Joseph; then he signs over the business to Morris and John and accepts Joseph's liabilities (and all rights to the tontine) for himself.

At Saranac during October 1887 Lloyd Osbourne began to write a story called "The Finsbury Tontine." After learning to use his stepfather's typewriter, the aspiring 19-year-old author completed the first draft in early December. Impressed by Lloyd's effort, Stevenson offered to revise the story for publication, and when Fanny left for San Francisco in March 1888, he started to rewrite entire sections of the story. Although he was penning *The Master of Ballantrae* during the same period, he continued to work on "The Finsbury Tontine" (which was retitled "A Game of Bluff" at one point) until May 1888, when all literary projects were postponed in lieu of the Pacific holiday. During his stay at Waikiki Beach in February 1889, his interest in the story resurfaced and by March the revised draft was completed. On March 8 he wrote to Charles Baxter: "Lloyd and I have finished a story, *The Wrong Box*. If it is not funny, I am sure I do not know what is. I have split over writing it."[1]

From Charles Scribner's Sons, Stevenson received an offer of $5,000 for the U.S. rights to the final, 128-page manuscript. On June 15, 1889, Scribner's (and Longmans, Green and Company of London) published the novel, giving Lloyd second billing on the title page. Stevenson had handwritten 105 pages and heavily revised the other 23 but he still remained faithful to his stepson's original plot and characters. Later in life, Lloyd recalled: "Louis had to follow the text very closely, being unable to break away without jeopardizing the succeeding chapters. He breathed into it, of course, his own incomparable power, humour and vivacity, and forced the thing to live as it had never lived before."[2]

Since its publication over a century ago, very little has been written about *The Wrong Box*. Most

Stevenson scholars have avoided it, and as J. R. Hammond notes, "it remains one of the few works by him which is almost completely unknown."[3] Initial sales of the novel were poor, a development that may have dissuaded Stevenson from further experimentation with black humor.

Most contemporary reviewers criticized the novel for its "vulgar" subject matter. The idea of wringing laughs from the concealment of a misidentified corpse was considered tasteless "and some commentators expressed surprise that Stevenson should have lent his name and reputation to such an enterprise."[4]

*The Wrong Box* is not *Treasure Island, Kidnapped,* or *The Master of Ballantrae,* but it was never meant to be on a par with these novels. In the preface to the original edition Louis and Lloyd clearly reveal their intent: "'Nothing like a little judicious levity,' says Michael Finsbury in the text; nor can any better excuse be found for the volume in the reader's hand. The authors can but add that one of them is old enough to be ashamed of himself, and the other young enough to learn better." Here Stevenson adds a humorous comment while simultaneously apologizing for being so absurd. To be sure, it is one of his lesser fictional works, but complex plotting, bizarre events, and moments of hilarious farce make it entertaining reading. All of the events are contrived to an obvious degree, but this stylistic technique lends the story its fantastic atmosphere.

Joseph Finsbury, the unpredictable and eccentric rover, emerges as a classic Stevensonian personality. His self-indulgent lectures tax the patience of all who hear them, but this obnoxious idiosyncrasy is tempered by loneliness and a desire to escape from avaricious relatives. Hammond writes, "for all his long-windedness, he is a genuine *character* reminiscent of the creations of Dickens or Wells."[5]

Stevenson's contributions to the Joseph character include some autobiographical references. The old man's poor health is mentioned several times, particularly in the early chapters, when the prescriptions of Sir Faraday Bond are reported meticulously. Like Stevenson, who was advised to leave the cool, damp Scottish climate, Joseph is ordered to seek "the purer air of Bournemouth" (the location of Skerryvore). The first paragraph of chapter two ("In Which Morris Takes Action") recalls the many remedies offered by Stevenson's various physicians:

> The weather was raw and changeable, and Joseph was arrayed in consequence according to the principles of Sir Faraday Bond, a man no less strict (as is well known) on costume than on diet. There are few polite invalids who have not lived, or tried to live, by that punctilious physician's orders. "Avoid tea, madam," the reader has doubtless heard him say, "avoid tea, fried liver, antimonial wine, and baker's bread. Retire nightly at 10:45; and clothe yourself (if you please) throughout in hygienic flannel. Externally, the fur of the marten is indicated. Do not forget to procure a pair of health boots at Messrs. Dall & Crumbie's." And he has probably called you back, even after you have paid your fee,

to add with stentorian emphasis: "I had forgotten one caution: avoid kippered sturgeon, as you would the very devil!"

Stevenson's nostalgia for Scotland is demonstrated subtly in chapter nine ("Glorious Conclusion of Michael Finsbury's Holiday"), when an aged woman serves supper to Michael:

> A spare old lady, with very bright eyes and a mouth humorously compressed, waited upon the lawyer's needs; in every line of her countenance she betrayed the fact that she was an old retainer; in every word that fell from her lips she flaunted the glorious circumstance of a Scottish origin; and the fear with which this powerful combination fills the boldest was obviously no stranger to the bosom of our friend.

Chapter 12 ("Positively the Last Appearance of the Broadwood Grand") reveals a humorous side of Louis and Lloyd's common interest in the tin whistle:

> It is singular enough that a man should be able to gain a livelihood, or even to tide over a period of unemployment, by the display of his proficiency on the penny whistle; still more so, that the professional should almost invariably confine himself to "Cherry Ripe." But indeed, singularities surround the subject, thick like blackberries. Why, for instance, should the pipe be called a penny whistle? I think no one ever bought it for a penny. Why should the alternative name be tin whistle? I am grossly deceived if it be made of tin. Lastly, in what deaf catacomb, in what earless desert, does the beginner pass the excruciating interval of his apprenticeship? We have all heard people learning the piano, the fiddle, and the cornet; but the young of the penny whistler (like that of the salmon) is occult from observation; he is never heard until proficient; and providence (perhaps alarmed by the works of Mr. Mallock) defends human hearing from his first attempts upon the upper octave.

Anyone who has attempted to play a tin whistle (or heard someone else try it) can appreciate the wit in this passage.

Morris's realization that his uncles are still living is one of the novel's most amusing events. Prior to reaching this conclusion, he assumes that Masterman is dead, mistakes the body of a stranger for that of Joseph, and stuffs the corpse into a barrel that is handled by at least eight people before it disappears altogether!

The ending, containing Michael's final conversation with Gideon Forsyth, is particularly droll:

> "And now, Mr. Forsyth," resumed Michael, turning to his silent guest, "here are all the criminals before you, except Pitman. I really didn't like to interrupt his scholastic career; but you can have him arrested at the Seminary: I know his hours. Here we are, then; we're not pretty to look at; what do you propose to do with us?
>
> "Nothing in the world, Mr. Finsbury," returned Gideon. "I seem to understand that this gentleman"—indicating Morris—"is the *fons et origo* of the trouble; and from what I gather, he has already paid through the nose. And really, to be quite frank, I do not see what is to gain by any scandal; not me, at least. And besides, I have to thank you for that brief."
>
> Michael blushed. "It was the

least I could do to let you have some business," he said. "But there's one thing more. I don't want you to misjudge poor Pitman, who is the most harmless being upon earth; I wish you would dine with me to-night, and see the creature on his native heath—say, at Verrey's?"

"I have no engagement, Mr. Finsbury," replied Gideon. "I shall be delighted. But—subject to your judgment—can we do nothing for the man in the cart? I have qualms of conscience."

"Nothing but sympathize," said Michael.

While Jenni Calder calls the novel "clumsy and heavy-handed,"[6] Richard Aldington makes the dubious assertion that its inferior quality can be attributed solely to Lloyd Osbourne: "Stevenson is not responsible for *The Wrong Box*. It was Lloyd's youthful indiscretion, and Stevenson wanted to help him and make it saleable by lending the book some of his style and his name.'"[7] Hammond, however, concludes that *The Wrong Box* is something more "than a light-hearted piece of buffoonery":

> It seems clear ... that Stevenson took the rather slight framework of his stepson's story and transformed it into a full-scale picaresque novel allowing scope for characterisation, description and narrative technique on a broad canvas.
>
> The novel provides many instances of his gift for creating powerful word-pictures of scenes and episodes. One thinks of the railway accident at Browndean; of the arrival of the luggage van at the home of Gideon Forsyth; of Morris's destruction of the statue of Hercules; of his attempt to cash a cheque bearing a forged signature.

These and other incidents are described with the eye for detail and narrative skill of a born novelist.[8]

The experience of working with Lloyd appealed to Stevenson, as he repeated the collaboration for *The Wrecker* and *The Ebb-Tide*. If *The Wrong Box* tells us anything about his literary skill, it clearly demonstrates his versatility and willingness to experiment with content and style.

The bizarre events and characters in *The Wrong Box* make it an ideal subject for the popular cinema. In the hands of a talented screenwriter and director, the novel could be transformed into an exciting and funny film. However, only two adaptations have been produced, perhaps suggesting that its convoluted plot and relative obscurity have discouraged would-be adapters.

In 1913 Solax Films released a one-reel silent version that touched upon a few characters and incidents. Like other early Stevenson adaptations, it is considered a lost film.

## *The Wrong Box* (Salamander-Columbia, 1966)

The only surviving screen version of *The Wrong Box* is a disappointing and tasteless British bastardization that wastes the talent of an excellent cast. Although writers Larry Gelbart and Burt Shevelove incorporated the general framework of the novel into their screenplay, they replaced most of its specific events and characterizations with absurd sight gags and vulgar innuendos.

The film begins with psychedelic 1960s titles and maintains a similarly incoherent style throughout. The opening scene, which depicts a pompous, gout-ridden official explaining the rules and provisions of the tontine to a group of young boys, demonstrates the general comic level: as the camera tracks in medium close-up around a long table at which the boys are seated, one of the disinterested lads casually picks his nose. Even a viewer unfamiliar with the novel should know that this is neither Stevenson and Osbourne nor entertainment of a very sophisticated caliber. (In 1889 the novel was criticized for its low humor, a quality that appears elegant when compared with the content of this film.)

The remaining 100 minutes contain material that some viewers will find banal and others will deem offensive. The signing of the tontine is followed by brief scenes depicting the subsequent fates of members, all of whom die in absurd ways: friendly fire warfare, a mauling by a pet falcon, a fall into the peak of a snow-capped mountain, a bludgeoning by a champagne bottle, and others too inane to mention. While the novel includes well-written black comedy, the film revels in overplayed gutter humor. When one of the members, now a disabled old man in a wheelchair, is pushed down a hill to his death, the effect on the viewer may be nausea rather than laughter.

Most of the novel's character names remain, but the personalities, with the exception of Joseph Finsbury, are altered greatly. Masterman Finsbury (John Mills), addressed as Michael Finsbury's *grand*father, is a one-dimensional buffoon who feigns illness while simultaneously trying to kill Joseph. Michael (Michael Caine) is not a lawyer but a medical student desperately in love with Julia (Nanette Newman), his cousin who lives with Joseph in an adjoining apartment. Morris Finsbury (Peter Cook) is a rapacious scoundrel who collects bird's eggs, while John Finsbury (Dudley Moore) is a sex maniac obsessed with "chambermaids and girls of the lower classes." Cook and Moore made their feature-film debuts here, and though the former gives a tolerable performance, the latter displays the hammy self-indulgence he would exploit in *Arthur* and other American films of the early 1980s. Both actors are best known in Great Britain for their comic partnership in such films as *Bedazzled* (1967), which they cowrote, *Those Daring Young Men in Their Jaunty Jalopies* (1969), and the perfectly atrocious *The Hound of the Baskervilles* (1978), a prime candidate for the worst Conan Doyle adaptation.

The most palatable aspect of the film is the performance of Sir Ralph Richardson, who captures the essence of the literary Joseph. Relaxed and self-assured, he is particularly good while delivering rambling lectures in the early scenes. His subtle comic touches in the train-wreck sequence provide a welcome contrast to the overblown theatrics that surround him. Here the screenwriters attempt to explain Morris's and John's misidentification of the body by including "the Bournemouth strangler," a wanted killer who dons Joseph's overcoat and deerstalker cap while the old man ducks into the water closet for a smoke. Escaping unscathed, Joseph wanders off and hitches a ride with a local farmer who is almost driven insane by the old man's biblical babble. After this scene fades away, the narrative focuses on the activities of Morris and John, and Joseph is relegated to a few brief, insignificant appearances.

Producer-director Bryan Forbes assembled an all-star cast of British character players, including Peter Sellers, who portrays the fabricated Dr. Pratt, a venereal disease specialist and signer of false death certificates. One of the film's most tasteless moments occurs when the inebriated doctor washes his hands and then dries them on the back of a black cat that is lounging beside the sink. After scrawling a sloppy signature on a certificate ordered by Morris, he recalls his earlier blunder by using a smaller black cat for a blotter.

In a comparatively restrained performance, Michael Caine does his best to improve a badly written characterization; possessing none of the shrewdness and skill of his literary counterpart, Michael Finsbury pines over Julia and interacts with Peacock (Wilfred Lawson), Masterman's aged and inarticulate butler. Morris's and John's activities also are limited by Gelbart's and Shevelove's screenplay: although they hide the supposed body of Joseph in the woods, Morris has nothing to do with packing the corpse in a barrel, and he assigns all of the dirty work to his brother before returning to London. Later John is seen at the train station, where he and two porters place a large barrel beside a packing case labeled "Finsbury, Albany Crescent, London." Here the "wrong box" contains a statue being returned to Michael by Lady Pitman; the novel's William Dent Pitman and the web of circumstances which arise from his involvement with the corpse are omitted. Instead, the statue is delivered to Morris at Joseph's residence, and the barrel containing the body suddenly turns up in Masterman's entryway. (At this point, about 40 minutes into the film, the plot becomes confusing. Many events are not shown but only alluded to in brief, disjointed sequences. The fact that the plot makes little sense, even after several viewings, suggests that other, more coherent, footage may have ended up on the cutting room floor.)

Anticipating Masterman's death, Michael clears the house of the old man's relics. When the barrel arrives, he assumes that it contains Lady Pitman's statue, but after kicking a hole in the side he finds a human arm and a label bearing Joseph Finsbury's name. Assuming that Masterman has murdered his brother, Michael pushes the corpse into a piano and seeks the advice of Peacock, who claims that there are unscrupulous men who may be hired to dispose of it.

In a subsequent scene Masterman rises from his bed and falls down the stairs. Two men (apparently hired by Michael) arrive and drag the unconscious old man out of the door and into a cart, but the following morning a group of Salvation Army women dredge him out of the Thames and carry him home. While workmen (hired by

*The Wrong Box* (1966). Joseph Finsbury (Ralph Richardson) and Michael Finsbury (Michael Caine) provide most of the interest in Salamander/Columbia's preposterous, disordered, and occasionally offensive adaptation.

Peacock) are carting the piano away, Julia, thinking that Masterman is dead, plans his funeral at a local mortuary. Morris returns home and instructs John to visit an undertaker while he plants the supposed Joseph's body at the foot of the stairs. After Morris finds a statue instead of the corpse, John arrives with a coffin, Masterman climbs out of a hearse, lawyer Patience (Thorley Walters) enters with the tontine money, and the police (who somehow have acquired the piano) make a timely appearance of their own! This confusion is followed by a Mack Sennett–style hearse chase, a vulgar interruption of a former tontine member's funeral, Masterman's attempt to bludgeon Joseph with a shovel, and Morris's acceptance of a reward for delivering the body of the Bournemouth Strangler to the authorities.

The first half of *The Wrong Box* is relatively faithful to the novel, but the remaining footage degenerates into a disordered farce. Forbes's attempt to integrate silent comedy techniques into a mid–1960s color film is a stylistic and narrative mess. His occasional use of title cards that repeat the action of certain scenes is visually cumbersome and dramatically superfluous. Since the screenplay was only "suggested by the novel of the same name by Robert Louis Stevenson and Lloyd Osbourne" (the credit is listed in fine print below the opening title), the viewer should not expect a faithful visualization of the text.

The most admirable technical aspect is the fluid and occasionally atmospheric cinematography of Gerry Turpin, whose other credits include *Seance on a Wet Afternoon* (1964), a Bryan Forbes–Richard Attenborough production directed by Forbes, and *Oh What a Lovely War* (1969), directed by Richard Attenborough and starring Ralph Richardson.

*The Wrong Box* premiered in London during the last week of May 1966, and was released in the United States two months later. Most critics published unfavorable reviews but praised Ralph Richardson and a few of the gags. *Variety*'s "Rich," who saw the film at the Columbia Theatre in London, commends Forbes for his attempt to salvage a bad script but criticizes his "maddening mixture of styles,"[9] while Bosley Crowther, in his review, writes:

> Robert Louis Stevenson and Lloyd Osbourne must be whirling in their graves, convulsed with astonishment and laughter at what a bunch of British actors have done in turning their humorous tale, "The Wrong Box," into an outlandish film. . . .
>
> Sure, the whole nutty business is tumbled together haphazardly in the script that has been written—or maybe scrambled—by Larry Gelbert *[sic]* and Burt Shevelove. Some sections and bits are funnier than others. Some are labored and dull. It is that sort of story, that sort of comedy. But it adds up to a lively lark. And, incidentally, the splendid color is mighty nice.
>
> Mr. Stevenson and Mr. Osbourne can rest contented that their story has been expertly vandalized.[10]

• SIXTEEN •

# The Commonplace Ghosts of Sailormen: *The Ebb-Tide: A Trio and Quartette* (1893)

> *"She's dead, right enough. Died of a bowel complaint. That was when I was away in the brig* Oregon. *She lies in Portland, Maine. 'Adar, only daughter of Captain John Davis and Mariar, his wife.' I had a doll for her on board. I never took the paper off'n that doll, Herrick; it went down the way it was, with the* Sea Ranger, *that day I was damned."*—CAPTAIN JOHN DAVIS, in *The Ebb-Tide*.

## Part 1: The Trio

Throughout the island world of the Pacific, scattered men of many European races and from almost every grade of society carry activity and disseminate disease. Some prosper, some vegetate. Some have mounted the steps of thrones and owned islands and navies. Others, again, must marry for a livelihood; a strapping, merry, chocolate-colored dame supports them in sheer idleness; and dressed like natives, but still retaining some foreign element of gait or attitude, still perhaps with some relic (such as a single spy-glass) of the officer and gentleman, they sprawl in palm-leaf verandas, and entertain an island audience with memoirs of the music-hall. And there are still others, less pliable, less capable, less fortunate, perhaps less base, who continue, even in these isles of plenty, to lack bread.

On the outskirts of Papeete "the three most miserable English-speaking creatures in Tahiti" sit huddled under a *purao* tree. Linked by common misfortune, they know little about each other's lives, "not even their true names." Robert Herrick, the Oxford-educated son of a successful London businessman, lost a clerkship in New York and in San Francisco "invested his last dollar" in a South Sea voyage that landed him in Papeete; "a little townward of the British Consulate," he shares an old calaboose with John Davis, an American sea captain, and Huish, a "wholly vile" Cockney clerk.

One morning the captain panhandles breakfast before setting off for town. He returns about 30 minutes later, produces note paper and three pencils, and demands that each of them write home. When Herrick is unable to put anything down, Davis charges, "If you had commanded the finest bark that ever sailed from Portland, Maine; if you had been drunk in your berth when she struck the breakers in Fourteen Island Group, and hadn't had the wit to stay there and drown, but come on deck, and given drunken orders, and lost six lives,—I could understand your talking then!"

That afternoon Davis meets the British consul and agrees to captain the *Farallone*, a 160-ton schooner bound for Sydney. Loaded with champagne, the ship was stranded in Tahiti after the captain, mate, and one hand died of smallpox. Finding only three Kanaka hands and a cook on board, the consul approached four other skippers, all of whom declined the commission. Davis selects Herrick as first mate, but the inexperienced landsman refuses when the captain reveals his plan to steal the ship: "In Peru, we'll sell that liquor off at the pier head, and the schooner after it, if we can find a fool to buy her, and then light out for the mines." Undaunted, Davis speaks of his needy family and Herrick's own situation: "Refuse this because you think yourself too honest, and before a month's out you'll be jailed for a sneak-thief."

During the early stages of the voyage Huish's insurgent attitude is augmented by his consumption of champagne. Davis also drinks heavily, but Herrick does his best to keep the ship on course and the crewmen at their posts.

Unable to maintain dead reckoning, Herrick asks the captain for help but is met with drunken bravado. Huish rallies to his side, but Herrick prefers the friendship of the native sailors. Taveeta (called "Uncle Ned" by Davis), describes the *Farallone*'s previous voyage, during which the drunken captain and mate allowed the ship to drift off course and land on a smallpox-infested island in the Paumotu (now Tuamotu) Archipelago.

Some days later the ship is menaced by a raging squall. When Herrick sees the crewmen running to their stations, he accuses the inebriated captain of negligence: "You lost the *Sea Ranger* because you were a drunken sot. Now you're going to lose the *Farallone*. You're going to drown here the same way you drowned others, and be damned." Scrambling to his feet, Davis shouts orders to the crew as the squall hits. Knee-deep in water, he struggles to remove the foresheet and, ten minutes later, the *Farallone* is sailing through a light breeze. When Herrick threatens to resign, Davis pledges to stay sober for the remainder of the voyage. His anger vented, Herrick pities his former friend.

In the cabin Davis informs Huish that they are sailing a teetotal ship, but the clerk ignores every word as he opens another champagne bottle and fills his mug with a still and colorless liquid. "W'y, wot's this? ... It's water!" he exclaims before handing the mug to his companions. Davis opens several cases, discovers that all the bottles have been filled with the tasteless liquid, and devises a plan to sink the schooner near an American consulate: "A day or so in the boat; the consul packs us home, at Uncle Sam's expense, to 'Frisco; and if that merchant don't put the dollars down, you come to me!" Davis chooses Samoa as their destination and orders Huish to write a bogus log entry.

A short time later Davis returns from the galley and threatens to shoot the cook for wasting the stores. Herrick insists that the captain's own drunkenness gave the natives free reign over the food and supplies, but when Huish begins a verbal attack he supports the captain, who again promises to stay sober. During a lull in the argument, one of the crewmen spots "a greenish, filmy iridescence" on the horizon.

## Part 2: The Quartette

Early the next morning the *Farallone* reaches a small island. The men see no signs of habitation but eventually sail within view of a large farm; a nearby hamlet, guarded by a ship's figurehead, appears deserted. As the ship passes a point of palms, a voice hails, "Schooner ahoy! . . . Stand in for the pier!" and a large man, attended by two oarsmen, steers his boat toward the dock; he introduces himself as "Attwater" and claims that he may have a commission for them, due to the lateness of his own schooner, the *Trinity Hall*. One of the island's four remaining inhabitants, Attwater reveals that 29 others died of smallpox, but he is reluctant to speak about his thriving pearl business. He invites them to dine with him at 6:30 P.M. but requests that Herrick appear at 4:00 P.M.

Suspecting that Attwater is a "firstrate, copper-bottomed aristocrat" hiding a fortune, Davis orders the wavering Herrick to talk him into bringing the goods aboard the *Farallone*. That afternoon Herrick learns three major facts: Attwater is a religious fanatic; he is storing a large number of pearls in an indoor safe; and he knows every detail of their criminal scheme. During dinner Attwater recalls an incident in which he hanged a native and drove another to suicide. Herrick breaks down and is escorted to the beach by Davis, who vows to kill their sinister host; but, on his way back to the veranda, the captain is ambushed by Attwater, who banishes them from the island.

Back on the *Farallone* Herrick jumps into the sea; unable to drown himself, he swims to the beach, where the rifle-toting Attwater meets him. Huish awakens with a severe hangover and devises a baleful plan to splash their enemy with vitriol. The captain first rejects such savagery but quickly capitulates. Hoping to appeal to Attwater's sense of mercy, Huish dictates a letter of apology before they return to the island.

Attwater and Herrick, armed with Winchesters, and the two servants, attired in divers' helmets, appear on the shore. Herrick hails the boat, delivers the letter to his new commander, and orders Davis to stand against the figurehead. Huish raises his hands and moves closer, but Attwater shoots him down, examines the vitriol, and turns toward the captain: "I give you sixty seconds to make your peace with God." Davis refuses, and the fanatic fires three shots into the figurehead. Throwing up his hands, the captain cries out to God and, after a brief fainting spell, pleads to be saved.

Two weeks later Davis kneels on the beach while Attwater barks orders to the *Farallone*'s Kanaka crew. As the captain's supplication creates "moods of piety and terror," Herrick rows out to the ship and sets her ablaze. Davis shrugs off his former mate's comments about the ship's fate and the impending arrival of the *Trinity Hall*, events that "don't amount to a hill of beans" in his new Christian philosophy: "But, O! why not be one of us? why not come to Jesus right away, and let's meet in yon beautiful land? That's just the one thing wanted; just say, 'Lord, I believe, help Thou mine unbelief!' and He'll fold you in His arms. You see, I know; I been a sinner myself."

During the spring of 1889 Lloyd Osbourne began writing "The Pearl Fisher," a novel set in the South Seas. After completing a draft of the first six chapters, he lost interest in the project, due, in large part, to Stevenson's constant criticisms: "try as I would I could not please R.L.S. I wrote and rewrote, and rewrote again, but always to have him shake his head. Finally, at his suggestion and in utter hopelessness, I laid the manuscript by, hoping to come back to it later with greater success. But I never did."[1]

Lloyd resumed working on "The Pearl Fisher" at Vailima in March 1890. In April Stevenson added his own material while cruising aboard the *Janet Nicoll*, but he grew tired of the idea three months later. The manuscript was abandoned for the next two and one-half years while he penned "The Beach of Falesa" and "The Isle of Voices," two South Seas tales that were paired with "The Bottle Imp" (written during the winter of 1889–90) and published as *Island Nights' Entertainments* in April 1893, and "The Waif Woman," a supernatural short story that remained unpublished until 1914.

Stevenson returned to "The Pearl Fisher" in February 1893 and, working at a frantic pace, wrote revision after revision, altering the length somewhat and, at one point, changing the title to "The Schooner Farallone." "But O, it has been such a grind!" he wrote to Sidney Colvin. "I break down at every paragraph ... and lie here and sweat, till I can get one sentence wrung out after another."[2] When he completed the final draft in early June 1893, he noted, "Well it's done. ... Those tragic 16 pp. are at last finished, and I ... have spent thirteen days about as nearly in Hell as a man could expect to live through."[3]

"The Ebb Tide. By Robert Louis Stevenson and Lloyd Osbourne" was published as 13 weekly installments in *To-day* 1 (November 11, 1893–February 3, 1894), and as six monthly installments in *McClure's Magazine* (February–July 1894). Having received £600 for the serial rights, Stevenson was offered £200 down on a 20 percent royalty by *McClure's*, who arranged publication with Stone and Kimball of Chicago. On July 15, 1894, *The Ebb-Tide: A Trio and Quartette* first appeared in book form. A British edition, published by William Heinemann of London, appeared on September 21, 1894.

Though it is one of Stevenson's lesser-known works, *The Ebb-Tide* is a coherent and fully realized work that demonstrates the enormous literary growth he experienced during the last two years of his life. Unfortunately, it was also the last of his fictional works to be published during his lifetime.

Most contemporary critics found Stevenson's pessimistic thematics and lowlife characters to be distasteful. Even Sidney Colvin disliked the majority of the tale but commented that the last two chapters had been written "with astonishing genius."[4] Israel Zangwill, writing in the New York *Critic*, praised Stevenson's stark examination of human disillusionment; he called it a "little masterpiece," "an enthralling romance," and "a subtle study of the psychology of blackguardism."[5]

The personalities of Stevenson's morally dubious characters constantly fluctuate: Their actions never become predictable, and their reliance upon one another often affects their respective attitudes. Huish's love of drink induces Davis to reclaim an alcoholic lifestyle, just as Herrick's sensitivity persuades the captain to give up booze and develop more tolerance for others. This psychological intricacy maintains a level of suspense throughout the novella.

Herrick, in particular, undergoes a series of mental transformations.

In the early chapters, set in Tahiti, he is a morally bankrupt failure who is too lethargic to improve his impoverished situation. Unable to accomplish anything on his own, Herrick is strengthened by Davis, whose ambition is the catalyst for many of his actions (writing a letter to his sweetheart, becoming first mate on the *Farallone*, and his participation in the plot against Attwater). His psychological complexity is demonstrated in chapter eight ("Better Acquaintance"), during his first meeting with Attwater:

> Herrick meanwhile resolved and resisted an immense temptation, to go up, to touch him on the arm, and breathe a word in his ear: "Beware, they are going to murder you." There would be one life saved; but what of the two others? The three lives went up and down before him like buckets in a well, or like the scales of balances. It had come to a choice, and one that must be speedy. For certain invaluable minutes the wheels of life ran before him, and he could still divert them with a touch to the one side or to the other; still choose who was to live and who was to die. He considered the men. Attwater intrigued, puzzled, dazzled, enchanted, and revolted him. Alive, he seemed but a doubtful good; and the thought of him lying dead was so unwelcome that it pursued him, like a vision, with every circumstance of color and sound. Incessantly he had before him the image of that great mass of man, stricken down, in varying attitudes and with varying wounds,— fallen prone, fallen supine, fallen on his side, or clinging to a doorpost, with the changing face and the relaxing fingers of the death agony. He heard the click of the

trigger, the thud of the ball, the cry of the victim; he saw the blood flow. And this building-up of circumstance was like a consecration of the man, till he seemed to walk in sacrificial fillets. Next he considered Davis, with his thick-fingered, coarse-grained, oat-bread commonness of nature; his indomitable valor and mirth in the old days of their starvation; the endearing blend of his faults and virtues; the sudden shining forth of a tenderness that lay too deep for tears; his children,—Ada and her bowel complaint; and Ada's doll. No, death could not be suffered to approach that head, even in fancy. With a general heat and a bracing of muscles, it was borne in on Herrick that Ada's father would find in him a son to the death. And even Huish shared a little in that sacredness; by the tacit adoption of daily life they were become brothers; there was an implied bond of loyalty in their cohabitation of the ship and of their past miseries, to which Herrick must be a little true or wholly dishonored. Horror of sudden death for horror of sudden death, there was here no hesitation possible: it must be Attwater. And no sooner was the thought formed (which was a sentence) than the whole mind of the man ran in a panic to the other side; and when he looked within himself, he was aware only of turbulence and inarticulate outcry.

Here Stevenson continues by explaining the metaphor in his title: "In all this there was no thought of Robert Herrick. He had complied with the ebb-tide in man's affairs, and the tide had carried him away; he heard already the roaring of the maelstrom that must hurry him under. And in his bedeviled and dishonored soul there was no thought of self."

After Herrick becomes acquainted with the authoritarian Attwater, he breaks down and, in his greatest moment of weakness, contemplates suicide. While swimming in the lagoon, he wrestles with his moral dilemma: "There were men who could commit suicide: there were men who could not; and he was one who could not." Perhaps motivated by fear, he decides to support Attwater—an experience from which he emerges with greater emotional stability.

Davis has a positive effect on Herrick but fails to live up to the standard he advocates for others. Prior to boarding the *Farallone*, he appears confident and courageous, but the uncertain nature of the voyage and the influence of Huish take their toll after the schooner sails from Tahiti. Affected by alcohol, he relies on Herrick, who has no previous sailing experience. On the island he vacillates between bravado and fear before losing his identity altogether.

Obnoxious and irresponsible in the early chapters, Huish becomes an apathetic drunkard on board the schooner, but he later proves his mettle when Davis fails to devise an effective plan. His attempt to murder Attwater with vitriol is the most courageous action performed by any member of the trio.

Unlike *Treasure Island*, wherein the *Hispaniola* and the island provide the settings for sweeping adventure, *The Ebb-Tide*'s ship and island perform a more symbolic function. Before Herrick, Davis, and Huish board the *Farallone*, they work together as a trio; but shortly after the voyage begins, they become self-interested and ineffective. In chapter six ("The Partners") each blames the others for their sorry state of affairs, and a violent altercation is avoided only when Uncle Ned spots the island. Here the three men escape the closed quarters of the schooner, only to discover an equally claustrophobic existence: even an obscure South Sea island cannot provide escape from oppression and frustration.

J. R. Hammond expertly analyzes the dual personality of the island god:

> Attwater, one of Stevenson's most profound characterizations, gives an outward impression of urbanity and confidence: he appears to be the embodiment of an English gentleman. It becomes apparent, however, that the facade of civilisation conceals a ruthless and authoritarian nature. He is a man who will brook no interference in his domain, who dispenses a puritanical order of justice over the native population and who will go to any lengths to conceal the secret of his island treasure. He magnetises the three men with the overpowering force of his personality and, whilst all three are soon consumed with hatred, it is a hatred inseparably overshadowed by fear.[6]

Attwater's evangelical Christianity is a vehicle for Stevenson's thoughts about religion; although political discussions are included in his earlier works, *The Ebb-Tide* contains his first major effort to examine religion in a novelistic context. Like the political arguments between Alan Breck and David Balfour, the debate between the fanatical Attwater and the agnostic Herrick is an outgrowth of their characterizations, not a philosophical statement grafted onto the story. Attwater's fervor is not apparent when the trio arrives but is drawn out by Herrick after the two meet on his estate; when the former attempts to describe how divine intervention affects people's lives, the latter offers a more realistic explanation:

> "Well, I saw these machines come up dripping and go down again, and come up dripping and go down again, and all the while the fellow inside as dry as toast," said Attwater; "and I thought we all wanted a dress to go down into the world in, and come up scatheless. What do you think the name was?" he inquired.
> "Self-conceit," said Herrick.
> "Ah, but I mean seriously," said Attwater.
> "Call it self-respect then," corrected Herrick, with a laugh.
> "And why not grace? Why not God's grace, Hay?" asked Attwater. "Why not the grace of your Maker and Redeemer, He who died for you, He who upholds you, He whom you crucify daily afresh? There is nothing here"—striking on his bosom—"nothing there"—smiting the wall—"and nothing there"—stamping—"nothing but God's grace! We walk upon, we breathe it; we live and die by it; it makes the nails and axles of the universe; and the puppy in pyjamas prefers self-conceit!" The huge dark man stood over against Herrick by the line of divers' helmets, and seemed to swell and glow; and the next moment the life had gone from him. "I beg your pardon," said he; "I see you don't believe in God."
> "Not in your sense, I am afraid," said Herrick.

"I never argue with young atheists or habitual drunkards," said Attwater, flippantly. "Let us go across the island to the outer beach."

Attwater's assertion about young atheists rings untrue, however, as he soon begins to argue with Herrick after the latter claims to despise himself. Advising Herrick to "fall on his knees" before God, Attwater becomes the crusading evangelist:

> He spread out his arms like a crucifix; his face shone with the brightness of a seraph's; in his voice, as it rose to the last word, the tears seemed ready.
>
> Herrick made a vigorous call upon himself. "Attwater," he said, "you push me beyond bearing. What am I to do? I do not believe. It is living truth to you; to me, upon my conscience, only folklore. I do not believe there is any form of words under heaven by which I can lift the burden from my shoulders. I must stagger on to the end with the pack of my responsibility; I cannot shift it. Do you suppose I would not, if I thought I could? I cannot—cannot—cannot—and let that suffice!"
>
> The rapture was all gone from Attwater's countenance; the dark apostle had disappeared, and in his place there stood an easy, sneering gentleman, who took off his hat and bowed. It was pertly done, and the blood burned in Herrick's face.

The last two chapters include several unforgettable images, but Herrick's sighting of Davis as he kneels in prayer is perhaps the most powerful. Here, the once colorful and venturesome sea captain becomes a timid creature enslaved by Attwater's religious extremism. While Herrick may choose to return to civilization, Davis is unable to make his own decisions. In chapter 11 ("David and Goliath"), the captain's acceptance of an evangelical moral code is a product of coercion, but such a transformation does fit into his general nature; a few pages before the fateful encounter, Stevenson foreshadows the outcome in a brilliantly written paragraph:

> The captain had come upon this errand for any one of a dozen reasons, the last of which was desire for its success. Superstition rules all men; semi-ignorant and gross natures, like that of Davis, it rules utterly. For murder he had been prepared; but this horror of the medicine in the bottle went beyond him, and he seemed to himself to be parting the last strands that united him to God. The boat carried him on to reprobation, to damnation; and he suffered himself to be carried, passively consenting, silently bidding farewell to his better self and his hopes.

The geographical and physical detail in *The Ebb-Tide* often serves a dark, metaphorical purpose. Like the familiar Scottish topography that enhances *Kidnapped* and *The Master of Ballantrae,* the settings are literary equivalents of locales that Stevenson visited during his years in the South Seas—environments which reflect the disappointment he sometimes experienced. Robert Kiely writes:

> When one recalls the boyish eagerness with which Stevenson looked forward to the health, simplicity, and natural morality of the Pacific islands it is not surprising that he was profoundly disillusioned, almost staggered, by his

first-hand sight of leprosy, influenza, and smallpox; appalled by the realities of cannibalism, devil worship, fetishism, sexual license; and revolted by the natural phenomenon of life feeding upon life in the very coral rock which supported him.[7]

The settings are an autobiographical element, as are many of the characters' personality traits. Herrick's disappointment with foreign travel and his longing to see his native England parallel the growing nostalgia Stevenson felt for Scotland. Early in chapter two ("Morning on the Beach") Stevenson's interest in the songs of Robert Burns is recalled when Davis sings to the Kanaka crew on board the dinghy schooner. A rare moment of optimism, this passage provides one of the novella's few humorous moments:

> "Tapena Tom *harry my*," said the spokesman, pointing.
> And the three beach-combers, following his indication, saw the figure of a man in pajama trousers and a white jumper approaching briskly from the town.
> "That's Tapena Tom, is it?" said the captain, pausing in his music. "I don't seem to place the brute."
> "We'd better cut," said the clerk. "'E's no good."
> "Well," said the musician, deliberately, "one can't most always generally tell. I'll try it on, I guess. Music has charms to soothe the savage Tapena, boys. We might strike it rich; it might amount to iced punch in the cabin."
> "Hiced punch?" Oh, my!" said the clerk. "Give him something 'ot, captain. 'Way down the Swanee River'; try that."
> "No, *sir!* Looks Scotch," said the captain; and he struck, for his life, into "Auld Lang Syne."
> Captain Tom continued to approach with the same businesslike alacrity; no change was to be perceived in his bearded face as he came swinging up the plank; he did not even turn his eyes on the performer.
>
> We twa hae paidled in the burn
> Frae morning tide till dine,
>
> went the song.
> Captain Tom had a parcel under his arm, which he laid on the house-roof, and then, turning suddenly to the strangers, "Here you!" he bellowed, "be off out of that!"

Attwater, whose intolerant religious and imperialist values are tempered by a complex psychology, is not a mere villain; in fact, Stevenson lent the megalomaniac a few of his own beliefs and interests. When Herrick observes some old sailing gear in chapter eight, Attwater comments, "You are like me—nothing so affecting as ships! . . . The ruins of an empire would leave me frigid, when a bit of an old rail that an old shellback leaned on in the middle watch would bring me up all standing." Some of Stevenson's motivations for exploring the Pacific are suggested when Herrick queries Attwater about the island:

> "What brought you here to the South Seas?" he asked.
> "Many things," said Attwater. "Youth, curiosity, romance, the love of the sea, and (it will surprise you to hear) an interest in missions. That has a good deal declined, which will surprise you less. They go the wrong way to work; they are too parsonish, too much of the old wife, and even the old apple-wife. *Clothes, clothes,* are their

idea; but clothes are not Christianity, any more than they are the sun in heaven, or could take the place of it! They think a parsonage with roses, and church bells, and nice old women bobbing in the lanes, are part and parcel of religion. But religion is a savage thing, like the universe it illuminates; savage, cold, and bare, but infinitely strong."

Like Stevenson, Attwater considers organized religion to be a facade that obscures the more positive aspects of Christianity, but he holds this belief for vastly different reasons. And the idea that Attwater's interest in Christian missions will surprise Herrick recalls Stevenson's own complex approach to the culture and society that he found in the South Seas. Kiely adds:

> [L]ike many commentators on the Pacific, Stevenson placed heavy blame for corruption and hardship on white settlers. He was well aware ... that several deadly and contagious diseases had been introduced to the islands by colonials, free-traders, and missionaries; that, because of them, whole village populations were threatened with extinction. ... But it is important to see that he quickly disabused himself of the oversimplified notion of a totally harmful civilization tainting a native Eden. He devoted much of his time in the South Seas to defending Christian missionaries and government officials as well as the rights of the island populace.[8]

Like "The Beach of Falesá," *The Ebb-Tide* incorporates Stevenson's perceptions of the racism he encountered in the Pacific. The exploitation of Kanakas, or South Sea natives, by white settlers is represented by the condescending attitudes displayed by Davis and Huish. Interestingly, Herrick, a well-educated Englishman, does not echo his companions' usage of the derogatory terms "nigger" and "pickaninny," and he treats the crew members with consideration: When the native whom Davis christens Uncle Ned insists that he be called Taveeta, his proper name, Herrick obliges and soon strikes up a friendship with him.

Stevenson features no significant females in *The Ebb-Tide*, only "a plump and pretty woman" whom Herrick notices in the doorway of Attwater's house: "'Too pretty,' said Attwater. 'That was why I had her married. A man never knows when he may be inclined to be a fool about women: so when we were left alone, I had the pair of them to the chapel and performed the ceremony. She made a lot of fuss. I do not take at all the romantic views of marriage,' he explained." Here Attwater displays a very Stevensonian view of marriage, a comment that recalls Mackellar's attitude toward women in *The Master of Ballantrae*.

Some events, such as the storm at sea and the climactic confrontation, are unforgettable. Stevenson's ability to imbue his scenes with a visual quality is demonstrated strikingly in chapter eight, when he simultaneously captures a general setting and a specific, elaborate body of detail:

> The storehouses were nearest him upon his right. The first was locked; in the second he could dimly perceive, through a window, a certain accumulation of pearl shell piled in the far end; the third,

which stood gaping open on the afternoon, seized on the mind of Herrick with its multiplicity and disorder of romantic things. Therein were cables, windlasses, and blocks of every size and capacity; cabin windows and ladders; rusty tanks; a companion hatch; a binnacle with its brass mountings, and its compass idly pointing, in the confusion and dusk of that shed, to a forgotten pole; ropes, anchors, harpoons; a blubber-dipper of copper, green with years; a steering-wheel; a tool-chest with the vessel's name upon the top, the *Asia,*—a whole curiosity-shop of sea curios, gross and solid, heavy to lift, ill to break, bound with brass and shod with iron. Two wrecks at least must have contributed to this random heap of lumber; and as Herrick looked upon it, it seemed to him as if the two ships' companies were there on guard, and he heard the tread of feet and whisperings, and saw with the tail of his eye the commonplace ghosts of sailormen.

This beautiful and haunting passage, with its combination of narrative description and character psychology, could be cinematically visualized through a series of close-ups and superimpositions, but the result would be a collection of interconnected images, rather than the unbroken, flowing portrait painted by Stevenson. It would be a mistake to claim that this paragraph could not be adapted faithfully by a talented filmmaker, but odds are that the filmic version would pale by comparison.

There are, however, many images in the story that could be transferred rigorously to film. Stevenson's depiction of the captain aboard ship in chapter five ("The Cargo of Champagne") appears tailor-made for the cinema:

The captain sat in the boat to windward, bellowing orders and insults, his eyes glazed, his face deeply congested, a bottle set between his knees, a glass in his hand, half empty. His back was to the squall, and he was first intent upon the setting of the sail. When that was done, and the great trapezium of canvas had begun to draw and to trail the lee-rail of the *Farallone* level with the foam, he laughed out an empty laugh, drained his glass, sprawled back among the lumber in the boat, and fetched out a crumpled novel.

The visual quality of the prose sometimes is represented by single sentences that describe an entire action. In chapter five, when Davis bellows a command to his crew during the storm, Stevenson delivers a powerful jolt: "But before it was well uttered, the squall shouted aloud and fell, in a solid mass of wind and rain commingled, on the *Farallone*, and she stooped under the blow, and lay like a thing dead."

Dialogue perfectly complements descriptive passages, particularly when it is used to develop the characterizations. In chapter seven ("The Pearl Fisher"), when Davis describes Attwater's behavior and reveals his own opinions about class divisions, Stevenson builds the character's individuality with word choice, punctuation, and dialect:

"Huish means the same as what I do," said Davis. "When that man came stepping around, and saying: 'Look here, I'm Attwater'—and you knew it was so, by God!—I sized him right straight up. Here's the real article, I said, and I don't like it; here's the real, firstrate, copper-bottomed aristocrat. *'Aw! don't know ye, do I? God d--n ye, did God make ye?'* No, that couldn't be nothing but genuine; a man's got to be born to that. And notice! smart as champagne and hard as nails; no kind of a fool; no, *sir!* not a pound of him! Well, what's he here upon this beastly island for? I said. *He's* not here collecting eggs. He's a palace at home, and powdered flunkies; and if he don't stay there, you bet he knows the reason why! Follow?"

The surprising changes in the characters' behavior and attitudes often are revealed through dialogue. In chapter 11, when Huish begins to contradict his formerly weak and apathetic nature, he offers a bold and perceptive view of murder: "'Look as long as you like,' Huish was going on. 'You don't see any green in my eye. I ain't afryde of Attwater, I ain't afryde of you, and I ain't afryde of words. You want to kill people, that's wot *you* want; but you want to do it with kid gloves, and it can't be done that w'y. Murder ain't genteel, it ain't easy, it ain't safe, and it takes a man to do it. 'Ere's the man.'"

In chapter eight an interesting parallel with "The Body-Snatcher" occurs when Attwater compares Herrick's personality with those of his two companions. Here Dr. Wolfe Macfarlane's concept of the lions and the lambs is rephrased in Attwater's own canine terminology:

> "I knew that you despised yourself," said Attwater. "I saw the blood come into your face to-day when you remembered Oxford. And I could have blushed for you myself, to see a man, a gentleman, with those two vulgar wolves."
>
> Herrick faced him with a thrill. "Wolves?" he repeated.
>
> "I said wolves, and vulgar wolves," said Attwater. "Do you know that to-day, when I came on board, I trembled?"
>
> "You concealed it well," stammered Herrick.
>
> "A habit of mine," said Attwater. "But I was afraid, for all that. I was afraid of the two wolves." He raised his hand slowly. "And now, Hay, you poor, lost puppy, what do you do with the two wolves?"

Attwater's comments recall those of Macfarlane, and the implementation of his own moral code on the island (taking whatever he wants from the environment and forcing others to live according to his sense of law and justice) also resembles the behavior of that erstwhile Edinburgh anatomist.

Though *The Ebb-Tide* has been neglected by many critics and readers, a few Stevenson scholars have ascertained its significance. Hammond claims that it "must be ranked as one of his most seminal works of fiction, a work which can be compared with Conrad's *Victory* as a penetrating study of the human condition."[9]

Stevenson did experience literary maturation during his final years, but his exploration of religion and other forms of organized moral codes in *The Ebb-Tide* is an expansion of themes that he had touched upon previously. His incorporation of these ideas into the characters' personae, rather than the use of a more polemical approach, is an admirable stylistic method and a tribute to his art. Kiely concludes:

It is a mark of the quality and depth of Stevenson's love for Samoa that it did not remain for long that of a foreign traveler in search of the picturesque. He found during his years in the Pacific, with its superstition, taboos, fear of death, envy, pride, lust, petty contentions, that the whole range of human wretchedness and human folly is neither the peculiar product nor the peculiar property of an anglicized Christian civilization in the nineteenth century, but perhaps the perennial and universal condition of man.[10]

## *Ebb Tide* (Paramount, 1922)

The first screen version of *The Ebb-Tide* is, like many other Stevenson adaptations, a Hollywood patchwork draped upon the bones of the original story. Screenwriter Waldemar Young not only added a female love interest for Herrick but he also threw in an exotic native dancer to increase the film's box-office appeal.

The film opens in Tahiti, where Robert Herrick (James Kirkwood), J. L. Huish (Raymond Hatton), and Captain Davis (George Fawcett) are beachcombing; but their desperate attempts to escape poverty in the novella are exchanged for a standardized movie device: Hired by men who want to cash in on an insurance indemnity, they become victims of sabotage (knowing that Davis is an alcoholic, the owners of the ship place enough champagne on board to ensure a successful wreck). After they weather a savage storm and reach an uncharted island, they meet—not an evangelical fanatic living with two servants and a native girl (who never speaks and is seen only once)—but Richard Attwater (Noah Beery), an island king who has murdered his wife and her lover. Currently living with his daughter, Ruth Attwater (Lila Lee), he forces the natives to dive for pearls in the nearby lagoon. Soon Herrick's amoral ways are overcome by his love for Ruth, and he refuses to aid Davis and Huish in the theft of Attwater's pearls. The others meet violent deaths, and the two young lovers embrace for the final fade-out, knowing that they will live happily ever after in the company of the liberated natives.

A critic for the *New York Times* who had never read the novella was wise enough to spot the hokum in the film's plot: "A stranger to the tale can only report that the picture seems to have more girl-and-virtue intensity than one is accustomed to find in the free-flung thrillers of the great narrator."[11] *Variety*'s "Fred" also wrote a lukewarm review:

> This started out as though it was going to be a whale of a picture, but simmered down, lost its punch and finished as one of the usual run of program features that the Paramount are releasing. Nothing out of the ordinary about it that will lift it above the class of the fair calibred box-office attractions, although it seemingly could have been turned into a sure-fire commercial hit.[12]

Not surprisingly, Young's screenplay avoids religious and social references and, particularly, Stevenson's downbeat denouement. At 80 minutes the film is overlong but features some fine underwater cinematography and a host of good

*Ebb Tide* (1937). Captain "Thorbecke" (Oscar Homolka), Huish (Barry Fitzgerald), and Herrick (Ray Milland), in the first Stevenson adaptation filmed in Technicolor. Unfortunately, the philosophical and psychological complexities of the novella are lost amid a string of Hollywood cliches.

performances. As Captain Davis, George Fawcett, a major character star who appeared in several films for D. W. Griffith, stands out in a cast of capable and well-known actors. Most reviewers found his performance, along with that of Raymond Hatton, to be the film's greatest asset.

## *Ebb Tide* (Paramount, 1937)

Paramount's 1937 remake of *The Ebb-Tide* was the first Stevenson adaptation to be shot in Technicolor. As scripted by Hollywood veteran Bertram Millhauser, this version is more faithful to the novella, but, once again, the studio could not resist adding a female love interest for Herrick. The narrative closely follows the story until Faith Wishart (Frances Farmer), daughter of the ship's deceased captain, joins the trio on their ocean voyage. When Herrick (Ray Milland) gets a good look at her, he abandons the plan developed by Captain Thorbecke (Oscar Homolka) and Huish (Barry Fitzgerald) to sell the ship and champagne in Peru. After the group (not the trio of the novella, but a quartet at this point) reach the uncharted island, they meet Attwater (Lloyd Nolan), who murders both Huish and the captain, leaving Herrick and Miss Wishart to go about their romantic business.

The basic outline and a few specific passages from the novella are included, but, as with the 1922 version, the substance and significance of the tale are touched upon only vaguely. The romantic subplot again interferes with the efforts of Huish and the captain, and, worse yet, the tormented Herrick becomes a one-dimensional, predictable Hollywood hero. The direction of James Hogan, who specialized in B programmers during the 1930s and early 1940s, is pedestrian, and the Technicolor compositions of Ray Rennahan and Leo Tover (which include some out-of-focus close-ups) often contribute to the stilted and unrealistic atmosphere.

Lloyd Nolan offers a glimpse of Attwater's complex personality, but the deliberate histrionics of Oscar Homolka (who made his American film debut here) transform the captain into an implausible caricature. Ray Milland makes a valiant effort but cannot overcome the superficial nature of his characterization.

Frances Farmer, who had appeared in six Hollywood productions prior to receiving second billing here, is pleasant window dressing but embarrassingly out of place. When the film premiered in October 1937, most reviewers singled out her performance and the romantic subplot as "secondary" and "cavalier" (which is not surprising, since none of this material appears in the novella). While *Variety*'s "Char." noted that the love interest "isn't the kind that guarantees satisfaction,"[13] Frank S. Nugent, writing in the *New York Times*, criticized Millhauser for "tossing" it into the plot—a plot, he claimed, that did not deserve much consideration: "A love interest, in itself, would have been no heresy, for 'The Ebb Tide' is only on the classical shelf by courtesy or contagion."[14] Nugent's comment (and subsequent two-sentence synopsis) suggests that either he neglected to read the novella or he shared the opinions of earlier literary critics who considered the subject matter to be "distasteful." However, he did join "Char." in praising the talents of Barry Fitzgerald:

> He plays him as Stevenson drew him: a poisonous, corrupt, amoral little toad; drink-sodden, foul-mouthed, conscienceless; blustering one moment, cringing the next, treacherous and sycophantic by turns. So outrageous a villain is he that he becomes somehow lovable—like Peter Lorre without the undercurrent of menace. Mr. Fitzgerald's Huish is one of the really great performances of the year.[15]

Fitzgerald's interpretation of Huish is actually a slight variation on a character that he played throughout his career: a hard-drinking, witty, and occasionally obnoxious Irish priest or friend of the protagonist. Born in Dublin on March 10, 1888, he landed the role of Huish after making his Hollywood debut in the John Ford–directed *The Plough and the Stars* the previous year. His performances usually border on caricature, and his Huish, although lauded at the time, is no exception. He won a best supporting actor Academy Award for his role as Father Fitzgibbon in the Leo McCarey–directed *Going My Way* in 1944, but is best remembered for his work in other John Ford productions, including *The Long Voyage Home* (1940), *How Green Was My Valley* (1941), and *The Quiet Man* (1952).

The film features a large number of fabricated characters, including several women. Some of the Kanaka crew members, including Taveeta (here called Tahiera [Harry Field]) and Sally Day (George Piltz), appear but are portrayed primarily by brown-tinted white actors. The most absurd component is Ralph Rainger and Leo Robin's syrupy choral "special title number" called "Ebb Tide" that surges onto the soundtrack during the closing credits.

## *Adventure Island* (Paramount, 1947)

Not satisfied with two adaptations of *The Ebb-Tide*, Paramount produced yet another cinematic version in 1947. Why the studio bothered to film the story a third time is hard to imagine, considering that screenwriter Maxwell Shane basically paraphrased the 1937 script used by James Hogan. Again, Faith Wishart, the deceased captain's daughter (Rhonda Fleming, who "is eye-appealing in some scant costumes"[16]), remains aboard ship to fall in love with Herrick (an incredibly wooden Rory Calhoun), but Mr. Huish (John Abbott) and the captain (called Donald Lochlin and played by Paul Kelly this time around) do dip into the champagne and discover the water-filled bottles. For some reason, Shane and director Peter Stewart excised the storm sequence and substituted a weak scene of the captain dropping anchor at an uncharted island to restock the ship's dwindling supplies.

On the island the group encounters Attwater (Alan Napier), a madman who actually believes he is God. As written by Shane and portrayed by Napier, Attwater is no longer the complex character of the novella, but a stock, horror-film villain. As proof of his cartoon-like insanity, he murders both Huish and the captain before falling into his own snakepit! The clichéd ending reaches the pinnacle of Hollywood hokum when Herrick and the lovely Miss Wishart sail off into the sunset.

*Variety*'s "Brog." considered the film to be "nifty pulp fiction for adventure-lovers,"[17] while "A.W." of the *New York Times* called it "pretty sad" and "dull, incredible and slowly paced."[18] Running a mere 66 minutes, this final entry in Paramount's *Ebb Tide* trilogy benefits from the rich Cinecolor camerawork of Jack Greenhaigh, but too much fabrication and caricature creates yet another disappointing adventure. Considering that the complex and little-known novella is difficult, if not impossible, to adapt, perhaps it should be left for those readers willing to locate the original in a bookstore or on a dusty library shelf.

## *The Ebb-Tide* on Television

In 1952 the BBC aired an English television adaptation of *The Ebb-Tide*. To date, this abridged effort remains the sole small-screen version.

• SEVENTEEN •

# No Bagatelle: *St. Ives* (1896)

> *"Rowley, you need have no fear. By how much I love my own honour, by so much I will take care to protect yours. We are but fraternising at the outposts, as soldiers do. When the bugle calls, my boy, we must face each other, one for England, one for France, and may God defend the right!"*—ANNE DE KEROUAL DE SAINT-YVES, in *St. Ives*.

In May 1813 Monsieur le Vicomte Anne de Keroual de Saint-Yves, a private in Napoleon Bonaparte's army, is imprisoned in Edinburgh Castle. Joining several hundred "very ignorant" comrades, the noble Frenchman masquerades as Champdivers, a common soldier. Engaged as an interpreter by some of the officers, he assists Major Chevenix, who combines French lessons with his morning meals.

Though the prisoners are forced to live on inadequate rations and wear unattractive, mustard yellow uniforms, they are allowed weekly visitations by local citizens. During a succession of Saturday visits, St. Ives becomes acquainted with Flora Gilchrist, a beautiful young woman, and her brother, Ronald.

After his second meeting with Flora, St. Ives is accosted by Philippe Goguelat, a fellow prisoner and "brute of the first water," who insults the young woman's honor. St. Ives challenges him to a duel and mortally wounds him with a scissor tied to a wooden pole. Fearing an investigation, the other prisoners vow to withhold all information pertaining to the incident.

Three days afterward the dying Goguelat whispers to St. Ives: "Trust me ... I'll take it to hell with me, and tell the devil." Chevenix then reveals his knowledge of the duel and suggests that the fracas was prompted by a lady.

One morning after Goguelat's death St. Ives is visited by Daniel Romaine, a London solicitor employed by Count de Keroual, St. Ives's great-uncle who had left pre-Revolutionary France for a life of luxury in England. Displeased with the conduct of St. Ives's cousin, Monsieur le Vicomte Alain de Saint-Yves, a Bonapartist spy, the ailing count has authored a new will bequeathing all interests to his more gentlemanly great-nephew. Romaine gives St. Ives money, informs him that he must escape to collect the inheritance, and suggests that he contact Burchell Fenn, a Wakefield gentleman who smuggles French prisoners out of England.

About three days later the Gilchrists pay another visit. In love with Flora, St. Ives reveals his true identity and asks to know the location of their home. Flora escorts St. Ives to the southern side of the fortress and points to Swanston Cottage near the Pentland Hills. The next morning Chevenix compliments St. Ives on his taste in women.

Some time later the prisoners in St. Ives's squad complete a tunnel near the "Devil's Elbow," the southwest corner of the "abominable precipice." Appointed as leader, St. Ives climbs down a rope as a thick sea-fog envelops the castle. Thirty minutes later, he reaches the ground and signals for the others to follow.

Before sunrise St. Ives reaches Swanston, and Flora ushers him into a nearby hen house. Early the next morning he is allowed to wash, change clothes, and eat in the cottage, where Flora's aunt is sleeping upstairs. Later the old woman regrets hiding a French prisoner under her roof, but provides him with Scottish currency and transportation.

In the company of Mr. Sim and Mr. Candlish, two cattle drovers, the fugitive makes his way south. One evening they are attacked by three men, but St. Ives scares them off when he bludgeons one with a cudgel. He then crosses the border, leisurely treks along the Great North Road, and arrives in the neighborhood of Wakefield, where he meets Burchell Fenn and joins forces with two French officers planning to escape from England.

At an alehouse in Bedfordshire, St. Ives is annoyed by Thomas Dudgeon, an attorney's clerk employed by Daniel Romaine. Shortly after noon the next day he hires a chaise and heads toward Amersham Place, the home of his great-uncle. At the estate he is given a private room and introduced to his valet, Rowley, a garrulous boy of about 16. After dinner he is ushered into the dying count's bedroom, where he receives a dispatch box containing paper notes and gold coins valued at £10,000. When Alain arrives to contest the inheritance, Romaine threatens to expose his treasonable activities. Accompanied by Rowley, St. Ives ventures into the snowy night with the dispatch box, a case of pistols, two valises, and the address of Mr. Robbie, an Edinburgh attorney.

The following morning St. Ives purchases a claret-colored chaise from the postmaster at Aylesbury; spotting Alain and two redcoats, he and Rowley make a quick exit. On the road near Gretna Green they run across a couple in the midst of an elopement: St. Ives rescues the 17-year-old, "pretty as an angel" girl from the arguments of Mr. Bellamy, "a half-bred hawbuck," and offers her a seat in the chaise. Determined to have his way, Bellamy, accompanied by two post-boys, follows on horseback. During the pursuit the girl introduces herself as Dorothy Greensleeves, before St. Ives blunderingly reveals his name. When the driver turns onto a southbound road, Bellamy gallops up to the chaise and fires a shot through the window; the bullet grazes St. Ives's forearm and lodges in a left-hand panel. Congratulated by Dorothy's father, the gallant hero and his valet resume their journey.

At an inn in Kirkby Lonsdale, St. Ives attempts to sell the chaise but barely escapes from the inquisitive innkeeper. After renting a room in Edinburgh, he sets out for Swanston, where he speaks to Flora through a barred window. During his declaration of love, he describes the duel with Goguelat and gives her "eight thousand odd pounds" in paper money.

On the way back to Edinburgh the following morning, he meets Mr. Robbie, the lawyer recommended by Romaine. The next day he learns that the drovers were not convicted for assaulting Mr. Faa, who has recovered from his wounds.

On Tuesday Rowley is unable to withdraw their funds from a guarded bank in George Street. Later St. Ives reads a newspaper report about his reappearance in the city. He then attempts to retrieve the money from Flora but is repelled by Major Chevenix, Ronald Gilchrist, and a "monster" dog.

At 8:00 P.M. on Thursday St. Ives attends an assembly ball at Mr. Robbie's home. When Flora arrives, accompanied by her aunt, Ronald, and Chevenix, he describes his desperate situation. Soon Alain appears, and after the two cousins confront each other, St. Ives sneaks into the Gilchrists' carriage.

In the wet and windy countryside near Swanston, St. Ives awaits the dawn. Shortly after 8:00 A.M. he meets Flora at an old quarry, and as the strains of "The Caledonian Hunt's Delight" waft over the hill, he stumbles upon a hot-air balloon demonstration in the meadow below. When Chevenix, Ronald, Alain, and other pursuers arrive, he climbs aboard the car of the balloon, joining Mr. Byfield, the owner, and Sheepshanks, a stowaway. Dalmahoy, a fourth passenger, comes aboard after he entangles himself in a depending rope.

Twenty hours later, the "incomplete aeronauts" ditch the balloon near a brig in Bristol channel. Making the acquaintance of Captain Colenso and his crew, St. Ives joins their voyage to Massachusetts (where he hopes to locate a French-bound vessel), while the other three agree to be dropped at Falmouth; in haste, St. Ives writes a letter to Flora and entrusts it to Mr. Byfield. Off the U.S. East Coast Colenso is killed by officers who claim that he reneged on a pledge to return American prisoners to the United States. Aided by the French Consul, St. Ives sails for Bordeaux on February 2, 1814.

On March 10 St. Ives reaches France and by March 30 is near the gates of Paris. As the Cossacks and Prussians invade the city, he witnesses the last stages of the Napoleonic conflict. At the home of Madame Jupille, he is told that Romaine will deliver a missive from Flora, so he patiently waits until April 5, when Alain arrives and threatens to turn him over to the police. In the nick of time Romaine enters and informs them that Chevenix has cleared St. Ives of the "murder."

At Dover, St. Ives is reunited with Rowley, and after a brief stay in London, they head to Edinburgh and Swanston Cottage. Following an early June wedding, St. Ives and Flora settle at Amersham Place, where the former Bonapartist enjoys a life of "inaction." As Flora expects her first child, the happy couple visits Edinburgh, where Ronald, now a soldier in the British Army, prepares to join the Duke of Wellington's forces.

Stevenson began dictating *St. Ives* to Isobel Strong at Vailima in January 1893. A month later he abandoned it for *The Ebb-Tide*, which he had put aside two and one-half years earlier. After completing the final draft of the latter in early June 1893, he corrected the proofs for *Catriona* before returning to *St. Ives* in late August. He again took advantage of his amanuensis and dictated the first 30 chapters at an erratic pace before shelving the novel in September 1894. In June of that year he had mentioned it in a letter to Bob Stevenson: "I have got to a crossing place, I suppose; the present book, *Saint Ives*, is nothing; it is in no style in particular, a tissue of adventures, the central character not very well done, no philosophic pith under the yarn."[1]

From September until December 1894 Stevenson dictated *Weir of Hermiston* (then known as "The Justice-Clerk"), which he had worked on intermittently since October 1892. After his death, the *St. Ives* manuscript was entrusted to Arthur T. Quiller-Couch, who wrote six additional chapters. Stevenson failed to complete the story, but he had outlined the remainder for Isobel, who relayed the information to Quiller-Couch.

From November 1896 to November 1897 the completed manuscript, *St. Ives: Being the Adventures of a French Prisoner in England*, was published as 13 monthly installments in London's *Pall Mall Magazine*. In the United States it ran as nine monthly installments in the March–November 1897 issues of *McClure's Magazine* and was first published in book form on October 2, 1897, by Charles Scribner's Sons. A full-length British version was published by London's William Heinemann in 1898.

Not surprisingly, *St. Ives* is Stevenson's weakest novel. Due to his half-hearted interest and untimely death, the narrative is rife with contrivances, but it does include several well-written characters, exciting adventure passages, and, most impressively, his amazingly detailed memories of Edinburgh and environs. Like many of his other stories, it is set within a specific historical milieu; some references are vague, but the Napoleonic era is a presence felt throughout.

By May 1813 the Napoleonic Wars (including the French Revolutionary War) had been raging for more than two decades. Except for an official cessation of hostilities in 1802-03 (The Peace of Amiens, signed by Britain and

France on March 25, 1802) and other peace treaties between France and Russia (July 7, 1807), and France and Prussia (July 9, 1807), warfare was the general rule of the day until Napoleon's defeat at Waterloo induced him to surrender on July 15, 1815.

Stevenson situates St. Ives's imprisonment during a period in which Napoleon was experiencing difficulties with his exhausted troops and a new alliance between Russia and Prussia. At the end of April 1813 Napoleon's new *Grande Armée,* numbering 145,000 men and 400 guns, prepared to invade Germany. At Bautzen on May 20, the emperor marched into a two-day battle in which 13,000 French and 20,000 allied soldiers were killed. On May 30, 1,600 French troops and a convoy of artillery were captured by a raiding German and Cossack party, and Napoleon was forced to sign an armistice agreement at Pleischwitz on June 4. By late summer Napoleon was at war with nearly every European nation and his prospects were dismal indeed. On March 10, 1814, the day that the fictitious St. Ives reaches France, Napoleon was engaged in a losing battle with Russian, Prussian, and Austrian troops near Laon.

*St. Ives* is a first-person narrative, but unlike *Treasure Island* and *Kidnapped,* it features an imprisoned adult who finds himself in dangerous (and often tedious) situations, rather than an inexperienced youth transported by exciting, fast-paced events. Due to the erratic and unfinished manuscript, the protagonist is never developed fully, and his early life is not touched upon until midway through the story, when Stevenson integrates historical material: St. Ives tells his uncle, "My story begins at the foot of the guillotine."

Interestingly, St. Ives is a displaced Frenchman who masquerades as a Scotsman and an Englishman. Born a Scotsman, Stevenson lived in England and France, and by the time he began *St. Ives,* he had lived as a voluntary exile for several years. He often felt nostalgic, but his physical detachment from Scotland allowed him to draw less subjective impressions of familiar traditions and customs. David Daiches writes:

> By the device of bringing an English-speaking Frenchman to Edinburgh, Stevenson was able to provide the reader with an objective picture of the city and its environs through the hero's natural reactions and to introduce without artificiality comments on the Scottish and English character of the kind that hitherto had appeared only in his essays. ... Stevenson is looking back to Scotland from Vailima; St. Ives, the Frenchman, the prisoner looking out on Edinburgh from the Castle, is a symbol of Stevenson looking back on the city from the South Seas.[2]

On several occasions Stevenson uses St. Ives and his countrymen to depict the prejudicial beliefs that existed during the Napoleonic era. Early in chapter one ("A Tale of a Lion Rampant"), the imprisoned Frenchman narrates:

> It chanced I was the only gentleman among the privates who remained. A great part were ignorant Italians, of a regiment that had suffered heavily in Catalonia. The rest were mere diggers of the soil,

treaders of grapes or hewers of wood, who had been suddenly and violently preferred to the glorious state of soldiers. We had but one interest in common: each of us who had any skill with his fingers passed the hours of his captivity in the making of little toys and *articles of Paris;* and the prison was daily visited at certain hours by a concourse of people of the country, come to exult over our distress, or—it is more tolerant to suppose—their own vicarious triumph. Some moved among us with a decency of shame or sympathy. Others were the most offensive personages in the world, gaped at us as if we had been baboons, sought to evangelise us to their rustic, northern religion as though we had been savages, or tortured us with intelligence of disasters to the arms of France. Good, bad, and indifferent, there was one alleviation to the annoyance of these visitors; for it was the practice of almost all to purchase some specimen of our rude handiwork. This led, amongst the prisoners, to a strong spirit of competition. Some were neat of hand, and (the genius of the French being always distinguished) could place upon sale little miracles of dexterity and taste.

In chapter 11 ("The Great North Road"), St. Ives witnesses a late-night procession during which a suicide victim is impaled with a sharpened steak and buried in the middle of the road—a practice he attributes to the vulgarity of the English people:

> It appeared this was a wretch who had committed many barbarous murders, and being at last upon the point of discovery fell of his own hand. And the nightmare at the cross-roads was the regular punishment, according to the laws of England, for an act which the Romans honored as a virtue! Whenever an Englishman begins to prate of civilisation (as, indeed, it's a defect they are rather prone to), I hear the measured blows of a mallet, see the bystanders crowd with torches about the grave, smile a little to myself in conscious superiority—and take a thimbleful of brandy for the stomach's sake.

As in some of his earlier stories, Stevenson sporadically puts Scottish and English phrases into the mouths of non–British characters. Although St. Ives's French mannerisms and speech are maintained with consistency (considering that the manuscript was left unfinished and uncorrected), he sometimes utters expressions such as "the capers we cut" and "every dog hangs by his own tail." (Stevenson utilizes many different dialects, noting the differences between the educated classes and commoners with amazing accuracy and fidelity; St. Ives's masquerades as a Scot and an Englishman account for some of his Britishisms.)

Like Alan Breck (another fugitive who flees through the countryside), St. Ives gives voice to a song now and then. As he walks with Thomas Dudgeon in chapter 15 ("The Adventure of the Attorney's Clerk"), he longs to hear the sounds of musicians and dancers:

> In the exhilaration of my heart I took the music on myself—
>
> "Merrily danced the Quaker's wife, And merrily danced the Quaker."
>
> I broke into that animated and appropriate air, clapped my arm about Dudgeon's waist, and away down the hill at a dancing step!

Here St. Ives and Dudgeon are clearly a later incarnation of Alan Breck and David Balfour. Earlier, in chapter eight ("The Hen-House"), Flora refers to the period in which *Kidnapped* is set, a remark that also parallels St. Ives with Alan:

> "My dear Miss Flora, you cannot make an omelette without breaking eggs," said I, "and it is no bagatelle to escape from Edinburgh Castle. One of us, I think, was even killed."
> "And you are as white as a rag, too," she exclaimed, "and can hardly stand! Here is my shawl; sit down upon it here in the corner, and I will beat your eggs. See, I have brought a fork, too; I should have been a good person to take care of Jacobites or Covenanters in old days!"

St. Ives has been criticized as a typical adventure-story protagonist,[3] but he is not a one-dimensional, infallible hero. He makes numerous mistakes and often appears dissatisfied with his behavior. At the end of chapter 24 ("The Innkeeper of Kirkby-Lonsdale"), the disgusted fugitive affirms: "It was none of my business to attend to broken chaises or shipwrecked travellers. I had my hands full of my own affairs; and my best defence would be a little more natural selfishness and a trifle less imbecile good-nature." St. Ives is another complicated creation; he is a Napoleonic soldier, but his political convictions consistently fluctuate, and his affection for Rowley offsets his comments about foreigners and the lower classes. Following Alain's departure from Amersham Place in chapter 20 ("After the Storm"), St. Ives offers an interesting assessment of heroism:

> No sooner was the house clear of my cousin, than I began to reckon up, ruefully enough, the probable results of what had passed. Here were a number of pots broken, and it looked to me as if I should have to pay for all! Here had been this proud, mad beast goaded and baited both publicly and privately, till he could neither hear nor see nor reason; whereupon the gate had been set open, and he had been left free to go and consider whatever vengeance he might find possible. I could not help thinking it was a pity that, whenever I myself was inclined to be upon my good behaviour, some friends of mine could always determine to play a piece of heroics and cast me for the hero—or the victim—which is very much the same. The first duty of heroics is to be of your own choosing. When they are not that, they are nothing. And I assure you, as I walked back to my own room, I was in no very complaisant humour: thought my uncle and Mr. Romaine to have played knuckle-bones with my life and prospects; cursed them for it roundly; had no wish more urgent than to avoid the pair of them; and was quite knocked out of time, as they say in the ring, to find myself confronted with the lawyer.

The St. Ives cousins are another example of Stevenson's fascination with the dual personality. While Anne is semi-heroic, Alain is thoroughly evil (and, perhaps, ranks as the novel's most one-dimensional character). The above passage demonstrates the complex feelings that Anne often expresses. (He also looks like Alain and wears his clothes on one occasion.) Edwin M. Eigner writes:

Alain's feelings about Anne are simple and straightforward—"I warn you that the day when I set my foot on your neck, the spine shall break." But Anne's reactions are more complicated. He would like, first of all, to deny the association with Alain entirely. His cousin's appearance upsets him. ... Anne is, at first, reluctant to admit his cousin's physical resemblance to himself. ... Yet when Anne sees his cousin humiliated and disinherited ... his identification with Alain is immediate.[4]

The novel's major female characters often overshadow the hero. Although J. R. Hammond claims that "Flora is simply a recreation of Catriona Drummond,"[5] she is not. Flora may share some qualities with Catriona, but she is more than a love interest for St. Ives. Near the end of chapter 28 ("Events of Monday: The Lawyer's Party"), when St. Ives asks for "her private thought upon the war," she replies with vigorous candor:

> "War is a subject that I do not think should be talked of to a girl. I am, I have to be—what do you call it?—a non-combatant? And to remind me of what others have to do and suffer: no, it is not fair!"
> "Miss Gilchrist has the tender female heart," said Chevenix.
> "Do not be too sure of that!" she cried. "I would love to be allowed to fight myself!"

A short time later St. Ives describes Chevenix's chauvinistic attitude:

> "Your man is very ambitious, sir," said I, "and very much of a hero! Mine is a humbler, and, I would fain think, a more human dog. He is one with no particular trust in himself, with no superior steadfastness to be admired for, who sees a lady's face, who hears her voice, and, without any phrase about the matter, falls in love. What does he ask for, then, but pity?—pity for his weakness, pity for his love, which is his life. You would make that women always the inferiors, gaping up at your imaginary lover; he, like a marble statue, with his nose in the air! But God has been wiser than you; and the most steadfast of your heroes may prove human, after all. We appeal to the queen for judgement," I added, turning and bowing before Flora.

Unfortunately, Flora's tendency to rise above a stereotypical characterization is marred by Stevenson's overlong and excessively florid love scenes.

The most impressive women are Flora's aunt, Miss Gilchrist, and Mrs. McRankine, the stolid and persuasive Edinburgh landlady. Miss Gilchrist has never married, guards her home with an eagle eye, and arranges a successful escape for St. Ives. Dominating several passages, Bethiah McRankine upholds a strict code of behavior (including the Calvinistic religious lifestyle that so exasperated Stevenson) and cares for Rowley after St. Ives flees from the assembly ball.

Amid some of the novel's more tedious adventure passages, Rowley emerges as a memorable character. Like earlier Stevenson youths, he is forced to mature in the face of adversity and impending violence. In chapter 21 ("I Become the Owner of a Claret-Coloured Chaise"), St. Ives praises Rowley's admirable adolescent qualities:

> Which of you considerate fellows would have done a thing at once so foolhardy and so wise as to make a

confidant of a boy in his teens, and positively smelling of the nursery? And when had I cause to repent it? There is none so apt as a boy to be the adviser of any man in difficulties such as mine. To the beginnings of virile common sense he adds the last lights of the child's imagination; and he can fling himself into business with that superior earnestness that properly belongs to play. And Rowley was a boy made to my hand. He had a high sense of romance, and a secret cultus for all soldiers and criminals.

Rowley makes an occasional blunder, due to his inexperience in matters outside the traditional upper-class lifestyle, but he often aids St. Ives and injects welcome humor into the story. In chapter 30 ("Events of Wednesday: The University of Cramond"), St. Ives finds Rowley in a stuporous state:

> I got easily forth of the chamber, which reverberated with the voices of these merry and laughing gentlemen, and breathed a long breath. I had passed an agreeable afternoon and evening, and I had apparently escaped scot-free. Alas! when I looked into the kitchen, there was my monkey, drunk as a lord, toppling on the edge of the dresser, and performing on the flageolet to an audience of the house lasses and some neighboring ploughmen.
> I routed him promptly from his perch, stuck his hat on, put his instrument in his pocket, and set off with him for Edinburgh. His limbs were of paper, his mind quite in abeyance; I must uphold and guide him, prevent his frantic dives, and set him continually on his legs again. At first he sang wildly, with occasional outbursts of causeless laughter. Gradually an inarticulate melancholy succeeded; he wept gently at times; would stop in the middle of the road, say firmly "No, no, no," and then fall on his back: or address me solemnly as "M'lord," and fall on his face by way of variety.

Stevenson's description of Rowley's drunkenness (and his use of the beloved flageolet) is one of many well-visualized passages in the novel (scenes that appear ideally suited for cinematic adaptation). The duel with Goguelat in chapter two, the harrowing escape in chapter six, the battle in which St. Ives defends the drovers in chapter ten, the impending fight with the attorney's clerk in chapter fifteen, and the chase through the English countryside with the runaway couple in chapter 23 are rousing, unforgettable and, occasionally, brutal events.

Stevenson's use of the Pentland Hills and Swanston Cottage as settings is indicative of the nostalgia he experienced while dictating the story. His remarkable description of Swanston in chapter seven ("Swanston Cottage") is matched by the many views of Edinburgh that are interspersed throughout the novel: his recollections of the castle and the imposing rock, with its sheer cliffs, upon which it sits; Princes Street, the "promenade to the fashionable inhabitants," and the lamplighters making their way through the dusk; and the "myriad of roofs" and "thirty leagues of sea and land" that are viewed from atop the castle.

The landscape of the Borders between Edinburgh and the Tweed is faithfully rendered on several occasions, particularly during St. Ives's journey with the drovers:

Edinburgh Castle, viewed from Princes Street. "The cliff went down before me almost sheer, but mantled with a thicket of climbing trees; from farther down, an outwork raised its turret; and across the valley I had a view of that long terrace of Princes Street which serves as a promenade to the fashionable inhabitants of Edinburgh." (1990 photograph by S. A. Nollen.)

A continual succession of insignificant shaggy hills, divided by a course of ten thousand brooks, through which we had to wade, or by the side of which we encamped at night; infinite perspectives of heather, infinite quantities of moor-fowl; here and there, by a stream-side, small and pretty clumps of willows or the silver birch; here and there, the ruins of ancient and inconsiderable fortresses—made the unchanging characters of the scene. Occasionally, but only in the distance, we could perceive the smoke of a small town or of an isolated farmhouse or cottage on the moors; more often, a flock of sheep and its attendant shepherd, or a rude field of agriculture perhaps not yet harvested.

The most self-reflective event occurs in chapter ten, when St. Ives and the drovers, traveling "among sites which have been rendered illustrious by the pen of Walter Scott," meet "a tall, stoutish, elderly gentleman" on the road. After St. Ives narrates this encounter, in which the gentleman tells a story about the area's early inhabitants, he proudly adds:

Years after it chanced that I was one day diverting myself with a Waverly Novel, when what should I come upon but the identical narrative of my green-coated gentleman upon the moors! In a moment the scene, the tones of his voice, his northern accent, and the very aspect of the earth and sky and temperature of the weather, flashed back into my mind with the reality of dreams. The unknown in the green coat had been the Great Unknown! I had met Scott; I had heard a story from his lips; I should have been able to write, to claim acquaintance, to tell him that his legend still tingled in my ears. But the discovery came too late, and the great man had already succumbed under the load of his honours and misfortunes.

Here Stevenson's depiction of St. Ives is highly autobiographical. Sir Walter Scott's appearance is contrived, but the incident adds a whimsical tone to one of the novel's better chapters.

Aside from the stilted love scenes, there are several improbable events that mar the pace and believability of the story: St. Ives's chance reunion with an English soldier who, during the war, had stolen his musket on a Castile battlefield (chapter 11); his encounter with Burchell Fenn's coach as he looks for Fenn's home (chapter 12); the adventure with Daniel Romaine's clerk (chapter 15); his fortuitous meeting with Mr. Robbie as he sets off for Robbie's home (chapter 27); and Alain's tendency to appear wherever Anne would go. Stevenson's erratic interest in the novel is most evident in chapter 28, when St. Ives refers to the two drovers as "Todd" and "Candlish"; in the earlier chapters they are called *Sim* and Candlish. Arguably, Stevenson could have corrected these problems had he lived to complete the manuscript, but since he had grown dissatisfied with the story before turning to *Weir of Hermiston*, it is likely that some of these problems would remain.

The six chapters written by Arthur T. Quiller-Couch are vastly inferior to any of Stevenson's material. Although Quiller-Couch worked from the outline provided by Isobel Strong, he wrote an additional 105 pages of drawn-out, melodramatic situations. Stevenson created many contrivances in the first 30 chapters, but Quiller-Couch's conclusion is a disappointing mixture of implausible incidents and pseudo–Stevensonian actions and dialogue. His use of the hot-air balloon, the drunken stowaway, and the frantic crowd of people gathered to see Professor Byfield's demonstration creates a sharp transition in tone and style from Stevenson's prose and would be more believable in a farce like *The Wrong Box*. The second-rate quality of Quiller-Couch's material can be attributed, in part, to his own derisive assessment of the novel. In an October 8, 1924, letter to W. Courthope Forman, he writes: "*St. Ives* is the sort of R.L.S. that a man can do his little best with and not hurt anybody. Had it been 'Weir of Hermiston' or stuff of that quality, of course I should not have looked at the job."[6]

Discounting Quiller-Couch's additions, *St. Ives* is one of Stevenson's longest fictional works. The story's flaws cannot be attributed wholly to its unfinished status, and it is perhaps unfortunate that so much precious time was dedicated to it. As Eigner has concluded, "It is foolish to wish that Stevenson had finished so bad a story as *St. Ives;* he did much better to drop it and work instead on *Weir of Hermiston*."[7]

## The Secret of St. Ives
## (Columbia, 1949)

*The Secret of St. Ives*, directed by Philip Rosen in 1949, is the sole cinematic adaptation of *St. Ives*. Running only 75 minutes, the film stresses the novel's heavy dependence on dialogue but fails to include many of its exciting adventure passages. Perhaps Columbia was dead set on mining unfilmed Stevenson (after all, the studio produced *The Black Arrow* and the weird western *Adventures in Silverado* the previous year), but it seems unusual that such an overlong and vacillatory novel was chosen as resource material.

Eric Taylor's screenplay omits most of the story, but the pace still drags interminably. Referred to as "Anatole de Keroual," St. Ives (Richard Ney) leads the escape from Edinburgh Castle and then visits "Floria" Gilchrist (Vanessa Brown), his fiancée, who immediately accompanies him on a journey to London, where he plans to claim an inheritance from his dying uncle, Count St. Ives (Jean Del Val). Incredibly, Daniel Romaine (Aubrey Mather) conspires with "Allan" St. Ives (Douglas Walton) to rob him of the riches and property! After St. Ives and Floria endure a series of stereotypical adventures, he is recaptured but manages to escape the hangman's noose.

Unlike the novel, *The Secret of St. Ives* depicts a hero whose main objective is to rejoin Napoleon's army. His primary obstacle, Major Edward "Chevenish" (Henry Daniell), does appear, as do several fabricated characters who stand in his path. Unfortunately, the character of Rowley is omitted entirely, and Miss Gilchrist, Flora's aunt (here called "Annie" and portrayed by Phyllis Morris) is scripted as a one-dimensional old maid.

Rosen, who began his career as a cameraman for Edison in 1912, graduated to director status in 1920. During the silent era he helmed some big-budget productions, including *Abraham Lincoln* (1924), a 12-reel depiction of the sixteenth president's life from the early Illinois years to the 1865 assassination, but he spent the majority of his directorial career churning out B films for Monogram. He is best remembered for two atrocious Bela Lugosi vehicles (*Spooks Run Wild* [1941] and *Return of the Ape Man* [1944]) and six of Monogram's Charlie Chan programmers (1944–45). Unable to inject much excitement into Taylor's stilted script, he helped to make *The Secret of St. Ives* one of his last directorial efforts.

Most contemporary critics ignored the film, and those who bothered to go to local theatres dismissed it as a tedious low-budget effort. In the *Variety* review "Brog." writes:

> *The Secret of St. Ives* is strictly for minor bookings. A cloak-and-sworder with a minimum of swashbuckling, it barely gets by as a programmer. Picture is overlength, at 75 minutes, for the lowercase position it will occupy on secondary twin bills. ... Plot is based upon a Robert Louis Stevenson story about a group of French soldiers captured by the British during the war with Napoleon. Such a setup is a rather ambitious undertaking for a budget production; costum-

ing, sets and other physical properties reflect corner-cutting. ... More sword play and physical clashes would have helped immeasurably in giving the footage some dash. Instead it plods along and the players give stock reading to the lines. ... Rudolph C. Flothow's production guidance is standard for secondary product and technical credits strike the same level.[8]

## *St. Ives* on Television

Three British television adaptations of *St. Ives* have been aired by the BBC. The first version, a six-part serial broadcast in 1955, was followed by feature versions in 1960 and 1967.

## • Eighteen •
# Dr. Jekyll's Potion: A Conclusion

*I saw rain falling and the rainbow drawn*
*On Lammermuir. Hearkening I heard again*
*In my precipitous city beaten bells*
*Winnow the keen sea wind. And here afar,*
*Intent on my own race and place, I wrote.*
    *Take thou the writing: thine it is. For who*
*Burnished the sword, blew on the drowsy coal,*
*Held still the target higher, chary of praise*
*And prodigal of counsel—who but thou?*
*So now, in the end, if this the least be good,*
*If any deed be done, if any fire*
    *Burn in the imperfect page, the praise be thine.*
    —STEVENSON's dedication to his wife, *Weir of Hermiston.*

The motion picture medium has not been very faithful to Robert Louis Stevenson. Though David Daiches notes that "the whole attitude displayed by Stevenson to his art is thoroughly congenial to the modern mind,"[1] the modern art of the cinema, born during the year in which Stevenson died, rarely has accommodated that attitude. His distinguished, varied, and timeless works have been bastardized more flagrantly than those of Edgar Allan Poe and Sir Arthur Conan Doyle. His acute perception of human behavior has been represented adequately by only a few film adaptations, namely Paramount's *Dr. Jekyll and Mr. Hyde* (1931), RKO-Radio's *The Body Snatcher,* and Agamemnon/TNT's *Treasure Island.*

Of the 45 feature-length theatrical and television adaptations discussed in the preceding chapters, only four may be called excellent examples of filmmaking, whether judged as visualizations of literature or strictly on their own terms: the three titles mentioned above and Paramount's *Dr. Jekyll and Mr. Hyde* (1920). Walt Disney's *Kidnapped* is well acted and faithfully scripted but is marred by some technical defects, while HTV's admirable, visually impressive *The Master of Ballantrae* suffers from a few structural and dramatic flaws. Five other titles rank as well made, entertaining, and reasonably faithful productions: Paramount's *The White Circle*, Monogram's *Kidnapped*, Columbia's *The Black Arrow*, Omnibus's *Kidnapped*, and Amicus's *I, Monster*.

Six adaptations (Columbia's *Trouble for Two*, 20th Century–Fox's *Kidnapped*, MGM's *Dr. Jekyll and Mr. Hyde*, Universal-International's *The Strange Door*, Salamander/Columbia's *The Wrong Box*, and the Disney Channel's *Black Arrow*) are undeniably bad, while two are nearly unwatchable (Pioneer's *Dr. Jekyll and Mr. Hyde* and National General's *Treasure Island*). The rest are mediocre films that may pass the time for young viewers or older folks who have nothing better to do. Of these, several have been overrated as "classics" by popular movie critics and the public at large; in particular, the MGM and Walt Disney versions of *Treasure Island* have achieved unwarranted reputations.

The four "continuations" of Stevenson stories are generally dreadful, but *Long John Silver's Return to Treasure Island* is the most watchable. The other three *(The Son of Dr. Jekyll, Return to Treasure Island,* and *Daughter of Dr. Jekyll)* range from insipid to abominable and will prove difficult viewing for even the most devoted fans of bad cinema. Responsible for producing and writing all three, Jack Pollexfen (who shared these credits with Aubrey Wisberg on *Return to Treasure Island* and cowrote the *Son of Dr. Jekyll* script with Mortimer Braus) had a short-term career as a Stevenson degrader. In fact, his series of artistic blunders could convict him of second-degree "cinemacide."

Except Warner Bros., all of the major Hollywood studios produced Stevenson adaptations during the golden age. In 1953 Warners released *The Master of Ballantrae* to utilize frozen English assets, but the studio did not include any of his stories in their excellent adventure series of the 1930s. All told, nine of Stevenson's novels, five of his short stories, and one of his travel books have inspired feature-length adaptations. Aside from the novels, Stevenson completed 21 short stories, coauthored with his wife *More New Arabian Nights: The Dynamiter,* a collection of 13 interconnected episodes, and penned a collection of 19 short "Fables."[2]

Screenwriters often have added new material to short stories or have combined two or more tales into multipart films such as Universal's *Flesh and Fantasy* (1943) and American International's *Tales of Terror* (1962), a three-episode Edgar Allan Poe adaptation. It is not likely that any of Stevenson's unfilmed tales will reach the theatrical screen, but there are at least 12 that could be adapted into atmospheric and exciting productions.

The novellas "The Misadventures of John Nicholson" and "The Beach of Falesa" are lively tales remarkable for their strong central characters and Stevenson's effortless integration of style and content. The former focuses on a disinherited young Scot who experiences emigration, homelessness, and murder before he is reconciled with his stern Calvinist father. It is a fast-paced tale augmented by Stevenson's autobiographical references (including his brilliant descriptions of Edinburgh) and refreshing wit; never one to portray a faultless protagonist, he opens the story with a satirical observation: "John Varey Nicholson was stupid; yet, stupider men than he are now sprawling in Parliament, and lauding themselves as the authors of their own distinction." Conceived while Stevenson was clearing the woods behind Vailima, the latter story is a gritty portrait of greed, colonial oppression, and bigotry that climaxes with one of his most suspenseful episodes. In this South Seas tale Stevenson presents a coarse and unremittingly prejudiced central character who saves his native wife and other islanders from a manipulative and murderous white trader, but later refers to his children as inferior beings: "there's nobody thinks less of half-castes than I do; but they're mine, and about all I've got."

Other adaptable stories could be linked together in multipart presentations (or be filmed as separate episodes for a television series.)[3] Two French tales, "A Lodging for the Night," an adventurous vignette set in 1456 Paris that concludes with a political debate between the frostbitten François Villon and the comfortable Lord of Brisetout, and "Providence and the Guitar," a beautifully written and whimsical tale of a destitute troubadour, are both amusing and meaningful, while "Will o' the Mill," an elegant allegory of unrealized ambitions, and "The Merry Men," a tale of youthful desire, shipwreck, and tragic madness set on Earraid, are moody and dramatic pieces filled with cinematic possibilities.

For nearly a century filmmakers with a taste for the macabre have turned to *The Strange Case of Dr. Jekyll and Mr. Hyde* as resource material, and only one other Stevenson thriller, "The Body-Snatcher," has appeared on the screen; but his six other "crawlers" (as he referred to them) deserve equal time before the public: "Thrawn Janet" is a spine-chilling account of a small Scottish community's persecution of a witch; "Markheim" (1885), one of his most famous short stories, is an eerie allegory about a criminal's guilty conscience; "Ollala," a haunting tale of horror, beauty, love, and sadness, is reminiscent of Edgar Allan Poe's "The Fall of the House of Usher"; and "The Bottle Imp," "The Isle of Voices," and the posthumously published "The Waif Woman" are fantastic fables in which materialism is conquered by supernatural forces. (The first two, set in the South Seas, involve a hellish genie and a wizard, respectively, while the third, set in Iceland, features a revengeful corpse.)[4] "Markheim" and "Ollala" are arguably the best of Stevenson's atmospheric thrillers, and as one critic has written, the latter "must be counted in the handful of truly great horror stories in the English language."[5] If faithfully adapted, any of these stories could give today's senseless horror genre a qualitative shot in the arm.

"An Old Song" (1877), a virtual blueprint for *The Master of Ballantrae* that was not attributed to Stevenson until 1982,[6] "The Story of a

Lie" (1879), a tale of love, misunderstanding, and class prejudice, and "The Rajah's Diamond" (1878) are among his weakest stories, and may not work well as film narratives. *The Dynamiter*, a disjointed series of episodes prompted by Stevenson's disgust for the Fenian bombings of the 1880s, includes moments of suspense and wit but is hampered by "Story of the Destroying Angel" and "Story of the Fair Cuban," two overlong digressions written by Fanny. But "When the Devil Was Well" (1875), an eventful story of love, royal oppression, and civil conflict in fifteenth-century Italy, could have been adapted when the adventure genre was at its height, and the "Fables" dealing with utopianism, race prejudice, religious intolerance, greed, and the cyclic nature of existence, could have been mined when short films were still popular.

The complexities of Stevenson's novels often have confounded screenwriters intending to attract a mass audience, so it is not surprising that *Prince Otto: A Romance*, *The Wrecker*, and the unfinished *Weir of Hermiston* have been neglected. *Prince Otto*, his third novel, is an opulent mixture of love and politics set in the "bygone" European state of Grunewald. Otto Johann Friedrich, grandson of King Florizel the first of Bohemia (a link with *New Arabian Nights*), is an irresponsible ruler threatened by the court intrigue of his young wife, Princess Amalia Seraphina, and her consort, Baron Gondremark, who plans to usurp the throne with the aid of a revolutionary army. Influenced by commoners, Otto evaluates his shortcomings, affirms his love for his reputedly unfaithful mate, and is imprisoned by the Princess and Gondremark just as the revolution begins. When Seraphina learns that the baron has used her as a pawn in his lust for power, she stabs him and escapes into the forest. Later Otto is freed through the influence of Gondremark's mistress, the Countess von Rosen, and finally is reunited with the princess as the new republic is declared.

*Prince Otto* is filled with elegant writing but is bogged down by excessively florid imagery in book two, chapter one ("Princess Cinderella"). Here Stevenson's descriptions of the forest divert the reader's attention from Seraphina's plight. Though the novel was admired in its day, it has been criticized as an example of Stevenson's infatuation with style. While the first half of "Princess Cinderella" supports this argument, the remainder of the novel features several well-developed characters and events. The political plot is primarily a stage on which the drama of Otto and Seraphina's complicated relationship is played. Book one ("Prince Errant") introduces Otto, book two ("Of Love and Politics") poses the characters' personal feelings and needs against their duty to the state, and book three ("Fortunate Misfortune") presents the revolutionary event from the points of view of Seraphina, Otto, and Countess von Rosen (in chapters one, two, and three, respectively).

*Prince Otto* includes two major female characters, an aspect that refutes the critical claim that Stevenson failed to feature significant women in his stories. Princess Seraphina and Countess von Rosen are motivating factors in the novel: they contribute to Otto's dilemma but eventually rescue him from ruin. While Seraphina's attempted murder of Gondremark recalls the actions of Shakespeare's Lady Macbeth, the countess is one of Stevenson's strongest females. The princess ultimately provides the love that Otto seeks, but von Rosen gives him a new life after Grunewald falls to the revolutionaries. In book two, chapter nine ("The Price of River Farm"), Otto, intending to aid a destitute farmer by purchasing his land, asks the countess to rob the treasury of 3,000 crowns; rather than committing a crime, she gives him 3,200 from her personal fortune and later persuades Seraphina to sign an order for Otto's release. Without the countess's able and intelligent efforts, Otto would lose his livelihood and his love. When she meets Otto to deliver the money, she wears a man's attire—an androgynous element that echoes the masculine behavior of Joanna Sedley/Matcham in *The Black Arrow*.

*Prince Otto* is set in a Germanic state, but Grunewald is actually a conglomeration of various European cultures. Stevenson incorporates the German words "burgher" and "schloss," but he also includes Scottish words and phrases such as "bonnet," "greymare's tail," "for all that," "glen," "haughs" and "burn." Otto even masquerades as an English traveler at one point, and his jailer, Colonel Gordon, is an amiable Scot from Aberdeen who, upon releasing his captive, accepts some poetry that the prince has written in his cell. Enthusiastically reading the verses, Gordon remarks, "I declare, they remind me of Robbie Burns!"

In book two, chapter four ("While the Prince is in the Anteroom"), Stevenson varies the animal imagery he first used in "The Body-Snatcher" and later revamped for *The Ebb-Tide*. The lions and lambs of the former story are here the "lions" and "wolves," terminology that the countess uses to label the opposing types of human beings. *Prince Otto* contains more politics and philosophy than Stevenson's other adventure tales—elements that would make a successful film adaptation difficult to achieve.

Stevenson and Lloyd Osbourne began writing *The Wrecker* on board the *Equator* during the summer of 1889. Intrigued by the disappearance of the brigantine *Wandering Minstrel* and by various stories about wrecked ships, the two authors planned the novel as a joint effort. "We had long been at once attracted and repelled by that very modern form of the police novel or mystery story," Stevenson wrote.[7] Unimpressed by the "airless, elaborate mechanism" that mystery writers relied on, he chose to situate a detective plot within a realistic context. Rather than depicting crime and investigation in a straightforward manner, *The Wrecker* focuses on Loudon Dodd, an American art student who becomes entangled in the mysterious fate of an English brig, the *Flying Scud*. Working from an elaborate outline, Louis and Lloyd each wrote specific chapters and collaborated on others, but it was

Stevenson who completed the final draft in Samoa in November 1891.

*The Wrecker* begins at Tai-o-hae in the Marquesas Islands, where Dodd meets with a "leisurely Englishman" who inquires about his involvement in a famous wrecking incident. Dodd opens his "queer yarn" by describing his commercial education in "the State of Muskegon," his visit to his mother's family in Edinburgh, and his experiences as a student in Paris's Latin Quarter. When his finances run out, he teams with Jim Pinkerton, a fellow artist and entrepreneur from San Francisco, who wishes to purchase the *Flying Scud*, which lies wrecked on the shore of Midway Island. Believing that the ship's cargo contains a cache of opium, Dodd and Pinkerton outbid Bellairs, a shyster, at the auction; while Pinkerton remains behind to keep his business afloat, Dodd and a small crew sail for Midway. Although 240 pounds of the drug are discovered, Pinkerton declares bankruptcy. Soon Dodd inherits a sizable fortune from his deceased uncle and, after establishing a new trade for Pinkerton, becomes obsessed with solving the mystery of the brig.

Dodd follows Bellairs to Europe and meets Norris Carthew, owner of the *Currency Lass*, a weathered ship that was dismasted near Midway. Faced with an ultimatum by Captain Trent, skipper of the *Flying Scud*, Carthew and his shipmates murdered the captain and his crew but failed to pilot the ship outside the island's coral reef. Though they were rescued by the crew of the *Tempest*, a British man-o'-war, they escaped prosecution. Pleased with Carthew's revelations, Dodd moves on.

Stevenson and Osbourne conceived *The Wrecker* as the first in a series of "South Sea Yarns" that was to include "The Pearl Fisher" (which became *The Ebb-Tide*) and "The Beachcombers" (a story that was never completed). *The Wrecker* is one of Stevenson's longest and most complex tales, and unlike his other novels, it is a discursive, slow-moving, and somewhat confusing amalgam of diverse narrative strands; the principal characters are introduced at various points and "the reader is carried forward by the incidents surrounding a secret which is kept to the last."[8] The first seven chapters comprise an autobiography of Dodd, while the major mystery plot begins in chapter eight ("Faces on the City Front").

Though Stevenson revised the final draft, the presence of two separate creators often is apparent. Unlike *The Ebb-Tide*, *The Wrecker* is a stylistic and structural experiment in which several stories are interconnected. It is a novel whose parts are greater than the whole: Stevenson's depiction of student life in Paris (based on his own experiences of 1874–77), Dodd's visits to Edinburgh, and the atmospheric scenes set in San Francisco; and Osbourne's brilliant description of a storm at sea and the massacre of the *Flying Scud*'s crew, an incident that delivers a powerful and unexpected jolt.

Dodd and Pinkerton are fully realized creations, and their complex relationship is a highlight: They rarely agree with one another, but their disparate personalities bind their friendship together. Stevenson based Dodd on his friend Will Low, but the character's attitudes and experiences often resemble his own: his eschewal of the family business in favor of an artistic life, his acceptance of a stipend from his father, his visits to dives and associations with lowlife individuals, and his adventures in Edinburgh, Paris, Barbizon, Hawaii, the Marquesas, San Francisco, Calistoga, Nebraska, and Council Bluffs, Iowa (where Dodd changes trains). Dodd also shares the youthful enthusiasm, adventurous spirit, and fallibility displayed by earlier Stevenson protagonists, particularly Jim Hawkins and David Balfour (who also inherits a fortune from a rich Scottish uncle). Other autobiographical elements are literary in nature: Dodd's references to Shakespeare, Scott, and Mary Shelley's *Frankenstein*, and other characters' comments about Dickens and Hawthorne. Sociocultural prejudices, particularly those of Scots and Americans, enhance the realistic atmosphere of the novel; on occasion, Dodd's didacticism is reminiscent of Stevenson the essayist.

Although the various threads sometimes fail to cohere, there are individual passages that rank among Stevenson's finest. Ironically, one of the novel's truly unforgettable images, that of a sailor struggling to gain a bearing during a raging storm, occurs in chapter 12 ("The 'Norah Creina'"), a section attributed to Osbourne, who demonstrates an impressive integration of description, movement, and nonverbal communication. But the most dramatically devastating incident appears in chapter 15, when Dodd and his crew are attacked by sea birds as they rifle a cargo of rice in which the opium is hidden. These events are indicative of *The Wrecker*'s cinematic potential, but its length and complex plotting would necessitate truncation or an ambitious miniseries.

Stevenson intended *The Wrecker* to differ from his earlier novels and the work of popular mystery writers. In his epilogue, he notes: "After we had invented at some expense of time this method of approaching and fortifying our police novel, it occurred to us it had been invented previously by someone else, and was in fact—however painfully different the results may seem—the method of Charles Dickens in his later work." As *The Wrong Box* had demonstrated previously, Stevenson's collaborations with Lloyd Osbourne allowed him to alter his own style, and *The Wrecker* proved to be a successful and profitable experiment.

Many scholars agree that *Weir of Hermiston* is Stevenson's masterpiece. As Paul Binding has written, this Scottish tale, even in its unfinished state, "is complete in spirit and is one of the most persistently overlooked first-rate novels in our language."[9] Although Stevenson worked on it sporadically over a period of two years, every word and sentence of its nine chapters "has been considered and refined to achieve an effect of fluidity and tension unusual in his fiction."[10] He dictated the story to Isobel Strong with a feverish intensity that taxed him emotionally and physically, and his efforts on the morning of December 4, 1894, may have triggered the brain hemorrhage that ended his life later that day.

The novel focuses on the tragic conflict between Adam Weir, a widowed justice-clerk known as "the Hanging Judge," and his rebellious son, Archie. After Archie attends the execution of a criminal sentenced to death by his father, he publicly criticizes capital punishment. Adam then exiles Archie to the family estate at Hermiston, where he lives with Kirstie Elliot, an old-maid housekeeper. The young laird soon falls in love with the maid's niece, Christina ("Kirstie") Elliott, who resides at neighboring Caldstaneslap. Due to the pressures exerted by the elder Kirstie and Frank Innes, a self-indulgent friend, Archie jeopardizes his relationship with Christina during a quarrel. Stevenson died at this dramatic juncture, but his outline for the remainder of the story was provided by Isobel when Sidney Colvin took the manuscript to England; at the request of Henry James, Chatto and Windus published it on May 20, 1896. Apparently, Archie and Christina effect a partial reconciliation, but after the girl is seduced and impregnated by Innes, Archie kills him. Arrested and jailed by his father, Archie is freed by Christina's legendary "Four Black Brothers," who have learned the truth about the murder. After the young couple escapes to the United States, old Adam, filled with regret, dies.

While dictating to Isobel on September 24, 1894, Stevenson told her, "Belle, I see it all so clearly! The story unfolds itself before me to the least detail—there is nothing left in doubt. I never felt so before in anything I ever wrote. It will be my best work; I feel myself so sure in every word."[11] Stylistically and thematically, *Weir of Hermiston* is a flawless work: Stevenson's fusion of economical, flowing prose with Scottish history and language, autobiography (particularly the complex ideological conflicts between father and son), psychological duality (the two Kirsties and the opposing personalities of Archie and Frank Innes), full-blooded characters who breathe with life, vivid description and dialogue, and passionate and violent confrontations creates a "novel of epic stature which can be seen as a summation of his creative endeavour."[12]

Though Stevenson had not seen Scotland since 1887, he uncannily integrated settings, historical events, and the Scots dialect into his inspired dictation. Written many seas away from his homeland, *Weir of Hermiston* is the most Scottish of his novels, a refined and profound exploration of human emotion and conflict set amid the moorlands of the Caledonian past. Referring to Archie and the elder Kirstie's nocturnal conversations, part three of chapter five ("Winter on the Moors") begins:

Such an unequal intimacy has never been uncommon in Scotland, where the clan spirit survives; where the servant tends to spend her life in the same service, a helpmeet at first, then a tyrant, and at last a pensioner; where, besides, she is not necessarily destitute of the pride of birth, but is, perhaps, like Kirstie, a connection of the master's, and at least knows the legend of her own family, and may count kinship with some illustrious dead. For that is the mark of the Scot of all classes: that he stands in an attitude toward the past unthinkable to Englishmen, and remembers and cherishes the memory of his forebears, good or bad; and there burns alive in him a sense of identity with the dead to the twentieth generation.

Stevenson based Adam Weir on Robert MacQueen, Lord Braxfield (1722–99), a formidable Scottish criminal judge; as Archie passes Holyroodhouse he envisions "old radiant stories" of Mary Stuart and Bonnie Prince Charlie; Adam champions the "fower quarters of John Calvin"; the Four Black Brothers pursue the murderers of their father "hot foot for Edinburgh by the way of the Pentland Hills"; and Andrew "Dand" Elliott, one of the brothers, achieves fame as a local bard, is credited with a contribution to Walter Scott's *Milstrelsy*, and claims, "I'll die young, like Robbie Burns." Ironically, like Burns, who, according to legend, passed away from "the drink" at the age of 37 (several scholars now agree that endocarditis ended his life), Stevenson was soon to die young himself.

Unforgettable phrases abound, often injecting a uniquely Scottish wit into the tragic story. In chapter five the Elliotts speedily hunt the murderous rogues: "It was three miles to Broken Dykes, down hill, and a sore road. Kirstie has seen men from Edinburgh dismounting there in plain day to lead their horses. But the four brothers rode it as if Auld Hornie were behind and Heaven in front." Stevenson's descriptions of the Scottish countryside surpass those in *Kidnapped*. When he offers an image of nature imbued with human characteristics in chapter six ("A Leaf from Christina's Psalm-Book"), the setting becomes a character, and not just a backdrop, in the narrative: "The grey, Quakerish dale was still only awakened in places and patches from the sobriety of its wintry colouring; and he wondered at its beauty; an essential beauty of the old earth it seemed to him, not resident in particulars but breathing to him from the whole." Rural images such as this are preceded by urban scenes set in Edinburgh and within the confines of the Weir household. Chapter three ("The Hanging of Duncan Jopp") contains one of Stevenson's most powerful images, a passage in which Archie walks into the Weir study and is ensnared by his father's rigid moral code. Here Stevenson unites style and the protagonist's psychological state in a single sentence paragraph that foreshadows Adam's letter-of-the-law treatment of his son: "The lamp was shaded, the fire trimmed to a nicety, the table covered deep with orderly documents, the backs of law books made a frame upon all sides that was only broken by the window and the doors." The writing of *Weir of Hermiston* took its toll on Stevenson, but he was confident that his literary power was at its height. At one point he admitted that the ease with which the story poured from his mind frightened him, and he worried that he would not be able to maintain this state long enough to complete it. One evening Louis read the first few chapters to a group of dinner guests; while many were quick to praise his efforts, Lloyd Osbourne was struck speechless by the brilliance of what he had heard. When Stevenson cried out that his stepson's lack of response was "like a blow in the face," Lloyd attempted to express his admiration:

> We were in the dark. I could not see his face. But I believe he listened with stupefaction. The reaction when it came was too great for his sorely strained nerves; tears rained from his eyes—and mine, too, streamed. Never had I known him to be so moved; never had I been so moved myself; and in the all-pervading darkness we were for once free to be ourselves, unashamed. Thus we sat, with our arms about each other, talking far into the night. Even after thirty years, I should not care to divulge anything so sacred as those confidences; the revelation of that tortured soul; the falterings of its Calvary. ... To me his heroism took on new proportions, and I now was thankful I had refused an important post to stay with him. "It will not be for long," he said.[13]

It is fortunate that *Weir of Hermiston* was left unfinished after Stevenson's death; even if another author had completed it according to the outline, its magnificence certainly would have been compromised. (*St. Ives* pales in the shadow of *Weir*, but Arthur Quiller-Couch's completion of the former proves that unfinished works should be left that way; and no filmmaker with any literary sense should attempt an adaptive completion of the latter, although some British television writers have tried.)

For every good Stevenson adaptation, there are at least ten bad ones, but if terrible films like MGM's *Dr. Jekyll and Mr. Hyde* and National General's *Treasure Island* can inspire viewers to read the original stories, they have served a useful purpose. None of the four stage dramas Stevenson cowrote with W. E. Henley have been filmed, but the stilted style and limited success of these plays account for their obscurity. In 1905 Fanny Stevenson theorized about these collaborations: "My husband's view of play-writing was to make a literary *tour de force*, built on the old conventions, Mr. Henley's to startle the public. It is possible that either, alone, might have been successful, but together they were too much at cross purposes."[14]

Rarely has an author been graced with the efforts of so many outstanding artists and performers; only William Shakespeare, Charles Dickens, and Sir Arthur Conan Doyle have inspired the endeavors of a similar "who's who" of the film and theatrical worlds. The fact that many individuals failed to create or interpret valid impressions of Stevenson's work does not prove that faithful cinematic adaptations of literature are impossible, but it does demonstrate that an effective transformation from page to screen is very difficult. And some of these transformations have been like the metamorphosis undergone by Dr. Jekyll: Often the screenwriter's efforts have been the potion that created a cinematic equivalent of the evil Mr. Hyde.

A few filmmakers and actors have captured fragments of Stevenson's vivid imagination and admirable philosophy, but a close study of his stories and their corresponding film versions proves that, in this specific case, literature is the preferable art form. Long after most of the films are forgotten, Stevenson's stories will be read and enjoyed by readers of all ages and persuasions. For Stevenson clearly understood the complexity of the human animal and the fact that there are no simple solutions to complicated problems. He often preferred the wisdom and enthusiasm of young people over the unpredictable and unreliable behavior of adults, and most importantly, he believed that literature should "embody character, thought, or emotion in some act or attitude that shall be remarkably striking to the mind's eye."[15] He felt that fiction is "not a transcript of life," but "a simplification of some side or point of life, to stand or fall by its significant simplicity."[16]

Stevenson's art is diverse, yet it remains true to his axiom that a book should enthrall and transport its reader away from his "homekeeping fancy." His romances often do stand by their simplicity, but they are not simplistic. The conflict, pessimism, and tragedy of existence are there, but Stevenson asks us to appreciate life's pleasures, to enjoy the quest while we can. For these reasons there will always be those who long, at least for a few hours, to be Jim Hawkins sailing alongside Long John Silver, or David Balfour fleeing through the heather with Alan Breck.

• APPENDIX A •

# Published Prose Writings, 1873–94

Following is a complete listing of Stevenson's prose writings that were published during his lifetime. Included for each entry are the original book or periodical title, the dates during which the work was written, the name of the publisher, and the date of publication, as well as information pertaining to any major reprints—including two major editions, the Edinburgh edition (1895–98), edited by Sidney Colvin, and the 35-volume Tusitala edition (1924), edited by Lloyd Osbourne.

1. "On the Thermal Influence of Forests" (lecture). Delivered May 19, 1873, to the Royal Society of Edinburgh; published in *Proceedings of the Royal Society of Edinburgh* 8 (November 1872–July 1875): 114–25, and in 50 offprints (Edinburgh: Neill); reprinted in the Tusitala edition, 28 (1924).

2. "Roads" (essay). Written August–September 14, 1873, under the pseudonym L. S. Stoneven; published in *The Portfolio* 4 (December 1873): 185–88; reprinted in the Tusitala edition, 25 (1924).

3. "Ordered South" (essay). Written late November 1873–February 5, 1874; published in *Macmillan's Magazine* 30 (May 1874): 68–73; included in *Virginibus Puerisque* (1881); reprinted in the Tusitala edition, 25 (1924).

4. "Victor Hugo's Romances" (essay). Written spring–May 4, 1874; published in *Cornhill Magazine* 30 (August 1874): 179–94; included in *Familiar Studies of Men and Books* (1882); reprinted in the Tusitala edition, 27 (1924).

5. "Lord Lytton's Fables in Song" (essay). Written May 2–15, 1874; published in *Fortnightly Review* 15 (June 1874): 817–23; reprinted in the Tusitala edition, 28 (1924).

6. "Notes on the Movements of Young Children" (essay). Written late June–July 1874; published in *The Portfolio* 5 (August 1874): 115–17; reprinted in the Tusitala edition, 25 (1924).

7. "The Ballads and Songs of Scotland" (review). Written July 1874; published in *The Academy* (August 8, 1874): 142–43;

reprinted in the Tusitala edition, 28 (1924); a review of J. Clark Murray's *The Ballads and Songs of Scotland, in View of Their Influence on the Character of the People* (London: Macmillan, 1874).

8. "Scottish Rivers" (review). Written July 1874; published in *The Academy* (August 15, 1874): 173; reprinted in the Tusitala edition, 28 (1924); a review of Sir Thomas Dick Lauder's *Scottish Rivers* (Edinburgh: Edmonston and Douglas, 1874).

9. "On the Enjoyment of Unpleasant Places" (essay). Written late August–September 11, 1874; published in *The Portfolio* 5 (November 1874): 173–76; reprinted in the Tusitala edition, 25 (1924).

10. "An Appeal to the Clergy of the Church of Scotland" (pamphlet). Written late August, September 1874–February 1875; printed as *An Appeal to the Clergy of the Church of Scotland with a Note for the Laity* (Edinburgh and London: William Blackwood and Sons, 1875); reprinted in the Tusitala edition, 26 (1924).

11. "John Knox and His Relations to Women" (essay). Written September–November 1874; published as two installments in *Macmillan's Magazine* 32 (September 1875): 446–56, and 33 (October 1875): 520–31; included in *Familiar Studies of Men and Books* (1882); reprinted in the Tusitala edition, 27 (1924).

12. "A Quiet Corner of England" (review). Written November 1874; published in *The Academy* 5 (December 1874): 602–3; reprinted in the Tusitala edition, 28 (1924); a review of Basil Champney's *A Quiet Corner of England: Studies of Landscape and Architecture in Winchelsea, Rye, and the Romney Marsh* (London: Seeley, Jackson, and Halliday, 1874).

13. "An Autumn Effect" (essay). Written December 1874–January 1875; published in *The Portfolio* 6 (April 1875): 53–58; reprinted in the Tusitala edition, 30 (1924).

14. "The Works of Edgar Allan Poe" (review). Written December 1874; published in *The Academy* (January 2, 1875): 1–2; reprinted in the Tusitala edition, 28 (1924); a review of John H. Ingram's *The Works of Edgar Allan Poe* (London and Edinburgh: Adam and Charles Black, 1874–75).

15. "Forest Notes" (essay). Written spring 1875–January 1876; published in *Cornhill Magazine* 33 (May 1876): 545–61; reprinted in the Tusitala edition, 30 (1924).

16. "Pierre Jean de Beranger" (essay). Written summer 1875; published in *The Encyclopaedia Britannica*, 9th edition (1875), 3: 581–82; reprinted in the Tusitala edition, 30 (1924).

17. "Charles of Orleans" (essay). Written summer 1875–July 1876; published in *Cornhill Magazine* 34 (December 1876): 695–717; included in *Familiar Studies of Men and Books* (1882); reprinted in the Tusitala edition, 27 (1924).

18. "The Charity Bazaar" (pamphlet). Written September–November 1875; privately printed four-page folder, distributed at a bazaar benefit for the Zenana Missions of the Church of Scotland (printed without listings of place, publisher, or date); reprinted in the Edinburgh edition, 28 (1898): 1–4, and in the Tusitala edition, 5 (1924).

19. "The Measure of a Marquis" (review). Published in *Vanity Fair: A Weekly Show of Political, Social, and Literary Wares* (November 25, 1875): 303–6; a review of the Marquess of Lorne's *Guido and Lita: A Tale of the Riviera* (London: Macmillan, 1875).

20. "Mr. Browning Again!" (review). Published in *Vanity Fair: A Weekly Show of Political, Social, and Literary Wares* (December 11, 1875): 332–33; reprinted (abridged form) in *Notes and Queries* (February 12, 1944): 102–3; a review of Robert Browning's *The Inn Album* (London: Smith, Elder, 1875).

21. "Walking Tours" (essay). Written January–February 1876; published in *Cornhill Magazine* 33 (June 1876); included in *Virginibus Puerisque* (1881); reprinted in the Tusitala edition, 25 (1924).

22. "The Poets and Poetry of Scotland" (review). Published in *The Academy* (February 12, 1876): 138–39; a review of James Grant Wilson's *The Poets and Poetry of Scotland: From the Earliest to the Present Time . . . Period: From Thomas the Rhymer to Richard Gall* (London: Blackie and Son, 1876).

23. "Salvini's Macbeth" (review). Written April 1876; published in *The Academy* (April 15, 1876): 366–67; reprinted in the Tusitala edition, 28 (1924); a review of Tommasso Salvini's first performance of Shakespeare's *Macbeth*.

24. "Virginibus Puerisque" (essay). Written before May 18, 1876; published in *Cornhill Magazine* 34 (August 1876): 169–76; included in *Virginibus Puerisque* (1881); reprinted in the Tusitala edition, 25 (1924).

25. "Jules Verne's Stories" (review). Written May 1876; published in *The Academy* (June 3, 1876): 532; reprinted in the Tusitala edition, 28 (1924); a review of eight novels by Jules Verne (London: Sampson Low, 1876).

26. "An Apology for Idlers" (essay). Written July 1876; published in *Cornhill Magazine* 36 (July 1877): 80–86; included in *Virginibus Puerisque* (1881); reprinted in the Tusitala edition, 25 (1924).

27. "The Comedy of the Noctes Ambrosianae" (review). Published in *The Academy* (July 22, 1876): 76; reprinted in the Tusitala edition, 28 (1924); a review of John Skelton's edition of the essays of John Wilson, first collected as *Noctes Ambrosianae* (1822–35).

28. "Some Portraits by Raeburn" (essay). Written October 1876; included in *Virginibus Puerisque* (1881).

29. "On Falling in Love" (essay). Written November 1876; published in *Cornhill Magazine* 35 (February 1877): 214–20; included in *Virginibus Puerisque* (1881); reprinted in the Tusitala edition, 25 (1924).

30. "Our City Men. No. I.—A Salt Water Financier" (essay). Written January 1877; published in *London* (February 3, 1877): 9–10.

31. "The Book of the Week. Mr. Tennyson's 'Harold'" (review). Written January 1877; published in *London* (February 3, 1877): 18–19.

32. "In the Latin Quarter. No. I.—A Ball at Mr. Elsinare's" (essay). Written February 1877; published in *London* (February 10, 1877): 41–42; reprinted in *The Stevensonian: The Journal of the Robert Louis Steven-*

son Club, London 2 (August 1965): 2–7.

33. "In the Latin Quarter. No. II.—A Studio of Ladies" (essay). Written February 1877; published in London (February 17, 1877): 64.

34. "The Paris Bourse" (essay). Written February 1877; published in London (February 24, 1877): 88; reprinted in *The Stevensonian: The Journal of the Robert Louis Stevenson Club, London* 2 (August 1965): 2–7.

35. "The Book of the Week. Wallace's Russia" (review). Written February 1877; published in *London* (February 24, 1877): 92–93.

36. "An Old Song" (story). Originally written as "The Two Falconers of Cairnstane" in November 1874; rewritten February–March 1877; published as 4 weekly installments in *London* (February 24–March 17, 1877); first published under Stevenson's own name in *An Old Song and Edifying Letters of the Rutherford Family* (Paisley, Scotland: Wilfion Books; and Hamden, Conn.: Archon Books, 1982): 31–79.

37. "François Villon, Student, Poet, Housebreaker" (essay). Written spring 1877; published in *Cornhill Magazine* 36 (August 1877): 215–34; included in *Familiar Studies of Men and Books* (1882); reprinted in the Tusitala edition, 27 (1924).

38. "A Lodging for the Night: A Story of François Villon" (short story). Written spring–summer 1877; published in *Temple Bar* 51 (October 1877): 197–212; included in *New Arabian Nights* (1882); reprinted in the Tusitala edition, 1 (1924).

39. "Will o' the Mill" (short story). Written June–July 1877; published in *Cornhill Magazine* 37 (January 1878): 41–60; included in *The Merry Men and Other Tales* (1887); reprinted in the Tusitala edition, 8 (1924).

40. "Crabbed Age and Youth" (essay). Written July–August 1877; published in *Cornhill Magazine* 37 (March 1878): 351–59; included in *Virginibus Puerisque* (1881); reprinted in the Tusitala edition, 25 (1924).

41. "New Novels" (review). Written July 1877; published in *The Academy* (August 4, 1877): 108–09; reviews of James Walter Ferrier's *Mottiscliffe: An Autumn Story* (Edinburgh and London: William Blackwood and Sons, 1877), Ernte Ariel Wolfe's *Shamrock and Rose* (London: Remington, 1877), Mrs. Fetherstonhaugh's *Kilcorran* (London: R. Bentley and Son, 1877), and Annie L. Walker's *Against Her Will* (London: Samuel Tinsley, 1877).

42. "The Sire de Maletroit's Door" (short story). Written August 1877; published in *Temple Bar* 52 (January 1878): 53–69; included in *New Arabian Nights* (1882); reprinted in the Tusitala edition, 1 (1924).

43. *An Inland Voyage* (journalistic book). Originally written (in journal form) September 1876; rewritten November 1877–January 1878; published April 28, 1878 (London: C. Kegan Paul, 1878; second edition: 1881), and June 1883 (Boston: Roberts Brothers, 1883); the first 5 pages of Stevenson's original notebook were published in *Hitherto Unpublished Prose Writings* (Boston: Bibliophile Society, 1921): 37–47; reprinted in the Tusitala edition, 17 (1924).

44. "The English Admirals" (essay). Written late 1877; published in *Cornhill Magazine* 38 (July 1878): 36–43; included in *Virginibus Puerisque*

(1881); reprinted in the Tusitala edition, 25 (1924).

45. "Latter-Day Arabian Nights: The Suicide Club" (three stories). Written March–September 1878 (with "The Rajah's Diamond"); published as 8 weekly installments in *London* (June 8–July 27, 1878); included in *New Arabian Nights* (1882); reprinted in the Tusitala edition, 1 (1924).

46. "Latter-Day Arabian Nights: The Rajah's Diamond" (four stories). Written March–September 1878 (with "The Suicide Club"); published as 10 weekly installments in *London* (August 3–August 17, August 31–September 14, September 28, and October 12–26, 1878); included in *New Arabian Nights* (1882); reprinted in the Tusitala edition, 1 (1924).

47. "Aes Triplex" (essay). Published in *Cornhill Magazine* 37 (April 1878): 432–37; included in *Virginibus Puerisque* (1881); reprinted in the Tusitala edition, 25 (1924).

48. "A Plea for Gas Lamps" (essay). Published in *London* (April 27, 1878): 304–05; included in *Virginibus Puerisque* (1881); reprinted in the Tusitala edition, 25 (1924).

49. "Pan's Pipes" (essay). Published in *London* (May 4, 1878): 328; included in *Virginibus Puerisque* (1881); reprinted in the Tusitala edition, 25 (1924).

50. "El Dorado" (essay). Published in *London* (May 11, 1878): 352; included in *Virginibus Puerisque* (1881); reprinted in the Tusitala edition, 25 (1924).

51. "Edinburgh: Picturesque Notes" (essays). Written June–September 1878; published as 7 monthly installments in *The Portfolio* 9 (June–December 1878), and as *Edinburgh: Picturesque Notes*, in December 1878 (London: Seeley, Jackson, and Halliday, 1879); reprinted in the Tusitala edition, 26 (1924); a partial version of Stevenson's draft of "The Pentland Hills" was published in W. H. Arnold, "My Stevensons," *Scribner's Magazine* 71 (January 1922): 60–61; for the Seeley book version, Stevenson added the chapters "The Parliament Close," "The Villa Quarters," and "To the Pentland Hills."

52. "Child's Play" (essay). Written summer 1878; published in *Cornhill Magazine* 38 (September 1878): 352–59; included in *Virginibus Puerisque* (1881); reprinted in the Tusitala edition, 25 (1924).

53. "The Gospel According to Walt Whitman" (essay). Written summer 1878; published in *New Quarterly Magazine* 10 (October 1878): 461–81; included in *Familiar Studies of Men and Books* (1882); reprinted in the Tusitala edition, 27 (1924).

54. *Travels with a Donkey in the Cévennes* (journalistic book). Originally written (in journal form) September 22–October 2, 1878; rewritten December 1878–January 1879; published June 2, 1879 (London: C. Kegan Paul, 1879), and in June 1879 (Boston: Roberts Brothers, 1879); reprinted in the Tusitala edition, 27 (1924); selections from the journal were published in *Hitherto Unpublished Prose Writings* (Boston: Bibliophile Society, 1921): 92–94, and in W. H. Arnold, "My Stevensons," *Scribner's Magazine* 71 (January 1922): 57–62; the entire journal was published as Gordon Golding (and Robin Hill), ed., *The Cévennes Journal: Notes on a Journey Through the French Highlands* (Edinburgh: Mainstream, 1978), and (French translation) Jacques Poujol, ed., *Journal de*

*Route en Cévennes* (Toulouse: Edouard Privat for the Club Cevenol, 1978).

55. "Providence and the Guitar" (short story). Written October–November 1878; published as "Leon Berthelini's Guitar," in 4 weekly installments in *London* (November 2–23, 1878); included in *New Arabian Nights* (1882); reprinted in the Tusitala edition, 1 (1924).

56. *Deacon Brodie* (stage play). Cowritten (with W. E. Henley) October 1878–January 1880 and at various times through 1887; printed as *Deacon Brodie, or, The Double Life: A Melodrama, Founded on Facts in Four Acts and Ten Tableaux,* December 1879–January 1880 (Edinburgh: T. and A. Constable, 1880); revised edition printed as *Deacon Brodie or the Double Life: A Melodrama in Five Acts and Eight Tableaux by William Ernest Henley and Robert Louis Stevenson* (Edinburgh: T. and A. Constable, Edinburgh University Press, 1888); published (book form) with *Admiral Guinea* and *Beau Austin* in *Three Plays by W. E. Henley and R. L. Stevenson* (London: David Nutt, 1892); the 1880 edition was reprinted in C. C. Bigelow and Temple Scott, eds., *The Works of Robert Louis Stevenson,* 10 volumes (New York: Lamb, 1906), 8: 249–322; the 1888 revised edition was reprinted in the Tusitala edition, 24 (1924); first performed December 28, 1882, at Pullan's Theatre of Varieties, Bradford; later performances: Her Majesty's Theatre, Aberdeen (April 1883), Prince's Theatre, London (July 1884), and New York (1887).

57. "The Late Sam Bough, R. S. A." (essay). Written late November 1878; published in *The Academy* (November 30, 1878): 530–31.

58. "The Pavilion on the Links" (short story). Written November 1878–November 1879; published as 2 installments in *Cornhill Magazine* 42 (September 1880): 307–27, and 42 (October 1880): 430–51; included in *New Arabian Nights* (1882); reprinted in the Tusitala edition, 1 (1924).

59. "Truth of Intercourse" (essay). Written January 1879; published in *Cornhill Magazine* 39 (May 1879): 585–90; included in *Virginibus Puerisque* (1881); reprinted in the Tusitala edition, 25 (1924).

60. "Some Aspects of Robert Burns" (essay). Written May–August 1879; published in *Cornhill Magazine* 40 (October 1879); included in *Familiar Studies of Men and Books* (1882); reprinted in the Tusitala edition, 27 (1924).

61. "The Story of a Lie" (story). Written July–August 1879; published in *New Quarterly Magazine* 25 (October 1879): 307–55; reprinted in the Tusitala edition, 14 (1924).

62. *The Amateur Emigrant* (journalistic book). Written September 1879–June 1880; published (abridged form) as "Across the Plains: Leaves from the Notebook of an Emigrant Between New York and San Francisco" in 2 installments in *Longman's Magazine* 2 (July 1883): 285–304, and 2 (August 1883): 372–86; published (unabridged form) as *The Amateur Emigrant,* in the Edinburgh edition, 3 (1895): 1–166; 1895 edition reprinted in the Tusitala edition, 18 (1924); in James D. Hart, ed., *From Scotland to Silverado* (Cambridge, Mass.: Harvard University Press, 1966): 1–147, and in Roger D. Swearingen, ed., *The Amateur Emigrant,* 2 volumes (Ashland: Lewis Osborne, 1976–77).

63. Contributions to *The Monterey Californian* (15 articles and announcements). Written October 7–December 23, 1879; published in *The Monterey Californian*, weekly (October 7–December 23, 1879); "San Carlos Day" was reprinted in *Scribner's Magazine* 68 (August 1920): 209–11, and in James D. Hart, ed., *From Scotland to Silverado* (Cambridge, Mass.: Harvard University Press, 1966): 168–71.

64. "Padre Dos Reales" (broadsheet). Written late November 1879; printed (121 words of text on 200 broadsheet copies) by Crevole M. Bronson, publisher of *The Monterey Californian;* reprinted in James D. Hart, ed., *From Scotland to Silverado* (Cambridge, Mass.: Harvard University Press, 1966): xxvii–xxviii.

65. "Henry David Thoreau: His Character and Opinions" (essay). Written December 1879–January 1880; published in *Cornhill Magazine* 41 (June 1880): 665–82; included in *Familiar Studies of Men and Books* (1882); reprinted in the Tusitala edition, 27 (1924).

66. "Yoshida-Torajiro" (essay). Written before January 23, 1880; published in *Cornhill Magazine* 41 (March 1880): 327–34; included in *Familiar Studies of Men and Books* (1882); reprinted in the Tusitala edition, 27 (1924).

67. "Samuel Pepys" (essay). Written June 1880 and at intervals through 1881; published in *Cornhill Magazine* 44 (July 1881): 31–46; included in *Familiar Studies of Men and Books* (1882); reprinted in the Tusitala edition, 27 (1924).

68. "The Old Pacific Capital" (essay). Written summer or autumn 1880; published in *Fraser's Magazine* 131 (November 1880): 647–57; included in *Across the Plains* (1892); reprinted, with "A Modern Cosmopolis" (1883), as "The Old and New Pacific Capitals" in the Edinburgh edition, 3 (1895): 169–91, and in the Tusitala edition, 18 (1924).

69. *Virginibus Puerisque* (essay collection). Collected and augmented late 1880; published, as *Virginibus Puerisque and Other Papers*, in mid–April 1881 (London: C. Kegan Paul, 1881), and in later editions (London: Chatto and Windus, beginning 1884).

70. "Health and Mountains" (essay). Published in the *Pall Mall Gazette* (February 17, 1881); reprinted in *Essays and Criticisms by Robert Louis Stevenson* (Edinburgh: Herbert B. Turner, 1903), in *Essays of Travel* (London: Chatto and Windus, 1905), and in the Tusitala edition, 30 (1924).

71. "Davos in Winter" (essay). Published in the *Pall Mall Gazette* (February 21, 1881); reprinted in *Essays and Criticisms by Robert Louis Stevenson* (Edinburgh: Herbert B. Turner, 1903), in *Essays of Travel* (London: Chatto and Windus, 1905), and in the Tusitala edition, 30 (1924).

72. "Alpine Diversions" (essay). Published in the *Pall Mall Gazette* (February 26, 1881); reprinted in *Essays and Criticisms by Robert Louis Stevenson* (Edinburgh: Herbert B. Turner, 1903), in *Essays of Travel* (London: Chatto and Windus, 1905), and in the Tusitala edition, 30 (1924).

73. "The Stimulation of the Alps" (essay). Published in the *Pall Mall Gazette* (March 5, 1881); reprinted in *Essays and Criticisms by Robert Louis Stevenson* (Edinburgh: Herbert B. Turner, 1903), in *Essays of Travel*

(London: Chatto and Windus, 1905), and in the Tusitala edition, 30 (1924).

74. "The Misgivings of Convalescence" (essay). Published in the *Pall Mall Gazette* (March 17, 1881).

75. "The Morality of the Profession of Letters" (essay). Written early 1881; published in *Fortnightly Review* n.s. 157 (April 1881): 513–20, and in *The Academy* (April 9, 1881): 261; reprinted in the Tusitala edition, 28 (1924).

76. "The Morality of the Profession of Letters" (letter). Written April 27, 1881; published in *The Academy* (May 7, 1881): 339; Stevenson's reply to criticism that appeared in *The Academy* (April 9, 1881): 261.

77. "Thrawn Janet" (short story). Written June 1881; published in *Cornhill Magazine* 44 (October 1881): 436–43; included in *The Merry Men and Other Tales and Fables* (1887); reprinted in the Tusitala edition, 8 (1924).

78. "The Body-Snatcher" (short story). Written June–July 1881; published in the *Pall Mall Christmas Extra* 13 (December 1884): 3–12; reprinted in the Tusitala edition, 11 (1924).

79. "The Merry Men" (story). Written June–July 1881; published in *Cornhill Magazine* 45 (June 1882): 646–95, and 46 (July 1882): 56–73; included in *The Merry Men and Other Tales and Fables* (1887); reprinted in the Tusitala edition, 8 (1924).

80. *Treasure Island* (novel). Written September–November 1881; published as "Treasure Island; or, The Mutiny of the Hispaniola. By Captain George North" in 17 weekly installments in *Young Folks* 19–20 (October 1, 1881–January 28, 1882); published (book form) as *Treasure Island*, November 14, 1883 (London: Cassell, 1883), in February 1884 (Boston: Roberts Brothers, 1884), and in August 1885 (London: Cassell, 1885); reprinted (New York: Charles Scribner's Sons, 1902), and in the Tusitala edition, 3 (1924).

81. *Familiar Studies of Men and Books* (essay collection). Collected autumn 1881, while writing the "Preface, by Way of Criticism"; published February 22, 1882 (London: Chatto and Windus, 1882); reprinted in the Tusitala edition, 27 (1924).

82. "Young Rob Roy" (letter). Published in the *Stirling Observer* (October 21, 1881), and in the *Stirling Observer*'s *Local Notes and Queries* (1883): 287–88; reprinted in J. A. MacCulloch, *Robert Louis Stevenson and the Bridge of Allan* (1927): 83–85, and in D. B. Morris, *Robert Louis Stevenson and the Scottish Highlanders* (1929): 69–72.

83. "Byways of Book Illustration: Bagster's *Pilgrim's Progress*" (essay). Written October–November 1881; published in *The Magazine of Art* 5, n.s. part 16 (February 1882): 169–74; reprinted in the Tusitala edition, 28 (1924); a commentary on the illustrations in *Pilgrim's Progress* (London: Samuel Bagster and Sons, undated).

84. *The Silverado Squatters* (journalistic book). Originally written (in journal form) 1880; rewritten early 1882–late April 1882; published as "The Silverado Squatters: Sketches from a California Mountain" in 2 installments in *Century Illustrated Monthly Magazine* 27 (November 1883): 27–39, and 27 (December 1883): 183–93; published (book form) January 8, 1884 (London:

Chatto and Windus, 1883), and in January 1884 (Boston: Roberts Brothers, 1884); portions of Stevenson's journal were published as "The Silverado Diary," in the Vailima edition, 2 (1922): 579–608; the complete journal was published in John E. Jordan, ed., *Robert Louis Stevenson's Silverado Journal* (1954); *The Silverado Squatters* and "The Silverado Diary" were reprinted in the Tusitala edition, 18 (1924); *The Silverado Squatters* was reprinted in James D. Hart, ed., *From Scotland to Silverado* (Cambridge, Mass.: Harvard University Press, 1966): 189–287.

85. "The Foreigner at Home" (essay). Written winter 1881–82; published in *Cornhill Magazine* 45 (May 1882): 534–41; included in *Memories and Portraits* (1887); reprinted in the Tusitala edition, 29 (1924).

86. "Talk and Talkers" (essay). Written winter 1881–82; published in *Cornhill Magazine* 45 (April 1882): 410–18; included in *Memories and Portraits* (1887); reprinted in the Tusitala edition, 29 (1924).

87. "Byways of Book Illustration: Two Japanese Romances" (essay). Written (approximately) early 1882; published in *The Magazine of Art* 5, n.s. part 25 (November 1882): 8–15; reprinted in the Tusitala edition, 28 (1924); a commentary on the illustrations in Frederick V. Dickins, translator, *Chiushingura; or the Loyal League* (1876; new edition, London: Allen, 1880), and in Bernard-Henri Gausseron, translator, *Les Fideles Ronins* (Paris: A. Quantin, 1882).

88. "A Gossip on Romance" (essay). Written February 1882; published in *Longman's Magazine* 1 (November 1882): 69–79; included in *Memories and Portraits* (1887); reprinted in the Tusitala edition, 29 (1924).

89. "A Modern Cosmopolis" (essay). Written spring 1882; published in *The Magazine of Art* 6, n.s. part 31 (May 1883): 272–76; reprinted, with "The Old Pacific Capital," as "The Old and New Pacific Capitals" in the Edinburgh edition, 3 (1895): 169–91, and in the Tusitala edition, 18 (1924).

90. *New Arabian Nights* (story collection). Collected in spring 1882; published in 2 volumes, July 17, 1882 (London: Chatto and Windus, 1882); volume 1 contains the 7 stories published as "Latter-Day Arabian Nights" in *London* (June 8–October 26, 1878); volume 2 contains "The Pavilion on the Links," "A Lodging for the Night," "The Sire de Maletroit's Door," and "Providence and the Guitar"; reprinted in the Tusitala edition, 1 (1924).

91. "Talk and Talkers (A Sequel)" (essay). Written spring 1882; published in *Cornhill Magazine* 46 (August 1882): 151–58; included in *Memories and Portraits* (1887); reprinted in the Tusitala edition, 29 (1924); a long critique, "The Restfulness of Talk," *Spectator* (April 1, 1882): 420–21, prompted Stevenson to extend his earlier essay, "Talk and Talkers."

92. "The Treasure of Franchard" (story). Written August–November 1882; published as 2 installments in *Longman's Magazine* 1 (April 1883): 672–94, and 2 (May 1883): 83–112; included in *The Merry Men and Other Tales and Fables* (1887); reprinted in the Tusitala edition, 8 (1924).

93. "Plagiarism" (letter). Written October 16, 1882; published in *The Athenaeum* (October 21, 1882): 531, and in the *New York Tribune* (October 28, 1882): 12.

94. *Across the Plains* (journalistic book). Originally written September 1879–June 1880; rewritten early 1883; published as 2 installments in *Longman's Magazine* (July, August 1883); Stevenson slightly revised the final 7 chapters of "The Amateur Emigrant" for this publication.

95. "The Character of Dogs" (essay). Written spring–midsummer 1883; published in *The English Illustrated Magazine* 5 (February 1884): 300–05; included in *Memories and Portraits* (1887); reprinted in the Tusitala edition, 29 (1924).

96. "Fontainebleau: Village Communities of Painters" (essay). Written spring 1883; published as 2 installments in *The Magazine of Art* 7, n.s. part 43 (May 1884): 265–72, and 7, n.s. part 44 (June 1884): 340–45; reprinted in the Tusitala edition, 30 (1924).

97. *Prince Otto* (novel). Written April 10–December 1883 (and at intervals before and after); published as 7 monthly installments in *Longman's Magazine* 5–6 (April–October 1885); published (book form) November 1, 1885, as *Prince Otto: A Romance* (London: Chatto and Windus, 1885); reprinted in the Tusitala edition, 4 (1924).

98. *The Black Arrow* (novel). Written May 26–July 1883; published as "The Black Arrow, A Tale of Tunstall Forest. By Captain George North" in 17 weekly installments in *Young Folks* 22–23 (June 30–October 20, 1883); published (book form) June 16, 1888, as *The Black Arrow: A Tale of the Two Roses* (New York: Charles Scribner's Sons, 1888), and August 2, 1888 (London: Cassell, 1888); reprinted in the Tusitala edition, 9 (1924).

99. "A Note on Realism" (essay). Written summer 1883; published in *The Magazine of Art* 7 (November 1883): 24–28; reprinted in the Tusitala edition, 28 (1924).

100. "Old Mortality" (essay). Written autumn–winter 1883; published in *Longman's Magazine* 4 (May 1884): 74–81; included in *Memories and Portraits* (1887); reprinted in the Tusitala edition, 29 (1924).

101. "A Penny Plain and Twopence Coloured" (essay). Written autumn 1883; published in *The Magazine of Art* 7, n.s. part 42 (April 1884): 227–32; included in *Memories and Portraits* (1887); reprinted in the Tusitala edition, 29 (1924).

102. *More New Arabian Nights: The Dynamiter* (story collection). Cowritten (with Fanny Stevenson) spring 1884–February 1885; published April 28, 1885 (London: Longmans, Green, 1885); reprinted in the Tusitala edition, 3 (1924); includes "Zero's Tale of the Explosive Bomb" (by Stevenson), "Story of the Destroying Angel" and "The Story of the Fair Cuban" (both by Fanny Stevenson), and "Prologue of the Cigar Divan," "Challoner's Adventure: The Squire of Dames," "The Squire of Dames [concluded]," "Somerset's Adventure: The Superfluous Mansion," "Narrative of the Spirited Old Lady," "The Superfluous Mansion [continued]," "Desborough's Adventure: The Brown Box," "The Brown Box" (concluded), and "Epilogue of the Cigar Divan" (written as collaborations between them).

103. *Admiral Guinea* (stage play). Cowritten (with W. E. Henley) summer or early autumn 1884; printed as

*Admiral Guinea: A Melodrama in Four Acts*, by William Ernest Henley and Robert Louis Stevenson, September 1884 (Edinburgh: private printing, R. and R. Clark, 1884); published (book form), with *Deacon Brodie* and *Beau Austin*, in *Three Plays by W. E. Henley and R. L. Stevenson* (London: David Nutt, 1892); published separately as *Admiral Guinea: A Drama in Four Acts by W. E. Henley and R. L. Stevenson* (London: William Heinemann, 1897); reprinted in Tusitala edition, 24 (1924); first performed (posthumously) November 29, 1897, at the Avenue Theatre, London.

104. *Beau Austin* (stage play). Cowritten (with W. E. Henley) summer or early autumn 1884; printed as *Beau Austin: A Play in Four Acts*, by William Ernest Henley and Robert Louis Stevenson, September 1884 (Edinburgh: private printing, R. and R. Clark, 1884); published (book form), with *Deacon Brodie* and *Admiral Guinea*, in *Three Plays by W. E. Henley and R. L. Stevenson* (London: David Nutt, 1892); published separately as *Beau Austin: A Drama in Four Acts by W. E. Henley and R. L. Stevenson* (London: William Heinemann, 1897); reprinted in the Tusitala edition, 24 (1924); first performed November 17, 1890, at the Theatre Royal, London, with H. Beerbohm Tree as Beau Austin.

105. "A Humble Remonstrance" (essay). Written autumn 1884; published in *Longman's Magazine* 5 (December 1884): 139–47; included in *Memories and Portraits* (1887); reprinted in the Tusitala edition, 29 (1924); a reply to Henry James's "The Art of Fiction," *Longman's Magazine* (September 1884).

106. "The Bell Rock Lighthouse" (two letters). Written October 3, 20, 1884; published in *The Athenaeum* (October, 11, 1884): 465, and (October 25, 1884): 529; a critical review of Frederick Whymper's *The Sea: Its Stirring Story of Adventure, Peril and Heroism*, 4 volumes, 2d edition (London: Cassell, 1882–85).

107. "Markheim" (short story). Written late November 1884; revised 1885; published in Henry Norman, ed., *The Broken Shaft: Tales in Mid-Ocean* (London: T. Fisher Unwin, 1886 [for 1885]): 27–38; included in *The Merry Men and Other Tales and Fables* (1887); reprinted in the Tusitala edition, 8 (1924).

108. "On Style in Literature: Its Technical Elements" (essay). Written December 1884; published in *The Contemporary Review* 47 (April 1885): 548–61; reprinted in the Tusitala edition, 28 (1924).

109. *Macaire* (stage play). Cowritten (with W. E. Henley) autumn and winter 1884–85; printed as *Macaire: A Melodramatic Farce in Three Acts*, by William Ernest Henley and Robert Louis Stevenson (Edinburgh: private printing, R. and R. Clark, 1885); published (posthumously) in *The Chap Book* (Chicago: June 1, 1895): 43–71, and (June 15, 1895): 92–101, and in *The New Review* 12 (June 1895): 685–706; published (book form) as *Macaire: A Melodramatic Farce by Robert Louis Stevenson and William Ernest Henley* (Chicago: Stone and Kimball, 1895), and as *Macaire: A Melodramatic Farce in Three Acts by W. E. Henley and R. L. Stevenson* (London: William Heinemann, 1897); reprinted in the Tusitala edition, 24 (1924); first performed (posthumously) November 4, 1900, at the Strand Theatre, London; first reading given December 12, 1887, at the Athenaeum Hall, Godolphin Road, Shepherd's Bush, London.

110. "Professor Fleeming" (obituary). Written mid–June 1885; published in *The Academy* (June 20, 1885): 441.

111. "Memoir of Fleeming Jenkin" (essay). Written autumn 1885–summer 1887; published in Sidney Colvin and J. A. Ewing, eds., *Papers Literary, Scientific, & c. by the Late Fleeming Jenkin, F. R. S., L. L. D. Professor of Engineering in the University of Edinburgh*, 2 volumes (London and New York: Longman's, Green, 1887), 1: xi–cliv; published separately as *Memoir of Fleeming Jenkin*, January 7, 1888 (New York: Charles Scribner's Sons, 1888); reprinted in the Tusitala edition, 19 (1924).

112. *The Strange Case of Dr. Jekyll and Mr. Hyde* (novella). Written September–October 1885; published January 5, 1886 (New York: Charles Scribner's Sons, 1886), and January 9, 1886 (London: Longmans, Green, 1886); reprinted in the Tusitala edition, 5 (1924).

113. "The Misadventures of John Nicholson" (story). Written November 1885, December 1886; published as "The Misadventures of John Nicholson: A Christmas Story" in *Yule Tide ... Cassell's Christmas Annual* (December 1887): 3–12; reprinted in the Tusitala edition, 13 (1924).

114. "Ollala" (short story). Written November–December 1885; published in *Court and Society Review* (Christmas 1885): 3–15; included in *The Merry Men and Other Tales and Fables* (1887); reprinted in the Tusitala edition, 8 (1924).

115. *Kidnapped* (novel). Written spring 1885; January–April or May 1886; published as "Kidnapped: or The Lad with the Silver Button. By Robert Louis Stevenson" in 14 weekly installments in *Young Folks* 28–29 (May 1–July 31, 1886); published (book form) July 14, 1886 (London: Cassell, 1886; and New York: Charles Scribner's Sons, 1886); reprinted in the Tusitala edition, 6 (1924).

116. "American Rights and Wrongs" (essay). Written March 15, 1886; published in *The Academy* (March 20, 1886): 203.

117. "Honour and Chastity" (letter). Written July 22, 1886; published in *Court and Society Review* (July 29, 1886): 677–78; reprinted in *The Stevensonian: The Journal of the Robert Louis Stevenson Society of London* 3 (August 1967): 3–7.

118. "Rodin and Zola" (letter). Written September 1886; published in *The Times* (London, September 6, 1886): 8.

119. "Some College Memories" (essay). Written autumn 1886; published in *The New Amphion: Being the Book of the Edinburgh University Union Fancy Fair...* (Edinburgh: David Douglas, 1886): 221–40; included in *Memories and Portraits* (1887); reprinted in the Tusitala edition, 29 (1924).

120. *The Merry Men and Other Tales and Fables* (story collection). Collected late 1886; published February 9, 1887 (London: Chatto and Windus, 1887), and February 19, 1887 (New York: Charles Scribner's Sons, 1887); portions of the draft preface were first published in Graham Balfour, *The Life of Robert Louis Stevenson* (London: Charles Scribner's Sons, 1901), 1: 189; the complete draft preface was published in *Hitherto Unpublished Prose Writings* (Boston: Bibliophile Society, 1921): 73–76, and in the Vailima edition, 26 (1923): 477–78; reprinted in

the Tusitala edition, 8 (1924); includes "The Merry Men," "Will o' the Mill," "Markheim," "Thrawn Janet," "Ollala," and "The Treasure of Franchard."

121. *Memories and Portraits* (essay collection). Collected late 1886, augmented 1887; published November 21, 1887 (London: Chatto and Windus, 1887), and December 2, 1887 (New York: Charles Scribner's Sons, 1887); reprinted in the Tusitala edition, 29 (1924).

122. *The Hanging Judge* (stage play). Cowritten (with Fanny Stevenson) winter 1886–87; printed as *The Hanging Judge: A Drama in Three Acts and Six Tableaux. By Robert Louis Stevenson and Fanny Van De Gript* [sic] *Stevenson*, March or June 1887 (Edinburgh: private printing, R. and R. Clark, 1887), and in 1914 (private printing for Thomas J. Wise); reprinted in the Vailima edition, 6 (1922): 316–414; and in the Tusitala edition, 24 (1924).

123. "Pastoral" (essay). Written spring 1887; published in *Longman's Magazine* 9 (April 1887): 596–602; included in *Memories and Portraits* (1887); reprinted in the Tusitala edition, 29 (1924).

124. "The Day After To-morrow" (essay). Written spring 1887; published in *The Contemporary Review* 51 (April 1887): 472–79; reprinted in the Tusitala edition, 26 (1924).

125. "Life of Fleeming Jenkin" (letter). Written March 28, 1887; published in *Nature* (April 12, 1887): 559; a commentary on the March 8, 1887, *Nature* review (433–35) of *Papers Literary, Scientific, & c. by the Late Fleeming Jenkin* (1887).

126. "International Copyright" (letter). Written March 31, 1887; published in *The Times* (London, April 2, 1887): 6.

127. "The Manse: A Fragment" (essay). Written spring 1887; published in *Scribner's Magazine* 1 (May 1887); included in *Memories and Portraits* (1887); reprinted in the Tusitala edition, 29 (1924).

128. "Books Which Have Influenced Me" (essay). Written April or early May 1887; published in *British Weekly* (May 13, 1887): 17–19, and (book form, with 11 other contributions to the series) as *"British Weekly" Extras, No. I. Books Which Have Influenced Me*, August 1887 (London: British Weekly, 1887): 3–16; reprinted in the Tusitala edition, 28 (1924).

129. "Thomas Stevenson: Civil Engineer" (essay). Written late May 1887; published in *The Contemporary Review* 51 (June 1887): 789–93; included in *Memories and Portraits* (1887); reprinted in the Tusitala edition, 19 (1924).

130. "A College Magazine" (essay). Written spring–summer 1887; published in *Memories and Portraits* (1887); reprinted in the Tusitala edition, 29 (1924); an introduction to "An Old Scotch Gardener," the reprint of Stevenson's March 1871 *Edinburgh University Magazine* essay.

131. "Memoirs of an Islet" (essay). Written spring–summer 1887; published in *Memories and Portraits* (1887); reprinted in the Tusitala edition, 19 (1924).

132. "A Gossip on a Novel of Dumas's" (essay). Written spring–summer 1887; published in *Memories and Portraits* (1887); reprinted in the Tusitala edition, 19 (1924); an essay on Alexandre Dumas's *Dix ans plus*

*tard, ou le vicomte de Bragelonne* (1848–50).

133. "A Chapter on Dreams" (essay). Written early October 1887; published in *Scribner's Magazine* 3 (January 1888): 122–28; included in *Across the Plains* (1892); reprinted in the Tusitala edition, 30 (1924).

134. "The Lantern-Bearers" (essay). Written early or mid–October 1887; published in *Scribner's Magazine* 3 (February 1888): 251–56; included in *Across the Plains* (1892); reprinted in the Tusitala edition, 30 (1924).

135. "Beggars" (essay). Written October–November 1887; published in *Scribner's Magazine* 3 (March 1888): 380–84; included in *Across the Plains* (1892); reprinted in the Tusitala edition, 25 (1924).

136. "Pulvis et Umbra" (essay). Written November–December 1887; published in *Scribner's Magazine* 3 (April 1888): 509–12; included in *Across the Plains* (1892); reprinted in the Tusitala edition, 26 (1924).

137. *The Master of Ballantrae* (novel). Written early December 1887–May 1889; published as 12 monthly installments in *Scribner's Magazine* 4–6 (November 1888–October 1889); published (book form) as *The Master of Ballantrae: A Winter's Tale*, September 20, 1889 (London: Cassell, 1889), and September 21, 1889 (New York: Charles Scribner's Sons, 1889); the preface was first published (posthumously) in the Edinburgh edition, 28 (1898): 48–51; the preface and note to *The Master of Ballantrae* were reprinted in the Tusitala edition, 10 (1924).

138. "Gentlemen" (essay). Written January or early February 1888; published in *Scribner's Magazine* 3 (May 1888): 635–40; reprinted in the Tusitala edition, 26 (1924).

139. "Some Gentlemen in Fiction" (essay). Written February 1888; published in *Scribner's Magazine* 3 (June 1888): 764–68; reprinted in the Tusitala edition, 26 (1924).

140. "Popular Authors" (essay). Written February or March 1888; published in *Scribner's Magazine* 4 (July 1888): 122–28; reprinted in the Tusitala edition, 28 (1924).

141. "Epilogue to 'An Inland Voyage'" (essay). Written March 1888; published in *Scribner's Magazine* 4 (August 1888): 250–56; included in *Across the Plains* (1892); reprinted in the Tusitala edition, 17 (1924).

142. "A Letter to a Young Gentleman Who Proposes to Embrace the Career of Art" (essay). Written March or April–May 1888; published in *Scribner's Magazine* 4 (September 1888): 377–81; included in *Across the Plains* (1892); reprinted in the Tusitala edition, 17 (1924).

143. "Contributions to the History of Fife: Random Memories" (essay). Written spring 1888; published in *Scribner's Magazine* 4 (October 1888): 507–12; included as "Random Memories" in *Across the Plains* (1892), and as "Random Memories: The Coast of Fife" in the Edinburgh edition, 1 (1894); reprinted in the Tusitala edition, 30 (1924).

144. "The Education of an Engineer" (essay). Written spring 1888; published in *Scribner's Magazine* 4 (November 1888): 636–40; included as "Random Memories Continued" in *Across the Plains* (1892), and as "Random Memories: The Education of an Engineer" in the Edinburgh

edition, 1 (1894); reprinted in the Tusitala edition, 30 (1924).

145. "A Christmas Sermon" (essay). Written spring 1888; published in *Scribner's Magazine* 4 (December 1888): 764–68; included in *Across the Plains* (1892); reprinted in the Tusitala edition, 26 (1924).

146. *The Wrong Box* (novel). Cowritten (with Lloyd Osbourne) March–May 1888, February–March 1889; originally written (by Lloyd Osbourne) October–November 1887; published June 15, 1889 (New York: Charles Scribner's Sons, 1889), and (London: Longmans, Green, 1889); reprinted in the Tusitala edition, 11 (1924).

147. "Recent German Doings in Samoa" (letter). Written February 10, 1889; published in *The Times* (London, March 11, 1889): 10; reprinted under the title "Letters to the 'Times,' 'Pall Mall Gazette,' Etc." in the Edinburgh edition, 25 (1897): 249–311, and in the Tusitala edition, 21 (1924).

148. *The Wrecker* (novel). Cowritten (with Lloyd Osbourne) summer 1889–November 1891; published as "The Wrecker. By Robert Louis Stevenson and Lloyd Osbourne" in 12 monthly installments in *Scribner's Magazine* 10–12 (August 1891–July 1892); published (book form) June 25, 1892 (London: Cassell, 1892), and June 27, 1892 (New York: Charles Scribner's Sons, 1892); reprinted in the Tusitala edition, 12 (1924).

149. *The South Seas* (journalistic book). Originally written June 1888–July 1890; rewritten October 1889–autumn 1891; printed (a 22-copy limited edition) as *The South Seas: A Record of Three Cruises*, November 12, 1890 (London: Cassell, 1890); published as "The South Seas: Life Under the Equator: Letters from a Leisurely Traveller" in 34 installments in *The Sun* (a New York weekly, February 1–December 13, 1891, except the weeks of February 2–March 8, July 19–August 30, and November 29–December 8), and as "The South Seas: A Record of Three Cruises" in 27 installments in *Black and White* (a London weekly, irregular intervals, February 6–December 19, 1891); all chapters were published together (posthumously) as *In the South Seas* in the Edinburgh edition, 20 (1896), September 26, 1896 (New York: Charles Scribner's Sons, 1896), and December 11, 1900 (London: Chatto and Windus, 1900); additional material was published in the Swanston edition, 18 (1912); various portions of the whole were published in Graham Balfour, *The Life of Robert Louis Stevenson* (London: Charles Scribner's Sons, 1921), 2: 96–101, in *Hitherto Unpublished Prose Writings* (Boston: Bibliophile Society, 1921): 116–56, 177–83, in the Vailima edition, 25 (1923), and 26 (1923): 425–76, and in the Tusitala edition, 20–21 (1924).

150. "The Bottle Imp" (story). Written December 1889–January 1890 (possibly begun at Honolulu, May or June 1889); published as 4 weekly installments in the *New York Herald* (February 8–March 1, 1891), as 2 installments in *Black and White* (London, March 28 and April 4, 1891) and *The Herald* (London, December 13, 20, 1891); translated into Samoan by Rev. Arthur E. Claxton and published as "O Le Fagu Altu: O le tala lenel a le Tusitala" in 7 monthly installments in *O Le Sulu Samoa* (May–August, October–December 1891); included in *Island Nights' Entertainments* (1893); reprinted in the Tusitala edition, 13 (1924).

151. "Father Damien" (letter). Written February 25, 1890; printed as *Father Damien: An Open Letter to the Reverend Doctor Hyde of Honolulu from Robert Louis Stevenson,* late February and March 1890 (Sydney, Australia: 1890); published as "Father Damien. An Open Letter to the Reverend Dr. Hyde of Honolulu" in 2 installments in *The Scots Observer* (May 3, 1890): 659–61, and (May 10, 1890): 687–89; published (book form) as *Father Damien: An Open Letter to the Reverend Doctor Hyde of Honolulu from Robert Louis Stevenson,* July 16, 1890 (London: Chatto and Windus, 1890); reprinted in the Tusitala edition, 21 (1924).

152. "The Beach of Falesa" (story). Written November 1890, April–September 1891; published as "Uma; or The Beach of Falesa. (Being the Narrative of a South Sea Trader)" in 6 weekly installments in *Illustrated London News* (July 2–August 6, 1892); published (book form) as *The Beach of Falesa,* July 1892 (London: Cassell, 1892); included in *Island Nights' Entertainments* (1893); reprinted in the Tusitala edition, 13 (1924).

153. "Samoa" (letter). Written October 12, 14, 1891; published in *The Times* (London, November 17, 1891): 7; reprinted under the title "Letters to the 'Times,' 'Pall Mall Gazette,' Etc." in the Edinburgh edition, 25 (1897): 249–311, and in the Tusitala edition, 21 (1924).

154. *A Footnote to History* (journalistic book). Written early 1890, November 1891–May 1892; published as *A Footnote to History: Eight Years of Trouble in Samoa,* August 8, 1892 (New York: Charles Scribner's Sons, 1892), and (London: Cassell, 1892); chapter 10 was published separately as "The Hurricane: March 1889" in *National Observer* (May 21, 1892): 12–15; reprinted in the Tusitala edition, 21 (1924).

155. *Across the Plains* (essay collection). Collected late 1891; published as *Across the Plains with Other Memories and Essays,* April 6, 1892 (London: Cassell, 1892; and New York: Charles Scribner's Sons, 1892); reprinted in the Tusitala edition, 18, 25, 28, 30 (1924); this edition includes 12 essays, 9 of which were published in *Scribner's Magazine* (1888); the remaining 3 essays ("Across the Plains," "The Old Pacific Capital," and "Fontainebleau") were featured in other publications during the early 1880s.

156. "Two Tahitian Legends" (essay). Written early 1892; published as "Two Tahitian Legends. I. Of the Making of Pai's Spear. ... II. Honours and the Weird Women" in *Longman's Magazine* 19 (March 1892): 568–72.

157. *Catriona* (aka *David Balfour*) (novel). Written February 13–September 30, 1892; published as "David Balfour: Memoirs of His Adventures at Home and Abroad" in 10 monthly installments in *Atalanta* 6 (December 1892–September 1893); published (book form) as *Catriona: A Sequel to "Kidnapped" Being Memoirs of the Further Adventures of David Balfour at Home and Abroad...,* September 1, 1893 (London: Cassell, 1893), and as *David Balfour: Being Memoirs of His Adventures at Home and Abroad...,* September 1, 1893 (New York: Charles Scribner's Sons, 1893); reprinted in the Tusitala edition, 7 (1924).

158. "The Latest Difficulty in Samoa" (letter). Written April 9 and 12, 1892; published in *The Times* (London, June 4, 1892): 18; reprinted under the title "Letters to the

'Times,' 'Pall Mall Gazette,' Etc." in the Edinburgh edition, 25 (1897): 249–311, and in the Tusitala edition, 21 (1924).

159. "Samoa" (letter). Written June 22, 1892; published in *The Times* (London, July 23, 1892): 12; reprinted under the title "Letters to the 'Times,' 'Pall Mall Gazette,' Etc." in the Edinburgh edition, 25 (1897): 249–311, and in the Tusitala edition, 21 (1924).

160. "Mr. Stevenson and Samoa" (letter). Written July 19, 1892; published in *The Times* (London, August 19, 1892): 4; reprinted under the title "Letters to the 'Times,' 'Pall Mall Gazette,' Etc." in the Edinburgh edition, 25 (1897): 249–311, and in the Tusitala edition, 21 (1924).

161. "Scott's Voyage on the Lighthouse Yacht: Note" (introductory note). Written July 31, 1892; published in *Scribner's Magazine* 14 (October 1893): 492–94; an introduction to "Reminiscences of Sir Walter Scott, Baronet," a manuscript by Robert Stevenson (RLS's grandfather) describing Scott's tour of lighthouses in northern Scotland in 1814.

162. "An Object of Pity" (collaborative story). Written (with Fanny Stevenson, Isobel Strong, Graham Balfour, Lady Jersey, and Rupert Leigh) late August 1892; printed as *An Object of Pity: or, The Man Haggard, a Romance. By Many Competent Hands,* in October 1892 (Sydney, Australia: private printing, 1892); privately printed (posthumously) in November 1898 (Edinburgh); reprinted in a 110-copy limited edition in 1900 (New York: Dodd, Mead, 1900), and in C. C. Bigelow and Temple Scott, eds., *The Works of Robert Louis Stevenson*, 10 volumes (New York: Lamb, 1906).

163. "Mr. Stevenson and Samoa" (letter). Written September 14, 1892; published in *The Times* (London, October 17, 1892): 7; reprinted under the title "Letters to the 'Times,' 'Pall Mall Gazette,' Etc." in the Edinburgh edition, 25 (1897): 249–311, and in the Tusitala edition, 21 (1924).

164. "The Isle of Voices" (story). Written autumn 1892; published as 4 weekly installments in *National Observer* (February 4–25, 1893); included in *Island Nights' Entertainments* (1893); reprinted in the Tusitala edition, 13 (1924).

165. *Island Nights' Entertainments* (collection of three stories). Collected late 1892; published April 1, 1893 (New York: Charles Scribner's Sons, 1893), and April 6, 1893 (London: Cassell); reprinted in the Tusitala edition, 13 (1924); includes "The Beach of Falesá," "The Bottle Imp," and "The Isle of Voices."

166. *The Ebb-Tide* (novella). Final version (written by Stevenson) February–early June 1893; original version (begun by Lloyd Osbourne) spring 1889; resumed (by Osbourne) March 1890; resumed (by Stevenson) April–July 1890; published as "The Ebb Tide. By Robert Louis Stevenson and Lloyd Osbourne" in 13 weekly installments in *To-day* 1 (November 11, 1893–February 3, 1894), and as 6 monthly installments in *McClure's Magazine* (February–July 1894); published (book form) as *The Ebb-Tide: A Trio and Quartette*, July 15, 1894 (Chicago: Stone and Kimball, 1894), and September 21, 1894 (London: William Heinemann, 1894); reprinted in the Tusitala edition, 14 (1924).

167. "Missions in the South Seas" (article). Written March 1893; published in *The Presbyterian* (Sidney,

March 18, 1893); reprinted in Graham Balfour, *The Life of Robert Louis Stevenson* (London: Charles Scribner's Sons, 1901), 2: 193–95.

168. "My First Book: *Treasure Island*" (essay). Written spring or early summer 1893; published in *The Idler* 6 (August 1894): 2–11, and in *McClure's Magazine* 3 (September 1894): 283–93; included in Jerome K. Jerome, ed., *My First Book* (London: Chatto and Windus, 1894): 297–309; reprinted in the Tusitala edition, 2 (1924).

169. "War in Samoa" (letter). Written September 4, 1893; published in *The Pall Mall Gazette*, 8877 (September 1893): 1–2; reprinted under the title "Letters to the 'Times,' 'Pall Mall Gazette,' Etc." in the Edinburgh edition, 25 (1897): 249–311, and in the Tusitala edition, 21 (1924).

170. Untitled (letter). Written October 6, 1893; published in the *Daily Pacific Commercial Advertiser* (Honolulu, October 7, 1893): 2; reprinted in Arthur Johnstone, *Recollections of Robert Louis Stevenson in the Pacific* (1905): 108–09, in Eleanor Rivenburgh, "Stevenson in Hawaii—III," *The Bookman* 46 (New York, December 1917): 458, in Martha M. McGaw, *Stevenson in Hawaii* (1950): 130–31, and in the Honolulu *Advertiser* (November 20, 1970): A-17; a defense of the Sans Souci Seaside Resort in Honolulu.

171. "Speech to the Scottish Thistle Club, Honolulu" (address). Delivered mid–October 1893; published (in a newspaper version) mid–October 1893 (perhaps the *Pacific Commercial Advertiser*, Honolulu); reprinted in Arthur Johnstone, *Recollections of Robert Louis Stevenson in the Pacific* (1905): 114–19.

172. "The Deadlock in Samoa" (letter). Written April 23, 1894; published in *The Times* (London, June 2, 1894): 17–18; reprinted under the title "Letters to the 'Times,' 'Pall Mall Gazette,' Etc." in the Edinburgh edition, 25 (1897): 249–311, and in the Tusitala edition, 21 (1924).

173. "Mr. Stevenson on Samoa" (letter). Written May 22, 1894; published in *The Times* (London, June 30, 1894): 6; reprinted under the title "Letters to the 'Times,' 'Pall Mall Gazette,' Etc." in the Edinburgh edition, 25 (1897): 249–311, and in the Tusitala edition, 21 (1924).

• APPENDIX B •

# Posthumously Published Prose Writings

Following is a listing of Stevenson's prose works that were published after his death in December 1894.

1. "The History of Moses" (essay). Dictated (to Margaret Stevenson) November 23–December 21, 1856; privately printed as *The History of Moses* in 1919 for A. Edward Newton (Daylesford, Penn.); published in the Vailima edition, 25 (1923): 5–13.

2. "The Book of Joseph" (essay). Dictated (to Margaret Stevenson) February 20–April 10, 1857; published in the Vailima edition, 25 (1923): 14–23, and the Tusitala edition, 28 (1924).

3. Untitled (stories dictated at Colinton Manse) (stories). Dictated late 1850s; partly quoted in Graham Balfour, *The Life of Robert Louis Stevenson*, 1 (London: Charles Scribner's Sons, 1901): 45.

4. Untitled (dictations to Alison Cunningham) (observations). Dictated January 7–February 25, 1863; quoted in R. T. Skinner, ed., *Cummy's Diary* (1926): 8, 79.

5. "The School Boys Magazine" (four stories). Written October 1863; quoted in Graham Balfour, *The Life of Robert Louis Stevenson*, 1 (London: Charles Scribner's Sons, 1901): 65–66.

6. "Monmouth: A Tragedy" (essay). Written April–September 1868; included in Charles Vale, ed., *Monmouth: A Tragedy* (New York: William Edwin Rudge, 1928).

7. Untitled (Journal written aboard the *Pharos*). Written June 18–22, 1869; published in "The Letters of Robert Louis Stevenson," Sidney Colvin, ed., *Scribner's Magazine* 25 (January 1899): 41–48.

8. "Sketches" (essays). Written late 1860s–1870s; published in the Edinburgh edition, 21 (1896): 31–48.

9. Untitled (A retrospective) (essay). Written early 1870s; published in the Edinburgh edition, 21 (1896): 89–101.

10. "Reminiscences of Colinton Manse" (essay). Written early 1870s; published (abridged form) in Graham Balfour, *The Life of Robert Louis Stevenson*, 1 (London: Charles Scribner's Sons, 1901): 40–47.

11. Untitled (Journal written as a law clerk) (journal entries). Written

May 9–June 5, 1872; published in W. H. Arnold, "My Stevensons," *Scribner's Magazine* 71 (January 1922): 54–55; excerpts quoted in M. M. Black, *Robert Louis Stevenson* (1898): 72–74, and Graham Balfour, *The Life of Robert Louis Stevenson*, 1 (London: Charles Scribner's Sons, 1901): 105.

12. Untitled (Speculative Society valedictory address) (address). Delivered March 25, 1873; published in "The Last Unpublished Robert Louis Stevenson," *The Outlook* (February 19, 1898): 71–73; address delivered to the Speculative Society at the University of Edinburgh.

13. Untitled (Notes of childhood) (reminiscences). Written May 18, 1873; published (abridged form) in Graham Balfour, *The Life of Robert Louis Stevenson*, 1 (London: Charles Scribner's Sons, 1901): 31–34, 40.

14. "Cockermouth and Keswick" (essay). Written before August 1873; published in the Edinburgh edition, 21 (1896): 101–14, and the Tusitala edition, 30 (1924).

15. "Edifying Letters of the Rutherford Family" (story). Written 1873; published in *An Old Song and Edifying Letters of the Rutherford Family* (Paisley, Scotland: Wilfion Books, 1982; and Hamden, Conn.: Archon Books, 1982): 83–102.

16. "Grand Hotel Godam" (parody). Written winter 1873–74; published in E. V. Lucas, *The Colvins and Their Friends* (1928): 84–85.

17. Untitled (selections from his notebook) (notes). Written 1874–75; published in the Vailima edition, 25 (1923).

18. "When the Devil Was Well" (story). Written winter 1874, January–February 1875; published as *When the Devil Was Well* (Boston: Bibliophile Society, 1921), in the Vailima edition, 26 (1923): 417–76, and in the Tusitala edition, 5 (1924).

19. Untitled (prose fragments: A French legend, A note at sea, A night in France). Written spring 1875; published in *Hitherto Unpublished Prose Writings* (Boston: Bibliophile Society, 1921): 77–89, in the Vailima edition, 24 (1923): 36–40, and in the Tusitala edition, 25, 30 (1924).

20. "Sunday Thoughts," "Good Content" and "A Summer Night" (prose poems). Written May–June 1875; "Sunday Thoughts" and "Good Content" published in *San Francisco Call* (April 14, 1895): 14, and in A. H. Japp, *Robert Louis Stevenson*... (1905): 166–69; "A Summer Night" published in *Scribner's Magazine* 52 (November 1912): 593–94.

21. "A Winter's Walk in Carrick and Galloway" (essay). Written after January 17, 1876; published in *The Illustrated London News* (summer 1896): 13–15, *The Chap Book* (Chicago, June 15, 1896): 108–19, and the Tusitala edition, 30 (1924).

22. "A Mountain Town in France" (essay). Written September 1878; published in *The Studio* (winter 1896–97): 3–17; as a limited edition book, *A Mountain Town in France* (New York and London: John Lane, Bodley Head, 1897), and the Tusitala edition, 17 (1924).

23. "The Cévennes Journal: Notes on a Journey through the French Highlands" (essay). Written September–October 1878; published as *The Cévennes Journal: Notes on a Journey Through the French Highlands* (Edinburgh: Mainstream, 1978); a manuscript journal of Stevenson's walking

tour through France's Cévennes mountains which formed the basis for *Travels with a Donkey in the Cévennes*.

24. "On the Choice of a Profession" (essay). Written January 1879; published in *Scribner's Magazine* 57 (January 1915): 66–69, and the Tusitala edition, 28 (1924).

25. "An April Day: or, Autocyclus in Service" (stage play). Written February 1879, early 1883; published in Nancy Blonder Schiffman, "A Critical Edition of Robert Louis Stevenson's Unpublished Play Autocyclus in Service" (Ph.D. dissertation, University of South Carolina, 1973).

26. "Lay Morals" (essay). Written March 1879, October 1883; 1879 edition published in the Edinburgh edition, 21 (1896): 313–77, the Tusitala edition, 26 (1924): 5–49, and (excerpts) in *Hitherto Unpublished Prose Writings* (Boston: Bibliophile Society, 1921): 59–61, and the Tusitala edition, 26 (1924): 3–4; preface to the 1883 edition published in *Hitherto Unpublished Prose Writings* (Boston: Bibliophile Society, 1921): 55–59, and the Tusitala edition, 26 (1924): 1–3.

27. "Memoirs of Himself" (autobiography). Written 1880 (augmented later); published (for private distribution only) in 1912 (Philadelphia), *The Cornhill Booklet* 4 (Christmas 1914): 55–68, and the Vailima edition, 26 (1923): 203–24.

28. "Essays, Reflections and Remarks on Human Life" (essays). Written January–February 1880; published in the Edinburgh edition, 28 (1898): 26–41, and the Tusitala edition, 26 (1924).

29. "Simoneau's at Monterey" (essay). Written winter 1880–81; published in *From Scotland to Silverado,* James D. Hart, ed. (Cambridge, Mass.: Harvard University Press, 1966): 172–78.

30. Untitled ("Protest on behalf of Boer independence") (essay). Written winter 1880–81; published in *Hitherto Unpublished Prose Writings* (Boston: Bibliophile Society, 1921): 97–99, and the Tusitala edition, 28 (1924).

31. Untitled ("A mock trial") (satire). Written March or April 1881; published in Louis L. Cornell, "A Literary Joke by R.L.S.: Interpretation and Commentary," *Columbia Library Columns* 17 (February 1968): 17–26.

32. "Stevenson at Play" (war games correspondence). Written winter 1881–82; published in *Scribner's Magazine* 24 (December 1898): 709–19, and the Tusitala edition, 30 (1924); "facetious journalistic accounts" of war games that Stevenson and Lloyd Osbourne conducted at Davos (1880–82).[1]

33. "The Great North Road" (story). Written late 1884–June 1885; published in *Illustrated London News* (Christmas 1895): 5–14; as 2 installments in *The Cosmopolitan* (New York) 20 (December 1895): 147–57, and 20 (January 1896): 289–300, and the Tusitala edition, 16 (1924).

34. "Thomas Stevenson" (biography). Written (circa) autumn 1885; quoted in Graham Balfour, *The Life of Robert Louis Stevenson,* 1 (London: Charles Scribner's Sons, 1901): 16–20.

35. "Confessions of a Unionist" (essay). Written January 1888; printed as *Confessions of a Unionist: An Unpublished "Talk on Things Current" by Robert Louis Stevenson* (Cambridge, Mass.: private printing, 1921).

36. Untitled (A malaga in Samoa) (observations). Written December 1889–January 1890; partly published in Graham Balfour, *The Life of Robert Louis Stevenson*, 2 (London: Charles Scribner's Sons, 1901): 85–88.

37. "Cannonmills" (unfinished story). Written August–September 1890; published in the Vailima edition, 25 (1923): 377–79, and the Tusitala edition, 16 (1924); Stevenson intended "Cannonmills" as a love story that "everybody will think ... dreadfully improper."[2]; the entire manuscript runs only 1½ pages.

38. "Our Samoan Adventure" (essay). Written September 1890–December 1894; published as *Our Samoan Adventure,* Charles Neider, ed. (London: Weidenfeld and Nicolson, 1956); transcription of a diary kept by Stevenson and Fanny during their residence in Samoa.

39. "The Shovels of Newton French" (unfinished novel). Written early 1891–late 1892; published in the Vailima edition, 25 (1923): 309–57, and the Tusitala edition, 16 (1924); Stevenson intended "The Shovels of Newton French" as "a strange kind of novel," a historical romance spanning the years 1660 to about 1830[3]; after revising 3 chapters, Stevenson abandoned it in late 1892.

40. "Prayers" (collection of prayers). Written summer 1891–December 1894; published as "Prayers written for Family Use at Vailima" in the Edinburgh edition, 21 (1896): 379–88, and as "Vailima Prayers" in Graham Balfour, *The Life of Robert Louis Stevenson,* 2 (London: Charles Scribner's Sons, 1901): 196–200; two additional prayers were published as "Prayers at Vailima" in *Hitherto Unpublished Prose Writings* (Boston: Bibliophile Society, 1921): 193–95; two additional prayers were published in W. H. Arnold, "My Stevensons," *Scribner's Magazine* 71 (January 1922): 60; 20 prayers (including 14 from the Edinburgh edition, 2 from the Bibliophile volume, and 4 additional) were published collectively in the Vailima edition, 26 (1923): 138–63.

41. "Records of a Family of Engineers" (family history). Written August 1891; June–August 1893 (conceived as early as 1887–88); published in the Edinburgh edition, 18 (1896): 187–389, and (book form) as J. Christian Bay, ed., *The Manuscripts of Robert Louis Stevenson's Records of a Family of Engineers: The Unfinished Chapters* (Chicago: Walter M. Hill, 1929); only Stevenson's introduction and 3 chapters were completed to any extent; he began work on chapters 4, 5, and 6, but passed away before much progress was made.

42. "The Young Chevalier" (unfinished novel). Planned January–March 1892; begun May 1892; published in the Edinburgh edition, 26 (1897): 63–83, and the Tusitala edition, 16 (1924).

43. *Weir of Hermiston* (unfinished novel). Written October 1892–December 1894; published as 4 monthly installments in *Cosmopolis* 1 (January–April 1896), in the *Edinburgh Edition* 26 (1897): 123–291, and as 8 daily installments in the *Chicago Tribune* 5–12 (April 1896); published (book form), as *Weir of Hermiston: An Unfinished Romance,* May 20, 1896 (London: Chatto and Windus, 1896, and New York: Charles Scribner's Sons, 1896).

44. "The Waif Woman" (story). Written autumn 1892 (possibly earlier); published as "The Waif Woman: A Cue—From a Saga" in *Scribner's Magazine* 56 (December 1914): 687–701; (book form) as *The*

*Waif Woman,* November 1, 1916 (London: Chatto and Windus, 1916), and in the Tusitala edition, 5 (1924).

45. Untitled (Letter to the *Samoa Times and South Sea Advertiser*). Written November 18, 1892; original publication details unavailable; reprinted in H. J. Moors, *With Stevenson in Samoa* (1910): 173.

46. *St. Ives* (unfinished novel). Written January 1893–September 1894 (chapters 31–36 written by Arthur T. Quiller-Couch); published as "St. Ives: Being the Adventures of a French Prisoner in England" in 13 monthly installments in *Pall Mall Magazine* (November 1896–November 1897), and as 9 monthly installments in *McClure's Magazine* (United States) 8–10 (March–November 1897); published (book form) as *St. Ives: Being the Adventures of a French Prisoner in England,* October 2, 1897 (New York: Charles Scribner's Sons, 1897), in 1898 (London: William Heinemann, 1898), and in the Tusitala edition, 15 (1924).

47. "Fables" (short stories). Final versions written 1893–94 (begun as early as 1874); published as 2 installments in *Longman's Magazine* 26 (August 1895): 362–79, and 26 (September 1895): 472–89; *includes:* "The Sinking Ship," "The Two Matches," "The Sick Man and the Fireman," "The Devil and the Innkeeper," "The Penitent," "The Yellow Paint," "The House of Eld," "The Four Reformers," "The Man and His Friend," "The Reader," "The Citizen and the Traveller," "The Distinguished Stranger," "The Cart Horses and the Saddle Horse," "The Tadpole and the Frog," "Something in It," "Faith, Half Faith and No Faith at All," "The Touchstone," "The Poor Thing," "The Song of the Morrow"; "The Touchstone" published separately in *Mc-*

*Clure's Magazine* 6 (February 1896): 300–03; published (book form) as *The Strange Case of Dr. Jekyll and Mr. Hyde with Other Fables,* March 16, 1896 (London: Longmans, Green, 1896), September 26, 1896 (New York: Charles Scribner's Sons, 1896), and the Tusitala edition, 5, 2 (1924).

48. "Rosa Quo Locorum" (essay). Written March 1893; published in the Edinburgh edition, 21 (1896): 302–12, and the Tusitala edition, 30 (1924).

49. "The Owl" (story). Written April 1893; published in the Vailima edition, 25 (1923): 359–74, and the Tusitala edition, 16 (1924).

50. "Heathercat" (unfinished novel). Written July 1893–summer 1894; published in the Edinburgh edition, 26 (1897): 87–118, and the Tusitala edition, 16 (1924).

51. "Note to *The Master of Ballantrae*" (essay). Written late 1893; revised early 1894; published as "The Genesis of 'The Master of Ballantrae'" in the Edinburgh edition, 21 (1896): 297–302; five paragraphs from the revised version published in *Hitherto Unpublished Prose Writings* (Boston: Bibliophile Society, 1921): 63–70, and the Vailima edition, 26 (1923): 479–81.

52. "Note to *Kidnapped*" (essay). Written early 1894; published in W. H. Arnold, "My Stevensons," *Scribner's Magazine* 71 (January 1922): 65.

53. "Address to the Samoan Chiefs" (address). Written October 1894; published (partial form) in *Bookman* (London) 7 (February 1895): 136, and (complete) as "Robert Louis Stevenson's Address

to the Samoan Chiefs" in *McClure's Magazine* 5 (July 1895): 173–76.

54. "Early Memories" (reminiscences). Written October–November 1894; quoted in Graham Balfour, *The Life of Robert Louis Stevenson*, 1 (London: Charles Scribner's Sons, 1901): 50–51.

55. "On Time" (essay). Date unknown; published in the Vailima edition, 24 (1923): 34–35, and the Tusitala edition, 25 (1924).

56. "On Morality" (essay). Date unknown; published in the Vailima edition, 24 (1923): 36–37, and the Tusitala edition, 26 (1924).

57. "Diogenes in London" and "Diogenes at the Savile Club" (satirical essays). Date unknown; published as *Diogenes in London* (San Francisco: Edwin and Robert Grabhorn for John Howell, 1920), and *Diogenes at the Savile Club* (Chicago: Frank M. Morris, printed by Edwin and Robert Grabhorn for David G. Joyce, June 1921); published (from above sources) in the Vailima edition, 26 (1923): 7–15, 15–18, and the Tusitala edition, 5 (1924).

58. "Robin Run-the-Hedge" (unfinished story). Date unknown (possibly early 1880s); published in the Vailima edition, 26 (1923): 9–11, and the Tusitala edition, 16 (1924); after outlining 6 chapters, Stevenson completed one before he was forced to abandon the idea altogether; in a letter to Adelaide Boodle dated September 1, 1890, he remarked that "some nefarious person pre-empted the name"[4]; here he was referring to Annette Lyster's *Robin-Run-the-Hedge* (1884).

59. "The Ideal House" (unfinished essay). Date unknown (possibly early 1880s); published in the Edinburgh edition, 28 (1898): 42–47, and the Tusitala edition, 25 (1924).

60. "Story of a Recluse" (story). Date unknown (possibly late 1880s); published in *Hitherto Unpublished Prose Writings* (1921): 102–8, the Vailima edition, 25 (1923): 301–08, and the Tusitala edition, 16 (1924).

61. "The Ethics of Crime" (essay). Date unknown (possibly 1887–88); published in the Vailima edition, 24 (1923): 274–78, and the Tusitala edition, 26 (1924).

62. "The Castaways of Soledad" (unfinished story). Date unknown (possibly early 1880s); printed as *The Castaways of Soledad* (Buffalo: private printing for Thomas B. Lockwood, 1928); Stevenson completed 3 chapters and 1 page of chapter 4 before abandoning the story.

63. "Stevenson's Companion to the Cook Book: Adorned with a Century of Authentic Anecdotes" (anecdotes). Date unknown (possibly begun in 1888-89); published in the Vailima edition, 26 (1923), and the Tusitala edition, 5 (1924); intending to release the "Companion" as a book, Stevenson and Fanny created this series of articles about cookery for S. S. McClure; in a letter to Charles Baxter dated March 26, 1894, Stevenson complained that McClure had cut out all of Fanny's recipes: "he has published the plums and left out the cookery."[5]

# • APPENDIX C •
# Published Poetry

Following is a listing of Stevenson's published poetry. *Collected Poems*, a comprehensive edition, was first published in 1950. Untitled poems are identified with the first line of verse.

1. *A Child's Garden of Verses*. Published (in book form) March 1885; some verses were published earlier in the *Magazine of Art;* includes: "Bed in Summer," "A Thought," "At the Sea-Side," "Young Night Thought," "Whole Duty of Children," "Rain," "Pirate Story," "Foreign Lands," "Windy Nights," "Travel," "Singing," "Looking Forward," "A Good Play," "Where Go the Boats?" "Auntie's Skirts," "The Land of Counterpane," "The Land of Nod," "My Shadow," "System," "A Good Boy," "Escape at Bedtime," "Marching Song," "The Cow," "Happy Thought," "The Wind," "Keepsake Mill," "Good and Bad Children," "Foreign Children," "The Sun's Travels," "The Lamplighter," "My Bed Is a Boat," "The Moon," "The Swing," "Time to Rise," "Looking-Glass River," "Fairy Bread," "From a Railway Carriage," "Winter-time," "The Hayloft," "Farewell to the Farm," "North-West Passage" ("Good Night," "Shadow March," "In Port"), "The Child Alone" ("The Unseen Playmate," "My Ship and I," "My Kingdom," "Picture-Books in Winter," "My Treasures," "Block City," "The Land of Story-Books," "Armies in the Fire," "The Little Land"), "Garden Days" ("Night and Day," "Nest Eggs," "The Flowers," "Summer Sun," "The Dumb Soldier," "Autumn Fires," "The Gardener," "Historical Associations"), "Envoys" ("To Willie and Henrietta," "To My Mother," "To Auntie," "To Minnie," "To My Name-Child," "To Any Reader").

2. *Underwoods*. Published (in book form) July 1887; some verses were published earlier in the *Magazine of Art, Cornhill Magazine, Atlantic Monthly*, and others; includes: "Book I (In English)": "Envoy," "A Song of the Road," "The Canoe Speaks," "It is the season now to go," "The House Beautiful," "A Visit from the Sea," "To a Gardener," "To Minnie," "To K. de M.," "To N. V. de G. S.," "To Will H. Low," "To Mrs. Will H. Low," "To H. F. Brown," "To Andrew Lang," "Et Tu in Arcadia Vixisti," "To W. E. Henley," "Henry James," "The Mirror Speaks," "Katharine," "To F. J. S.," "Requiem," "The Celestial Surgeon," "Our Lady of the Snows," "Not yet, my soul, these friendly fields desert," "It is not yours, O mother, to complain," "The Sick Child," "In Memoriam F. A. S.,"

"To My Father," "In the States," "A Portrait," "Sing clearlier, Muse, or evermore be still," "A Camp," "The Country of the Camisards," "Skerryvore," "Skerryvore: the Parallel," "*My house*, I say. But hark to the sunny doves," "My body which my dungeon is," "Say not of me that weakly I declined," "Dedicatory Poem"; "Book II (In Scots)": "The Maker to Posterity," "Ille Terrarum," "Where aince Aprile has fairly come," "A Mile an' a Bittock," "A Lowden Sabbath Morn," "The Spaewife," "The Blast—1875," "The Counterblast—1886," "The Counterblast Ironical," "Their Laureate to an Academy Class Dinner Club," "Embro Hie Kirk," "The Scotsman's Return from Abroad," "Late in the nicht in bed I lay," "My Conscience!" "To Doctor John Brown," "It's an owercome sooth for age an' youth."

3. *Songs of Travel and Other Verses*. Written 1887-91; published (in book form) August 1896; some verses were previously printed in the *P. M. Gazette, New Review,* the *Scots Observer,* and others; the collection was first printed in book form in volume 14 of the Edinburgh edition (December 1895); includes: "The Vagabond," "Youth and Love—I," "Youth and Love—II," "The Unforgotten—I," "The Unforgotten—II," "The infinite shining heavens," "Plain as the glistering planets shine," "To you, let snow and roses," "Let Beauty awake in the morn from beautiful dreams," "I know not how it is with you," "I will make you brooches and toys for your delight," "We Have Loved of Yore," "Ditty," "Mater Triumphans," "Bright is the ring of words," "In the highlands, in the country places," "Home no more home to me, whither must I wander," "To Dr. Hake," "To—," "The morning drum—call on my eager ear," "I have trod the upward and the downward slope," "He hears with gladdened heart the thunder," "The Lost Occasion," "If This Were Faith," "My Wife," "Winter," "The stormy evening closes now in vain," "To an Island Princess," "To Kalakaua," "To Princess Kaiulani," "To Mother Maryanne," "In Memoriam, E. H.," "To My Wife," "To the Muse," "To My Old Familiars," "The tropics vanish, and meseems that I," "To S. C.," "The House of Tembinoka," "The Woodman," "Tropic Rain," "And End of Travel," "We uncommiserate pass into the night," "The Last Sight," "Sing me a song of a lad that is gone," "To S. R. Crockett," "Evensong."

4. *Ballads*. Published (in book form) December 1890; several ballads were published earlier in *Scribner's Magazine* and the *Scots Observer;* includes: "The Song of Rahero: A Legend of Tahiti" ("The Slaying of Tamatea," "The Venging of Tamatea"), "Rahero," "The Feast of Famine: Marquesan Manners" ("The Priest's Vigil," "The Lovers," "The Feast," "The Raid"), "Ticonderoga: A Legend of the West Highlands" ("The Saying of the Name," "The Seeking of the Name," "The Place of the Name"), "Heather Ale: A Galloway Legend," "Christmas at Sea."

5. *New Poems*. Includes: "Summer Night," "I sit up here at midnight," "Lo! in thine honest eyes I read," "Though deep indifference should drowse," "My heart, when first the blackbird sings," "I dreamed of forest alleys fair," "Verses Written in 1872," "To H. C. Bunner," "From Wishing Land," "The Well-Head," "The Mill-House," "St. Martin's Summer," "All influences were in vain," "The old world moans and topes," "I am like one that has sat alone," "The whole day thro', in contempt and pity," "The old

Chimaeras, old receipts," "Dedication," "Prelude," "The Vanquished Knight," "Auld Reekie," "Athole Brose," "Over the Water wi' Chairlie," "To the Commissioners of Northern Lights," "After reading 'Antony and Cleopatra'," "The relic taken, what avails the shrine," "About the sheltered garden ground," "I know not how, but as I count," "Take not my hand as mine alone," "The Angler rose, he took his rod," "Spring-Song," "Thou strainest through the mountain fern," "The summer sun shone round me," "You looked so tempting in the pew," "Love's Vicissitudes," "The moon is sinking—the tempestuous weather," "Death," "Duddingstone," "Stout marches lead to certain ends," "Away with funeral music," "To Sydney," "Had I the power that have the will," "O, dull cold northern sky," "Apologetic postscript of a year later," "To Marcus," "To Ottilie," "This gloomy, northern day," "To a Youth," "John Cavalier," "Praise and Prayer," "Hopes," "I have a friend: I have a story," "Link your arm in mine, my lad," "The wind is without there and howls in the trees," "A Valentine's Song," "Hail! Childish slaves of social rules," "Swallows travel to and fro," "To Mesdames Zassetsky and Garschine," "To Madame Garschine," "Music at the Villa Marina," "Fear not, dear friend, but freely live your days," "Let love go, if go she will," "I do not fear to own me kin," "I am like one that for long days had sate," "Sit doon by me, my canty freend," "Here he comes, big with statistics," "Voluntary," "O now, although the year be done," "Ad Se Ipsum," "In the green and gallant spring," "Death, to be dead forevermore," "To Charles Baxter," "The look of death is both severe and mild," "Her name is as a word of old romance," "In autumn when the woods are red," "Light as my heart was long ago," "Gather ye roses while ye may," "Poem for a Class Re-Union," "I saw red evening through the rain," "Last night we had a thunderstorm in style," "O lady fair and sweet," "If I had wings, my lady, like a dove," "Rondels," "Eh, man Henley, you're a don," "All night through, raves or broods," "The rain is over and done," "There where the land of love," "Love is the very heart of spring," "On His Pitiable Transformation," "I, who all the winter through," "Love—what is love?" "Soon our friends perish," "As one who having wandered all night long," "Strange are the ways of men," "The wind blew shrill and smart," "Man sails the deep a while," "The cock's clear voice into the clearer air," "Now when the number of my years," "What man may learn, what man may do," "The Susquehanna and the Delaware," "If I could arise and travel away," "Good old ale, mild or pale," "Nay, but I fancy somehow, year by year," "My wife and I, in one romantic cot," "At morning on the garden seat," "Small is the trust when love is green," "Know you the river near to Grez," "It's forth across the roaring foam," "Dedication," "Farewell," "The Fine Pacific Islands," "Topical Song," "Student Song," "An English Breeze," "To Miss Cornish," "To Rosabelle," "As in their flight the birds of song," "Prayer," "The Piper," "Epistle to Albert Dew-Smith," "Of schooners, islands, and maroons," "To Mrs. Macmarland," "Yes, I remember, and still remember wailing," "Tales of Arabia," "Behold, as goblins dark of mein," "Still I love to rhyme, and still more, rhyming, to wander," "Long time I lay in little ease," "Flower God, God of the spring, beautiful, bountiful," "Come, my beloved, hear from me," "Since years ago forevermore," "For Richmond's Garden Wall," "Here Lies Erotion," "To Priapus," "Aye mon, it's true; I'm no' that weel," "Hail, guest, and enter freely!" "Lo, now, my guest, if aught amiss were said," "So live, so love, so use that fragile hour," "Before this little gift was come," "Go, little book—the ancient phrase," "My love was warm: for that I crossed," "Come, my little children, here are songs for you," "Home from the daisied meadows, where you linger yet," "Early in the morning I hear on your piano," "Fair isle at sea—thy lovely name," "Loud and low in the chimney," "I love to be warm by the red fireside," "Mine eyes were swift to know thee," "Fixed is the doom: and to the last of years," "Men are heaven's piers, they evermore," "Spring Carol," "To what shall I compare her," "When the sun comes after the rain," "Late, O miller," "To friends at home, the lone, the admired, the lost," "I, whom Apollo sometimes visited," "The Far-Farers," "Far over seas an island is," "On the gorgeous hills of morning," "Rivers and winds among the twisted hills," "Tempest tossed and sore afflicted," "I, now, O friend, whom noiselessly the snows," "Since thou hast given me this good hope, O God," "God gave to me a child in part," "Over the land is April," "Light as a linnet on my way I start," "Come, here is adieu to the city," "It blows a snowing gale in the winter of the year," "Ne Sit Ancillae Tibi Amor Pudori," "To all that love the far and blue," "Now bare to the beholder's eye," "The Bour-Tree Den," "Sonnets," "The Family," "Air of Diabelli's," "De Erotio Puella," "I look across the ocean," "I am a hunchback, yellow faced," "Song," "The New House," "Men marvel at the works of man," "To Master Andrew Lang," "To the Stormy Petrel," "The indefensible impulse of my blood," "Who would think, herein to look," "Epistle to Charles Baxter," "Ad Martialem," "De M. Antonio," "Not roses to the rose, I trow," "To a Little Girl," "To Miss Rawlinson," "The pleasant river gushes," "To H. F. Brown," "To H. E. Henley," "O, Henley, in my hours of ease," "All things on earth and sea," "On Some Ghostly Companions at a Spa," "To Charles Baxter," "To Henry James," "Here you rest among the valleys, maiden known to but a few," "And thorns, but Did the sculptor spare," "My brain swims, empty and light," "The Light-Keeper," "The Daughter of Herodias," "The Cruel Mistress," "Storm," "Stormy Nights," "Song at Dawn," "Sole scholar of your college I appear," "Dark women," "A Valentine," "To a Midshipman," "The faces and forms of yore," "The Consecration of Braille," "Burlesque Sonnet," "To Teuila," "To Ko Ung," "To Ko Ung, the Goddess," "In Lupum," "In Charidemum," "Ad Nepotem," "Epitaphium Erotii," "Ad Quintilianum," "De Hortis Julii Martialis," "In Maximum," "Ad Olum," "De Coenatione Micae," "Ad Piscatorem."

6. Additional Poems. Two poems, "The Gods Are Dead" and "Lord Nelson and the Tar," were first published in the second edition of *Collected Poems* in 1971.

## • APPENDIX D •
# Silent Film Adaptations

Following is a listing of Anglo-American and European silent films directly adapted from Stevenson's novels and stories.

1. *Dr. Jekyll and Mr. Hyde* (1908). CREDITS: Directed by Sidney Olcott; based on the novella *The Strange Case of Dr. Jekyll and Mr. Hyde;* released by Kalem. CAST: Gene Gauntier, Frank Rose.

2. *Dr. Jekyll and Mr. Hyde* (1908). CREDITS: Alternate title: *The Modern Dr. Jekyll;* directed by Otis Turner; based on the novella *The Strange Case of Dr. Jekyll and Mr. Hyde* and the play by Luella Forepaugh; released by Selig Polyscope; running length, 1,035 feet. CAST: Hobart Bosworth, Betty Harte.

3. *Treasure Island* (1908). CREDITS: Based on the novel *Treasure Island;* released by Vitagraph Pictures.

4. *Dr. Jekyll and Mr. Hyde* (1909). CREDITS: Danish title: *Den Skaebnesvangre Opfindelse;* directed by August Blom; produced by Ole Olson; screenplay by August Blom; based on the novella *The Strange Case of Dr. Jekyll and Mr. Hyde;* released by Nordisk (Great Northern), Copenhagen, Denmark. CAST: Alvin Neuss (Dr. Jekyll/Mr. Hyde), Emilie Sannon, Oda Alstrup.

5. *The Suicide Club* (1909). CREDITS: Based on the short story trilogy "The Suicide Club"; released by American Mutoscope-Biograph.

6. *The Duality of Man* (1910). CREDITS: Based on the novella *The Strange Case of Dr. Jekyll and Mr. Hyde;* released by Wrench Films, Great Britain.

7. *Dr. Jekyll and Mr. Hyde* (1911). CREDITS: Directed by Lucius Henderson; based on the novella *The Strange Case of Dr. Jekyll and Mr. Hyde;* released by Thanhouser; running length, 1 reel. CAST: James Cruze (Dr. Jekyll), Harry Benham (Mr. Hyde), Marguerite Snow (Muriel Carew).

8. *Treasure Island* (1912). CREDITS: Directed by J. Searle Dawley; based on the novel *Treasure Island;* released by Edison.

9. *Dr. Jekyll and Mr. Hyde* (1913). CREDITS: Directed by Herbert Brenon; produced by Carl Laemmle; based on the novella *The Strange Case of Dr. Jekyll and Mr. Hyde;* released by Imp; running length, 2 reels. CAST: King Baggot (Dr. Jekyll/Mr. Hyde), Jane Gail (Alice), Matt Snyder (Alice's father), Howard Crampton (Dr. Lanyon), William Sarell (Utterson).

10. *Dr. Jekyll and Mr. Hyde* (1913). CREDITS: Based on the novella *The Strange Case of Dr. Jekyll and Mr. Hyde;* photographed in 2-strip color; released by Kineto-Kinemacolor Corporation, Great Britain; running length, 2 reels.

11. *The Wrong Box* (1913). CREDITS: Based on the novel *The Wrong Box* by Stevenson and Lloyd Osbourne; released by Solax.

12. *The Suicide Club* (1914). CREDITS: Directed by Maurice Elvey; based on the short story trilogy "The Suicide Club"; released by British and Colonial Kinematograph Company, Great Britain; running length, 4 reels. CAST: Montagu Love, Elizabeth Risdon, Fred Groves, M. Gray Murray.

13. *Horrible Hyde* (1915). CREDITS: Directed by Arthur Hotaling; based on the novella *The Strange Case of Dr. Jekyll and Mr. Hyde;* released by Lubin. CAST: Jerold T. Horner, Billy Reeves, May Hotely.

14. *Miss Jekyll and Madame Hyde* (1915). CREDITS: Directed by Charles L. Gaskill; suggested by the novella *The Strange Case of Dr. Jekyll and Mr. Hyde;* released by Vitagraph. CAST: Helen Gardner, Paul Scardon.

15. *Kidnapped* (May 1917). CREDITS: Directed by Alan Crosland; screenplay by Sumner Williams; based on the novel *Kidnapped;* released by Forum/Edison; running length, 5 reels. CAST: Raymond McKee (David Balfour), Joseph Burke (Ebenezer Balfour), Robert Cain (Alan Breck), William Wadsworth (Angus Bankeillor), Ray Hallor (Ransome, the Cabin Boy), Walter Craven (Riach), John Nicholson (Shuan), Franklin Hanna (Captain Hoseason), Sam Niblack (Cluny McPherson), Horace Hain (Colin Campbell), James Levering.

16. *Treasure Island* (January 1918). CREDITS: Directed by C. M. and S. A. Franklin; based on the novel *Treasure Island;* released by Fox Pictures ("Kiddie" series); running length, 6 reels. CAST: Francis Carpenter (Jim Hawkins), Virginia Lee Corbin (Virginia), Violet Radcliffe (Long John Silver), Lloyd Pearl.

17. *Unheimliche Geschicten* (1919). CREDITS: Based on the short story trilogy "The Suicide Club"; produced in Germany.

18. *Dr. Jekyll and Mr. Hyde* (early April 1920). CREDITS: Directed by John S. Robertson; screenplay by Clara S. Beranger; based on the novella *The Strange Case of Dr. Jekyll and Mr. Hyde;* photographed by Roy Overbaugh; released by Paramount Pictures; running length, 7 reels. CAST: John Barrymore (Dr. Henry Jekyll/Mr. Oscar Hyde), Martha Mansfield (Millicent Carew), Brandon Hurst (Sir George Carew), Charles Lane (Dr. Richard Lanyon), J. Malcolm Dunn (John Utterson), Cecil Clovelly (Edward Enfield), Nita Naldi (Miss Gina [also called Therese]), George Stevens (Poole), Louis Wolheim (Music Hall Owner).

19. *Dr. Jekyll and Mr. Hyde* (late April 1920). CREDITS: Produced by Louis B. Mayer; based on the novella *The Strange Case of Dr. Jekyll and Mr. Hyde;* released by Pioneer Film Corporation; running length, 4 reels. CAST: Sheldon Lewis (Dr. Jekyll/Mr. Hyde), Alexander Shannon (Dr. Lanyon), Dora Mills Adams (Mrs. Lanyon), Gladys Field (Bernice Lanyon), Harold Forshay (Edward Utterson), Leslie Austin (Danvers Carew).

20. *Der Januskopf* (1920). CREDITS: U.S. titles, *The Head of Janus, Janus-*

*Faced, Love's Mockery;* directed by F. W. Murnau; screenplay by Hans Janowitz; based on the novella *The Strange Case of Dr. Jekyll and Mr. Hyde;* photographed by Karl Freund, Carl Hoffman, and Carl Weiss; art direction by Heinrich Richter; a Lipow Film production; released by Decla-Bioscop, Berlin, Germany. CAST: Conrad Veidt (Dr. Warren/Mr. O'Connor), Margarete Schlegel, Magnus Stifter, Willi Kaiser-Heyl, Bela Lugosi (Dr. Warren's Butler), Margarete Kupfer, Gustav Botz, Jaro Furth, Marga Reuter, Lansa Rudolph, Danny Gurtler.

21. *Treasure Island* (April 1920). CREDITS: Directed by Maurice Tourneur; screenplay by Stephen Fox (Jules Furthman); based on the novel *Treasure Island;* photographed by Rene Guissart; released by Paramount Pictures; running length, 6 reels. CAST: Shirley Mason (Jim Hawkins), Josie Melville (Mrs. Hawkins), Al Filson (Billy Bones), Wilton Taylor (Black Dog), Lon Chaney (Blind Pew/George Merry), Charles Ogle (Long John Silver), Joseph Singleton (Israel Hands), Bull Montana (Morgan), Harry Holden (Captain Smollett), Sydney Dean (Squire Trelawney), Charles Hill Mailes (Dr. Livesey).

22. *The White Circle* (September 1920). CREDITS: Directed by Maurice Tourneur; screenplay by Jules Furthman and Jack (John) Gilbert; based on the short story "The Pavilion on the Links"; photographed by Alfred Ortlieb; released by Paramount Pictures; running length, 5 reels. CAST: Janis Wilson (Clara Huddlestone), Jack Gilbert (Frank Cassilis), Spottiswoode Aitken (Bernard Huddlestone), Harry B. Northrup (Northmour), Jack McDonald (Gregorio), W. Barry (Ford).

23. *Ebb Tide* (November 19, 1922). CREDITS: Directed by George Melford; screenplay by Waldemar Young; based on the novel *The Ebb-Tide;* photographed by Bert Glennon; released by Famous Players–Lasky/Paramount Pictures; running length, 8 reels. CAST: Noah Beery (Richard Attwater), Lila Lee (Ruth Attwater), James Kirkwood (Robert Herrick), Raymond Hatton (J. L. Huish), George Fawcett (Captain Davis), Jacqueline Logan (Tehura).

• APPENDIX E •

# Sound Film Adaptations

Following is a listing of English-language and European sound feature films directly adapted from Stevenson's novels, stories, and travelogues.

1. *Dr. Jekyll and Mr. Hyde* (December 31, 1931). CREDITS: Directed and produced by Rouben Mamoulian; screenplay by Samuel Hoffenstein and Percy Heath; based on the novella *The Strange Case of Dr. Jekyll and Mr. Hyde;* photographed by Karl Struss; edited by William Shea; art direction by Hans Drier; costumes by Travis Benton; makeup by Wally Westmore; song, "Champagne Ivy," performed by Miriam Hopkins; copyrighted in late 1931; presented by Adolph Zukor; released by Paramount Pictures; running time, 97 minutes. CAST: Fredric March (Dr. Henry Jekyll/Mr. Hyde), Miriam Hopkins (Ivy Pierson), Rose Hobart (Muriel Carew), Holmes Herbert (Dr. Lanyon), Edgar Norton (Poole), Halliwell Hobbes (Brigadier General Carew), Arnold Lucy (Utterson), Tempe Pigott (Mrs. Hawkins), Colonel McDonnell (Hobson), Eric Wilton (Briggs), Douglas Walton (Student), John Rogers (Waiter), Murdock MacQuarrie (Doctor), Major Sam Harris (Dance Extra).

2. *Unheimliche Geschichten* (1932). CREDITS: Based on the short story trilogy "The Suicide Club"; produced in Germany.

3. *Treasure Island* (August 17, 1934). CREDITS: Directed by Victor Fleming; produced by Hunt Stromberg; screenplay by John Lee Mahin, Leonard Praskins, and John Howard Lawson; based on the novel *Treasure Island;* photographed by Ray June, Harold Rosson, and Clyde DeVinna; edited by Blanche Sewell; musical score by Herbert Stothart; art direction by Cedric Gibbons, Merrill Pye, and Edwin B. Willis; costume designer/technical adviser, Dwight Franklin; released by Metro-Goldwyn-Mayer Pictures; running time, 109 minutes. CAST: Wallace Beery (Long John Silver), Jackie Cooper (Jim Hawkins), Lionel Barrymore (Billy Bones), Otto Kruger (Dr. Livesey), Lewis Stone (Captain Alexander Smollett), Nigel Bruce (Squire Trelawney), Charles "Chic" Sale (Ben Gunn), William V. Mong (Pew), Charles McNaughton (Black Dog), Dorothy Peterson (Mrs. Hawkins), Douglas Dumbrille ("Ugly Israel" Hands), Edmund Breese (Anderson), Olin Howard (Dick), Charles Irwin (Abraham Gray), Edward Pawley (O'Brien), Richard Powell (William Post), James Burke (George Merry), John Anderson (Harry Sykes), Charles Bennett (Dandy Dawson), J. M. Kerrigan

(Tom Morgan), Westcott Clark (Allan), Yorke Sherwood (Mr. Arrow), Harry Cording (Henry), Tom Mahoney (Redruth), Sidney D'Allbrook (Joyce), Frank Dunn (Hunter), Robert Adair (Tom, Seaman), Cora Sue Collins (Child at Inn), Howard Entwistel (Ship's Chandler), Harold Wilson (Oldster), Bernice Beatty (Woman at Inn), Vernon Downing (Boy at Inn), Bobby Bolder (Mild Man at Inn), Edith Kingdon (Wife at Inn), Wilson Benge (Friend at Inn), Shirlee Simpson (Woman Friend at Inn), Matt Gillman, Bob Anderson, A. B. Lane, John Kerr, Tom Wilson, James Mason, Edwin J. Brady, Frank Hagney, Bill Booley, Bob Stevenson, Red Burger, Jack Hill, King Mojave (Pirates), Kay Deslys, Jane Tallent, Ethel Ransome, Jill Bennett (Streetwalkers).

4. *Trouble for Two* (May 29, 1936). CREDITS: British title, *The Suicide Club;* directed by J. Walter Ruben; produced by Louis D. Lighton; screenplay by Manuel Seff and Edward E. Paramore, Jr.; based on the short story trilogy "The Suicide Club" in *New Arabian Nights;* photographed by Charles Clarke; edited by Robert J. Kern; musical score by Franz Waxman; art direction by Cedric Gibbons; released by Metro-Goldwyn-Mayer Pictures; running time, 75 minutes. CAST: Robert Montgomery (Prince Florizel), Rosalind Russell (Miss Vandeleur [Princess Brenda]), Frank Morgan (Colonel Geraldine), Reginald Owen (Dr. Franz Noel, President of the Club), Louis Hayward (Young Man with Cream Tarts), E. E. Clive (The King), Walter Kingsford (Malthus), Ivan Simpson (Collins), Tom Moore (Major O'Rook), Robert Grieg (Fat Man), Guy Bates Post (Ambassador), Pedro de Cordoba (Sergei), Leyland Hodgson (Captain Rich), Pat Flaherty (Ship Captain), Frank Darien (King's Aide), Tom Ricketts (Excited Club Member), Pat O'Malley (Purser), Leonard Carey (Valet), Bill O'Brien (Club Waiter), Paul Porcasi (Cafe Proprietor), Sidney Bracey (Henchman), Frank McGlynn, Jr. (Club Member), Larry Steers (Officer), Olaf Hytten (Butler), Edgar Norton (Herald), Fred Graham (Club Guard), David Holt (Florizel as a Child), Virginia Weidler (Miss Vandeleur as a Child).

5. *Treasure Island* (1937). CREDITS: Directed by Vaynstok; based on the novel *Treasure Island;* produced and released in the USSR. CAST: Osip Abdulov (Long John Silver).

6. *Ebb Tide* (October 1937). CREDITS: Directed by James Hogan; produced by Lucien Hubbard; screenplay by Bertram Millhauser; based on the novel *The Ebb-Tide* by Stevenson and Lloyd Osbourne; photographed in Technicolor by Ray Rennahan and Leo Tover; edited by LeRoy Stone; music score by Ralph Rainger and Leo Robin; costumes designed by Edith Head; special effects by Gordon Jennings; released by Paramount Pictures; running time, 91 minutes. CAST: Oscar Homolka (Captain Thorbecke), Frances Farmer (Faith Wishart), Ray Milland (Robert Herrick), Lloyd Nolan (Attwater), Barry Fitzgerald (Huish), Charles Judels (Port Doctor), David Torrence (Tapena Tom), Lina Basquette (Attwater's Servant), Harry Field (Tahiera), George Piltz (Sally Day), Manuella Kalili (Fiji Islander), Jim Spencer (Cook), Arthur Allen, Joe Molina (Native Sailors), Sonny Chorre (Attwater's Guard), David Hope (Sailor), Leonard Sues (Native Boy), Inez Palange (Native Woman), Gloria Williams, Nancy Chaplin (Women), Jacques Vanaire (Assistant Port Doctor), Antrim Short, Don Wayson, Bob Haines (Men), Bernard Siegal (Waiter), Al Kikume (Native Policeman), Stella Francis (Woman

Tourist), Olaf Hytten (English Tourist), Eugene Beday (Port Officer), Jack George (Band Leader), Jack Clark, Elizabeth Hartman (Tourists).

7. *Kidnapped* (May 1938). CREDITS: Directed by Alfred Werker; produced by Darryl F. Zanuck and Kenneth MacGowan; screenplay by Sonya Levien, Eleanor Harris, Ernest Pascal, and Edwin Blum; based on the novel *Kidnapped;* photographed by Gregg Toland; edited by Allen McNeil; musical score and direction by Arthur Lange; previewed May 17, 1938, at Grauman's Chinese Theatre; released by 20th Century–Fox; running time, 93 minutes. CAST: Warner Baxter (Alan Breck), Freddie Bartholomew (David Balfour), Arleen Whelan (Jean MacDonald), C. Aubrey Smith (Duke of Argyll), Reginald Owen (Captain Hoseason), John Carradine (Gordon), Nigel Bruce (Neil MacDonald), Miles Mander (Ebenezer Balfour), Ralph Forbes (James), H. B. Warner (Rankeiller), Arthur Hohl (Riach), E. E. Clive (Minister MacDougall), Halliwell Hobbes (Dominie Campbell), Montagu Love (English Officer), Donald Haines (Ransome), Moroni Olsen (Douglas), Leonard Mudie (Red Fox), Mary Gordon (Mrs. MacDonald), Forrester Harvey (Innkeeper), Clyde Cook (Cook), Russell Hicks (Bailiff), Billy Watson (Bobby MacDonald), Eily Malyon (Mrs. Campbell), Kenneth Hunter (Captain Fraser), Charles Irwin (Sergeant Ellis), John Burton (Lieutenant Stone), David Clyde (Blacksmith), Holmes Herbert (Judge), Brandon Hurst (Donnelly), Vernon Steele (Captain), C. Montague Shaw (Scotch Salesman), R. T. Noble (Warden).

8. *Dr. Jekyll and Mr. Hyde* (July 1941). CREDITS: Directed and produced by Victor Fleming; screenplay by John Lee Mahin; based on the novella *The Strange Case of Dr. Jekyll and Mr. Hyde;* photographed by Joseph Ruttenberg; edited by Harold F. Kress; musical score by Franz Waxman; art direction by Cedric Gibbons and Daniel B. Cathcart; set decorations by Edwin B. Willis; costumes by Adrian and Gile Steele; makeup by Jack Dawn; special effects by Warren Newcombe and Peter Ballbusch; choreography by Ernst Matray; released by Metro-Goldwyn-Mayer Pictures; running time, 127 minutes. CAST: Spencer Tracy (Dr. Harry Jekyll/Mr. Hyde), Ingrid Bergman (Ivy Peterson), Lana Turner (Beatrix Emery), Donald Crisp (Sir Charles Emery), Ian Hunter (Dr. John Lanyon), Barton MacLane (Sam Higgins), C. Aubrey Smith (The Bishop), Peter Godfrey (Poole), Sara Allgood (Mrs. Higgins), Frederic Worlock (Dr. Heath), William Tannen (Intern Fenwick), Frances Robinson (Marcia), Denis Green (Freddie), Billy Bevan (Dr. Weller), Forrester Harvey (Old Prouty), Lumsden Hare (Colonel Weymouth), Lawrence Grant (Dr. Courtland), John Barclay (Constable), Doris Lloyd (Mrs. Marley), Gwen Gaze (Mrs. French), Hillary Brooke (Mrs. Arnold), Mary Field (Wife), Aubrey Mather (Inspector), Alec Craig.

9. *The Body Snatcher* (March 1945). CREDITS: Directed by Robert Wise; produced by Val Lewton; executive producer, Jack J. Gross; screenplay by Philip MacDonald and Carlos Keith (Val Lewton); based on the short story "The Body-Snatcher"; photographed by Robert De Grasse; edited by J. R. Whittredge; art direction by Albert S. D'Agostino and Walter Keller; set decoration by Darrell Silvera and John Sturtevant; musical score by Roy Webb; musical direction by Constantin Bakaleinikoff; sound direction by Baily Fesler and Terry Kellum; first assistant director, Harry Scott; second assistant

director, Nate Levinson; camera operator, Charles Burke; assistant cameraman, Tex Wheaton; costumes by Rene; men's wardrobe, Hans Bohnstedt; ladies' wardrobe, Mary Tate; makeup by Frank LaRue; hairdresser, Fay Smith; gaffer, Leo Green; best boy, Frank Healy; first grip, Marvin Wilson; second grip, Harry Dagleish; first prop man, Milt James; second prop man, Dean Morgan; boom man, D. Dent; laborers, Joe Farquhar, Fred Kenny; painter, Joe Haecker; dialogue director, Mrs. Charlot; filmed October 25–November 17, 1944; released by RKO-Radio Pictures; running time, 78 minutes. CAST: Boris Karloff (John Gray), Bela Lugosi (Joseph), Henry Daniell (Dr. MacFarlane), Edith Atwater (Meg Camden), Russell Wade (Donald Fettes), Rita Corday (Mrs. Marsh), Sharyn Moffet (Georgina Marsh), Donna Lee (Street Singer), Robert Clarke (Richardson), Carl Kent (Gilchrist), Jack Welch (Boy), Larry Wheat (Salesman), Mary Gordon (Mrs. Mary McBride), Jim Moran (Horse Trader), Ina Constant (Maid), Bill Williams (bit).

10. *Adventure Island* (August 8, 1947). CREDITS: Directed by Peter Stewart; produced by William Pine and William Thomas; screenplay by Maxwell Shane; based on the novel *The Ebb-Tide* by Stevenson and Lloyd Osbourne; photographed in Cinecolor by Jack Greenhaigh; edited by Howard Smith; music score by Darrell Calker; released by Paramount Pictures; running time, 66 minutes. CAST: Rory Calhoun (Mr. Herrick), Rhonda Fleming (Faith Wishart), Paul Kelly (Captain Lochlin), John Abbott (Mr. Huish), Alan Napier (Mr. Attwater).

11. *Adventures in Silverado* (March 25, 1948). CREDITS: Directed by Phil Karlson; produced by Ted Richmond and Robert Cohn; screenplay by Kenneth Gamet, Tom Kilpatrick, and Joe Pagano; suggested by the journalistic book *The Silverado Squatters;* photographed by Henry Freulich; edited by Henry Batista; art direction by Harold MacArthur; set decorations by George Montgomery; musical direction by Mischa Bakaleinikoff; copyrighted March 24, 1948; released by Columbia Pictures; running time, 75 minutes. CAST: William Bishop (Bill Foss), Gloria Henry (Jeanie), Edgar Buchanan (Dr. Henderson/"The Monk"), Forrest Tucker (Zeke), Edgar Barrier (Robert Louis Stevenson), Irving Bacon, Joseph Crehan (Sheriff), Paul E. Burns, Patti Brady (Lucy), Fred Sears, Joe Wong, Charles Kane, Eddy Waller, Netta Parker, Trevor Bardette.

12. *The Black Arrow* (June 1948). CREDITS: Directed by Gordon Douglas; produced by Grant Whytock; screenplay by Richard Schayer, David P. Sheppard, and Thomas Seller; based on the novel *The Black Arrow;* photographed by Charles Lawton, Jr.; edited by Jerome Thoms; art direction by Stephen Gooson and A. Leslie Thomas; set decorations, Wilbur Menefee and James Crowe; assistant director, Carl Hiecke; gowns by Jean Louis; makeup for Louis Hayward by Don Cash; musical score by Paul Sawtell; sound engineer, Lambert Day; fencing master, Fred Cavens; previewed June 28, 1948; an Edward Small Production; released by Columbia Pictures; running time, 76 minutes. CAST: Louis Hayward (Richard Shelton), Janet Blair (Joanna Sedley), George Macready (Sir Daniel Brackley), Edgar Buchanan (Lawless), Rhys Williams (Bennett Hatch), Walter Kingsford (Sir Oliver Oates), Lowell Gilmore (Duke of Gloucester), Halliwell Hobbes (Bishop of Tilsbury), Paul Cavanagh (Sir John

Sedley), Ray Teal (Nick Appleyard), Russell Hicks (Sir Harry Shelton), Leslie Denison (Sir William Catesby), Betty Fairfax (Dame Carter), William "Billy" Bevan (Jailer).

13. *Kidnapped* (September 1948). CREDITS: Directed by William Beaudine; produced by Lindsley Parsons; associate producers, Roddy McDowall and Ace Herman; screenplay by W. Scott Darling; based on the novel *Kidnapped;* photographed by William Sickner; edited by Leonard W. Herman; musical score and direction by Edward J. Kay; art direction by Dave Milton; previewed September 2, 1948; released by Monogram Pictures; running time, 81 minutes. CAST: Roddy McDowall (David Balfour), Sue England (Aileen Fairlie), Dan O'Herlihy (Alan Breck), Roland Winters (Captain Hoseason), Jeff Corey (Shuan), Houseley Stevenson (Ebenezer), Erskine Sanford (Rankeillor), Alex Fraser (Fairlie), Winefried McDowall (Innkeeper's Wife), Bobby Anderson (Ransome), Janet Murdoch (Janet Clouston), Olaf Hytten (The Red Fox), Erville Anderson (Mungo).

14. *The Secret of St. Ives* (May 1949). CREDITS: Directed by Philip Rosen; produced by Rudolph C. Flothow; screenplay by Eric Taylor; based on the novel *St. Ives* by Stevenson and Arthur T. Quiller-Couch; photographed by Henry Freulich; edited by James Sweeney; musical score by Mischa Bakaleinikoff; art direction by Cary Odell; set decoration by Sidney Clifford; makeup by Bob Shiffer; released by Columbia Pictures; running time, 75 minutes. CAST: Richard Ney (Anatole de Keroual), Vanessa Brown (Floria Gilchrist), Henry Daniell (Major Edward Chevenish), Edgar Barrier (Sergeant Carnac), Aubrey Mather (Daniel Romaine), Luis Van Rooten (Clausel), John Dehner (Couguelat), Paul Marion (Amiot), Douglas Walton (Allan St. Ives), Jean Del Val (Count St. Ives), Phyllis Morris (Annie Gilchrist), Maurice Marsac (Portuguese Joe), Harry Cording (Innkeeper), Alex Fraser (Swindow), Tom Stevenson (Flint), Billy Bevan (Douglas), Guy de Vestal (Dubois), Charles Andre (Rene).

15. *Treasure Island* (July 19, 1950). CREDITS: Directed by Byron Haskin; produced by Perce Pearce; screenplay by Lawrence E. Watkin; based on the novel *Treasure Island;* photographed in Technicolor by F. A. Young; edited by Alan L. Jaggs; musical score by Clifton Parker; musical direction by Muir Matheson; music performed by the Royal Philharmonic Orchestra; production executive, Fred Leahy; production manager, Douglas Pierce; production designer, Thomas Morahan; matte artist, Peter Ellenshaw; assistant director, Mark Evans; location directors, Russell Lloyd and Alex Bryce; location cameramen, L. Cave Chinn and Stanley Sayre; camera operator, Skeets Kelly; continuity, Joan Davis; technicolor consultant, Joan Bridge; makeup by Tony Sforzini; hairstyling by Vivienne Walker; sound engineer, Jack Locke; sound editor, Kenneth Healey Ray; a Walt Disney Production; released by RKO-Radio Pictures; running time, 96 minutes. CAST: Bobby Driscoll (Jim Hawkins), Robert Newton (Long John Silver), Basil Sydney (Captain Smollett), Walter Fitzgerald (Squire Trelawney), Denis O'Dea (Dr. Livesey), Ralph Truman (George Merry), Finlay Currie (Captain Bones), John Laurie (Pew), Francis de Wolff (Black Dog), Geoffrey Wilkinson (Ben Gunn), David Davies (Arrow), Andrew Blackett (Gray), Paddy Brannigan (Hunter), Ken Buckle (Joyce), John Gregson (Redruth), Howard Douglas (Williams), Geoffrey Keen (Israel Hands), William Devlin (Tom

Morgan), Diarmuid Kelly (Bolen), Sam Kydd (Cady), Eddie Moran (Jack Bart), Harry Locke (Haggott), Harold Jamieson (Scully), Stephen Jack (Job Anderson), Jack Arrow (Norton), Jim O'Brady (Wolfe), Chris Adcock (Pike), Reginald Drummond (Vane), Gordon Mulholland (Durgin), Patrick Troughton (Roach), Leo Phillips (Spotts), Fred Clark (Bray), Tom Lucas (Upson), Bob Head (Tardy).

16. *The Strange Door* (December 9, 1951). CREDITS: Directed by Joseph Pevney; produced by Ted Richmond; screenplay by Jerry Sackheim; based on the short story "The Sire de Maletroit's Door"; photographed by Irving Glassberg; edited by Edward Curtiss; special effects by David S. Horsley; art direction by Bernard Herzbrun and Eric Orbom; set decoration by Russell A. Gausman and Julia Heron; musical direction by Joseph Gershenson; sound recording by Leslie J. Carey and Glenn E. Anderson; makeup by Bud Westmore; costumes by Rosemary Odell; assistant director, Jesse Hibbs; previewed October 29, 1951; released by Universal-International Pictures; running time, 81 minutes. CAST: Charles Laughton (Sire Alan de Maletroit), Boris Karloff (Voltan), Sally Forrest (Blanche de Maletroit), Richard Stapley (Denis de Beaulieu), Michael Pate (Talon), Paul Cavanagh (Edmond de Maletroit), Alan Napier (Count Grassin), William Cottrell (Corbeau), Morgan Farley (Rinville), Charles Horvath (Turec), Edwin Harker (Moret).

17. *El Extraneo Caso del Hombre y la Bestia* (1951). CREDITS: Italian title, *Il Doctor Jekyll;* U.S. title, *The Doctor Jekyll;* directed by Mario Soffici; based on the novella *The Strange Case of Dr. Jekyll and Mr. Hyde;* produced and released in Argentina. CAST: Mario Soffici (Dr. Jekyll/Mr. Hyde), Anna Maria Campoy, Jose Cibrian.

18. *The Treasure of Lost Canyon* (February 7, 1952). CREDITS: Directed by Ted Tetzlaff; produced by Leonard Goldstein; screenplay by Brainerd Duffield and Emerson Crocker; based on the story "The Treasure of Franchard"; photographed in Technicolor by Russell Metty; edited by Milton Carruth; musical direction by Joseph Gershenson; art direction by Bernard Herzbrun and Alexander Golitzen; released by Universal-International Pictures; running time, 82 minutes. CAST: William Powell (Doc Homer Brown), Julia Adams (Myra Wade), Charles Drake (Jim Anderson), Henry Hull (Lucius Cooke), Rosemary de Camp (Samuella Brown), Tommy Ivo (David), Chubby Johnson (Baltimore Dan), John Doucette (Gyppo), Marvin Press (Paddy), Frank Wilcox (Stranger), Griff Barnett (Judge Wade), Virginia Mullen (Mrs. Crabtree), Paul "Tiny" Newlan (Coach Driver), Jimmy Ogg (Guard), Hugh Prosser (Fire Captain), George Taylor (Clem), Philo McCullough, Ed Hinkle (Miners), Edward Rickard (bit), Jack Perrin (Sheriff).

19. *The Master of Ballantrae* (July 1953). CREDITS: Directed by William Keighley; screenplay by Herb Meadow; additional dialogue by Harold Medford; based on the novel *The Master of Ballantrae;* photographed in Technicolor by Jack Cardiff; edited by Jack Harris; musical score by William Alwyn; musical direction by Muir Mathieson; art direction by Ralph Brinton; costumes designed by Margaret Furse; makeup by George Frost; sound engineer, Harold King; assistant director, Frank Mattison; fencing master, Patrick Crean; technicolor consultant, Joan Bridge; loca-

tion scenes filmed in Scotland, England, and Sicily; previewed July 14, 1953; released by Warner Bros. Pictures; running time, 89 minutes. CAST: Errol Flynn (Jamie Durisdeer), Roger Livesey (Colonel Francis Burke), Anthony Steel (Henry Durisdeer), Beatrice Campbell (Lady Alison), Yvonne Furneaux (Jessie Brown), Felix Aylmer (Lord Durisdeer), Mervyn Johns (MacKellar), Charles Goldner (Mendoza), Ralph Truman (Major Clarendon), Francis de Wolff (Matthew Bull), Jacques Berthier (Arnaud), Moultrie Kelsall (MacCauley), Charles Carson (Colonel Banks), Gillian Lynne (Marianne), Jack Taylor, Stephen Vercoe.

20. *Le Testament du Doctor Cordelier* (September 1959). CREDITS: U.S. title, *The Will of Doctor Cordelier;* directed by Jean Renoir; screenplay by Jean Renoir; an updated adaptation of the novella *The Strange Case of Dr. Jekyll and Mr. Hyde;* photographed by Georges Leclere; edited by Renee Lichtig; a Sofirad production, Paris, France; premiered theatrically at the 1959 Venice Film Festival; released theatrically by Pathe; broadcast premiere, November 16, 1961, on Radio-Television Française, Paris; running time, 90 minutes. CAST: Jean-Louis Barrault (Dr. Cordelier/Mr. Opale), Michel Vitold (Severin), Teddy Bilis (Joly), Jean Topart (Desire), Gaston Modot (Blaise).

21. *Kidnapped* (March 25, 1960). CREDITS: Directed by Robert Stevenson; associate producer, Hugh Attwooll; screenplay by Robert Stevenson; based on the novel *Kidnapped;* photographed in Technicolor by Paul Beeson, B.S.C.; camera operator, Alan Hume; special photographic effects by Peter Ellenshaw; musical score by Cedric Thorpe Davie; music conducted by Muir Matheson; art direction by Carmen Dillon; costumes designed by Margaret Furse; set decorator, Vernon Dixon; story sketches by Don Da Gradi; edited by Gordon Stone; production manager, Frank Ernst; assistant director, Peter Manley; makeup by Stewart Freeborn; hair stylist, Florrie Hyde; continuity by Pamela Carlton; casting by Maude Spector; dialect adviser, John Breslin; sound edited by Lionel Selwyn; sound recorded by Leo Wilkins and Bill Daniels; filmed spring 1959 on location in Scotland at Ardgour, Glen Nevis, Onich Falls, Oban, and Ballachulish; a Walt Disney Production; released by Buena Vista Distribution; previewed February 24, 1960; running time, 97 minutes. CAST: Peter Finch (Alan Breck Stewart), James MacArthur (David Balfour), Bernard Lee (Captain Hoseason), Niall MacGinnis (Shuan), John Laurie (Uncle Ebenezer), Finlay Currie (Cluny MacPherson), Peter O'Toole (Robin Oig MacGregor), Miles Malleson (Mr. Rankeillor), Oliver Johnston (Mr. Campbell), Duncan MacRae (The Highlander), John Pike (Cabin Boy), Andrew Cruikshank (Colin Roy Campbell), Abe Barber (Donald Dhu MacLaren), Eileen Way (Jennet Clouston), Alex MacKenzie (The Ferryman).

22. *The Two Faces of Dr. Jekyll* (October 1960). CREDITS: U.S. title, *House of Fright;* directed by Terence Fisher; produced by Michael Carreras; screenplay by Wolf Mankowitz; based on the novella *The Strange Case of Dr. Jekyll and Mr. Hyde;* production designer, Bernard Robinson; photographed in color by Jack Asher; camera operator, Len Harris; musical director, John Hollingsworth; songs composed by Monty Norman and David Heneker; associate producer, Anthony Nelson-Keys; sound by Jock May; production manager, Clifford Parkes; makeup by Roy Ashton; cos-

tumes by Molly Arbuthnot; assistant director, John Peverall; second assistant director, Hugh Harlow; casting by Dorothy Holloway; hairdresser, Ivy Emmerton; dance director, Julies Mendes; still photographer, Tom Edwards; assistant art director, Don Mingaye; filmed at Bray Studios, England; a Hammer production; released by Columbia Pictures (England) and American International Pictures (United States); running time, 89 minutes. CAST: Paul Massie (Dr. Henry Jekyll/Mr. Edward Hyde), Dawn Addams (Kitty Jekyll), Christopher Lee (Paul Allen), David Kossoff (Ernest Litauer), Francis de Wolff (Inspector), Norma Marla (Maria), Magda Miller, Joy Webster (Sphinx Girls), William Kendall (Clubman), Helen Goss (Nannie), Pauline Shepherd (Girl in Gin Shop), Percy Cartwright (Coroner), Janini Faye (Jane), Joe Robinson (Corinthian), Arthur Lovegrove (Cabby), Oliver Reed (bit).

23. *Treasure Island* (1965). CREDITS: An animated adaptation of the novel *Treasure Island;* released by UPA.

24. *The Wrong Box* (May 1966). CREDITS: Directed and produced by Bryan Forbes; screenplay by Larry Gelbart and Burt Shevelove; suggested by the novel *The Wrong Box* by Stevenson and Lloyd Osbourne; photographed in Eastmancolor by Gerry Turpin; edited by Alan Osbiston; musical score and direction by John Barry; song, "Light of Head," by Clifford Bevan; art direction by Ray Simm; set design by Peter James; costumes designed by Julie Harris; makeup by Paul Rabiger and Basil Newall; a Salamander Film Production; released by BLC (Great Britain) and Columbia Pictures (United States); running time, 107 minutes. CAST: John Mills (Masterman Finsbury), Ralph Richardson (Joseph Finsbury), Michael Caine (Michael Finsbury), Peter Cook (Morris Finsbury), Dudley Moore (John Finsbury), Nanette Newman (Julia Finsbury), Tony Hancock (The Detective), Peter Sellers (Dr. Pratt), Wilfred Lawson (Peacock), Thorley Walters (Lawyer Patience), Cicely Courtneidge (Major Martha), Peter Graves (Military Officer on Train), Irene Handl (Mrs. Hackett), Gerald Sim (First Undertaker), John Le Mesurier (Dr. Slattery), Norman Bird (Clergyman), Hilton Edwards (Lawyer), Norman Rossington (First Rough), Diane Claire (Mercy, Salvation Army Girl), Tutte Lemkow (Bournemouth Strangler), Charles Bird (Bonn's Vanman), Joseph Behrman (Vanman's Mate), Marianne Stone (Spinster on Train), Michael Bird (Countryman), Thomas Gallagher (Second Rough), Timothy Bateson (Clerk), Reg Lye (Third Undertaker), John Junkin (First Engine Driver), Roy Murray (First Stoker), Tony Thawnton (Second Undertaker), George Selway (Railway Vanman), Gwendolyn Watts (Maid), Vanda Godsell (Mrs. Goodge, Bournemouth Landlady), Donald Tandy (Ticket Collector), Lionel Gamlin (Second Engine Driver), Martin Terry (Second Stoker), George Spence (Workman in Road), Jeremy Lloyd (Brian Allen Harvey, Artillery Officer), James Villiers (Sydney Whitcombe Sykes, Falconer), Graham Stark (Ian Scott Fife, Mountaineer), Dick Gregory (Leicester Young Fielding), Nicholas Parsons (Alan Fraser Scrope), Willoughby Goddard (James White Wragg, Mine Owner), Valentine Dyall (Oliver Pike Harmsworth), Leonard Rossiter (Vyuyan Alastair Montague, Duel Umpire), Hamilton Dyce (Derek Lloyd Peter Digby), Donald Oliver (Gunner Sergeant), Totti Truman-Taylor (Lady at Launching), Jeremy Roughton (Bu-

gler), Frank Singuineau (Native Bearer), Michael Lees (Young Digby, Bathchair Pusher), Andre Morell (Club Butler), Avis Bunnage (Queen Victoria), Penny Brahms, Maria Kazan (Twittering Females on Moors), Freddy Clark, George Hillsden (Constables), Alf Mangun, Norman Morris (Gravediggers), Arthur Sandiford, Louise Noland (Mourners), John Tateham (Verger), Sarah Harrison (Governess), Peggy Ray (Child with Governess), John Parker, John Fitch, Norman Hibbert, Jimmy Scott, Alistair Dick (Undertaker's Assistants), Dan Cressey (Judas), Lindsay Hooper (Matthew), Dorothy Ford, Unity Greenwood (Salvation Army Girls), John Morris (Sotheby's Assistant), The Temperance Seven (Themselves), Denis Cowles (Sotheby's Partner), Patsy Snell, Andrea Allen (Girls on Train), Phillip Stewart (Elderly Man on Train), Rita Tobin (Elderly Woman on Train).

25. *Kidnapped* (1968). CREDITS: Directed by Seemann; based on the novel *Kidnapped;* produced and released in East Germany. CAST: Thomas Weisberger (Alan Breck), Werner Kanitz (David Balfour).

26. *Treasure Island* (1970). CREDITS: Directed by Zoran Janzic; an animated adaptation of the novel *Treasure Island;* produced and released in Australia.

27. *Dr. Jekyll and Sister Hyde* (October 1971). CREDITS: Directed by Roy Ward Baker; produced by Albert Fennell and Brian Clemens; screenplay by Brian Clemens; suggested by the novella *The Strange Case of Dr. Jekyll and Mr. Hyde;* photographed in Technicolor by Norman Warwick; edited by James Needs; musical score by David Whitaker; musical direction by Philip Martell; song, "He'll Be There," composed by Brian Clemens; art direction by Robert Jones; sound editor, Charles Crafford; costumes designed by Robert Jones; wardrobe by Rosemary Burrows; wardrobe mistress, Kathleen Moore; makeup by John Wilcox; hairdresser, Bernie Ibbetson; continuity by Sally Ball; casting by Jimmy Liggat; filmed at MGM/EMI Studios, Elstree, England; a Hammer production; released by EMI (Great Britain) and American International Pictures (United States); running time, 97 minutes. CAST: Ralph Bates (Dr. Jekyll), Martine Beswick (Sister Hyde), Gerald Sim (Professor Robertson), Lewis Fiander (Howard), Dorothy Alison (Mrs. Spencer), Neil Wilson (Older Policeman), Ivor Dean (Burke), Paul Whitsun-Jones (Sergeant Danvers), Philip Madoc (Byker), Tony Calvin (Hare), Susan Brodrick (Susan), Dan Meaden (Town Crier), Virginia Weatherell (Betsy), Geoffrey Kenion (First Policeman), Irene Bradshaw (Yvonne), Anna Brett (Julie), Jackie Poole (Margie), Rosemary Lord (Marie), Petula Portell (Petra), Pat Brackenbury (Helen), Liz Romanoff (Emma), Will Stampe (Mine Host), Roy Evans (Knife Grinder), Derek Steen (First Sailor), John Lyons (Second Sailor), Jeanette Wild (Jill), Bobby Parr (Young Apprentice), Julia Wright (Street Singer).

28. *Kidnapped* (December 1971). CREDITS: Directed by Delbert Mann; produced by Frederick H. Brogger; associate producer, Hugh Attwooll; screenplay by Jack Pulman; based on the novels *Kidnapped* and *Catriona;* photographed in Panavision by Paul Beeson, B.S.C.; color by Movielab; music composed and conducted by Roy Budd; song, "For All My Days," lyrics by Jack Fishman, performed by Mary Hopkin; production manager, Robin Douet; art direction by Vetchinsky; edited by Peter Boita; costumes designed by Olga Lehmann; assistant to the producer, Stuart

Elliott; sound mixed by Danny Daniel and Ken Barker; set dresser, Arthur Taksen; special effects by Cliff Cully; makeup by Billy Partleton and Roy Ashton; hairdressers, A. G. Scott and Stella Rivers; filmed on location in Oban, Scotland; an Omnibus Production; released by American International Pictures; running time, 100 minutes. CAST: Michael Caine (Alan Breck), Trevor Howard (Lord Advocate), Jack Hawkins (Captain Hoseason), Donald Pleasence (Ebenezer Balfour), Gordon Jackson (Charles Stewart), Vivien Heilbron (Catriona), Lawrence Douglas (David Balfour), Freddie Jones (Cluny), Jack Watson (James Stewart), Andrew McCulloch (Andrew), Eric Woodburn (Doctor), Roger Booth (Duke of Cumberland), Russell Waters (Lord Advocate's Secretary), John Hughes (Simon Campbell), Claire Nielsen (Barbara Grant), Geoffrey Whitehead (Lieutenant Duncansby), Peter Jeffrey (Riach), Terry Richards (Mungo Campbell).

29. *I, Monster* (1971). CREDITS: Directed by Stephen Weeks; produced by Max J. Rosenberg and Milton Subotsky; screenplay by Milton Subotsky; based on the novella *The Strange Case of Dr. Jekyll and Mr. Hyde;* photographed in Eastmancolor by Moray Grant; camera operator, Robert Kindred; edited by Peter Tanner; musical direction by Carl Davis; art direction by Tony Curtis; makeup by Harry Frampton and Peter Frampton; sound editor, Michael Redbourne; sound mixer, Buster Ambler; production manager, Theresa Bolland; assistant director, Al Burgess; filmed in 1970 at Shepperton Studios, England; released in 1971 (Great Britain) and 1973 (United States); an Amicus production, in association with British Lion Films; released by Cannon Films (United States); running time, 75 minutes. CAST: Christopher Lee (Dr. Charles Marlowe/Mr. Edward Blake), Peter Cushing (Utterson), Mike Raven (Dr. Enfield), Richard Hearndell (Lanyon), George Merritt (Poole), Kenneth J. Warren (Dean), Susan Jameson (Diane), Margie Lawrence (Annie), Aimee de la Main (Landlady), Michael Des Barres (Boy in Alley).

30. *Treasure Island* (1971). CREDITS: Directed by Basylev; based on the novel *Treasure Island;* produced and released in the USSR. CAST: Boris Andreyev (Long John Silver), Aare Laanemets (Jim Hawkins), L. Norika (Dr. Livesey), A. Massulis (Squire Trelawney), A. Pikialis (Israel Hands).

31. *Treasure Island* (October 1972). CREDITS: Directed by John Hough; produced by Harry Alan Towers; screenplay by Wolf Mankowitz and O. W. Jeeves (Orson Welles); based on the novel *Treasure Island;* photographed in Eastmancolor by Cecilio Paniagua and Ginger Gemell; edited by Nicholas Wentworth; musical score by Natal Massara; art direction by Frank White; set decoration by Jose Maria Alarcon; sound engineer, Gerry Humphreys; assistant director, Julio Sempere; a Massfilms-Eguiluz-FDL-CCC production (Great Britain/Spain/France/Germany); released by National General Pictures (United States); running time, 94 minutes. CAST: Orson Welles (Long John Silver), Kim Burfield (Jim Hawkins), Walter Slezak (Squire Trelawney), Lionel Stander (Billy Bones), Paul Muller (Blind Pew), Maria Rohm (Mrs. Hawkins), Angel Del Pozo (Doctor Livesey), Michel Garland (George Merry), Rik Battaglia (Captain Smollett), Jean Lefebvre (Ben Gunn), Aldo Sambrell (Israel Hands), Alibe (Mrs. Silver), Chinchilla (Anderson).

32. *The Black Arrow* (1972). CREDITS: Directed by Leif Gram; an animated adaptation of the novel *The Black Arrow;* produced and released in Australia.

33. *Kidnapped* (1972). CREDITS: Directed by Leif Gram; an animated adaptation of the novel *Kidnapped;* produced and released in Australia.

34. *The Strange Case of Dr. Jekyll and Mr. Hyde* (1987). CREDITS: Directed by Orlov; based on the novella *The Strange Case of Dr. Jekyll and Mr. Hyde;* produced and released in the USSR. CAST: Innokenti Smoktunovsky (Dr. Jekyll), Alexander Feklistovh (Mr. Hyde).

35. *Treasure Island* (January 22, 1990). CREDITS: Directed, produced, and screenplay by Fraser C. Heston; executive producer, Peter Snell; associate producer, Ted Lloyd; production managers, Gladys Pearce and Linda McGowan; production manager (Jamaica), Natalie Thompson; production coordinator, Sally Hayman; photographed by Robert Steadman; camera operator, Jimmy Turrell; edited by Eric-Boyd Perkins, A.C.E.; additional editing by Bill Parnell and Gregory Gontz; musical score composed by Paddy Moloney; musical score performed by The Chieftains; music supervisor, John Stronach; production designer, Tony Woollard; art direction by Ricky Eyres; assistant art director (Jamaica), Sue Henzell; set decoration by Joanne Woollard; special effects supervisor, John Richardson; senior special effects technicians, Chris Corbould and Ken Morris; special effects technicians, Daniel Dark and Andrew Williams; supervising sound editors, Samuel R. Crutcher, M.P.S.E., and Norval D. Crutcher, M.P.S.E.; sound mixers, Wayne Artman, Tom Beckert, and Tom Dahl; wardrobe supervisor, Tiny Nicholls; wardrobe master, Brian Cox; chief makeup, Daniel Parker; chief hairdresser, Jan Dorman; location manager (U.K.), John Southwood; location manager (Jamaica), Jeremy Francis; first assistant director, Terry Needham; second assistant director, Michael Stevenson; assistant to director, Beverly Winston; assistant to Charlton Heston, Carol Lanning; script supervisor, Sally Jones; focus, Stephen Murray and David Watkins; clapper/loaders, Robert Stilwell and Robert Wright; chief electrician, Frank Heeney; best boy, George Vince; grip, Ray Hall; production mixer, Roy Charman; boom operator, David Pearson; sound maintenance, John Pitt; transport manager, Poy Farr; property master, Barry Wilkinson; supervising property, Joseph Dipple; c/h dressing property, Reg Wheeler; dressing property, Kevin Wheeler; construction manager (U.K.), Vic Simpson; construction manager, Leroy Grant; supervising carpenter, J. V. Hammerton; stunt arranger, Peter Diamond; casting director, Rebecca Howard; production accountant, John Wall; *Bounty* coordinators, Captain John Rumsey and Laura Stoye; *second unit (Jamaica)*, director, Joe Canutt; director of photography, Tony Westman; first assistant director, Kevin de la Noy; second assistant directors, Adam Somner, Joel Wein, and Gina Tamburine; unit manager, Michael London; marine manager, Greg Newman; continuity, Ilene Pickus; focus, Robert Peterson; clapper/loader, Emil Leto; grip, Perry Jones; best boy, Rick LaCoste; filmed at Pinewood Studios, England, and on location in Baysingstoke and Devon, England, Florida, and Jamaica; an Agamemnon Films Production, in association with British Lion; premiered January 22, 1990, on Turner Network Television; released theatrically by Turner Pictures (outside

the United States); running time, 130 minutes. CAST: Charlton Heston (Long John Silver), Christian Bale (Jim Hawkins), Julian Glover (Dr. Livesey), Richard Johnson (Squire Trelawney), Oliver Reed (Captain Billy Bones), Christopher Lee (Blind Pew), Clive Wood (Captain Smollett), John Benfield (Black Dog), Isla Blair (Mrs. Hawkins), Robert Putt (Job Anderson), Michael Thomas (Hunter), James Coyle (Tom Morgan), Nicholas Amer (Ben Gunn), John Abbott (Joyce), Brett Fancy (Young Tom), Steven MacKintosh (Dick), Richard Beale (Mr. Arrow), Michael Halsey (Israel Hands), Peter Postlethwaite (George Merry), William Sloan (Scarface).

# • APPENDIX F •
# Film "Continuations"

Following is a listing of films that are "continuations" of events in *Treasure Island* and *The Strange Case of Dr. Jekyll and Mr. Hyde*.

## *Treasure Island*

1. *Return to Treasure Island* (late June 1954). CREDITS: Directed by E. A. Dupont; produced by Aubrey Wisberg and Jack Pollexfen; screenplay and story by Aubrey Wisberg and Jack Pollexfen; photographed in Pathecolor by William Bradford; edited by Fred Feitshans, Jr.; musical score by Paul Sawtell; previewed June 18, 1954; released by United Artists Pictures; running time, 75 minutes. CAST: Tab Hunter (Clive Stone), Dawn Addams (Jamesina Hawkins), Porter Hall (Maximilian Harris), James Seay (Felix Newman), Harry Lauter (Parker), William Cottrell (Cookie), Henry Rowland (Williams), Lane Chandler (Cardigan), Dayton Lummis (Captain Flint), Robert Long (Long John Silver), Ken Terrell (Thompson).

2. *Long John Silver's Return to Treasure Island* (December 1954). CREDITS: Alternate title: *Long John Silver;* directed by Byron Haskin; produced by Joseph Kaufman; screenplay by Martin Rackin; photographed in Cinemascope and Eastmancolor by Carl Guthrie; camera operators, Ross Wood and Karl Kayser; edited by Manuel Del Campo; production designer, William Constable; musical score by David Buttolph; music performed by the Sydney Symphony Orchestra; production executive, Mark Evans; assistant directors, Maurie Power and Hans Von Alderstein; sound engineers, Hans Wetzel and Alan Allen; chief electrician, Warren Mearns; set construction, Charles Woolveridge; assistant designer, Desmonde Downing; continuity, Valerie Frost; makeup by Dimitry Ustrizoff and Nesta Tait; costumes by John Wayne; wigs by Edward Bower; hairdresser, Elsie Dayne; premiered December 15, 1954, Rialto Theatre, London, England; presented by Treasure Island Pictures, Australia; released by Distributors Corporation of America (DCA); running time, 108 minutes. CAST: Robert Newton (Long John Silver), Kit Taylor (Jim Hawkins), Connie Gilchrist (Purity Pinker), Eric Reiman (Trip Fenner), Syd Chambers (Ned Shill), Grant Taylor (Patch), John Brunskill (Old Stingley), Harry Hambleton (Big Eric), Henry Gilbert (Billie Bowlegs), Elwyn Daniel (Dodd Perch), Al Thomas (Harry Grip), Harvey Adams (Governor Strong), Muriel Steinbeck (Lady Strong), Lloyd Berrell (Mendoza), Tony Arpino

(Kling), Billy Kay (Ironhand), Frank Ransom (Sentry), Don McNiven (Sergeant Cover), Charles McCallum (Elderly Naval Officer), Rodney Taylor (Israel Hands), Hans Stern (Father Monaster), Thora Smith (Elizabeth Strong), George Simpson Little (Captain McDougal), John Pooley (Young Naval Officer).

## The Strange Case of Dr. Jekyll and Mr. Hyde

1. *The Son of Dr. Jekyll* (October 1951). CREDITS: Directed by Seymour Friedman; screenplay by Mortimer Braus and Jack Pollexfen; photographed by Henry Freulich; edited by Gene Havlik; musical score by Paul Sawtell; musical direction by Morris Stoloff; art direction by Walter Holscher; previewed September 28, 1951; released by Columbia Pictures; running time, 77 minutes. CAST: Louis Hayward (Edward Jekyll), Jody Lawrence (Lynn), Alexander Knox (Dr. Curtis Lanyon), Lester Matthews (John Utterson), Gavin Muir (Richard Daniels), Paul Cavanagh (Inspector Stoddard), Rhys Williams (Michaels), Doris Lloyd (Lottie Sarelle), Claire Carleton (Hazel Sarelle), Patrick O'Moore (Joe Sarelle), James Logan, Leslie Denison (Constables), Robin Camp (Willie Bennett), Bruce Lester (Reporter), Holmes Herbert (Local Constable), Matthew Boulton (Inspector Grey), Pat Aherne (Landlord), Wheaton Chambers (Magistrate), Vesey O'Davoren (Butler), Harry Martin (Plainclothesman), Olaf Hytten (Prosecutor), Stapleton Kent.

2. *Daughter of Dr. Jekyll* (August 1957). CREDITS: Directed by Edgar G. Ulmer; produced by Jack Pollexfen; screenplay by Jack Pollexfen; photographed by John F. Warren; edited by Holbrook N. Todd; musical supervision by Melvyn Lenard; art direction by Theobold Holsopple; previewed August 12, 1957; released by Allied Artists Pictures; running time, 67 minutes. CAST: John Agar (George Hastings), Gloria Talbot (Janet Smith), Arthur Shields (Dr. Lomas), John Dierkes (Jacob), Martha Wentworth (Mrs. Merchant), Mollie McCart (Maggie).

# • APPENDIX G •
# Jekyll-and-Hyde Parodies

Following is a listing of comedy films that are direct parodies of *The Strange Case of Dr. Jekyll and Mr. Hyde.*

## Silent Shorts

1. *Dr. Jekyll and Mr. Hyde* (1914). CREDITS: Released by Starlight.

2. *Dr. Jekyll and Mr. Hyde Done to a Frazzle* (1914). CREDITS: Released by Warner Bros.; running length, 1 reel.

3. *Dr. Jekyll and Mr. Hyde* (1920). CREDITS: Released by Arrow Film Corporation. CAST: Hank Mann (Dr. Jekyll/Mr. Hyde).

4. *When Quackel Did Hyde* (1920). CREDITS: Released by Aywon.

5. *Dr. Jekyll and Mr. Hyde* (1925). CREDITS: Released by Standard.

6. *Dr. Pyckle and Mr. Pryde* (1925). CREDITS: Directed by Percy Pembroke; produced by Joe Rock; running length, 2 reels. CAST: Stan Laurel (Dr. Pyckle/Mr. Pryde).

## Sound Shorts

1. *Doctor Jekyll's Hide* (1932). CREDITS: Directed and produced by Albert De Mond; screenplay by Albert De Mond; incorporating footage from Imp's *Dr. Jekyll and Mr. Hyde* (1913); released by Snappy (Universal) Pictures; running time, 20 minutes.

## Sound Features

1. *Abbott and Costello Meet Dr. Jekyll and Mr. Hyde* (August 1953). CREDITS: Directed by Charles Lamont; produced by Howard Christie; screenplay by Lee Loeb and John Grant; based on the screen story by Sidney Fields and Grant Garrett, and the novella *The Strange Case of Dr. Jekyll and Mr. Hyde;* photographed by George Robinson; edited by Russell Schoengarth; special effects by David S. Horsley; art direction by Bernard Herzbrun and Eric Orbom; set decoration by Russell A. Gausman; musical direction by Joseph Gershenson; dance direction by Kenny Williams; dialogue direction by Milt Bronson; sound recording by Leslie I. Carey; makeup by Bud Westmore; costumes by Rosemary Odell; previewed July 21, 1953; released by Universal-International Pictures; running time, 77 minutes. CAST: Bud Abbott (Slim), Lou Costello (Tubby), Boris Karloff (Dr. Henry Jekyll), Craig Stevens (Bruce Adams), Helen Westcott (Vicky Edwards), Reginald Denny (Inspector), John Dierkes (Batley), Patti McKaye, Lucille Lamarr (Cancan Dancers),

Harry Corden (Javanese Actor), Camden de Lavallade (Javanese), Marjorie Bennett (Militant Woman), Harry Cording (Rough Character), Arthur Gould-Porter (Bartender), Clyde Cook, John Rogers (Drunks in Pub), Herbert Deans (Victim), Judith Brian (Woman on Bike), Gil Perkins (Man on Bike), Hilda Plowright (Nursemaid), Keith Hitchcock (Jailer), Donald Kerr (Chimney Sweep), Clive Morgan, Tony Marshe, Michael Hadlow (Bobbies).

2. *The Ugly Duckling* (1959). CREDITS: Directed by Lance Comfort; produced by Tommy Lyndon-Hayes; executive producer, Michael Carreras; screenplay by Sid Colin and Jack Davies; photographed by Michael Reed; edited by James Needs and John Dunsford; musical score by Douglas Gamley; art direction by Bernard Robinson; a Hammer Film production, Great Britain; released by Columbia Pictures (United States); running time, 84 minutes. CAST: Bernard Bresslaw (Henry Jekyll/Teddy Hyde), Reginald Beckwith (Reginald), Jon Pertwee (Victor Jekyll), Maudie Edwards (Henrietta Jekyll), Jean Muir (Snout), Richard Watts (Barclay), Elwyn Brook-Jones (Dandy), Michael Ripper (Benny), David Lodge (Peewee), Harold Goodwin, Norma Marla, Keith Smith, Michael Ward, John Harvey, Jess Conrad, Mary Wilson, Geremy Phillips, Vicky Marshall, Jill Carson, Cyril Chamberlain, Alan Coleshill, Jean Driant, Nicholas Tanner, Shelagh Dey, Ian Wilson, Verne Morgan, Sheila Hammond, Ian Ainsley, Reginald Marsh, Roger Avon, Richard Statman, Robert Desmond, Alexander Dore.

3. *Dr. Black and Mr. Hyde* (1976). CREDITS: Alternate title, *The Watts Monster;* original title, *Dr. Black and Mr. White;* directed by William Crain; produced by Charles Walker; screenplay by Larry LeBron; photographed in Metrocolor by Tak Fujimoto; edited by Jack Horger; musical score by Johnny Pate; released by Dimension Pictures; running time, 87 minutes. CAST: Bernie Casey (Dr. Pride/Mr. Hyde), Rosalind Cash (Dr. Billie Worth), Marie O'Henry (Linda), Ji-Tu Cumbuka (Lieutenant Jackson), Milt Kogan (Lieutenant O'Connor), Stu Gilliam (Silky).

4. *Dr. Heckyl and Mr. Hype* (1980). CREDITS: Directed by Charles B. Griffith; produced by Menaham Golan and Yoram Globus; screenplay ("with apologies to Robert Louis Stevenson") by Charles B. Griffith; photographed in Metrocolor by Robert Carras; edited by Skip Schoolnik; musical score by Richard Band; production designer, Maxwell Mendes; art direction by Bob Ziembiki; set decoration by Maria Delia Javier; filmed in England; released by Cannon; running time, 99 minutes. CAST: Oliver Reed (Dr. Heckyl/Mr. Hype), Mel Welles (Dr. Hinkle), Jackie Coogan (Sergeant Fleacollar), Corinne Calvet (Pizelle Puree), Sunny Johnson (Coral Careen), Virgil Frye (Lieutenant Mac Druck "Il Topo"), Maia Danziger (Miss Finebaum), Kedrick Wolfe (Dr. Lew Hoo), Dick Miller (Irsil/Orson), Sharon Compton (Mrs. Quivel), Charles Howerton (Clutch Cooger), Lucretia Love (Debra Kate), Jack Warford (Herringbone Flynn), Denise Hayes (Liza Rowne), Ben Frommer (Sergeant Gurnisht Hilfn), Jacque Lynn Colton (Mrs. Fran van Crisco), Lisa Zebro (Mrs. van Crisco), Stan Ross (Flash Flud), Michael Fox (Mrs. Fritz L. Pitzle), Steve Ciccone (Dum-Dum), Duane Thomas (Bad William's Ideal), Joe Anthony Cox (Bad Williams), Michael Ciccone (Hollowpoint), Candi Brough (Teri Tailspin), Randi Brough (Toni Tailspin), Yehuda

Efroni (Bull Quivel), Dan Sturkie (Naso Rubico, the Wino), Herta Ware (Old Lady on Bus), Dana Feller (Nurse Pertbottom), Carin Berger (Nurse Lushtush), Cindy Riegel (Nurse Rosenrump), Katherine Kirkpatrick (Nurse Nietkiester), Merle Ann Taylor (Nurse Talltale), Samuel Livner (Acutucklic Patient), Christina Ann Saul (Blinkin'), Ed Randolph (Midnight Eaglehead), Jessica Griffith (Policeman's Daughter).

5. *Jekyll and Hyde . . . Together Again* (1982). CREDITS: Directed by Jerry Belson; produced by Lawrence Gordon; screenplay by Monica Johnson, Harvey Miller, Jerry Belson, and Michael Lesson; photographed in Metrocolor by Philip Lathrop; edited by Billy Weber; music score by Barry DeVorzon; production designer, Peter Wooley; costumes designed by Marilyn Kay Vance; special effects by Michael Boddiker and D. G. Grigg; makeup by John M. Elliot, Jr., and Mark Bussan; released by Paramount Pictures; running time, 87 minutes. CAST: Mark Blankfield (Jekyll/Hyde), Bess Armstrong (Mary), Krista Errickson (Ivy), Tim Thomerson (Dr. Lanyon), Michael McGuire (Dr. Carew), Neil Hunt (Queen), Cassandra Peterson (Busty Nurse), Jessica Nelson (Barbara), Peter Brocco (Hubert), Michael Klingher, Noelle North, David Murphy (Students), Mary McCusker (Patient), Liz Sheridan (Mrs. Larson), Alison Hong (Asian Girl), Walter Janowitz (Elderly Man), Belita Moreno (Nurse Gonzales), Leland Sun (Wong), George Wendy (Injured Man), Glen Chin (Sushi Chef), Dan Barrows (Customer), Virginia Wing (Madame WooWoo), Jesse Goins (Dutch), Jack Collins (Baron), Michael Ensign (Announcer), John Dennie Johnston (Macho Kid), David Ruprecht (Brigham), Clarke Coleman (Box Boy), Sam Whipple (Produce Man), Nancy Lenehan (Mother), Barret Oliver (Child), Tony Cox, Selwyn Emerson Miller (Lawn Jockeys), Art LaFleur (Clockman), Bernadette Birkett (Mrs. Simpson), Lin Shaye (Nurse), Madelyn Cates (Helen), George Chakiris (Himself), Sheila Rogers, Gerald Saunderson Peters, Bud Davis, Jose Borcia, Maher Bouros, Kate Fitzmaurice, Howard George.

## Cartoons

1. *Mighty Mouse Meets Jekyll and Hyde Cat* (1944). CREDITS: Directed by Mannie Davis; produced by Paul Terry; a Terrytoon Technicolor cartoon.

2. *Dr. Jekyll and Mr. Mouse* (1947). CREDITS: Directed by William Hanna and Joseph Barbera; produced by Fred Quimby; musical score by Scott Bradley; a Metro-Goldwyn-Mayer Technicolor cartoon; running time, 8 minutes.

3. *Doctor Jerkyll's Hide* (1955). CREDITS: Story by Warren Foster; a Warner Bros. "Looney Tunes" Technicolor cartoon; running time, 7 minutes.

## • APPENDIX H •
# Films Inspired by *Treasure Island* and *The Strange Case of Dr. Jekyll and Mr. Hyde*

Following is a listing of films that incorporate elements from *Treasure Island* and *The Strange Case of Dr. Jekyll and Mr. Hyde*.

### Treasure Island

1. *Scalawag* (mid–October 1973). CREDITS: Directed by Kirk Douglas; produced by Anne Douglas; screenplay by Albert Maltz and Sid Fleischman; photographed in Technicolor by Jack Cardiff; edited by John Howard; art direction by Sjelco Senecic; musical score by John Cameron; assistant director, Bata Maricic; filmed in Yugoslavia; an Inex-Oceania/Bryna production; released by Paramount Pictures; running time, 93 minutes. CAST: Kirk Douglas (Peg), Mark Lester (Jamie), Neville Brand (Brimstone/Mudhook), George Eastman (Don Aragon), Don Stroud (Velvet), Lesley-Anne Down (Lucy-Ann), Danny De Vito (Fly Speck), Mel Blanc (Barfly the Parrot), Phil Brown (Sandy), Davor Antolic (Rooster), Stole Arandjelovic (Beanbelly), Fabijan Sovagovic (Blackfoot), Shaft Douglas (Beau the Dog).

### The Strange Case of Dr. Jekyll and Mr. Hyde

#### SILENT FILMS

1. *Der Andere [The Other]* (1913). CREDITS: Directed by Max Mack; based on a play by Paul Lindau; a Vitaskop production, Germany. CAST: Albert Basserman, Emmerich Hanus, Relly Ridon, Hanni Weise, Leon Rosemann, Otto Collot, C. Lengling, Paul Passarge.

2. *Luke's Double* (1916). CREDITS: Released by Pathe Phunfilm.

#### SOUND FILMS

1. *Der Andere [The Other]* (1930). CREDITS: Directed by Robert Wiene; based on a play by Paul Lindau; filmed in Germany.

2. *Sing, Baby, Sing* (1936). CREDITS: Directed by Sidney Lanfield; produced by Darryl F. Zanuck; screenplay by Milton Sperling, Jack Yellen, and Harry Tugend; based on

a story by Milton Sperling and Jack Yellen; photographed by Peverell Marley; edited by Barbara McLean; musical direction by Louis Silvers; art direction by Mark-Lee Kirk; set decoration by Thomas Little; costumes designed by Royer; released by 20th Century–Fox; running time, 90 minutes. CAST: Alice Faye (Joan Warren), Adolphe Menjou (Bruce Farraday), Gregory Ratoff (Nicky), Ted Healey (Al Craven), Patsy Kelly (Fitz), Michael Whalen (Ted Blake), The Ritz Brothers (Themselves), Montagu Love (Robert Wilson), Dixie Dunbar (Telephone Operator), Douglas Fowley (Mac), Paul Stanton (Brewster), Tony Martin (Tony Renaldo), Virginia Field (Farraday's Nurse), Paul McVey (Doctor), Carol Tevis (Tessie), Cully Richards (Joe), Lynn Bari.

3. *Shado Kalo* (1953). CREDITS: Directed by Amal Bose; produced by Basu Mitra; photographed by Dibyenda Ghose; filmed in India. CAST: Sipra, Sisir, Gurudas, Pahari Sanyal, Biren Chatterjee.

4. *The Haunted Strangler* (June 1958). CREDITS: British title, *Grip of the Strangler;* directed by Robert Day; produced by John Croydon; executive producer, Richard Gordon; screenplay by Jan Read and John C. Cooper; based on a story by Jan Read; photographed by Lionel Banes; edited by Peter Mayhew; musical score by Buxton Orr; musical direction by Frederick Lewis; special effects by Les Bowie; art direction by John Elphick; sound recording by Peter Davies; previewed May 23, 1958; released by Metro-Goldwyn-Mayer Pictures; running time, 78 minutes. CAST: Boris Karloff (James Rankin), Jean Kent (Cora Seth), Elizabeth Allan (Barbara Rankin), Anthony Dawson (Superintendent Burk), Vera Day (Pearl), Tim Turner (Kenneth McColl), Diane Aubrey (Lily), Dorothy Gordon (Hannah), Peggy Ann Clifford (Kate), Leslie Perrins (Prison Governor), Michael Atkinson (Styles), Desmond Roberts (Dr. Johnson), Jessie Cairns (Maid), Roy Russell (Medical Superintendent), Derek Birch (Superintendent), George Hirste (Lost Property Man), John G. Heller (Male Nurse), George Spence (Hangman), Joan Elvin (Can-Can Girl).

5. *Il Mio Amico Jeckyll* (1960). CREDITS: U.S. titles, *My Friend, Dr. Jekyll, Casanova Jekyll, My Friend Jeckyll, My Pal, Dr. Jekyll;* directed by Marino Girolami; a Union/MG-Cei production, Italy. CAST: Ugo Tognazzi, Abbe Lane, Raimondo Vianello, Carlo Croccolo.

6. *Corridors of Blood* (April 1963). CREDITS: Directed by Robert Day; produced by John Croydon and Charles Vetter; executive producer, Richard Gordon; associate producer, Peter Mayhew; screenplay and story by Jean Scott Rogers; photographed by Geoffrey Faithfull; camera operator, Frank Drake; edited by Peter Mayhew; art direction by Anthony Masters; production manager, George Mills; musical score by Buxton Orr; musical direction by Frederick Lewis; sound recording by Cyril Swern and Maurice Askew; dubbing editor, Peter Musgrave; continuity, Susan Dyson; makeup by Walter Schneiderman; hairdresser, Eileen Warwick; dress designer, Emma Selby-Walker; wardrobe mistress, Doris Turner; filmed in Great Britain at MGM, Boreham Wood, in 1958; released by Metro-Goldwyn-Mayer Pictures; running time, 85 minutes. CAST: Boris Karloff (Dr. Thomas Bolton), Betta St. John (Susan), Finlay Currie (Dr. Matheson), Christopher Lee (Resurrection Joe), Francis Matthews (Dr. Jonathan Bolton), Adrienne Corri (Rachel), Francis de Wolff (Black Ben), Basil Dignam

(Chairman), Frank Pettingell (Dr. Blount), Marian Spencer (Mrs. Matheson), Carl Bernard (Ned the Crow), Yvonne Warren (Rosa), Charles Lloyd Pack (Hardcastle), Robert Raglan (Wilkes), John Gabriel (Dispenser), Nigel Green (Inspector Donovan), Howard Lang (Chief Inspector), Julian D'Albie (Bald Man), Roddy Hughes (Man with Watch), Bernard Archard, Charmion Eyre, Anthea Holloway, Frank Sieman.

7. *The Nutty Professor* (May 1963). CREDITS: Directed by Jerry Lewis; produced by Jerry Lewis and Ernest D. Glucksman; screenplay by Jerry Lewis and Bill Richmond; based on a story by Jerry Lewis; photographed in Technicolor by W. Wallace Kelley; edited by John Woodcock; musical score by Walter Scharf; song, "We've Got a World That Swings," by Louis Y. Brown and Lil Mattis; art direction by Hal Pereira and Walter Tyler; set decoration by Sam Comer and Robert R. Benton; costumes designed by Edith Head; special effects by Paul K. Lerpal; makeup by Wally Westmore; assistant director, Ralph Axness; released by Paramount Pictures; running time, 107 minutes. CAST: Jerry Lewis (Professor Julius Ferris Kelp/Buddy Love), Stella Stevens (Stella Purdy), Del Moore (Dr. Hamius R. Warfield), Kathleen Freeman (Millie Lemmon), Ned Flory, Skip Ward, Norman Alden (Football Players), Howard Morris (Father Kelp), Elvia Allman (Mother Kelp), Milton Frome (Dr. Leevee), Buddy Lester (Bartender), Marvin Kaplan (English Boy), David Landfield, Celeste Yarnall, Francine York, Julie Parrish, Henry Gibson (College Students), Dave Willock (Bartender), Doodles Weaver (Rube), Mushy Callahan (Cab Driver), Gavin Gordon (Salesman Clothier), Joe Forte (Faculty Member), Terry Higgins (Cigarette Girl), Murray Alper (Judo Instructor), Gary Lewis (Boy), Les Brown and His Band of Renown (Themselves).

8. *El Secreto del Dr. Orloff* (1964). CREDITS: U.S. titles, *Mistresses of Dr. Jekyll*, *Brides of Dr. Jekyll*, *Dr. Orloff's Monster*; directed by Jesus Franco; a Leo production, Spain/Austria; released by American International Pictures. CAST: Jose Rubio, Agnes Spaak, Hugo Glanco, Perla Cristal.

9. *Dr. Sexual and Mr. Hyde* (1971).

10. *Dr. Jekyll y el Hombre Lobo* (1971). CREDITS: U.S. title, *Dr. Jekyll and the Wolfman*; directed by Leon Klimovsky; produced by Jose Frade; screenplay by Jacinto Molina (Paul Naschy); an Arturo Gonzalez production, Spain; released by International Cinema Films (United States). CAST: Paul Naschy (Waldemar Daninsky), Shirley Corrigan, Jack Taylor.

11. *The Man with Two Heads* (1972). CREDITS: Directed, written, and photographed by Andy Milligan; produced by William Mishkin; music and lyrics by David Tike; art direction by Elaine; costumes designed by Rafine; makeup by Lois Marsh; released by Mishkin Pictures; running time, 80 minutes. CAST: Denis De Marne (Dr. William Jekyll/Mr. Blood), Julia Stratton (April Conners), Gay Feld (Mary Ann Marsden), Jacqueline Lawrence (Carla), Berwick Kaler (Smithers), Bryan Southcombe (Oliver Marsden), Jennifer Summerfield (Vicky).

12. *The Adult Version of Dr. Jekyll and Mr. Hyde* (1972). CREDITS: Directed by B. Ron Eliot; an Entertainment Ventures production. CAST: Jack Buddliner, Jane Tsentas.

13. *The Jekyll and Hyde Portfolio* (1972). CREDITS: Directed by Eric Jeffrey; a Xerxes production. CAST:

Sebastian Brook, Mady McGuire, Don Greer.

14. *The Switch* (1974). CREDITS: A Magenta Films production; released by Scotia International. CAST: Veronica Parrish.

15. *Dr. Jekyll and Miss Osbourne* (1981). CREDITS: Directed by Wladimir Borowczyk; filmed in France. CAST: Udo Kier (Dr. Jekyll), Marino Pierro (Miss Osbourne), Patrick Magee, Howard Vernon, Clement Haragi.

16. *Dr. Jekyll's Dungeon of Death* (1982). CREDITS: Directed, produced, photographed, and edited by James Wood; screenplay by James Mathers; musical score by Marty Allen; choreography by Rick Alemany. CAST: James Mathers (Dr. Jekyll), John Kearney, Tom Nicholson, Dawn Carver Kelly, Nadine Kalmes.

17. *Edge of Sanity* (1989). CREDITS: Directed by Gerard Kikoine; produced by Edward Simons and Harry Alan Towers; screenplay by J. P. Felix and Ron Raley; photographed in Eastmancolor by Tony Spratling; edited by Malcolm Cooke; musical score by Fredric Talgorn; production designer, Jean Charles Dedieu; art direction by Fred Carter and Tivadar Bertalan; costumes by Valerie Lanee; makeup by Gordon Kaye; filmed in England and Budapest, Hungary; released by Millimeter–Allied/Allied Vision; running time, 86 minutes. CAST: Anthony Perkins (Dr. Jekyll/Mr. Hyde), Glynis Barber (Elisabeth Jekyll), Sarah Maur-Thorp (Susannah), David Lodge (Underwood), Ben Cole (Johnny, the Pimp), Ray Jewers (Newcomen), Jill Melford (Flora), Lisa Davis (Maria), Noel Coleman (Egglestone), Briony McRoberts (Ann Underwood), Mark Elliot (Lanyon), Harry Landis (Coroner), Jill Pearson (Mrs. Egglestone), Basil Hoskins (Mr. Bottingham), Ruth Burnett (Margo), Carolyn Cortez (Maggie), Cathy Murphy (Cockney Prostitute), Claudia Udy (Liza).

• APPENDIX I •

# Television Adaptations

Following is a listing of television programs directly adapted from Stevenson's novels, stories, and poems.

1. "Treasure Island" (1947). CREDITS: Adapted by Fletcher Markle; based on the novel *Treasure Island*; network, Canadian Broadcasting Corporation.

2. "Kidnapped" (1949). CREDITS: Adapted by Andrew Allan; based on the novel *Kidnapped*; network, Canadian Broadcasting Corporation.

3. "Suspense": "Dr. Jekyll and Mr. Hyde" (September 20, 1949). CREDITS: Directed and produced by Robert Stephens; based on the novella *The Strange Case of Dr. Jekyll and Mr. Hyde*; network, CBS. CAST: Ralph Bell (Dr. Jekyll/Mr. Hyde), Pamela Conroy (Esther), Gage Clarke, Ivan Simpson.

4. "The Strange Case of Dr. Jekyll and Mr. Hyde" (1950). CREDITS: Produced by Fred O'Donovan; adapted by John Keir Cross; based on the novella *The Strange Case of Dr. Jekyll and Mr. Hyde*.

5. "The Master of Ballantrae" (1950). CREDITS: Adapted by Andrew Allan; based on the novel *The Master of Ballantrae*; network, Canadian Broadcasting Corporation.

6. "For the Children": "Treasure Island" (1951). CREDITS: Based on the novel *Treasure Island*; network, BBC 1, Great Britain.

7. "Treasure Island" (1951; 7-part serial). CREDITS: Based on the novel *Treasure Island*; network, BBC 1, Great Britain.

8. "Fun with Books": "Kidnapped" (1951). CREDITS: Based on the novel *Kidnapped*; network, Canadian Broadcasting Corporation.

9. "The Sire de Maletroit's Door" (1951). CREDITS: Based on the short story "The Sire de Maletroit's Door"; network, BBC 1, Great Britain.

10. "Kidnapped" (1952; serial). CREDITS: Based on the novel *Kidnapped*; network, Canadian Broadcasting Corporation.

11. "The Ebb-Tide" (1952). CREDITS: Based on the novel *The Ebb-Tide* by Stevenson and Lloyd Osbourne; network, BBC, Great Britain.

12. "Markheim" (1952). CREDITS: Based on the short story "Markheim."

13. "More Stories in Verse" (1953). CREDITS: Based on several poems; network, BBC 1, Great Britain.

14. "On Camera": "The Bottle Imp" (1954). CREDITS: Adapted by Richard Denis; based on the short story "The Bottle Imp"; network, Canadian Broadcasting Corporation.

15. "Climax": "Dr. Jekyll and Mr. Hyde" (July 28, 1955). CREDITS: Directed by Allen Reisner; teleplay by Gore Vidal; based on the novella *The Strange Case of Dr. Jekyll and Mr. Hyde;* hosted by William Lundigan and Mary Costa; network, CBS; running time, 50 minutes. CAST: Michael Rennie (Dr. Jekyll/Mr. Hyde), Sir Cedric Hardwicke, Mary Sinclair, Lowell Gilmore, John Hoyt.

16. "St. Ives" (1955; 6-part serial). CREDITS: Based on the novel *St. Ives* by Stevenson and Arthur T. Quiller-Couch; network, BBC 1, Great Britain.

17. "The Adventures of Long John Silver" (1956; 26-episode series). CREDITS: produced by Isola del'Oro and Joseph Kaufman; executive producer, Mark Evans; music by David Buttolph; filmed in Australia; network, syndicated; running time, 25 minutes (each episode). CAST: Robert Newton (Long John Silver), Kit Taylor (Jim Hawkins), Connie Gilchrist (Purity Pinker), Harvey Adams (Governor Strong), Lloyd Berrell (Mendoza), Grant Taylor (Patch), Rodney Taylor (Israel Hands), Henry Gilbert (Billy Bowledge).

18. "For the Children": "Kidnapped" (1956; 6-part serial). CREDITS: Based on the novel *Kidnapped;* network, Canadian Broadcasting Corporation.

19. "Kidnapped" (1956). CREDITS: Based on the novel *Kidnapped;* network, BBC. CAST: John Laurie (Ebenezer Balfour).

20. "On Camera": "Markheim" (1957). CREDITS: Adapted by Alfred Harris; based on the short story "Markheim"; network, Canadian Broadcasting Corporation.

21. "For the Children": "The Old Buccaneer" (1957). CREDITS: Based on the novel *Treasure Island;* network, BBC 1, Great Britain.

22. "Treasure Island" (March 5, 1960). CREDITS: Directed by Daniel Petrie; produced by David Susskind; associate producer, Audrey Gellen; teleplay by Michael Dyne; settings designed by Otis Riggs; musical score by the Clancy Boys and Tommy Makem; technical director, Ted Miller; lighting director, Ralph Holmes; background film by Alan Villers; program staff, Virginia Gray, Ruth Conforte, and Emaline Mechanic; production supervisor, Murray Susskind; talent coordinator, Rose Tobias; costumes designed by Sal Anthony; associate to the producer, Maureen Hesselroth; assistant director, Frank Leicht; makeup by Dick Smith; a Talent Associates Production; network, CBS; running time, 75 minutes. CAST: Hugh Griffith (Long John Silver), Max Adrian (Blind Man), Michael Gough (Dr. Livesey), Boris Karloff (Billy Bones), Barry Morse (Captain Smollett), Richard O'Sullivan (Jim Hawkins), Douglas Campbell (Squire Trelawney), George Rose (Ben Gunn), John Colicos (Mr. Arrow), George Mathews (Black Dog), Tim O'Connor (Morgan), Tom Clancy (Israel Hands), Betty Sinclair (Mrs. Hawkins), Woodrow Parfrey.

23. "St. Ives" (1960). CREDITS: Based on the novel *St. Ives* by Stevenson and Arthur T. Quiller-Couch; network, BBC 1, Great Britain.

24. "Le Testament du Docteur Cordelier" (November 16, 1961). (See Appendix E, no. 20.)

25. "The Master of Ballantrae" (1962). CREDITS: Based on the novel *The Master of Ballantrae;* broadcast in Scotland.

26. "St. Ives" (1967). CREDITS: Based on the novel *St. Ives* by Stevenson and Arthur T. Quiller-Couch; network, BBC 1, Great Britain. CAST: David Sumner (St. Ives), Gay Hamilton (Flora Gilchrist).

27. "The Strange Case of Dr. Jekyll and Mr. Hyde" (January 7, 1968). CREDITS: Directed by Charles Jarrott; produced by Dan Curtis; adapted by Ian McLellan Hunter; based on the novella *The Strange Case of Dr. Jekyll and Mr. Hyde;* art direction by Trevor Williams; musical score by Robert Cobert; network, Canadian Broadcasting Corporation (U.S. network, ABC); running time, 150 minutes. CAST: Jack Palance (Dr. Jekyll/Mr. Hyde), Leo Genn (Lanyon), Oscar Homolka (Stryker), Billie Whitelaw (Gwyn), Tessie O'Shea (Tessie O'Toole), Torin Thatcher (Sir John Turnbull), Denholm Elliot (Devlin), Gillie Fenwick (Poole).

28. "Billy Bones" (1968; series). CREDITS: Based on the novel *Treasure Island;* network, BBC 1, Great Britain.

29. "Treasure Island" (1969; 13-part serial). CREDITS: Based on the novel *Treasure Island;* produced by Franco London Films; network, Canadian Broadcasting Corporation.

30. "Markheim" (1970). CREDITS: Adapted by Tom Wright; based on the short story "Markheim"; network, BBC 1, Great Britain.

31. "Dr. Jekyll and Mr. Hyde" (1972). CREDITS: network, BBC 1, Great Britain.

32. "Dr. Jekyll and Mr. Hyde" (March 7, 1973). CREDITS: Directed by David Winters; produced by Burt Rosen; executive producers, David Winters and Burt Rosen; associate producer, David W. Orton; associate director, Christopher Barry; conceived by David Winters; teleplay by Sherman Yellen; a musical adaptation of the novella *The Strange Case of Dr. Jekyll and Mr. Hyde;* music and lyrics by Lionel Bart, Mel Mandel, and Norman Sachs; photographed by Dick Bush, B.S.C.; edited by Robert Best; music arranged and conducted by Irwin Kostal; additional orchestrations by Eric Rogers; choreography by Eleanor Fazan; art direction by Jack Shampan; costumes designed by Emma Porteu; makeup by Neville Smallwood; hairdresser, Biddy Chrystal; production manager, David Anderson; production assistant, Mary Ellis; post-production supervisor, Patricia Berlly; production coordinator, Joel Douglas; executive in charge of production, Ernest D. Glucksman; filmed at Shepperton Studios, London, England; video facilities at Lion Television Services, London, England; a Winters/Rosen Production; distributed by ABR Entertainment Company; network, NBC; running time, 79 minutes. CAST: Kirk Douglas (Dr. Jekyll/Mr. Hyde), Susan George (Annie), Susan Hampshire (Isabel), Michael Redgrave (Danvers), Donald Pleasence (Smudge), Stanley Holloway (Poole), Geoffrey Chater (Lanyon), Judi Bowker (Tupenny), Nicholas Smith (Hastings), John Moore (Utterson), Geoffrey Wright (Wainwright).

33. "Weir of Hermiston" (1973; serial). CREDITS: Adapted by Tom Wright; based on the unfinished novel *Weir of Hermiston;* network, BBC 2, Great Britain.

34. "Treasure Island" (1974). CREDITS: Based on the novel *Treasure*

*Island;* network, New Zealand Television.

35. "Kidnapped" (1975; animated). CREDITS: Based on the novel *Kidnapped;* network, New Zealand Television.

36. "Treasure Island" (1977; 4-part serial). CREDITS: Produced by Barry Letts; adapted by John Lucarotti; based on the novel *Treasure Island;* network, BBC 1, Great Britain. CAST: Alfred Lynch, Anthony Bate, Patrick Troughton, Jack Watson.

37. "Weir of Hermiston" (1977). CREDITS: Compilation based on the unfinished novel *Weir of Hermiston;* network, BBC Scotland.

38. "Around Scotland" (1977). CREDITS: Including a segment based on the novel *Kidnapped;* network, New Zealand Television.

39. "The Silverado Squatters" (1977). CREDITS: Based on the journalistic book *The Silverado Squatters;* network, BBC Scotland.

40. "The Rajah's Diamond" (1979). CREDITS: Operatic adaptation; produced by J. Mervyn Williams; based on the short story "The Rajah's Diamond"; libretto by Myfanwy Piper; music by Alun Hoddinott; introduced by Humphrey Burton; commissioned by the BBC in association with the Welsh Arts Council; network, BBC 2, Great Britain.

41. "Kidnapped" (1980). CREDITS: Produced by Tom Cotter; based on the novel *Kidnapped;* network, BBC Scotland.

42. "Kidnapped" (1980; serial). CREDITS: Based on the novel *Kidnapped;* network, BBC Scotland.

43. "The Strange Case of Dr. Jekyll and Mr. Hyde" (1980). CREDITS: Directed by Alistair Reid; produced by Jonathan Powell; teleplay by Gerald Savory; based on the novella *The Strange Case of Dr. Jekyll and Mr. Hyde;* music by David Greenslade; filmed in England; network, BBC 2, Great Britain (U.S. network, PBS, "Mystery," January 6, 13, 1981); running time, 100 minutes. CAST: David Hemmings (Dr. Jekyll/Mr. Hyde), Toyah Willcox (Janet), Lisa Harrow (Ann Coggeshall), Ian Bannen (Oliver Utterson), Diana Dors (Kate Winterton), Clive Swift (Hastie Lanyon), Roland Curram (Poole), Gaye Brown (Diane), Seville Delofski (Fifi), Gretchen Franklin (Cook), Anna Faye (Mary), Roger Davidson (Bradshaw), Jane Slaughter (Gwen), Sheelah Wilcocks (Mrs. Willoughby), Angela Catherall (Dollymop), Terry Downes (Prisoner), Kenteas Brine (Argyll Prostitute), Tim Calver (Argyll Pimp), Ashley Knight (Boy Prostitute).

44. "Treasure Island" (1981; serial). CREDITS: Based on the novel *Treasure Island;* network, New Zealand Television.

45. "Black Arrow" (1984). CREDITS: directed by John Hough; produced by Harry Alan Towers and Michael John Biber; assistant producers, Andres Vincente Gomez and Maria Rohm; screenplay by David Pursall and Peter Welbeck; based on the novel *The Black Arrow;* photographed by John Cabrera; edited by Geoffrey Foot; musical score by Stanley Myers; casting by Sue Watnough; art direction by Jose Maria Alarcon; assistant director, Luis Valdivieso; camera operator, Ricardo Navarrete; stunt director, Jose Luis Chinchilla; assistant editor, Gary Dishman; dubbing editor, Michael Campbell; assistant, Terry Busby; costumes by Bermans and Nathans;

titles and processing by Kay Laboratories, London; sound by Cine-Lingual Sound Studios; production accountant, Gerry Wheatley; a Pan-atlantic Picture; network, the Disney Channel; running time, 93 minutes. CAST: Benedict Taylor (Richard), Georgia Stowe (Joanna), Oliver Reed (Sir Daniel), Fernando Rey (Warwick), Stephan Chase (Black Arrow), Donald Pleasence (Oates), Roy Boyd (Lawless), Aldo Sambrell (Scar), Carol Gotell (Hannah), Robert Russell (Appleyard).

46. "The Master of Ballantrae" (January 31, 1984). CREDITS: Directed by Douglas Hickox; produced by Hugh Benson and Peter Graham Scott; executive producer, Larry White; teleplay by William Bast; based on the novel *The Master of Ballantrae;* photographed by Bob Edwards; edited by Geoff Shepherd; musical score by Bruce Broughton; production designed by John Biggs; art direction by Derek Nice; costumes designed by Olga Lehmann; casting director, Esta Charkham; production supervisor, Keith Webber; production manager, Jake Wright; assistant director, John O'Connor; assistant art director, Richard Hornsby; costume supervisor, Brenda Dabbs; wardrobe master, Daryl Bristow; makeup supervisor, Jane Pearce; camera operator, Roger Pearce; sound mixer, Gordon Kethro; boom operator, Gus Lloyd; second unit director, Peter Graham Scott; second unit cameraman, Brian Morgan; stunt supervisor, Peter Diamond; key grip, Steve O'Connor; gaffer, Alan Gibbs; special effects, Mike Collins; horsemaster, Mike Irish; executive consultant, William Bast; (for HTV Limited) supervising executive producer, Patrick Dromgoole; producer, Peter Graham Scott; filmed on location in England, Scotland, and Wales; a Larry White/Hugh Benson production, in association with HTV Limited, Great Britain; distributed by Columbia Pictures Television; network, CBS ("Hallmark Hall of Fame"); running time, 151 minutes. CAST: Richard Thomas (Henry Durie), Michael York (James Durie), John Gielgud (Lord Durrisdeer), Timothy Dalton (Colonel Francis Burke), Ian Richardson (Andrew MacKellar), Nickolas Grace (Secundra Dass), Finola Hughes (Alison Graeme), Brian Blessed (Captain Teach), Kim Hicks (Jessie Broun), Donald Eccles (John Paul), Pavel Douglas (Prince Charles), James Cosmo (Lone Horseman), Brian Pettifer (Andy Broun), Robert James (Macconochie), James Coyle (Grady the Pirate), Jeremy Bulloch (Warship First Officer), John Aliberi (Warship Captain), Eddie Tagoe (Roberts the Pirate), Nick Brimble (Chew), Cornelius Garrett (French Soldier), Lapana Sengupta (First Indian Dancer), Gigi Chowdhury (Second Indian Dancer), Katya Mirza (Indian Girl Attendant), Esmail Sheikh (Tabla Player), Mick Taylor (Sitar Player), Leonard McGuire (The Sin Eater), Conrad Phillips (Man in Paris Salon), Andrew Panton (Alexander), Paul McDowell (Governor General Clinton), John Hallam (Captain Harris), Brian Coburn (John Mountain), Ed Bishop (Pinkerton), Don Henderson (Hicks), Arua Taylor (Indian Cipaye Boy).

47. "Return to Treasure Island" (1985; 10-part series). CREDITS: Directed by Piers Haggard; produced by Alan Clayton; executive producer, Patrick Dromgoole; assistant producer, Manny Wessels; teleplays by John Goldsmith; series based on a storyline by Ivor Dean; a continuation of the novel *Treasure Island;* series developed by Robert S. Baker; director of photography, Tony Impey; lighting cameraman, Peter Thornton; camera operators, Robin

Higginson, Mike Matthews, and Howard Rockliffe; edited by Tim Wallis and Bob Freeman; editing supervision by Geoff Shepherd; assistant editors, David Scobbit, Richard Dunford, and John Parr; assistant directors, Alex Kirby and Alan Clayton; production designers, Doug James and Phil Williams; musical score by Terry Oldfield and Tom McGuinness; musical supervision by Ray Williams; art direction by Richard Hornsby and Kate Barnett; costumes designed by Aideen Morgan; sound mixers, Alan Jones, Barrie White, and Paul Gaydon; graphics by Rae Lambert; production buyers, Barry Greaves, Peter Smith, and George Noonan; production accountant, David Aubrey; makeup supervisors, Barbara Southcott and Pam Mullins; key grip, Alan Imeson; prop man, Roger Grocott; gaffer electricians, Len Tyler, Ray Telling, and Bill Usher; chargehand riggers, Paul O'Neill and Martin Duckett; casting director, Michael Barnes; local casting, Laura Cairns; horse manager, Marla Bisset; armory special effects, Ken Lailey Studios; stunt arranger, Alf Joint; production assistants, Carol Evans and Barbara Thomas; location manager, Alan Pinniger; location assistant directors, Chris Dando, Paddy Carpenter, and Tony Dyer; production managers, Peter Richardson, Dennis Morgan, Artie Thomas, and Trevor Gittings; production secretaries, Cathy Long and Sarah Anderson; production controller, Dave Bartle; ship, the *Saracen*, provided by Square Sail; produced for video and the Disney Channel by HTV in association with Primetime Television Ltd.; episode titles include: "The Map," "The Mutiny," "The Island of the Damned," "Jamaica"; network, the Disney Channel; running time, 55 minutes (each episode). CAST: Brian Blessed (Long John Silver), Christopher Guard (Jim Hawkins), Reiner Schone (Van Der Bracken), Ken Colley (Ben Gunn), Deborah Poplett (Isabella), Artro Morris (Reverend Morgan), Bruce Purchase (Squire Trelawney), Peter Copley (Dr. Livesey), Richard Beale (Captain Smollett), Charlotte Mitchell (Mrs. Hawkins), John Tordoff (Gadney), Tony Osoba (Joe), Geoffrey Greenhill (Hockley), Willoughby Goddard (Sir Solomon Pridham), John Hallam (Captain Parker), Forbes Collins (Gridley), Jean Faulds (Miss Macphail), Mark Colleano (Moxon), Declan Mulholland (Cook), Roy Pattison (Baker), Roger McKern (Jake), Graham McTavish (Ned), Eddie Blackstone (Bill), Stephen Lyons (Richards), Roy Heather (Simpson), Phil Rowlands (Roberts), Alan Haider (Spanish Captain), Hubert Tucker (Tom the Coachman), Martyn Colborn (Bradle), Brian Bowes, Terry Cade, Gerry Crampton, Terry Forestal, Nick Hobbs, James Lodge, Val Musetti, Doug Robinson (Stuntmen), Peter Lloyd, Aixa Moreno.

48. "Treasure Island" (1987; animated). CREDITS: Executive producer, Tom Stacey; animation director, Warwick Gilbert; director studio 2, Geoff Collins; assistant director, Janey Dunn; animators, Jamil Ahmad, Sue Beak, Patrick Burns, Jon Ellis, Bun Heang Ung, Greg Ingram, Vic Johnson, Peter Jones, Dwayne Labbe, Cynthia Leech, Paul Maron, Neil McCann, Wally Micati, Astrid Nordheim, Mike Stapleton, and Maria Szemenyei; storyboards, Alex Nicholas, Glen Lovett, and Steve Lyons; character design, Simon O'Leary; timing, Jean Tych; animation checkers, Kim Craste, Carla Daley, Renee Robinson, Margot Goslett, Kim Marden, Mark D'Arcy-Irvine, and Tim Adlide; painting supervisor, Jenny Schowe; color stylist, Angela Bodini; preproduction, Alex Nicholas; layout

supervisor, Glen Lovett; layout artists, Yashiko Barry, Rory Baxter, Joanne Beresford, David Cook, Andi Sutherland, Andrew Szemenyei, and Pere Van Reyk; background layouts, David Skinner, Yaroslav Horak, Yashiko Barry, and Glen Lovett; background artists, Beverly McNamara, Paul Pattie, and Jerry Liew; camera operators, Gary L. Page and Tanya Viskich; editors, Peter Jennings and Caroline Neave; voice track director, George Stephenson; stereo sound mixing, Palm Studios; postproduction supervisor, Steve Simon; cmx editor, Eric Christiansen; tape operator, Eddie Schultz; production manager, Roddy Lee; production coordinators, Joy Craste and Fraser McDonald; a Burbank Films (Australia) production; distributed worldwide by ABR Entertainment Company; running time, 50 minutes.

49. "Jekyll and Hyde" (January 21, 1990). CREDITS: Directed and written by David Wickes; produced by Nick Elliott, David Wickes, and Gerald Abrams; based on the novella *The Strange Case of Dr. Jekyll and Mr. Hyde;* music by John Cameron; a production of David Wickes Television, in association with London Weekend Television and King Phoenix Entertainment; network, ABC; running time, 95 minutes. CAST: Michael Caine (Jekyll/Hyde), Cheryl Ladd, Ronald Pickup, Joss Ackland, Lionel Jeffries, Margaret Rawlings, Kim Thomson, Miriam Karlin, Lee Montague, Kevin McNally, David Schofield, Frank Barrie, John Heal.

50. "The Strange Case of Dr. Jekyll and Mr. Hyde" (1990). CREDITS: Directed by Michael Lindsay-Hogg; produced by Bridget Terry; executive producer, Shelley Duvall; teleplay by J. Michael Straczynski; based on the novella *The Strange Case of Dr. Jekyll and Mr. Hyde;* photographed by Ron Vargas; edited by Roy Watts; production designer, Jane Osmann; musical score by Stephen Barber; costume designer, Robert Blackman; unit production manager, Thom Anable; first assistant director, Jim Charleston; second assistant director, Jack Cash; assistant producer, Christopher Toyne; casting by Vicki Hillman; art director, Jack Crosby; assistant art director, Philip Tubach; set decorators, Joyce Gilstrap and Susana Cruciana; graphic designer, Bob Engelsiepen; construction coordinator, Jim Young; set dresser, Sara Andrews; makeup, Sheryl Leigh Ptak; hair stylist, Rachel Dowling; assistant makeup, Ron Wild; assistant costume designer, Camille Argus; key costumer, Cheryl Mitchell; set costumer, Elizabeth Gower; property master and special effects, Eugene McCarthy; assistant property master, Katie Carmichael; script supervisor, Christena Alcorn; first assistant camera operator, Amanda Thompson; second assistant camera operator, Cynthia Pushek; Steadicam operator, Guy Norman Bee; second unit camera operator, Michael Delahoussaye; stills photographer, Lynn Houston; sound mixer, Morteza Rezvani; boom operator, Steve Mackey; music supervisor, Rob Meurer; sound supervisor, Barney Cabral; rerecording mixer, David Fluhr; supervising coordinator, Carla Fry; production coordinator, Rosemary Mitchell; assistant to the producer, Linda Engelsiepen; location manager, Wallace Uchida; casting assistant, Glenn Nash; production secretary, Ginger Lyvere; production accountant, Josh Brown; transportation coordinator, John W. Barbee; production assistants, Alan Ravick, Kevin Bell, Joe Canepa, Greg Elder, Minna Fry, Patty Harbeck, and Jay Schmidt; gaffer, Allan Brennecke; best boy electric, Brian R. Lukas; electricians, Brian Berlin, Taki Ohno,

Peter Hutchinson, and Leo Mendoza; key grip, J. C. Cole; best boy grip, Rachel Flores; grips, Steve Lube and Garrett McTerna; unit publicist, Jeanmarie Murphey-Burke; assistant editor, Beth Spiegel; stand-ins, Maggie Mills and Hugh Milstein; first aid/craft services, John Acevedo; costumes, The Center Theatre Group; stunt coordinator, Ernie Orsatti; extra casting, Judy's Casting and Cenex Casting; caterers, The Gourmet Chabar; completion guaranty, The Completion Bond Company; camera equipment, Otto Nementz; grip and electric equipment, Keylight PSI; laboratory, Foto-Kem/Foto-Tronics; negative cutter, Magic Film Works; opticals, T and T Optical Effects; postproduction, Compact Sound Services; executive in charge of production, Wayne Morris; network, Showtime; running time, 55 minutes. CAST: Anthony Andrews (Dr. Henry Jekyll/Edward Hyde), Laura Dern (Rebecca Laymon), Nicholas Guest (Richard Utterson), George Murdock (Professor Laymon), Rue McClanahan (Madam), Gregory Cooke, I. M. Hobson, Lisa Langlois, Mary Kohnert, Elizabeth Gracen.

51. "Treasure Island" (1990). (See Appendix E, no. 35.)

52. "Treasure Island" (1991; animated). CREDITS: Executive producer, Jerald E. Bergh; produced by Winston Richard; musical score by Haim Saban and Shuki Levy; a Fuji Television production; released on videocassette by International Services; running time, 29 minutes.

The following television program was inspired by the novella *The Strange Case of Dr. Jekyll and Mr. Hyde:*

"Star Trek": "The Enemy Within" (October 6, 1966). CREDITS: Directed by Leo Penn; produced by Gene Roddenberry and Gene L. Coon; executive producer, Gene Roddenberry; associate producers, Robert H. Justman and John D. F. Black; teleplay by Richard Matheson; script consultant, Steven W. Carabatsos; photographed by Jerry Finnerman; edited by Robert L. Swanson, Fabian Tjordmann, Frank P. Keller, A.C.E., and Bruce Schoengarth; theme music by Alexander Courage; musical score by Sol Kaplan; music editors, Robert H. Raff and Jim Henrickson; assistant to the producer, Edward K. Milkis; assistant directors, Gregg Peters and Michael S. Glick; set decoration by Carl F. Biddiscombe and Marvin March; costumes created by William Ware Theiss; post-production executive, Bill Heath; sound editors, Joseph G. Sorokin and Douglas H. Grindstaff; sound mixers, Jack F. Lilly and Cameron McCulloch; sound by Glen Glenn Sound Company; script supervisor, George A. Rutter; music consultant, Wilbur Hatch; music coordinator, Julian Davidson; photographic effects, Howard A. Anderson Company; special effects, Jim Rugg; property master, Irving A. Feinberg; gaffer, George H. Merhoff; head grip, George Rader; production supervisor, Bernard A. Widin; makeup by Fred B. Phillips, S.M.A.; wardrobe mistress, Margaret Makau; casting by Joseph D'Agosta; filmed middle and late June 1966; a Desilu production, in association with Norway Corporation; executive in charge of production, Herbert F. Solow; distributed by Paramount Pictures; network, NBC; running time, 50 minutes. CAST: William Shatner (Captain James T. Kirk), Leonard Nimoy (Mr. Spock), DeForest Kelley (Dr. Leonard McCoy), James Doohan (Lieutenant Commander Montgomery Scott), George Takei (Mr. Sulu), Grace Lee Whitney (Yeoman Janice Rand), Jim Goodwin (Lieutenant John Farrell),

Edward Madden (Technician Fisher), Garland Thompson (Technician Wilson), Don Eitner (Shatner's Double).

The following program includes a parody of the novella *The Strange Case of Dr. Jekyll and Mr. Hyde:*
"Jack Benny": "Dr. Jekyll and Mr. Hyde" skit (March 22, 1953). CREDITS: Network, CBS. CAST: Jack Benny (Dr. Jekyll/Mr. Hyde), Dennis Day (Mr. Hyde), Jeanne Cagney (Nurse), Bob Crosby (Intern), Don Wilson (Bobby), Iris Adrian (Old Woman), Mel Blanc (voices).

The following program is a dramatization in which Stevenson appears as a character:
"Heather on Fire" (circa 1970). CREDITS: Network, BBC Scotland. CAST: Lawrence Douglas (Robert Louis Stevenson).

• APPENDIX J •

# Radio Programs

Following is a listing of English-language radio programs (1926–81) that have included adaptations of Stevenson's prose, poetry, and essays.

1. "Dr. Jekyll and Mr. Hyde" (October 31, 1926). Director/writer, Dailey Paskman; based on the novella *The Strange Case of Dr. Jekyll and Mr. Hyde;* network, WGBS, New York. CAST: Howard Kyle (Dr. Jekyll/Mr. Hyde).

2. "Markheim" (1928). Based on the short story "Markheim"; Daventry, England.

3. "The Wrecker" (1930). Writer, Michael Talbot; based on the novel *The Wrecker* by Stevenson and Lloyd Osbourne; Daventry, England.

4. "Admiral Guinea" (1932). Based on the play *Admiral Guinea* by Stevenson and W. E. Henley; Great Britain.

5. "Markheim" (1932). Writer, Ursula Branston; based on the short story "Markheim"; London, England.

6. "The Bottle Imp" (1933). Based on the short story "The Bottle Imp"; Great Britain.

7. "Weir of Hermiston" (1935). Writer, Halbert Talbot; based on the unfinished novel *Weir of Hermiston;* Scotland.

8. "Treasure Island" (1936). Writer, E. M. Delafield; based on the novel *Treasure Island;* Great Britain.

9. "Treasure Island" (1936). Writer, Olive Dehn; based on the novel *Treasure Island;* Great Britain.

10. "Kidnapped" (1937). Based on the novel *Kidnapped;* Great Britain.

11. "The Suicide Club" (1937). Writer, Ursula Branston; based on the short-story trilogy "The Suicide Club"; Great Britain.

12. "Senior English 6": "Book Talk" (1938). Based on the novella *The Strange Case of Dr. Jekyll and Mr. Hyde;* Great Britain (schools program).

13. "Markheim" (1938). Writer, Francis Dillon; based on the short story "Markheim"; Great Britain.

14. "St. Ives" (1938; 4-part series). Writer, Sybil Clarke; based on the novel *St. Ives* by Stevenson and Arthur T. Quiller-Couch; Great Britain.

15. "Weir of Hermiston" (1943). Writer, Moultrie Kelsall; based on

Appendix J     411

the unfinished novel *Weir of Hermiston;* Scotland.

16. "This Is My Best": "The Master of Ballantrae" (1945). Director, Dave Titus; producer, Homer Fickett; writer, Robert Tallman; music, Bernard Katz; host, Edward Arnold; network, CBS, United States; sponsor, Cresta Blanca Wines; running time, 30 minutes. CAST: Orson Welles, Ray Collins, Agnes Moorehead.

17. "Weird Circle": "Dr. Jekyll and Mr. Hyde" (circa 1945). Based on the novella *The Strange Case of Dr. Jekyll and Mr. Hyde;* network, NBC, United States; running time, 30 minutes.

18. "Tell It Again": "Kidnapped" (1948). Director, Ralph Rose; music, Del Castillo; network, CBS, United States; running time, 30 minutes. CAST: Marvin Miller.

19. "The Beach of Falesa" (1950). Based on the story "The Beach of Falesa"; Scotland.

20. "The Bottle Imp" (1950). Writer, James MacGregor; based on the short story "The Bottle Imp"; Great Britain.

21. "Dr. Jekyll and Mr. Hyde" (1950). Writer, Barbara Burnham; based on the novella *The Strange Case of Dr. Jekyll and Mr. Hyde;* Great Britain.

22. "Scottish Heritage" (1950). Based on the novel *Kidnapped;* Scotland.

23. "This Is My Country" (1950). A reading of "The Tale of Tod Lapraik" from the novel *Catriona;* Scotland.

24. "The Master of Ballantrae" (1950; serial). Producer, James Crampsey; writer, R. J. B. Sellar; based on the novel *The Master of Ballantrae;* Great Britain.

25. "This Is My Country" (1950). Readings of several poems and songs; Scotland.

26. "Thrawn Janet" (1950). A reading of the short story "Thrawn Janet"; reader, Harold Wightman; Scotland.

27. "Treasure Island" (1950). Producer, Thurston Holland; based on the novel *Treasure Island;* Great Britain.

28. "How Treasure Island Came to Be Written" (1950). Commentary on the novel *Treasure Island;* producer, James Crampsey; writer, E. J. B. Mace; Scotland.

29. "May We Recommend?" "Children's Hour" (1953). Readings from the novel *Kidnapped;* Scotland.

30. "Edinburgh: Picturesque Notes" (1954). Readings from the essay "Edinburgh: Picturesque Notes"; reader, Richard Baker; Great Britain.

31. "In the South Seas" (1954). Readings from the journalistic book *In the South Seas;* Great Britain.

32. "Island Nights' Entertainments" (1954). Readings from the short story collection *Island Nights' Entertainments;* Great Britain.

33. "The Autumn Garden" (1954). A reading of the poem "A Lowden Sabbath Morn"; Scotland.

34. "Arts Review" (1954). Readings from the novel *The Master of Ballantrae;* Scotland.

35. "May We Recommend?" (1954). Readings from the novel *The Master of Ballantrae;* Great Britain.

36. "The Master of Ballantrae" (1954). Readings from the novel *The Master of Ballantrae;* Great Britain.

37. "St. Ives" (1954; 8-part series). Based on the novel *St. Ives* by Stevenson and Arthur T. Quiller-Couch; Great Britain.

38. "Travels with a Donkey in the Cévennes" (1954). Readings from the journalistic book *Travels with a Donkey in the Cévennes;* Scotland and Northern Ireland.

39. "Senior English 1": "The Old Buccaneer and Treasure Island" (1954). Readings from the novel *Treasure Island;* Great Britain.

40. "Poetry Reading" (1955). Poetic readings from *A Child's Garden of Verses;* Scotland.

41. "Woman's Hour" (1955). A reading of the letter "To S. R. Crockett"; Great Britain.

42. "May We Recommend?" (1955). Readings from the journalistic book *Travels with a Donkey in the Cévennes;* Great Britain.

43. "Scottish Heritage" (1955; serial). Based on the novel *Treasure Island;* Scotland.

44. "St. Andrew's Children" (1955). A reading of the poem "The Vagabond"; Scotland.

45. "Admiral Guinea" (1956). Arranger, Cyril Wood; based on the play *Admiral Guinea* by Stevenson and W. E. Henley; Great Britain.

46. "Annals of Scotland" (1956). A reading of the poem "The Counterblast"; Scotland.

47. "Curtain Up!" (1956). Based on the novella *The Strange Case of Dr. Jekyll and Mr. Hyde;* Great Britain.

48. "This Is My Country" (1956). A reading from the novel *Catriona;* Scotland.

49. "May We Recommend?" (1956). Readings from the novel *Treasure Island;* Great Britain.

50. "Senior English 2" (1956). Readings from the novel *Treasure Island;* Great Britain.

51. "Party Pieces" (1956). A reading of the poem "The Vagabond"; Scotland.

52. "Arts Review—Theatre" (1956). Commentary on the unfinished novel *Weir of Hermiston;* Scotland.

53. "Lighten Our Darkness" (1957). A reading of the poem "The Celestial Surgeon"; Great Britain.

54. "Scottish Heritage": "Smout" (1957). Writer, Derek Walker; based on poems in *A Child's Garden of Verses;* Scotland.

55. "Senior English 1" (1957). A reading of the poem "Christmas at Sea"; Great Britain.

56. "Listen with Mother" (1957). A reading of the poem "The Cow"; Great Britain.

57. "Enjoying Literature": "Fifth and Sixth Forums" (1957). A reading from the novel *Kidnapped;* Scotland.

58. "Adventures in English" (1957). Readings of several poems; Great Britain.

59. "Poets and Poetry (No. 6)": "Robert Louis Stevenson" (1957). Readings of several poems; Scotland and Northern Ireland.

60. "Rain" (1957). A reading of the poem "Rain"; Great Britain.

61. "Scottish Heritage" (1957). Based on the novel *St. Ives* by Stevenson and Arthur T. Quiller-Couch; Scotland.

62. "Before We Sleep" (1957). Readings from the journalistic book *Travels With a Donkey in the Cévennes;* Great Britain.

63. "Out of Term" (1957). A discussion on the writing of the novel *Treasure Island;* Great Britain.

64. "In Praise of Walking" (1957). Readings from the essay "Walking Tours"; England and Northern Ireland.

65. "Weir of Hermiston" (1957). Writer, R. J. B. Sellar; based on the unfinished novel *Weir of Hermiston;* Scotland.

66. "Repertory in Britain" (1957). Commentary on the unfinished novel *Weir of Hermiston;* Scotland.

67. "The Arrow Strikes" (1958; serial). Based on the novel *The Black Arrow;* Great Britain.

68. "This Is My Country" (1959). Based on the short story "The Bottle Imp"; Scotland.

69. "My Kingdom" (1959). A reading of the poem "My Kingdom," from *A Child's Garden of Verses;* Great Britain.

70. "Children's Hour" (1959). Poetic readings from *A Child's Garden of Verses;* Great Britain.

71. "This Is My Country" (1959). Based on the novella *The Strange Case of Dr. Jekyll and Mr. Hyde;* Scotland.

72. "This Is My Country" (1959). Based on the short story "The Merry Men"; Scotland.

73. "The Wrong Box" (1959). Based on the novel *The Wrong Box* by Stevenson and Lloyd Osbourne; Great Britain.

74. "Home This Afternoon" (1960). Poetic readings from *A Child's Garden of Verses;* commentator, Elizabeth Seagar; Great Britain.

75. "In the Steps of David Balfour" (1961). Producer, Ian Nimmo; based on the novel *Kidnapped;* Great Britain.

76. "Scottish Heritage" (1963). Writer, Barbara Kerr; based on the novel *Kidnapped;* Scotland.

77. "Late Night Bookshelf" (1963). A reading of the short story "Markheim"; Scotland.

78. "Late Night Bookshelf" (1963). Readings from the journalistic book *Travels with a Donkey in the Cévennes;* Scotland.

79. "Late Night Bookshelf" (1964). Readings from the story *The Misadventures of John Nicholson;* Scotland.

80. "Travels with a Donkey in the Cévennes" (1964). A discussion about 5 Bristol students who planned to retrace the route Stevenson documented in his journalistic book *Travels with a Donkey in the Cévennes;* host, Michael Vickers; guest, Clive Critchley; Wales.

81. "The Sire de Maletroit's Door" (1965). Based on the short story "The Sire de Maletroit's Door"; Great Britain.

82. "Ideas in Education (No. 4)": "A Second Start: Children and Fiction" (1965). Readings from the novel *Treasure Island;* Great Britain.

83. "Schools Programme" (1966). Based on the short story "The Bottle Imp"; Scotland.

84. "Story Time": "Two Island Tales, No. 1" (1966). Based on the short story "The Bottle Imp"; Great Britain.

85. "Fireside Sunday School" (1966). A reading of 7 poems from *A Child's Garden of Verses;* Scotland.

86. "Fireside Sunday School" (1966). A reading of the poem "The Cow"; reader, James Crampsey; Great Britain.

87. "Mid-Week Theatre" (1966). Based on the novella *The Strange Case of Dr. Jekyll and Mr. Hyde;* Great Britain.

88. "Springboard": "Trains" (1966). A reading of the poem "From a Railway Carriage"; Great Britain.

89. "Story Time" (1966). A reading of the short story "The Isle of Voices"; Great Britain.

90. "The Art of the Short Story" (1966). A reading of the short story "A Lodging for the Night"; Great Britain.

91. "Things I Have Done" (1966). A reading of the poem "My Shadow"; Great Britain.

92. "The Suicide Club": "The Young Man with the Cream Tarts" (1966). Based on the first part of "The Suicide Club"; Scotland.

93. "Home This Afternoon" (1966). A discussion with a man who retraced, on bicycle, the route documented by Stevenson in his journalistic book *Travels with a Donkey in the Cévennes;* host, Michael Gilliam; guest, Fred Ablethorpe; Great Britain.

94. "Ten to Eight, By Request": "Poems of Today, First Series" (1967). A reading of the poem "The Celestial Surgeon"; Great Britain.

95. "Escape at Bedtime" (1967). A reading of the poem "Escape at Bedtime"; reader, John Betjeman; Great Britain.

96. "Story Time" (1967; 7-part serial). Writer, Aileen Mills; based on the novel *Treasure Island;* Great Britain.

97. "Scottish Studies" (1968). Based on the novella *The Strange Case of Dr. Jekyll and Mr. Hyde;* Scotland (schools program).

98. "Story Time": "Children's Hour" (1968). Writer, Gordon Emslie; based on the novel *Kidnapped;* Scotland. CAST: Bryden Murdoch, Calum Mill.

99. "Travels with a Donkey in the Cévennes" (1968; 2-part drama). Based on the journalistic book *Travels with a Donkey in the Cévennes;* Scotland.

100. "Stories and Rhymes" (1969). A reading of the poem "The Dumb Soldier"; network, Radio 4, Great Britain.

101. "Story Time" (1969). Readings from the journalistic book

*Travels with a Donkey in the Cévennes;* network, Radio 4, Great Britain.

102. "Six Stories": "The Body-Snatcher" (1970). Based on the short story "The Body-Snatcher"; Scotland.

103. "Story Time": "Children's Programmes" (1970). Based on the novel *The Master of Ballantrae;* network, Radio 4, Great Britain.

104. "Further Education": "Classics of Psycho-Horror" (1971). A discussion of the novella *The Strange Case of Dr. Jekyll and Mr. Hyde;* host, Dr. Christopher Evans; guest, J. G. Ballard; network, Radio 3, Great Britain.

105. "Schools Programme" (1971). A reading of the poem "Foreign Children"; network, Radio 4, Great Britain.

106. "Markheim" (1971). Writer, Tom Wright; based on the short story "Markheim"; network, Radio 4, Great Britain.

107. "Serial Reading for Children": "The Old Sea Dog at Admiral Benbow Inn" (1972). A reading from the novel *Treasure Island;* network, Radio 4, Great Britain.

108. "Readings for Children": "Treasure Trove" (1972). A reading from the novel *Treasure Island;* network, Radio 4, Great Britain.

109. "Christmas Afternoon Theatre" (1972). Based on the novel *Treasure Island;* network, Radio 4, Great Britain.

110. "Sunday Theatre Series" (1972). Writer, Ronald Hambleton; based on the short story "The Treasure of Franchard"; network, Radio 4, Great Britain.

111. "Weir of Hermiston" (1972). A discussion concerning an operatic adaptation of the unfinished novel *Weir of Hermiston;* host, Penny Craig; guest, Robin Orr; network, Radio 3, Great Britain.

112. "Saturday Night Theatre" (1972). Based on the novel *The Wrong Box* by Stevenson and Lloyd Osbourne; network, Radio 4, Great Britain.

113. "The Beach of Falesa" (1974). Writer, Alun Hoddinott; a 3-act opera based on the story "The Beach of Falesa"; a Welsh National Opera Company production; network, Radio 3, Great Britain.

114. "Story Time" (1974). Readings from the story *The Misadventures of John Nicholson;* network, Radio 4, Great Britain.

115. "For Better for Worse" (1974). Readings from the essay collection *Virginibus Puerisque* selected by April Cantelo; reader, Richard Hurndall; network, Radio 3, Great Britain.

116. "Night Hath No Wings" (1975). Readings of poems from *A Child's Garden of Verses;* network, Radio 3, Great Britain.

117. "Poetry Prom" (1975). A reading of the poem "Christmas at Sea"; network, Radio 4, Great Britain.

118. "The Master of Ballantrae" (1975; serial). Writer, D. Bancroft; based on the novel *The Master of Ballantrae;* reader, Ian Cuthbertson; network, Radio 4, Great Britain.

119. "The Pavilion on the Links" (1975). Writer, Neville Teller; based

on the story "The Pavilion on the Links"; reader, Ian Cuthbertson; network, Radio 4, Great Britain.

120. "The Philosophy of Nomenclature" (1975). A reading of the essay "The Philosophy of Nomenclature"; reader, Patricia Hughes; network, Radio 3, Great Britain.

121. "Miscellaneous Poems" (1975). A reading of 5 poems; reader, John Curle; network, Radio 3, Great Britain.

122. "Hermiston: An Opera in Three Acts" (1975). Libretto, William Bryden; music, Robin Orr; based on the unfinished novel *Weir of Hermiston;* network, Radio 3, Great Britain.

123. "Nurses" (1976). A reading of the essay "Nurses"; network, Radio 3, Great Britain.

124. "Kaleidoscope" (1976). Based on the novel *Treasure Island;* network, Radio 4, Great Britain.

125. "The Body Snatcher" (1977). Writer, David Pinner; based on the short story "The Body-Snatcher"; network, Radio 4, Great Britain.

126. "Story Time" (1977). A 5-part reading of the novella *The Strange Case of Dr. Jekyll and Mr. Hyde;* reader, Leonard Maguire; network, Radio 4, Great Britain.

127. "Bestseller No. 4" (1978). Producer, Stanley Williamson; a reading of the novella *The Strange Case of Dr. Jekyll and Mr. Hyde;* network, Radio 4, Great Britain.

128. "Interval Programme" (1978). Readings from the journalistic book *An Inland Voyage;* network, Radio 3, Great Britain.

129. "Interval Programme" (1978). Readings from the essay "A Winter's Walk in Carrick and Galloway"; reader, Malcolm Ruthven; network, Radio 3, Great Britain.

130. "Good and Bad Children" (1979). Producer, Cormac Rigby; a reading of the poem "Good and Bad Children"; reader, Peter Barker; network, Radio 3, Great Britain.

131. "Interval Programme": "Sleep Beneath the Stars" (1979). Readings from several works; reader, Jon Curle; network, Radio 3, Great Britain.

132. "An Anthology of Animals" (1980). A reading of the poem "The Cow"; reader, Jon Curle; network, Radio 3, Great Britain.

133. "An Inland Voyage" (1980). Producer, Cormac Rigby; readings from the journalistic book *An Inland Voyage;* reader, Donald Price; network, Radio 3, Great Britain.

134. "Across the Plains" (1980). Producer, Pat Trueman; writer, Alanna Knight; based on "Across the Plains," from the journalistic book *The Amateur Emigrant;* network, Radio 4, Great Britain.

135. "Woman's Hour" (1981). A reading from the novel *Catriona;* reader, June Knox-Mawer; network, Radio 4, Great Britain.

136. "Treasure Island" (1981). A discussion on the centenary of the writing of the novel *Treasure Island* at Braemar; host, Ken Bruce; guest, Alanna Knight; network, Radio 4, Great Britain.

## • APPENDIX K •
# Educational Films

Following is a listing of educational films based on, or chronicling, Stevenson's life and works.

1. *Kidnapped* (1973; animated). Based on the novel *Kidnapped;* running time, 49 minutes.

2. *Treasure Island Revisited* (1973; animated). Based on the novel *Treasure Island.*

3. *Kidnapped* (1979). Produced by MRA; based on the novel *Kidnapped;* recommended for ages 12–17; running time, 28 minutes.

4. *Treasure Island* (1979). Produced by MRA; based on the novel *Treasure Island;* recommended for ages 9–14; running time, 30 minutes.

5. *Treasure Island* (1983). Based on the novel *Treasure Island;* running time, 22 minutes.

6. *Treasure Island Compilation* (1985; animated). Based on the novel *Treasure Island;* running time, 30 minutes.

7. *Kidnapped* (1988; animated). Based on the novel *Kidnapped;* running time, 50 minutes.

8. *Treasure Island* (1988; animated). Based on the novel *Treasure Island;* running time, 50 minutes.

9. *Meet the Authors:* "Robert Louis Stevenson" (short documentary). Running time, 22 minutes.

# • APPENDIX L •

# Television and Radio Documentaries

Following is a listing of British and Canadian television and radio programs that have featured historical, biographical, and critical material pertaining to Stevenson's life and work.

## Television Programs

1. "An American Gentleman" (1953). A play based on Stevenson's life; network, BBC 1.

2. "Focus": "Stamp Collection, Stevenson" (1958). Network, BBC 1.

3. Untitled (1964). A film showing Stevenson relics in the home of Lady Stair, Lawnmarket, Edinburgh; network, BBC 1.

4. "The Day It Is" (1968). An interview with Jorge Luis Borges about Stevenson; network, Canadian Broadcasting Corporation.

5. "Around Scotland": "A Scottish Writer: Robert Louis Stevenson" (1977). Producer/writer, Tom Cotter; network, BBC Scotland (schools program).

6. "Spectrum": "Another Child, Far, Far Away" (1978). Network, BBC Scotland (schools program).

7. "Penny Whistles of Robert Louis Stevenson" (1979). A "musical evening"; producer, David Rose; network, BBC 2. CAST: Mike Maran (Robert Louis Stevenson), David Sheppard (Thomas Stevenson).

8. "Around Scotland": "Read All About It" (1979). A literary quiz on Stevenson; presenter, David Daiches; network, BBC Scotland.

9. "Great Railway Journeys of the World" (1980). A retracing of Stevenson's 1879 rail journey from New Jersey to California; director, Gerry Troyna; host, Ludovic Kennedy; network, BBC 2.

## Radio Programs

1. Untitled (1924). A talk about Stevenson; network, 2LO.

2. "Workshops of Famous Men": "Stevenson at Samoa" (1924). Writer, Caroline Buchan; network, 2LO.

3. "Modern English Poetry": "Stevenson and Henley" (1925). Writers, J. C. Stobart and Mary

Somerville; network, 2LO (schools program).

4. Untitled (1926). Arranger, C. A. Lewis; network, 2LO.

5. "Children's Hour": "The Childhood of R. L. Stevenson" (1944); Scotland.

6. "Robert Louis Stevenson" (1950). Writer, Richard Hughes; network, BBC Home Service.

7. Untitled (1950). Producer, Robin Richardson; writer, John Keir Cross; network, BBC Home Service.

8. "This Is My Country" (1950). Stevenson biography, part 1; Scotland.

9. "Prose Readings" (1954). Readings from various works; network, Radio 3.

10. "Prose Readings" (1954). Readings from letters to Sidney Colvin; network, Radio 3.

11. "Life and Letters" (1956). Readings from letters; network, BBC Home Service.

12. "Life and Letters": "The Unforgotten" (1956). Readings from letters; network, BBC Home Service.

13. "This Is My Country" (1956). Stevenson biography, part 2; Scotland.

14. "The Ivory Lighthouse": "R. L. Stevenson and the Samoan Imbroglio, 1890–94" (1956). Writer, Eric Evans; network, Radio 3.

15. "Adventures in English": "Teller of Tales" (1956). Short Stevenson biography.

16. "Today": "Life as a Cook-Houseboy for R. L. S." (1958). Writer, Charles Howard; network, BBC Home Service.

17. "I Remember" (1959). Interview with Charles Howard; network, BBC Home Service.

18. "To Travel Hopefully" (1959). Readings from various works; network, BBC Home Service.

19. "The Eye Witness" (1960). Report on Swanston cottages being restored by Edinburgh Corporation; network, BBC Home Service.

20. "Two of a Kind": "On the Road of the Loving Heart" (1961). A discussion about Samoan islanders' opinions of Stevenson; narrator, Elizabeth Bryson; network, BBC Home Service.

21. "Scottish Life and Letters" (1963). Interview with Jorge Luis Borges by George Bruce; Scotland.

22. "Today" (1963). Interview with Charles Howard; network, BBC Home Service.

23. "Scottish Heritage": "Samoa Days" (1963). Discussion of Stevenson's love of Samoan islanders; writer, Derek Walker; Scotland.

24. "The Eye Witness" (1964). Interview with Mrs. M. Merrilees about the auction of Stevenson's Edinburgh home, by Geoffrey Cameron; network, BBC Home Service.

25. "Indian Summer" (1964). Interview with Charles Howard by Jack Singleton; network, BBC Home Service.

26. "Scottish Life and Letters" (1964). Interview with Helen Barclay

and Ethel Blair-Wilson; interviewer, George Bruce; Scotland.

27. "R. L. S. in Bournemouth" (1965). Talk by Vincent Waite; network, BBC Home Service.

28. "Home This Afternoon" (1965). Talk by George Nash; Northern Ireland.

29. "The Living Voice" (1965). Interview with Bella Lunan and Ethel Blair-Wilson; Scotland.

30. "Town and Country" (1966). Talk by Ernest Marwick; Scotland.

31. "Ten to Eight" (1966). Reading of prayers written at Vailima, Samoa; reader, Peter Barker.

32. "Scottish Studies" (1967). A 2-part biography of Stevenson; writer, Phillipa Pierce; Scotland.

33. "Shape of Childhood Series" (1968). Readings from various Stevenson works; network, Canadian Broadcasting Corporation.

34. "Home This Afternoon" (1970). Interview with Charles Howard by Anthea Cameron; network, Radio 4.

35. "Woman's Hour" (1970). Discussion by Cicely Williams and Keith Brace; network, Radio 4.

36. "Story Time": "Strange Tales from Scotland" (1971). Readings from various Stevenson works; network, Radio 4.

37. "The Adventures of Robert Louis Stevenson and Marcel Schwob" (1972). Talk by Michael Sadler; network, Radio 4, Scotland.

38. "Scottish News" (1973). Interview with Alanna Knight, author of *The Private Life of Robert Louis Stevenson;* interviewer, Allan Rogers; network, Radio 4, Scotland.

39. "Kaleidoscope": "R. L. Stevenson" (1974). Discussion of James Pope Hennessy's biography by David Daiches and Nigel Nicholson; network, Radio 4.

40. "Memories of Robert Louis Stevenson" (1975). Interview with Helen Barclay and Ethel Blair-Wilson; interviewer, George Bruce; network, Radio 4, Scotland.

41. "Interval Programme" (1976). Readings from various Stevenson works; reader, Patricia Hughes; network, Radio 3.

42. "Kaleidoscope": "The Illustrated Robert Louis Stevenson" (1977). Review of Roy Gasson's book, by Antonia Byatt; network, Radio 4.

43. "P.M. Reports": "Penny Whistles" (1977). Interview about the musical *Penny Whistles of Robert Louis Stevenson;* interviewer, Rosalind Morris; network, Radio 4.

44. "Tusitala and Swift Cloud" (1978). Biography of Robert Louis and Fanny Stevenson; writer/presenter, June Knox-Mawer; network, Radio 4.

45. "Round Midnight" (November 13, 1979). Writer/host, Richard Garrett; network, Radio 4.

46. "Kaleidoscope": "R. L. S.: A Life Study" (1980). Review of Jenni Calder's book by Christopher Stace; network, Radio 4.

47. "Stevenson and Victorian Edinburgh" (1980). Interview with Jenni Calder; interviewer, Jack Reagan; network, Radio 4.

48. "Late Night Bookshelf": "Robert Louis Stevenson" (1981). Network, Radio 4.

## • APPENDIX M •
# Record Albums

Following is a listing of record albums containing performances of Stevenson's prose and poetry.

*Treasure Island*

1. *Treasure Island.* Read by Ian Richardson; Caedmon TC 2075 (two records).

2. *The Cambridge Treasury of English Prose: Dickens to Butler.* Read by Cambridge University Members; includes an excerpt from *Treasure Island,* along with excerpts from the works of Charles Dickens, William Makepeace Thackeray, John Ruskin, Walter Pater, John Henry Newman, Matthew Arnold, George Eliot, Thomas Hardy, Lewis Carroll, George Meredith, and Samuel Butler; Caedmon TC 1058.

*The Strange Case of Dr. Jekyll and Mr. Hyde*

3. *The Strange Case of Dr. Jekyll and Mr. Hyde* (1944). Produced as a "talking book" by the American Foundation for the Blind; read by John Brewster; RCA Manufacturing, Camden, New Jersey (six records).

4. *The Strange Case of Dr. Jekyll and Mr. Hyde* (1969). Read by Anthony Quayle; Caedmon TC 1283.

5. *Fredric March Starring as Dr. Jekyll and Mr. Hyde* (1975). Read by Fredric March; Triple Cross DJH 4806.

6. *The Strange Case of Dr. Jekyll and Mr. Hyde.* A "talking book" by the Sound Recording Committee; read by Major J. R. T. Mathews; London Decca Record, Great Britain (three records).

7. *Dr. Jekyll and Mr. Hyde.* Directed by Christopher Casson; narrated by Robert Somerset; Spoken Arts SA 3005. CAST: Aiden Grennell (Dr. Jekyll/Mr. Hyde), Peter O'Connell (Lanyon).

*Kidnapped*

8. *Kidnapped* (abridged). Read by Douglas Fairbanks, Jr.; Caedmon TC 1636.

Poetry and Essays

9. *Robert Louis Stevenson: His Poetry, Prose and the Story of His Life.* Read by George Rose; Caedmon TC 1448.

10. *A Child's Garden of Verses.* Read by Dame Judith Anderson; Caedmon TC 1077.

11. *Victorian Poetry.* Read by Max Adrian, Claire Bloom, and Alan

Howard; includes "Requiem" and "The Vagabond," along with poems by John Henry, Cardinal Newman, Elizabeth Barrett Browning, Edward Fitzgerald, Alfred Lord Tennyson, William Makepeace Thackeray, Robert Browning, Edward Lear, Charlotte Brontë, Emily Brontë, Arthur Hugh Clough, Charles Kingsley, George Eliot, Matthew Arnold, George Meredith, Dante Gabriel Rossetti, Lewis Carroll, James Thomson, Algernon Charles Swinburne, Thomas Hardy, Gerard Manley Hopkins, Coventry Patmore, Robert Bridges, William Ernest Henley, Oscar Wilde, A. E. Housman, Francis Thompson, George Santayana, Arthur Symons, and Rudyard Kipling; Caedmon, TC 3004 (three records).

12. *The Art of the Essay.* Read by Ian Richardson; includes "On Falling in Love," along with essays by Francis Bacon, Joseph Addison, Charles Lamb, James Henry Leigh Hunt, and Stephen Leacock; Caedmon TC 2071 (two records).

13. *Meditations for the Modern Classroom.* Read by Dame Judith Anderson and Ed Begley; includes "Requiem," along with excerpts from the poetry and prose of Edwin Markham, Marcus Aurelius, Benjamin Franklin, Howard Arnold Walker, Thomas Carlyle, Henry Van Dyke, Edgar A. Guest, Jesse Stuart, John Oxenham, James Russell Lowell, William Shakespeare, M. G. Gosselink, Lao-Tse, Theodore Roosevelt, Louise Driscoll, J. Allen, Eleanor Farjeon, Walter A. Cutter, Richard Armour, Ralph Waldo Emerson, Henry David Thoreau, George Washington, Henry Wadsworth Longfellow, Arthur Guiderman, Lord Thomas Babington Macaulay, Clare Tree Major, John Greenleaf Whittier, E-Yeh-Shure, Kate Walker Grove, Hamlin Garland, Alfred Lord Tennyson, William Ernest Henley, Walt Whitman, William Tyler Page, Edward Everett Hale, Abraham Lincoln, Oliver Wendell Holmes, Thomas Jefferson, Emily Dickinson, John Masefield, Harry Behn, Jane Taylor, Sara Teasdale, Thomas Paine, Charles Loundsberry, Thomas Nash, Langston Hughes, John Milton, Percy Bysshe Shelley, Virgil, James S. Tippett, Dixie Wilson, Thomas Bailey Aldrich; Caedmon TC 2029 (two records).

• APPENDIX N •

# Further Manifestations

Following is a listing of works in various media that have been inspired by, or contain references to, Stevenson's stories, characters, and poetry.

## "The Pavilion on the Links" (1880)

As mentioned in the text, Sir Arthur Conan Doyle openly admitted his admiration for Stevenson's fiction. Also born in Edinburgh (on May 22, 1859), he mentions Stevenson in his 1924 autobiography, *Memories and Adventures,* and he earlier wrote the essay "Methods of Robert Louis Stevenson in Fiction." He may have been inspired by "The Pavilion on the Links," as some of the story's elements turn up in at least two of his Sherlock Holmes tales.

In Conan Doyle's "The Adventure of the Six Napoleons" (1904), the character of "Beppo," an Italian thief and murderer, recalls Stevenson's Beppo, the trustworthy Italian sailor. Another Holmes story, "The Adventure of the Empty House" (1903), features the infamous Von Herder air rifle fired by Colonel Sebastian Moran, a weapon perhaps inspired by the air gun utilized by Stevenson's *carbonari*. (More Conan Doyle parallels are covered in the section on *Treasure Island* below.)

## "The Body-Snatcher" (1881)

RKO Radio's *The Body Snatcher* is the only film directly adapted from Stevenson's short story. However, several other films have dealt with the Burke and Hare murders. Not surprisingly, these productions vary in historical accuracy and technical quality: *The Flesh and the Fiends* (1960), a Hammer film directed by John Gilling and starring Peter Cushing as Dr. Robert Knox, George Rose as Burke, and Donald Pleasence as Hare; *The Anatomist* (1961), directed by Leonard William from a play by James Bridie and starring Alistair Sim; and *Burke and Hare* (1971), directed by Vernon Sewell and starring Harry Andrews as Dr. Knox, Derren Nesbitt as Burke, and Glynn Edwards as Hare.

Billed as a true story, *The Doctor and the Devils* (1985) was produced by master of schtick Mel Brooks and directed by British horror veteran Freddie Francis. Originally written by Dylan Thomas in 1953, the screenplay was revamped by Ronald Harwood and transforms the identity of Knox to "Dr. Thomas Rock" (Timothy Dalton). Set in London, the film is not historically accurate, but it features a surprisingly faithful version of the murderous activities of Burke and Hare and a few elements apparently lifted from Stevenson's tale (the relationship between Dr.

Rock and his assistant, for example). The most misleading aspect of the film is its depiction of Dr. Rock as a freethinking humanitarian anatomist who often shows his concern for the downtrodden. This characterization is a far cry from the elitist and racist Dr. Robert Knox, who believed that destitute and "debased" individuals deserved to die.

A 1958 British film, *The Doctor from Seven Dials* (released in the United States as *Corridors of Blood* in 1963), also includes a pair of murderers (Francis de Wolff and Christopher Lee) who supply a London anatomist with fresh corpses. Obtaining death certificates from Dr. Thomas Bolton (Boris Karloff), a surgeon and research scientist, they smother their victims in a seedy tavern and then deliver the bodies to the hospital where the doctor works and teaches. (See Appendix H, no. 6, for filmographic information.)

## *Treasure Island* (1881)

It would take an entire volume to document the countless media and commercial references to this novel and, particularly, the character of Long John Silver. One of the most famous names in Western literature, Silver (along with J. M. Barrie's Captain Hook) has provided the physical qualities for the stereotype of the vicious pirate scoundrel in pulp fiction, films, radio and television programs, cartoons, comic books, and advertising.

In *Coasts of Treasure Island* Harold Francis Watson provides a lengthy discussion of the similarities between Stevenson's novel and Conan Doyle's *The Sign of Four* (1890), "The Gloria Scott" (1893), and other, non–Holmes stories. Fanny Stevenson's "Story of the Avenging Angel" in *The Dynamiter,* an episode that deals with Utah's Mormons, may have inspired a similar subplot in Conan Doyle's first Sherlock Holmes novel, *A Study in Scarlet* (1887). And Stevenson repays Conan Doyle's admiration when he mentions Holmes in chapter seven of *Weir of Hermiston!*

Many television shows and cartoons have bastardized Silver for their own ends. "Buccaneer Bunny," a vintage Warner Bros. "Looney Tunes" entry, features pirate Yosemite Sam's efforts to overcome Bugs Bunny: Sam sings the "Dead Man's Chest" song and paraphrases the "Dead men don't bite" remark.

In the United States Silver's name has been commercialized by the "Long John Silver's Sea Food Shoppe" franchise, a fast-food restaurant that sells deep-fried fish and chicken. Unlike most appropriations of artistic works by commercial concerns, this organization perhaps can justify its name: Stevenson's Silver is a cook who operates his own restaurant. But it is unlikely that the founders of the company were familiar with the fictional character: in the 1970s their signs featured a peg-legged, eye-patched pirate who displayed an unbelievable look of ignorance—definitely *not* Stevenson's Silver. Surprisingly, television commercials for this franchise have yet to tie in the "Barbecue" nickname.

Another fast-food usage is a McDonald's animated version of *Treasure Island* available on videocassette for about $10. An example of how companies disguise advertising as children's programming (toy companies have produced films and Saturday morning cartoons to "indirectly" sell their products), this 30-minute adaptation awkwardly works Ronald McDonald into the plot.

Children also have added Silver to their toy collections: In 1990 the Imperial Toy Corporation marketed the character as one of the "Pirates of the

High Seas," a collection of six plastic action figurines that includes Blackbeard, Captain Kidd, and Captain Hook. Imperial's packaging includes several errors, including the comment that "Long John's distinguishing characteristic was his peg leg"!

More reverent and artistic references to Silver have turned up in contemporary musical compositions. The folk-rock movement, most popular in Great Britain and the United States during the early to mid–1970s, has often incorporated maritime motifs and tales of the sea. Canadian musician Gordon Lightfoot's "High and Dry" mentions Silver in a verse about pirates, and the salty ditty "Ghosts of Cape Horn" and the *Child's Garden*–like "Pony Man" would have pleased Stevenson.

Scotsman Ian Anderson's "Mother Goose," featured on the 1971 Jethro Tull album *Aqualung*, includes a narrator who refers to himself as Long John Silver, and several of his other atmospheric songs have a certain Stevensonian flavor. When asked if Stevenson or Robert Burns had influenced his work, Anderson wrote in 1991: "I have never read any of the works of R. L. Stevenson, and although I have been acquainted with a few of the works of Robert Burns, it was a long time ago while at primary school in Edinburgh at the age of about ten. I suppose it is just possible that "One Brown Mouse" [a 1978 song] might have origins in some half-remembered Burns poem, as well as a line in the song "Aqualung" but any other suppositions on your part would, particularly in the case of Stevenson, be overly wishful thinking."[1]

Here Anderson proves that Long John Silver (like many other literary characters) has been utilized by those who have never experienced the original creation. (Mary Shelley's Frankenstein Monster, Bram Stoker's Dracula, and Conan Doyle's Sherlock Holmes are three obvious examples of characters that are familiar to moviegoers and television viewers who have not read the stories.) After a character "evolves" into the broader context of folklore, it takes on a life outside its literary setting and may not retain any of its original characteristics. In Anderson's case the "Stevensonian" references come from the Scottish culture in which he was raised.

## *The Strange Case of Dr. Jekyll and Mr. Hyde*

It would be impossible to list even a small percentage of media references to this story, considering that "Jekyll and Hyde" is a standard entry in any modern English-language dictionary. Perhaps the names of Stevenson's dual-personality character have been uttered more times in Western society than that of any other literary creation (excepting perhaps the three famous characters listed in the entry above). Other than being mentioned in hundreds of films, television and radio programs, stories, magazine articles, newspapers, and comic books, the doctor has shown only his evil side in many instances. A popular model kit called "Dr. Jekyll as Mr. Hyde" was first marketed by Aurora in the early 1960s; this horror series also included the Frankenstein Monster (simply called "Frankenstein"), Dracula, the Mummy, the Wolfman, and King Kong.

## Poetry and Songs

Several of Stevenson's poems and songs have been set to music by distinguished composers, including Ralph Vaughan Williams, who wrote melodies for seven of the *Songs of Travel* in 1905–07, and Alan Reid, who added his own melody and chorus to "A Mile an'a Bittock" for the 1982 Battlefield Band album, *There's a Buzz*. Some of the songs and tunes mentioned in Stevenson's stories and essays have been recorded by U.K. and Irish folk artists, including the Tannahill Weavers ("Johnnie Cope" and "Auld Lang Syne"), the Chieftains ("Lillibulero" and "Over the Sea to Skye") Gordon Mooney ("The Twa Corbies"), Connie Dover ("Siúil a Rúin" ["Shule Aroon"]) and Fairport Convention ("Sir Patrick Spens").

# Glossary

Following are English translations and definitions of Scots words and terms used in the text.

| | | | |
|---|---|---|---|
| ain | own | couldnae | could not |
| ane | one | crofter | a tenant farmer |
| auld | old | dine | dinner |
| Auld Hornie | the devil | dow | do |
| awa' | away | eldritch | strange; unearthly |
| ayont | beyond | evermair | evermore; forever |
| bairn | child | frae | from |
| bane | bone | gang | go |
| blaw | blow | gloaming | twilight; dusk |
| bonny | pretty; beautiful | Gude | God |
| bouman | a tenant who buys stock from a landlord and then shares the profit with him; a man who has charge of cattle on a farm | hae | have |
| | | hame | home |
| | | haugh | a low-lying meadow in a river valley |
| | | Hielands | Highlands |
| | | Hogmanay | New Year's Eve |
| | | jo | sweetheart; joy |
| brae | hillside | ken | know |
| braw | fine | kirk | church |
| brig | bridge | lang | long |
| brogues | heavy leather shoes | maun | must |
| burn | a small stream | nae | no |
| cairn | a mound of stones erected as a landmark or memorial | nane | none |
| | | nicht | night |
| | | paidle | to paddle; to wade |
| callant | a young lad | philabeg | the Highlander's kilt |
| cam' | came | pibroch | a traditional dirge for the Highland bagpipes |
| cannae | cannot | | |
| Cantyre | Kintyre | | |
| Chairlie | Charlie (Charles Edward Stewart; Bonnie Prince Charlie) | sall | shall |
| | | scaur | rock; stone |
| | | sair | sore; painful |
| clachan | village | soutar | shoemaker |
| clouted | patched | strath | a wide, flat river valley |
| corbie | carrion crow; raven | syne | since; then |

| | | | |
|---|---|---|---|
| **tautit** | neat; trim | **waur** | worse |
| **tenty** | careful | **wha'll** | who'll |
| **thrawn** | crooked; misshapen; gnarled | **whaur** | where |
| | | **wouldnae** | would not |
| **twa** | two | | |

# Notes

## Preface
    1. *Variety,* February 17, 1960.

## Introduction
    1. Richard A. Rice, *Stevenson: How to Know Him,* p. 27.
    2. Paul Maixner, ed., *Robert Louis Stevenson: The Critical Heritage,* pp. 42–43.
    3. Robert Kiely, *Robert Louis Stevenson and the Fiction of Adventure,* p. 3.
    4. J. R. Hammond, *A Robert Louis Stevenson Companion,* p. ix.

## Chapter One: Fiction into Film
    1. George Bluestone, *Novels into Film,* p. viii.
    2. *Ibid.,* p. 6.
    3. *Ibid.,* p. 34.
    4. *Ibid.,* p. 62.
    5. Joy Gould Boyum, *Double Exposure: Fiction into Film,* p. 8.
    6. *Ibid.,* p. 9.
    7. *Ibid.,* p. 15.
    8. *Ibid.*
    9. David Wheeler, ed., *No, But I Saw the Movie,* p. xiv.
    10. *Ibid.*
    11. Gabriel Miller, *Screening the Novel: Rediscovered American Fiction in Film,* p. x.
    12. Wheeler, p. xviii.

## Chapter Two: Robert Louis Stevenson
    1. David Daiches, *Robert Louis Stevenson and His World,* p. 5.
    2. Jenni Calder, *Robert Louis Stevenson: A Life Study,* p. 32.
    3. James Pope Hennessy, *Robert Louis Stevenson,* p. 26.
    4. Calder, p. 12.
    5. David Daiches, *Robert Louis Stevenson,* pp. 19–20.
    6. *Ibid.,* p. 21.
    7. Moray McLaren, *Stevenson and Edinburgh: A Centenary Study,* p. 79.
    8. Calder, p. 16.
    9. Daiches, *Robert Louis Stevenson and His World,* p. 27.
    10. Calder, p. 60.

11. *Ibid.*, p. 61.
12. *Ibid.*, p. 80.
13. Hennessy, p. 68.
14. *Ibid.*
15. *Ibid.*
16. Robert Louis Stevenson, letter to E. R. Crosby, October 7, 1873.
17. Hennessy, p. 98.
18. *Ibid.*, p. 99.
19. *Ibid.*, p. 103.
20. *Ibid.*, p. 128.
21. James D. Hart, Introduction, in *From Scotland to Silverado*, p. xxii.
22. *Ibid.*, p. xxiii; and Robert Louis Stevenson, *Robert Louis Stevenson's Letters to Charles Baxter*, pp. 68–69.
23. Hart, p. xxx.
24. Hennessy, p. 138.
25. Hart, p. xxxi.
26. Calder, pp. 90–91.
27. *Ibid.*, p. 171.
28. Hennessy, p. 160.
29. *Ibid.*
30. Lloyd Osbourne, "Stevenson at Thirty-Seven," in Robert Louis Stevenson, *Strange Case of Dr. Jekyll and Mr. Hyde, Fables—Other Stories*, pp. x, xi.
31. Calder, p. 224.
32. *Ibid.*, p. 202.
33. Fanny Stevenson, Preface, in Robert Louis Stevenson, *Strange Case of Dr. Jekyll and Mr. Hyde, Fables—Other Stories*, p. xix.
34. Osbourne, pp. xiv–xv.
35. Hennessy, p. 184.
36. J. C. Furnas, *Voyage to Windward: The Life of Robert Louis Stevenson*, p. 261.
37. *Ibid.*, pp. 261–62.
38. Richard Aldington, *Portrait of a Rebel: The Life and Work of Robert Louis Stevenson*, p. 212.
39. Hennessy, p. 189.
40. Calder, p. 233.
41. Hennessy, p. 192.
42. *Ibid.*, p. 195.
43. Furnas, pp. 342–43.
44. Aldington, p. 212.
45. *Ibid.*, p. 217.
46. Calder, p. 273.
47. Aldington, p. 209.
48. Daiches, *Robert Louis Stevenson*, p. 168.
49. Robert Louis Stevenson, letter to Sidney Colvin, August 23, 1893.
50. Joseph W. Ellison, *Tusitala of the South Seas: The Story of Robert Louis Stevenson's Life in the South Pacific*, p. 280.

## Chapter Three: The Art of RLS

1. Robert Louis Stevenson, "A Gossip on Romance," in *Selected Poetry and Prose of Robert Louis Stevenson*, ed. Bradford A. Booth, p. 56.

2. James M. Barrie, in *Robert Louis Stevenson: The Critical Heritage*, ed. Paul Maixner, p. 323.
3. David Daiches, "Stevenson and the Art of Fiction," p. 10.
4. Joseph Conrad, *Life and Letters*, volume 1, ed. G. Jean-Auby (New York: 1927), p. 147.
5. Daiches, p. 11.
6. *Ibid.*, p. 7.
7. Edwin M. Eigner, *Robert Louis Stevenson and Romantic Tradition*, p. 246.
8. Stevenson, pp. 65, 66.
9. Henry James, "Robert Louis Stevenson," *Century Magazine* 35 (April 1888): 869–79.
10. Robert Louis Stevenson, "A Gossip on Dumas' Novels" (Edinburgh: Swanston edition, 1911–12), 9: 129.
11. Robert Kiely, *Robert Louis Stevenson and the Fiction of Adventure*, p. 34.
12. Robert Louis Stevenson, letter to Marcel Schwob, August 19, 1890.
13. Robert Louis Stevenson, letter to Sidney Colvin, January 31, 1892.
14. Gordon Donaldson and Robert S. Morpeth, *Who's Who in Scottish History*, p. 241.
15. Robert Louis Stevenson, "Edinburgh: Picturesque Notes," in *The Travels and Essays of Robert Louis Stevenson*, pp. 312–13.
16. *Ibid.*, pp. 333, 341.
17. Battlefield Band, *Celtic Hotel*.

## Chapter Four: "The Sire de Maletroit's Door"

1. Richard A. Rice, *Stevenson: How to Know Him*, p. 178.

## Chapter Five: "The Suicide Club"

1. Robert Kiely, *Robert Louis Stevenson and the Fiction of Adventure*, p. 114.
2. *Ibid.*, p. 155.
3. *Variety*, June 3, 1936.
4. Frank S. Nugent, *New York Times*, May 30, 1936, p. 7.

## Chapter Six: "The Pavilion on the Links"

1. David Daiches, *Robert Louis Stevenson*, p. 13.
2. *Variety*, September 3, 1920.

## Chapter Seven: "The Body-Snatcher"

1. Robert G. Carlsen, "A Word to the Reader," *Dr. Jekyll and Mr. Hyde and Other Stories*.
2. Owen Dudley Edwards, *Burke and Hare*, pp. 135–36.
3. Reginald Horsman, *Race and Manifest Destiny: The Origins of American Racial Anglo-Saxonism*, p. 73.
4. Edwards, p. 135.
5. *Ibid.*, p. 123.
6. Thomas Schatz, *The Genius of the System: Hollywood Filmmaking in the Studio Era*, p. 180.

## Chapter Eight: *Treasure Island*

1. Robert Louis Stevenson, "My First Book," in *The Essays of Robert Louis Stevenson*, p. 453.
2. *Ibid.*, pp. 454–55.
3. David Daiches, *Robert Louis Stevenson and His World*, p. 55.
4. Harold Francis Watson, *Coasts of Treasure Island*, p. 19.
5. *Ibid.*
6. *Ibid.*, p. 20.
7. *Ibid.*, p. 21.
8. *Ibid.*, p. 56.
9. *Ibid.*
10. *Ibid.*, p. 86.
11. *Ibid.*, p. 95.
12. Robert Louis Stevenson, *Letters and Miscellanies of Robert Louis Stevenson*, p. 378.
13. Watson, p. 124.
14. Stevenson, "My First Book," p. 457.
15. Paul Maixner, ed., *Robert Louis Stevenson: The Critical Heritage*, p. 125.
16. Robert Kiely, *Robert Louis Stevenson and the Fiction of Adventure*, p. 68.
17. James D. Hart, Introduction, *From Scotland to Silverado*, p. xlix.
18. Watson, pp. 151, 152.
19. J. R. Hammond, *A Robert Louis Stevenson Companion*, p. 105.
20. David Daiches, *Robert Louis Stevenson*, p. 47.
21. Dennis Butts, *Robert Louis Stevenson*, p. 35.
22. Kiely, p. 79.
23. Hammond, p. 103.
24. Daiches, *Robert Louis Stevenson*, pp. 40–41.
25. *Ibid.*, p. 49.
26. J. C. Furnas, *Voyage to Windward: The Life of Robert Louis Stevenson*, p. 440.
27. Tony Thomas, *The Great Adventure Films*, p. 27.
28. *New York Times*, April 12, 1920, p. 13.
29. *Ibid.*
30. *Variety*, August 21, 1934.
31. *Ibid.*
32. Perry Nodelman, "Searching for Treasure Island," in *Children's Novels and the Movies*, Douglas Street, ed., p. 60.
33. Leonard Maltin, *The Disney Films*, p. 99.
34. *Ibid.*, pp. 99, 100.
35. *Ibid.*, p. 99.
36. *Ibid.*, pp. 99–100.
37. *Ibid.*, p. 100.
38. *Ibid.*
39. *Long John Silver* pressbook, p. 4.
40. *Ibid.*, p. 5.
41. *Variety*, November 1, 1972.
42. Nodelman, p. 61.
43. *Variety*, October 24, 1973.
44. *Treasure Island* presskit.
45. *Ibid.*
46. *TV Guide* 38, no. 27 (July 7, 1990): 9.

47. *Ibid.*, 39, no. 12 (March 23, 1991): 147.
48. *Treasure Island* presskit.
49. *Ibid.*
50. *Ibid.*
51. *Ibid.*
52. *Ibid.*
53. *Ibid.*
54. "The Chieftains," *Hancher Presents*, p. 2.

## Chapter Nine: *The Silverado Squatters*

1. James Hart notes: "Tiburcio Vasquez, who had a long career of crime, ranging from robberies to murder, had been hanged just four years before Stevenson arrived in Monterey, but he had already become a legend as a romantic leader of a band of highwaymen and a kind of local Robin Hood. Although he may have had a few followers, Vasquez did not command any troops." From James D. Hart, ed., *From Scotland to Silverado*, p. 162 n. 2.

2. Hart notes: "Isaac Pocock's two-act melodrama *The Miller and His Men* (1813) deals with a villainous miller who is also the leader of a band of scoundrels. It is one of the dramas that Stevenson staged as a child in the toy theater he celebrates in "A Penny Plain and Twopence Coloured." The character of Grindoff would naturally have delighted the creator of Deacon Brodie and of Dr. Jekyll and Mr. Hyde." From *ibid.*, p. 196 n. 4.

3. Hart notes: "As Stevenson points out in his *Journal* (p. 79), the date to reclaim the mine had somehow been overlooked so that 'for a month back it had been anyone's to jump who chose.' Yet he also makes clear that it was jumped the day after the visit from the former owner, rather than on the later date indicated in the book. The little newspaper that young Sam (Lloyd Osbourne) printed in the Chinaman's house declares: 'The Silverado mine was jumped on the 27th of June by Rufe Hanson for water purposes, No bloodshed expected.'" From *ibid.*, p. 274 n. 6.

4. Hart notes: "The adventure of Sam Weller's father is narrated by Dickens in *The Posthumous Papers of the Pickwick Club*, I, xiii; and the elder Weller is described (I, x) by his son: 'My father, sir, wos a coachman. A widower he wos, and fat enough for anything—uncommon fat, to be sure ... wery smart—top boots on—nosegay in his button-hole, broad-brimmed tile—green shawl—quite the gen'lm'n.'" From *ibid.*, p. 197 n. 5.

## Chapter Ten: "The Treasure of Franchard"

1. David Daiches, *Robert Louis Stevenson*, pp. 13–14.
2. James Pope Hennessy, *Robert Louis Stevenson*, p. 189.
3. Robert Louis Stevenson, *Letters and Miscellanies of Robert Louis Stevenson*, ed. Sidney Colvin, p. 236.
4. Paul Maixner, ed., *Robert Louis Stevenson: The Critical Heritage*, p. 254.
5. *Variety*, February 13, 1952.

## Chapter Eleven: *The Black Arrow*

1. Robert Louis Stevenson, letter to Sidney Colvin, October 1883.
2. Robert Louis Stevenson, letter to William Archer, March 27, 1894.

3. J. R. Hammond, *A Robert Louis Stevenson Companion*, p. 143.
4. Jeremy Potter, *Good King Richard?* p. 31.
5. *Ibid.*, p. 141.
6. Stevenson, letter to Colvin.
7. J. C. Holt, *Robin Hood*, p. 186.
8. *Ibid.*, p. 190.
9. Hammond, p. 143.
10. *The Black Arrow* pressbook (Columbia Pictures Corp., 1948), p. 14.

## Chapter Twelve: *The Strange Case of Dr. Jekyll and Mr. Hyde*

1. Lloyd Osbourne, "Stevenson at Thirty-Seven," in Robert Louis Stevenson, *Strange Case of Dr. Jekyll and Mr. Hyde, Fables—Other Stories*, p. xii.
2. *Ibid.*, p. xiii.
3. Jenni Calder, *Robert Louis Stevenson: A Life Study*, p. 222.
4. Fanny Stevenson, Preface, in Robert Louis Stevenson, *Strange Case of Dr. Jekyll and Mr. Hyde, Fables—Other Stories*, pp. xx–xxi.
5. Richard A. Rice, *Stevenson: How to Know Him*, p. 249.
6. J. R. Hammond, *A Robert Louis Stevenson Companion*, p. 122.
7. Harry M. Geduld, *The Definitive Dr. Jekyll and Mr. Hyde Companion*, p. 3.
8. *Ibid.*, p. 10.
9. Edwin M. Eigner, *Robert Louis Stevenson and Romantic Tradition*, p. 154.
10. *Ibid.*, p. 161.
11. Moray McLaren, *Stevenson and Edinburgh: A Centenary Study*, pp. 157–58.
12. *Ibid.*, p. 159.
13. William Winter, *Life and Art of Richard Mansfield*, 1: 67.
14. Paul Wilstach, *Richard Mansfield: The Man and the Actor*, p. 159.
15. William Veeder and Gordon Hirsch, eds., *Dr. Jekyll and Mr. Hyde after One Hundred Years*, p. 166.
16. *Ibid.*, p. 167.
17. *Ibid.*, p. 163.
18. *Ibid.*, p. 168.
19. Winter, p. 207.
20. Wallace Palmer, letters to author, July 24, 1991, and August 5, 1991.
21. Tino Balio, ed., *The American Film Industry*, p. 27.
22. James Kotsilibas-Davis, *The Barrymores: The Royal Family in Hollywood*, p. 24.
23. *Ibid.*, p. 25.
24. Lionel Barrymore, as told to Cameron Shipp, *We Barrymores*, p. 191.
25. *Moving Picture World*, April 10, 1920, p. 239.
26. *Ibid.*, p. 300.
27. Kotsilibas-Davis, p. 28.
28. *Moving Picture World*, April 24, 1920, p. 599.
29. Fred Lawrence Guiles, *Stan: The Life of Stan Laurel*, p. 88.
30. Ephraim Katz, *The Film Encyclopedia*, p. 786.
31. Richard J. Anobile, ed., *Rouben Mamoulian's Dr. Jekyll and Mr. Hyde*, p. 6.
32. Veeder and Hirsch, p. 175.
33. *Ibid.*, p. 181.
34. *Ibid.*, pp. 176–77.
35. *Ibid.*, p. 174.

Notes (pp. 190–232)                                    435

36. Janice R. Welsch, "The Horrific and the Tragic in Rouben Mamoulian's *Dr. Jekyll and Mr. Hyde*," in *The English Novel and the Movies*, ed. Michael Klein and Gillian Parker, p. 169.
37. *Ibid.*, p. 171.
38. Veeder and Hirsch, p. 175.
39. Welsch, p. 177.
40. Veeder and Hirsch, p. 178.
41. Anobile, p. 7.
42. Alan Frank, *Horror Films*, p. 32.
43. William K. Everson, *Classics of the Horror Film*, p. 74.
44. Veeder and Hirsch, p. 180.
45. *Ibid.*, pp. 179–80.
46. Denis Gifford, *A Pictorial History of Horror Movies*, p. 92.
47. Leslie Halliwell, *Halliwell's Hundred*, p. 71.
48. Veeder and Hirsch, pp. 181–82.
49. *Variety*, January 10, 1931, p. 2.
50. *Ibid.*, December 29, 1931, p. 8.
51. *Ibid.*, January 5, 1932.
52. Veeder and Hirsch, p. 177.
53. Larry Swindell, *Spencer Tracy . . . A Biography*, p. 171.
54. Halliwell, p. 69.
55. *New York Times*, August 13, 1941, p. 13.
56. Swindell, p. 173.
57. *Ibid.*
58. Ingrid Bergman and Alan Burgess, *Ingrid Bergman: My Story*, pp. 98–99.
59. Lawrence J. Quirk, *The Films of Ingrid Bergman*, pp. 84–85.
60. Bergman and Burgess, pp. 101–02.
61. *New York Times*, August 13, 1941, p. 13.
62. *Variety*, August 28, 1957.
63. Frank, p. 91.
64. Robert W. Pohle, Jr., and Douglas C. Hart, with the participation of Christopher Lee, *The Films of Christopher Lee*, pp. 79–80.
65. John Brosnan, *The Horror People*, pp. 235–38.
66. Pohle and Hart, p. 150.
67. Brosnan, p. 222.
68. *Variety*, September 28, 1949.
69. *Ibid.*, September 16, 1959.

## Chapter Thirteen: *Kidnapped* and *Catriona*

1. J. R. Hammond, *A Robert Louis Stevenson Companion*, p. 133.
2. Jenni Calder, Introduction, *Kidnapped*, pp. xi–xii.
3. Robert Louis Stevenson and Henry James, *Henry James and Robert Louis Stevenson: A Record of Friendship and Criticism*, ed. Janet Adam Smith, p. 149.
4. Descended from Breton Celts, the Stewarts ascended the throne in 1371, when Robert Stewart, grandson of Robert the Bruce, was crowned King Robert II of Scotland. The French spelling, Stuart, was first used during the reign of Mary, Queen of Scots, who ruled 1561–67; considered a threat by Queen Elizabeth of England, she was executed in 1587. Both spellings, as well as a third, Steuart, were used by the family after Mary's reign. In the text each individual is accompanied by his/her respective spelling, but to maintain consistency, the family, or clan, is referred to with the original spelling.

5. Bruce Lenman, *The Jacobite Cause*, p. 34.
6. *Ibid.*, p. 35.
7. *Ibid.*, p. 38.
8. *Ibid.*, p. 87.
9. Eric Linklater, *The Prince in the Heather*, p. 134.
10. David Daiches, *The Paradox of Scottish Culture: The Eighteenth Century Experience*, p. 16.
11. Linklater, pp. 120–22.
12. David N. Mackay, ed., *James Stewart (The Appin Murder)*, p. xxi.
13. *Ibid.*, p. x.
14. The historical display at the Western Highlands Museum in Fort William includes a rifle claimed to be the weapon used in the murder of Colin Roy Campbell. The information panel displayed with the rifle identifies Allan Breck as the possible murderer and Stevenson's novel as the best-known fictionalization of the event.
15. David Daiches, *Robert Louis Stevenson*, pp. 67–68.
16. *Ibid.*, pp. 70–71.
17. Daiches, *The Paradox of Scottish Culture*, p. 35.
18. Calder, p. xiii.
19. *Ibid.*, p. xvii.
20. Linklater, p. 65.
21. Calder, p. xvi.
22. Robert Kiely, *Robert Louis Stevenson and the Fiction of Adventure*, p. 89.
23. Jenni Calder, Introduction, *Catriona*, pp. x–xi.
24. *Ibid.*, p. xvi.
25. *Ibid.*, p. xvii.
26. Robert B. Connelly, ed., *Silent Film, 1910–1936*, in *The Motion Picture Guide*, 10:136.
27. *Variety*, May 11, 1917.
28. *New York Times*, May 28, 1938, p. 9.
29. John Russell Taylor, ed., *Graham Greene on Film: Selected Film Criticism, 1935–1940*, p. 197.
30. *Variety*, September 8, 1948.
31. *Kidnapped* pressbook (1960), p. 3.
32. *Ibid.*, p. 2.
33. Leonard Maltin, *The Disney Films*, p. 168.
34. *Variety*, February 17, 1960.
35. *Ibid.*
36. *Kidnapped* pressbook (1971), p. 18.
37. W. M. von Zharen, "*Kidnapped*—Improved Hodgepodge?" in Douglas Street, ed., *Children's Novels and the Movies*, p. 87.
38. *Ibid.*, p. 91.

## Chapter Fourteen: *The Master of Ballantrae*

1. Robert Louis Stevenson, "The Genesis of *The Master of Ballantrae*," *Scribner's Magazine*, 1891.
2. *Ibid.*
3. J. R. Hammond, *A Robert Louis Stevenson Companion*, p. 149.
4. *Ibid.*
5. David Daiches, *Robert Louis Stevenson*, p. 75.

6. M. R. Ridley, Introduction, *The Master of Ballantrae and Weir of Hermiston*, p. ix.
7. James Pope Hennessy, *Robert Louis Stevenson*, p. 194.
8. Ridley, p. xi.
9. Stevenson.
10. Hammond, p. 159.
11. Stevenson.
12. Hammond, p. 156.
13. B. Allen Bentley, Introduction, in *The Master of Ballantrae*, p. 3.
14. *The Master of Ballantrae* pressbook, p. 13.
15. *Ibid.*, p. 15.
16. Charles Higham, *Errol Flynn: The Untold Story*, p. 301.
17. *Ibid.*, pp. 301–02.
18. *The Master of Ballantrae* pressbook, p. 16.

## Chapter Fifteen: *The Wrong Box*

1. J. R. Hammond, *A Robert Louis Stevenson Companion*, p. 162.
2. *Ibid.*
3. *Ibid.*
4. *Ibid.*, p. 166.
5. *Ibid.*, p. 164.
6. Jenni Calder, *Robert Louis Stevenson: A Life Study*, p. 279.
7. Richard Aldington, *Portrait of a Rebel: The Life and Work of Robert Louis Stevenson*, p. 189.
8. Hammond, pp. 164–65.
9. *Variety*, June 1, 1966.
10. *New York Times*, July 20, 1966, p. 46.

## Chapter Sixteen: *The Ebb-Tide*

1. Alanna Knight, ed., *The Robert Louis Stevenson Treasury*, p. 54.
2. J. R. Hammond, *A Robert Louis Stevenson Companion*, p. 175.
3. *Ibid.*
4. Knight, p. 55.
5. Hammond, p. 176.
6. Hammond, p. 178.
7. Robert Kiely, *Robert Louis Stevenson and the Fiction of Adventure*, p. 186.
8. *Ibid.*, p. 187.
9. Hammond, pp. 182, 184.
10. Kiely, p. 192.
11. *New York Times*, November 20, 1922.
12. *Variety*, November 24, 1922.
13. *Variety*, October 13, 1937.
14. *New York Times*, October 18, 1937, p. 27.
15. *Ibid.*
16. *Variety*, August 13, 1947.
17. *Ibid.*
18. *New York Times*, October 20, 1947, p. 29.

## Chapter Seventeen: *St. Ives*

1. Robert Louis Stevenson, *Letters and Miscellanies of Robert Louis Stevenson,* ed. Sidney Colvin.
2. David Daiches, *Robert Louis Stevenson,* pp. 95–96.
3. Edwin M. Eigner, *Robert Louis Stevenson and Romantic Tradition,* p. 168.
4. *Ibid.,* p. 169.
5. J. R. Hammond, *A Robert Louis Stevenson Companion,* p. 186.
6. George L. McKay, "Some Notes on Robert Louis Stevenson: His Finances and His Agents and Publishers," p. 39.
7. Eigner, p. 169.
8. *Variety,* June 1, 1949.

## Chapter Eighteen: Conclusion

1. David Daiches, "Stevenson and the Art of Fiction," p. 7.
2. An additional story, "The Banker's Ward," was included in *The Sunbeam Magazine,* an amateur school publication, in early 1866. Stevenson was only 15 when he wrote it, but at least one bibliographer lists the tale as one of his legitimate works. An additional fable, "The Persons of the Tale," was published with *Treasure Island.*
3. Several "unfilmed" stories have been adapted for radio.
4. "Markheim" and "The Bottle Imp" have been dramatized for British television.
5. Michael Hayes, ed., Introduction, *The Supernatural Stories of Robert Louis Stevenson.*
6. "An Old Song" was published anonymously in *London* in 1877. While reading issues of the magazine at Yale University's Beinecke Rare Book and Manuscript Library, scholar Roger Swearingen realized that the story corresponded with a Stevenson manuscript fragment he had seen in the library years before. After confirming his discovery, he published the story, along with an unpublished Stevenson fragment, in *An Old Song and Edifying Letters of the Rutherford Family* (Hamden, Conn.: Archon Books, 1982).
7. Robert Louis Stevenson and Lloyd Osbourne, *The Wrecker* (New York: Dover Publications, 1982), p. 425.
8. George E. Brown, *A Book of R.L.S.,* p. 285.
9. Paul Binding, Introduction, in Robert Louis Stevenson, *Weir of Hermiston and Other Stories,* p. 48.
10. J. R. Hammond, *A Robert Louis Stevenson Companion,* p. 194.
11. *Ibid.,* p. 193.
12. *Ibid.,* p. 194.
13. Binding, p. 8.
14. Fanny Stevenson, Preface, in Robert Louis Stevenson, *Strange Case of Dr. Jekyll and Mr. Hyde, Fables—Other Stories,* p. xviii.
   Stevenson cowrote an additional play, *The Hanging Judge,* a forerunner to *Weir of Hermiston,* with Fanny; it was privately printed in Edinburgh in 1887.
15. Robert Louis Stevenson, "A Gossip on Romance," in Bradford A. Booth, ed., *Selected Poetry and Prose of Robert Louis Stevenson,* p. 59.
16. Robert Louis Stevenson, "A Humble Remonstrance," in Booth, pp. 74–75.

## Appendix B: Posthumously Published Prose Writings

1. Roger G. Swearingen, *The Prose Writings of Robert Louis Stevenson: A Guide*, p. 74.
2. *Ibid.*, p. 153.
3. *Ibid.*, pp. 157–58.
4. Robert Louis Stevenson, letter to Adelaide Boodle, September 1, 1890.
5. Swearingen, p. 122.

## Appendix N: Further Manifestations

1. Ian Anderson, letter to author, April 8, 1991.

# Bibliography

## Primary Sources

### LETTERS BY STEVENSON

Stevenson, Robert Louis. *Letters and Miscellanies of Robert Louis Stevenson.* 2 volumes. Edited by Sidney Colvin. New York: Charles Scribner's Sons, 1918.
―――――. *Robert Louis Stevenson's Letters to Charles Baxter.* Edited by DeLancey Ferguson and Marshall Waingrow. Oxford: Oxford University Press, 1956.
―――――. *Vailima Letters, Being Correspondence by Robert Louis Stevenson to Sidney Colvin (November 1890–December 1894).* 2 volumes. New York: Greenwood, 1969.
―――――, and Henry James. *Henry James and Robert Louis Stevenson: A Record of Friendship and Criticism.* Edited by Janet Adam Smith. London: Rupert Hart-Davis, 1948.

### ESSAYS BY STEVENSON

Stevenson, Robert Louis. *The Essays of Robert Louis Stevenson.* London: MacDonald, 1950.
―――――. *The Travels and Essays of Robert Louis Stevenson.* New York: Charles Scribner's Sons, 1918.

### MEMOIRS ABOUT STEVENSON

Guthrie, Lord (Charles). *Robert Louis Stevenson: Some Personal Recollections.* Edinburgh: W. Green and Son, 1920.
Osbourne, Lloyd. "Stevenson at Thirty-Seven," in Robert Louis Stevenson, *Strange Case of Dr. Jekyll and Mr. Hyde, Fables—Other Stories.* New York: Charles Scribner's Sons, 1925.
Stevenson, Fanny. Preface in Robert Louis Stevenson, *Strange Case of Dr. Jekyll and Mr. Hyde, Fables—Other Stories.* New York: Charles Scribner's Sons, 1925.

### PRESSBOOKS AND PRESSKITS

*The Black Arrow.* Columbia Pictures Corporation, 1948.
*House of Fright.* American International Pictures, 1960.
*Jekyll and Hyde ... Together Again.* Paramount Pictures Corporation, 1982.
*Kidnapped.* Walt Disney Productions, 1960.
*Kidnapped.* American International Pictures, 1971.

*Long John Silver*. Distributors Corporation of America, 1954.
*The Master of Ballantrae*. Warner Bros. Pictures Distributing Corporation, 1953.
*Treasure Island*. Turner Network Television, 1990.

## AUTOBIOGRAPHIES

Barrymore, Lionel, as told to Cameron Shipp. *We Barrymores*. New York: Appleton-Century-Crofts, 1951.
Bergman, Ingrid, and Alan Burgess. *Ingrid Bergman: My Story*. New York: Delacorte, 1980.

## BOOKS ABOUT THE AMERICAN AND BRITISH CINEMA

Behlmer, Rudy, ed. *Memo from David O. Selznick*. New York: Viking, 1972.
Taylor, John Russell, ed. *Graham Greene on Film: Selected Film Criticism, 1935–1940*. New York: Simon and Schuster, 1972.

## BOOKS ABOUT AMERICAN RADIO AND TELEVISION

*Variety Television Reviews*. Volume 13 (1983–86).

## NEWSPAPERS AND TRADE PAPERS

*Moving Picture World*, April 10, 1920–April 24, 1920.
*New York Times*, April 12, 1920–July 20, 1966.
*Variety*, May 11, 1917–November 1, 1972.
*Variety Obituaries, Volume 4 (1948–1950)*. New York: Garland, 1988.

## TRAVEL PUBLICATIONS

"Fort William and Lochaber 1990." In *The Scottish Highlands and Islands*. Fort William: Fort William and Lochaber Tourist Board, 1990.
"Inverness, Loch Ness, and Nairn." In *The Scottish Highlands and Islands*. Inverness, 1990.
"Ordnance Survey: Routeplanner of Britain." Devon: Pilgrim's Progress, 1988.
"The Silverado Museum Devoted to Robert Louis Stevenson (1850–1894)." St. Helena, California, 1991.

## Secondary Sources

### BIOGRAPHIES OF STEVENSON

Aldington, Richard. *Portrait of a Rebel: The Life and Work of Robert Louis Stevenson*. London: Evans Brothers, 1957.
Balfour, Graham. *The Life of Robert Louis Stevenson*. New York: Charles Scribner's Sons, 1912.
Butts, Dennis. *Robert Louis Stevenson*. London: Bodley Head, 1966.
Calder, Jenni. *Robert Louis Stevenson: A Life Study*. New York: Oxford University Press, 1980.

Caldwell, Elsie Noble. *Last Witness for Robert Louis Stevenson*. Norman: University of Oklahoma Press, 1960.
Carre, Jean Marie. *The Frail Warrior (A Life of Robert Louis Stevenson)*. New York: Coward-McCann, 1930.
Chesterton, G. K. *Robert Louis Stevenson*. London: Hodder and Stoughton, 1929.
Cruse, Amy. *Robert Louis Stevenson*. New York: Frederick A. Stokes, 1915.
Daiches, David. *Robert Louis Stevenson and His World*. London: Thames and Hudson, 1973.
Dalglish, Doris N. *Presbyterian Pirate: A Portrait of Stevenson*. London: Oxford University Press, 1937.
Ellison, Joseph W. *Tusitala of the South Seas: The Story of Robert Louis Stevenson's Life in the South Pacific*. New York: Hastings House, 1953.
Furnas, J. C. *Voyage to Windward: The Life of Robert Louis Stevenson*. New York: William Sloane, 1951.
Hennessy, James Pope. *Robert Louis Stevenson*. London: Jonathan Cape, 1974.
Mackenzie, Compton. *Robert Louis Stevenson*. London: Morgan-Grampian, 1968.
Rice, Edward. *Journey to Upolu: Robert Louis Stevenson, Victorian Rebel*. New York: Dodd, Mead, 1974.

### PAPERS AND LECTURES ABOUT STEVENSON AND HIS WORK

Daiches, David. "Stevenson and the Art of Fiction." New York: privately printed, 1951.
McKay, George L. "Some Notes on Robert Louis Stevenson: His Finances and His Agents and Publishers." New Haven, Conn.: Yale University Library, 1958.

### GENERAL REFERENCES ABOUT STEVENSON AND HIS WORK

Knight, Alanna, ed. *The Robert Louis Stevenson Treasury*. London: Shepheard-Walwyn, 1985.

### EDITIONS OF STEVENSON'S WORKS

Bentley, B. Allen, ed. Introduction. In *The Master of Ballantrae*. New York: Airmont, 1964.
Binding, Paul. Introduction. In *Weir of Hermiston and Other Stories*. Harmondsworth, England: Penguin, 1979.
Booth, Bradford A. Introduction. In *Selected Poetry and Prose of Robert Louis Stevenson*. Boston: Houghton Mifflin, 1968.
Calder, Jenni. Introduction. In *Catriona*. Edinburgh: W and R Chambers, 1980.
―――. Introduction. In *Kidnapped*. Edinburgh: W and R Chambers, 1980.
―――, ed. Introduction. In *Dr. Jekyll and Mr. Hyde and Other Stories*. London: Penguin, 1979.
Carlsen, Robert G. "A Word to the Reader." In *Dr. Jekyll and Mr. Hyde and Other Stories*. New York: Scholastic Magazines, 1963.
Fraser, G. S. Afterword. In *Treasure Island*. New York: New American Library, 1981.
Hart, James D., ed. Introduction. In *From Scotland to Silverado*. Cambridge, Mass.: Harvard University Press, 1966.
Hayes, Michael, ed. Introduction. In *The Supernatural Stories of Robert Louis Stevenson*. London: John Calder, 1976.

Letley, Emma. Introduction. In *Kidnapped* and *Catriona*. Oxford: Oxford University Press, 1986.
Ridley, M. R., ed. Introduction. In *The Master of Ballantrae* and *Weir of Hermiston*. London: J. M. Dent and Sons, 1989.
Royle, Trevor. Introduction. In *Travels with a Donkey, An Inland Voyage, The Silverado Squatters*. London: J. M. Dent and Sons, 1992.
Smith, Janet Adam, ed. Introduction. In *Collected Poems*. Second edition. New York: Viking, 1971.
Swearingen, Roger G., ed. Introduction. In *An Old Song and Edifying Letters of the Rutherford Family*. Hamden, Conn.: Archon, 1982.

## GUIDES TO STEVENSON'S PROSE WRITINGS

Swearingen, Roger G. *The Prose Writings of Robert Louis Stevenson: A Guide*. Hamden, Conn.: Archon, 1980.

## BOOKS ABOUT STEVENSON'S PROSE WRITINGS

Brown, George E. *A Book of R.L.S.* London: Methuen, 1919.
Daiches, David. *Robert Louis Stevenson*. New York: James Laughlin, 1947.
Eigner, Edwin M. *Robert Louis Stevenson and Romantic Tradition*. Princeton, N.J.: Princeton University Press, 1966.
Hammond, J. R. *A Robert Louis Stevenson Companion*. London: Macmillan, 1984.
Kiely, Robert. *Robert Louis Stevenson and the Fiction of Adventure*. Cambridge, Mass.: Harvard University Press, 1964.
Maixner, Paul, ed. *Robert Louis Stevenson: The Critical Heritage*. London: Routledge and Kegan Paul, 1981.
Rice, Richard A. *Stevenson: How to Know Him*. Indianapolis: Bobbs-Merrill, 1916.
Ricklefs, Roger, ed. *The Mind of Robert Louis Stevenson: Selected Essays, Letters, and Prayers*. New York: Thomas Yoseloff, 1963.

## BOOKS ABOUT DR. JEKYLL AND MR. HYDE

Geduld, Harry M. *The Definitive Dr. Jekyll and Mr. Hyde Companion*. New York: Garland, 1983.
Veeder, William, and Gordon Hirsch, eds. *Dr. Jekyll and Mr. Hyde after One Hundred Years*. Chicago: University of Chicago Press, 1986.

## BOOKS ABOUT PIRACY AND THE ADVENTURE STORY

Watson, Harold Francis. *Coasts of Treasure Island*. San Antonio: Naylor, 1969.

## BOOKS ABOUT STEVENSON AND SCOTLAND

Calder, Jenni, ed. *Stevenson and Victorian Scotland*. Edinburgh: Edinburgh University Press, 1981.
McLaren, Moray. *Stevenson and Edinburgh: A Centenary Study*. London: Chapman and Hall, 1950.

# Bibliography

## BOOKS ABOUT SCOTTISH HISTORY

Carney, Seamus. *The Killing of the Red Fox: An Investigation into the Appin Murder.* Moffat, Scotland: Lochar, 1989.
Daiches, David. *The Paradox of Scottish Culture: The Eighteenth Century Experience.* London: Oxford University Press, 1964.
Donaldson, Gordon, and Robert S. Morpeth. *Who's Who in Scottish History.* Oxford: Basil Blackwell, 1973.
Edwards, Owen Dudley. *Burke and Hare.* Edinburgh: Polygon, 1980.
Fry, Plantagenet, and Fiona Somerset Fry. *The History of Scotland.* London: Routledge and Kegan Paul, 1982.
Hanley, Clifford. *The Scots.* New York: Times Books, 1980.
Kemp, Hilary. *The Jacobite Rebellions.* London: Almark, 1975.
Lenman, Bruce. *The Jacobite Cause.* Glasgow: Richard Drew, 1986.
Linklater, Eric. *The Prince in the Heather.* London: Grafton, 1976.
Mackay, David N., ed. *James Stewart (The Appin Murder).* Edinburgh: William Hodge, 1931.
McLynn, Frank. *Charles Edward Stuart: A Tragedy in Many Acts.* London: Routledge, 1988.
―――. *The Jacobites.* London: Routledge and Kegan Paul, 1985.

## BOOKLETS ABOUT SCOTTISH HISTORY

Archibald, Sally. *The West Highland Museum, Fort William.* Derby, England: Pilgrim, 1988.
Bold, Alan. *Bonnie Prince Charlie.* North Way, Scotland: Pitkin Pictorials, 1973.
Sked, Phil. *Culloden.* Edinburgh: National Trust for Scotland, 1987.

## BOOKS ABOUT THE HISTORY OF SCOTTISH MUSIC

Donaldson, William. *The Jacobite Song: Political Myth and National Identity.* Aberdeen: Aberdeen University Press, 1988.

## BOOKS ABOUT EUROPEAN, BRITISH, AND UNITED STATES HISTORY

Glover, Michael. *The Napoleonic Wars: An Illustrated History, 1792–1815.* New York: Hippocrene, 1979.
Holt, J. C. *Robin Hood.* London: Thames and Hudson, 1982.
Horsman, Reginald. *Race and Manifest Destiny: The Origins of American Racial Anglo-Saxonism.* Cambridge, Mass.: Harvard University Press, 1981.
Potter, Jeremy. *Good King Richard?* London: Constable, 1983.
Ross, Charles. *Richard III.* Berkeley: University of California Press, 1981.
Seward, Desmond. *The Hundred Years War: The English in France, 1337–1453.* New York: Atheneum, 1978.
―――. *Richard III: England's Black Legend.* London: Hamlyn, 1983.
Wilson, Derek. *The Tower: The Tumultuous History of the Tower of London from 1078.* New York: Charles Scribner's Sons, 1979.

## BOOKS ABOUT FILM ADAPTATIONS OF LITERATURE

Bluestone, George. *Novels into Film*. Berkeley: University of California Press, 1957.
Boyum, Joy Gould. *Double Exposure: Fiction into Film*. New York: Universe, 1985.
Klein, Michael, and Gillian Parker. *The English Novel and the Movies*. New York: Frederick Ungar, 1981.
Miller, Gabriel. *Screening the Novel: Rediscovered American Fiction in Film*. New York: Frederick Ungar, 1980.
Sinyard, Neil. *Filming Literature: The Art of the Screen Adaptation*. London: Croom Helm, 1986.
Street, Douglas, ed. *Children's Novels and the Movies*. New York: Frederick Ungar, 1983.
Wheeler, David, ed. *No, But I Saw the Movie*. New York: Penguin, 1989.

## BIOGRAPHIES ABOUT THEATER AND FILM PERSONALITIES

Higham, Charles. *Errol Flynn: The Untold Story*. Garden City, N.Y.: Doubleday. 1980.
Kotsilibas-Davis, James. *The Barrymores: The Royal Family in Hollywood*. New York: Crown, 1981.
Swindell, Larry. *Spencer Tracy . . . A Biography*. New York: World Publishing, 1969.
Thomas, Tony. *Errol Flynn: The Spy Who Never Was*. Secaucus, N.J.: Citadel, 1991.

## BOOKS ABOUT THE AMERICAN THEATER

Wilstach, Paul. *Richard Mansfield: The Man and the Actor*. New York: Charles Scribner's Sons, 1908.
Winter, William. *Life and Art of Richard Mansfield*. 2 volumes. New York: Moffat, Yard, 1910.

## BOOKS ABOUT THE AMERICAN AND BRITISH CINEMA

Adams, Les, and Buck Rainey. *Shoot-Em-Ups*. New Rochelle, N.Y.: Arlington House, 1978.
Anobile, Richard J., ed. *Rouben Mamoulian's Dr. Jekyll and Mr. Hyde*. New York: Avon, 1975.
Balio, Tino, ed. *The American Film Industry*. Revised edition. Madison: University of Wisconsin Press, 1985.
Benson, Michael. *Vintage Science Fiction Films, 1896–1949*. Jefferson, N.C.: McFarland, 1985.
Brosnan, John. *The Horror People*. New York: New American Library, 1976.
Connelly, Robert B., ed. *Silent Film, 1910–1936*. Volume 10 of *The Motion Picture Guide*. Chicago: Cinebooks, 1986.
Curtis, James. *James Whale*. Metuchen, N.J.: Scarecrow, 1982.
Dooley, Roger. *From Scarface to Scarlett: American Films in the 1930s*. New York: Harcourt Brace Jovanovich, 1981.
Everson, William K. *Classics of the Horror Film*. Secaucus, N.J.: Citadel, 1974.
Fell, John L., ed. *Film Before Griffith*. Berkeley: University of California Press, 1983.
Frank, Alan. *Horror Films*. London: Hamlyn, 1977.

Gifford, Denis. *A Pictorial History of Horror Movies*. London: Hamlyn, 1973.
Guiles, Fred Lawrence. *Stan: The Life of Stan Laurel*. New York: Stein and Day, 1980.
Halliwell, Leslie. *The Filmgoer's Companion*. Sixth edition. New York: Avon, 1977.
———. *Halliwell's Film and Video Guide*. Fourth edition. New York: Charles Scribner's Sons, 1983.
———. *Halliwell's Hundred*. New York: Charles Scribner's Sons, 1982.
Hardy, Phil. *The Western*. New York: William Morrow, 1983.
Hurst, Walter E., and William Storm Hall. *Film Superlist for 1940–1949: Motion Pictures in the U.S. Public Domain*. Hollywood: Seven Arts, 1979.
Katz, Ephraim. *The Film Encyclopedia*. New York: Thomas Y. Crowell, 1979.
Lentz, Harris M., III, ed. *Science Fiction, Horror and Fantasy Film and Television Credits*. Volume 2. Jefferson, N.C.: McFarland, 1983.
Maltin, Leonard. *The Disney Films*. New York: Crown, 1973.
Mank, Gregory William. *Karloff and Lugosi: The Story of a Haunting Collaboration*. Jefferson, N.C.: McFarland, 1990.
Naha, Ed. *Horrors from Screen to Scream*. New York: Avon, 1975.
Nash, Jay Robert, and Stanley Ralph Ross. *The Motion Picture Guide*. 9 volumes. Chicago: Cinebooks, 1985–87.
Nollen, Scott Allen. *Boris Karloff: A Critical Account of His Screen, Stage, Radio, Television and Recording Work*. Jefferson, N.C.: McFarland, 1991.
Palmer, Scott. *A Who's Who of British Film Actors*. Metuchen, N.J.: Scarecrow, 1981.
Pitts, Michael R. *Western Movies: A TV and Video Guide to 4200 Genre Films*. Jefferson, N.C.: McFarland, 1986.
Pohle, Robert W., Jr., and Douglas C. Hart, with the participation of Christopher Lee. *The Films of Christopher Lee*. Metuchen, N.J.: Scarecrow, 1983.
Quirk, Lawrence J. *The Films of Ingrid Bergman*. Secaucus, N.J.: Citadel, 1970.
Schatz, Thomas. *The Genius of the System: Hollywood Filmmaking in the Studio Era*. New York: Pantheon, 1988.
Thomas, Tony. *The Cinema of the Sea: A Critical Survey and Filmography, 1925–1986*. Jefferson, N.C.: McFarland, 1988.
———. *The Great Adventure Films*. Secaucus, N.J.: Citadel, 1976.
———, Rudy Behlmer, and Clifford McCarty. *The Films of Errol Flynn*. Secaucus, N.J.: Citadel, 1969.

## BOOKS ABOUT THE GERMAN CINEMA

Kracauer, Siegfried. *From Caligari to Hitler: A Psychological History of the German Film*. Princeton, N.J.: Princeton University Press, 1947.

## BOOKS ABOUT AMERICAN RADIO AND TELEVISION

Asherman, Allan. *The Star Trek Compendium*. New York: Pocket, 1981.
Buxton, Frank, and Bill Owen. *The Big Broadcast (1920–1950)*. New York: Viking, 1972.
Gianakos, Larry James. *Television Drama Series Programming: A Comprehensive Chronicle, 1947–1984*. 5 volumes. Metuchen, N.J.: Scarecrow, 1984.
Marill, Alvin H. *Movies Made for Television: The Telefeature and the Mini-Series (1964–1986)*. New York: New York Zoetrope, 1987.

McNeil, Alex. *Total Television: A Comprehensive Guide to Programming from 1948 to the Present.* New York: Viking Penguin, 1984.

Terrace, Vincent. *Encyclopedia of Television Series, Pilots and Specials (1937–1973).* Volume 1. New York: New York Zoetrope, 1986.

Trimble, Bjo. *The Star Trek Concordance.* New York: Ballantine, 1976.

## PERIODICALS ABOUT THE AMERICAN AND BRITISH CINEMA

Klemensen, Richard, ed. *Little Shoppe of Horrors* 4 (April 1978).

## PERIODICALS ABOUT AMERICAN TELEVISION

*TV Guide* 38, number 27 (July 7, 1990), and 39, number 12 (March 23, 1991).

## PERFORMANCE PROGRAMS

"The Chieftains." *Hancher Presents.* Iowa City: Iowa Center for the Arts, 1987.

## RECORDINGS

Battlefield Band. *Celtic Hotel.* Temple, COMD 2002, 1987.
Battlefield Band. *There's a Buzz.* Temple, COMD 2007, 1982.
The Chieftains. *Reel Music: The Film Scores.* RCA Victor, 60412-2-RC, 1991.
Dover, Connie. *The Wishing Well.* Taylor Park Music, TPMD 0201, 1994.
Fairport Convention. *Full House.* Carthage, CGCD 4417, 1970.
Galway, James, and the Chieftains. *Over the Sea to Skye.* RCA Victor, 60424-2-RC, 1990.
Jethro Tull. *Aqualung.* Chrysalis, VK 41044, 1971.
Lightfoot, Gordon. *Gord's Gold Volume II.* Warner Bros., 25784-2, 1988.
Mooney, Gordon. *O'er the Border.* Temple, COMD 2031, 1989.
Silly Wizard. *A Glint of Silver.* Green Linnet, GLCD 1070, 1986.
The Tannahill Weavers. *The Best of the Tannahill Weavers.* Green Linnet, GLCD 1100, 1989.
———. *Cullen Bay.* Green Linnet, GLCD 1108, 1990.
———. *Dancing Feet.* Green Linnet, GLCD 1081, 1987.

# Index

*Numbers in* **boldface** *refer to pages with photographs. A black dot ( • ) indicates a work by Robert Louis Stevenson.*

Abbott, Bud 208–10, 394
Abbott, John 324, 383
*Abbott and Costello Meet Dr. Jekyll and Mr. Hyde* (1953 film) 207–10, **209**, 211, 394–95
*Abbott and Costello Meet Frankenstein* (1948 film) 208
Abdulov, Osip 98, 381
*Abraham Lincoln* (1924 film) 336
*The Absent-Minded Professor* (1961 film) 269
*The Academy* (periodical) 19
"Across the Plains" • 20
Act of Settlement (Great Britain) 233
Act of Union (Great Britain) 234
Adams, Dora Mills 176, 378
Adams, Julia 136, 385
Addams, Dawn 106, 107, 212, 387, 392
*The Adult Version of Dr. Jekyll and Mr. Hyde* (1972 film) 399
*Adventure Island* (1947 film) 324, 383
*The Adventures of Don Juan* (1949 film) 290
"The Adventures of Long John Silver" (1955–56 television series) 117, 402
*The Adventures of Robin Hood* (1938 film) 148, 153, 198, 293
"Aes Triplex" • 36–37, 353
Agamemnon Films 111, 115, 118, 338, 390
Agar, John 211, 393
Agee, James 62
Ager, Cecilia 204
Aitken, Spottiswoode 66, 67, 379
Alarcon, Jose Maria 153, 389, 404
Alberoni, Cardinal Giulio 235

Aldington, Richard 304
Alibe 109, 389
Allan, Andrew 280, 295, 401
Allied Artists Pictures 210, 211, 263, 291, 393
Alstrup, Oda 168, 377
*The Amateur Emigrant* • 20, 23, 354, 416
American Broadcasting Company (ABC) 224, 226, 403, 407
American International Pictures (AIP) 276, 279, 387, 388, 389, 399
American Mutoscope 58, 377
Amicus Productions 214, 215–16, 339, 389
"Anastasia: The Mystery of Anna" (1986 television miniseries) 114
*The Anatomist* (1961 film) 423
Anderson, Bobby 265, 384
Anderson, Ian 425
Andrews, Anthony 226, 408
Andreyev, Boris 108, 389
*Anglicae Historiae* (book) 146
"Annie Laurie" (song) 30
Anobile, Richard J. 180, 194
*The Ape Man* (1943 film) 264
Appin murder 240–42, 250–52, 253, 269, 274, 279, 285
*Applause* (1929 film) 180
Archer, William 28, 143
Arrow Films 178, 394
*Arthur* (1981 film) 305
*Atalanta* (periodical) 249
Attenborough, Richard 308
Atwater, Edith 75, 81, 383
"Auld Lang Syne" (song) 317, 426
Austin, Leslie 177, 378

449

# 450 Index

Avery, Henry ("Long Ben") 86
Aylmer, Felix 292, 386
Aywon company 178, 394

**B**abington, The Rev. Churchill 17
*Back Street* (novel) 269
*Back Street* (1941 film) 269
Baggot, King 169, 377
Baker, Roy Ward 219, 221, 388
Bale, Christian 113, 114, 391
Balfour, George (uncle of RLS) 28
Balfour, Inspector General John (uncle of RLS) 287
Balfour, Lewis (grandfather of RLS) 10, 11
Balfour, Maud (cousin of RLS) 17
*Ballad of the Irish Horse* (1985 television show) 117
Bandmann, Daniel 165–66
Bannockburn (battle) 11
Barker, Abe 273, 274, 386
Barrault, Jean-Louis 222, 386
Barrie, Sir James M. 39, 424
Barrier, Edgar 125–26, 128, 383, 384
*Barry Lyndon* (1976 film) 117
Barrymore, John 165, 169–74, **175, 176,** 256, 378
Barrymore, Lionel 94, 169–70, 380
Bart, Lionel 225, 403
Bartholomew, Freddie 257, 258, **259,** 263, 382
Barton, Charles T. 208
Bast, William 295, 296, 405
Bate, Anthony 118, 404
Bates, Ralph 219, **220,** 221, 388
Battlefield Band 46, 426
Baxter, Charles 21, 24, 26, 30, 249, 301, 375
Baxter, Warner 257, 258–59, 263, **264,** 272, 275, 382
Bazin, Andre 6
"The Beach of Falesa" • 34, 40, 42, 312, 318, 339–40, 364, 411, 415
Beale, Richard 118, 406
Beaudine, William 264, 265, 268, 384
*Bedazzled* (1967 film) 305
*Bedlam* (1946 film) 74
Beery, Noah 321, 379
Beery, Wallace 95, 97, 98, **99,** 380
Beeson, Paul 275, 279, 386, 388
*Bela Lugosi Meets a Brooklyn Gorilla* (1952 film) 264

Bell, Derek 117
Bell, Ralph 222, 401
Benelli, Sam 170
Benham, Harry 168, 377
Benny, Jack 222, 409
Beranger, Clara S. 171, 173, 174, 378
Bergman, Ingrid 200–01, 203, 204–05, 382
Berthier, Jack 292, 386
Beswick, Martine 219, **220,** 221, 388
Bevan, Billy 153, 382, 384
Biber, Michael John 154, 404
"Billy Bones" (1968 television series) 118, 403
*Billy the Kid vs. Dracula* (1966 film) 264
Binding, Paul 344
Biograph 58, 377
*The Birth of a Nation* (1915 film) 67
Bishop, William 126, 383
*The Black Arrow* • 26, 42, 138–54, 255, 342, 358, 383, 390, 404, 413
*The Black Arrow* (1948 film) 150–53, **152,** 336, 383
*The Black Arrow* (1972 animated film) 390
"Black Arrow" (1984 television film) 153–54, 339, 404–05
*The Black Cat* (1934 film) 63, 210
*Blackbeard's Ghost* (1968 film) 269
*Blackenstein* (1973 film) 221
*Blacula* (1972 film) 221
Blair, Isla 116, 391
Blair, Janet 150, 151–52, **152,** 383
Blanc, Mel 110, 397, 409
Blankfield, Marc 222, 396
Blessed, Brian 118, 295, 405, 406
Bloch, Robert 223
Blom, August 168, 377
*Blood and Sand* (1941 film) 184
*Bluebeard* (1944 film) 210
Bluestone, George 5
Blum, Edwin 256, 262, 382
"The Body-Snatcher" • 45, 68–82, 220, 320, 339, 342, 356, 382, 415, 416, 423–24
*The Body Snatcher* (1945 film) 73–82, **76,** 113, 208, 272, 338, 382–83
Bonaparte, Napoleon 329, 336
"The Bonnets of Bonnie Dundee" (song) 82, 232, 264, 266, 268
"The Bonnie House of Airlie" (song) 246
"The Book of Joseph" • 11

# Index

Booth, Edwin 174
Borges, Jorge Luis 418, 419
Bosworth, Hobart 168, 377
Bothwell Brig (battle) 9–10
"The Bottle Imp" • 312, 340, 363, 402, 410, 411, 413, 414
*The Bowery* (1932 film) 97, 114
The Bowery Boys 264
Bowker, Judi 226, 403
Boyum, Joy Gould 6
Bradford, William 107, 392
Brady, Patti 126, 383
Braus, Mortimer 206, 339, 393
Breslin, John 272, 386
Bresslaw, Bernard 212, 395
Brett, Jeremy 168
Breuer, Josef 161
*Bride of the Monster* (1955 film) 107
"Bright Is the Ring of Words" • 9, 374
Brimble, Nick 295, 405
British and Colonial Kinematograph Company 58
British Broadcasting Corporation (BBC) 54, 63, 114, 117, 118, 129, 225, 226, 280, 324, 337, 401, 402, 403, 404, 409, 418, 419, 420
British East India Company 10
Brodie, Deacon 160
Brodrich, Susan 219, 388
Bronson, Crevole 23
Bronte, Charlotte 269, 422
Brooks, Mel 423
*The Brothers Rico* (1957 film) 128
Broughton, Bruce 297, 405
Brown, Vanessa 336, 384
Bruce, Nigel 96, 98, 198, 258, 380, 382
Bruce, Robert (King of Scotland) 11, 435
buccaneers 85–86
Buchanan, Edgar 126, 128, 150, 153, 383
*A Bucket of Blood* (1959 film) 221
Burfield, Kim 108, 109, 389
Burke, William 69–70, 71, 74, 75, 77, 81, 82, 220, 423
*Burke and Hare* (1971 film) 423
Burlingame, E. L. 28, 134
Burney, S. H. 87
Burns, Robert 2, 27, 42–43, 45, 46, 279, 317, 342, 346, 354, 425
Burrows, J. C. 165
Bush, George 3
Butts, Dennis 90

*The Cabinet of Dr. Caligari* (1919 film) 169
Cabrera, John 153, 404
Cade, Jack ("John Amend-All") 148
Cain, Robert 256, 378
Caine, Michael 226, 276, **277, 278,** 279, 305, 306, **307,** 387, 389, 407
Calder, Jenni ix, 11, 15, 17, 27, 33, 231, 246–47, 248, 250, 304, 420
Calhoun, Rory 324, 383
Calistoga Gold and Silver Mine (Silverado) 89, 120
Calvet, Corinne 222, 395
Calvin, John 346
Calvin, Tony 219, 388
Cambridge University (England) 15, 18, 269
Cameron, Beatrice 164, 165
Cameron, John 110, 397, 407
Campbell, Beatrice 292, 294, 386
Campbell, Sir Colin (royal sheriff) 233
Campbell, Colin Roy ("The Red Fox") 240–43, 250, 253, 257, 263, 269, 271, 272, 274, 279
Campbell, Douglas 117, 402
Campbell, John (2nd Duke of Argyll) 234, 235
Canadian Broadcasting Corporation (CBC) 117, 118, 223, 280, 295, 401, 402, 403, 420
Cannon, Alexander 232
Canova, Antonio 189, 197
Capone, Al 181
Capone, Sidney 181
*Captain Blood* (1935 film) 117, 198, 290
*Captain Kyd, or the Wizard of the Sea* (novel) 87
Cardiff, Jack 294, 385
Carney, Seamus 242
Carpenter, Francis 93, 378
Carr, Comyns 166
Carreras, Sir James 221
Carreras, Michael 212, 386, 395
Casey, Bernie 221, 395
Cassell and Company 88, 143, 230, 249, 283
*Cat People* (1942 film) 74
*Catriona* • 32, 34, 44, 249–56, 261, 265, 266, 267, 268, 274, 276, 277, 279, 280, 328, 364, 388, 411, 412, 416
Cavanagh, Paul 52, **53,** 54, 150, 153, 206, 383, 385, 393
Cavens, Fred 151, 383

452 Index

*Century Illustrated Monthly Magazine* 124
*The Champ* (1931 film) 97
Chandler, Helen 179
Chaney, Lon, Jr. 211
Chaney, Lon, Sr. 94, **95, 96,** 174, 379
Chaplin, Charles 107
Charles I (King of England) 232
Charles II (King of England) 9, 232
Charles VII (King of France) 49
Charles Scribner's Sons 143, 159, 230, 250, 283, 301, 328
Charlie Chan (film series) 264, 265, 336
"Charlie Is My Darling" (song) 246
Chase, Stephen 154, 405
Chatto and Windus 124, 345
The Chieftains 116–17, 390, 426
*A Child's Garden of Verses* • 2, 26, 373, 412, 413, 414, 415, 421, 425
"A Christmas Sermon" • 33–34, 363
*Citizen Kane* (1941 film) 79, 108
*City Streets* (1931 film) 180–81
The Clancy Brothers 118, 402
Clemens, Brian 219–21, 388
"Climax" (television series) 222, 402
Clive, Colin 192
Clive, E. E. 59, 257, 381, 382
Coburn, Brian 295, 405
Cockburn, Henry 70
Colin, Sid 212, 395
Colley, Ken 118, 406
Columbia Broadcasting System (CBS) 222, 295, 402, 409, 411
Columbia Pictures 125, 128, 150, 153, 206, 297, 304, 307, 336, 339, 383, 384, 387, 393, 395
Colvin, Sidney 18, 28, 34, 42, 87, 143, 147, 285, 312, 313, 345, 419
"Come Lasses and Lads" (song) 89
Comfort, Lance 212, 395
Compton, W. H. 165
Conan Doyle, Sir Arthur 5, 58, 134, 162, 168, 305, 338, 347, 423, 424, 425
Conneff, Kevin 117
Conrad, Joseph 2, 39, 320
Constant, Benjamin 15
Coogan, Jackie 222, 395
Cook, Peter 305, 387
Cooper, Gary 180
Cooper, Jackie 94, 95, 97–98, **99,** 380
Cooper, James Fenimore 87
Cope, General Sir John ("Johnnie Cope") 236
Copley, Peter 118, 406
Corbin, Virginia Lee 93, 378
Corday, Rita 74, 383
Cording, Harry 153, 210, 384, 395
Corey, Jeff 265, 384
Corman, Roger 215, 221
*Cornhill Magazine* 19, 49, 65
*Corridors of Blood* (1963 film) 398–99, 424
Costello, Lou 208–10, 394
Costner, Kevin 164
Cotter, Tom 280, 404
Coulter, Frazer 164–65
*Court and Society Review* (periodical) 159
Covenanters 9, 14, 20, 44, 46, 331
Coyle, James 116, 391
"Crabbed Age and Youth" • 39, 352
Crampton, Howard 169, 377
*The Crater* (novel) 87
*The Creature from the Haunted Sea* (1960 film) 221
Crisp, Donald 200, 203, 205, 382
Crocker, Emerson 136, 385
Cromwell, Oliver 232
Crosby, E. R. 18
Crosland, Alan 256, 378
Cross, John Keir 222, 401, 419
Crowther, Bosley 308
Cruikshank, Andrew 271, 386
Cruze, James 168, 377
Culloden (battle) 237, 238, 272, 281, 285, 292, 296
Cunningham, Alison ("Cummy") 11, 12, 367
Cunningham, Allan 87
Currie, Finlay 99, 271, 384, 386, 398
*The Curse of Frankenstein* (1957 film) 211
*Curse of the Cat People* (1944 film) 74
Curtis, Dan 223, 403
Cushing, Peter 211–12, 214, **215,** 389, 423
Custer, General George Armstrong 286
*The Cyclops* (1957 film) 211

**D**abbs, Brenda 297, 405
Daft, Jamie 69, 81
Daiches, David ix, 14, 15, 33, 39, 66, 89–90, 91, 132, 133, 238, 242, 245, 284, 329, 338, 418, 420

# Index    453

Dalglish, Doris N. 1
Dalrymple, Sir John (Master of Stair) 233
Dalton, Timothy 295, 405, 423
Daniell, Henry 74, **76,** 77, 269, 336, 383, 384
*Darby O'Gill and the Little People* (1959 film) 269
Darien scheme 10
Darling, W. Scott 265, 266, 267, 268, 384
Darwin, Charles 14, 70
*Daughter of Dr. Jekyll* (1954 film) 107, 210–11, 339, 393
*David Balfour* • see *Catriona*
Davie, Cedric Thorpe 275, 386
Davies, Jack 212, 395
Dawley, J. Searle 93, 377
Dawn, Jack 202, 382
*Deacon Brodie* • 65, 160, 354
Dean, Ivor 219, 388
de Camp, Rosemary 136, 385
de Cordoba, Pedro 59, 381
Defoe, Daniel 87
De Grasse, Robert 78, 81, 382
del Oro, Isola 117, 402
Del Val, Jean 336
Denny, Reginald 208, 394
*Den Skaebnesvangre Opfindelse* (1909 film) 168, 377
De Quincey, Thomas 160
*Der Andere* (1913 film) 397
*Der Andere* (1930 film) 397
*Der Januskopf* (1920 film) 169, 378–79
Dern, Laura 226, 408
*Detour* (1946 film) 210
de Veuster, Father Damien 30, 33, 363–64
De Vito, Danny 110, 397
de Wolff, Francis 99, 384, 386, 387, 398, 424
Dickens, Charles 2, 5, 6, 106, 302, 344, 347, 421
Dierkes, John 208, 211, 393, 394
Disney, Walt 98–99, 101, 103, 107, 112, 268–69, 270, 274, 275, **276,** 384, 386
Distributors Corporation of America (DCA) 98, 104, 105, 392
Docherty, Mary 69
*The Doctor and the Devils* (1985 film) 423
*Dr. Black and Mr. Hyde* (1976 film) 221, 395

*Dr. Freckle and Mr. Snide* (1887 play) 165
*Dr. Heckyl and Mr. Hype* (1980 film) 221–22, 395
*The Doctor Jekyll* (1951 film) 205–06, 385
*Dr. Jekyll and Miss Osbourne* (1981 film) 400
*Dr. Jekyll and Mr. Hyde* (1887 play) 163–66, 168
*Dr. Jekyll and Mr. Hyde* (1888 play) 165–66
*Dr. Jekyll and Mr. Hyde* (1897 play) 168, 377
*Dr. Jekyll and Mr. Hyde* (1902–03 touring play) 166
*Dr. Jekyll and Mr. Hyde* (1908 Kalem film) 168, 377
*Dr. Jekyll and Mr. Hyde* (1908 Polyscope film) 168, 377
*Dr. Jekyll and Mr. Hyde* (1911 film) 168, 377
*Dr. Jekyll and Mr. Hyde* (1913 Imp film) 169, 377, 394
*Dr. Jekyll and Mr. Hyde* (1913 Kineto-Kinemacolor film) 168–69, 378
*Dr. Jekyll and Mr. Hyde* (1914 film) 169, 394
*Dr. Jekyll and Mr. Hyde* (1920 Arrow film) 178, 394
*Dr. Jekyll and Mr. Hyde* (1920 Paramount film) 165, 169–74, **175, 176,** 181, 193, 212, 214, 338, 378
*Dr. Jekyll and Mr. Hyde* (1920 Pioneer film) 174–78, 339, 378
*Dr. Jekyll and Mr. Hyde* (1923 play) 166
*Dr. Jekyll and Mr. Hyde* (1925 film) 179, 394
*Dr. Jekyll and Mr. Hyde* (1927 play) 166
*Dr. Jekyll and Mr. Hyde* (1931 play) 166
*Dr. Jekyll and Mr. Hyde* (1931 film) ix, 179–99, **185, 186, 193,** 200–05, 214, 223, 224, 225, 272, 338, 380
*Dr. Jekyll and Mr. Hyde* (1941 film) 185, 199–205, **201,** 225, 262, 339, 347, 382
"Dr. Jekyll and Mr. Hyde" (1949 television show) 222, 401
"Dr. Jekyll and Mr. Hyde" (1955 television show) 222, 402
"Dr. Jekyll and Mr. Hyde" (1972 television film) 225, 403
"Dr. Jekyll and Mr. Hyde" (1973 television film) 225–26, 403

*Dr. Jekyll and Mr. Hyde Done to a Frazzle* (1914 film) 169, 394
*Dr. Jekyll and Mr. Mouse* (1947 cartoon) 396
*Dr. Jekyll and Sister Hyde* (1971 film) 219–21, **220**, 388
*Dr. Jekyll y el Hombre Lobo* (1971 film) 399
*Dr. Jekyll's Dungeon of Death* (1982 film) 400
*Dr. Jekyll's Hide* (1932 film) 394
*Dr. Jerkyll's Hyde* (1955 cartoon) 396
*Dr. Pyckle and Mr. Pryde* (1925 film) 178, 394
*Dr. Sexual and Mr. Hyde* (1971 film) 399
*Dr. Terror's House of Horrors* (1964 film) 215
*Don Juan* (1926 film) 256
Donat, Robert 203
Doohan, James 223, 408
Douglas, Anne 110, 397
Douglas, Kirk 110, 111, 225–26, 397, 403
Douglas, Laurence 276, **277**, 279, 389, 409
Dover, Connie 426
Down, Lesley-Anne 110–11, 397
*Dracula* (novel) 169, 212, 223, 425
*Dracula* (1931 film) 179
*Dracula* (1974 television film) 223
*Dracula's Daughter* (1936 film) 63, 205
Drake, Charles 136, 385
Driscoll, Bobby 99, 100, 101, **102**, 106, 118, 384
*The Duality of Man* (1910 film) 168, 377
Duffield, Brainerd 136, 385
Dumas, Alexandre 41, 361–62
Dumbrille, Douglas 98, 380
Dupont, E. A. 107, 392
"Dupont Show of the Month" (television series) 117

**E**ast Side Kids 264
Eastman, George 110
*Ebb Tide* (1922 film) 321–22, 379
*Ebb Tide* (1937 film) 322–24, **322**, 381
*The Ebb Tide* • 32, 34, 40, 304, 309–24, 328, 342, 343, 365, 379, 381, 383, 401

"The Ebb Tide" (1952 television show) 324, 401
Eccles, Donald 295, 405
*Edge of Sanity* (1989 film) 400
"Edinburgh: Picturesque Notes" • 20, 44–45, 46, 71, 353, 411
Edison Company 93, 256, 336, 377, 378
Edward III (King of England) 144
Edward IV (King of England) 144, 147
Edward V (King of England) 147
Edwards, Bob 295, 405
Edwards, Owen Dudley 70
Egan, Pierce 148
Eigner, Edwin M. 40, 160, 331–32, 335
*El Extraneo Caso del Hombre y la Bestia* see *The Doctor Jekyll*
*El Secreto del Dr. Orloff* (1964 film) 399
Elliott, Denholm 223, 403
Elstree Studios 293
Elvey, Maurice 58, 378
*Empire of the Sun* (1987 film) 114
"The Enemy Within" (1966 "Star Trek" episode) 223, 408–09
England, Sue 266, 267, 384
Erskine, John (6th Earl of Mar) 234, 235
Everson, William K. 194
Evesson, Isabelle 164


"**F**ables" • 132, 339, 371
Fairport Convention 426
Falkirk (battle) 237
"The Fall of the House of Usher" (short story) 134, 340
Famous Players–Lasky 170, 379
Farmer, Frances 322, 323, 381
Fawcett, George 321, 322, 379
Fay, Martin 117
Feklistovh, Alexander 222, 390
Fennell, Albert 221, 388
Fenwick, Gillie 224, 403
Fergusson, Robert 46
Ferrier, Walter 160
Fiander, Lewis 219, 388
Field, Gladys 177, 378
Field, Harry 324, 381
Fields, Sidney 208, 394
Finch, Peter 269, **270**, **271**, 272–73, **273**, 274, **276**, 386

Fish, George F. 168
Fisher, Terence 211–12, 214, 386
Fitzgerald, Barry **322,** 323–24, 381
Fitzgerald, Walter 100, 384
*Five Against the House* (1955 film) 128
Fleischman, Sid 110, 397
Fleming, Rhonda 324, 383
Fleming, Victor 97, 199–205, 380, 382
*Flesh and Fantasy* (1943 film) 339
*The Flesh and the Fiends* (1960 film) 423
Flothow, Rudolph C. 337
*The Flying Dutchman or a Legend of the High Seas* (novel) 87
Flynn, Errol 117, 148, 290–95, **291, 293,** 386
Fontaine, Joan 269
"For the Children" (television series) 117, 280, 401, 402
Forbes, Bryan 306, 307, 308, 387
Forbes, Ralph 257, 382
"The Foreigner at Home" • 44
Forepaugh, Luella 168, 377
Forman, W. Courthope 335
Forrest, Sally 52, 385
Forshay, Harold 176, 378
Fox Film Corporation 93, 378
Francis, Freddie 423
Franco London Films 118
Frank, Alan 194, 214
*Frankenstein* (novel) 160, 161–62, 223, 285, 344, 425
*Frankenstein* (1931 film) 179, 192, 199
*Frankenstein* (1972 television film) 223
Frankenstein film series 205, 206
*Frankenstein Must Be Destroyed* (1969 film) 219
Franklin, Benjamin 24, 422
Franklin, C. M. 93, 378
Franklin, S. A. 93, 378
Fraser, Simon (12th Lord Lovat) 252
Fraser, Simon (legal counsel) 252
Frazer, Alex 266, 384
French Revolution 328
Freud, Sigmund 161, 162, 185, 202, 214, 216, 217, 218
Freund, Karl 136, 169, 379
"From the Clyde to Sandy Hook" • 20
Fulton, A. R. 168, 377
"Fun with Books" (television series) 280
Furnas, J. C. ix, 28, 93
Furneaux, Yvonne 292, 295, 386
Furthman, Jules 66, 93–94, 379

Gail, Jane 169, 377
Gainsborough 269
Gardner, Helen 169, 378
Garfunkel, Art 110
Garrett, Grant 208, 384
Gaskill, Charles L. 169, 378
Gauguin, Paul 30, 109
Gaumont-British 269
Gauntier, Gene 168, 377
Geduld, Harry M. 160, 161
Gelbart, Larry 304, 306, 308, 387
Genn, Leo 223, 403
George, Duke of Clarence (brother of Richard III) 147
George, Susan 225, 403
George I (King of England and Scotland) 234
George II (King of England and Scotland) 262, 281, 292, 293
George Eastman Theatre 179
*The Ghost Ship* (1943 film) 74
*Ghosts on the Loose* (1943 film) 264
*The Ghoul* (1933 film) 63
Gielgud, Sir John 295, 405
Gilbert, John 66, 67, 379
Gilbert, William 163
Gilchrist, Connie 104, 117, 392, 402
Gilmore, Lowell 150, 383, 402
Gilstrap, Captain MacRae 293
Gladstone, William 88
*Glen or Glenda?* (1953 film) 107
Glencoe massacre 233
Glidden, Helen 164
Globus, Yoram 221, 395
Glover, Julian 114, 115, 391
Godfrey, Peter 200, 382
*Going My Way* (1944 film) 323
Golan, Menahem 221, 395
"The Gold Bug" (story) 87, 88, 134
Goldner, Charles 292, 294, 386
*Gone with the Wind* (novel) 74
Gordon, Mary 81, 266, 382, 383
"A Gossip on Romance" • 38, 40, 357
Gough, Michael 117, 402
Grace, Nikolas 295, 405
*The Graduate* (1967 film) 110
Graham, General John of Claverhouse (Viscount Dundee; "Bonnie Dundee") 232
Grant, Gerald 116
Grant, John 208, 394
Grant, William (Lord Advocate of Scotland) 250
Gray, James 75

*Great Expectations* (novel) 6
*Great Expectations* (1946 film) 6
Greene, Graham 62, 263
Greenhaigh, Jack 324, 383
*The Grey Fox* (1982 film) 117
Griffith, Charles B. 221, 395
Griffith, D. W. 67, 180, 322
Griffith, Hugh 117, 402
Groves, Fred 58
Guard, Christopher 118, 406
Guiles, Fred Lawrence 179
Guissart, Rene 94, 379
Gun, Benjamin 89
*Guy Mannering* (novel) 41

"Hail! Childish slaves of social rules" • 15–16, 375
Haines, Donald 260
Hall, Porter 106, 392
Hallam, John 296, 405, 406
Halliwell, Leslie 198
"Hallmark Hall of Fame" (television series) 295, 405
Halsey, Michael 116, 391
*Hamlet* (play) 174
Hammer Films 211–12, 213, 215, 219–21, 386, 388, 395, 423
Hammond, J. R. 2, 91, 144, 150, 160, 284, 288, 290, 302, 304, 315, 320, 332
Hampshire, Susan 225, 403
Hanna, Franklin 256, 378
Hardwicke, Sir Cedric 222, 402
Hardy, Oliver 178
Hardy, Thomas 27, 421, 422
Hare, William 69–70, 71, 74, 77, 82, 220, 423
Harkins, D. H. 165
Harris, Eleanor 256, 262, 382
Harrison, Louis Reeves 178
Hart, James 23, 24
Harte, Betty 168, 377
Haskin, Byron 98, 100, 101, 102–03, 104, 384, 392
Hatton, Raymond 321, 322, 379
*The Haunted Strangler* (1958 film) 398
"Hawaii Five-O" (television series) 272
Hawkins, Jack 276, 279, 389
Hawthorne, Nathaniel 344
Hayes, Helen 272
Haynes, Stanley 106

Hayward, Louis 60, 150, 151, **152**, 206, 381, 383, 393
Hayworth, Rita 184
Hearndell, Richard 214, 389
"Heart of the Country" (BBC television film) 114
Heath, Percy 181, 183, 380
"Heather on Fire" (BBC television show) 279, 409
"Heathercat" • 46, 371
Heilbron, Vivien 276, 279, 389
Hemingway, Mariel 63
Hemmings, David 226, 404
Henderson, James 143
Henderson, Lucius 168, 377
Henley, W. E. 18, 26, 27, 44, 65, 89, 160, 347, 375, 410, 422
Hennessy, James Pope ix, 17, 18, 19, 24, 25, 28, 286, 420
Henry, Gloria 126, 383
Henry IV (King of England) 144
Henry V (King of England) 144
*Henry V* (play) 105
*Henry V* (1944 film) 105
Henry VI (King of England) 144, 147, 148
Henry VII (King of England) 146
Hepburn, Katharine 204
Herbert, Holmes 181, **193**, 198, 380, 382, 393
Heston, Charlton 111, 113–14, **115**, 116, 272, 391
Heston, Fraser C. 111–12, 113, 114, 390
Hickox, Douglas 295, 405
Hicks, Kim 295, 405
Hinds, Anthony 212
*The History of King Richard the Third* (More) 146
"The History of Moses" • 11
Hitchcock, Alfred 7, 63
Hobart, Rose 182, 380
Hobbes, Halliwell 153, 182, 199, 257, 380, 382, 383
Hoddinott, Alun 63, 404
Hoffenstein, Samuel 181, 183, 380
Hoffman, Carl 169, 379
Hogan, James 323, 324, 381
Hogarth, William 252
Holloway, Stanley 225, 403
Holt, J. C. 148
Homolka, Oscar 224, **322**, 323, 381, 403
Hopkins, Miriam 182, **186**, 198, 203, 204, 380

## Index

Horner, Jerold T. 169, 378
Horner, William George 167
*Horrible Hyde* (1915 film) 169, 378
*Horror of Dracula* (1958 film) 212
Hotely, May 169, 378
Hough, John 108, 389, 404
*The Hound of the Baskervilles* (1959 film) 212
*The Hound of the Baskervilles* (1978 film) 305
*How Green Was My Valley* (1941 film) 268, 324
Howard, Trevor 278, 279, 389
Howison, John 87
HTV Limited 297, 338, 405, 406
Hudson, Alfred 165
Hughes, Finola 295, 296, 297, 405
Hugo, Victor 40
Hull, Henry 136, 385
"A Humble Remonstrance" • 5, 40, 43, 359
*The Hunchback of Notre Dame* (1923 film) 94, 178
The Hundred Years War 49, 51, 133
Hunter, Ian 200, 205, 382
Hunter, Ian McLellan 223, 224, 403
Hunter, Tab 106, 107, 392
Hurst, Brandon 171, 186, 378, 382
Hurst, Fanny 269
Hutton, R. H. 135
Huygens, Christian 167
Hyde, Anne 232
Hyde, The Reverend C. M. 33
Hytten, Olaf 265, 381, 382, 384, 393

"*I* Am a Hunchback, Yellow Faced" • 16, 376
*I, Mobster* (1959 film) 215
*I, Monster* (1971 film) 214–18, **215**, 217, 224, 339, 389
*I Walked with a Zombie* (1943 film) 74
*Il Mio Amico Jekyll* (1960 film) 398
"In the Gloaming" (song) 30–31
*In the South Seas* • 32, 363, 411
Independent Motion Picture Company (IMP) 169, 377
Ingraham, Joseph Holt 87
*An Inland Voyage* • 1, 19, 20, 362, 416
*Intolerance* (1916 film) 67
*The Invisible Man* (1933 film) 198
Irving, Henry 166, 174
Irving, Washington 88

"The Island" (short story) 87
*Island Nights' Entertainments* • 312, 365, 411
*Isle of the Dead* (1945 film) 74
"The Isle of Voices" • 340, 365, 414
*Ivanhoe* (novel) 148
Ivo, Tommy 136, **137**, 385

Jack the Ripper 219, 221, 223
Jackson, Gordon 278, 389
Jacobite Rebellion of 1689 232–33
Jacobite Rebellion of 1708 234
Jacobite Rebellion of 1715 (the '15) 11, 234–35
Jacobite Rebellion of 1719 (the '19) 235
Jacobite Rebellion of 1745 (the '45) 27, 29, 46, 47, 231–32, 236–37, 275, 276, 281, 285, 287, 288, 292, 295, 296
Jacobites 11, 14, 27, 29, 45, 47, 117, 231–38, 245, 252, 266, 268, 275, 276, 279, 281, 285, 288, 292, 331
James, Henry 27, 40, 41, 231, 250, 345, 376
James, Robert 295, 405
James II (King of England and Ireland) and VII (King of Scotland) 232, 233
Jameson, Susan 217, 389
*Jane Eyre* (novel) 269
*Jane Eyre* (1944 film) 269
Jannings, Emil 179
Janowitz, Hans 169
Jarrott, Charles 223, 403
*The Jazz Singer* (1927 film) 256
"Jekyll and Hyde" (1990 television film) 226, 407
*The Jekyll and Hyde Portfolio* (1972 film) 399–400
*Jekyll and Hyde ... Together Again* (1982 film) 222, 395
Jenkin, Fleeming 18, 20, 71, 360, 361
*Jessie James Meets Frankenstein's Daughter* (1966 film) 264
*The Jest* (1919 play) 170
Jethro Tull 425
Joan of Arc 49
John Amend-All *see* Cade, Jack
"Johnnie Cope" (song) 246, 247, 426
*Johnny Tremain* (1957 film) 269
Johns, Mervyn 292, 386
Johnson, Richard 114, 115, 391
Jones, Freddie 278, 279, 389
June, Ray 94, 97, 380

Kalakaua (King of Hawaii) 30, **31**
Kalem Company 168, 377
Kanitz, Werner 276, 388
Karloff, Boris 52, **53**, 54, 63, 74, 75, **76,** 77, 78, 81, 113–14, 118, 179, 197–98, 207–10, **209**, 269, 272, 383, 385, 394, 398, 402, 424
Karlson, Phil 128–29, 383
Katz, Ephraim 179
Kaufman, Joseph 117, 392, 402
Kay, Edward J. 268
Keane, Sean 117
Keaton, Buster 177
Keen, Geoffrey 100, **102**, 384
Keighley, William 293–94, 385
Kelley, DeForrest 223, 408
Kelly, Paul 324, 383
Kelsall, Moultrie 292, 386
Kidd, William ("Captain Kidd") 86, 89
*Kidnapped* • ix, 2, 20, 26, 40, 44, 45, 124, 227–80, 284, 285, 286, 289, 290, 302, 316, 329, 346, 360, 371, 378, 382, 384, 386, 388, 390, 401, 402, 404, 410, 411, 412, 413, 414, 417, 421
*Kidnapped* (1917 film) 256, 378
*Kidnapped* (1938 film) 256–63, **259, 264,** 265, 266, 267, 268, 339, 382
*Kidnapped* (1948 film) 263–68, 384
"Kidnapped" (1949 television show) 280, 401
"Kidnapped" (1951 television show) 280, 401
"Kidnapped" (1951 television serial) 280, 401
"Kidnapped" (1956 television show) 280, 402
"Kidnapped" (1956 television serial) 280, 402
*Kidnapped* (1960 film) ix, 268–75, **270, 271, 273, 276,** 338, 386
*Kidnapped* (1968 film) 276, 388
*Kidnapped* (1971 film) 276–80, **277, 278,** 339
"Kidnapped" (1975 television film) 280, 404
"Kidnapped" (1980 television film) 280, 404
"Kidnapped" (1980 television serial) 280, 404
Kiely, Robert 2, 42, 58, 88, 90, 248, 316–17, 318, 320–21
Killiecrankie (battle) 232

Kineto-Kinemacolor 168, 378
*A King in New York* (1957 film) 107
*King Kong* (1933 film) 221
Kingsford, Walter 150, 153, 381, 383
Kingsley, Charles 88, 422
Kirkwood, James 321, 379
Knight, Alanna ix, 416, 420
Knight, Arthur 275
Knox, Alexander 206, 393
Knox, Dr. Robert 69, 70, 74, 77, 81, 220, 423–24
Koerner, Charles 74
Korngold, Erich Wolfgang 117
Kossoff, David 213, 387
Kruger, Otto 97, 380

Laanemets, Aare 108, 389
Ladd, Cheryl 226, 407
*The Lady from Shanghai* (1949 film) 108
Laemmle, Carl, Sr. 63, 169, 179, 377
*Lafitte, the Pirate of the Gulf* (novel) 87
Lamont, Charles 208, 394
Lane, Charles 171, 378
Lang, Fritz 136
Laughton, Charles 51, 52, 53, 385
Laurel, Stan 178–79, 394
Laurie, John 99, 271, **276,** 280, 384, 386, 402
Lawson, Wilfred 306, 387
Lean, David 6, 106
Lee, Anna 269
Lee, Bernard **270,** 271, 386
Lee, Christopher 115–16, 211–18, **213, 215, 217,** 224, 387, 389, 391, 398, 424
Lee, Donna 74, 383
Lee, Lila 321, 379
Lee, Rowland V. 151
Lefebvre, Jean 108, 389
Lehmann, Olga 297, 388, 405
Lenman, Bruce 233, 235
Leonardo da Vinci 167
*The Leopard Man* (1943 film) 74
Lester, Mark 110, 397
Letts, Barry 118, 404
Levien, Sonya 256, 262, 382
Lewis, Sheldon 175–76, 178, 200, 226, 378
Lewton, Val 73–74, 75, 76, 77, 78, 81, 82, 382
*The Life of Emile Zola* (1937 film) 198
*The Light in the Forest* (1958 film) 272
Lightfoot, Gordon 425

Liliuokalani (Hawaiian princess) 31
"Lillibulero" (tune) 89, 117, 426
Linklater, Eric 238, 248
Lister, Joseph 18
*Little Annie Rooney* (1925 film) 264
*Little Caesar* (1930 film) 180
*The Little Shoppe of Horrors* (1960 film) 221
Livesey, Roger 292, 386
"Loch Lomond" (song) 258, 261, 262
"Lochaber No More" (song) 245
"A Lodging for the Night: A Story of Francois Villon" • 49, 57, 340, 352, 414
Loeb, Lee 108, 394
*London* (periodical) 20, 49, 57
Long, Robert 106, 392
*Long John Silver's Return to Treasure Island* (1954 film) 98, 103–04, **105**, 117, 339, 392–93
*The Long Voyage Home* (1940 film) 324
Longmans, Green and Company 159, 166, 301
*Longman's Magazine* 132
Lorentz, Pare 62
Lorre, Peter 323
Louis XIV (King of France) 233, 234
Love, Montagu 58
*The Love Bug* (1969 film) 269
Low, Will H. 30, 344
Lubin 169, 378
Lucarotti, John 118, 404
Lugosi, Bela 63, 74, **76**, 81, 169, 179, 210, 223, 264, 336, 379, 383
*Luke's Double* (1916 film) 397
Lummis, Dayton 106, 392
*Lust for a Vampire* (1971 film) 219
Lynch, Alfred 118, 404
Lyndon, Barre 103
Lynne, Gillian 294, 386


MacArthur, Charles 272
MacArthur, James 269, **270**, **271**, 272, **276**, 386
*Macbeth* (play) 57
McCarey, Leo 323
McCarthy, Joseph 209
McClanahan, Rue 226, 408
McClure, Sam 29, 372
*McClure's Magazine* 312, 328
MacDonald, Alexander 236
MacDonald, Alisdair 233

MacDonald, Flora 248
MacDonald, John ("Long John") 87
MacDonald, Philip 73, 74, 75, 382
MacDonalds of Glencoe (Clan Ian Abrach) 233
MacDougal, Helen 69
McDowall, Roddy 264, 265, 268, 384
MacGinnis, Niall 271, 386
Macgregor, James More 246, 270
Macgregor, Rob Roy 252, 356
Macgregor, Robin Oig 246, 270
McKee, Raymond 256, 378
MacKenzie, Alex 271, 386
MacKintosh, Steven 116, 391
McLaren, Moray 14, 162
*MacMillan's Magazine* 19
McNeill, Allen 257, 382
Macpherson, Ewan (Cluny) 239, 271
MacQueen, Robert (Lord Braxfield) 346
MacRae, Duncan 271, 386
Macready, George 150, 383
Mahin, John Lee 97, 98, 200, 380, 382
*Maid Marian* (novel) 148
Malleson, Miles 274, 386
Malloy, Matt 117
Maltin, Leonard 101–02, 103, 111
Maltz, Albert 110, 397
Mamoulian, Rouben 179–99, 201, 205, 216, 380
*The Man in the Iron Mask* (1939 film) 151
*The Man Who Changed His Mind* (1936 film) 269
*The Man with Two Heads* (1972 film) 399
Mandel, Mel 225, 403
Mander, Miles **259**, 382
Mankowitz, Wolf 108, 212, 214, 386, 389
Mann, Delbert 276, 279, 280, 388
Mann, Hank 178, 394
Mansfield, Martha 171, **175**, 378
Mansfield, Richard 162–66, 168
March, Fredric 181, **185**, **186**, **193**, 197–98, 204, 224, 225, 272, 380, 421
*Mardi* (novel) 87
*Mark of the Vampire* (1935 film) 198
"Markheim" • 340, 359, 401, 402, 403, 410, 413, 415
Markle, Fletcher 117, 401
Marla, Norma 212, 214, 387, 395

460    Index

Marryat, Captain Frederick 87, 283
Mary, Queen of Scots 346, 435
*Mary Poppins* (1964 film) 269
Mason, Shirley 93, **96,** 379
Massara, Natal 109, 110, 389
Massie, Paul 212, **213,** 214, 387
*The Master of Ballantrae* • 29, 30, 40, 43, 45, 281–97, 301, 302, 316, 318, 340, 362, 371, 385, 401, 403, 405, 411, 412
"The Master of Ballantrae" (1950 television show) 295, 401
*The Master of Ballantrae* (1953 film) 290–95, **291, 293,** 339, 385–86
"The Master of Ballantrae" (1962 television show) 295, 403
"The Master of Ballantrae" (1984 television film) 295–97, 338–39, 405
Mather, Aubrey 336, 382, 384
Matheson, Richard 223
Mathieson, Muir 275, 384, 385, 386
Matthews, Lester 206, 393
Maugham, W. Somerset 203
Mayer, Carl 169
Mayer, Louis B. 98, 174–75, 178, 200, 378
Meadow, Herb 292, 295, 385
Medford, Harold 292, 295, 385
Melville, Herman 2, 87
Merritt, George 214, 389
"The Merry Men" • 40, 45, 69, 256, 339, 356, 411
*The Merry Men and Other Tales and Fables* • 132, 135, 360
Metro-Goldwyn-Mayer Pictures (MGM) 58, 62, 63, 67, 94, 97, 99, 107, 112, 185, 194, 199, 200, 201, 203, 206, 207, 290, 339, 347, 380, 381, 382, 398
Metty, Russell 136, 385
*Mighty Mouse Meets Jekyll and Hyde Cat* (1944 cartoon) 396
"A Mile an' a Bittock" • 374, 426
Milland, Ray **322,** 323, 381
Miller, Gabriel 7
Millhouser, Bertram 322, 381
Mills, John 305, 387
Milton, John 284
*Minstrelsy of the Scottish Border* (ballad and poetry collection) 346
"The Misadventures of John Nicholson" • 27, 43, 45, 339–40, 360, 413, 415
*Miss Jekyll and Madame Hyde* (1915 film) 169, 219, 378

Mitchell, Charlotte 118, 406
Mitchell, Margaret 74
*Moby Dick* (novel) 87
Modena, Mary 232
*The Modern Dr. Jekyll* see *Dr. Jekyll and Mr. Hyde* (1908)
Moffet, Sharyn 74, 383
Moloney, Paddy 116–17, 390
Moncreiff, Sir James 70
Mong, William V. 94, 380
Monogram Pictures 263–64, 268, 336, 339, 384
*Monterey Californian* (newspaper) 23
Montgomery, Robert 59, 381
Mooney, Gordon 426
Moore, Dudley 305, 387
Moore, John 225, 403
More, Sir Thomas 146
*More New Arabian Nights: The Dynamiter* • 339, 341, 358, 424
Morgan, Frank 59, 381
Morgan, Helen 180
Morricone, Ennio 110
Morris, Phyllis 336
Morse, Barry 117, 402
Moscow Art Theatre 179
"MS Found in a Bottle" (short story) 87
Mudie, Leonard 257
Muir, Gavin 206, 393
Muller, Paul 109, 389
Mullins, Darby 89
*The Mummy* (1959 film) 212
Munro, Professor Alexander 70, 71
"Murders in the Rue Morgue" (short story) 134
Murdoch, Janet 265, 384
Murnau, F. W. 136, 169, 210
Murray, Lieutenant General Lord George 236, 237
Murray, M. Gray 58
*Mutiny on the Bounty* (1962 film) 112
"My First Book" • 88, 366
"Mystery" (television series) 226, 404
*Mystery of the Wax Museum* (1933 film) 198

**N**aldi, Nita 174, 214, 378
Napier, Alan 324, 383, 385
Napoleonic Wars 328–29
*The Narrative of Arthur Gordon Pym* (novella) 87

# Index

National Broadcasting Corporation (NBC) 114, 226, 403, 408
National General Pictures 107, 108, 339, 347, 389
Neale, Nelson 87
*The Neanderthal Man* (1953 film) 107
*Network* (1976 film) 272
*New Arabian Nights* • 57, 63, 65, 132, 341, 357
New York Theatre Guild 179–80
*New York Times* (newspaper) 62, 93, 170, 174, 203, 205, 321, 323, 324
*New York World* (newspaper) 29, 204
New Zealand Television 118, 280, 404
Newman, Felix 106
Newman, Nanette 305, 387
Newton, Robert 100, 100–03, 104–06, **105**, 111, 114, 117, 118, 384, 392, 402
Ney, Richard 336, 384
Nice, Derek 297, 405
Nimoy, Leonard 223, 408
Nodelman, Perry 97, 108
Nolan, Lloyd 322, 323, 381
Nordisk Company (Great Northern) 168, 377
Northrup, Harry B. 66, 379
Norton, Edgar 187, 199, 380, 381
*Nosferatu* (1921 film) 169
Nugent, Frank S. 62, 63, 262, 323
*The Nutty Professor* (1963 film) 399

**O**dd Man Out (1947 film) 105
O'Dea, Denis 99, 384
O'Donovan, Fred 222, 401
"O'er the Sea to Skye" (tune) 45, 266, 426
"O'er the Water to Charlie" (song) 45
Ogle, Charles 94, 114, 379
*Oh What a Lovely War* (1969 film) 308
O'Herlihy, Dan 265, 272, 384
Olcott, Sidney 168, 377
"The Old Buccaneer" (1957 television show) 117, 402
"An Old Scotch Gardener" • 21
"An Old Song" • 18, 20, 49, 340, 352
*Old Yeller* (1957 film) 269
Oliphant, Caroline (Lady Nairne) 46
*Oliver Twist* (novel) 6, 106
*Oliver Twist* (1948 film) 6, 106
Olivier, Sir Laurence 105, 272
"Ollala" • 159, 340, 360
Omnibus 276, 277, 279, 339

*Omoo* (novel) 87
"On Falling in Love" • 19–20, 351, 422
Ortlieb, Alfred 67, 379
Osbourne, Hervey 19
Osbourne, Isobel (stepdaughter of RLS) 19, 30, **33**, 34, 35, 328, 335, 344–45
Osbourne, Samuel 23
Osbourne, Samuel Lloyd (stepson of RLS) 19, 24, 26, 27, 28, **29**, 30, **33**, 35, 85, 120, 123, 124, 158–59, 164, 301, 302, 304, 307, 308, 312, 342–43, 344, 346–47, 369, 378, 381, 383, 387, 401, 410, 413
O'Sullivan, Adjutant General John 237
O'Sullivan, Richard 117, 402
Otis, Captain A. H. 30
O'Toole, Peter 270, **273**, 274, 386
"Over the Water wi' Chairlie" • 45, 375
Overbaugh, Roy 173, 378
Owen, Reginald 60, 168, 260, 381, 382

**P**alance, Jack 223–24, 403
*Pall Mall Christmas Extra* (periodical) 69
*Pall Mall Magazine* (periodical) 328
Pallette, Eugene 153
Paniagua, Cecilio 109, 389
Pankhurst, Emmeline 210
Panton, Andrew 295, 405
*Paradise Lost* (book) 284
Paramore, Edward E., Jr. 59, 60, 61, 62, 63, 381
Paramount Pictures ix, 66, 93, 94, 95, 103, 110, 165, 169, 170, 174, 178, 179, 180, 193, 194, 199, 200, 201, 212, 214, 222, 321–24, 338, 339, 379, 380, 381, 383, 396, 397, 408
Parker, Clifton 101, 384
Parker, Edwin 209
Pascal, Ernest 256, 262, 381
Paterson, David 69, 81
Paterson, Mary 69, 81
*Paul Jones* (novel) 87
"The Pavilion on the Links" • 3, 23, 57, 64–67, 354, 379, 415–16, 423
Peace of Amiens (treaty) 328–29
Peace of Ryswick (treaty) 86
Peacock, Thomas Love 148
Pembroke, Percy 178, 394

## 462 Index

Penn, Sir William 24
Pepys, Samuel 355
Pevney, Joseph 52, 54, 223
*The Phantom of the Opera* (1925 film) 94
*The Phantom Ship* (novel) 87, 283
*The Phenix City Story* (1955 film) 128
Phillips, Alfred R. 143
*Photoplay* (periodical) 170
Pichel, Irving 181
Pickford, Mary 264
*The Picture of Dorian Gray* (novel) 171, 173, 212, 213–14
Pierce, Jack P. 197–98
Pigott, Tempe 187, 380
*The Pilot* (novel) 87
Piltz, George 324, 381
Pinewood Studios 112, 269, 270, **276**, 390
Pioneer Film Corporation 174, 200, 339, 378
Piper, Myfanwy 63, 404
*The Pirate* (novel) 87
*The Pirate Queen* (novel) 87
pirates 86
*Plan 9 from Outer Space* (1959 film) 107
Plateau, Joseph 167
*Plays of the Year* 166
Pleasence, Donald 154, 225–26, 276, 389, 403, 405, 423
*The Plough and the Stars* (1936 film) 323
Poe, Edgar Allan 5, 51, 57, 87, 88, 124, 134, 338, 339, 340, 350
Pollexfen, Jack 106, 107, 206, 210, 211, 339, 392, 393
Polyscope Company 168, 377
Poole, Howard 164
*Porgy* (1927 musical) 180
Porter, Jane 87
*The Portfolio* (periodical) 19
Postlethwaite, Peter 116, 391
Potter, Jeremy 144, 146
Powell, William 136, **137**, 385
Power, Tyrone 184
Prestonpans (battle) 236, 240, 246
*The Prince and the Pauper* (1937 film) 293
*Prince Otto* • 23, 26, 40, 42, 61, 134, 255, 341–42, 358
Production Code of 1934 179, 197, 201, 206
"Providence and the Guitar" • 57, 340, 354

Public Broadcasting System (PBS) 224, 226, 404
Pulman, Jack 276, 279–80, 388
Purchase, Bruce 118, 406
Pursall, David 154, 404
Putnam, Boyd 164

*The Quiet Man* (1952 film) 324
Quiller-Coach, Arthur T. 328, 335, 347, 384, 402, 403, 410, 412, 413

*Races of Men* (book) 70
Rackin, Martin 104, 392
Radcliffe, Violet 93, 378
Rainger, Ralph 324, 381
Rains, Claude 148
"The Rajah's Diamond" • 57, 63, 341, 404
"The Rajah's Diamond" (1979 television opera) 63, 404
Ramsay, Allan 46, 245
Rathbone, Basil 98, 148, 198
Raven, Mike 214, 389
"Red Is the Rose" (song) 258
*The Red Rover* (novel) 87
*Redburn: His First Voyage* (novel) 87
Redgrave, Sir Michael 225, 403
Reed, Carol 105
Reed, Oliver 114–15, 154, 221, 387, 391, 395, 405
Reeves, Billy 169, 378
Reid, Alan 425–26
Reid, Alistair 226, 404
Reid, Denis 30–31
Reisner, Allen 222, 402
Rennahan, Ray 323, 381
Rennie, Michael 222, 402
Renoir, Jean 222, 386
Republic Pictures 290
"Requiem" • 24, 36, 373, 422
*Return of the Ape Man* (1944 film) 336
*Return to Treasure Island* (1954 film) 106–07, 111, 210, 339, 392
"Return to Treasure Island" (1985 television series) 118–19, 295, 405–06
Reudi, Dr. Karl 25
*The Revenge of Frankenstein* (1958 film) 212
Rey, Fernando 154, 405
Rice, Richard A. 1, 51, 159

# Index

Richard, Duke of York (father of Richard III) 144, 147
Richard II (King of England) 144
Richard III (King of England) 146–47, 153
Richards, Terry 276
Richardson, Ian 295, 405, 421, 422
Richardson, Sir Ralph 305, **307**, 308, 387
Ridley, M. R. 286
Risdon, Elizabeth 58
RKO-Radio Pictures 73, 74, 76, 81, 98, 272, 338, 383, 384
Robert I *see* Bruce, Robert
Robert II (King of Scotland) 232
Robertson, John S. 172, 378
Robin, Leo 324, 381
*Robin Hood and Little John* (novel) 148
Robin Hood legends 127, 144, 148, 153, 257
Robinson, George 209, 394
*Robinson Crusoe* (novel) 87
Roch, Valentine 26, 28, **29**, 30
Rock, Joe 178, 394
Rose, Frank 168, 377
Rosen, Burt 225, 403
Rosen, Philip 336, 384
Rosenberg, Max J. 214, 389
Rousseau, Jean Jacques 86
Ruben, J. Walter 60, 62, 381
Russell, Rosalind 59, 381
Russian Repertory Theatre 179
Ruttenberg, Joseph 203, 382
Ryan, Kate 164

Sachs, Norman 225, 403
Sackheim, Jerry 51, 52, 53, 385
Saint-Gaudens, Augustus 262
*St. Ives* • 34, 110, 325–37, 347, 371, 384, 402, 403, 410, 412, 413
"St. Ives" (1955 television serial) 337, 402
"St. Ives" (1960 television film) 337, 402
"St. Ives" (1967 television film) 337, 403
Salamander company 304, 307, 339, 387
Sambrell, Aldo 108, 109, 389
Sanchez, Adulpho 23
Sanford, Erskine 267, 384
Sannon, Emilie 168, 377

Sarell, William 169, 377
Savile Club 18
Savory, Gerald 226, 404
*Scalawag* (1973 film) 110–11, 397
"Scarborough Fair" (song) 109–10
*Scarface* (1932 film) 180
Schayer, Richard 150, 383
Schlegel, Margarete 169, 379
Schulberg, Ben 179
Schwob, Marcel 133
Scott, Sir Walter 2, 12, 15, 40–41, 82, 148, 231, 232, 264, 334–35, 344, 346, 365
Scott, The Reverend William A. 24
*Scribner's* (periodical) 28, 134, 283
*The Sea Hawk* (1940 film) 117
*Seance on a Wet Afternoon* (1964 film) 308
*The Secret of St. Ives* (1949 film) 336, 384
Seff, Manuel 59, 60, 61, 62, 63, 381
Selig, Colonel William 168
Seller, Thomas 150, 383
Sellers, Peter 306, 387
Selznick, David O. 74, 179, 204, 269
Selznick International Pictures 74
Sennett, Mack 307
*The Seventh Victim* (1943 film) 74
*Shado Kalo* (1953 film) 398
Shakespeare, William 18, 57, 105, 146–47, 172, 342, 344, 347, 422
Shane, Maxwell 324
Shannon, Alexander 176, 378
Shatner, William 223, 408
Shea, William 196, 380
Shelley, Mary Wollstonecraft Godwin 161, 223, 285, 287, 344, 425
Shelley, Percy Bysshe 39, 287
Shelley, Sir Percy Florence 287
Sheppard, David P. 150, 383
Shepperton Studios 216, 389, 403
Sheridan, Emma 164, 165
Sherlock Holmes (1939–46 film series) 98, 198, 205
Sherlock Holmes stories (Conan Doyle) 58, 134, 423, 424, 425
Sherriffmuir (battle) 11, 235
Shevelove, Larry 304, 306, 308, 387
Shields, Arthur 211, 393
*The Shipwreck* (novel) 87
Showtime cable network 226, 407
"Shule Aroon" (song) 288, 426
Sickner, William 265, 268, 384
Sidney, Sylvia 180

*The Sign of Four* (novel) 424
*The Silverado Squatters* • 24, 120–29, **122,** 132, 356, 383, 404
Sim, Gerald 219, 388
Simon, Paul 110
Simpson, Sir Walter 18, 19
*Sing, Baby, Sing* (1936 film) 397–98
"Sing me a song of a lad that is gone" • 47, 374
*Sir Edward Seaward's Narrative of His Shipwreck* ... (novel) 87
"Sir Patrick Spens" (song) 426
"The Sire de Maletroit's Door" • 20, 48–54, 57, 71, 133, 136, 352, 384, 401, 414
"The Sire de Maletroit's Door" (1951 television show) 54, 401
Sitwell, Bertie 18
Sitwell, Frances ("Fanny") 17–18
Small, Edward 150, 151, 153, 383
Smith, Sir C. Aubrey 199–200, 382
Smoktunovsky, Innokenti 222, 390
Snow, Marguerite 168, 377
Snyder, Matt 169, 377
Sobieska, Maria Clementina 235
Soffici, Mario 206, 385
"Some Aspects of Robert Burns" • 42–43, 46, 354
*The Son of Dr. Jekyll* (1951 film) 151, 206–07, 339, 393
*Son of Flubber* (1963 film) 269
*The Son of Monte Cristo* (1940 film) 151
*Songs of Travel and Other Verses* • 9, 374, 425
Sophia, Electress of Hanover 234
*The Spanish Galleon, or the Pirate of the Mediterranean* (novel) 87
*Sparrows* (1926 film) 264
*Spectator* (periodical) 135
Speculative Society ("Spec") 15
Spielberg, Steven 114
"Spit Song" (song) 82
*Spooks Run Wild* (1941 film) 336
Stander, Lionel 108, 109, 389
Stapley, Richard 51, 53, 385
"The Star of County Down" (song) 116
"Star Trek" (television series) 223, 408–09
Starlight company 169, 394
Starrett, Charles 88
Steadman, Robert 116, 390
Steel, Anthony 292, 386
Steiner, Max 116
Stephens, Robert (director) 222, 401

Stevens, Craig 208, 394
Stevens, George (actor) 172, 378
Stevenson, Alan (uncle of RLS) 26
Stevenson, Frances Matilda Vandegrift Osbourne ("Fanny," wife of RLS) 13, 18–19, 20, 23, 24, 25, 26, 27, 28, **29,** 30, **31,** 32, **33,** 34, 35–36, 120, 121, **122,** 123, 124, 128, 143, 158–59, 161, 338, 347, 370, 372, 420, 424
Stevenson, Houseley 265, 384
Stevenson, Katherine (cousin of RLS) 12, 155
Stevenson, Margaret Isabella Balfour (mother of RLS) 9, 11, 25, 28, 29, 30, 32, **33,** 35, 367
Stevenson, Robert (grandfather of RLS) 9, 10
Stevenson, Robert ("Bob," cousin of RLS) 12, 15, 18, 19, 27, 58, 328
Stevenson, Robert (director) 268–69, 270, 274, 275, 386
Stevenson, Robert Louis Balfour: birth 9, **10;** ancestry 9–10; residences 9, **10,** 11, **12, 13,** 23, 24, 25, 28, **29,** 32, 328, 340; name change 10; nickname of "Smout" 10, 11; illnesses 10–11, 23–24, 25, 26, 27, 28–29, 34, 41, 43; early education 11, 12; and religion 11, 15, 16–17, 18, 315–18, 320; early literary efforts 11, 12, 16, 19; childhood holidays 11, 12; at Edinburgh University 12, 14–15, 18; travels 12, 15, 18–19, 20–21, 22–26, 28, 29, 30–32, 46, 65, 120–25, 283, 301; interest in Scottish history and culture 13–14, 25, 38, 41, 44–47, 65, 71, 121, 125, 231–32, 238–40, 250, 256, 284, 285, 287, 303, 345–46; bohemian lifestyle 14–16; interest in French history and culture 14, 20, 49, 343; early sexual experiences 14, 17; drinking habits 14, 17, 87; conflict with father 15, 17, 18; use of drugs 17; admission to Scottish bar 18; on marriage 19–20, 25; in the United States 20, 22–25, 28–30, 120–25, 127–28, 162–64, 287; on emigration 20; in Chicago 20; at Swanston Cottage 21; in Iowa 22; in Nebraska 22; on racism 22, 318, 340; on Native Americans 22, 287; marriage 24, 120; honeymoon 24, 120–25; on women 25, 134; interest in Celtic music 26–27, 30–31, 32, 82, 89, 116, 125, 245–46, 288–89, 303,

317, 333, 349–50; and Ireland 27; on wealth 28; South Seas voyages 29, 30–32, **31**, 283, 301, 312, 316–17; at the Molokai leper colony 30; and Samoan politics 32, 33, 364–65; Samoan name, "Tusitala" 32; death 34–35, 344–45; funeral 35; on Percy Bysshe Shelley 39; on Sir Walter Scott 40–41; use of female characters 42, 164, 254–55, 318, 332, 341–42; use of Scots dialect 45, 46; on Robert Burns 42–43, 46; on *Treasure Island* 85, 87–88, 89, 143–44; use of young protagonists 41–42, 90–91, 92, 134; in California 120–25, 127–28; on *The Black Arrow* 143–44; on William Shakespeare 147; on *Weir of Hermiston* 345
Stevenson, Thomas (father of RLS) 9, 11, 12, 13, 14, 15, 17, 21, 24, 25, 26, 27–28, 85, 361, 369
Stewart, Alexander 241
Stewart, Allan Breck 44, 240–42, 253, 279, 285, 436
Stewart, Allan Oig 242
Stewart, Charles (Laird of Ardshiel) 240
Stewart, Charles (notary) 253
Stewart, Douglas 87
Stewart, James ("James of the Glens") 240–42, 250–51, 253, 257, 263, 274, 276, 279, 280
Stewart, Paul 324
Stewart dynasty 232, 435
Stoddard, Charles Warren 24
Stoker, Bram 169, 212, 223, 425
Stoloff, Morris 206, 393
Stone, Lewis 96, 98, 380
Stone and Kimball 313
"The Story of a Lie" • 341, 354
"Story of the Destroying Angel" 341
"Story of the Fair Cuban" 341
Stothart, Herbert 97, 380
Stowe, Georgia 154, 405
*The Strange Case of a Hyde and Seekyl* (1886 play) 165
*The Strange Case of Dr. Jekyll and Mr. Hyde* • 2, 26, 27, 41, 155–226, 230, 284, 290, 340, 360, 377, 378, 379, 380, 382, 386, 388, 389, 390, 393, 394–96, 397–400, 401, 402, 403, 404, 407, 408, 409, 410, 411, 412, 413, 414, 415, 416, 421, 425
"The Strange Case of Dr. Jekyll and Mr. Hyde" (1951 television show) 222, 401
"The Strange Case of Dr. Jekyll and Mr. Hyde" (1968 television film) 223–24, 403
"The Strange Case of Dr. Jekyll and Mr. Hyde" (1980 television film) 226, 404
*The Strange Case of Dr. Jekyll and Mr. Hyde* (1987 film) 222, 390
"The Strange Case of Dr. Jekyll and Mr. Hyde" (1990 television show) 226, 407–08
*The Strange Door* (1951 film) 51–54, **53**, 136, 208, 223, 339, 385
Strauss, Richard 116
Strong, Austin 31, 32, **33**
Strong, Isobel *see* Osbourne, Isobel
Strong, Joe 30, 32, **33**, 34, 122, 123
Struss, Karl 181, 194, 196, 199, 380
Stuart, Anne (Queen of England and Scotland) 234
Stuart, Charles Edward ("The Young Pretender"; "Bonnie Prince Charlie") 44, 45, 46, 47, 235–39, 248, 265, 266, 273, 281, 285, 288, 292, 295, 346
Stuart, James Francis Edward ("The Old Pretender") 232, 233, 234, 235
Stuart, Mary (daughter of King Charles I) 232
Stuart, Mary (wife of William of Orange/Queen of England) 232
Stuart, Mary *see* Mary, Queen of Scots
*A Study in Scarlet* (novel) 424
Subotsky, Milton 214, 215–16, 218, 389
"The Suicide Club" • 2, 55–63, 377, 378, 380, 381, 410, 414
*The Suicide Club* (1909 film) 58, 377
*The Suicide Club* (1914 film) 58, 378
*The Suicide Club* (1987 film) 63
Sullivan, John T. 165
Sullivan, Thomas Russell 163–66, 168
Sullivan, William 163
*Sunset Boulevard* (1950 film) 137
"Suspense" (television series) 222, 401
Susskind, David 117, 118, 402
Swanston Cottage 21, 333, 419
Swearingen, Roger G. ix
Swinburne, Algernon Charles 58, 422
Swindell, Larry 203–04
Swinnerton, Frank 1
*Swiss Family Robinson* (1960 film) 272

*The Switch* (1974 film) 400
Sydney, Basil 100, 384
Symonds, John Addington 159

Talbot, Gloria 210-11, 393
*Tales of Terror* (1962 film) 339
Tannahill Weavers 426
Taylor, Benedict 154, 405
Taylor, Eric 336, 384
Taylor, Kit 104, 117, 392, 402
Taylor, Rod (Rodney) 104, 117, 392, 402
Tchaikovsky, Pyotr Ilich 117
Teach, Edward ("Blackbeard") 86, 286
Teal, Ray 150, 384
Tembinoka (South Sea despot) 31
*Temple Bar* (periodical) 49
*The Test of Honor* (1919 play) 170
*Le Testament du Doctor Cordelier* (1959 film) 222-23, 386, 403
Tetzlaff, Ted 106, 136, 385
Tew, Thomas 89
*That Darn Cat* (1964) 269
*The Theatre* (periodical) 164, 165, 166
*Third Man on the Mountain* (1959 film) 272
Thomas, Richard 295, 296, 405
Thomas, Tony 93
Thomas the Rhymer (Thomas of Erceldoune) 281
Thoreau, Henry David 24, 355, 422
*Those Daring Young Men in Their Jaunty Jalopies* (1969 film) 305
*A Thousand and One Nights* (book) 58
"Thrawn Janet" • 40, 45, 69, 256, 339, 356, 411
"Ticonderoga" • 28, 374
*To-Day* (periodical) 312
Toland, Gregg 258, 382
Tolstoy, Leo 27
*Tom Brown's School Days* (1940 film) 269
Tory party 237
*Touch of Evil* (1958 film) 108
Tourneur, Maurice 66, 93, 94, **96**, 379
Tover, Leo 323, 381
Towers, Harry Alan 154, 389, 404
Tracy, Spencer 200, 201-02, **201**, 203-05, 226, 382
*The Tragedy of Richard III* (play) 146-47, 172, 174

*Travels with a Donkey in the Cévennes* • 20, 65, 353-54, 368-69, 412, 413, 414, 415
*Treasure Island* • ix, x, 2, 25, 40, 69, 83-119, 124, 132, 134, 143, 144, 231, 242, 284, 286, 289, 302, 314, 329, 356, 366, 377, 378, 379, 380, 384, 388, 389, 390, 402, 403, 404, 405, 406, 408, 410, 412, 413, 414, 415, 416, 417, 421, 423, 424-25
*Treasure Island* (1908 film) 93, 377
*Treasure Island* (1912 film) 93, 377
*Treasure Island* (1918 film) 93, 378
*Treasure Island* (1920 film) 93-94, **95, 96,** 97, 379
*Treasure Island* (1934 film) 94-98, **99,** 100, 107, 111, 112, 200, 262, 339
*Treasure Island* (1937 film) 98, 381
"Treasure Island" (1947 television show) 117, 401
*Treasure Island* (1950 film) 98-103, **102,** 107, 111, 112, 268, 271, 339, 384-85
"Treasure Island" (1951 television show) 117, 401
"Treasure Island" (1951 serial) 117, 401
"Treasure Island" (1960 television show) 117-18, 208, 402
*Treasure Island* (1965 educational film) 387
"Treasure Island" (1969 television serial) 118, 403
*Treasure Island* (1970 educational film) 388
*Treasure Island* (1971 film) 107-08, 389
*Treasure Island* (1972 film) 107-10, 212, 339, 347, 389
"Treasure Island" (1974 television film) 118, 403-04
"Treasure Island" (1977 television serial) 118, 404
"Treasure Island" (1981 television serial) 118, 404
*Treasure Island* (1987 animated film) 406
*Treasure Island* (1990 film) 111-17, **115,** 272, 295, 338, 390-91, 408
*Treasure Island* (1991 educational film) 408
"The Treasure of Franchard" • 42, 130-37, 357, 385, 415
*The Treasure of Lost Canyon* (1951 film) 135-37, **137,** 385

# Index

*Trouble for Two* (1936 film) 58–63, 151, 262, 339, 381
Troughton, Patrick 118, 404
Truman, Harry S 166
Truman, Ralph 103, 384, 386
Tucker, Forrest 126, 383
Turner, Lana 200, **201,** 203, 204, 205, 382
Turner, Otis 168
Turner, Ted 112
Turner Network Television (TNT) 111, 115, 295, 390
Turpin, Gerry 308, 387
*TV Guide* (periodical) 111
"Twa Corbies" (song) 289, 426
Twain, Mark 2, 5, 29
*Twelfth Night* (play) 18
Twentieth Century–Fox Pictures 98, 256, 262, 264, 268, 290, 339, 382, 398
*The Two Admirals* (novel) 87
*The Two Faces of Dr. Jekyll* (1960 film) 212–14, **213,** 386–87
*Typee* (novel) 87

*The Ugly Duckling* (1959 film) 212, 395
Ulmer, Edgar G. 210, 211, 393
*Unheimliche Geschichten* (1919 film) 58, 380
*Unheimliche Geschichten* (1932 film) 58, 380
United Artists Pictures 106, 291, 392, 380
Universal Pictures 51, 54, 63, 73, 94, 98, 128, 135, 136, 178, 198, 206, 207–08, 209, 210, 211, 269, 290, 339, 385, 394
Universum Film Aktien Gesellschaft (UFA) 269
Urban, Charles 168

*The Valley of Fear* (novel) 58
Valli, Frankie 111
*The Vampire Lovers* (1970 film) 219
Van Sloan, Edward 192
Vandegrift, Nellie 23
*Vanity Fair* (periodical) 19
*Variety* (1925 film) 107
*Variety* (trade paper) 62, 94, 108, 137, 198, 199, 204, 211, 222, 256, 268, 275, 308, 321, 323, 324, 336
Veldt, Conrad 169, 379
"A Vendetta in the West" • 23
Vergil, Polydore 146
Verne, Jules 351
*Victory* (novel) 320
Vidal, Gore 222, 402
Vietnam War 279
Villon, Francois 340, 352
Vitagraph 93, 169, 219, 377, 378
von Zharen, W. M. 279, 280
*Voodoo Man* (1944 film) 264
Vorkapitch, Slavko 202

**W**ade, General George 236
Wade, Russell 74, 81, 383
"The Waif Woman" • 312, 339, 370–71
Walt Disney Studios ix, 98, 105, 118, 153–54, 268, 269, 270, 272, 280
Walters, Thorley 307, 387
Walton, Douglas 336, 380, 384
"Wandering Willie" (song) 45, 288–89
*War of the Worlds* (novel) 103
*War of the Worlds* (1953 film) 103
Warner, Jack 294
Warner Bros. Pictures 116, 169, 290–95, 339, 386, 394, 424
Wars of the Roses 144–45, 147–48
Watkin, Lawrence E. 99, 100, 101, 102, 108, 384
Watson, Harold Francis 86, 87, 88, 424
Watson, Jack 118, 276, 389, 404
*The Watts Monster* see *Dr. Black and Mr. Hyde*
*Waverly* (novel) 231, 334
Waxman, Franz 62, 199, 380, 382
Wayne, John 110
*We Barrymores* (memoir) 170
Webb, Roy 81, 82, 382
"We'd Better Bide a Wee" (song) 82
Weeks, Stephen 216, 218, 389
*Weir of Hermiston* • 34, 40, 42, 43, 46, 328, 335, 338, 341, 344–47, 370, 403, 404, 410, 411, 412, 413, 415, 416, 424
Weisberger, Thomas 276, 389
Weiss, Carl 169, 379
Weitzel, Edward 170, 174
Welbeck, Peter 154, 404

Welch, Jack  82, 383
Weller, Sam  128
Welles, Orson  108–09, 212, 269, 389
Wells, H. G.  103, 162, 302
Welsch, Janice  190, 191
Welsh Arts Council  63, 404
Werker, Alfred  257, 382
West, Adam  220
Westcott, Helen  208, 394
Westmore, Bud  209, 385, 394
Westmore, Wally  194, 198, 380
Whale, James  63, 151, 179
"Wha'll Be King But Cherlie?" (song)  45–46
Wheeler, David  7, 8
Whelan, Arleen  258, **264**, 382
*When Quackel Did Hyde* (1920 film)  178, 394
"When the Devil Was Well"  •  341
"When Ye Gang Awa', Jamie" (song)  82
Whig party  233, 238, 323
*The White Circle* (1920 film)  66–67, 339, 379
"The White Cockade" (tune)  117, 274, 275
*White Jacket* (novel)  87
Whitechapel murders  221
Whitelaw, Billie  223, 403
Whitman, Walt  353
Wickes, David  226, 403, 407
Wiene, Robert  169, 397
Wilde, Oscar  58, 162, 171, 212, 422
Wilder, Billy  137
Wilkinson, Geoffrey  100, 384
"Will o' the Mill"  •  20, 49, 132, 340, 352
"Will Ye No Cam Back Again?" (song)  82
William, Duke of Cumberland ("The Butcher")  236, 237, 240
William Heinemann company  313, 328
William Marshall Productions  291
William of Orange, King of England and Scotland  232, 233
Williams, J. Mervyn  63, 404
Williams, Ralph Vaughan  425
Williams, Rhys  150, 153, 383, 393
Williams, Sumner  256, 378

Wilson, Janis  67, 379
*The Window* (1948 film)  106
Winter, William  165
Winters, David  225, 226, 403
Winters, Roland  384
Wisberg, Aubrey  106, 107, 339, 392
Wise, Robert  75, 79, 382
"Wolf in the Fold" ("Star Trek" episode)  223
Wood, Clive  113, 391
Woollard, Tony  112, 390
Women's Social and Political Union  210
*Wonderful World of Disney* (television series)  103
Wood, Edward D., Jr.  107
World Films  106, 107
Worlock, Frederic  200, 382
*The Wrecker*  •  31, 32, 304, 341, 342–44, 363, 410
Wrench Films  168, 377
*The Wrong Box*  •  30, 44, 135, 283, 298–308, 335, 344, 363, 378, 387, 413, 415
*The Wrong Box* (1913 film)  304, 378
*The Wrong Box* (1966 film)  304–08, 307, 339, 387

*Year of the French* (1982 television show)  117
Yellen, Sherman  225–26, 403
York, Michael  295, 296, 297, 405
Young, F. A.  98, 384
Young, Margaret Dickson  21
Young, Robert (gardener at Swanston)  21
Young, Robert (son)  21
Young, Waldemar  321, 379
"The Young Chevalier"  •  46–47, 370
*Young Folks* (periodical)  88, 143, 230
*The Young Stranger* (1957 film)  272

Zangwill, Israel  313
Zanuck, Darryl F.  256, 258, 262, 263, 382, 397
Zukor, Adolph  170, 380

www.ingramcontent.com/pod-product-compliance
Lightning Source LLC
Chambersburg PA
CBHW021332230426
43666CB00006B/275